LAND LAW

A PROBLEM-BASED APPROACH

REBECCA KELLY AND EMMA HATFIELD

Routledge Problem–Based Learning Series

A new textbook series that creates a fresh approach to learning through the use of integrated realistic case studies designed to simulate how the law works in practice. Unlike other textbooks, books in the Problem–Based Learning series integrate a thorough exposition of the legal rules with applied problem-solving opportunities, highlighting the legal issues and providing essential context for the law.

AVAILABLE NOW:

Equity & Trusts: A Problem-Based Approach, Judith Riches
Land Law: A Problem-Based Approach, Rebecca Kelly and Emma Hatfield

FORTHCOMING TITLES:

Tort Law: A Problem-Based Approach, Neil Stanley

LAND LAW

A PROBLEM-BASED APPROACH

REBECCA KELLY AND EMMA HATFIELD

Routledge
Taylor & Francis Group

LONDON AND NEW YORK

First published 2018
by Routledge
2 Park Square, Milton Park, Abingdon, Oxon OX14 4RN

and by Routledge
711 Third Avenue, New York, NY 10017

Routledge is an imprint of the Taylor & Francis Group, an informa business

© 2018 Rebecca Kelly and Emma Hatfield

British Library Cataloguing in Publication Data
A catalogue record for this book is available from the British Library

Library of Congress Cataloging in Publication Data
Names: Kelly, Rebecca, (Law teacher), author. | Hatfield, Emma, (Law teacher), author.
Title: Land law: a problem-based approach / Rebecca Kelly, Emma Hatfield.
Description: New York, NY: Routledge, 2017. | Includes bibliographical references and index.
Identifiers: LCCN 2016052366 | ISBN 9780415844895 (hardback) | ISBN 9780415844901 (pbk.) | ISBN 9781317802426 (epub) | ISBN 9781317802419 (mobipocket)
Subjects: LCSH: Real property–Great Britain.
Classification: LCC KD829.K45 2017 | DDC 346.4104/3–dc23
LC record available at https://lccn.loc.gov/2016052366

ISBN: 978-0-415-84489-5 (hbk)
ISBN: 978-0-415-84490-1 (pbk)
ISBN: 978-1-315-81373-8 (ebk)

Typeset in Bembo, Bell, Avenir
by Wearset Ltd, Boldon, Tyne and Wear

Visit the companion website: www.routledge.com/cw/kelly

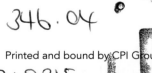

346.04

269315

1·19

Printed and bound by CPI Group (UK) Ltd, Croydon, CR0 4YY

The authors of this book would like to thank their families. In particular Rebecca would like to thank her Mum and Dad for all their help and support. Emma would like to say a big thank you to her boys Harry and Tom for being patient whilst Mum was busy. 'I love you both very much and remember anything is possible.'

CONTENTS

DETAILED CONTENTS

WHAT IS PROBLEM-BASED LEARNING?

Problem-based learning (PBL) is a method of learning which always begins with a problem which is designed to stimulate the interest of the reader. Its key ingredients are:

[A] *problem description*, which invites further active deliberation; *prior knowledge* that is activated by the process of thinking through the problem; *questions* raised by the problem and the need – or *motivation* – to look for further information relevant to the problem at hand. When other students, who are also interested in the problem, *share* in the process of active deliberation and all this takes place *under the guidance of a tutor*, the essential elements of problem-based learning are in place.[1]

At a very basic level, the PBL learning cycle could therefore be summarised according to Figure 0.1.

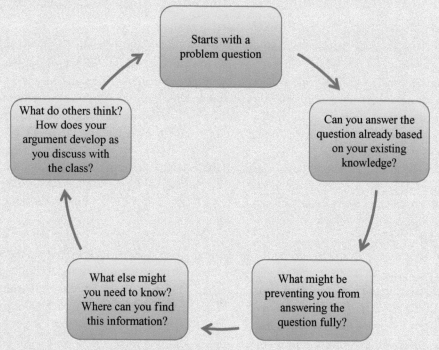

Figure 0.1 The problem-based learning cycle

---

1 Jos Moust, P Bouhuijs and Hans Schmidt, *Introduction to Problem-Based Learning* (Routledge, 2007) 10

PBL was initially introduced, as a method of tuition, in the Medical School of McMaster University, Canada in 1969. Whilst the method is especially popular in medicine, it is increasingly used in other disciplines such as law, psychology, engineering, economics and the humanities.

HOW DOES PBL WORK?

PBL usually takes place in the context of an individual module but may be applied to an entire degree course. Most commonly, students are divided into small groups – for example, of between five and ten. In their first group meeting, students are given a problem which forms the focus of the learning process. At this stage, students have no prior knowledge based on lectures or textbooks. The problem is then discussed whilst the tutor acts as facilitator. The group discussion should raise questions regarding the problem.

- Has the group been able to identify all of the legal issues presented by the problem?
- Which issues might require further clarification?
- Are there any issues that are not understood and need to be researched further by the group?

These questions form *learning objectives* which each student pursues individually over the next few days by conducting further research (they may choose to look for information by consulting books, academic articles, media reports or online material, or by consulting the teaching staff). Following the research phase, students meet together in their allotted group to share what they have learned and to evaluate the extent to which they have achieved an improved understanding of the problem.

PBL contrasts with the traditional approach to law-school tuition which is based on transmitting information to students in lectures, supported by textbook-based reading. Students are directed to information which is selected and delivered by the teaching staff.

In PBL, learning always begins with a problem (or case study) which kick-starts the learning process. Students engage with a problem at the outset of each topic studied. This stands in stark contrast to traditional higher-education tuition in which a seminar problem, to test a student's understanding of the law and his/her ability to apply it to a problem, comes at the end of the learning process.

WHAT ARE THE BENEFITS OF A PROBLEM-BASED APPROACH?

Why are more and more law schools adopting a problem-based approach to teaching and what are the benefits to you as a student?

One of the main benefits of problem-based learning is that it helps students to learn to be more independent in their studies, just as they will be in the world of employment. Moust et al[2] argue that a PBL approach leads to deeper understanding: 'Learning – that is the acquisition, retention and recall of knowledge – within a specified context and related to particular problems is more effective than the acquisition of facts and information simply gleaned from reading a book from cover to cover.'
What does this mean for the student?

- First, you will learn to **analyse** the question and **identify** the relevant legal issues. Often when faced with problem questions in coursework or exam situations, students are able to identify only some of the legal issues that the question presents and lose marks as a result. Following a PBL approach will help you to hone those skills of analysis so that you are able to distinguish more readily what is relevant from what is unimportant. The tutor tips in this book will help to highlight examples of where additional marks could be lost or gained.
- You will notice your ability to **reason** and to **solve problems** within your area of study will develop and improve. By considering how the law can be applied to resolve the issues under consideration, you will begin to acquire a much deeper understanding of the law than you would from lectures or textbooks alone.
- You will improve your **research** skills, digging deeper and wider to find the information you need to resolve all of the legal issues presented by the problem.
- You will benefit from working as part of a team, **sharing** knowledge and **collaborating** with the group to **communicate** what you have learned and discuss the legal issues.

Above all though, problem-based learning is an *active* approach to learning. This means that you will only achieve these benefits if you embrace this style of learning and commit (see Figure 0.2).

OUR PROBLEM-BASED APPROACH

In common with traditional PBL, this textbook focuses upon the centrality of the problem as a learning tool; however, in contrast to traditional PBL, study of the legal issues is supported through substantive coverage of the law. The textbook, in our opinion, is an efficient means of setting out the law which students must understand

---

2 ibid 11

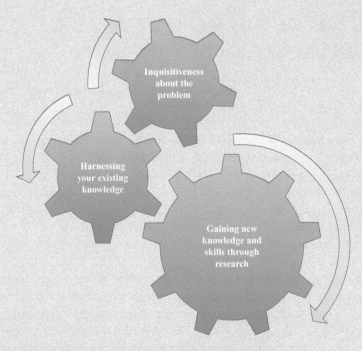

Figure 0.2 Embracing the problem-based learning approach

and be able to apply to a set of facts. In our version of PBL, group work, as opposed to individual study, is reserved for seminars. A key strength of our approach is that it enables students to *apply* legal principles in a structured manner to a series of case study problems *before* they tackle problems in the context of a seminar. The opportunity to apply the law to the case studies and alternative scenarios contained in each chapter is intended to provide students with greater confidence when making contributions to subsequent seminar discussions.

The ability to apply the law (or rules generally) to 'solve' a problem is a skill prized by a wide range of potential employers. Your career will almost certainly involve some form of problem-solving, and this is especially true if you intend to practise law as a solicitor or barrister. In any profession you will need to keep up to date with developing knowledge in your chosen profession. This will inevitably require you to be a self-directed learner as you cannot rely on others to spoon-feed you a summary of the new knowledge in your profession.

Our problem-based approach creates a fresh approach to learning through the use of integrated and realistic case studies. Each case study is designed to stimulate the reader's interest in how the law is applied in practice to a real-life factual scenario. Unlike other textbooks, in addition to detailed coverage of land law this book combines an exposition of the legal rules with applied problem-solving opportunities.

The book's goal is to familiarise students with a more active and practical approach to land law that will deepen their knowledge and understanding. Written in a clear and concise style but without sacrificing detail or analysis, Rebecca Kelly and Emma Hatfield not only provide students with a full and wide-ranging account of the law, but also assist them to develop the analytical and problem-solving skills they will need to succeed in their studies and beyond.

Key features include:

- **Case Studies** in each chapter provide real-world context to each topic and help you to familiarise yourself with typical legal problems you may encounter in a higher-education assessment, or possibly, in legal practice;
- **Apply Your Learning** boxes invite you to reflect and consolidate on the content covered in order to apply the law back to each case study;
- **Consider This** boxes present variations of the case studies and alternative scenarios to challenge you to take their application of the law to the next level;
- **Key Cases and Statutes** boxes reinforce the essential role of cases and legislation in the development and application of land law and help you to identify key sources of legal authority for revision purposes;
- **Tutor Tips** highlight important issues which you should note especially relating to assessments; and
- **Preparing for Assessments** sections are ideal for revision and offer opportunities to bring it all together and practise exam technique.

Neil Stanley
Leeds
June 2016

GUIDE TO THE WEBSITE

All the books in the *Problem-Based Learning* series are supported by a companion website which offers a suite of resources designed to extend learning and provide practical support for assessments, as well as guidance for lecturers on how to implement a problem-based learning approach in the classroom.

FOR STUDENTS

Reading lists – Looking to get the very best marks? Reading around the subject will help you to deepen and expand your understanding. Here you will find a list of both print and electronic sources for taking your study further, hand-picked and recommended by the authors.

Problem Scenarios – Can you apply the law? Improve your ability to identify legal issues and apply the law with these advanced multiple-choice questions. For each of the problems put forward, you must employ your understanding of the law and legal reasoning to select from multiple solutions.

Flash Cards – Do you know your legal authority? Practice your recall of the key principles of major cases and statutes to help you cite legal authority more accurately.

FOR ADOPTERS

Instructor's Guide – A guide to using the books and a problem-based approach in the classroom, including two sample problem-based tutorials, to help support those teaching as part of a team and outside of their area of primary expertise, as well as those new to the idea of using problem questions in their teaching.

Mooting scenarios – Mooting is a great way to put problem-based learning into practice. Here you will find some sample mooting scenarios to help you set up an informal moot with your students.

TABLE OF CASES

TABLE OF STATUTES

STATUTORY INSTRUMENTS

FOREIGN LEGISLATION

1

CHAPTER 1
AN INTRODUCTION

STUDYING LAND LAW

Land law has the reputation of being a 'challenging' subject, governed by a system of sometimes technical rules and involving a number of complex and abstract concepts. This book is designed to make the subject both accessible and enjoyable, using realistic problem scenarios to develop an understanding and appreciation of the development, relevance and application of those rules and concepts. You will already know more than you may realise; everyone needs and uses land and so will come to the subject having some knowledge on its nature. This book gradually adds layers of knowledge, with topics building upon and reinforcing knowledge gained earlier. As a subject, land law demands coherence, since the answer to many questions requires an understanding of a number of interrelated issues or topics of study. A calm, structured approach both to study of the key principles and to answering questions will help you a great deal. The law covered in this text applies to England and Wales – Scotland and Northern Ireland have their own separate systems of land law.

As your studies progress, it will become apparent that to understand land law you must move beyond viewing it as simply a system of technical rules. You must be aware of the needs and issues that land generates, then the rules can be understood as a response to those challenges and be both appreciated and criticised. Land law is about the relationships which people and the state have with land. Nobody can live without land, and most people have to share it, creating competing rights. England and Wales have a limited supply of land and (at least in towns and cities) a dense population, so disputes about rights over land are common. The system of rules must regulate the use of land and take account of the needs and the culture of the society in which it operates.

Land can be a commercial financial asset but there are wider considerations relating to access to land and land as a home. In a market-based society land must be freely tradable, with security and guarantees for its owners, but there must also be recognition of those with lesser rights or interests in the land. Many land law problems will involve not just two but three sets of competing interests: those of a buyer of the land, a seller of the land, and a third party who has some lesser interest in the land (e.g. a right to live there for life, a loan secured against it, or the right to walk across it).

Land law has its own peculiar language and concepts that must be grasped before the complexities of the law in action can be addressed and understood. Thus the first part of the book explains the basic building blocks of the law, covering the meaning of property and ownership, the definition of land and the relationship between law and equity. It then moves on to how to transfer and create rights in land and to the role of unregistered and registered land systems. The book then explores the principal transactions that people get involved with in their occupation and use of land, namely leases, licences, mortgages, easements and restrictive covenants. It explores also the rights arising outside of agreed transactions, such as resulting and constructive trusts, adverse possession and proprietary estoppel.

USING THE PROBLEM-BASED LEARNING APPROACH IN LAND LAW

Traditionally, land law is taught by way of transmission of information concerning rules and concepts, followed by discussion and analysis of real-life application and the wider social and moral debates. Problem-based learning (PBL) reverses this, with learning centred on realistic scenarios from the very start. You are supported in thinking independently about the problems and issues raised and about how the material covered relates to the issues and objectives. Using this approach you will develop the confidence to conduct research into problems and to produce advice, with a solid foundation of knowledge concerning how the land law system works.

Effective use of PBL requires you to assume major responsibility for your own learning. It is important that you engage fully with each problem scenario. Research shows that learning the legal rules in context rather than in the abstract provides a deeper understanding and better recall. It is also more realistic in developing the practical skills you need as a lawyer, as well as being more enjoyable and engaging. Be aware that you should not expect to be able to answer a problem from the outset – each one raises new concerns and builds upon prior understandings. This can be challenging, but it will promote creative and original thinking and ensure that the points made in the text are better appreciated and more fully considered.

One of the primary aims of PBL is to develop 'active learning' skills among participants, in other words promoting the concept that responsibility for learning belongs to the student. Tutor Tips are used to direct students, with elements of the book requiring the students to engage actively via the Apply Your Learning activities throughout the chapters. These provide the opportunity to think about what has been read, consolidate those thoughts and to prepare for the Discussion section. These opportunities are all designed to reinforce, elaborate upon or introduce you to the issues raised in the PBL scenarios presented at the chapter outset. The best way to get the most from all these additional activities is to keep the PBL scenario in mind and see if you are able to relate the material you are given to the scenario, to supplement, deepen and enhance your understanding of the issues you have identified as arising from it.

FEATURES OF THIS BOOK

This book aims to cover the syllabus of land law at an undergraduate and GDL/CPE conversion level, using a PBL approach integrated throughout the text. As identified earlier, this approach is particularly relevant where the subject matter can be explained best via the real-world context. The aim of this book in using this approach is to:

- Engage students' interest so that they want to learn about the topic and cultivate: independence, curiosity and skills for self-directed, life-long learning.
- Embed learning in a realistic setting, integrating knowledge with practice.
- Trigger existing knowledge and understanding which enables students to build upon what they already know.
- Promote self-motivation and self-responsibility to learn.
- Facilitate more enjoyable and more effective learning in land law.
- Encourage learning from experience, allowing students to use and organise what has been learnt to understand problems.
- Facilitate reflection, transition and self-assessment.

HOW TO USE THIS BOOK

1   Chapter Aims and Objectives – enable students to focus on the outcomes for the chapter, including knowledge, skills and essential cases and statutes.
2   Case Studies – provide realistic and detailed problem scenarios, featuring several strands or sets of circumstances which will be referred to as the chapter progresses and provide structure and focus for learning.
3   Apply Your Learning – enables students to apply/engage with content which they have covered by linking it back to the case studies.
4   Tutor Tips – pointers to help focus learning through highlighting key points, directing studies and highlighting how to avoid common mistakes.
5   Consider This – a case study may be modified to explore the implications of an alternative scenario.
6   Key Cases – contain extracts from judgments allowing students to familiarise themselves with the legal authority.
7   Discussion – pulls together issues which might feature in a discursive essay question, including a summary of the main critical debates, policy issues or problematic areas of law that might be open for reform.
8   End of Chapter Summary – a summary of the key points from the chapter.
9   Questions – sample examination-style essay and problem questions to allow the student to practise writing responses. Note that Chapter 17 has only an essay question, but it is of a practical bent.
10 Further Reading – further sources relevant to the law identified and the points for discussion developed in the chapter.
11 Companion Website – answers to Apply Your Learning boxes, answers to the Consider This questions, annotated answers to the end of chapter discussion questions, self-test questions and updates.

2

CHAPTER 2
PROPERTY RIGHTS IN LAND

CHAPTER AIMS AND OBJECTIVES

In this chapter we will explore the underlying concepts fundamental to an understanding of land law. The first consideration is what is meant when lawyers refer to 'property'. The second is the definition of land as a particular division of property.

By the end of this chapter you should be able to:

- understand the concept of property rights as rights over a thing;
- explain the relevance of a claim being classed as a property right as opposed to a personal right;
- appreciate the relevance of the classification of property as either real (rights relating to land) or personal;
- identify, using relevant statutes, the various elements of the definition of land including:
  - the distinction between corporeal and intangible incorporeal hereditaments
  - how to distinguish fixtures forming part of the land and chattels as personal possessions
  - the difference between tenure and estate;
- apply the above to the case study and learning tasks.

CASE STUDY – ONE

Philip has various questions in relation to Meadow Cottage, a property he informs you he legally 'owns':

(a) One of his neighbours has begun regularly flying model aircraft over Meadow Cottage's gardens, at low altitude. Philip is unsure whether he can require his neighbour to stop.

(b) When Philip purchased Meadow Cottage last year, he had assumed that a number of items would be included in the sale: a fitted kitchen, an easily movable greenhouse in the garden, and a large framed picture attached to the living room wall with screws. All the objects were removed by the previous owners on the day they vacated. They also dug up and removed a range of the more expensive plants from the garden, as well as taking with them some expensive rose specimens growing in pots which had been resting on the garden path. Philip wonders whether they should have done so.

(c)   While visiting Meadow Cottage, Philip's brother found a modern gold necklace resting on the surface of the grass at the front of the house. While digging in the back garden to help assist in the preparation to lay a new patio, Philip's brother unearthed a modern bronze ring from just below the surface. Philip believes he has a better claim than his brother to both items.

(d)   The previous owners of Meadow Cottage allowed the children of a friend to play in its gardens whenever they wanted to. Philip is unsure whether he is required to respect the permission given by his predecessors.

(e)   Meadow Cottage has no direct access to the road, but there is a driveway leading to it which runs over a neighbouring property. The owner of that land granted the right of way to the previous owners of Meadow Cottage. Philip is worried that his neighbour now plans to block the driveway.

(f)   Philip is planning on building a double garage. But a neighbour has informed him of a promise made by the previous owners of Meadow Cottage; they covenanted not to erect any structures without express permission from the neighbour. Philip wants to know whether such an agreement could bind him.

Consider Philip's concerns.

PROPERTY RIGHTS

Philip has made reference to Meadow Cottage belonging to him, so our starting point is to consider what is meant when people refer to their 'property'.

Your initial instinct may be to respond by saying my property is a thing (an object or resource). However, if you dig deeper the limitations of perceiving property as the thing itself become apparent.

First, the actual relevance or usefulness of your claim rests upon an ability to assert it against others. Second, the notion of a single owner with an unlimited claim over a thing is often insufficient.

As a lawyer, property is better understood as meaning the rights you have in regards to a thing. The word property is from the Latin *proprietas*, which means the right or fact of possession.

To be a property or proprietary right, the type of power you hold must be sufficient to penetrate and subsist in relation to the thing itself. The property in the thing survives even when you cease to physically possess it. For example, if you have purchased this book then you are now its owner with the right to its possession. That property right remains over the book even if it were to be lost or stolen tomorrow. Only you as the owner can abandon or transfer that ownership to another.

KEEP IN MIND

- What does Philip mean when he refers to 'owning' the property named Meadow Cottage?
- What does Meadow Cottage itself comprise as a piece of land?
- Is it just that the previous owners took the listed items with them when they moved?
- Can Philip's brother keep the objects he found?
- Why might it be useful and sometimes necessary for a landowner to have rights over a piece of land owned by someone else?
- Why does it matter whether the rights claimed are classed as property rights or personal rights?

The greatest property right is that of ownership. Ownership typically gives rights to use the thing to the exclusion of others, to enjoy its fruits and to deal with it (including the ability to transfer your ownership to another individual).

APPLY YOUR LEARNING – TASK 1

We will need to explore what ownership means in relation to land, but you can now start to consider what this means for Philip. He can expect some control over the use of his property – how could that be relevant to the situation with the aircraft and the items found by his brother?

While less than ownership, there are a large range of rights over a thing owned by another which are still classified as property or proprietary.

APPLY YOUR LEARNING – TASK 2

We will consider some of the rights recognised over land later in this chapter, for now look at the right of way over the property neighbouring Meadow Cottage and the promise restricting development of Meadow Cottage. Can you see how they have an effect on a piece of land owned by another?

These property rights are also called rights *in rem* (a right in respect of a *rem*, *rem* meaning thing in Latin). By attaching themselves to the thing, anyone taking possession of it in the future may still be bound by such rights. In contrast, personal rights or rights *in personam* are only enforceable against some specific person.

The practical significance of this distinction is illustrated by considering the consequences when third parties become involved. We will begin with a simple example from outside of land law.

CONSIDER THIS – 1

Suppose that Daniel purchases a painting from an art gallery. He is now the owner of that object. Daniel then leaves his property in the custody of the gallery to care for it until it can be delivered to his house. Should the gallery pretend to still own the painting and sell it to Sandra for a higher price, Daniel has a claim against Sandra because he has a property right or a right *in rem* in the painting.

Alternatively, if Daniel paid only a deposit to secure the painting until he is paid next week, he has only a contract to buy the painting from the gallery. The contract creates only a purely personal right or a right *in personam*. He has a right enforceable against the gallery but no right in the painting itself. Were the gallery to sell to Sandra instead, he would have no rights against her and would be limited to a claim against the gallery for breach of contract.

The first part of the scenario raises another important element of property law, the relevance of possession and title. When Daniel asserts his rights against Sandra as the 'owner' of the painting, what he is really arguing is that he can prove he has a better right to possession of the property or the stronger 'title'. He had possession before her, and had not relinquished his claim. Against anyone other than Daniel, Sandra's title would be the stronger (assuming that there is no one with an earlier and better claim than Daniel himself).

Just how much evidence of ownership is normally required depends on the type of property. Neither Daniel nor Sandra are likely to have asked for formal evidence of ownership when making a relatively inexpensive purchase from a shop. The shop's physical possession would most likely have been seen as proof enough. When it comes to expensive pieces of land, it is unsurprising that we find a formal system for proof of ownership and various grades of title, so purchasers can be more certain of what claim they are acquiring.

The focus of our efforts in this book is in relation to land and does not extend to other types of property, so having introduced the general concept of property as opposed to personal rights, we will now move to consider land as a particular type of property.

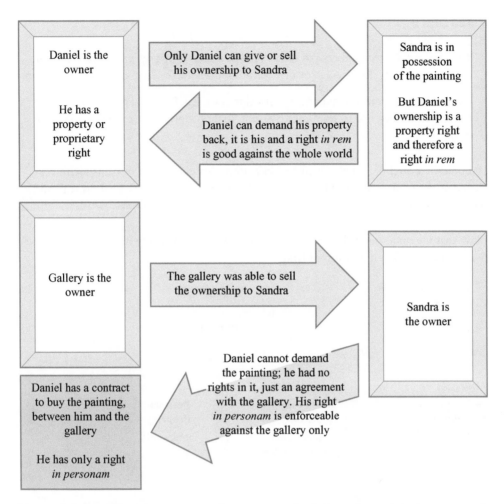

Figure 2.1 Daniel's rights contrasted: a contract of sale (creating a right *in personam*) versus a sale (transferring a right *in rem*)

CLASSIFICATION OF PROPERTY

Property is divided into two categories, real property and personal property. The distinction is based upon the historical remedy prescribed to a person wrongfully dispossessed of property.

In early law, a 'real action' entitled a person to recover the property. Only land could be so recovered, it being permanent and 'immovable'. Recovery was not available for all other types of 'movable' property, for which only a 'personal action' for financial compensation was available. As a result, land became known as real property and is still classified as such in modern law. Everything else is personal property.

It should be noted here that, for historical reasons, leasehold land remains technically classed as personal property. However, leaseholds are referred to as 'chattels real' and modern law treats them in practice as real property (as will this book).

Now that we understand that references to real property or realty mean land, the next point is to provide a definition of land.

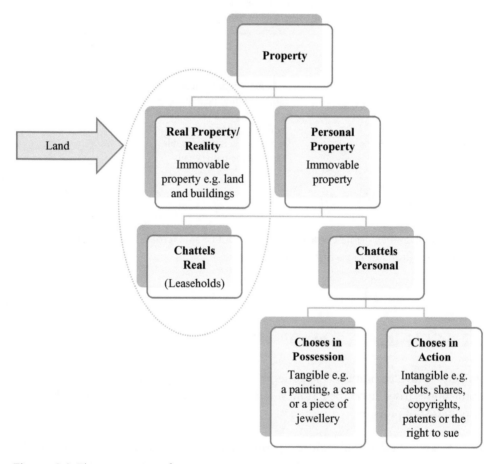

Figure 2.2 The categories of property

THE DEFINITION OF LAND

When first asked to think about what we mean by the term 'land', it is perfectly normal for students to start with a somewhat limited definition referring to a particular plot of ground. For example, the plot upon which a house or a factory is built, or an area used as an allotment or for farming. It is, after all, the most obvious starting point and we see it all around us every day.

With further consideration, often prompted by a tutor asking questions about what else they see and would really expect to be included should they purchase one of these plots, many students independently begin to think about other elements. The features that may need to form part of the definition necessary for the plot to be used and enjoyed. You will have noticed the types of features that make Meadow Cottage more than just a plot of earth.

> **CONSIDER THIS – 2**
>
> Before we begin to explore the concept of 'land', take some time to consider your own definition.

The starting point is the definition of 'land' in the Law of Property Act 1925 (LPA 1925) at s 205(1)(ix):

> Land includes land of any tenure, and mines and minerals, whether or not held apart from the surface, buildings or parts of buildings (whether the division is horizontal, vertical or made in any other way) and other corporeal hereditaments ... and other incorporeal hereditaments, and an easement, right, privilege, or benefit in, over, or derived from land ...

Notice that this is only a partial definition and not exhaustive. It shows that land has a very wide meaning and includes many different types of right.[1] As you can see in the section itself, these rights can be classified as either corporeal or incorporeal hereditaments (a hereditament, from the Latin *h r dit mentum*, means property that can be inherited).

- A corporeal hereditament is a tangible object, something which can be physically possessed, such as the land itself, plants growing in it, materials (such as minerals and timber) and buildings.
- An incorporeal hereditament is an intangible or invisible right against the land. Examples include easements, profits and rentcharges.

---

1 Section 132(1) of the Land Registration Act 2002 expands the definition to include 'land covered with water'.

When you made your own list, you may well have thought of the corporeal elements first. The intangible ones are, however, absolutely necessary as land is expensive, an essential part of life and limited in its availability. We need ways to allow any one physical plot of land and the objects that form a physical part of it to be used to its maximum potential. The less physical and more abstract elements of the definition of land allow, for example, rights to use property owned by another, to restrict how the owner uses their land, to use land as security for a loan, and even to have more than one owner of a particular plot at the same time.

Having considered the broad distinction between the incorporeal and corporeal, we will now consider some of the different aspects of the statutory definition.

LAND OF ANY TENURE

At this stage only note the reference to 'land of any tenure'. Tenure will be defined and discussed later in this chapter when we explore what 'ownership of land' really means.

For now, we will focus on what the definition tells us first about the corporeal or physical characteristics of land as extending beyond the surface area, and second about the role of the incorporeal rights that are not physical at all.

THE SURFACE

The instinctive starting point for defining land is to think of boundaries dividing the surface area of England and Wales into separate properties, for example the boundaries of Meadow Cottage. Indeed, we are familiar with the sight of physical boundary structures such as walls or hedges and can easily move from that concept to the idea of an imaginary line dividing one person's property from neighbouring land.

Such mapping is essential to enable landownership. As we shall see in our studies, the use of Ordnance Survey mapping with marked boundaries is a key element in creating and identifying rights.[2] However, it is clear from the statutory definition that the surface area is not the extent of territory which can be owned as land. It may be held 'apart from the surface' and include 'mines and minerals'. Philip's use of Meadow Cottage requires control over more than just the surface.

The often-referenced Latin maxim *cujus est solum ejus est usque ad coelum et ad inferos* (the landowner owns everything up to the heavens and to the centre of the earth) in theory appears to give an unqualified claim over airspace and the subterranean space below. Land would be defined by only vertical boundaries. Do you think that practical considerations regarding the needs of other landowners and of the general public might necessitate recognition of some limitations on how far claims beyond the surface really extend?

....

2 While a useful guide, it is important to note that markings on the Ordnance Survey do not conclusively fix boundaries and that disputes are not infrequent.

ABOVE THE SURFACE

The landowner does not own 'up to the very heavens'. Case law relating to the ownership of airspace above the property has demonstrated a limitation on the applicability of the maxim.

It is now accepted that a landowner is entitled only to the portion of immediate superjacent airspace, effective control over which is necessary for the landowner's reasonable enjoyment of his land at ground level. Should there be an infringement of such ownership rights, usually an injunction will be awarded by the courts. Case law demonstrates that the courts have to seek to balance the rights of the landowner and those of the general public who, as well as the landowner, have an interest in the use of airspace.

> **KEY CASE:** *BERNSTEIN V SKYVIEWS AND GENERAL LTD* [1978] QB 479; [1977] 2 ALL ER 902
>
> The case concerned defendants flying over the plaintiff's land and taking aerial photograph of his house. The plaintiff claimed this amounted to trespass. In rejecting the claim, Griffiths J explained:
>
>> The problem is to balance the rights of an owner to enjoy the use of his land against the rights of the general public to take advantage of all that science now offers in the use of air space. This balance is in my judgment best struck in our present society by restricting the rights of an owner in the air space above his land to such height as is necessary for the ordinary use and enjoyment of his land and the structures upon it

Control over the airspace above land is restricted to such height as is necessary for the ordinary use and enjoyment of land and structures upon it. Of course, what is reasonable and necessary is a factual matter that needs to be decided on a case by case basis, taking into consideration the alleged infringing activity and surrounding regulations imperative to such activity.

While this means claims over airspace are not unlimited and available only where there is really some interference with possession of land, it does provide clarity regarding protection against trespass into airspace at the height which may interfere with the ordinary user of the land. It prevents the erecting of overhanging structures by adjoining landowners or passing over land, without the need for the claimant to make any argument that damage or annoyance is being caused.

> **KEY CASE:** *KELSEN V IMPERIAL TOBACCO CO* [1957] 2 QB 334; [1957] 2 ALL ER 343
>
> An advertisement sign projecting from an adjoining building and extending in to the airspace above a shop by four inches gave rise to trespass. The claimant sought an injunction to force the defendants to remove the sign. The defendants argued that it was necessary for the claimant to prove that the presence of the sign caused a detriment. However, the court held that the invasion of airspace immediately above land is trespass and therefore it was not necessary for the claimants to prove harm. The injunction was awarded, forcing the defendants to remove the sign.

In *John Trenberth v National Westminster Bank* [1979],[3] the defendant needed to repair his building because it was unsafe. The claimant refused to allow scaffolding to be erected on his land, but the defendant proceeded anyway. The claimant was granted an injunction to prevent this. Similarly, in *Laiqat v Majid* [2005],[4] an extractor fan at about 4.5 m above ground level protruded 750 mm into the claimant's garden. The court held that it was a trespass to the claimant's airspace and it did not matter that the fan had not actually interfered with the claimant's normal use of his garden.

From the above cases, it is apparent that a landowner's claim to airspace should be restricted to such height as is necessary for him to enjoy in an ordinary way the land that he owns and the structures that are placed upon it. Beyond that, he has no more of a claim to airspace than any other member of the public.

The airspace above land is also regulated by statute. For example, s 76 of the Civil Aircraft Act 1982 gives aircraft the general right to fly over land at a height which is reasonable under the circumstances. Furthermore, the Rules of the Air Regulations 1996 (SI 1996/1393) sch 1, reg 5(1)(e) denote that no aircraft may fly closer than 500 feet to any person, vessel, vehicle or structure.

The rights of a landowner are thereby limited to such a height as is necessary for the ordinary use and enjoyment of the land and above that height the landowner has no greater rights than any other member of the public. The landowner's right to bring a claim against potential trespass have to be limited; otherwise the law would be unbalanced.

APPLY YOUR LEARNING – TASK 3

How does defining land as including airspace relate to Philip and the model aircraft? Could he claim trespass?

---

3 [1979] 39 P & CR 104.
4 EWHC 1305 (QB); [2005] All ER (D) 231 (Jun).

BELOW THE SURFACE

The ownership of land below the surface has not been interpreted as being restricted to what is necessary for its ordinary use and enjoyment. The owner of the surface of land owns the strata beneath it, including mines and minerals contained in it, unless there had been an alienation of them by a conveyance, at common law or by statute[5] to someone else.

KEY CASE: *BOCARDO SA V STAR ENERGY UK ONSHORE LTD* [2010] UKSC 35; [2011] 1 AC 380

Star Energy drilled diagonally at a depth of up to 2,900 feet under Bocardo's land to search for and extract a natural reservoir of petroleum and gas. (The oil itself belonged to the Crown, with the argument about ownership of the strata surrounding it.) Bocardo asserted this amounted to trespass and claimed for damages. In response, Star Energy argued that there must be a stopping point whereupon the depth of the earth became too deep for the landowner's interest in his land to be affected.

Lord Hope in the Supreme Court accepted that, although the maxim *cujus est solum ejus est usque ad coelum et ad inferos* is still good law, there must indeed be some practical limits with a point where it would become absurd to argue about the strata belonging to anybody. However, in considering the oil wells that stopping point had not been reached, Lord Hope reasoned that although the drilling was at such depths that it did not interfere with Bocardo's own use of its land, the fact that the petroleum could be reached by human activity raised the question of who owned the petroleum and who owned the land being drilled to reach the petroleum. He concluded:

> The fact that there were substances at that depth which can be reached and got by human activity is sufficient to raise the question as to who, if anybody, is the owner of the strata where they are to be found. The Crown has asserted ownership of the petroleum, but it does not assert ownership of the strata that surround it. The only plausible candidate is the registered owner of the land above

---

The drilling was therefore held to be an actionable trespass and Bocardo was awarded damages.

---

5 For example, coal, oil and gas are under state ownership by virtue of the Coal Industry Act 1994 and the Petroleum Act 1998.

BUILDINGS AND PARTS OF BUILDINGS

Buildings become part of the land, so the house on Meadow Cottage will form part of it. Note also from the statutory definition it is possible for a particular part of a building to be a separate piece of land through a vertical or horizontal division. For example, the top floor of a block of flats may be owned by an individual without that individual owning any of the flats below.

In the same manner that buildings may be part of land, other things may become part of it.

TREES AND PLANTS

Plants growing in the land generally become part of it whether wild or cultivated. However, commercially grown crops may belong to the planter.

WATER

Water passing through the soil through an undefined channel is incapable of ownership.

Water running through a defined channel such as a river or a stream is still incapable of ownership, but the owner of the soil or bed over which the water flows will have certain rights to use that water including fishing and reasonable abstraction for domestic household purposes and agricultural use.

Where a river borders two plots of land, each owner will own the bed up to the mid-point of the river (with the exception of tidal rivers, owned by the Crown).

When owning land next to a river, stream or ditch, however, a number of responsibilities come with the ownership. Such owners are known as a 'riparian landowner'. As a riparian landowner you must ensure that the water flows onto or under your land in its natural quantity and quality. This means that water should not be taken out of a watercourse if it could lead to a lack of water for those who need it downstream. It also means that a person cannot carry out activities that could lead to pollution of the water and therefore reduce the natural water quality within a watercourse. As a landowner, though, you do have the right to protect your property from flooding, and your land from erosion.

WILD ANIMALS

Wild creatures, such as birds or fish, do not belong to anyone. But a landowner does have the right to capture and hunt such animals on his land and, if a creature is captured or killed on his land, it belongs to the landowner.

FIXTURES

Items can become so affixed to land or buildings that they cease to be chattels (movable personal property) and are treated instead as part of the land. Items so attached are referred to as fixtures. A Latin maxim useful in this situation is *quicquid plantatur solo, solo cedit*, which means whatever is attached to the land becomes part of the land. In the Meadow Cottage scenario this means the various objects listed as being at the property prior to the sale to Philip need to have their status checked to see if they formed part of it.

Determining whether an object forms part of land is particularly important when land is being sold. While a seller may take away any items that remain mere chattels or fittings, once a contract is in place fixtures may no longer be removed (unless the seller specifically excludes them from the sale in the contract). Under s 62 of the LPA 1925, the title to the land which passes on to the new purchaser will include all fixtures because they are regarded as being part of the land or building.

The test for determining whether an item affixed to land or a building remains a chattel or has become a fixture considers both the degree of annexation and the purpose of that annexation.[6]

Degree of annexation
The degree of annexation concerns the manner of an item's attachment to land. The (rebuttable) presumption is that an object attached to the land other than by its own weight is a fixture. The firmer that attachment, the stronger the presumption created.

---

6 In regard to sales, a standard Fixtures, Fittings and Contents Form is normally used to avoid uncertainty and make it clear to buyers what items will be included in the sale. The form lists items found in or around property, and allows the vendor to confirm whether each item is included in the sale, excluded, or not at the property.

Conversely, an object unattached the land other than by its own weight or only superficially connected (such as an appliance plugged into an electricity socket or a poster attached to the wall with a drawing pin) is presumed to remain a mere chattel. For example, in *Berkley v Poulett* [1977][7] a very heavy marble statue on a plinth, and a large sundial resting on a stone baluster were not fixtures which passed to the purchaser of a house but mere chattels that the vendor could remove. However, the degree and mode of annexation creates only a *prima facie* initial inference (a rebuttable presumption).

KEY CASE: *HOLLAND V HODGSON* (1872) LR 7 CP 328

The owner of a mill attached looms to the stone floor by nails driven into wooden beams. They could easily be removed. In determining whether the looms were fixtures or chattels, Blackburn J explained:

> Perhaps the true rule is, that articles not otherwise attached to the land than by their own weight are not to be considered as part of the land, unless the circumstances are such as to shew that they were intended to be part of the land, the onus of shewing that they were so intended lying on those who assert that they have ceased to be chattels, and that, on the contrary, an article which is affixed to the land even slightly is to be considered as part of the land, unless the circumstances are such as to shew that it was intended all along to continue a chattel, the onus lying on those who contend that it is a chattel.

It is not only the degree of annexation, but also the purpose or object of annexation which determines status. It was held that the looms had become fixtures.

The mere fixation of a thing to land is not the only criterion by which it is determined whether it is removable. Think about this. Many objects that you might feel are not part of a sale of land would otherwise be included, for example a picture or ornament fixed to a wall with screws to better view and enjoy.

Equally, objects that you might naturally assume form part of land could be excluded by virtue of being free-standing. In *Holland v Hodgson* (1872), the example was given by Blackburn J that:

> [B]locks of stone placed on top of another without any mortar or cement for the purpose of forming a dry stone wall would become part of the land, though the same stones, if deposited in a building yard and for convenience sake stacked on top of each other in the form of a wall, would not.

---

7 [1977] 1 EGLR 86.

For an object resting on the ground by its own weight alone, it may still be found to be a fixture, if it is so heavy that there is no need to tie it into a foundation, and if it were put in place to improve the land.

This instinctive idea that degree of annexation is not alone sufficient is reflected in the other element of the test for fixtures, the purpose of annexation. Indeed, it was suggested in *Hamp v Bygrave* [1983][8] that this second consideration of the test is now the dominant one. After reviewing the authorities on the question of when items become fixtures as opposed to mere chattels, Boreham J concluded that the paramount concern nowadays is the purpose of annexation.

Purpose of annexation
The purpose of annexation relates to why an object was annexed, or the link between the item and the land or building.

If the purpose was so that the chattel may be better enjoyed as a chattel, it will remain a mere chattel or fitting.

KEY CASE: *LEIGH V TAYLOR* [1902] AC 157

Valuable tapestries were affixed by a tenant for life to the walls of a house. In deciding whether they were fixtures, it was determined that they were attached to the building for the purpose of ornament and the better enjoyment of them as chattels. In this case, the manner of the attachment was a consideration in understanding the purpose, with the attachment being such that they could be removed without doing any structural injury.

Similarly, in *Berkley v Poulett* [1977],[9] pictures fixed in the recesses of the panelling of rooms were held to be mere chattels.

If, however, the purpose was to improve the land or building itself, the chattel will then become a fixture.

KEY CASE: *D'EYNCOURT V GREGORY* (1866) LR 3 EQ 382

Tapestries hanging on the walls of a house, ornamental statues resting in the hall, staircase and gardens, stone garden seats and garden vases were held to form part of the land. They were fixtures, forming part of the architectural design of the property. Lord Romilly MR explained:

---

8 [1983] 1 EGLR 174, 266 Estates Gazette 720; [1983] EGD 1000.
9 [1977] 1 EGLR 86.

> I think it does not depend on whether any cement is used for fixing these articles, or whether they rest on their own weight, but upon this--whether they are strictly and properly part of the architectural design for the hall and staircase itself and put in there as such, as distinguished from mere ornaments to be afterwards added.
>
> The case establishes that items resting of their own weight may still be fixtures.

Similarly, in *Vaudeville Electric Cinema Ltd v Muriset* [1923],[10] the items in dispute were seats secured to the floor of a cinema hall. Usually, free-standing seats would be considered chattels. Here, however, they were affixed to make the hall more convenient as a cinema and were held to be fixtures.

The test is whether an item has been brought on the land to be enjoyed or to enhance the land permanently. It is important to note that all cases will depend upon their facts. This leads to the result that the same object may constitute a fixture in one case, but a chattel in another.

Note that in *Elitestone Ltd v Morris* [1997][11] the court expressly cautioned that the intention of the parties is relevant only to the extent that it can be derived from the degree and object of the annexation. The subjective intention of the parties cannot affect the question whether the chattel has become part of the land.

KEY CASE: *BOTHAM V TSB BANK PLC (1997) 73 P & CR D1*

The bank obtained possession of a flat following its owner failing to repay a mortgage and argued that all 109 items were fixtures and so formed part of the land. The case is a useful illustration of how the degree and the purpose of annexation test is applied to determine the status of any item.

Roch LJ affirmed that it is the purpose of annexation which is the key issue, with the degree of annexation serving only as a reminder that there must be some physical annexation before a chattel can become part of land. In terms of discerning the purpose of annexation, he said:

> If the item viewed objectively, is, intended to be permanent and to afford a lasting improvement to the building, the thing will have become a fixture. If the attachment is temporary and is no more than is necessary for the item to be used and enjoyed, then it will remain a chattel.

---

10 [1923] 2 Ch 74.
11 [1997] 2 All ER 513; [1997] 1 WLR 687.

In essence, is an item attached to make a permanent improvement to the land or building, or rather to enhance the enjoyment of the item itself?

The bathroom fittings (including larger items such as the bath and basin and ironmongery such as towel rails, soap dishes and toilet roll holders) were held to be fixtures. The attachment to the building demonstrated a 'significant connection' showing an intention to effect a 'permanent improvement'. They were also necessary to enable the room to be used as a bathroom, and not to be enjoyed in their own right.

The kitchen units, work surfaces and sink were also held to be fixtures, with the degree of annexation making it difficult to remove the fitted units without causing damage to the property.

The fitted carpets, curtains and blinds were held to have remained chattels. The annexation to the land was insubstantial with no indication of an intention to effect a permanent improvement. The method of keeping them in place was no more than required for enjoyment of the items themselves.

With regard to light fittings, gas fires and kitchen appliances it was suggested that much would depend on how they were attached. For example, in relation to the more substantial kitchen appliances, such as hobs, refrigerators, ovens and dishwashers, these may often be integrated into the kitchen as fixtures by design (as opposed to being free-standing, which would suggest they remained chattels). Smaller items such as an electric kettle or a food mixer, which are all normally 'plugged in' would likely be fittings given the slight attachment as necessary for normal use.

Buildings

Houses built into land are clearly attached and so fixtures. However, this does not fit with how they are ordinarily viewed. Buildings themselves are not commonly thought of as fixtures, but rather as part of the land.

To better reflect the more everyday understanding, a threefold classification of chattels, fixtures or a 'part and parcel of the land itself' may be used.

KEY CASE: *ELITESTONE LTD V MORRIS* [1997] 2 ALL ER 513; [1997] 1 WLR 687

The House of Lords when considering the status of a wooden bungalow resting by its own weight on concrete pillars, preferred the threefold classification. Lord Lloyd of Berwick explained this reasoning, saying that:

The nature of the structure is such that it could not be taken down and re-erected elsewhere. It could only be removed by a process of demolition. This, as will appear later, is a factor of great importance in the present case. If a structure can only be enjoyed in situ, and is such that it cannot be removed in whole or in sections to another site, there is at least a strong inference that the purpose of placing the structure on the original site was that it should form part of the realty at that site, and therefore cease to be a chattel. ...

For my part I find it better in the present case to avoid the traditional two-fold distinction between chattels and fixtures, and to adopt the three-fold classification set out in *Woodfall, Landlord and Tenants* ...

> 'An object which is brought onto land may be classified under one of three broad heads. It may be (a) a chattel; (b) a fixture; or (c) part and parcel of the land itself. Objects in categories (b) and (c) are treated as being part of the land.'

So the question in the present appeal is whether, when the bungalow was built, it became part and parcel of the land itself. The materials out of which the bungalow was constructed ... were all, of course, chattels when they were brought onto the site. Did they cease to be chattels when they were built into the composite structure? The answer to the question ... depends on the circumstances of each case, but mainly on two factors, the degree of annexation to the land, and the object of the annexation ...

Many different tests have been suggested, such as whether the object which has been fixed to the property has been so fixed for the better enjoyment of the object as a chattel, or whether it has been fixed with a view to effecting a permanent improvement of the freehold. This and similar tests are useful when one is considering an object such as a tapestry ... These tests are less useful when one is considering the house itself. In the case of the house the answer is as much a matter of common sense as precise analysis. A house which is constructed in such a way so as to be removable ... may well remain a chattel ... But a house which is constructed in such a way that it cannot be removed at all, save by destruction, cannot have been intended to remain as a chattel. It must have been intended to form part of the realty ...

... In *Deen v Andrews* the question was whether a greenhouse was a building so as to pass to the purchaser ... it was not ... It is obvious that a greenhouse which can be moved from site to site is a long way removed from a two bedroom bungalow which cannot be moved at all without being demolished.

The outcome in *Elitestone v Morris* [1997] is usefully contrasted with that in *Chelsea Yacht and Boat Co Ltd v Pope* [2001],[12] which concerned a houseboat moored to the bank of the Thames and connected to various facilities.[13] The houseboat could be untied, the services disconnected, and then it could be towed to a new location. It was held that it did not form part of the land. As Tuckey LJ explained:

> [T]he houseboat rested periodically on the river bed below it and was secured by ropes, and perhaps to an extent the services, to other structures … all these attachments could simply be undone. The houseboat could be moved quite easily without injury to itself or the land

APPLY YOUR LEARNING – TASK 5

Could some of the items the previous owners of Meadow Cottage removed from the house be considered as part of the land purchased by Philip? What about the greenhouse, kitchen and the specimen roses in the garden?

We begin by considering whether an agreement has been made, either in verbal or in written form that specifically states that the items in dispute were to be included in the sale of the property. If there are no indications by way of conveyance, the general test to decide whether an item is a fixture or chattel is laid down in *Holland v Hodgson* (1872). Explore each item individually and select cases which are materially most similar to the dispute.

Take note of the following questions and principles:

- Did the vendor originally affix or bring the items in question onto the property?
- If it is fixed to the land, however slightly, then it is to be classified as a fixture unless there is good reason to classify it as remaining a chattel. Intention to the contrary must be proved. If it is not attached, the presumption is reversed: it is to be classified as a chattel unless there is good reason to classify it as a fixture.
- Was the item brought on the land to be enjoyed or to enhance the land permanently?
- If there is such a degree of physical annexation that an object cannot be removed without serious damage to, or some destruction of, the realty, then there is a strong case for the item to be classified as a fixture. Even if the items were not affixed to the ground, were they on the land for an architectural purpose?

---

12 [2001] 2 All ER 409; [2000] 1 WLR 1941.
13 A more recent example of a case considering the status of houseboats is found in *Tristmire Ltd v Mew* [2011] EWCA Civ 912; [2012] 1 WLR 852.

CONSIDER THIS – 4

Would it make a difference if the kitchen units at Meadow Cottage were free-standing or if the greenhouse could be easily moved without causing its destruction or significant damage?

Exceptions to Quicquid plantatur solo credit

It is possible that a person who is selling land may include a provision in the contract for sale that gives a right to remove fixtures. Exceptions also arise where the person who has affixed the object is a tenant, though they must make good any damage caused by removal of the fixture.

Tenant's fixtures

A tenant under a lease occupies land for a limited period only and when the limited period comes to an end, he will have to return the land to the landlord at the end of the tenancy. This is known as yielding up. The rule is that if a tenant attaches a fixture to the property, it forms part of the land and as such will have to be left at the end of the lease term. It may only be removed if the tenant is still lawfully in possession of it. In order to ensure that this happens the items must be classified as tenant's fixtures to enable the tenant to remove then at the end of the lease.

Tenant's fixtures consist of domestic and ornamental items affixed to the land for the purpose of rendering it more convenient. Stoves, shelves and lighting equipment are types of domestic fixtures, whilst curtains, blinds and beds fastened to walls are ornamental fixtures.

In relation to commercial properties it is even more important that the tenant clearly defines and documents all fixtures to be classified as tenant's fixtures to ensure that they can be removed when the property is yielded up (i.e. returned to the landlord) at the end of the lease.

Trade fixtures

A tenant is entitled to remove fixtures he has installed for the purposes of carrying out his particular trade (*Poole's Case* [1703][14]). They encompass those items that are annexed to the premises to facilitate the storage, handling and display of their stock such as booths, bars, display cases and lights. For example, machinery and equipment in a factory or the fittings of a public house.

So in, *Smith v City Petroleum* [1940],[15] a tenant was entitled to remove petrol pumps from the land because they were trade fixtures and could easily be removed since they were

14 91 ER 320.
15 [1940] 1 All ER 260.

only bolted to the land. In *Young v Dalgety plc* [1987],[16] a tenant who had laid carpets and installed lighting was able to remove them because they were trade fixtures attached to render the premises convenient for the tenant's business use. Or, more recently, in *Peel Land and Property (Ports No 3) Ltd v TS Sheerness Steel Ltd* [2014],[17] heavy industrial plant items installed on site during the term of its lease for use as a steel-making plant.

Agricultural fixtures

Agricultural fixtures are articles that are annexed for the purpose of farming. They can also be viewed as trade fixtures. Farm tenants are given statutory rights under s 8 of the Agricultural Holdings Act 1995, to remove any fixture they have affixed to the land.

LOST ITEMS

The Meadow Cottage scenario raises a number of items which have been misplaced on or in the property. We need to explore whether Philip, as the landowner, has a claim to them and if so the strength of that claim in different circumstances.

Unattached items found on land

For items found lying on the surface of land which are lost or abandoned, the finder of the object will acquire title to it by the fact of possession. The landowner will have a better claim only if the finder was not on the land lawfully, or the landowner acquired an earlier title by manifesting an intention to exercise control over both the land and objects which might be found upon it.

> **KEY CASE:** *PARKER V BRITISH AIRWAYS BOARD* [1982] QB 1004; [1982] 1 ALL ER 834
>
> ----
>
> The case concerned a gold bracelet found on the floor of the executive lounge at an airport, and a dispute about title to the property between the finder and British Airways.
>
> Donaldson LJ began by explaining that should the 'true' owner of property come forward they would have the best claim. He then continued by considering the basis of the finder's claim, that the act of finding a chattel gives the finder rights to it. This was accepted as an argument supported by common law (*Armory v Delamirie* (1722) 1 Strange 505) but with some important qualifications to the general proposition explained:
>
>> [O]ne who 'finds' a lost chattel in the sense of becoming aware of its presence, but who does no more, is not a 'finder' for this purpose and does not, as such, acquire any rights.

----

16 [1987] 1 EGLR 116.

17 [2014] EWCA Civ 100; [2014] 2 P & CR 8. The court noted that any contractual restriction on a tenant's right to remove tenant's fixtures must be clearly stated and without any ambiguity.

Some qualification has also to be made in the case of the trespassing finder. The person vis à vis whom he is a trespasser has a better title. The fundamental basis of this is clearly public policy. Wrongdoers should not benefit from their wrongdoing … Accordingly, the common law has been obliged to give rights to someone else, the owner ex hypothesi being unknown. The obvious candidate is the occupier of the property upon which the finder was trespassing

Donaldson LJ next moved to consider whether a landowner may have stronger title even where an object is found lawfully. Such a claim must be based on the landowner having pre-existing rights in relation to the property immediately before it was found. This required the landowner to manifest an intention to control the land or building and the things which may be upon it or in it. Applying this to the facts of the case, it was determined that the finder had the stronger claim.

The plaintiff was not a trespasser and, in taking the bracelet into his care and control was acting honestly. Prima facie he had a full finder's rights. The defendants could not assert any title as a chattel attached to a building; the bracelet was lying loose on the floor. Their claim must, in his view, be based upon a 'manifest intention to exercise control over the lounge and all things which might be in it'. Donaldson LJ reasoned:

> The evidence is that they claimed the right to decide who should and who should not be permitted to enter and use the lounge, but their control was in general exercised upon the basis of classes or categories of user and the availability of the lounge in the light of the need to clean and maintain it … But this control has no real relevance to a manifest intention to assert custody and control over lost articles. There was no evidence that they searched for such articles regularly or at all …

> It was suggested in argument that in some circumstances the intention of the occupier to assert control over articles lost on his premises speaks for itself. I think that this is right. If a bank manager saw fit to show me round a vault containing safe deposits and I found a gold bracelet on the floor, I should have no doubt that the bank had a better title than I, and the reason is the manifest intention to exercise a very high degree of control. At the other extreme is the park to which the public has unrestricted access during daylight hours. During those hours there is no manifest intention to exercise any such control. In between these extremes are the forecourts of petrol filling stations, unfenced front gardens of private houses, the public parts of shops and supermarkets as part of an almost infinite variety of land, premises and circumstances.

> This lounge is in the middle band and in my judgment, on the evidence available, there was no sufficient manifestation of any intention to exercise control over lost property before it was found

Further illustration of the relevance of control over the land comes from *Hannah v Peel* [1945].[18] Mr Hannah, a lance corporal in the Second World War, was stationed in Mr Peel's house. There he found a brooch lodged near a window frame and gave it to the police. Since no one came forward to claim the item, the item was returned to the landowner, Mr Peel, who kept it. Mr Hannah claimed he had the better title to the brooch. The court concluded that Mr Hannah should have the brooch, reasoning that a landowner does not automatically acquire ownership of items found on his land.

The court used the decision of *Bridges v Hawkesworth* [1851],[19] in which banknotes were found on the floor in a shop; it was held that the banknotes were never in the custody of the landowner and found no reason to deviate from the general rule that the finder of a lost article is entitled to it against all others except the real owner.

In *Hannah v Peel*, the landowner had no knowledge of the item until it was brought to his attention by the police and had not exerted any degree of control or care over the item.

APPLY YOUR LEARNING – TASK 6

Do you think that Philip's brother is entitled to keep the gold necklace he found resting on the grass if its true owner cannot be found?

He was not a trespasser when he found it, and there is no suggestion that Philip was even aware of the item before his brother noticed it.

Philip would need to show he had manifested an intention to exercise control of the land and the things on it. The grass at the front of the house falls somewhere between the 'extremes'. It is not a public park, but nor is it within the house itself. We would need to learn more about factors such as whether the garden is fenced off and how access to the front garden was controlled.

What difference would it make if Philip was taking part in a village 'open garden' day at the time?

CONSIDER THIS – 5

Would it make a difference if the finder of such an item did so in the course of his employment?

South Staffordshire Water Co v Sharman [1896] 2 QB 44; [1895–99] All ER Rep 259 involved two gold rings found by employees cleaning a pool. In holding that the rings did not belong to the finders, Lord Russell of Killowen CJ said:

18 [1945] 1 KB 509; [1945] 2 All ER 288.
19 [1851] 21 LJ QB 75.

The general principle within which the case falls seems to me to be that where there is possession of a house or land, with a manifest intention to exercise control over it, and the things in or upon it, and with control over that particular locus in quo, then if something is found on it by a person who is either a stranger or a servant, the presumption is that the possession of the thing so found is in the owner of that locus in quo. For these reasons I think judgment must be for the plaintiffs.

Items attached to or underneath land

Where an item is found beneath or attached to the land, there is no need for the landowner to manifest an intention to control. The presumption is that the landowner has the better title to the object than the finder. A somewhat dramatic illustration of the principle comes from a prehistoric boat which that was found six feet below the surface of the land being held to belong to the landowner.[20] The possible reasons for this distinction have gradually emerged through case law.

KEY CASE: *WAVERLEY BOROUGH COUNCIL V FLETCHER* [1996] QB 334

The case concerned a park owned by the council, to which members of the public had free access. The council had posted notices prohibiting the use of metal detectors within the park, but they had been torn down. A member of the public lawfully present in the park and unaware of the council's policy, used his metal detector to locate a medieval gold brooch buried in the ground and excavated the soil to a depth of nine inches to recover it. The case was to settle ownership as between the council and the finder.

It is interesting to note from the judgment of Auld LJ that the reasoning behind presuming items beneath the surface are owned by the landowner is not clear. It may be based upon the idea of ownership of land extending to include everything down to the centre of the earth or on the basis that to remove buried objects would be trespass, unless permission was given to start digging. He explained that, with regard to the distinction between things which are on land and things which are attached to or under it:

> In my view, the authorities reveal a number of sound and practical reasons for the distinction.
>
> First, as Donaldson LJ said in *Parker v. British Airways Board* [1982] QB 1004, 1010, an object in land 'is to be treated as an integral part of the realty as against all but the true owner' or that the finder in detaching the object would, in the absence of licence to do so, become a trespasser ... It is also consistent with Chitty J.'s reasoning in the Elwes case, 33 ChD 562, 567, which I have quoted...

---

20 *Elwes v Brigg Gas co* (1886) 33 ChD.

Second, removal of an object in or attached to land would normally involve interference with the land and may damage it…

Third, putting aside the borderline case of a recently lost article which has worked its way just under the surface, in the case of an object in the ground its original owner is unlikely in most cases to be there to claim it. The law, therefore, looks for a substitute owner, the owner or possessor of the land in which it is lodged. Whereas in the case of an unattached object on the surface, it is likely in most cases to have been recently lost, and the true owner may well claim it. In the meantime, there is no compelling reason why it should pass into the possession of the landowner as against a finder unless he, the landowner, has manifested an intention to possess it

CONSIDER THIS – 6

How would the principles apply to a ring found just under the surface of the sand on a beach?

If we apply the principle that an owner of land owns all that is in or attached to it, then the owner of the beach has a right superior to that of the finder. Is there any permission to remove the object because they are entitled to enjoy the beach?

APPLY YOUR LEARNING – TASK 7

Do you think that Philip's brother is entitled to keep the bronze ring found beneath the surface in the back garden?

Treasure

Found items which are classed as treasure under the Treasure Act 1996 belong to the Crown. Any finds which may reasonably be believed to include such items must be reported to the Coroner for Treasure within 14 days in accordance with s 8. A failure to report is a criminal offence punishable by imprisonment and/or a fine.

The definition of treasure was expanded by the Treasure Act 1996, which replaced the narrow protection afforded by the common law. At common law, a treasure trove was limited to objects made substantially of gold or silver and deliberately hidden with the intention of recovery. This meant many valuable items of historical and cultural importance could be appropriated by private finders, rather than preserving them for the nation.

Sections 1–3 of the Treasure Act 1996 removed the need for the object to have been deliberately hidden and widened the meaning of treasure to include:

- Items other than a single coin which are at least 300 years old and contain at least 10 per cent by weight of gold or silver.
- Ten or more coins (whatever the precious metal content) from the same find where at least one is more than 300 years old.
- Anything which would have been a treasure trove under the common law.
- Items designated by the Secretary of State.

Using the powers under s 2(1) of the Treasure Act, the Secretary of State had designated further objects as treasure. The Treasure (Designation) Order 2002 (SI 2002/2666) extends the designation of treasure to include:

(a) any object (other than a coin), any part of which is base metal, which, when found is one of at least two base metal objects in the same find which are of prehistoric date;

(b) any object (other than a coin), which is of prehistoric date, and any part of which is gold or silver.

The Coroner will investigate the status of the object as treasure. If the object is found to be treasure and is to be transferred to a museum, normally the finder and/or the landowner will be paid a reward in line with the Treasure Act 1996 Code of Practice, the latest of which is from 2002.

Rewards where the finder is deliberately searching for artefacts with permission are normally divided equally between the landowner and the finder. Where the finder was not searching for artefacts but made a chance find with permission, again the normal practice is to be divided between the landowner and finder on a 50:50 basis. Where there was no permission, the individual circumstances will be taken into account.

APPLY YOUR LEARNING – TASK 8

How does this relate to the lost items found by Philip's brother?

CONSIDER THIS – 7

What difference could it make if the ring were silver and appeared to be very old?

INCORPOREAL HEREDITAMENTS

There are a range of rights over land which do not give any physical possession, but are still recognised as proprietary. Looking again at the Meadow Cottage scenario, there are rights allowing access over land belonging to another and restricting the use of land belonging to another. We must determine whether they have proprietary status as real property. Despite the importance of the question whether an entitlement creates a property right or merely a personal right, the reasoning behind settled classifications does not provide for absolute answers.

In a somewhat circular argument, the approach adopted to the recognition of property rights is to consider whether they are currently understood to have the effects of a right *in rem*. As Lord Wilberforce explained in *National Provincial Bank Ltd v Ainsworth* [1965]:[21]

> Before a right or interest can be admitted into the category of property, or of a right affecting property, it must be definable, identifiable by third parties, capable in its nature of assumption by third parties, and have some degree of permanence or stability.

In this book, we will in any event identify and explain the key rights you need to learn in relation to land and whether they have been classified as property rights or personal rights. It is still, however, useful at this point to consider some examples of rights falling short of proprietary status, to show you that for such claims the characteristics limiting them to rights *in personam* may already be apparent to you. Keep in mind the factors set out by Lord Wilberforce above.

CONSIDER THIS – 8

Take inviting a neighbour to your house for lunch. The permission is informal and may be easily cancelled. Their right is only a bare licence and entirely personal between the two of you.

Even something that has more formality and creates clearer expectations of some use of land may instinctively not be enough to reach the threshold of giving an interest in land. If you booked a venue in advance for a party on a particular night and paid a deposit, would you expect a new owner of the premises to be bound by your booking? Was this one-off event something with the necessary degree of permanence or stability? This would be a contractual licence, again only a personal right between the parties to the contract.

---

21 [1965] AC 1175; [1965] 2 All ER 472.

APPLY YOUR LEARNING – TASK 9

How does this apply to Philip and the children playing in the garden? Applying the factors set out by Lord Wilberforce, do you think the permission given by the previous owners would amount to a property right?

Remember a property right would have been attached to the estate he purchased, whereas a personal agreement would not.

In contrast, we will next consider two rights that do enjoy recognised proprietary status.

The first is an 'easement', which appears in the statutory definition of land. This is a definite right over one piece of land for the benefit of another piece of land, such as a right of way to cross it by foot or by car or the right to run pipes under its surface. You can see that this right has more than a fleeting relevance to the use of the benefited land, and poses a limit on the use of the burdened land substantial enough to instinctively feel sufficient to pass the threshold to be property.

APPLY YOUR LEARNING – TASK 10

Consider the impact of the recognition of an easement as a property right in relation to Philip and the driveway. Can he argue that the land he purchased had the benefit of the easement attached to it?

CONSIDER THIS – 9

Could it make a difference if Meadow Cottage had its own access to the road and the previous owners of Meadow Cottage were given only temporary verbal permission to use the driveway should wintery weather block their own route?

The second is a restrictive covenant, a promise made in a deed by one owner of land to another not to use it in a certain way. For example, not to use a property for commercial purposes. Again, the benefits and the limits of such an arrangement have been found to meet the threshold to be recognised as proprietary property rights.

APPLY YOUR LEARNING – TASK 11

Consider the impact of the recognition of restrictive covenants as property right in relation to Philip's ability to build his garage. Could the land he purchased have the burden of the covenant attached to it?

OWNERSHIP OF LAND

Technically, all land is owned by the Crown. The concept of tenure recognises that people merely 'hold' a particular piece of land. However, people can 'own' the right to possess, use, enjoy and deal with land by virtue of an estate.

TENURE

After the Norman Conquest, a system of tiered landholding was introduced with the Crown owning all land. Use of the land was distributed between the king's supporters, who held land as his tenants. In return, they pledged the king loyalty and duties, composed of money and services.

The immediate tenants of the king would then grant away rights over the land to subtenants, who would in turn swear oaths to their lord. This process was called subinfeudation. The subtenant could then further subinfeudate. The feudal system thus created was a pyramid of power, with the king at the top and a growing number of lords between him and the tenants at the bottom. They were called mesne lords.

The relationship of service pledged to the king or mesne lord by such a tenant was called tenure. Tenures historically included different types of service – military, spiritual and agricultural. Tenures within this feudal system were free, the tenants having taken them up as a result of choice. Unfortunately, the majority of the population had no status within that system and were not considered to be free (being bound to work as labourers for their lord).

The process of subinfeudation was prohibited in 1290 by the Statute of Quia Emptores, also called the Third Statute of Westminster. The statute halted the growth of the feudal pyramid, and gradually most tenancies came to be held from the Crown. The decline of tenure as a system with any practical importance occurred over time as society developed. First, it became common to extract money in place of services in kind. Next, money too ceased to be collected as payments were fixed and inflation made the amounts so insignificant it became uneconomical to collect. The decline was furthered by the Tenures Abolition Act 1660, which converted most free tenures into 'free and common socage'. Socage tenures have no military or spiritual requirements. The Law of Property Acts 1922 and 1925 completed the process by converting all tenures into socage.

Today, almost all tenants now hold directly from the Crown. While land may at some point have been subject to a mesne lordship created before 1290, it is now highly unlikely such a claim can be made. In the absence of contrary evidence, a tenant is assumed to hold directly of the Crown. The passage of time and the reduction in both the forms of tenure and the very usefulness of enforcing terms of service means any evidence of lordships has all but disappeared. So, while it is still true to say that a landowner holds his land from the Crown, in practice they are most likely unaware of it and the relationship itself is of very little significance.

ESTATES

When Philip makes reference to owning land, what is meant is an estate in land. An estate gives its owner possession of a piece of land to enjoy it for a particular period of time.

Estates are what interests, such as the easements and the restrictive covenants referred to earlier, are granted against for the benefit of another.

> TUTOR TIP – 2
> ....
>
> The terms tenure and estate are often confused. Remember that tenure relates to the conditions of landholding and estates to the nature and duration of possession or enjoyment of a piece of land.
>
> While studying land, you will be most interested in estates as tenure has negligible practical significance in modern law.

The legal estates recognised in land before 1925 are as follows:

Fee Simple – In theory a fee simple can last indefinitely, and is therefore the greatest estate possible and closest thing possible to absolute ownership of land. A fee simple in land will come to an end only if the current owner dies without a will and without next of kin. If there is no will and no next of kin it reverts to the Crown *bona vacantia* (this literally translates from the Latin as 'ownerless goods').

Entail – The entail, or fee tail, lasts as long there is a certain class of descendant of the original grantee (the person to whom the grant was made). Should the line of descendants run out, the entail terminates.

Life Estate – A life estate, really a life interest, lasts for the lifetime of some person and comes to an end upon their death. They are normally granted for the lifetime of the grantee, but can be linked to the lifetime of another person.[22]

Lease or Term of Years – In a lease over land, or term of years absolute, the maximum duration is fixed and the estate will come to an end once that time expires.

> TUTOR TIP – 3
> ....
>
> Students sometimes make the mistake of thinking that a piece of land can only have one owner. In fact the concept of the estate allows one piece of land to have several 'owners'.

....

22 Since 1925, the life estate can no longer be recognised at law and so may only now be an equitable interest arising under a trust. It should now, therefore, always be referred to as a life interest but do not be surprised if the older terminology is sometimes used.

> For example, if Philip owns the fee simple to Meadow Cottage he can grant a lease over all of the property or just part of it in favour of another person (Sam). The owner of that lease can potentially in turn then grant somebody else (Ben) a shorter lease out of their leasehold estate.
>
> Philip (fee simple) → Sam (20-year lease)
> ↓
> Ben (2-year sublease)

While all of the estates listed were once recognised at law, in order to simplify the ownership of land the Law of Property Act 1925 (LPA 1925) reduced the number of legal estates to two.

The two legal estates are set out in s 1(1) of the LPA 1925:

> The only estates and interests in land which are capable of subsisting or of being conveyed or created at law are –
>
> (a) an estate in fee simple absolute in possession;
> (b) a term of years absolute.

The fee simple absolute in possession (more commonly referred to as a 'freehold estate') and the term of years or leasehold estate are the only ways you can be said to own land in law.

APPLY YOUR LEARNING – TASK 12

When Philip refers to being the legal owner of Meadow Cottage, he must be the owner of either the freehold estate or a leasehold estate.

The point to be made will not fully make sense until you read the next chapter explaining the role in land played by a system called equity. For now, note that the other estates still have a role to play but as confirmed by s 1(3) of the LPA 1925: 'All other estates, interests, and charges in or over the land take effect as equitable interests.'

So, the entails and life estates we considered above are only capable of recognition in equity. Also, the only type of free simple legally recognised is one in possession.

TUTOR TIP – 4

Students are often confused by the difference between the fee simples.

A fee simple can be a fee simple absolute in possession (which has legal status as an estate) or a fee simple in reversion or remainder (which can only be equitable interests).

In possession means that the owner has physical possession of the land (or is in receipt of rents of profits or the rights to receive the same – i.e. where they have granted a lease). In remainder means that there is currently no possession but only a future entitlement to it, because there is some prior interest such as a life interest.

For example, Philip may grant a life interest in the fee simple to Meadow Cottage. (This could once have created a lifetime estate in law, but since 1925 could only be an equitable 'life interest'.)

If Philip created a life interest in favour of his daughter (Beth) then that settlement does not exhaust the fee simple. Therefore, upon the daughter's death, the possession will revert to Philip (or, if he is also dead, the next people entitled). Philip has a fee simple in reversion. This could have been a legal estate prior to 1925, but may now only be an equitable 'interest in reversion'.

   Beth (life interest) → Philip (fee simple in reversion/interest in reversion)

If Philip left the fee simple for life to his widow (Joanne), thereafter to his daughter (Beth) in fee simple, then the daughter has a fee simple in remainder. This could have been a legal estate prior to 1925, but may now only be an equitable 'interest in remainder'.

   Joanne (life interest) → Beth (fee simple in remainder/interest in remainder)

Each of the parties does have an interest in Meadow Cottage. While they do not have physical possession of Meadow Cottage, they have future right to it and all of these interests may be owned, bought and sold from the date they are created.

However, since 1925, they are only recognised in equity and are enforceable as equitable interests. We will explore the role played by equity in the next chapter.

DISCUSSION

The definition of land is extensive, including a range of tangible and intangible elements.

CONSIDER THIS – 10

Having considered the statutory definition of land, how does your answer in defining 'land' differ for your initial view?

A common question asked of students is to consider just how useful and accurate the maxim *cujus est solum ejus est usque ad coelum et ad inferos* is.

The physical extent of a piece of land can itself be difficult to settle, but in any event what we are really concerned with are the rights people may have in land. These rights allow the use of land to be sliced into sections of time, via estates, and for various claims to be made over it which cannot be seen but are of real benefit to its enjoyment.

The need for such a range of rights is because of the nature of land; it is expensive, essential and limited in its availability. The difficulty is that it sometimes makes it hard to spot some of the more abstract elements. As we move away from the centre starting point of the physical plot of land, the rights cannot be seen just by looking at the corporeal.

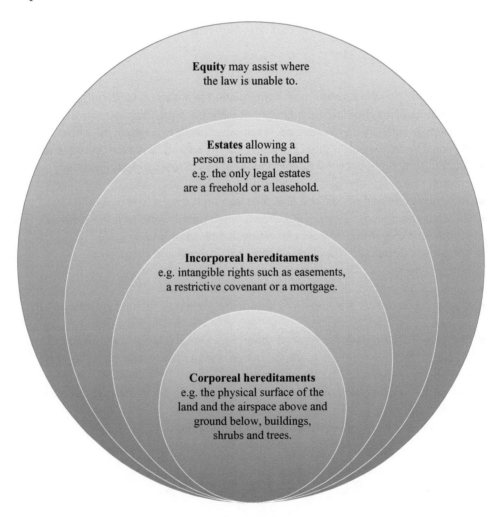

Equity may assist where the law is unable to.

Estates allowing a person a time in the land e.g. the only legal estates are a freehold or a leasehold.

Incorporeal hereditaments e.g. intangible rights such as easements, a restrictive covenant or a mortgage.

Corporeal hereditaments e.g. the physical surface of the land and the airspace above and ground below, buildings, shrubs and trees.

Figure 2.3 Defining land: beyond the tangible

CONSIDER THIS – 11

What issues might such a wide and somewhat abstract definition result in for purchasers of land? They cannot see the existence, nature and extent of rights just by looking at the property.

Keep this in mind throughout our exploration of land law in this book, as we discover how these difficulties have been mitigated by formalities for creating and proving real property rights and consider where problems persist.

END OF CHAPTER SUMMARY

- The starting point in providing advice in relation to a claim is to identify whether the individual may hold a property right or personal right.
- Property/proprietary rights are rights *in rem* which are good against the whole world.
- Personal rights are only right *in personam*, good only against a particular person.
- The property rights we will be exploring are those in real property (including chattels real or leasehold).
- An action in respect of land will give the claimant the right to recover the land.
- All land is held on tenure from the Crown; when people refer to themselves as landowners they mean they own an estate in a piece of land.
- Land is widely defined to include a range of corporeal and incorporeal hereditaments.
- Common law and equity are both applied in relation to land.
- Sometimes it can be challenging to determine when an item has become attached or affixed to the land.
- The owner of land does not have a better claim than the finder to items found on it unless they have manifest an intention to exercise control over both the land and objects which might be found upon it.
- The owner of land does have a better claim to items found in the land (beneath the surface).
- There are only two legal estates, freehold and leasehold.

PREPARING FOR ASSESSMENTS
QUESTIONS

ESSAY QUESTION

To what extent can prospective purchasers of an estate in land be certain which buildings and other elements form part of it and of its boundaries?

PROBLEM QUESTION

While setting off for a walk, Alan noticed a necklace stuck in the branches of a bush planted in his garden but overhanging into the garden of his neighbour. To reach the necklace, he had to reach over the fence dividing the two properties. The owner of the house, Brian, a very private person, saw him take the necklace. He alleges that Brian was trespassing and that the item was found on his property so must be returned to him.

Alan's walk led him into a park open to the public. On the main path in the park, he spotted a £20 note and picked it up. He then saw something small and shiny resting at the bottom of a shallow stream running through the park. Upon digging away the mud in which the majority of the object was embedded, Alan realised it was a gold ring and quickly put it in his pocket along with the money. A park attendant saw both events, and now the park owners are challenging his claim to the property.

Determine who has the stronger titles.

FURTHER READING

- Bray, J, 'The Law on Treasure from a Land Lawyer's Perspective' [2013] Conv 265. Considers the complex rules regarding claims to a find of treasure.
- Bridge, S, 'Part and Parcel: Fixtures in the House of Lords' (1997) 56 CLJ 498. Considers the case *Elitestone Ltd v Morris* [1997] 1 WLR 687 and whether a chalet which rested on concrete pillars and was not attached to ground was fixture or chattel.
- Gray, K, 'Property Rights in Thin Air' (1991) 50 CLJ 252. An analysis of meaning of 'property', from a jurisprudential perspective.
- Haley, M, 'The Law of Fixtures: An Unprincipled Metamorphosis?' [1998] Conv 137. Examines the application of tests of method and degree of annexation and object and purpose of annexation in determining whether items are fixtures or chattels, considering the case of *Botham v TSB Bank plc* [1996] EG 149 (CS) (CA (Civ Div)).
- Hoath, DC, 'Some Conveyancing Implications of "Finding" Disputes' [1990] Conv 348. Explores the law surrounding conflicting claims to items found by an occupier of land.
- Nugee, E, 'The Feudal System and the Land Registration Acts' (2008) 124 LQR 586. An argument that the feudal system still largely exists in England and Wales.

3

CHAPTER 3
COMMON LAW AND EQUITY

CHAPTER AIMS AND OBJECTIVES

In this chapter we will consider the two sets of rules or systems which apply to landownership: common law and equity. The limitations of the common law system will be considered first, followed by an explanation of the development of equity and the evolution of the 'trust'. The impact of legal and equitable interests and remedies specifically in relation to land will then be explored and applied.

By the end of this chapter, you should be able to:

- appreciate the development and inadequacies of the common law system;
- understand the role of equity in resolving the deficiencies of the common law;
- explain the evolution and nature of the trust;
- distinguish between rights recognised by equity or equitable interests and rights recognised by law or legal interests;
- apply the above to the case study and learning tasks.

CASE STUDY – ONE

Emily was the legal owner of the freehold title to Woodland Cottage. She transferred the property to her friend, Marie, on trust for her disabled nephew, Charlie. Marie has now decided to sell Woodland Cottage to Matthew. Consider the implications for Matthew of the following:

(a) Matthew has been told about the interest of Charlie in Woodland Cottage.
(b) Alternatively, Matthew has not been informed about Charlie, but Charlie is currently living at Woodland Cottage.
(c) While still the legal owner of the property, Emily entered into the following transactions:

   (i) An agreement with a neighbour purporting to grant him a five-year lease over a section of Woodland Cottage's garden for use as an allotment, with a right of way by foot to cut across the property's garden to reach it. The neighbour has a document containing all the terms, dated and signed by both parties.
   (ii) A covenant with a neighbour preventing use of Woodland Cottage for anything other than residential purposes.

COMMON LAW AND EQUITY

To understand the nature and impact of the various property rights or interests affecting Woodland Cottage, we need to distinguish between legal and equitable rights. While no longer administered by separate courts, the rules governing the availability and effect of legal, as opposed to equitable, interests and remedies remain clearly distinct.

THE COMMON LAW

Before the Norman Conquest, local law and customs governed different parts of England and Wales. After the Conquest a system of uniform law was created that applied generally rather than varying locally and so became known as 'common law', enforced in the courts of the king. The courts would interpret and uphold the king's law, a practice which over time developed into the modern understanding of common law as being judge-made law. Later still, it was settled that common law may be altered or ended by an Act of Parliament and new laws created.

The common law system had a number of inadequacies, including that:

- An action could only be commenced if an appropriate royal writ was available and after 1258 the Provisions of Oxford prevented any further expansion by the courts of the writ system to cover new forms of action.
- The common law remedy of damages was often unsuitable for responding to the particular needs of plaintiffs.
- The common law was preoccupied with formalities or 'form', ignoring the 'substance' of agreements between and the behaviour of parties.

> TUTOR TIP – 1
>
> Having an appreciation of the historic development of the common law is useful to understanding its role and nature. For the purposes of your land law course, however, the meaning of common law (usually referred to simply as Law) can be summarised as judge-made law as amended by Acts of Parliament.

THE DEVELOPMENT OF EQUITY

The deficiencies in common law resulted in appeals to the king personally, asking that justice be done. The number of petitions meant they began to be passed to the Lord Chancellor, a cleric able to apply principles of justice and good conscience. Eventually, the practice became to send appeals directly to the Lord Chancellor. From this the Court of Chancery evolved.

The different origins of the Court of Chancery and the common law courts led to clear differences between them, creating distinctions in legal and equitable entitlement which still apply today:

■ The focus of equity is on what is just and fair, looking to the substance or reality behind the intentions and actions of parties not just at whether the right formalities were followed. The law is instead strictly concerned with whether the right formalities and procedures were adhered to. Equity has developed its own maxims (principles that guide its operation) such as:

  ■ *Equity will not suffer a wrong without a remedy*
  ■ *Equity looks to substance not form*
  ■ *Equity will not permit a statute to be used as an instrument of fraud*
  ■ *Equity sees as done that which ought to be done*

■ The application of these maxims has resulted in a range of equitable remedies beyond the mere award of damages available through law, most notably, for our purposes, injunctions ordering the defendant to desist or refrain from a particular action and specific performance ordering the defendant to carry out a promise.
■ Equity has created new rights unavailable at law, including the institution of the trust.
■ The award of equitable remedies is at the discretion of the court, whereas the legal remedy of damages is available as of right (can be demanded) so long as the case is proved.
■ Whereas legal rights are good against the world and so may be enforced against anyone who acquires the land irrespective of whether they knew about it, equitable rights are enforceable against anyone except a bona fide purchaser without notice of the right. We will explore the implications of this and the term 'bona fide' shortly; it means those who purchase property genuinely in good faith.

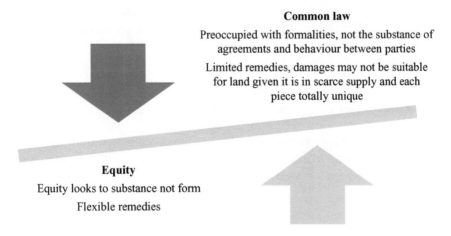

Common law

Preoccupied with formalities, not the substance of agreements and behaviour between parties

Limited remedies, damages may not be suitable for land given it is in scarce supply and each piece totally unique

Equity

Equity looks to substance not form

Flexible remedies

Figure 3.1 The differences between the law and equity

Unpredictability in equitable decisions was reduced when the office of the Lord Chancellor began to be awarded to lawyers rather than ecclesiastics; prior to that change Lord Chancellors often had differing views on what justice and good conscience demanded. The appointment of lawyers as Lord Chancellors gradually resulted in less of such variations and the systemisation of equity into a set of relatively rigid rules. While modern equitable principles are still more flexible than those of the law, there are now settled rules governing the exercise of the court's discretion.

The problems caused by rivalry and duplication between the two courts was not resolved until the Judicature Acts of 1873 and 1875. The court system was completely reorganised and the old higher courts were abolished and a new Supreme Court of Judicature created. The split in the court system between common law and equity was fused, with the Supreme Court able to award both legal and equitable remedies on any matter that comes before it. From that point, the law and equity have continued to be applied under one roof. Section 25 of the Judicature Act 1873 also provides that in the case of a conflict between the rules of law and equity, equity shall prevail.[1]

> TUTOR TIP – 2
> ....
>
> While law and equity are now administered in the same court, the rules applied to determine legal rights and remedies still differ from those in equity. The key implication of this for the study of land is that in relation to any piece of property, there can exist both legal and equitable rights.
>
> A good tip is to remember that you always start by considering the position at law before moving to equity, as reflected by the important equitable maxim that *Equity follows the law.*

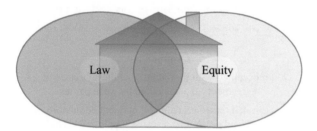

The court will apply both the law and equity to resolve a dispute in relation to property.

It will start with the law but if the principles and remedies in equity provide a fairer result, remember that equity prevails.

Figure 3.2 Equity operating alongside the law

Now that you have an appreciation of the broad distinctions between law and equity, the next stage in advising Matthew is to consider the status of each of the property rights raised in the scenario as legal or equitable.

LEGAL INTERESTS IN LAND

We saw in the last chapter that property rights in land are divided into estates and rights that exist over the land of another. We also considered that, in order to simplify the ownership of land, the Law of Property Act 1925 (LPA 1925) reduced the number of

---

1   See also *Earl of Oxford's Case* (1616) 1 Rep Ch 1.

estates recognised at law to two; freehold and leasehold. For the same reasons, the LPA 1925 also limited the number of legal interests in land. Section 1(2) of LPA 1925 provides:

> The only interests or charges in or over land which are capable of subsisting or of being conveyed or created at law are—
>
> (a) An easement, right, or privilege in or over land for an interest equivalent to an estate in fee simple absolute in possession or a term of years absolute;
> (b) A rentcharge in possession issuing out of or charged on land being either perpetual or for a term of years absolute;
> (c) A charge by way of legal mortgage;
> (d) … any other similar charge on land which is not created by an instrument;
> (e) Rights of entry exercisable over or in respect of a legal term of years absolute, or annexed, for any purpose, to a legal rentcharge.

Any interest of a type not listed in s 1(2) and granted for a period equivalent to one of the two legal estates (i.e. a freehold or leasehold) can never be legal. However, s 1(3) of the LPA 1925 provides that it may still be recognised as an equitable interest: 'All other estates, interests, and charges in or over land take effect as equitable interests.'

Equity only recognises a limited range of such interests, which we will explore in the next section. First, we need to outline the legal interests listed in s 1(2).

EASEMENTS AND PROFITS (S 1(2)(A))

An easement is a right over piece of land for the benefit of another, such as a right of way or rights to drainage or support.

A 'profit à prendre' (profit) is a right to enter the land of another and to take something from it, such as wild game or timber.

TUTOR TIP – 3

As profits are not expressly referred to in s 1(2) of the LPA 1925, students sometimes forget that they are one of the legal interests recognised in land. Their inclusion is implicit in the wording of s 1(2)(a) 'an easement, right or privilege'.

Easements and profits are covered in detail in Chapter 12.

RENTCHARGES (S 1(2)(B))

An annual or periodic payment by the owner of a freehold estate to the owner of the rentcharge. If payment is not made, the owner of the rentcharge has a right of entry to the land to enforce it.

It was once common for vendors of land to impose rentcharges to produce continuing income after sale. The Rentcharges Act 1977 prohibits the creation of any new rentcharges of that type but makes an exception for 'estate rentcharges'. An estate rentcharge allows for collection of service charges for repairs or other benefits to the land affected by the rentcharge. Services could include the upkeep of shared facilities such as estate roads or providing landscaping. These rentcharges may be used to enforce the performance of positive covenants in freehold land, a point which will be discussed in Chapter 14.

> ## TUTOR TIP – 4
>
> Students often mistake a rentcharge for the rent paid under the terms of a lease. Remember that a rentcharge relates to freehold estates.

CHARGE BY WAY OF LEGAL MORTGAGE (S 1(2)(C))

A mortgage charges an estate with the repayment of a debt. The mortgage provides the lender with security for the loan, giving them an estate or interest in the property enabling them to take possession and sell it should the loan not be repaid. Mortgages will be explored fully in Chapter 13.

ANY OTHER SIMILAR CHARGE ON LAND WHICH IS NOT CREATED BY AN INSTRUMENT (S 1(2)(D))

Rarely of relevance today and discussed no further.

RIGHTS OF ENTRY (S 1(2)(E))

Rights of entry are commonly included in leases enabling landlords to re-enter leased property should the tenant breach their obligations.

They are also attached to rentcharges, allowing the owner of the rentcharge to enter and take possession of the property if it is not paid.

> ### APPLY YOUR LEARNING – TASK 1
>
> The lease is potentially legal, as leasehold is one of the two legal estates under s 1(1) LPA 1925. Can you identify which one of the legal interests under s 1(2) is raised by the right of way by foot over Woodland Cottage?

THE REQUIREMENT OF A DEED

The creation or transfer of a legal estate or interest normally requires a deed to be used. Section 52(1) of the LPA 1925 provides: 'All conveyances of land or any interest therein are void for the purpose of conveyancing or creating a legal estate unless made by deed.'

An exception to this is short leases under s 54(2) of the LPA 1925. To qualify, the lease must be of no more than three years, with immediate possession (i.e. the tenant is to occupy right away) at the best rent which can be reasonably obtained (i.e. a market rent), without taking a fine (a lump sum payment). Short leases do not have to be in writing at all.

If a deed was not used when required, the next best which can be claimed is an equitable interest. The possibility of this is considered in the next section, on equitable rights in land.

Whether the requirements for a valid deed were met depends upon when the estate or interest was created or transferred. For deeds executed before 31 July 1990, the deed was required to be signed, sealed and delivered. For deeds created on or after 31 July 1990, the requirement for a seal (historically in red wax) was abolished. A document is now required only to make clear on its face that it is a deed, be signed by the grantor executing the deed, witnessed and delivered.

The modern requirements are set out in ss 1(2) and (3) of the Law of Property (Miscellaneous Provisions) Act 1989 (LP(MP)A 1989). Section 1(2) provides:

An instrument shall not be a deed unless—

(a) it makes it clear on its face that it is intended to be a deed by the person making it or, as the case may be, by the parties to it (whether by describing itself as a deed or expressing itself to be executed or signed as a deed or otherwise); and
(b) it is validly executed as a deed by that person or, as the case may be, one or more of those parties.

Section 1(3) continues:

An instrument is validly executed as a deed by an individual if, and only if—

(a) it is signed—

   (i) by him in the presence of a witness who attests the signature; or
   (ii) at his direction and in his presence and the presence of two witnesses who each attest the signature; and

(b) it is delivered as a deed by him or a person authorised to do so on his behalf.

EQUITABLE INTERESTS IN LAND

Equity has created interests that are incapable of being recognised by the common law. The most important to note in relation to land are set out below.

THE TRUST

The development of the trust enables land to be held by one person for the benefit of another. To better understand the vital role played by trusts, it is useful for us to start by briefly exploring the origins of trusts and then to consider the modern institution.

At the time of the Crusades, it became common practice for knights to transfer their ownership of land to a trusted person (the transferee) on the understanding that they would use the land to benefit the wife and children of the knight while he was away. The common law recognised the transferee as the legal owner but then had no means of enforcing the promise made to manage the property for the family.

To prevent the transferee acting unconscionably by ignoring his undertaking, equity intervened by ordering the transferee to carry out its terms. The terminology was that the transferee held as a 'feoffee to uses', with the transfer of the land (or feoffment) to him having certain conditions. The result was that while the transferee was the owner at common law, the people he held for the benefit of had equitable ownership of the same piece of land. The equitable title to the land gave the right to the enjoyment of it and to compel performance according to the directions and obligations imposed in the transfer.

The modern terminology no longer makes reference to uses, instead referring to trusts. But the effect remains the same, with ownership of land being split into a position in law and one in equity. The holder of the legal title (called the trustee) must deal with the estate for the benefit of a person or persons who hold the equitable title (called beneficiaries).

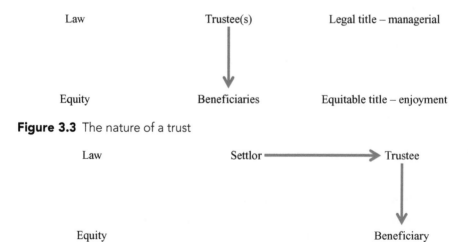

Law   Trustee(s)   Legal title – managerial

Equity   Beneficiaries   Equitable title – enjoyment

Figure 3.3 The nature of a trust

Law   Settlor ⟶ Trustee

Equity   Beneficiary

Figure 3.4 Constituting a trust, with another to act as the trustee

Express trusts

Express trusts enable property owners (called the settlor) to vest legal title and thereby administrative and management powers in trustees; the property can be used upon particular terms to provide for beneficiaries unable to deal with it themselves. A common example is to create on behalf of children, until they are old enough to receive it.

The settlor may either declare himself a trustee or transfer the property to a third party who has agreed to act as trustee.

An express declaration of trust must be evidenced in writing, according to s 53(1)(b) of the LPA 1925: 'A declaration of trust respecting any land or any interest therein must be manifested and proved by some writing signed by some person who is able to declare such trust or by his will.'

> **APPLY YOUR LEARNING** – TASK 2
>
> Can you identify who is the current legal owner of Woodland Cottage, and who has the equitable ownership? Draw a diagram identifying the trustee and beneficiary. What requirements will have been followed by Emily in creating the express trust? Would an oral declaration be sufficient?

Implied trusts

Trusts also arise by implication, based either upon the presumed intention of the settlor (resulting trusts) or when imposed by the courts as it would be unconscionable of the owner of property not to hold it on trust for someone else (constructive trusts). These trusts may be implied in a range of circumstances; for now it is useful to introduce briefly some of the key ways in which they operate in relation to land.

A presumed resulting trust occurs in favour of a person who makes a contribution to the purchase price of an estate but is not then registered as a legal owner. The beneficial share in the property will be in proportion to their contribution.[2]

Constructive trusts are based upon the 'common intention' between parties to hold the beneficial ownership of land jointly. One may arise if a party relies upon the intention to their detriment.[3] The common intention may be express or can be inferred from the conduct of the parties in making direct financial contributions to the purchase price or mortgage. The beneficial share is not, however, dependent on the proportion contributed, but rather upon the conduct of the parties taking into account a wide range of factors.[4]

---

2 *Dyer v Dyer* [1788] EWHC Exch J8; (1788) 2 Cox Eq Cas 92.
3 *Lloyds Bank plc v Rosset* [1990] UKHL 14; [1991] 1 AC 107; [1990] 1 All ER 1111.
4 *Stack v Dowden* [2007] UKHL 17; [2007] 2 AC 432; [2007] 2 All ER 929.

A constructive trust can also be created by entering into a binding contract for the sale of land. Once there is a valid contract, the vendor becomes a trustee for the purchaser of the property.[5] They should, for example, maintain the property until the sale is completed.

Both resulting and constructive trusts are exempted by s 53(2) of the LPA 1925 from the formalities of requiring writing.

CONSIDER THIS – 1

The Woodland Cottage scenario raises an express trust.

How could you argue an implied trust if the facts were instead that, while not a legal owner:

(a) Charlie contributed half of the purchase price when Emily first acquired the legal title, or
(b) Charlie was allowed to move in after the purchase and assured by Emily that the house was 'as much his as hers'. In reliance upon that agreement, Charlie contributed to mortgage payments.

We will look at both the creation of trusts as well as structure and the rights of beneficiaries in much more detail in Chapters 9, 10 and 11.

RESTRICTIVE COVENANTS

Freehold covenants are imposed by sellers of land to either limit how it will be used (for example, preventing building work) or to require the purchaser to carry out a particular activity (for example, erecting a boundary fence). They are often used where a landowner is only selling part of his land, and therefore wants to control what happens next door.

Where limits are imposed (as opposed to a positive duty) the undertaking is called a restrictive covenant. In equity, such promises may be enforceable not only between the original parties to the agreement, but also between successors in title. So, for example, a purchaser of the land with the benefit of the covenant could enforce the undertaking and a purchaser of the land with the burden of the covenant would be subject to the restriction.

---

5 *Shaw v Foster* (1871–72) LR 5 HL 321.

APPLY YOUR LEARNING – TASK 3

Is the covenant in relation to Woodland Cottage restrictive and what would that mean about its potential to bind Matthew should he purchase it?

The enforcement of freehold covenants is discussed in depth in Chapter 14.

INFORMALLY CREATED INTERESTS

Potentially legal estates and interests require certain formalities to be completed, in order to create them at law, for example the requirement for a deed. Where the legal formalities are not complied with, equity may still view that an interest has been created provided there is an enforceable agreement. This has given rise to equitable equivalent interests such as leases, easements, profits à prendre and mortgages.

KEY CASE: *PARKER V TASWELL* (1858) 22 JP 432, 2 DE G & J 559; (1858) 44 ER 1106

An agreement purporting to grant a lease did not create a legal lease (it lacked the formalities of the deed required to do so), but it did create an equitable equivalent interest based on there being an enforceable contractual agreement. Equity would give the remedy of specific performance, requiring that the lease be granted as promised. However, if we now think back to the maxim *Equity sees as done that which ought to be done*, what the court was actually able to hold was that there has been an equitable lease from the date of the contract. A lease of the same duration and with the same terms, an equivalent lease in equity.

In order for a failed attempt to create a legal estate or interest to create an equitable interest, there must be an enforceable contract in accordance with the criteria in s 2 of the LP(MP)A 1989. The requirements of this Act were in fact introduced as a response to the difficulties cases such as *Parker v Taswell* (1858) caused; to reduce uncertainty about when a binding agreement has been reached and also what the terms of the agreement are. In order to be effective, land contracts are now required to be in writing, to incorporate all the terms and to be signed by the parties:

(1) A contract for the sale or other disposition of an interest in land can only be made in writing and only by incorporating all the terms which the parties have expressly agreed in one document or, where contracts are exchanged, in each.
(2) The terms may be incorporated in a document either by being set out in it or by reference to some other document.
(3) The document incorporating the terms or, where contracts are exchanged, one of the documents incorporating them (but not necessarily the same one) must be signed by or on behalf of each party to the contract.

TUTOR TIP – 5

Remember that where the land contract relates to the creation or conveyance of a legal estate in land (i.e. freehold or leasehold) or to an option to purchase or rights of pre-emption, it is called an 'estate contract'.

APPLY YOUR LEARNING – TASK 4

The agreement in relation to Woodland Cottage purporting to grant a five-year lease and an easement fails to satisfy the requirements for a deed, but could the contracts comply with s 2 of the LP(MP)A 1989?

If you are satisfied that there is possibly a valid land or estate contract, there is another step before equity will assist. Specific performance, as are all equitable remedies, is discretionary. The first condition that must be met is that the contract complies with s 2 as above. The second, is that the claimant has given consideration because *Equity will not assist a volunteer* forms another maxim. The third, required the claimant to come with 'clean hands' so not fraudulently or dishonestly.

Assuming the neighbour has paid for the lease and easement and is not doing anything that would cause him to have 'dirty hands', there is no reason for specific performance not to be available.

AGREEMENTS TO GRANT INTERESTS

Agreements to grant an estate of interest in the future ('I promise to grant you') may also be enforceable in equity, provided the agreement is contained in a valid contract complying with s 2 of the LP(MP)A 1989 as set out above.

KEY CASE: *WALSH V LONSDALE* (1882) LR CH D 9

While a contractual agreement to grant a seven-year lease could not create a legal lease (for which a grant by deed was required), it did create an equitable equivalent seven-year lease based on the enforceable agreement. The court would order specific performance of the contract and *Equity sees as done that which ought to be done.*

The doctrine of *Walsh v Lonsdale* (1882) is not limited to creating equitable leases, so could this be used to assist with both the lease and the right of way relating to Woodland Cottage?

APPLY YOUR LEARNING – TASK 5

Based on the contractual agreement for a lease and an easement, what would be the outcome if specific performance is available and the maxim *Equity sees as done that which ought to be done* is applied? Would the doctrine of *Walsh v Lonsdale* create legal rights or equitable rights equivalent to what was agreed?

TIME

Any interest not granted for a period equivalent to one of the two legal estates (i.e. a freehold or leasehold) can never be legal. So if, for example, a right of way was created for someone's lifetime it could only ever be recognised in equity.

EXCEPTIONS TO THE REQUIREMENTS OF S 2 OF THE LP(MP)A 1989

The purpose of s 2 of the LP(MP)A 1989 is to avoid uncertainty about when an enforceable land contract has been entered into, as before that stage neither side can sue the other for specific performance. Yet, notable exceptions are made. These include:

- Contracts to grant short leases (s 2(5)(a) of the LP(MP)A 1989).
- Collateral contracts, separate to the disposition in land.[6]
- Where a proprietary estoppel is upheld.
- Where a resulting or constructive trust may be imposed (s 2(5)(c) of the LP(MP)A 1989).

The arguments of estoppel or constructive trust have proved to be particularly controversial, given it may allow agreements to be upheld in the absence of the contractual certainty s 2 is designed to ensure. As a result, the courts have demonstrated that while willing to apply estoppel and to impose constructive trusts they will do so cautiously. In circumstances where a contract would still have been expected to settle expectations, a finding that the person making the claim in equity was assured of some right will be difficult to argue. In Chapter 16 on Proprietary Estoppel we will consider a number of cases and the view expressed on the relationship with s 2. In relation to constructive trusts, a common intention trust may arise after the owner of an estate in land enters into an agreement with a claimant that they will have a beneficial interest in respect of that estate which the claimant then relies upon to his detriment. Chapter 9, 'Express, Resulting and Constructive Trusts', explores common intention trust in depth. For now, one example will suffice.

6 For a recent example of the difficulties determining when this may be argued, see *Keay v Morris Homes (West Midlands) Ltd* [2012] EWCA Civ 900; [2012] 1 WLR 2855. The terms of the agreement relating to the land have to be in writing, and verbal terms may not be recognised.

KEY CASE: *YAXLEY V GOTTS* [2000] CH 162; [1999] 3 WLR 1217

An oral agreement by the owner of land to grant a builder ownership of the ground floor of a house, in exchange for him undertaking significant work on the property, was held to be enforceable as a constructive trust after the builder fulfilled the arrangement.

ENFORCEMENT OF EQUITABLE INTERESTS

As we discussed in Chapter 2, property rights may bind anyone taking possession of land in the future (as opposed to personal rights or rights *in personam*, enforceable only against some specific person). The actual conditions for proprietary rights to bind in this manner depend on whether the right is classed as legal or equitable.

Legal estates and interests fit clearly into the category of rights *in rem*, being rights that are 'good against the world' and thereby binding everyone. Anyone taking possession of the burdened land would have to respect the legal interest. So, Matthew will purchase Woodland Cottage subject to the legal rights.

Equitable interests are much harder to categorise, but we must do so in order to provide advice to Matthew on the impact of those interests which exist in equity. Certainly the origins and underlying rationale of equity are personal as reflected in the often cited maxim *Equity acts in personam*. Equity's remedies and the interests created are indeed based upon an individual acting according to justice and good conscience. However, the effect of equitable interests has developed beyond that of purely rights *in personam*. Equitable rights have the ability to bind third parties, such as a future purchaser of the burdened estate.

The best illustration of this for our purposes is a trust, under which the beneficiary's ownership is potentially good against persons other than the original owner of the legal estate who first created the trust in their favour. This is far removed from the original personal jurisdiction of equity. However, such equitable interests are more vulnerable than legal ones given they will only bind certain people and not the whole world. The new owner of a land will take free of an equitable right if they are a *bona fide purchaser of a legal estate for value without notice*, as defined below.

BONA FIDE

Acting bona fide means in good faith.

PURCHASER FOR VALUE

This requires that some sort of consideration must be given for the land.

LEGAL ESTATE

This includes the purchase of a legal freehold estate, a leasehold estate and also a mortgage.

WITHOUT NOTICE

The test for notice developed through case law, but is now set out in s 199(1)(ii) of the LPA 1925:

> A purchaser shall not be prejudicially affected by notice of … any other instrument or matter or any fact or thing unless—
>
> (a) it is within his own knowledge, or would have come to his knowledge if such inquiries and inspections had been made as ought reasonably to have been made by him; or
> (b) in the same transaction with respect to which a question of notice to the purchaser arises, it has come to the knowledge of his counsel, as such, or of his solicitor or other agent, as such, or would have come to the knowledge of his solicitor or other agent, as such, if such inquiries and inspections had been made as ought reasonably to have been made by the solicitor or other agent.

Three different forms of notice are included, any of which will prevent the purchaser taking free of the equitable right. These are considered in detail in Chapter 4, 'Unregistered Land'.

Actual notice

A purchaser has actual notice if he knew about the right at the time of purchase.

Constructive notice

A purchaser is deemed to have constructive notice if he would have known about the right were reasonable inquiries and inspections carried out. This includes investigating the title deeds and visiting the property to make a physical inspection of it.

Imputed notice

A purchaser has imputed knowledge of all things his legal agent (for example, his solicitor) has actual or constructive notice of.

APPLY YOUR LEARNING – TASK 6

What type of notice may be arguable (note Tutor Tip 6, highlighting the diminishing importance of this form of the doctrine of notice in modern land law) in relation to Matthew as a purchaser of Woodland Cottage, where he (a) was told about the beneficial interest of Charlie and (b) was not told, but could have seen that Charlie is living there if a visit to the property were made?

> **TUTOR TIP – 6**
>
> ....
>
> These types of notice have dwindling relevance in land law today. Students tend to remember the doctrine of notice, as it is covered early in courses, and often raise it when it cannot be applied. As the book progresses, make sure you note how it has been replaced to remove the uncertainty it used to cause. What follows is a brief summary of how its role has reduced.
>
> The title to the majority of land is now registered (registered land is a centralised system for recording the ownership of land and other interests, both legal and equitable). The doctrine plays no role in that system; equitable interests are protected through notices or restrictions and sometimes through actual occupation.
>
> For increasingly scarce unregistered land, there is a separate system of registration of land charges, which in effect replace the doctrine of notice for equitable interests (although trusts continue to be governed by the doctrine of notice).
>
> Chapters 4 and 5 explore the rules governing unregistered and registered land in depth.

THE 1925 PROPERTY LEGISLATION

The Law of Property Act 1925 and its role in reducing the number of legal estates and interests in land has been referred to already. However, this was only one piece in a raft of new legislation in 1925 designed to simplify the process of purchasing land. The main complications addressed were proving title to the land being conveyed and identifying both legal and equitable interests held by other people over the land being purchased.

The Land Registration Act 1925 introduced a system of compulsory, nationwide registration of title. We will explore this system, now governed by the Land Registration Act 2002, in detail in Chapter 5, 'Registered Land'. For now you simply need to be aware of its overall aim of requiring (1) ownership of an estate to be proved through registering the title, and (2) both legal and equitable interests in land to be registered in order to bind future purchasers of the property.

For titles not yet on the registered title system, referred to as unregistered land, a system for registered equitable interests was introduced in the Land Charges Act 1925. This replaced the different types of notice outlined above. Interests registrable as land charges are either registered, in which case a purchaser takes subject, or not registered, in which case a purchaser takes free. We will explore this system, now governed by the Land Charges Act 1972, in detail in Chapter 4, 'Unregistered Land'.

For now it is important to remember how legal and equitable interests are created.

DISCUSSION

The LPA 1925, along with other legislation, was introduced to modernise land law by simplifying conveyancing and facilitating the alienability of land.

CONSIDER THIS – 2

Section 1(1) LPA of the 1925 allows only freeholds (the fee simple absolute) and leaseholds (the term of years absolute) to be legal estates. Section 1(2) of the LPA 1925 limits legal interests with all others shifted to being equitable per s 3. Consider how this significantly reduced fragmentation of ownership into a multitude of estates and the legal interests that could be claimed against an estate, confining them to the commercial kind.

Think about the other matters to which the 1925 legislation also needed to respond.

One consequence is an increase in rights which could be recognised in equity. How did we determine whether an equitable right would bind a purchaser of the burdened estate and what were the weaknesses with that approach given the aim of making land more alienable? Consider whether the doctrine of notice is acceptable and, if not, how it could be replaced.

How do we go about proving legal ownership of an estate or the existence of a legal interest against an estate? They must have been created by deed, but what is the problem with relying on deeds to prove matters which, given the very nature of land as permanent may have happened a very long time ago? In terms of other means of identifying legal rights, remember that many are incorporeal and removed from things which may be readily physically apparent. Consider whether there may be a system less prone to problems caused by the passage of time or by lost or fraudulent documentation.

In Chapter 5, 'Registered Land', we will explore how the establishment of a title of register showing estate ownership and third-party interests, combined with overreaching, aims to resolve the issues caused by the complexity of dealings with land. In Chapter 4 on unregistered land we will explore the 'temporary' system put in place whilst land reaches this registered system. When reading those chapters keep in mind the overall question of whether the 1925 legislation achieved its aim of simplifying the sale of land.

END OF CHAPTER SUMMARY

- The starting point in providing advice in relation to claims in and over land is to identify whether the claim relates to a property/proprietary right or personal right, which gives a right *in personam* binding only on a particular person.
- For property a right, its status as legal or equitable must then be decided to determine the conditions for it binding others in the future, such as purchasers of the burdened estate.
- Legal property rights are rights *in rem* binding on the whole world.
- The number of estates and interests recognised at law are limited to those identified in s 1 of the LPA 1925.
- To have legal status, certain formalities must be followed in the creation and transfer of legal estates and interests such as the use of a deed under s 52(1) of the LPA 1925.
- Equitable rights bind everyone except for a bona fide purchaser of a legal estate for value without notice.
- Equitable interests may arise because the interest could not be recognised at law (for example, a restrictive covenant) or because of a lack of legal formality.
- A contract for the grant of a potentially legal estate or interest may give rise to an equitable equivalent if it meets the requirements under s 2 of the LP(MP)A 1989.
- Note that the doctrine of notice, in terms of inspection of title and of the land, plays much less of a role post the 1925 legislation and the introduction of registered title and registered land charges.

PREPARING FOR ASSESSMENTS
QUESTIONS

ESSAY QUESTION

The range of estates and interests and the divide between law and equity creates a complex picture of land in England and Wales. Analyse the development of the modern definition of land, and consider whether its elements combine to produce a fair and effective understanding.

PROBLEM QUESTION

Read through the narrative below and identify whether or not the rights referred to are potentially legal or equitable.

Forest Hall (freehold) is owned by Elizabeth. She has decided to sell the property because she is having difficulties repaying a loan of £500,000 which she borrowed to purchase the property (mortgage).

Elizabeth is reluctant to sell the property as she has always loved the rural setting – she will even miss reaching the house by crossing a bumpy driveway running across her neighbour's land (easement). That reminds her, she needs to make the annual £50 payment to her neighbour Shamus towards the upkeep of that route (rentcharge). Elizabeth loves to look out on to the field she owns where Shamus grazes his cattle (profit à prendre).

Elizabeth has agreed to sell the property to Richard, a local builder. Elizabeth has heard rumours that Richard is going to build several houses on the field and sell them on. She therefore decided to impose a condition of sale preventing any construction of other buildings on the land (restrictive covenant).

Richard is finishing another building project, which will take another six months, and so does not want to complete the sale right away. However, Elizabeth and Richard have already exchanged written contracts, incorporating the terms and signed by both parties, for completion of the sale in six months (estate contract).

FURTHER READING

- Garner, JF, 'Ownership and the Common Law' [1986] JPEL 404. Considers the meaning of ownership, as the ultimate relationship between a person and the object owned and the basic rights it confers.
- Howell, J, 'Informal Conveyances and Section 2 of the Law of Property (Miscellaneous Provisions) Act 1989' [1990] Conv 441. Explores s 2 LP(MP)A 1989 and its requirements for valid land contracts. Now the doctrine of part performance no longer applies to land contracts, the article considers the effect of s 2 on the enforcement in equity of a purported conveyance (or creation) of a legal interest, which fails to comply with the necessary formalities for the creation of legal interests.
- Mason, A, 'The Place of Equity and Equitable Remedies in the Contemporary Law World' (1994) 110 LQR 238. Analyses the role of equity, exploring of its principles and remedies.

4

CHAPTER 4
UNREGISTERED LAND

CHAPTER AIMS AND OBJECTIVES

Earlier chapters have explored the breadth of land law and introduced the 1925 legislation. In this chapter we now will explore the effect and impact of the 1925 legislation in more detail, considering in particular its role in simplifying the process of conveying land.

A main function of the 1925 legislation was to introduce a nationwide system of compulsory registration of title and now more than 86 per cent of the land mass in England and Wales is registered. This means that in practice you will work primarily with what is called 'registered land' on the registered system, the principles and operation of which are covered separately in Chapter 5.

However, as you can discern, that still leaves a significant proportion of land which has not yet made the transition to the registered system and remains unregistered. This chapter is concerned with equipping you to manage dealings with such 'unregistered land', post the 1925 property legislation.

By the end of this chapter, you should be able to:

- appreciate the reasons for the 1925 legislation reforms and the main aspects;
- understand the process for proving title to unregistered land;
- explain how legal interests in unregistered land are identified and bind purchasers;
- explain how equitable interests in unregistered land are identified and bind purchasers, including:
  - detachment of equitable interests by the mechanism of 'overreaching'
  - land charges registration
  - equitable interests still subject to the doctrine of notice;
- apply the above to the case study and learning tasks.

CASE STUDY – ONE

You have been instructed by Susan regarding the proposed purchase from Lorna of a freehold house 'Rosemary Hall' with outbuildings and a large garden. Lorna purchased the freehold in 1970, before the area became one of compulsory registration, and the title to the property is still unregistered. Susan has discovered (is aware of) the following:

(a) A restrictive covenant made in 1923 preventing the use of the property for anything other than domestic purposes and another made in 1979 preventing the construction of any more buildings.
(b) A grant made in 1982 creating a profit à prendre for 40 years to graze sheep.
(c) When Lorna purchased the freehold estate, her friend contributed half the purchase price, although the legal title was conveyed to Lorna alone. Lorna acknowledges she holds the house on trust for herself and her friend Maurice who has a beneficial interest in the land.
(d) Last year, Lorna leased one of the outbuildings to Olive for five years. A document was drawn up (not in the form of a deed) containing the terms of the agreement and both Lorna and Olive signed it.
(e) Earlier this year, Lorna orally granted a two-year lease of another outbuilding to Trevor. He rarely uses it.

Advise how Lorna's legal title to the property will be investigated and whether Susan may take subject to any of the interests listed above as a potential purchaser. She has agreed to pay just below the asking price.

KEEP IN MIND

- How legal title is proved in unregistered land.
- Whether the interests raised in the scenario are legal or equitable.
- That legal interests bind the whole world.
- That equitable rights bind everyone except a bona fide purchaser of the legal estate without notice of the right.
- How the status of a purchaser as bona fide is tested through the doctrine of notice.
- The effects of the 1925 legislation in reducing the role played by the doctrine of notice through the introduction of land charges and interests that are overreachable (avoidable).
- The effectiveness of the unregistered land system in reducing uncertainly for Susan as a purchaser and simplify the conveyancing process.

PROBLEMS WITH THE FORMER SYSTEM

Under the system prior to the 1925 property legislation, title to land was based on historical title deeds. Proof of ownership, for example Lorna's ownership of Rosemary Hall, required a time-consuming detailed inspection by the purchaser of the seller's deeds and other related documents, which were sometimes difficult to read and understand and could be lost, destroyed or tampered with. The exercise was hazardous, given the risk of missed issues or error, and the time-consuming exercise needed to be repeated afresh each time a conveyance occurred.

Determining ownership was also made problematic by the range of estates (remember, this equates to ownership giving the right to possess, use, enjoy and deal with land) which could subsist over one piece of land, including the potentially very complicated life estates, fees simple in remainder and entails (now rare) we noted in Chapter 2. This ability to divide ownership between so many people made it difficult for a purchaser to identify and resolve all the different possible ownership claims.

Also, there were many third-party proprietary interests which could exist over the land of another, as we considered in Chapter 3. For purchasers, in addition to further cluttering the property, identifying these interests could be difficult given the range of them and the fact that they may well have been created a very long time ago. You can see how the purchase of Rosemary Hall by Susan could be a somewhat risky business.

In summary, the two key problems identified in the conveyance or transfer of land which the 1925 legislation sought to resolve related to:

- proof of title to the land being purchased, and
- identifying third party rights in that land.

Let's explore the changes made by the 1925 legislation to try and improve the situation for purchasers such as Susan.

PROOF OF TITLE

A main objective of the 1925 legislation was to ultimately establish a national system where every title to land is registered. With that centrally kept register providing a guaranteed record of ownership, any need to locate and check historical title deeds is removed. Yet, despite more than 90 years having elapsed, that objective has still not been fully achieved. As we explained in the introduction, the number of unregistered titles remains far from insignificant.

Where title to land has not yet been registered, the residual principles of proof of ownership based upon title deeds continue to apply. However, the 1925 legislation had lessened the onerous task of examining title deeds by reducing the period of time a seller must produce documents for. In 1925, the period was set at 30 years by s 44(1) of the Law of Property Act 1925 (LPA 1925) but this was reduced to 15 years by s 23 of the Law of Property Act 1969 (LPA 1969).

So, a seller need only produce a document going back at least 15 years in order to establish what is referred to as a 'good root of title'. This will normally be a deed of conveyance.

APPLY YOUR LEARNING – TASK 1

The root of title is normally a deed of conveyance and dates back at least 15 years. Will the 1970 conveyance of Rosemary Hall suffice to show Lorna as its legal owner and comply with the root of title requirements?

THIRD-PARTY RIGHTS

In unregistered land, whether a purchaser will take subject to any third-party proprietary rights affecting land is dependent largely upon whether it is legal or equitable.

In Chapters 2 and 3, we explained that legal status affords the greatest security given legal rights are good against the whole world thereby affecting purchasers of a burdened estate automatically. In contrast, equitable claims will not bind the bona fide purchaser of the legal estate without notice of the right.

The 1925 legislation responded to the cluttering of land with rights which reduce its usability and marketability, by reducing the number of estates to two and interests to five recognised at law. The legal estates and legal interests were limited to the most 'commercial', the kind essential to the property market which form the ordinary dispositions. Everything else became equitable. The 1925 legislation also introduced an ability for purchasers to avoid taking subject to some equitable claims and a system for registering others and thereby effectively remove the uncertainty caused by the doctrine of notice.

Estates
Under s 1(1) of the LPA 1925, as explained in Chapter 2, only two legal estates are now recognised.

All other ownership rights (notably, life estates and fees simple in remainder) as 'family' interests may now exist in equity only under a trust.

To reduce the negative impact of these family-type claims (in contrast to those of a commercial kind, these interests are usually created in favour of family members) over

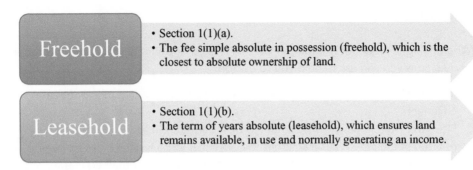

Figure 4.1 Freehold and leasehold: the two legal estates

property, a mechanism called overreaching was introduced to enable purchasers to detach any trust of land from the property upon a sale by two trustees. We will consider overreaching in a separate section later in this chapter.

Interests

Under s 1(2) of the LPA 1925, as explained in Chapter 3, there are now only five classes of interests recognised as having legal status.

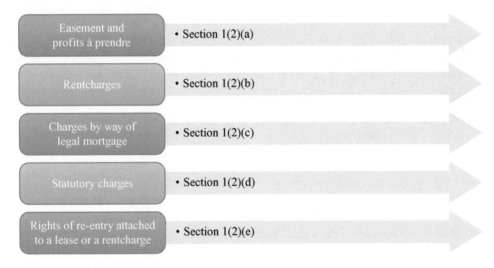

Figure 4.2 The five legal interests

Proving they have been created using the correct formalities, legal interests bind the world. This means that a purchaser of the burdened estate will take subject, irrespective of whether or not they knew about the legal interest.

All that is required is that the correct formalities are followed which, as considered in Chapter 3, generally involves creation by deed, which must be signed, witnessed and delivered. These deeds should be kept with the title deed, meaning that a purchaser should normally be able to discover the interest whilst inspecting title.

TUTOR TIP – 1

When trying to work out whether an interest is legal or equitable there are a number of questions you can ask to help you to decide.

1   Identify what your interest is. For example, is it an easement, a mortgage or a covenant?
2   Does the interest have the potential to be legal? I.e. is it listed in either s 1(1) or s 1(2) of the LPA 1925? If so it has the potential to be legal *if* it has followed the correct formalities. If not, it can never be anything other than equitable.
3   How has the interest been created?

If it had the potential to be legal *and* it has been created by deed in accordance with s 52(1) of the LPA 1925, the interest will be legal.

If it had the potential to be legal but it has been created by contract and is compliant with s 2 of the LP(MP)A 1989 then, provided specific performance is available, the interest is equitable.

APPLY YOUR LEARNING – TASK 2

The profit over Rosemary Hall is potentially legal, as profits are listed under s 1(2)(a) of the LPA 1925. It has also been created using the correct formalities, with the scenario identifying that a valid deed was used. What does its status as a legal interest mean for our purchaser, Susan, and whether she will take subject to it?

What are the other potentially legal estates and interests identified in the scenario, was a deed used?

One exception to legal estates and interests requiring no protection and which automatically bind the world is the 'puisne' mortgage. Though legal, it requires registration as a land charge in order to bind a purchaser for value. This will be explained in the section on the Land Charges Register.

Under s 1(3) of the LPA 1925, all other interests (such as those identified in Chapter 3, including the beneficial interest under a trust, restrictive covenants, estate contracts, informally created interests and the equitable right to redeem) now exist only in equity.

APPLY YOUR LEARNING – TASK 3

The Rosemary Hall scenario refers to restrictive covenants and to a trust. Given they are not listed in s 1 of the LPA 1925 could they ever have legal status? If not, would equity recognise them as equitable interests?

The five-year lease could potentially be legal. Leases are one of the two estates recognised by s 1(1) of the LPA 1925. But, at least for leases over three years, a deed is required for a legal creation (s 52(1) of the LPA 1925). The scenario confirms no deed was used; given that, could the five-year lease be legal? What is the relevance of the contract, complying with s 2 of the Law of Property (Miscellaneous Provisions) Act 1989 as explored in Chapter 3, to any argument of an equitable lease? Note that as it is a contract to create an estate, it is an estate contract.

The two-year lease looks to fall under the exception to s 52(1) of the LPA 1925. A grant of a lease for three years or less will be effective in law, regardless of how it was made, provided that it is to take effect immediately, there is no fine or premium and it is at the best rent (s 54(2) of the LPA 1925).

Under the old system, whether equitable interests would bind a purchaser depended upon the doctrine of notice. However, as we saw in Chapter 3, the doctrine of notice is unreliable and inappropriate for a commodity as essential, expensive and unique as land.

The 1925 legislation responded to this by requiring the equitable interests which often form the subject of financial transactions to be registered, thereby providing a means of discovery for a purchaser and removing the need to speculate about what a 'reasonable' purchaser should have discovered. This group of interests have been termed by some as 'commercial nature interests'.

For unregistered land, the owner of these commercial nature interests must register them on the Land Charges Register and a purchaser of the land is expected to carry out a search of that register. This method of registration is not without its problems, however, as the commercial nature interest is not registered against the property but instead again the estate owners who hold title at the time the interest is created.

TUTOR TIP – 2

Do not make the mistake of confusing the reference here to a limited 'registration' of equitable interests as land charges with the far more comprehensive registered land system.

As we shall see in Chapter 5, under the registered land system the title to land as well as both legal and equitable third-party interests affecting it are registered.

LAND CHARGES

To advise Susan whether, as a purchaser, she will take Rosemary Hall subject to the equitable interests we have identified, we must explore what land charges are available and determine the effect of registration and non-registration. The Land Charges Act 1925 was replaced by the Land Charges Act 1972 (LCA 1972), and to avoid confusion we will refer to the current Act only. However, the essential principles remain the same.

TUTOR TIP – 3

You will note from the following explanation of the Land Charges Register that trusts form a notable equitable interest omitted from the system. This may seem confusing given the major consequences for a purchaser, but remember that this is because of their family nature as discussed above and make sure that you explain they are instead covered by the mechanism of overreaching.

CATEGORIES OF LAND CHARGES

The Land Charges Register has six classes of entry (A–F), as set out in s 2 of the LCA 1972. The most important for you to note are:

B – charge imposed by statute

A Class B entry relates to a charge imposed by statute. An example of such a charge would be one imposed by the Legal Services Commission in favour of legal costs owed to the Legal Services Commission. Whilst public funding for legal matters is becoming increasingly limited, there may be historic charges, for example, a situation where a party in a divorce matter received public funding for the divorce and ancillary relief matters but was not in a position to repay the monies on completion of the matter. If the matrimonial home was received as part of the financial settlement, the Legal Services Commission may have placed a charge over the property to secure the outstanding monies to be repaid at some point in the future, i.e. when the matrimonial home is eventually sold.

How to deal with a Class B entry

If the charge remains upon completion of the sale, the buyer will take the property subject to those outstanding monies in the same way as an outstanding mortgage. The buyer's solicitor must therefore ask for an undertaking from the seller's solicitor that the monies will be redeemed from the sale proceeds upon completion and the entry removed upon completion with evidence of this sent to buyer to confirm its removal.

TUTOR TIP – 4

The term 'completion' means the date when the legal title to the property passes to the buyer, in unregistered land.

C(i) – the puisne mortgage

The first mortgagee (the person or business making the loan secured against the land) has the right to take possession of the title deeds as its security.[1] Where a mortgagee takes possession of the title deeds, the mortgage is not capable of registration as a land charge under s 2(4) of the LCA 1972. This creates a dilemma as only one set of title deeds will exist for the land; however, it is possible to create more than one legal mortgage. As only the first mortgagee can take possession of the title deeds, the other mortgagees need to protect their position and ensure that the mortgagor cannot sell the property without their outstanding monies being repaid. As such any legal mortgagee not in possession of the title deeds will protect their position by registering a Class C(i) puisne mortgage entry against all estate owners.

How to deal with a Class C(i) entry

When a Class C(i) entry is uncovered by a buyer on a land charges search it alerts the potential buyer to the fact there is a second or subsequent legal mortgage affecting the property. The buyer's solicitor would normally write to the seller's solicitor with a copy of the search asking him to certify to what the Class C(i) relates to, who the charge is in favour of and whether there are any monies still outstanding. It is possible that it is a mistake, that it is an old mortgage which has simply not been discharged or accidentally registered twice. If this is the case, then the seller's solicitor would apply to the Land Charges Department to remove the entry.

If the entry relates to a live mortgage with monies outstanding, the buyer's solicitor must ask for an undertaking from the seller's solicitor that the mortgage will be redeemed from the sale proceeds upon completion and that the vacated mortgage deed (i.e. evidence that it has been paid) will be sent upon receipt of it from the mortgagee.

If the purchase were completed without the mortgage being paid off, the purchaser would take subject to it. The solicitor acting for the buyer would be negligent and would have to pay it off at his/her firm's expense.

C(iii) – a general equitable charge

An equitable mortgage (for example, where a deed has not been used) must be protected under Class C(iii) if it was not secured by a deposit of the title deeds with the mortgagee. As with a puisne legal mortgage, if further investigation reveals the entry relates to a live mortgage with monies outstanding, the buyer's solicitor must ask for an undertaking from the seller's solicitor that the mortgage will be paid off.

C(iv) – estate contracts

As explained in Chapter 3, binding contracts may be entered into in relation to land. Where these relate to the informal creation or conveyance of an estate or to a future grant, they are classed as estate contracts. Examples are contracts to create or convey freehold and leasehold estates, options to purchase and rights of pre-emption (a right of first refusal).

---

1 S 85(1) of the LPA 1925.

How to deal with a Class C(iv) entry

When an estate contract entry is revealed it is important to make inquiries to ascertain when the contract was created, who was a party to the contract and what the terms of the contract were. If the current owner, the seller, lodged the land charge entry themselves then it should be removed easily. If it is a third party who has lodged the entry then this could cause problems. The buyer will require the seller to get the entry removed prior to completion and insert a term in the contract between the seller and buyer to that effect. If this does not happen then the buyer's solicitor should advise their client not to proceed with the transaction.

Class D(i) – HM Revenue and Customs charge

A Class D(i) entry is one imposed by HM Revenue and Customs (previously, the Inland Revenue) for unpaid Inheritance Tax and Capital Gains Tax. In such situations the buyer must check the contract to see whether the property is being sold subject to the charge.

How to deal with a Class D(i) entry

If there is no mention of the charge in the contract then the seller's solicitor should give a suitable undertaking to repay the monies from the proceeds of sale and to remove the entry on or before completion. Providing the seller pays the outstanding monies in full HM Revenue and Customs will have no grounds for refusing to remove the charge.

D(ii) – restrictive covenants

This only relates to restrictive covenants that have been created on/after 1 January 1926 between freeholders. As we will explain in Chapter 14, these are covenants imposed normally by the sellers of land to limit how it will be used.

How to deal with a Class D(ii) entry

The effect of a registered restrictive covenant is that the interest can be directly enforced against the current owner of the property at that time, even if they have not been the ones to directly breach the covenant themselves. If the sellers have made no mention of it in the contract they will be in breach of contract if a Class D(ii) entry is then revealed and the seller cannot secure its discharge on or before completion. As we will see in Chapter 14, such covenants can in theory subsist forever unless the person with the benefit releases the land from the covenants.

The first step is for the buyer to ascertain what the covenant is and whether it does relate to the land. If it does not then the seller should be asked to certify that the entry does not affect the land. Remember that land charges are registered against estate owners and not the land itself.

Restrictive covenants which have not been registered will not bind subsequent buyers, even if they have seen the deed with the restrictive covenants in. It is, however, important to always read the deeds for positive covenants as these may not be registered as either D(ii) charges or as notices in the charges register. They could still be directly binding (fencing obligations) or, more significantly, the buyer could be expected to give an indemnity to the seller in the conveyance/transfer for their future performance.

D(iii) – equitable easements

This relates to equitable easements created on or after 1 January 1926. While easements are capable of being legal, a lack of formality in their creation (i.e. failure to use a deed) or not being for period equivalent to a freehold or a leasehold estate may result in only an equitable easement or profit as we will see in Chapter 12 later. Equitable easements do not automatically bind the world in the same way legal easements do, they can only bind third parties in unregistered land if they have been registered against the estate owner as a class D(iii) entry.

> ### TUTOR TIP – 5
>
> As equitable profits are not specifically listed under s 2 of the LCA 1972, students may assume they cannot be protected with a land charge. In fact, Class D(ii) includes equitable profits as well as equitable easements.
>
> Please also remember that if the easement or profit is legal, it does not require registration as a land charge. This requirement is limited to those with only equitable status.
>
> So, in the Rosemary Hall scenario there would be no need for a land charge in relation to the profit. Only if there were, for example no deed, but a valid land contract in compliance with s 2 of the LP(MP)A 1989, or if the profit were not equivalent in duration to one of the two legal estates in land would a Class D(ii) charge be relevant.

F – statutory rights to occupy the family home

A spouse or civil partner under the Family Law Act 1996 or civil partner under the Civil Partnership Act 2004 has a right of occupation of the family home. The right of occupation applies to non-owning partners when they reside at the family home and their name does not appear on the deed. It is a method of protection for the spouse or partner, preventing the family home being sold without the removal of this entry.

How to deal with a Class F entry

Where a Class F entry appears on a land charges search then a buyer must ensure its removal before completion of the sale. If the seller does not remove the charge the buyer may be in a position to withdraw from the contract and claim damages. When acting for the seller in such situations, the solicitor must ensure that the non-owning spouse will sign the cancellation of the entry and also the contract to confirm they are happy for the property to be sold. The seller's solicitor, however, cannot advise the non-owning partner and must advise them to obtain independent legal advice. A Class F entry will automatically become ineffective upon death, divorce, court order or by voluntary agreement.

EFFECT OF REGISTRATION OR FAILURE TO REGISTER

Registration operates as actual notice of the interest to the world under s 198(1) of the LPA 1925:

(1) The registration of any instrument or matter … shall be deemed to constitute actual notice of such instrument or matter, and of the fact of such registration, to all persons and for all purposes connected with the land affected, as from the date of registration or other prescribed date and so long as the registration continues in force.

This means that any purchaser is bound by a registered right irrespective of whether they search the Land Charges Register.

Failure to correctly register a registrable right means that certain types of purchaser take free of the interest, whether they knew about it or not. Section 199(1)(i) of the LPA 1925 expressly removes the effect of notice in such situations:

(1)   A purchaser shall not be prejudicially affected by notice of—

   (i)   any instrument or matter capable of registration under the provisions of the Land Charges Act, 1925, or any enactment which it replaces, which is void or not enforceable as against him under that Act or enactment, by reason of the non-registration thereof…

The implication of this is that certain types of purchasers will take the land free from an interest if it has not been registered, even if they were aware of the interest. The type of purchaser is dependent upon the class of charge.

The courts have interpreted these provisions strictly, given that the very purpose of the LCA 1972 is to remove the role of the doctrine of notice. This reasoning was explained, by Harman J in *Hollington v Rhodes* [1951].[2] Here, the purchaser had actual

---

2 [1951] 2 TLR 691.

notice of and even agreed to take subject to an equitable lease which the tenant failed to protect with a class C(iv) land charge. Harman J explained:

> It appears at first glance wrong that a purchaser, who knows perfectly well of the rights subject to which he is expressed to take, should be able to ignore them. … It seems to me, however, that this argument cannot prevail having regard to the words in s 13(2) of the Land Charges Act 1925 [now s 4(6) of the LCA 1972] … The fact is that it was the policy of the framers of the 1925 legislation to get rid of equitable rights of this sort unless registered.

The case also established that occupiers of unregistered land have no equivalent protection to the overriding interest introduced for registered land by the Land Registration Act 1925 (LRA 1925). It also confirms that there is no requirement for the value of consideration to be adequate.

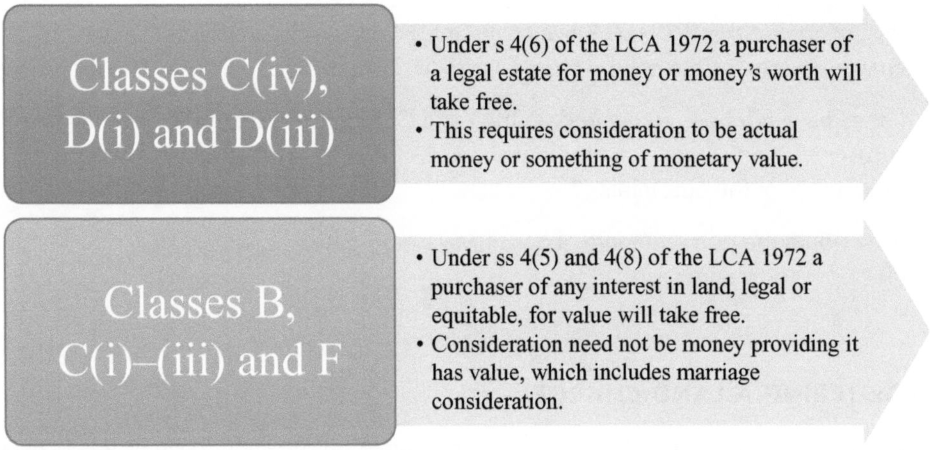

Classes C(iv), D(i) and D(iii)	• Under s 4(6) of the LCA 1972 a purchaser of a legal estate for money or money's worth will take free. • This requires consideration to be actual money or something of monetary value.
Classes B, C(i)–(iii) and F	• Under ss 4(5) and 4(8) of the LCA 1972 a purchaser of any interest in land, legal or equitable, for value will take free. • Consideration need not be money providing it has value, which includes marriage consideration.

Figure 4.3 Consequences of failure to register a land charge

KEY CASE: *MIDLAND BANK TRUST CO LTD V GREEN* [1981] AC 513; [1981] 1 ALL ER 153

The irrelevance of notice was confirmed even when the purchaser does not act in good faith. The case related to an option to purchase a farm given by a father to his son. As an estate contract, the son's interest was registrable as a class C(iv) land charge but he failed to register his interest. The father then, in a deliberate attempt to deprive his son, sold the farm to his wife who was aware of the option and paid just £500, which was considerably less than the farm was worth. It was estimated that the farm was worth £40,000 at this time.

The inadequacy of the consideration and her lack of good faith did not alter the mother being found a purchaser for money or money's worth and thereby taking free of the son's option. Lord Wilberforce said:

> The case is plain. The Act is clear and definite. Intended as it was to provide a simple and understandable system for the protection of title to land, it should not be read down or glossed: to do so would destroy the usefulness of the Act.

APPLY YOUR LEARNING – TASK 5

The case study identifies Susan as a purchaser of Rosemary Hall; she is paying just below the market price for the property and so will clearly fit into either definition as a purchaser for value or for money or money's worth.

Assuming that the 1979 restrictive covenant is registered as a Class D(ii) land charge and the estate contract as a Class C(iv) land charge, will Susan be bound?

If they have not been registered on the Land Charges Register, will Susan take subject to them? Does it matter that she is aware, or that Olive may be making regular use of the outbuilding?

How would the outcome differ if Susan was being gifted Rosemary Hall (as opposed to purchasing it)?

REGISTERING A LAND CHARGE

Under s 3(1) of the LCA 1972, interests are registered on the Land Charges Register by the person claiming to hold the right as a charge against the name of the owner of the burdened estate at the time the interest is created, known as the 'estate owner'. The estate owner is defined as 'the owner of the legal estate' under s 205(1)(v) of the LPA 1925. The entry records the nature of the interest and the name of the person claiming it. Mistakes may occur where sub-vendors and sub-purchasers are involved. For example, A (the legal owner of land) contracts to sell to B, and B (before completion) then contracts to sell to C.

The case of *Barrett v Hilton Developments Ltd* [1975] highlights the problems and possible confusion with the land charges system in such situations and the unfortunate outcome that results.

> **KEY CASE:** *BARRETT V HILTON DEVELOPMENTS LTD* [1975] CH 237
>
> A owned the land and contracted with B to sell the land to him. Before completion of this transaction, B contracted to sell the land to C. C wished to protect his interest which constituted an estate contract and registered a Class C (iv) entry against the name of B.
>
> The court held that the land charge entry registered by C was void, as at the time of registration the estate owner was still A not B. The effect of this was that the land charge entry and the interest in favour of C was invalid and not binding.

Even if the correct estate owner is used for the purposes of registering the land charge it is vital that the correct version and spelling of their name is used. The entry should be made against the name of the estate owner as it appears on the title deed (normally the deed of conveyance). Registration must be against the landowner's name exactly as it appears on the title deed, even if that is different from the name on their birth certificate. On this, see *Standard Property Investment plc v British Plastics Federation* [1987].[3]

> **APPLY YOUR LEARNING** – TASK 6
>
> In the Rosemary Hall scenario, if Lorna's title deed identifies her as Lorna Anne Johnston then that is the name land charges must be registered against. Would it matter if her birth certificate said her name is Lorna Anne Johnson or if people commonly refer to her as Annie Johnson?

Where a land charge is registered against an incorrect name, either the wrong person or an informal or wrong version of the name, it will not then bind a purchaser who as a result has made and obtained a clear search result.

> **KEY CASE:** *DILIGENT FINANCE CO LTD V ALLEYNE* (1972) 23 P & CR 346
>
> Erskine Owen Alleyne was the legal owner of a house and that was the name on the conveyance to him. His wife registered a Class F land charge against the name of Erskine Alleyne (missing the middle name). Mr Alleyne later mortgaged the property to Diligent Finance (a purchaser) who conducted a search in the correct name and obtained a clear result. The wife's interest was held not to bind them.

---

3 (1987) 53 P & CR 25.

Where a fair version of a name is used, the land charge will not bind if a search has been made against the correct name. If, however, the purchaser was also at fault in failing to search or searching against a wrong version of the name a charge will be effective provided it is registered against a fair version of the full names.

KEY CASE: *OAK CO-OPERATIVE BUILDING SOCIETY V BLACKBURN* [1968] CH 730; [1968] 2 ALL ER 117

Francis David Blackburn was the legal owner of a house which was conveyed to him in that name. The appellant claimed an estate contract over the house, which he registered as a land charge against the name Frank David Blackburn. Mr Blackburn later mortgaged the house to the building society (a purchaser), who searched the Land Charges Register against Francis Davis Blackburn and obtained a clear result. In determining whether the purchaser should take free given the incorrect registration, Russell LJ explained:

> But if there be registration in what may be fairly described as a version of the full names of the vendor, albeit not a version which is bound to be discovered on a search in the correct full names, we would not hold it a nullity against someone who does not search at all, or who (as here) searches in the wrong name.

SEARCHES BY THE PURCHASER

The purchaser should conduct a search of the Land Charges Register, checking against the names of previous owners of the land; to the period of time they were estate owners of the land. See Extract 1 at the end of this chapter for an example of the K15 Land Charges Form. A prudent solicitor will undertake this as part of their investigation of title prior to exchange of contracts by buyer and seller (once done the transaction is legally binding) and will undertake a search against every estate owner who appears or is mentioned from the root of title document to the present day. The solicitor will also undertake a further land charges search against the current estate owners shortly before completion. Under s 24 of the LPA 1969, the purchaser may withdraw from the contract should he discover a previously unknown land charge.

Undiscoverable land charges
The difficulty with this process is that the purchaser might miss interests created more than 15 years ago. Given a seller's need to produce a root of title going back only 15 years, he may be unable to identify all of the names against which to search.

Figure 4.4 The problem of pre-root land charges

Consider Figure 4.4. In this example, F, the buyer, only needs to go as far back as the 1989 conveyance in order to show good root of title. This satisfies s 23 of the LPA 1969 in relation to the 15-year rule. This does not alter the fact that a purchaser has actual notice and is therefore bound by a land charge, which has been correctly entered before that date. For example if the 1961 conveyance created a restrictive covenant that was not contained, mentioned or referred to in the 1989 conveyance and there was no way of knowing it existed, F would not be able to search for it. He therefore runs the risk of being bound by a charge that he could not have known about and was unable to discover. To reduce the problem of undiscoverable land charges, s 25 of the LPA 1969 provides for compensation by the state where the purchaser has suffered loss and can establish he had no actual knowledge of the charge and if the charge was registered against the owner of the estate who was not a party to any transaction in the current title.

OVERREACHABLE EQUITABLE INTERESTS

Land charges only relate to commercial nature interests. Equitable interests under a trust for sale or a strict settlement are not registerable as land charges. These are classified as 'family interests'. The Rosemary Hall scenario raises a trust in land, for which no land charge is available. There is, however, still help available to Susan. The mechanism of overreaching allows a purchaser to take free from certain equitable interests, the interest that is detached from the land then shifts to the purchase monies meaning the owner of the interest should not lose out.

Overreaching mainly relates to the beneficial interest under a trust or settlement. Other types of equitable interest, such as estate contracts, restrictive covenants and equitable easement and profits, are simply not suitable to take effect against money as they cannot exist without being attached to a piece of land.

> TUTOR TIP – 6
> ....
>
> The principle of overreaching applies to both unregistered and registered land, so remember to refer to it whenever you come across a beneficial interest under a trust. Note that a mortgage advance from a lender contitutes purchase monies for the purposes of overreaching.

Under ss 27(2) and 2(1)(ii) of the LPA 1925, to overreach, the purchaser must pay two or more trustees or a trust corporation. The difficulty with this is that, given trusts of land cannot be protected with a land charge, trusts remain subject to the unpredictability of the doctrine of notice and therefore the purchaser may not recognise the need to purchase from more than one legal owner. Two cases demonstrate the importance of this.

KEY CASE: *CITY OF LONDON BUILDING SOCIETY V FLEGG* [1988] AC 54; [1987] 3 ALL ER 435

A husband, wife and the wife's parents, the Fleggs, funded the purchase of a house. The husband and wife were registered as legal owners, holding it upon trust for themselves and the Fleggs. The two legal owners held as trustees, with themselves and the Fleggs sharing the beneficial interest. A second mortgage was taken out over the property (a purchase) by the two legal owners, with the building society paying the money to the two trustees. Despite the Fleggs occupying the property and being unaware of the mortgage, the result was that the trust was overreached and when the mortgage was defaulted upon they could not remain at the property.

KEY CASE: *WILLIAMS & GLYN'S BANK LTD V BOLAND* [1981] AC 487; [1980] 2 ALL ER 408

A husband was the sole owner of the legal title to the matrimonial home. Mrs Boland had made substantial contributions to the purchase price creating an equitable interest. Mr Boland mortgaged the house (a purchase) and defaulted on payments. The bank sought possession of the property, which Mrs Boland was occupying. Her beneficial interest was not overreached because the purchase monies had been advanced to only one trustee.

TUTOR TIP – 7

If in a question there is only one legal owner of the land, do not assume overreaching is unavailable.

Where there is only one trustee, a purchaser should require the appointment of a second trustee for the purpose of giving 'good receipt' i.e. for overreaching to apply. In practice, when this situation arises the seller's solicitor will normally appoint himself as the second trustee. This is a lot easier and less complicated than appointing a member of the seller's family and is a good way of ensuring that the beneficiary under the trust receives his or her money once the sale has been completed.

APPLY YOUR LEARNING – TASK 7

Susan has actual knowledge of the trust in the Rosemary Hall scenario, but it is suitable for overreaching. What must Susan do to ensure the mechanism operates? Note there is currently only one legal owner of the property.

EQUITABLE INTERESTS REMAINING SUBJECT TO THE DOCTRINE OF NOTICE

A small number of equitable interests are still subject to the doctrine of notice, most notably:

- overreachable interests
- restrictive covenants between freeholders created prior to 1 January 1926
- restrictive covenants contained in a lease
- equitable easements and equitable profits created prior to 1 January 1926
- interests arising by proprietary estoppel.

Remember, to satisfy the doctrine of notice the purchaser must establish that they are a bona fide purchaser of a legal estate for value without notice.

APPLY YOUR LEARNING – TASK 8

In the Rosemary Hall scenario, the 1923 restrictive covenant and the beneficial interest under the trust remain subject to the doctrine of notice. Susan has actual notice, but if the question had not confirmed that she was aware, what steps should have been taken to show that she had acted as a reasonable purchaser? Look back to Chapter 3 covering equity for details.

DISCUSSION

Where land remains unregistered, the system for dealings with it must minimise the shortcomings caused by the lack of a central register.

CONSIDER THIS – 1

Do you consider that the system for proof of ownership and protection of legal and equitable property rights in unregistered land provides an effective and fair balance? Remember to look at this question from the point of view of purchasers and the owner of a third-party interest in an estate.

Consider how shifting land onto the registered system with a central register may reduce some of the issues you identify. This will be explored in Chapter 5 on registered land.

END OF CHAPTER SUMMARY

- Legal estates and interests are good against the whole world and will bind a purchaser automatically. But note the puisne mortgage, which is registrable as a land charge.
- Many equitable interests are registrable as land charges under s 2 of the LCA 1972, including estate contracts, post-1925 restrictive covenants, post-1925 equitable easements and profits, and statutory rights to occupy the family home.
- Registrable interests must be correctly entered in order for them not to be void against certain types of purchaser under s 4 of the LCA 1972. Section 199(1)(i) of the LPA 1925 expressly removes the effect of notice in such situations.
- Correct registration, which is made against the name of the estate owner as it appears in the title deeds under s 3(1) of the LCA 1972, means the charge will bind all purchasers under s 198(1) of the LPA 1925.
- Some equitable interests may be overreached using the process under ss 27(2) and 2(1)(ii) of the LPA 1925. Note in particular beneficial rights under a trust of land and settlements. To overreach, the purchaser must pay two or more trustees or a trust corporation.
- A small number of equitable interests remain subject to the doctrine of notice, notably trusts, pre-1926 restrictive covenants, pre-1926 equitable easements and profits, and interests arising by proprietary estoppel.

PREPARING FOR ASSESSMENTS
QUESTIONS

ESSAY QUESTION

The land charges system was intended to eliminate the burdensome and unpredictable operation of the doctrine of notice in conveyances. How effectively does the system achieve that aim, and do you consider that it produces fair outcomes in all cases?

PROBLEM QUESTION

Tom has just purchased Cherry House from Tony, a freehold title that is unregistered. The following problems have now arisen:

(a) Tony's wife, Dorothy, did not contribute to the purchase price but there is a Class F land charge registered against Tony's name.
(b) Cherry House has a large grassed area and Jessie, a close personal friend of Tony and Dorothy, has been permitted to use it to exercise her dogs. She hopes that she will be allowed to continue to do so.
(c) Betty, Dorothy's sister, moved into the house three years ago and paid off the rest of the mortgage. Tony had been struggling with the repayments, and was

so grateful that he made a valid declaration of trust in her favour, which gave her a quarter of the beneficial estate. Betty likes to go on long holidays, and was on a three-month cruise when the survey of the property was conducted prior to the purchase.

(d) Peggy, a neighbouring landowner, has produced a valid deed granting her a five-year lease over a small gravelled area at the bottom of the garden that she uses to park her car. The grant of the lease includes details of a right of way, so that she can walk through the garden and reach her house.

(e) Natalie has a written document, signed by herself and by Tony, which gives her a four-year lease of a garage on the property.

Advise Tom whether any of these matters have created rights enforceable against him.

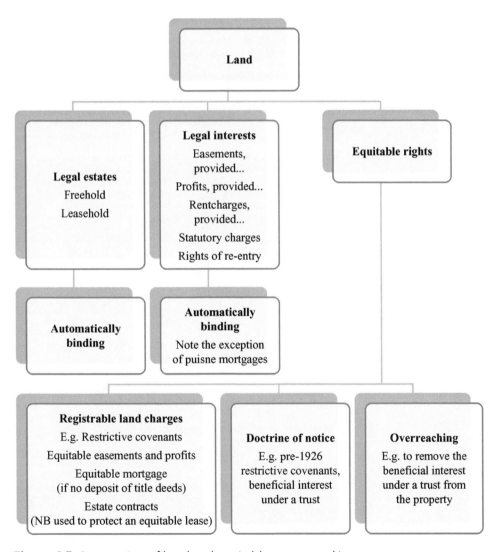

Figure 4.5 An overview of legal and equitable estates and interests

FURTHER READING

- Harpum, C, 'Overreaching, Trustee's Powers and the Reform of the 1925 Legislation' (1990) 49 CLJ 277. Examines the mechanism of overreaching, the process whereby a purchaser of property takes it free from any interests or powers, which attach instead to the proceeds of sale.
- Howell, J, 'Notice: A Broad View and a Narrow View' [1996] Conv 34. Considers the scale of awareness to constitute notice of an equitable right for the purpose of applying the doctrine of priority to a bona fide purchaser of legal estate without notice. From a narrow to a broader view of the doctrine.
- Howell, J, 'The Doctrine of Notice: An Historical Perspective' [1997] Conv 431. Explores the decline of influence of doctrine of notice culminating in the 1925 legislation and its application.
- Neild, S, 'Imputed Notice' [2000] Conv 196. Explores cases on the doctrine that a person has notice of knowledge possessed by his agent.
- Thompson, MP, 'The Purchaser as a Private Detective' [1986] Conv 283. Considers the impact of constructive notice of equitable interest upon a purchaser.
- Wade, HWR, 'Land Charge Registration Reviewed' (1956) 14 CLJ 216. An assessment of the success and limitations of the land charges system.

EXTRACT 1 FORM K15: LAND CHARGES FORM

Form K15   **Land Charges Act 1972**

Fee panel
Place "X" in the appropriate box. See Note 1 overleaf.
☐ A cheque or postal order for the correct fee accompanies this application.

☐ Please debit our Direct Debit under an authorised agreement with Land Registry.

APPLICATION FOR AN OFFICIAL SEARCH

NOT APPLICABLE TO REGISTERED LAND

Application is hereby made for an official search in the index to the registers kept pursuant to the Land Charges Act 1972 for any subsisting entries in respect of the undermentioned particulars.

IMPORTANT: Please read the notes overleaf before completing this form

For Official Use Only			NAMES TO BE SEARCHED *(Please use BLOCK LETTERS and see Note 4 overleaf)*	PERIOD OF YEARS *(see Note 5 overleaf)*	
SIX				From	To
			Forename(s)		
			SURNAME		
			Forename(s)		
			SURNAME		
			Forename(s)		
			SURNAME		
			Forename(s)		
			SURNAME		
			Forename(s)		
			SURNAME		
			Forename(s)		
			SURNAME		

COUNTY *(see Note 6 overleaf)*	
FORMER COUNTY	
DESCRIPTION OF LAND *(see Note 7 overleaf)*	
FORMER DESCRIPTION	

Particulars of Applicant *(See Notes 8, 9 and 10 overleaf)*		Name and address (including postcode) for despatch of certificate *(Leave blank if certificate is to be returned to applicant's address)*
KEY NUMBER	Name and address (including postcode)	

Applicant's reference	Date	**FOR OFFICIAL USE ONLY**

NOTES FOR GUIDANCE OF APPLICANTS

The following notes are supplied for assistance in making the application overleaf. Detailed information for the making of all kinds of applications to the Land Charges Department is contained in Practice Guide *63 – Land Charges – Applications for registration, official search, office copy and cancellation,* which is obtainable on application at the address shown below.

1. **Effect of search.** The official certificate of the result of this search will have no statutory effect in relation to registered land (see Land Registration Act 1925, s.59 and Land Charges Act 1972, s.14).

2. **Bankruptcy only searches.** Form K16 should be used for Bankruptcy only searches.

3. **Fees.** Fees must be paid by Direct Debit under an authorised agreement with Land Registry or by cheque or postal order made payable to "Land Registry" (see the Practice Guide referred to above).

4. **Names to be searched.** The forename(s) and surname of each individual must be entered on the appropriate line of the form. The name of a company or other body should commence on the forename line and may continue on the surname line (the words "Forename(s)" and "Surname" should be crossed through). If you are searching more than 6 names, use a second form.

5. **Period of years to be searched.** The inclusive period to be covered by a search should be entered in complete years, e.g. 1968-1975.

6. **County names.** This must be the appropriate name as set out in Appendix C to the Practice Guide referred to above. Searches affecting land within the Greater London area should state "GREATER LONDON" as the county name. ANY RELEVANT FORMER COUNTY SHOULD ALWAYS BE STATED. Appendix C as referenced above provides relevant guidance.

7. **Land description.** It is not essential to provide a land description but, if one is given, any relevant former description should also be given (see the guide referred to above).

8. **Key Number.** If you have been allocated a key number, please take care to enter this in the space provided overleaf, whether or not you are paying fees by Direct Debit.

9. **Applicant's name and address.** This need not be supplied if the applicant's key number is correctly entered in the space provided overleaf.

10. **Applicant's reference.** Any reference must be limited to 25 characters, including any oblique strokes and punctuation.

11. **Despatch of this form.** When completed, send this application to the address shown below, which is printed in a position so as to fit within a standard window envelope.

The Superintendent
Land Charges Department
Search Section
PO Box 292
PLYMOUTH PL5 9BY
DX 8249 PLYMOUTH (3)

5

CHAPTER 5
REGISTERED LAND

CHAPTER AIMS AND OBJECTIVES

The last chapter explored the property legislation of 1925 and its objective to simplify the transfer of land. The legislation provided for the extension of the 'registered land' system, with the aim of establishing a national system recording all landownership in England and Wales and the rights and interests attached to land. At present, more than 86 per cent of land is registered.

Each title to land is registered separately at the Land Registry. Registration of the title provides a state guarantee, meaning any subsequent purchaser can then rely on the accuracy of the register of title as a record of ownership. This removes the issues with proving a 'good root of title' to an estate, which we considered in the last chapter.

The registered system also reduces uncertainty for purchasers about any third-party proprietary interests affecting the land, the difficulties of which were explained in the last chapter. For most rights it is simply a question of whether it has or has not been recorded against the registered title. Rights entered on the register will bind a purchaser, if a right is not so protected then a purchaser will take free.

However, as we shall see, the realities of requiring the purchaser to look no further than the register could sometimes result in harsh outcomes for those claiming a right. The principle of registration has therefore been mitigated by recognising a small class of 'overriding interests'. These interests are so called as they are rights to which a purchaser will take subject, despite the fact they are not entered into the register of title. There is also the further exception provided for by the mechanism of 'overreaching' which, as we considered in the last chapter, operates to detach certain equitable interests from land.

By the end of this chapter, you should be able to:

- appreciate the aims of the Land Registration Acts;
- identify when the title to a freehold or leasehold estate must be registered;
- explain the process for transfer of a registered title (estate);
- explain how rights and interests over registered land are identified and bind purchasers, including:

  - entry into the register of title

- overriding interests
- overreachable interests;

- understand how alterations are made to the register;
- apply the above to the case study and learning tasks.

CASE STUDY – ONE

Miles is considering purchasing the registered freehold title to Lavender Lodge from James. Consider the following:

(a) James purchased Lavender Lodge in 1995, at the time Lavender Lodge was unregistered.

(b) James could not afford to purchase Lavender Lodge alone, so his partner Sarah paid just over half of the purchase monies. Sarah lives in the main house with James.

(c) Two months ago, James granted Alex a ten-year lease over a self-contained annex to the house. Alex's job requires her to work abroad regularly. While she is often away for several weeks at a time, she keeps her furniture and possessions in the annex.

(d) One month ago, James granted his neighbour Simon a lease of one of the property's garages for four years. Simon stores his prized classic car there.

(e) Simon was also granted an easement for eight years giving the right to park one car on a large area of concrete hardstanding outside the property's garages. He parks his everyday car there most nights.

(f) In exchange for a sum of money, James entered into a restrictive covenant with his neighbour Ian to use the property for residential purposes only.

KEEP IN MIND

- How legal title is proved in registered land.
- The interests raised in the scenario.
- The limits of protecting interests via registration. Requiring entry may be best for the purchaser but what about vulnerable people who did not realise registration was needed and are there some interests which are simply inappropriate for registration?
- How the registered land system responds. Consider for each of the interests whether it:

  - could have been entered on the title register
  - is potentially an overriding interest
  - is capable of being overreached.

- Overall, just how effective and fair is the registered land system for all of the parties?

THE AIMS OF THE LAND REGISTRATION ACTS

In the last chapter, we considered the main difficulties, which existed with the 'old' system for dealings with land as relating to:

- proof of title to the land being purchased, and
- identifying third-party rights in that land.

The response of the 1925 legislation was to expand a system of registered conveyancing, establishing a national Land Registry recording ownership and providing proof of title to land which could be relied upon by subsequent purchasers of it. By applying the registered land system to the Lavender Lodge scenario, we will see the advantages for Miles as a purchaser but also the limitations on his ability to completely rely on the register in practice.

> ## TUTOR TIP – 1
>
> It is not the land itself, but rather the various titles to it which are recorded.
>
> This means that one parcel of land may have several separately registered titles to it, each having its own register of title.
>
> For example, a piece of land may be 'owned' by a freeholder, a lessee (the owner of a leasehold), and a sub-lessee (a sublease is granted by a lessee). Each of these titles may be registrable.

The Land Registry Act 1862 and Land Transfer Act 1875 first introduced a system of land registration. The system, however, was voluntary and most titles (estates) remained unregistered. Compulsory registration upon the sale of property was provided for by the Land Transfer Act 1897, but only in designated areas and by the time of the 1925 legislation only London was covered.

The 1925 legislation was intended to gradually extend compulsory registration to all areas. However, the process proved slow and it was not until 1 November 1990[1] that it became universal, covering the whole of England and Wales. This process of gradual introduction is why the unregistered system, covered in the last chapter, continues to exist alongside. The number of unregistered titles is ever diminishing, given an increasing range of 'triggers' requiring a first registration of title in pursuit of the overall objective of a complete Land Register.

The Land Registration Act 1925 introduced the modern registered land system, which today is governed by the Land Registration Act 2002 (LRA 2002). The underlying aim remains the same and is based on three concepts: the mirror principle, the insurance principle and the curtain principle.

---

1 Registration of Title Order 1989, SI 1989/1347.

THE MIRROR PRINCIPLE

The register of title should be an accurate and authoritative statement of the title and the interests affecting the land. However, this fundamental idea of the register as a perfect reflection is undermined by a limited number of rights which do not appear on the register of title and yet may still bind a purchaser. These are known as overriding interests and, as a result, it is often said that the 'mirror is cracked'.

While it is arguably impractical and unfair to expect all interests to be registered, the objective of creating a register that is as comprehensive and transparent as attainable has resulted in a gradual reduction in the number of overriding interests. It is also notable that overriding interests are those which would normally be discoverable upon an inspection of the land.

THE CURTAIN PRINCIPLE

Certain equitable interests, such as the details of trusts of land, are not entered on the register and are hidden from a purchaser's view. As explained in the last chapter, such rights are considered as 'family' interests and any requirement for formal protection inappropriate for that type of claim. However, as also explained in the last chapter, the beneficial interest under a trust can be overreached and thereby detached from the land.

THE INSURANCE PRINCIPLE

The state guarantees the accuracy of the register. If the register is found to be inaccurate it will normally be altered or rectified. Any loss resulting from the alteration or rectification will normally be compensated by the payment of an indemnity (s 103 of the LRA 2002).

SUBSTANTIVELY REGISTRABLE TITLES

Only certain legal estates and interests are capable of 'substantive registration' in an individual register of title, with a unique title number and file describing the land, its ownership and the rights and interests affecting that particular parcel of land. Section 2 of the LRA 2002 makes provision for the substantive registration and clarifies which are affected.

The title to Lavender Lodge will be so registered. We will be considering only the substantive registration of title to freehold and leasehold estates in land. Note that only leases of more than seven years are capable of such registration (ss 3(3), 4(1)(c) and 27(2)(b)(i) of the LRA 2002).[2]

---

2 Leases for more than three years may, however, be noted. See ss 33, 34 and 35 of the LRA 2002.

Section 2(a)(i)

- Freehold estate
- Leasehold estate (with over 7 years to run)

Section 2(a)(ii)

- Rentcharge

Section 2(a)(iii)

- Franchise (a privilege granted from the Crown; the most common is the right to hold a market or fair).

Section 2(a)(iv)

- Profit à prende in gross (in gross means exercisable independently of ownership of dominant land).

Figure 5.1 Estates and interests capable of substantive registration

Other estates and interests in the land, such as the various rights and interests affecting Lavender Lodge, cannot normally be substantively registered but are entered into the register against the relevant title, the easement and the restrictive covenant, for example.

STRUCTURE OF THE REGISTER OF TITLE

Each registered title (estate) has an individual register of title comprising three parts: the property register, the proprietorship register and the charges register. The register of title for Lavender Lodge will be so divided.

> TUTOR TIP – 2
>
> ....
>
> Students are sometimes confused by the naming of the three parts as 'registers', they are not separate files but just parts of one overall register of title.

THE PROPERTY REGISTER

The property register describes the estate, indicating whether the title is freehold or leasehold (the duration of a lease will be included) and the geographical location of the land (usually the address) with reference to an official title plan based on the Ordnance Survey map.[3] It also includes the particulars of rights benefiting the land (where the land is dominant), such as easements and restrictive covenants.

THE PROPRIETORSHIP REGISTER

The proprietorship register states the quality or grade of title. There are three grades of title for freehold and four for leasehold as we will see later in this chapter. It also gives the name and address of the legal owner(s). These are the people who have the legal title vested in them. The proprietorship register will also show any restrictions on their power to deal with the land.

THE CHARGES REGISTER

The charges register contains the particulars of registrable interests to which the land is subject (where the land has the burden), such as mortgages and restrictive covenants, easements and leases. See Extract 1 at the end of this chapter for a sample register.

FIRST REGISTRATION OF TITLE

At some point, Lavender Lodge will have required first registration (i.e. the move from the unregistered land system to the registered one). First registration of the title to an estate can be voluntary or compulsory.

There are consequences of which you need to be aware in the event that a compulsory first registration event, known as a 'trigger', is not complied with and we will therefore begin with a consideration of compulsory registration.

COMPULSORY REGISTRATION

Section 4 of the LRA 2002 specifies the triggers for a first compulsory registration, including:

---

3 The boundaries shown on the plan, edged in red, are for the great majority of land in England and Wales only 'general' and do not determine the exact line of the boundary. Section 60 of the Land Registration Act 2002 states that: '(1) The boundary of a registered estate as shown for the purposes of the register is a general boundary, unless shown as determined under this section. (2) A general boundary does not determine the exact line of the boundary.' For an example of a case where the general border marked on the plan was out by several metres from the actual border, see *Drake v Fripp* [2011] EWCA Civ 1279; [2012] 1 P & CR 69. The borders were between four and five metres apart, and the landowner argued he should be compensated for a loss of land. However, as the boundary marked on the plan was for identification purposes only, providing no guarantee, and never the true boundary there was in reality no loss of land to him and so no compensation was given. A boundary may be fixed if determined (following a satisfactory application to the Land Registry, which will consider the evidence and any objections from neighbouring landowners) under s 60 of the Land Registration Act 2002.

- The transfer (whether as a gift, for consideration, by means of an assent, or in pursuance of a court order) of an unregistered legal freehold or of a leasehold that has more than seven years to run from the date of the grant.
- The grant of a leasehold of more than seven years.
- The grant of a lease of any duration to take effect in possession after a period of more than three months beginning with the date of the grant (such future leases are known as 'reversionary leases').
- The creation of a protected first legal mortgage (one that ranks in priority ahead of any other mortgages affecting the mortgaged estate) of a freehold estate or leasehold estate of more than seven years.

> TUTOR TIP – 3
> ....
>
> Note that it is not compulsory to register title to profits in gross, rentcharges and franchises. Registration of title to those interests is voluntary.
>
> Other incorporeal hereditaments, for example easements or restrictive covenants, can only be registered as appurtenant to registered land. It is a relatively common mistake for students to suggest that to grant an easement or a profit out of unregistered land, to be legal both a deed and first registration is required. Note this is not the case, they are not a trigger for first registration under s 4 of the LRA 2002. Look again at the list we have given above and then at the section itself to reinforce this point.

Section 6 of the LRA 2002 requires the transferee or grantee to make an application for first registration within two months, beginning with the date of completion of the trigger event. (In the case of a protected first legal mortgage, the mortgagee normally makes the application in the name of mortgagor. To be more precise, their solicitor will do so as a solicitor can work for both the lender and the buyer in the conveyancing process.)

If an application is not made within that period, the transfer or grant of a legal estate becomes void under s 7 of the LRA 2002.[4] The legal title reverts in the transferor or grantor, and the transferee or grantee is left with only an equitable estate:

- If the failure to register relates to a transfer, the legal estate (freehold or leasehold with more than seven years to run) reverts to the transferor, who will hold it on a bare trust for the transferee.
- If the failure to register relates to the grant of a lease or a protected first legal mortgage, it will be void but will take effect as if it were a contract for valuable consideration to grant the lease or mortgage concerned.

---

4 An application can be made to the registrar to extend the two-month period, an order will be made if there is good reason for doing so under s 6(5) of the LRA 2002. The transferee, lessee or mortgagee then recovers their legal estate, and is treated as having retained it all along (s 7(3) of the LRA 2002).

If the transaction has to be repeated to allow the title to be registered, then the cost will be borne by the person who failed to register on time.

VOLUNTARY REGISTRATION

The owner of an unregistered estate may decide to register voluntarily. This is provided for by s 3 LRA 2002. The legal estates and interests which can be voluntarily registered are set out in Figure 5.2.

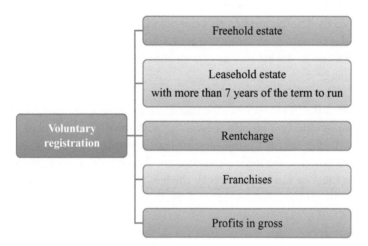

Figure 5.2 Estates and interests capable of voluntary first registration

To encourage voluntary registration, the fee payable to the Land Registry is reduced. Registering voluntarily has other benefits, such as giving state-backed proof of title. This eases future dealings with the land, and is particularly helpful should a purchaser or mortgager have concerns about the title, for example where the title deeds have been lost or destroyed. It also helps to protect land from fraud.

GRADES OF TITLE

James is registered as the owner of Lavender Lodge, but just how strong is his title?

When a title is first registered, applicants must provide all the deeds and documents relating to the title so they may be examined by the Land Registry. In unregistered conveyancing, as explained in the last chapter, showing a full documentary title commencing with a good root of title at least 15 years old should normally establish ownership. In a minority of cases, there may be questions about the strength of an applicant's claim to ownership. There are therefore different grades of title that the Land Registry may grant, with the assessment process principally determined by the quality of the documents proving title. There are currently seven grades of title prescribed by ss 9 and 10 of the LRA 2002.

ABSOLUTE FREEHOLD TITLE

An absolute title is the strongest grade, and is granted only where the supporting documents are in order and the registrar is satisfied that no one else may claim rights in the property.

ABSOLUTE LEASEHOLD TITLES

An absolute leasehold title is only to be granted if the registrar is satisfied of the validity not only of the lease itself but also of the title of the lessor who granted it (i.e. his title to the freehold estate or superior leasehold estate).

GOOD LEASEHOLD

If the registrar is not satisfied with the quality of the lessor's title, only a good leasehold title may be granted. Good leasehold title is normally due to the freehold title being unregistered, as such the Land Registry have not yet had sight of it to satisfy itself as to the quality of the lessor's title. This is normally the case where the lessor holds large areas of land, and is very common in certain geographical areas.

POSSESSORY TITLES

A possessory title is based on the applicant's actual possession of the land, where the documents proving title are inadequate or have been lost or destroyed. It is typically used by those claiming ownership through adverse possession, as covered in Chapter 15.

QUALIFIED TITLES

Qualified titles are rare. They are granted where there is some issue with the applicant's title, for example if the applicant's title to the estate has been established for a period of less of than 15 years.

UPGRADING THE TITLE

Sections 62, 63 and 64 of the LRA 2002 empower the registrar to upgrade titles if
certain procedures and requirements have been met. The Land Registry can upgrade
titles in a number of situations:

- *From good leasehold to absolute leasehold* if the Land Registry are satisfied 'as to the
  title to the freehold and the title to any intermediate leasehold'. As explained
  previously, good leasehold normally exists where the freehold title is still unregistered;
  as such it can be upgraded where the freehold title is produced for registration.
- *A possessory title can be upgraded to absolute freehold title* if the title has been
  registered as possessory for 12 years without challenge. It will be upgraded
  automatically or if the Land Registry is satisfied with the title for some other
  reason. This means that there is at least a period of 24 years in total from the
  granting of the possessory title to an upgrade of absolute title.
- Finally *a qualified title may be upgraded to absolute or good leasehold* if
  evidence is presented to the Land Registry to satisfy them that the title is sound.

DISPOSITIONS OF A REGISTERED TITLE

Once title has been registered, as Lavender Lodge now is, it is from that point onwards
governed by the LRA 2002 and the rules relating to unregistered land play no part.

Keeping in mind the mirror principle we considered above, the register is intended to
be a complete and accurate reflection of the state of the title to a registered estate at any
given time and so must be kept up to date. To achieve this, s 27(2) of the LRA 2002
lists various dispositions which must be completed by registration. Under s 27(1) of the
LRA 2002, registration is required in order for those dispositions to operate at law.

Section 27 of the LRA 2002 requires the transfer of a registered freehold or leasehold
estate to be registered, so that the new owner may be recorded. If this is not done, the

transfer of the title does not operate at law and the transferor will retain the legal title on bare trust for the transferee who will have only an equitable estate.

APPLY YOUR LEARNING – TASK 2

Consider the procedure for the transfer of the legal registered freehold title to Lavender Lodge from James to Miles.

We have already explained that the first requirement is a deed. For transfers of the whole of a registered estate, the Land Registry form TR1 must be used. This takes effect as a deed.

Miles must apply for registration, sending the completed TR1 form. What is the status of his estate until registration (keep in mind s 2(1) of the LRA 2002)?

Section 27 of the LRA 2002 also requires other dispositions to be registered on the register of title in order to take effect at law. Until registration, the interest does not operate at law and may only be equitable.

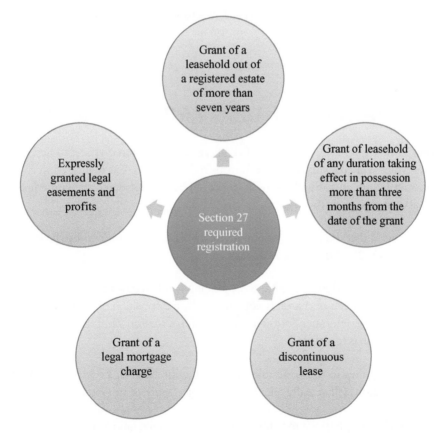

Figure 5.3 Dispositions required to be registered

APPLY YOUR LEARNING – TASK 3

In relation to the transfer or creation of estates and interest in registered land, there are three stages in considering whether a legal property right exists:

1   is it capable of being legal (s 1 of the LPA 1925);
2   did it require the use of a deed (s 52 of the LPA 1925); and
3   did it require registration (s 27 of the LRA 2002)?

In relation to the matters at Lavender Lodge there are three potentially legal rights:

■ The ten-year lease to Alex. The scenario confirms a grant (deed), but it does not say whether it has been registered. This is a lease for more than seven years and requires completion by registration. If it has, then this is a legal lease and will bind Miles. If it has not, then there may only be a ten-year lease in equity and we will need to consider the implications of this for Miles.
■ The four-year lease to Simon. A deed was used and the lease is for no more than seven years, meaning there was no need to register. It is a legal lease and will bind Miles.
■ The easement granted to Simon. A deed was used, but the question does not confirm whether it was registered. If it was registered, it has legal status and will bind Miles. If not, there may only be an equitable easement.

THIRD-PARTY RIGHTS IN REGISTERED LAND

We must now explore the treatment of rights against a registered estate, to determine whether Miles will take subject to the various rights and interests identified in relation to Lavender Lodge, in particular how they should be protected and the consequence if they do not appear on the register.

The basic rule is that the priority of any interest in land is determined by the order of creation. Section 28 of the LRA 2002 says:

(1)   Except as provided by ss 29 and 30, the priority of an interest affecting a registered estate or charge is not affected by a disposition of the estate or charge.
(2)   It makes no difference for the purposes of this section whether the interest or disposition is registered.

However, exceptions to this basic rule mean that a purchaser of a registered estate for value consideration will actually take the land subject only to interests which are:

■ protected by entry into the register of title concerning the land to which they relate; or
■ those which override the register.

If the burden is not registered then a purchaser of the title land for valuable consideration will take free[5] according to s 29(1) of the LRA 2002:

> If a registrable disposition of a registered estate is made for valuable consideration, completion of the disposition by registration has the effect of postponing to the interest under the disposition any interest affecting the estate immediately before the disposition whose priority is not protected at the time of registration.

CONSIDER THIS – 1

What if the scenario relating to Lavender Lodge told you that Miles had been informed about the restrictive covenant relating to the property when he made a visit but there was no entry in the charges register relating to it. Would Miles as a purchaser for valuable consideration take subject?

Where an interest has not been protected by an entry on the register to protect its priority against a purchaser upon a disposition of a registered estate, a way round the effect of s 29(1) of the LRA 2002 is to make an argument that the interest is overriding and therefore did not require an entry in order to bind (s 29(2)(a)(ii) of the LRA 2002). This brings us to a consideration of:

- the means for protecting the priority on an interest by making an entry in the register, and
- the routes for arguing overriding status.

PROTECTION BY ENTRY IN THE REGISTER

In order to bind a purchaser for value of the legal estate, third-party interests affecting a registered estate or charge must be protected by entry into the register of title (unless overriding, meaning a right which binds despite it not appearing on the register).

TUTOR TIP – 5

The term used under the LRA 1925, the predecessor to the LRA 2002, for interests not capable of being substantively registered or of overriding the register was 'minor interests'. The LRA 2002 does not use the term 'minor interest'. All interests affecting an estate or charge are instead defined simply under s 132(3)(b) of the LRA 2002 as 'an adverse right affecting the title to the estate or charge'. However, in practice it is still common language to make reference to rights as minor interests so please do not be confused if you come across it in your independent reading.

---

5 Whereas a non-purchaser (e.g. a gift or by will) would be bound by a pre-existing interest even if not protected with a notice or restriction. See *Halifax plc v Curry Popeck* [2008] EWHC 1692 (Ch); [2009] 1 P & CR DG3.

The LRA 2002 provides two methods of entry: notices and restrictions.

Notices

Notices are entries made in the respect of the burden of an interest affecting property (s 32 of the LRA 2002). The registration of a notice does not limit future dealings with the property, but means that a purchaser will take subject to the interest. Notices appear in the charges register section of the register of title relating to the burdened land. Think of the notice as the third party advertising his or her right to the world on a notice board, i.e. the Charges Register.

> TUTOR TIP – 6
> ....
>
> Please remember that the charges register is just one of the three parts of the register of title for the property: the property register, the proprietorship register and the charges register. It has nothing do with the 'land charges' system that we explored in relation to unregistered land. Similarly, notices are not the same as the 'doctrine of notice' also explored in relation to unregistered land.

Most interests can be protected by notice, so it is easier to remember those which are not. Rather than listing the rights which can be entered as a notice, s 33 of the LRA 2002 lists interests which cannot be protected in this way, including:

- Interests under a trust of land or settlement.
- Leases of no more than three years and taking effect in possession (i.e. not a reversionary lease as discussed above).
- Restrictive covenants entered into between a lessor and lessee (leasehold restrictive covenants).

This leaves a wide range of rights which can be entered as a notice. There are those interests we considered above which, if created over registered land, must be registered in order to operate at law. These include expressly created easements and profits, and the grant of a legal charge. Other interests which should be protected include:

- Estate contracts: remember these are contracts to grant a freehold or leasehold estate (equitable lease).
- Equitable easements and profits.
- Restrictive covenants between freehold estate owners (freehold restrictive covenants).
- Statutory rights to occupy the family home (for spouses and civil partners).[6]
- Equitable mortgages.
- Estoppel rights (discussed in Chapter 16 on Proprietary Estoppel).

---

6 By r 82 of the Land Registration Rules 2003, SI 2003/1417.

> ### TUTOR TIP – 7
>
> Do not make the mistake of suggesting that the entry of a notice proves the validity of the interest, all it does is make the claim to the interest binding against a purchaser. So if the claim is valid, the purchaser will then have to recognise the interest to which it relates.
>
> This is one reason for two kinds of notice being used.
>
> An agreed notice will be entered with the agreement of the registered proprietor of the land burdened.
>
> A unilateral notice can be entered without that consent, but the registered proprietor of the burdened land must be informed of the entry so he can apply for its cancellation under s 36 of the LRA 2002. Think of the unilateral notice as a hostile act.
>
> Make sure you refer to the different options in your responses.

APPLY YOUR LEARNING – TASK 4

In relation to Lavender Lodge, the ten-year lease (whether we find it is legal or equitable – remember the question of registration), the four-year lease, the easement (whether legal or equitable), and the restrictive covenant could all be protected with a notice.

Why is the trust not listed as something which could be protected in that way?

Restrictions

Restrictions are entries that prevent or regulate the registration of any dealings with a property (s 40 of the LRA 2002). Restrictions appear in the proprietorship register section of the register of title. The restriction limits the proprietor's ability to change, amend, add or delete entries from the register without the consent of the person with the benefit of the restriction.

The most common use of a restriction deals with a beneficial interest under a trust. The restriction ensures a purchaser complies with the requirements for overreaching by the payment of the purchase monies to two or more trustees (or a trust corporation) in accordance with the requirements for overreaching set by s 2(1)(ii) and 27(2) of the LPA 1925.

APPLY YOUR LEARNING – TASK 5

A notice could not be used to protect Sarah's trust (s 33 of the LRA 2002), but a restriction could. If Sarah has done so, it means Miles will have to comply with the restriction. By ensuring that Miles uses the mechanism of overreaching, Sarah will not lose her claim as it will move into the purchase funds.

If there is no restriction, someone in Sarah's position will need to rely on actual occupation, which can be uncertain.

TUTOR TIP – 8
....

Do not be surprised if you come across a reference to something called a 'caution' in your reading.

The LRA 2002, which came into force on 13 October 2003, simplified the methods of entry to the two types now available. Under the previous LRA 1925 there were three often-used types: notices, cautions and restrictions. The LRA 2002 abolished any new cautions, but those entered prior to the LRA 2002 coming into force remain valid.

A caution provides limited protection, merely securing the cautioner notification of any application for registration of dealings with the affected land. However, given that a purchaser is unlikely to risk a cautioner objecting to his future application for registration, in practice a purchaser will search for the existence of a caution and deal with it before proceeding.

OVERRIDING INTERESTS

While the mirror principle is fundamental to the registered land system, there are rights to which a registered title is subject even though they do not appear on the register. These are known as overriding interests. These 'cracks' in the mirror mean that Miles cannot completely rely on the register of title for Lavender Lodge, and are a hotly debated area for consideration in this topic.

The LRA 2002 reduced the number and scope of rights capable of overriding the register from the categories under s 70(1) of the LRA 1925. It was, however, considered that the entry of some interests still cannot be expected. For example, for rights created informally such as an equitable lease or a constructive trust it may be unreasonable to expect the person making the claim to have made an entry; here, the overriding rights of a person in actual occupation may be relied upon. For short leases, the workload involved in registration means it is arguably not sensible to require registration and may be unfair to vulnerable tenants.

The LRA 2002 distinguishes between first registration and registration of a disposition. Interests which override first registration are listed in sch 1 and those which override registered dispositions in sch 3.

Schedule 1 lists interests that override first registration (by virtue of s 11(4) or s 12(4) of the LRA 2002), as shown in Figure 5.4.

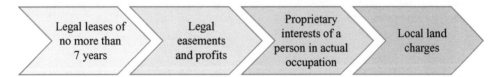

Figure 5.4 Overriding interests

> TUTOR TIP – 9
> ....
>
> Please remember that sch 1 of the LRA 2002 cannot be used to save an interest that has ceased to exist upon the unregistered conveyance.
>
> Once an interest is void, through lack of protection with a land charge or the operation of the doctrine of notice, it cannot be revived (*Wilkes v Spooner* [1911] 2 KB 473). You cannot, for example, argue actual occupation for an equitable lease or beneficial interests in a trust which has ceased to exist.

Schedule 3 lists interests that override registered dispositions (by virtue of ss 29(2) or 30(2) of the LRA 2002), the list is almost the same as that in sch 1 including also:

- Legal leases of no more than seven years (sch 3, para 1 of the LRA 2002).
- Legal easements and profits (sch 3, para 3 of the LRA 2002).
- Proprietary interests of a person in actual occupation (sch 3, para 2 of the LRA 2002).
- Local land charges (sch 3, para 6 of the LRA 2002).

Legal leases of no more than seven years

Legal leases of no more than seven years are automatically overriding, irrespective of whether there is in actual occupation of the property. Note that only legal leases and not equitable leases may override, a principle that was established in the case of *Permanent Building Society v Miller* [1952].[7] Actual occupation (explained below) may, however, be applied for equitable leases as they are proprietary in nature.

---

7 [1952] Ch 840; [1952] 2 All ER 621.

APPLY YOUR LEARNING – TASK 6

This means that while Simon could have protected his four-year legal lease with a notice, he did not need to as it will override anyway.

The status is limited to legal leases, so how would your advice on the advisability of using a notice differ if Simon's lease had not been created with a deed, but only a written contract?

For leases granted before the commencement of the LRA 2002 on 13 October 2003, in keeping with leases only of more than 21 years requiring registration under s 70(1)(k) of the LRA 1925, legal leases of no more than 21 years were overriding. Those leases continue to be overriding, per sch 12, para 12 of the LRA 2002.

Legal easements and profits

On first registration, any legal easement or *profit à prendre* is an overriding interest (sch 1, para 3 of the LRA 2002).

On registrable dispositions, the position for legal easements and profits à prendre was the same as for first registrations until 12 October 2006. Since 13 October 2006, an unregistered legal easement or profit will now only override registered dispositions if the purchaser had actual knowledge of the right, or it would have been obvious on a reasonably careful inspection of the land over which the easement or profit is exercisable, or it is proved to have been exercised in the year prior to the disposition (sch 3, para 3 of the LRA 2002).

However, for registered titles, remember that post the LRA 2002 the express creation of an easement in registered land requires not only a deed but also completion by registration in order to operate at law. As such, only legal easements created other than expressly (by implied grant or prescription, see Chapter 12 on easements) may be overriding in any event. Equitable easements and profits will always need to be protected through the entry of a notice.

For easements and profits created before the 13 October 2003, under s 70(1)(a) of the LRA 1925 all legal easements, no matter how they were created, and all profits were overriding. Under the LRA 1925, it was also possible for an equitable easement or profit to be an overriding interest if it was openly exercised and enjoyed (as a result of the High Court decision in *Celsteel Limited v Alton House Holdings Limited* [1985][8] as approved by the Court of Appeal in *Thatcher v Douglas* [1996][9]). These easements and

---

8 [1985] 2 All ER 562; [1985] 1 WLR 204.
9 (1996) 146 NLJ 282 (CA).

profits continue to be overriding, per sch 12, para 9 of the LRA 2002, but note that this applied only to preserve the overriding status of older existing equitable easements and profits of this kind. Also, it affects only registered land as only legal easements or profits can now override first registration.

APPLY YOUR LEARNING – TASK 7

The easement raised in relationship to Lavender Lodge must have been registered for it to have legal status and bind Miles. If not, it is equitable only and, given its creation post October 2003, cannot override.

Local land charges

When purchasing land, whether unregistered or registered, a search should be made with the local authority to identify any relevant local land charges. (This register of local land charges is not the same as the centralised Land Charges Register discussed in the last chapter.)

The local land charges register may contain a number of important rights; each district council in England and Wales will maintain a register of local land charges in its area. Examples include designation as a conservation area of architectural or historic interest, the making of tree preservation orders, details of money due to the local authority, designation as a smoke control area, or proposals for changes to roads such as widening.

Such local land charges are overriding and will bind a purchaser regardless of whether they knew about the entries or not so the local authority register must be carefully checked.

Proprietary interests of a person in actual occupation

In order to successfully claim this as an overriding interest, a person must establish two elements. First, that they have a proprietary interest in the land in question *and* second, that they are a person in actual occupation, as seen in Figure 5.5.

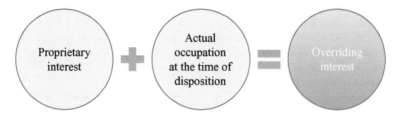

Figure 5.5 Interests of a person in actual occupation

A proprietary interest, whether legal or equitable, will have overriding status if its holder can prove they were in actual occupation of the burdened land at the time of the disposition. If the holder only occupies part of the land, the interest only overrides to the extent of that part and not the whole of it.[10]

The interests which may override are not listed; rather every interest which is a proprietary right in land is covered. The rationale is to assist those who are in occupation and may not have been aware they had to register their interest. This includes interests such as estate contracts, equitable leases and trusts, even though they could have been protected by an entry on the register, through a notice or a restriction.[11] A personal right, such as a bare licence[12] or the right of a spouse or civil partner to remain in the family home[13] would not be covered.

Certain kinds of interest are excluded from ever being overriding under sch 1, para 2 and sch 3, para 2 of the LRA 2002. These include an interest under a strict settlement (now very rare) and a leasehold estate in land granted to take effect in possession after the end of the period of three months beginning with the date of the grant and which has not taken effect in possession at the time of the disposition (this would need to be registered). Also, a spouse or civil partner's right of occupation under sch 11, para 34 of the LRA 2002.

More significantly, in relation to a registrable disposition under sch 3,[14] an interest will not override if either:

1   An inquiry is made of the holder of the interest and he fails to disclose it when he 'could reasonably be expected to do so' (sch 3, para 2(b) of the LRA 2002).

> TUTOR TIP – 10
> ....
>
> The difficulty is deciding whether it was unreasonable to expect the holder of a right to reveal it. Those lacking mental capacity is an example; this could include young children or those suffering from insanity or senility. This is an interesting critical point to raise in your responses.

2   The occupation would not have been obvious on a reasonably careful inspection of the land, and the purchaser did not have actual knowledge of the interest (sch 3, para 2(c) of the LRA 2002).

---

10 This represents a change, brought about by sch 3, para 2 of the LRA 2002, meaning *Ferrishurst v Wallcite* [1999] Ch 355; [1999] 1 All ER 977 is no longer good law. It had established that occupation of part of the land should be recognised as occupation of the whole of the land.

11 For example, a wife's beneficial under a trust for which a restriction was not entered was overriding in *Williams and Glyn's Bank Ltd v Boland* [1981] AC 487; [1980] 2 All ER 408.

12 Personal rights, such as a licence, cannot have overriding status. See *Strand Securities v Caswell* [1965] Ch 958; [1965] 1 All ER 820.

13 *National Provincial Bank Ltd v Ainsworth* [1965] AC 1175; [1965] 2 All ER 472. While the main purpose of the Family Law Act 1996 as amended by the Civil Partnership Act 2004 is to protect the right of a spouse or civil partner to occupy the home, it is not an overriding interest but constitutes a charge on the home that can be protected in the register by an agreed notice (r 82 of the Land Registration Rules 2003, SI 2003/1417).

14 This exception does not apply on first registration.

KEY CASES: *REASONABLY CAREFUL INSPECTION*

The question of what a reasonably careful inspection entails and what signs make an occupation obvious was considered in *Thomas v Clydesdale Bank plc* [2010] EWHC 2755 (QB); [2010] NPC 107. Ramsey J dismissed the relevance of the person inspecting having any particular knowledge and rejected any requirement of the person inspecting to make reasonable inquiries. He concluded that, 'it is the visible signs of occupation which have to be obvious on an inspection'.

What then of cases where the visible signs of occupation are hidden? The most controversial of such cases would be where the lack of visibility is not down to the holder of the interest, but a deliberate act by the legal owner of the burdened land to conceal the evidence. *Kingsnorth Trust Ltd v Tizard* [1986] 2 All ER 54; [1986] 1 WLR 783 raised such deception and a reasonable inspection was not found to include opening cupboards and drawers.

In relation to actual knowledge, *Thomas v Clydesdale Bank plc* [2010] held that 'actual knowledge of the facts giving rise to the interest' is sufficient. There need not be knowledge of the interest itself.

The phrase 'actual occupation' was not defined in the LRA 1925 and is not in the LRA 2002. It is to be given its ordinary meaning in plain English, a question of fact requiring nothing more than a physical presence.[15] This may sound simple enough, but in fact the wide range of circumstances that case law has been required to consider shows just how complex determining this issue of a fact can actually be. This is particularly difficult if the person said to be in actual occupation is not personally present on the land at the relevant time. How then is it to be shown that his occupation was manifested and accompanied by a continuing intention to occupy?

KEY CASE: *ABBEY NATIONAL BUILDING SOCIETY V CANN* [1991] 1 AC 56; [1990] 1 ALL ER 1085

This case confirmed that the physical presence requires some degree of permanence and continuity. But, as Lord Oliver highlighted, it was accepted that, 'even plain English may contain a variety of shades of meaning'.

---

15 Denning MR in *Williams and Glyn's Bank Ltd v Boland* [1979] Ch 312; [1979] 2 All ER 697, observed that actual occupation is a 'matter of fact, not matter of law'. Lord Wilberforce in *Williams and Glyn's Bank Ltd v Boland* [1981] AC 487; [1980] 2 All ER 408 said that: 'These words are ordinary words of plain English, and should, in my opinion, be interpreted as such ... Given occupation, i.e. presence on the land, I do not think that the word "actual" was intended to introduce any additional qualification ... it merely emphasises that what is required is physical presence'.

Mrs Cann had a constructive trust based on her contribution to the purchase price of a property purchased by her son (with the assistance of a mortgage) in his sole name. She intended to live there with him. On the date of completion, she was abroad on holiday but workmen moved in furniture and fitted carpets on her behalf 35 minutes before completion took place. The son defaulted on the mortgage, and the question arose whether she has an overriding binding the building by virtue of her being in actual occupation. Lord Oliver reasoned:

> In *Williams & Glyn's Bank Ltd. v Boland* [1981] AC 487, 504, Lord Wilberforce observed that these words should be interpreted for what they are, that is to say, ordinary words of plain English. But even plain English may contain a variety of shades of meaning…
>
> …It is, perhaps, dangerous to suggest any test for what is essentially a question of fact, for 'occupation' is a concept which may have different connotations according to the nature and purpose of the property which is claimed to be occupied. It does not necessarily, I think, involve the personal presence of the person claiming to occupy. A caretaker or the representative of a company can occupy, I should have thought, on behalf of his employer. On the other hand, it does, in my judgment, involve some degree of permanence and continuity which would rule out mere fleeting presence. A prospective tenant or purchaser who is allowed, as a matter of indulgence, to go into property in order to plan decorations or measure for furnishings would not, in ordinary parlance, be said to be occupying it, even though he might be there for hours at a time. … [I]in the instant case, there was, no doubt, on the part of the persons involved in moving Mrs. Cann's belongings, an intention that they would remain there and would render the premises suitable for her ultimate use as a residential occupier … [H]owever, I am unable to accept that acts of this preparatory character carried out by courtesy of the vendor prior to completion can constitute 'actual occupation'

This idea that the occupation must be such as to make it apparent is now formalised in the requirements of sch 3, para 2(c) of the LRA 2002 as we discussed above.

According to *Abbey National Building Society v Cann* [1991], the physical presence must be more than fleeting. So, for example, in *Epps v Esso Petroleum* [1973][16] the parking of a car at undefined times on a strip of undefined land was not actual occupation. Nor can the mere user of a right of way easement constitute actual occupation as it lacks the required intensity of use: *Celsteel Ltd v Alton House Holdings Ltd* [1985][17] and

---

16 [1973] 2 All ER 465; [1973] 1 WLR 1071.
17 [1985] 2 All ER 562; [1985] 1 WLR 204.

Chaudhary v Yavuz [2011].[18] Keeping furniture and belongs at a flat but not actually living there was also insufficient (see *Link Lending v Bustard* [2010]).[19]

The degree of physical presence required or manifestation will depend on the nature and the purpose of the property.

In *Abbey National Building Society v Cann* [1991], we saw that preparatory work prior to moving in such as decorating was not sufficient. This can be contrasted with cases where work is required on the property.

KEY CASE: *LLOYDS BANK V ROSSET* [1989] CH 350; [1988] 3 ALL ER 915

Work on the property was again undertaken some six weeks before completion of the purchase and the creation of a mortgage. This was again done with a view to moving, but the house was this time in a state of semi-dereliction. The person claiming the interest had spent a considerable amount of time at the property directing building work and decorating. The Court of Appeal held that this activity showed actual occupation because of the nature of the land, as explained by Nicholls LJ:

> [T]here was physical presence on the property by the wife and her agent of the nature, and the extent, that one would expect of an occupier having regard to the then state of the property, namely, the presence involved in actively carrying out the renovation necessary to make the house fit for residential use.

Actual occupation is not limited to dwelling houses. Take *Kling v Keston Properties Ltd* (1985)[20] in which the parking of a car in a garage was held sufficient, or *Malory Enterprises v Cheshire Homes* [2002][21] in which boarding up property, fencing it off and storing goods were all relevant factors for finding actual occupation of derelict land. Where land cannot be occupied for living in buildings, cultivating or use for recreational purposes other acts denoting physical presence, showing that the land as occupied and not abandoned, must be considered.

Even with the requisite degree of physical presence, there are also the issues of absences or lapses in that presence. At what point is the necessary 'degree of permanence and continuity' identified in *Abbey National Building Society v Cann* [1991] lost? Case law once more shows that a flexible approach must be taken based on the facts of the particular case whether occupation ceases to be continuing. Key considerations include not only the length of absence, but also the reason for it.

---

18 [2011] EWCA Civ 1314; [2013] Ch 249.
19 [2010] EWCA Civ 424; [2010] 2 EGLR 55.
20 (1985) 49 P & CR 212; [1984] LS Gaz R 1683.
21 [2002] EWCA Civ 151; [2002] Ch 216.

KEY CASE: *CHHOKAR V CHHOKAR* [1984] FLR 313

A short stay in hospital did not prevent a finding of actual occupation. There was a clear intention to return, the right holder's possessions remained in the house and the reason for absence was both temporary and justifiable.

KEY CASE: *STOCKHOLM FINANCE LTD V GARDEN HOLDINGS INC* [1995] NPC 162

A Saudi princess absent from her London home for 14 months was regarded as no longer continuing in actual occupation. Robert Walker LJ explained:

Whether a person's intermittent presence at a house which is fully furnished, and ready for almost immediate use, should be seen as continuous occupation marked (but not interrupted) by occasional absences, or whether it should be seen as a pattern of alternating periods of presence and absence, is a matter of perception which defies deep analysis. Not only the length of any absence, but also the reason for it, may be material (a holiday or a business trip may be easier to reconcile with continuing and unbroken occupation than a move to a second home, even though the duration is the same in each case). But there must come a point at which a person's absence from his house is so prolonged that the notion of his continuing to be in actual occupation of it becomes insupportable.

The relevance of a persistent and continuing intention to return can mean that even lengthy absences may be acceptable.

KEY CASE: *LINK LENDING V BUSTARD* [2010] EWCA CIV 424; [2010] 2 EGLR 55

At the time a legal mortgage charge was granted, Mrs Bustard was being detained while receiving compulsory treatment for a severe psychiatric condition. Despite the long-term nature of her care, she argued she was still in actual occupation of the house. In the Court of Appeal, Mummery LJ said:

Some of the primary facts point against Ms Bustard's actual occupation of the Property at the relevant date: she was not personally present in the Property on 29 February 2008; she had been in a residential care home since January 2007; she was incapable of living safely in the Property; and her visits to the Property were brief and supervised.

Some of the primary facts point to Ms Bustard's continuing actual occupation of the Property: it was her furnished home and the only place to which she genuinely wanted to return; she continued to visit the Property because she still considered it her home; those who had taken responsibility for her finances regularly paid the bills, such as the community charge, from her funds; she was in the process of making an application to the Mental Health Review Tribunal in order to be allowed to return home; and no-one took a final and irrevocable decision that she would not eventually be permitted to return home.

... The trend of the cases shows that the courts are reluctant to lay down, or even suggest, a single legal test for determining whether a person is in actual occupation. ... The degree of permanence and continuity of presence of the person concerned, the intentions and wishes of that person, the length of absence from the property and the reason for it and the nature of the property and personal circumstances of the person are among the relevant factors.

... It is clear ... that Ms Bustard's is not a case of a 'mere fleeting presence', or a case, like *Cann*, of acts preparatory to the assumption of actual occupation. It is also distinguishable from *Stockholm*, which involved the domestic living arrangements of a Saudi princess living with her mother in Saudi Arabia and owning a house in London, where there was furniture and clothing and caretaking arrangements in place, but where she had not lived for more than a year. In this case the new and special feature is in the psychiatric problems of the person claiming actual occupation. The judge was, in my view, justified in ruling, at the conclusion of a careful and detailed judgment, that Ms Bustard was a person in actual occupation of the Property. His conclusion was supported by evidence of a sufficient degree of continuity and permanence of occupation, of involuntary residence elsewhere, which was satisfactorily explained by objective reasons, and of a persistent intention to return home when possible, as manifested by her regular visits to the Property.

The difficulty with the relevance of an intention to return is that it is not something that will necessarily be physically visible; potentially causing significant trouble for the courts.

In *Thompson v Foy* [2009][22] Lewison J interestingly noted that even where an inspection has not been carried out at all the court can ask 'whether [hypothetically] occupation would have been obvious on a reasonably careful inspection'. If not then the failure to inspect will not disqualify the application of sch 3, para 2(c)(i) of the LRA 2002.

---

22 [2009] EWHC 1076 (Ch); [2010] 1 P & CR 16.

A final consideration is when a person other than the holder of the right can establish their occupation. The answer is yes provided that person actually is their agent. We have already explored such a case, in *Abbey National Building Society v Cann* [1991] with the builders. But where the person is not representing the right holder, their presence is of no consequence.

So, in *Strand Securities v Caswell* [1965],[23] occupation by a stepdaughter was insufficient. In *Hypo-Mortgage Services v Robinson* [1997],[24] it was decided that a parent could not rely on the occupation of young children. Children have no rights of occupation of their own, being there only because of their parent as 'shadows' of that occupation.

Note that the LRA 2002, in seeking to reduce the impact of overriding interests, has removed the category of a person in receipt of rents and profits from claiming an overriding interest. So, in *Strand Securities v Caswell* [1965], governed by s 70 of the LRA 1925, if the stepdaughter had have been paying rent it would have altered the outcome but it would not do so now.

APPLY YOUR LEARNING – TASK 8

If the easement over Lavender Lodge was not registered and is therefore only equitable, could the fact that Simon uses it frequently make it overriding? Is it ever possible to occupy an easement?

What is the relevance of Sarah living at the house to determining whether Miles may take subject?

If the ten-year lease was not registered and therefore is equitable, is the absence of Alex fatal to a claim of actual occupation? Consider why she was away, for how long, her intention to return and the presence of her clothes and possessions.

If the four-year lease had not been granted by deed, and was equitable based on an estate contract, would it be possible for Simon to claim actual occupation based on keeping the car there? What factors might be relevant, considering the nature of the property?

It is also worth considering how the outcome would differ if this were a question concerning unregistered land. Under that system, the trust would be dealt with by the doctrine of notice rather than actual occupation. An equitable lease would be protected with a land charge, and if no charge was entered a purchaser would then take free. There would be no back-up argument of actual occupation available.

---

23 [1965] Ch 958; [1965] 2 WLR 958; [1965] 1 All ER 820; (1965) 109 SJ 131.
24 [1997] 2 FLR 71.

The date of overriding interests and actual occupation

Under the LRA 2002, there is a period referred to as the 'registration gap' between the date of disposition (completion of the transaction) and the date of registration. Any unprotected interest affecting the estate immediately before the disposition is postponed (s 29(1) of the LRA 2002). However, there is notable exception to this in s 29(2)(a)(ii) of the LRA 2002 which gives priority to overriding interests even though they are not protected on the register. What then of new overriding interests created within the gap? Given that a purchaser will have carried out his inspection of the land and title looking for evidence of short leases, actual occupation or easements and profits, prior to completion, this is clearly an issue.

Regarding actual occupation, the date for showing occupation under the LRA 1925 was held by the House of Lords in *Abbey National Building Society v Cann* [1991] to be the date of the disposition (completion). Schedule 3, para 2 of the LRA 2002 now confirms that the relevant interest must belong at the date of disposition to a person in actual occupation. The reasoning in *Abbey National Building Society v Cann* was applied to the LRA 2002 in *Re North East Property Buyers Litigation* [2014].[25]

The duty to disclose overriding interests

Under s 71 of the LRA 2002 there is a general duty on an applicant for registration to disclose overriding interests. This enables a notice to be entered if appropriate. In keeping with this aim, those interests which do not require disclosure are those which could not be protected with a notice, including: interests under a trust of land or settlement, leases of no more than three years and taking effect in possession, and restrictive covenants entered into between a lessor and lessee.

Overreaching an overriding interest

As we know, overreaching is used predominantly to detach a beneficial interest under a trust from land. It was held in *City of London Building Society v Flegg* [1988][26] that actual occupation does not prevent the mechanism of overreaching operating.

PROCESS FOR TRANSFER OF REGISTERED LAND

Linking all of this information together, we can now consider the stages for the transfer of registered title such as Lavender Lodge to a purchaser such as Miles.

Pre-contract, a purchaser will view an official copy of the registered title.

---

25 [2014] UKSC 52; [2015] AC 385. It was determined that *Abbey National Building Society v Cann* [1991] 1 AC 56 applied to prevent the assertion of an equitable right that had arisen only on completion.

26 [1988] 1 AC 54; [1987] 3 All ER 435.

Post-contract, shortly before completion, the purchaser will get an official search certificate to check whether any new entries have been made since the issue of the official copy so far relied upon. The search certificate has a priority period of 30 working days; provided the application for registration is made within those 30 days the purchaser will not be bound by any new entries made within that time.

A land transfer document, or TR1 form from the Land Registry, is used for the transfer and take effect as a deed. A completed TR1 form is then included with the application for registration.

_____

ALTERING THE REGISTER

Alterations to the register can be made under s 65 of the LRA 2002, with the circumstances set out in sch 4. Alterations can be court ordered or made by the registrar for the purpose of:

- correcting a mistake;
- bringing the register up to date;
- giving effect to any estate, legal right or interest that is not affected by registration; or
- removing a superfluous entry (only by the registrar, not the court).

Many alterations are purely administrative, but some types of alterations are classified as 'rectifications' and treated differently. A rectification is a correction that prejudicially affects the title (for example, its value) of a registered proprietor. There is a statutory scheme to compensate anyone affected suffering a loss resulting from rectification or a refusal to rectify a mistake. Under sch 8 of the LRA 2002, indemnity may be payable when:

- the correction of a mistake on the register has caused loss;
- a mistake caused loss before it was rectified; or
- a mistake that is not rectified has caused loss.

There are restrictions on this right to indemnity:

- Lapse of time – a claimant will lose their right to apply to the court for indemnity after six years.
- Fraud – if the claimant's loss has been caused by his own fraud, then they lose the right to indemnity.
- Lack of proper care – a claimant loses the right to claim indemnity if his own lack of proper care caused their loss.
- Contributory negligence – a claimant who has partly contributed to his loss by their lack of proper care may have any indemnity payable reduced reflecting their share in the responsibility.

DISCUSSION

You should by now have an appreciation of the complexity of land, the resulting issues that arise in dealings with it, and possible solutions which encourage certainty and security though at the cost of flexibility. You should also understand the limitations of the system applied to unregistered land and how in comparison registered land simplifies conveyancing and facilitates the alienability of land.

> **CONSIDER THIS** – 2
>
> Consider the successes of the registered land system as it stands and its shortfalls. Can you think of any ways in which you would like to see it change?

The registered land system has a number of advantages:

- the ability to search a state-backed central register, allowing inspection of a particular registered title and official search certificate giving priority for 30 working days;
- assisting the ease of pre-contract searches, which can identify issues at an early stage; and
- well-established rules and procedures.

There are, however, criticisms that may be made:

- The retention of overriding interests, though do note the justifications for them, and that the number of such interests has been reduced by the LRA 2002, along with new conditions that must be met and a duty to register them upon discovery.
- The length of time between when an offer to purchase is informally accepted and completion remains very long.
- The lack of transparency and attendant problems in the chain in terms of delay and uncertainty.
- The potential for poor conveyancing standards given a continued reliance on paper-based systems.
- The 'registration gap' between completion and registration and the controversy about the consequences of interests created in that gap and issues related to the seller retaining legal title.

TUTOR TIP – 11

In evaluating the effectiveness of the land registration law, the reviews by the Law Commission are an invaluable source of information and critical analysis. Points from the two recent papers are set out below, but it is well worth reading the documents in full.

LAW COMMISSION, LAND REGISTRATION FOR THE TWENTY-FIRST CENTURY: A CONVEYANCING REVOLUTION (LAW COM NO 271, 2001)

The LRA 2002 followed from this report, which incorporated a draft Bill.

The report states [1.5]–[1.10]:

> The fundamental objective of the Bill is that, under the system of electronic dealing with land that it seeks to create, the register should be a complete and accurate reflection of the state of the title of the land at any given time, so that it is possible to investigate title to land on line, with the absolute minimum of additional inquiries and inspections.
>
> Although that ultimate objective may seem an obvious one, its implications are considerable, and virtually all the changes that the Bill makes to the present law flow directly from it …
>
> It should be noted that there are some interests in registered land, presently known as overriding interests, which are not protected in the register at all but which nonetheless bind any person who subsequently acquires an interest in the land affected. This is so whether or not that person knew of, or could readily have discovered, the existence of these interests.
>
> If it is to be possible to achieve the fundamental objective of the Bill …
>
> (1) all express dispositions of registered land will have to be appropriately protected on the register unless there are very good reasons for not doing so;
> (2) the categories of overriding interests will have to be very significantly reduced in scope; and
> (3) dispositions of registered land will have to be registered simultaneously, so that it becomes impossible to make most dispositions of registered land except by registering them …
>
> To achieve the goals stated … will also require a change in attitude.
>
> There is a widely-held perception that it is unreasonable to expect people to register their rights over land. We find this puzzling given the overwhelming prevalence of registered title. Furthermore, the law has long required compliance with certain formal requirements for the transfer of interests in land and for contracts to sell or dispose of such interests. The wisdom of these requirements is not seriously questioned. We cannot see why the further step of registration should be regarded as so onerous. In any event, under the system of electronic conveyancing that we envisage (and for which the Bill makes provision), not only will the process of registration become very much easier, but the execution of the transaction in electronic form and its simultaneous registration will be inextricably linked.

These changes will necessarily alter the perception of title to land. It will be the fact of registration and registration alone that confers title. This is entirely in accordance with the fundamental principle of a conclusive register which underpins the Bill.

The LRA 2002 has succeeded in furthering those objectives:

- Section 58 of the LRA 2002 guarantees the conclusiveness of registered estates and interests.
- Leases of more than seven years require compulsory registration; under the old system it was 21 years.
- Leases of no more than seven years are overriding; under the old system it was 21 years.
- Actual occupation will not make a right overriding (unless the purchaser is aware of it) if the, 'occupation would not have been obvious on a reasonably careful inspection of the land at the time of the disposition'.
- Only a legal easement will be an overriding interest.
- There is now a duty to disclose certain overriding interests.
- The new scheme for adverse possession (which is covered in Chapter 15) as contained in sch 6 to the LRA 2002, makes claims far more difficult.
- Progress has been made on some of the elements necessary for e-conveyancing.

There is still, however, further progress to be made:

- The register is sometimes inaccurate, hence the need for a process for rectification.
- E-conveyancing does not yet extend to cover the contract and transfer stage.
- E-conveyancing was envisaged as a way of enabling the limit for compulsory registration of leases to be further reduced to three years (in line with the lack of a requirement for a deed under the LPA 1925).
- E-conveyancing would also facilitate the removal of overriding interests, by requiring contracts to make a registrable disposition to be, themselves, registered. This would limit the application of the principle from *Walsh and Lonsdale* (1882) LR 21 Ch D 9.
- E-conveyancing would also remove the 'registration gap'.

The overall hope was that the introduction of e–conveyancing would reduce problems, making the process fully electronic and thereby faster, more reliable transparent and simultaneous completion and registration removing altogether the registration gap and its associated difficulties. However, as is explored in Chapter 18 which shows the routine complexity of the conveyancing process for a solicitor, to achieve that aim in practice would be very challenging. That the Law Commission itself is now questioning the impracticality of adopting a requirement of simultaneous completion and registration means that the project should, at least for now, be dropped. This is one of the points included in the consideration of the Law Commission's second paper on registered land law below.

LAW COMMISSION, UPDATING THE LAND REGISTRATION ACT 2002: A CONSULTATION PAPER (CONSULTATION PAPER NO 227, 2016)

At the time of writing, a new consultation by the Law Commission has closed for responses. The report and draft Bill is expected in late 2017. While we will not speculate on what the analysis of those responses will uncover, the issues considered in the conclusion paper reveals which aspects of the LRA 2002 were identified as areas for possible future improvement.

The issues considered include:

■ The reduction of length at which leases become registrable to three years.
■ The consultation provisionally proposes that there should be no reduction, as the advantages for tenants do not outweigh the disadvantages of additional regulation, cost and burdens for landlords when registering (or terminating) leases.
■ The lack of a requirement on the beneficiary of a unilateral notice to produce evidence in support of the right claimed.
■ The consultation suggests this may hamper attempts by the parties to negotiate a solution to any dispute. Further, any unresolved dispute must be referred by the Land Registry to the Land Registration Division of the Property Chamber of the First-tier Tribunal (the Tribunal) and registered proprietors may find themselves in Tribunal proceedings before any evidence is even produced on the right being claimed.
■ The consultation provisionally proposes amending the procedures for unilateral notices so that evidence must be produced at an earlier stage.
■ The undermining of the guarantee of title given in s 58 of the LRA 2002 by the possibility of rectification of the register.
■ The consultation suggests that the system could be improved so as to remove any issues of principle that are unresolved – for example: (1) Where a registered proprietor's name has been mistakenly or fraudulently removed should the land be returned to them or should they be satisfied with an indemnity; and (2) Should it matter how much time has passed since the fraud took place?
■ The consultation provisionally proposes: (1) Where the registered proprietor's name is removed (or omitted) from the register by mistake then the law should be weighted in favour of returning the land to him or her; (2) However, a registered proprietor in possession should be protected in determining who should retain the land as possession is an indication of who most needs or values land; (3) The introduction of a 'long stop' so that after ten years rectification of the register should generally cease to be available; and (4) that where a charge (a mortgage) is registered by mistake, then the chargee should be confined to receiving an indemnity as the chargee's interest is financial only.

- The practicality of moving directly from a paper-based conveyancing system to an electronic conveyancing model that provides for simultaneous completion and registration of an interest.
- The consultation provisionally proposes that the requirement of simultaneous completion and registration should be removed from the LRA 2002.
- Extending the special rules relating to priority under s 29 of the LRA 2002 so that they apply to competing interests that cannot be registered but can be recorded (e.g. an option to purchase or a restrictive covenant protectable with notices).
- The consultation provisionally proposes this extension.
- It would mean, for example, that the owner of an option to purchase created later in time than an earlier unprotected restrictive covenant would not be bound by that covenant provided they record their option with a notice first.
- Currently, even after entering a notice of the option, should the owner of the restrictive covenant enter a notice as any point prior to the purchase being completed (a registrable disposition protected by s 29) will be subject to the restriction even though it was not on the register when they made the decision to buy the land in the future.

END OF CHAPTER SUMMARY

- The features of registered land are the mirror principle, the insurance principle and the curtain principle. Together they work to introduce certainty and simplicity into the ownership and transfer of land.
- Each registered estate (notably freehold titles and leases of more than seven years) has its own title register consisting of three parts: the property register, the proprietorship register and the charges register.
- Security of title is state-backed, and compensation is available for loss suffered because of a mistake in the register.
- The register sets out all the rights that benefit and affect the title, other than certain overriding interests.
- Third-party rights must be entered in the register in order to bind a purchaser, except for overriding interests. Overriding interests are those which would be discoverable on a physical inspection.
- An entry on the register may be through a notice or a restriction.
- The beneficial interests under a trust may be overreached.

PREPARING FOR ASSESSMENTS QUESTIONS

ESSAY QUESTION

It is fundamental to the system of registered land that the mirror principle is upheld. Considering the significant number of overriding interests which remain, to what extent it is achieved and do you consider the crack in the mirror should be reduced?

PROBLEM QUESTION

You have been instructed by Adrian regarding the proposed purchase of freehold property from Bradley. Bradley purchased the freehold estate to the land upon which his house is built in 1988. The legal title to that estate (Thistle Hall) is unregistered. Bradley later purchased a plot to use as an allotment situated across the road. The title to that estate (the 'Allotment') is registered. Adrian is buying both.

The interests that potentially affect the unregistered Thistle Hall estate are as follows:

(a) Two years ago, Bradley granted a four-year lease over a garage on the land to Charles.
(b) Last year, Bradley granted by deed a nine-year lease of stable block standing on Thistle Hall to Donald. The deed was not registered. Donald keeps two horses in the stables, and visits every day to care for them.

You have carried out a land charges search against Bradley's full name. The search reveals that no interests have been registered against him.

The interests that potentially affect the registered Allotment estate are as follows:

(a) When Bradley purchased the freehold title, his sister Edith contributed quarter of the purchase price from her own savings. Bradley acknowledges that Edith has a beneficial interest in the land which he now holds on trust for her but the proprietorship register has no entry in relation to her. Edith is the more keen gardener and grows a variety of fruit and vegetable on the land, which requires her to work on it most weekends.
(b) Bradley's purchase was subject to a covenant not to keep or feed any animals on the property.
(c) Last month, after deciding the allotment area was far in excess of what he needed, Bradley contracted to transfer part of it to Frank who lives in a flat with no garden. Excited, Frank has been allowed to visit the plot on a few occasions prior to completion as he plans what to do with it.

Determine the legal or equitable status of the above and then advise to what extent each interest may bind Miles as a potential purchaser.

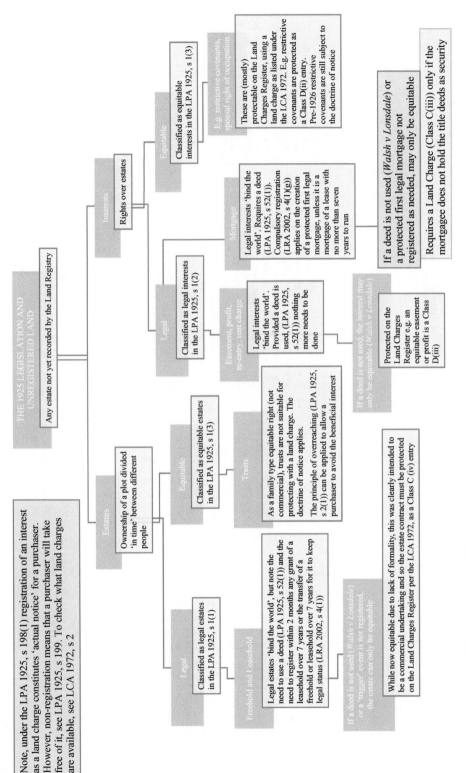

Figure 5.6 Overview of the unregistered land system

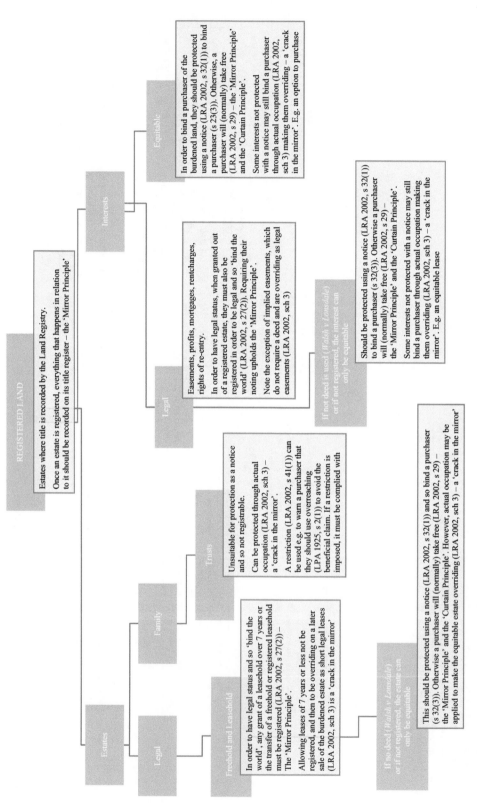

Figure 5.7 Overview of the registered land system

FURTHER READING

- Bevan, C, 'Overriding and Over-Extended? Actual Occupation: A Call to Orthodoxy' [2016] Conv 104. Evaluates the current judicial approach to determining the meaning, scope and operation of the actual occupation. Discusses the rationale and purpose of the actual occupation provisions. Calls for a return to the objective assessment of actual occupation.

- Bogusz, B, 'Defining the Scope of Actual Occupation Under the Land Registration Act 2002: Some Recent Judicial Clarification' [2011] Conv 268. Considers case law on what is meant by actual occupation. Discusses an apparent move to a more contextual approach, the relevance of the intention and wishes of the parties, and the necessity for a reasonable inspection.

- Bogusz, B, 'The Relevance of "Intentions and Wishes" to Determine Actual Occupation: A Sea Change in Judicial Thinking?' [2014] Conv 27. Examines the cases in which the courts have been prepared to take account of a party's expressed or implied intentions or wishes with regard to a property to determine if they were in actual occupation. Considers how objective and subjective criteria have been balanced in this decision-making.

- Dixon, M, 'The Reform of Property Law and the Land Registration Act: A Risk Assessment' [2003] Conv 136. Assesses the impact of the substantive changes in the Land Registration Act 2002, including the changes to the nature and types of categories of overriding interests and formalities for the creation and transfer of proprietary rights in registered land and the role of proprietary estoppel.

- Jackson, N, 'Title by Registration and Concealed Overriding Interests: The Cause and Effect of Antipathy to Documentary Proof' (2003) 119 LQR 660. Discusses the problem of inconclusiveness of the land register caused by overriding interests and the reforms made in the Land Registration Act 2002 including discoverability by the purchaser.

- Law Commission, *Land Registration for the Twenty-First Century: A Conveyancing Revolution* (Law Com No 271, 2001).

- Law Commission, *Updating the Land Registration Act 2002: A Consultation Paper* (Consultation Paper No 227, 2016).

EXTRACT 1 SAMPLE REGISTER OF TITLE

Land Registry
Official copy of
title plan

Title number **CS72510**
Ordnance Survey map reference **ST1680NE**
Scale **1:1250**
Administrative area **Cornshire: Maradon**

© Crown Copyright. Produced by Land Registry. Reproduction in whole or in part is prohibited without the prior written permission of Ordnance Survey. Licence Number 100026316.

This official copy issued on 23 July 2007 shows the state of this title plan on 23 July 2007 at 11:39:46. It is admissible in evidence to the same extent as the original (s.67 Land Registration Act 2002).
This title plan shows the general position, not the exact line, of the boundaries. It may be subject to distortions in scale. Measurements scaled from this plan may not match measurements between the same points on the ground. See Land Registry Public Guide 19 – Title plans and boundaries.
This title is dealt with by Land Registry, **Maradon Office**.

Land Registry

Official copy of register of title

Title number CS72510	Edition date 11.04.2007

- This official copy shows the entries in the register of title on 23 July 2007 at 11:39:46.
- This date must be quoted as the "search from date" in any official search application based on this copy.
- The date at the beginning of an entry is the date on which the entry was made in the register.
- Issued on 23 July 2007.
- Under s.67 of the Land Registration Act 2002, this copy is admissible in evidence to the same extent as the original.
- For information about the register of title see Land Registry website www.landregistry.gov.uk or Land Registry Public Guide *1 – A guide to the information we keep and how you can obtain it.*
- This title is dealt with by Land Registry Maradon office.

A: Property register
The register describes the registered estate comprised in the title.

CORNSHIRE : MARADON

1. (19.12.1989) The Freehold land shown edged with red on the plan of the above title filed at Land Registry and being 13 Augustine Way, Kerwick (PL14 3JP).

2. (19.12.1989) The land has the benefit of a right of way on foot only over the passageway at the rear leading into Monk's Mead.

3. (03.12.2003) The exact line of the boundary of the land in this title (between the points A – B in blue on the title plan) is determined under section 60 of the Land Registration Act 2002 as shown on the plan lodged with the application to determine the boundary dated 3 December 2003.

   Note: Plan filed.

B: Proprietorship register
This register specifies the class of title and identifies the owner. It contains any entries that affect the right of disposal.

Title absolute

1. (10.07.2000) PROPRIETOR: PAUL JOHN DAWKINS and ANGELA MARY DAWKINS both of 28 Nelson Way, Kerwick, Maradon, Cornshire PL14 5PQ and of pjdawkins@ail.com.

2. (10.07.2000) The price stated to have been paid on 2 June 2000 was £78,000.

Title Number CS72510]

3. (10.07.2000) RESTRICTION: No disposition by a sole proprietor of the registered estate (except a trust corporation) under which capital money arises is to be registered unless authorised by the Court.

4. (05.10.2002) Caution in favour of Mary Gertrude Shelley of 18 Cambourne Street, Kerwick, Maradon, Cornshire PL14 7AR and of Messrs Swan & Co of 25 Trevisick Street, Kerwick, Maradon, Cornshire PL14 6RE.

5. (28.11.2003) RESTRICTION: No disposition of the registered estate by the proprietor of the registered estate is to be registered without a written consent signed by the proprietor for the time being of the Charge dated 12 November 2003 in favour of Fast and Furious Building Society referred to in the Charges register.

C: Charges register

This register contains any charges and other matters that affect the registered estate.

1. (19.12.1989) The passageway at the side is included in the title is subject to rights of way on foot only.

2. (10.07.2000) A Transfer of the land in this title dated 2 June 2000 made between (1) John Charles Brown and (2) Paul John Dawkins and Angela Mary Dawkins contains restrictive covenants.

   NOTE: Original filed.

3. (01.08.2002) REGISTERED CHARGE dated 15 July 2002 to secure the moneys including the further advances therein mentioned.

4. (01.08.2002) Proprietor: WEYFORD BUILDING SOCIETY of Society House, The Avenue, Weyford, Cornshire CN12 4BD.

5. (28.11.2003) REGISTERED CHARGE dated 12 November 2003.

6. (28.11.2003) Proprietor: FAST AND FURIOUS BUILDING SOCIETY of Fast Plaza, The Quadrangle, Weyford, Cornshire CN14 3NW.

7. (03.12.2003) The parts of the land affected thereby are subject to the leases set out in the schedule of leases hereto.

Schedule of notices of leases

1.	*Registration date and Plan ref.*	*Property description*	*Date of lease and Term*	*Lessee's Title*
	03.12.2003	13 Augustine Way, Kerwick	12.11.2003 999 years from 10.10.2003	CS385372

End of register

6

CHAPTER 6
LEASEHOLD

CHAPTER AIMS AND OBJECTIVES

In this chapter we will explore the leasehold estate in land. We will consider what a lease is and what the essential characteristics of a lease are, noting in particular how to distinguish this proprietary estate from a personal licence. We then will look at the formalities of a lease, identifying what is required to create a legal lease and how equitable leases arise. We will establish how legal and equitable leases may bind third parties. Finally, we will examine the different ways that a lease may be brought to an early end. In particular, forfeiture will be analysed as the main means by which a landlord may insist on ending a lease before it expires.

By the end of this chapter, you should be able to:

- recognise the various means by which leases are created and the different types of lease that exist;
- know and understand the formal requirements of legal and equitable leases;
- know the methods used to protect legal and equitable leases in registered and unregistered land and understand the implications for third parties;
- understand the basic obligations and duties each party has under a lease;
- understand the means by which leases may be brought to an early end, particularly the use of forfeiture;
- know and understand the procedures required to forfeit a lease.

CASE STUDY – ONE

Elizabeth and her boyfriend, George, were living together in a one-bedroom flat when Elizabeth's aunt offered them the opportunity to move into a three-bedroomed cottage which she owns the freehold title to. It was agreed that:

- They could stay 'for as long as they should wish whilst ever I do not need the cottage to live in upon my retirement'.
- They would pay £300 a month rent.
- They would need to give one month's notice if they decided to leave.

Elizabeth's aunt retained a key in order to visit the property to check how the renovations and redecoration they promised to undertake were progressing.

> **KEEP IN MIND**
>
> - We know that there are only two legal estates in land, s 1(1) of the Law of Property Act 1925. The freehold (fee simple absolute in possession) and the leasehold (term of years absolute).
> - The case study makes it clear that the freehold title, the closest to absolute ownership of land, to the cottage belongs to the aunt.
> - Elizabeth and George may, however, be able to claim a leasehold estate for a period of time.
> - We know that there are formalities associated with creating any legal estate in land and so some of the informality suggested by the facts of the case study are likely to raise issues that we will need to respond to before giving any advice.

THE BASICS

As we have seen from earlier chapters there are two types of legal estate under the Law of Property Act 1925 (LPA 1925). It is important to remember the fundamental differences between the two.

THE TWO LEGAL ESTATES

Freehold

The freehold or fee simple absolute in possession is the larger of the two types of legal estate in land under s 1(1)(a) of the LPA 1925. As we have seen, the expression 'fee' indicates that it is inheritable therefore you can leave it to others in your will. The word 'absolute' means that it is not subject to any conditions. This is the best estate a person can have and potentially could last forever. So long as you have heirs or leave a will, the estate can continue to pass freely from one person to another. This is the nearest you can get to having absolute ownership. It is known as a freehold estate.

Leasehold

The second type of estate is a leasehold or term of years absolute under s 1(1)(b) of the LPA 1925. Unlike a freehold, you only hold a leasehold for a fixed period of time.

> TUTOR TIP – 1
>
> There are no limits to the number of legal leases that can be granted. There can however only be one legal freehold estate in a piece of land at any one time.

A lease is a document creating an interest in land for a specified period and usually in consideration of the payment of a rent. A lease is sometimes referred to as a 'demise' and the leased premises is called the 'premises demised'. You may also have heard people talk about having a tenancy for a house they are renting. A tenancy is also a lease but is a term often used for interests lasting for a relatively short period only. In everyday terminology, the term lease is usually indicates a longer, more enduring interest.

A term of years absolute is defined by s 205(xxvii) of the LPA 1925 and means: 'a term of years (taking effect either in possession or in reversion whether or not at a rent) … and either certain or liable to determination by notice, re-entry, operation of law, or in any other event'.

As we will see, a lease must have certain duration, which must be clearly defined before the lease starts as it is not possible for the lease to continue indefinitely. The lease does not however have to be in possession immediately. A term of years absolute can be created now (in possession) or in the future (in reversion).

ESSENTIAL TERMINOLOGY

Lease	A lease is a document creating an estate in land for a specified period of time, usually in consideration of the payment of a rent.
Demise	A lease is sometimes referred to as a demise and the premises in question as the 'premises demised'.
Tenancy	Used for estates lasting for a relatively short period only whilst a lease will usually indicate a more enduring interest.
Periodic tenancy	A lease that runs for a continuous periodic term, typically from month to month or less commonly from week to week or year by year. As opposed to a lease lasting for a fixed term such as six months or one year.
Landlord or lessor	The person who grants the lease.
Tenant or lessee	The person who has the benefit of the lease.
Reversion	On the granting of the lease the lessor retains the reversion. This can be sold, transferred or assigned to another person. Another way of looking at it is that once the lease comes to an end the property reverts back to them.
Sublease or underlease	Instead of assigning the lease (i.e. transferring the estate for the whole of the period for which it is held), the owner of the lease may grant a new 'sublease' (or underlease) for some shorter period.

ILLUSTRATING HOW LEASEHOLDS OPERATE

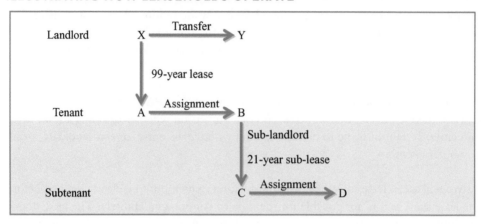

Figure 6.1 An example of a lease and sublease

The 99-year lease

In Figure 6.1, X owns the freehold estate in the property. Rather than sell and transfer the whole freehold estate to another person, X can grant a lease. In this example X granted a lease to A for a term of 99 years. A now owns a leasehold estate in the property for 99 years. At the end of the 99 years the property would have reverted back to X (if he had not already assigned his reversion) and A will no longer have an estate. X is the landlord and A is the tenant.

During the 99 years under the lease X and A will have obligations to each other in relation to the property. X will probably receive rent and profits in consideration of granting A the lease.

Although X has granted the lease to A, he still holds the freehold interest and can therefore assign this freehold interest in the property, which is known as the freehold reversion, to another person. Here X decides that he will sell his interest to Y. So now Y holds the freehold reversion and the property will in fact currently revert to Y at the end of the 99 years. Y is also the landlord during the remainder of the lease.

As A has an estate in land, he, too, can transfer his leasehold to another person. A can sell whatever time remains under the lease – here he sells the remaining time under the lease to B. B now holds the leasehold estate. Y is the landlord and B the tenant.

The 21-year lease

As a leasehold interest is an estate in land it is possible to grant a further lease out of one. As B holds a leasehold interest, B can grant a new, smaller lease to another person. This is acceptable providing B grants a lease for shorter time that he has remaining under his lease, because you cannot give more than you have. For example, here B can grant a lease of 21 years but cannot grant a lease of 150 years, because after the 99 years fully expires he will no longer have any interest in the property.

The first original lease is known as the head lease and X (then Y) is the head landlord and A (then B) is the head tenant.

The second lease for 21 years is known as the sublease or underlease and B is the sub-landlord and C the subtenant.

There are no limits on how many leases may be created, unless the original lease included a non-assignment clause, therefore C is entitled to grant a further lease out of his estate. The same rules apply here however as C cannot grant a lease for longer than 21 years or however many years actually remain at the time he acts.

THE IMPORTANCE OF DISTINGUISHING BETWEEN LEASES AND LICENCES

A leasehold is an estate in land and therefore a proprietary right. A licence, explored in depth in Chapter 8, is only a personal right.

TUTOR TIP – 2

Note that a property right, such as a lease, applies beyond the original parties and is capable of binding third-party successors. So, if you purchase a freehold estate to a house that is currently being rented for one year, you will have to honour that lease.

A licence is a personal right between the original parties only. So, should you purchase a freehold estate to a house that is currently subject to licence you would take free of it (in Chapter 8, we will see that in certain circumstances some clever argument may be made using constructive trusts and proprietary estoppel).

The argument of a lease is much more powerful and it is far better if a person can establish they have a lease rather than a licence. We must, therefore, be able to distinguish one from the other. The specific advantages of a lease include:

- A lessee can assign his interest in the land, which means he can sell the lease to another person. A licensee may be unable to do so.
- A successor in title to the landlord may take subject to the lease until it ends, in effect becoming the new landlord. A licence will not run.
- A lessee has security of tenure and therefore has the statutory protection, regulation of their rent and the right to enforce some covenants against the landlord, which are implied into the lease. A licensee has less protection.

ESSENTIAL CHARACTERISTICS OF A LEASE

Just like many other interests in land law, there are a number of essential characteristics that are required when establishing that a lease exists. The leading case of *Street v Mountford* [1985][1] developed a three-point definition of a lease. A common practice at the time was for those who might otherwise be considered as landlords to give the 'appearance' that they had granted only a licence. This was to avoid the statutory protection available to tenants under a lease, notably the Rent Act 1977. The parties to the agreement would often subjectively agree that a licence was in place, even though the actual characteristics objectively fitted with it being a leasehold.

KEY CASE: *STREET V MOUNTFORD* [1985] UKHL 4; [1985] AC 809; [1985] 2 ALL ER 289

In this case Mrs Mountford had signed an agreement, expressly referred to as a 'licence agreement' under which she was granted the right to occupy two rooms for a rent of £37 per week. At the bottom of the document she has signed it clearly stated: 'I understand and accept that a licence in the above form does not and is not intended to give me a tenancy protected under the Rent Acts.'

In this case the House of Lords, whose judgment was delivered by Lord Templeman, considered that an objective stance should be taken in determining what had been created by the parties' agreement.

The key element was identified as 'exclusive possession at a rent for a term'. If these elements were present then a tenancy had been created, not a licence, irrespective of what the parties had chosen to label it. Lord Templeman stated that: '[T]he manufacture of a five pronged implement for digging results in a fork even if the manufacturer, unfamiliar with the English language, insists that he intended to make and has made a spade!'

He continued:

> In my opinion in order to ascertain the nature and quality of the occupancy … the court must decide whether upon its true construction the agreement confers on the occupier exclusive possession. If exclusive possession at a rent for a term does not create a tenancy then the distinction between a contractual tenancy and a contractual licence of land becomes wholly unidentifiable.

So the means by which the parties describe the agreement is not the determining factor as to the nature of the transaction:

> The consequences in law of the agreement once concluded, can only be determined by consideration of the effect of the agreement. If the agreement satisfied all the requirements of a tenancy, then the agreement produced a tenancy and the parties cannot alter the effect of the agreement by insisting they created only a licence.

---

1 [1985] UKHL 4; [1985] AC 809; [1985] 2 All ER 289.

Put simply, if the three essential components are not present then a 'tenant' will not have a lease but a licence. The three essential components identified are shown in Figure 6.2.

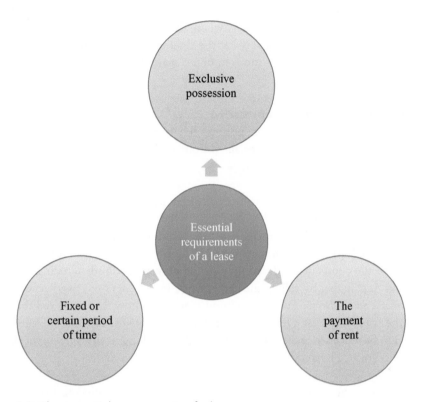

Figure 6.2 The essential components of a lease

> TUTOR TIP – 3
> ....
>
> While Lord Templeman identified rent as essential, we shall soon see that the courts later decided it is not. It is, however, an important thing to note that presence or absence of, given that a lack of payment may indicate that there was no intention to enter into legal relations. That would result in a court only finding a licence, which we will also explore in due course.

EXCLUSIVE POSSESSION

Exclusive possession is the most important of the three components. A tenant, unlike a licensee, will have the right to exclusive possession of the demised premises. Exclusive possession enables the tenant to exclude all other persons from the premises demised, including the landlord. As Lord Templeman explained in *Street v Mountford* [1985], exclusive possession is seen as territorial control, the tenant's ability 'to call the land his own' which gives rise to exclusory power and immunity from supervisory control. If a tenant has exclusive possession then the landlord has no right of entry unless he makes provision for this in the lease. Such provisions are normally limited to issues such as the right to inspect the property to ensure that it is in a good state of repair or a right to enter to repair. Exclusive possession cannot be established if the grantor has a right to re-enter at will. This will not be a lease but a mere licence, as was seen in *Interoven Stove Co Ltd v Hibbard* [1936].[2] Similarly, where the grantor remains in general control of the premises and the grantee merely has the right to use the premises for certain limited purposes e.g. a lodger or a room in hotel, again this is indicative of a licence rather than a lease.

The development of exclusive possession

The question as to whether exclusive possession has been given is determined by the intention of the parties, which is ascertained from all the circumstances of the case, rather than the language of the parties.

The distinction between a lease and a licence began in the 1960s when landlords attempted to avoid the effects of the Rent Acts, which gave tenants very substantial security of tenure. To avoid the Rent Acts many landlords attempted to give 'tenants' mere rights of occupancy, which were stated to be licences, though in reality they were leases. At first the courts decided that they would prevent landlords avoiding the effects of the Rent Acts simply by calling the agreement a lease as opposed to a licence. The decision in *Facchini v Bryson* [1952][3] is a good example of how the courts did this. In the case the court held that a lease had been created despite the fact that the agreement was stated to be a licence and contained a term that 'nothing in this agreement shall be construed to create a tenancy'.

During the 1970s, however, there was a change in attitude and the courts started to give greater importance to the parties' intentions rather than to the objective assessment of what had been created. This shift was possibly provoked by a reaction to the effects of the Rent Acts themselves, rather than a perceived change in the relationship between the parties. Originally the Rent Acts were seen as attempting to protect vulnerable tenants, but later they were regarded as an increasing burden to landlords. This resulted in a shortage of rented accommodation nationally. This change in attitude can be seen in the judgments of Lord Denning, who had previously sat in the case of *Facchini v Bryson*. In *Shell Mex and BP Ltd v Manchester Garages Ltd* [1971],[4] Denning gave primacy to the intentions of the parties in order to avoid the effects of the Rent Acts. He stated, 'I realise that this means that the parties can, by agreeing on a licence, get out of the Act; but so be it; it may be no bad thing'. This approach was subsequently followed in *Somma v Hazlehurst* [1978].[5]

---

2 [1936] 1 All ER 263.
3 (1952) 96 Sol Jo 395; [1952] 1 TLR 1386.
4 [1971] 1 All ER 841; [1971] 1 WLR 612.
5 [1978] 1 WLR 1014.

The new approach could at best be described as a subjective approach taking into consideration the expressed intentions of the parties rather than the substantive and objective reality of what the parties actually created.

KEY CASE: *SOMMA V HAZLEHURST* [1978] 1 WLR 1014

An unmarried couple entered into an agreement with the owner of a house for the use of a bedsit. The agreement was stated to be a licence and the couple were required to sign separate agreements. It was a term of the agreement that the licensees may be required to share their accommodation with 'such licensees or invitees whom the licensor shall from time to time permit to use the room'. This meant that they did not have the power to exclude anyone else from the premises. It was clear, however, that the couple really enjoyed exclusive occupation of the bedsit and that the agreement was calculated to avoid the effects of the Rent Acts. The couple later claimed that they had a lease but the Court of Appeal held that a mere licence had been created. Cumming-Bruce LJ stated:

> We can see no reason why an ordinary landlord should not be able to grant a licence to occupy an ordinary house. If that is what both he and the licensee intend and if they can frame any written agreement in such a way as to demonstrate that it is not really an agreement for a lease masquerading as a licence, we can see no reason in law or justice why they should be prevented from achieving that object. Nor can we see why their common intentions should be categorised as bogus or unreal or as a sham merely on the ground that the court disapproves of the bargain.

The decision does seem a little duplicitous when considering the facts of the case. The bedsit was a room measuring 22 ft × 18 ft and in reality it is hardly credible to suggest that the landlord could impose other occupiers on the couple in such a small space, or that the couple would have agreed to this. Similarly, if one of the occupiers left was it feasible for the landlord to allow or impose another occupier of a different sex on the remaining party?

The reality was of course that the landlord had no intention of doing either of these things. The arrangement in fact was a sham to avoid the provisions of the Rent Acts.

This subjective approach was finally ended in the case of *Street v Mountford* [1985] where the House of Lords, considered that an objective stance should be taken in determining what had been created by the parties' agreement. The key element was identified as 'exclusive possession at a rent for a term'. If these elements were present then a tenancy had been created, irrespective of what the parties had chosen to label it as. This approach was subsequently adopted.

Exclusive occupation or exclusive possession?

There are difficulties with the objective approach in *Street v Mountford* [1985] as the notion of exclusive possession is a legal concept not a factual one. This can be seen in the difference between exclusive occupation as opposed to exclusive possession.

A hotel guest will have exclusive occupation as he would not have to share his room with another guest. He will not, however, have exclusive possession as he cannot exclude the owner, his agents or employees from entering the room. Where there is exclusive occupation there may be exclusive possession, but where there is no exclusive occupation there can be no exclusive possession and any interest can only be a licence. The dividing line is very difficult to define and in truth it will depend 'upon a combination of factors' as seen in *Aslan v Murphy* [1989].[6]

If the grantor of the interest reserves genuine access at will to the presumed premise i.e. a right to re-enter at will, a lease is not created and the occupier cannot resist intrusion by the landlord. Examples of this have been seen in a number of cases such as a resident in an old people's home and where a landlord provides laundry services to the lodger.

In *Abbeyfield (Harpenden) Society Ltd v Woods* [1968][7] the grantee was described as sole occupant of a room in an old people's home. The grantor provided a housekeeper, meals and other services, in addition to reserving the right to take possession of the room at its discretion but promised to give a month's notice if this right was exercised. It was held that this arrangement was personal in nature and therefore only amounted to a licence.

In *Appah v Parncliffe Investments Ltd* [1964][8] individuals had occupation of a room, each room had a Yale lock and key, a gas ring and a gas meter. Bath and toilet facilities were communal. No meals were provided, but other services were provided which included daily cleaning of the rooms, the making of beds and the weekly supply of fresh linen, and cleaning of the staircase and other parts of the building in common use. The 'landlord' reserved a general right of entry of rooms entered once a month to clear the coin-box of the gas meter and displayed notices requiring visitors to leave by 10.30 p.m. The occupant was not required to give notice if he wished to quit his room providing he was not in arrears. It was held that there was no exclusive possession and again the occupier held a licence not a lease.

In both cases it was clear the individual did not have supervisory control of the property nor did they have the ability to exclude the landlord or his agents.

However, in *Family Housing Association v Jones* [1990][9] the retention of a key did not prevent the finding of a tenancy and in *Aslan v Murphy* [1989], Donaldson MR noted:

---

6 [1989] 3 All ER 130; [1990] 1 WLR 766.
7 [1968] 1 All ER 352n; [1968] 1 WLR 374.
8 [1964] 1 All ER 838; [1964] 1 WLR 1064.
9 [1990] 1 All ER 385; [1990] 1 WLR 779.

Provisions as to keys … do not have any magic in themselves. … A landlord may well need a key in order that he may be able to enter quickly in the event of an emergency … He may need a key to enable him … to read meters or to do repairs which are his responsibility. None of these underlying reasons would of themselves indicate that the true bargain between the parties was such that the occupier was a lodger [a licence]. On the other hand, if the true bargain is that the owner will provide genuine services which can be provided only by having keys, such as frequent cleaning, daily bed-making, the provision of clean linen at regular intervals … it is possible to infer that the occupier is a lodger rather than a tenant.

APPLY YOUR LEARNING – TASK 1

Do you consider the retention of the key by Elizabeth's aunt to be a problem to finding exclusive possession? Do you think she is providing a genuine service when she makes her inspections?

Multiple occupiers

The sharing of premises does not necessarily mean there is not exclusive possession. They may together have joint exclusive possession by either:

- holding separate tenancies for their particular parts of the property that they occupy, for example their own bedrooms, but may share other common areas; or
- holding as joint tenants sharing the whole of the property.

Whether occupiers have exclusive possession or are separate licensees depends on how they share.

KEY CASE: *AG SECURITIES V VAUGHAN* [1990] 1 AC 417; [1988] 2 ALL ER 173

Four people occupied a four-bedroom property. Each signed a separate agreement expressed to be a licence. The agreements were all made at different times and different rents were agreed. The actual occupants of the house varied over time as people left and were replaced. They were held to occupy as licensees. If the occupiers has been jointly entitled to exclusive possession then, on the death of one of them, the remaining three would have had to be entitled to joint and exclusive possession. It was, however, clear that in that situation the owner would have had the right to replace him and the occupiers could not have prevented him from so doing.

The requirement for an intention to create legal relations

While Lord Templeman, in *Street v Mountford* [1985], identified exclusive possession as central to the recognition of a lease he accepted that there are some situations in which, even though it is present, there can be no lease. When considering a 'combination of factors' to establish exclusive possession the courts will look at whether there was an intention to create a legal relationship.

A lease is a formal document creating a contract between the parties; as such there must be an intention to create legal relations between the parties. Consideration is given to:

- what circumstances gave rise to exclusive possession;
- did the grantor have the power to grant a lease; and
- was there anything that negated the party's intention to create a lease.

There are a number of situations that can cause particular difficulty with establishing an intention to create legal relations. Each is far removed from an apparently commercial motivation (Figure 6.3).

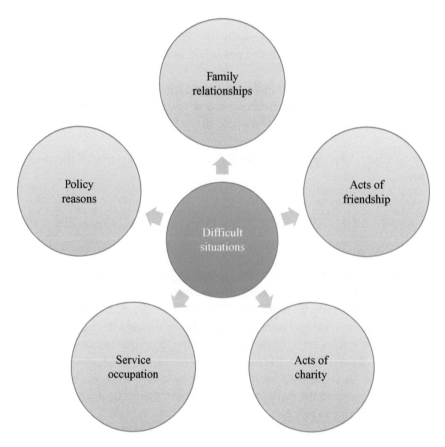

Figure 6.3 Situations suggesting no intention to create legal relations

Family relationships

Where there is occupation by reason of a family relationship this may also point to the absence of a tenancy. The rationale is that there is not normally an intention to create a legal relationship between family members and as such the family connection is likely to point to the absence of a tenancy. Informal arrangements within a family context are more likely than not to give rise to licences rather than leases, as was seen in the cases of *Cobb v Lane* [1952][10] and *Barnes v Barratt* [1970].[11] In *Barnes v Barratt* a couple were provided with exclusive occupation of three rooms in a house in return for them cooking and supplying other domestic services to the owner and their payment of certain household bills. The Court of Appeal held that this situation was 'closely akin to those produced by family arrangements to share a house' and therefore there was no intention to create a legal relationship between the parties giving rise to a lease. In *Errington v Errington* [1952][12] an arrangement was entered into in which a young couple occupied a house owned by the husband's father provided they paid the mortgage repayments. The courts held this to be a licence as the arrangement was informal and there was no intention to create legal relations.

Family situations do not, however, necessarily preclude a lease from arising. In the case of *Nunn v Dalrymple* [1989][13] a farm was owned by Mr Chapman and managed by his son Guy. Guy arranged with his parents-in-law, the defendants, to renovate a lodge on the estate and then occupy it. Upon completion of the renovations the defendants gave up a tenancy of a council property they had lived in for a number of years. Upon moving in to the property they made regular payments of rent. The farm was sold and the question was whether the defendants had a lease.

The Court of Appeal stated that even where there was exclusive occupation and the payment of rent it is possible to negate the existence of a lease in family situations. They were clear that this did not stop family relationships from creating leases but the bar would be high. There must be sufficient evidence to show that the parties intended to create the relationship of landlord and tenant. In this case the payment of rent and the defendants giving up the security of tenure on their council property were seen as strong evidence. Clearly, giving up a proprietary right on another property was a clear indicator that the occupier intended that the new occupation agreement should give her equally enforceable rights.

---

10 [1952] 1 All ER 1199, 96 Sol Jo 295.
11 [1970] 2 QB 657; [1970] 2 All ER 483.
12 [1952] 1 KB 290; [1952] 1 All ER 149.
13 (1989) 59 P & CR 231; [1990] Fam Law 65.

APPLY YOUR LEARNING – TASK 2

The family relationship between Elizabeth and her aunt could be a problem and must be considered. Given the payment or rent (as well as the promise to carry out renovations) and the formality of giving a month's notice before leaving, do you think you could argue this was the creation of a legal relationship?

Acts of friendship and charity

When occupation is granted on the basis of generosity or charity this also may indicate that there is not a tenancy but a licence as was the case in *Booker v Palmer* [1942].[14] In *Marcroft Wagons Ltd v Smith* [1951][15] a daughter lived with her mother who was a statutory tenant of a house. On the mother's death the daughter asked the landlord to transfer the tenancy to herself, which the landlord refused to do. He did, however, allow her to remain in occupation in return for the payment of rent. The Court of Appeal held that she was not a tenant but a mere licensee. Lord Evershed, MR, took the view that it would be wrong to give landlords a disincentive to acting out of 'ordinary human instincts of kindness and courtesy' because they were afraid that the occupant could not be removed. He reasoned,

> It seems to me that it would be quite shocking if, because a landlord allowed a condition of affairs to remain undisturbed for some short period of time, the law would have to infer that a relationship had arisen which made it impossible thereafter for the landlord to recover possession of the property.

Service occupation

A person who enjoys occupation by virtue of their employment will not enjoy a tenancy, for example a school caretaker or a security guard. In order to establish whether a service occupation exists *Smith v Seghill Overseers* (1875)[16] stated that the relevant test of service occupancy is whether the servant is required to occupy the premises to better perform his duties as a servant. This test was affirmed in *Norris (t/a J Davis & Son) v Checksfield* [1991][17] by Lord Woolf who stated: 'What is required is that there should be a sufficient factual nexus between the commencement of the occupation of the premises and the employment which would benefit from that occupation.'

In *Street v Mountford* [1985] Lord Templeman believed that a service occupation may be eliminated from the list of those creating leases as:

---

14 [1942] 2 All ER 674, 87 Sol Jo 30.
15 2 KB 496; [1951] 2 All ER 271.
16 (1875) LR 10 QB 422, 40 JP 228; [1874–80] All ER Rep 373.
17 [1991] 1 WLR 1241.

A service occupier is a servant who occupies his master's premises in order to perform his duties as a servant. In those circumstances the possession and occupation of the servant is treated as the possession and occupation of the master and the relationship of landlord and tenant is not created.

Policy reasons

There are certain types of public sector landlords who may be able to grant licences in circumstances where a private landlord could not. This has been seen in a number of cases including *Westminster City Council v Basson* (1990),[18] *Westminster City Council v Clarke* [1992],[19] *Ogwr Borough Council v Dykes* [1989][20] and *Camden London Borough Council v Shortlife Community Housing Ltd* (1992)[21] relating to local authority and housing association accommodation.

In *Westminster City Council v Clarke* [1992] the House of Lords held that an occupant of a council hostel for single homeless persons was a licensee, not a tenant, with the same rights as a lodger. Westminster City Council owned the premises, which were used as a hostel for single homeless men. The occupants had no exclusive rights of occupation and could be required by the local authority to change rooms or to share their room with another occupant. Occupants could not have visitors without prior approval and could have their 'licences' terminated on seven days' notice or forthwith if they were in breach of the hostel rules.

Lord Templeman, who had presided over *Street v Mountford* also sat on this case in the House of Lords. He held that the limitations placed upon each occupier:

> confirmed that the council retained possession of all the rooms of the hostel in order to supervise and control the activities of the occupiers, including Mr Clarke. Although Mr Clarke physically occupied the room he did not enjoy possession exclusively of the council.

Lord Templeman was clear, however, to distinguish this case from other landlord-and-tenant situations for policy reasons, accepting the provisions were genuine and necessary for the proper management of hostel but not for avoiding the Rent Acts. Lord Templeman explained:

> This is a very special case which depends on the peculiar nature of the hostel maintained by the council, the use of the hostel by the council, the totality, immediacy, and objectives of the powers exercisable by the council and the restrictions imposed on Mr Clarke. The decision in this case will not allow a landlord, private or public, to free himself from the Rent Acts or from the restrictions of a

---

18 (1990) 23 HLR 225; 62 P & CR 57.
19 [1992] AC 288; [1992] 1 All ER 695.
20 [1989] 2 All ER 880.
21 (1992) 90 LGR 358, 25 HLR 330.

secure tenancy merely by adopting or adapting the language of the licence to occupy. The provisions of the licence to occupy and the circumstances in which that licence was granted and continued, lead to the conclusion that Mr Clarke has never enjoyed that exclusive possession which he claims.

The curious case of Bruton

The doctrine of *nemo dat quod non habet* is long established within land law, meaning you cannot give away what you do not have. Indeed one of the points of consideration is establishing that the grantor had the power to grant a lease. The case of *Bruton v London & Quadrant Housing Trust* [1999],[22] however, flies in the face of this.

KEY CASE: *BRUTON V LONDON & QUADRANT HOUSING TRUST* [1999] UKHL 26; [2000] 1 AC 406; [1999] 3 ALL ER 481

The local authority granted London & Quadrant Housing Trust (LQHT) a licence to use council premises for the purposes of providing short-term accommodation to homeless people in the borough. LQHT then entered into the agreement with Mr Bruton granting him exclusive possession of a self-contained flat for a fee of £18 per week. LQHT granted this on the basis of a weekly licence ensuring there was no security of tenure. The plaintiff subsequently brought proceedings in the county court claiming that he was the tenant of the premises and seeking specific performance by the trust of an implied covenant to keep them in repair.

Despite the fact that LQHT had only been granted a licence by the local authority, the House of Lords held that Mr Bruton had a lease and not a licence. They concluded that given he was able to exclude everyone including the local authority and LQHT, the trust did not retain control over the premises and Mr Bruton could establish exclusive possession.

Justifying their position Lord Hoffman held that:

> [T]he term 'lease' or 'tenancy' describes a relationship between two parties who are designated landlord and tenant. It is not concerned with the question of whether the agreement creates an estate or other proprietary interest which may be binding upon third parties. A lease may, and usually does, create a proprietary interest called a leasehold estate or, technically, a 'term of years absolute.' This will depend upon whether the landlord had an interest out of which he could grant it. *Nemo dat quod non habet*. But it is the fact that the agreement is a lease which creates the proprietary interest. It is putting the cart before the horse to say that whether the agreement is a lease depends upon whether it creates a proprietary interest.

---

22 [1999] UKHL 26; [2000] 1 AC 406; [1999] 3 All ER 481.

Later Lord Hope of Craighead also explained:

> The present case does not depend upon the establishing of an estoppel nor does any problem arise from the fact that the housing trust did not have a legal estate. The case of Mr Bruton depends upon his establishing that his agreement with the housing trust has the legal effect of creating a relationship of tenant and landlord between them. That is all. It does not depend upon his establishing a proprietary title good against all the world or against the council. It is not necessary for him to show that the council had conveyed a legal estate to the housing trust.

In summary the House of Lords held:

- A 'lease' was not always an estate in the land, but could be a merely personal arrangement between 'landlord' and 'tenant'.
- This non-proprietary lease could be justified by exclusive possession of the 'tenant', even though the landlord could not grant the kind of exclusive possession (that is, of an estate in the land) that was so crucial in *Street v Mountford*.
- The House of Lords disagreed that the special nature of the trust (charitable body) was sufficient to take it out of the *Street v Mountford* rule.
- They rejected the argument that the trust could not create a lease because it had no estate in the land. Lord Hoffmann stated that the creation of an estate was usual to create a lease but not essential. The term lease, 'is not concerned with the question of whether the agreement creates an estate or other proprietary interest which may be binding upon third parties.'

Implications following Bruton

The ruling had immediate implications for LQTR, as they were deemed responsible for repairing obligations of the premises to Mr Bruton, despite not having a proprietary interest in the property themselves. Much more significantly *Bruton* had wider implications for land law as the ruling in *Bruton* created a second category of leases:

1. There is the proprietary lease creating an estate or interest in the land. This is how everyone viewed leases prior to *Bruton*
2. A non-proprietary lease which is contractual relationship between the parties, personal in nature and does not create an estate or interest in the land.

This second category of lease is confusing as its description appears the same as a licence. This new 'non-proprietary lease' also raises a number of important questions too, including:

1. When is a non-proprietary lease created?
2. How was a non-proprietary lease created?

3   What is the effect of a non-proprietary lease on third parties?
4   Do these contractual non-proprietary leases provide a tenant with statutory
     protection in the same way proprietary leases do?

There have been two cases since *Bruton* in which the reasoning was applied: *Kay v London Borough of Lambeth* [2005][23] and *London Borough of Islington v Green* [2005].[24] As with *Bruton* the cases involved housing associations who had been granted licences by a local authority enabling them to provide temporary accommodation to homeless and vulnerable people. In both cases, the courts made the point that a person with a *Bruton* tenancy does not have a proprietary interest in land binding against the freehold or any other third party. In *Green*, Blackburne J pointed out, 'it seems to me to follow that the fact that the tenants held *Bruton* tenancies did not enable them to say that they had estates in the properties that they occupied.'

Unfortunately, these two cases do not add a great deal to our understanding of *Bruton* and many of the questions raised by it still remain unanswered. It is difficult to make the distinction between the concepts of a contractual lease and the implications for the rule of *nemo dat quod non habet*, which would require that a lease cannot be granted by a party without an estate in land (a freehold or a longer lease).

FIXED OR CERTAIN PERIOD

The second requirement set out by Lord Templeman in *Street v Mountford* [1985] is that the lease must be for a certain period. If there is any uncertainty as to the commencement and duration of the lease it will fail. This has been a long-standing requirement of a lease and is intended to prevent the possibility of a lease being granted that would last forever, which in theory would make it a freehold. The case of *Lace v Chantler* [1944][25] first established this principle with a 'lease' granted to the tenant for 'the duration of the war'. It is obvious that nobody had any idea how long the war was going to last and as such the landlord and the tenant could not confirm the duration of the lease. The courts therefore held that the lease was invalid due to uncertainty.

The House of Lords decision in *Prudential Assurance Co Ltd v London Residuary Body* [1991][26] confirmed that the commencement and duration of a lease must be certain or capable of being rendered certain before the lease takes effect. Here the local authority had granted Prudential a lease of a property fronting Walworth Road, a busy road in London. The council had included a clause stating that 'the tenant shall continue until the ... land is required by the council for the purposes of widening of [the road].' The House of Lords stated that there was not a valid fixed-term lease as its duration could not be certain. As it happened, the widening of the road never actually took place.

....

23   [2005] QB 352.
24   [2005] EWCA Civ 56.
25   [1944] KB 368; [1944] 1 All ER 305.
26   [1991] UKHL 10; [1992] 2 AC 386; [1992] 3 All ER 504.

> ## TUTOR TIP – 4
>
> A fixed-term lease provides certainty of period; a lease for say 7, 20 or 100 years leaves no ambiguity.
>
> What of a periodic tenancy, which renews from period to period until the landlord or tenant give notice to bring it to any end? The majority will run from month to month. One cannot be sure at the outset whether a monthly tenancy will be renewed for six months or six years. Periodic tenancies are saved from uncertainty by having clear notice. As long as the notice period by which the lease may be brought to an end is clear, the duration of the lease need not be clear at the outset and certainty exists.
>
> There is also no need to be certain that the lease will continue for the full duration, so the inclusion of a break clause would not be a problem. Break clauses are commonplace in commercial leases, allowing parties to end the lease at different points. So if, for example, a tenant agrees to enter into a 15-year lease of a shop they could negotiate an option to walk away at the end of the fifth year. This is helpful if the business is struggling or indeed if it is thriving and bigger premises are needed.

PAYMENT OF RENT

Lord Templeman indicated in *Street v Mountford* [1985] that rent was an essential element of a lease. There has been some debate as to whether rent is a strict requirement. In *Ashburn Anstalt v Arnold* [1988][27] the Court of Appeal held that rent was not an essential criterion in establishing the existence of a lease. This decision is consistent with the definition of a lease in s 205(1)(xxvii) of the LPA 1925 where a term of years absolute is defined as a 'term of years (taking effect in possession or in reversion whether or not at a rent)'. In *Bostock v Bryant* [1990][28] a grant by 'Uncle Joe' of part of his house to the defendants, who paid no rent but contributed to the outgoings in terms of fuel bills, was held not to create a tenancy, but a licence. The payment of the fuel bills did not constitute rent. Whilst in *Foster v Robinson* [1950][29] a retiring employee surrendered a Rent Act tenancy in return for an undertaking to allow him to remain in the cottage rent-free for the rest of his life. His daughter claimed the tenancy on his death by virtue of the Rent Acts. It was held that she merely had a licence.

By contrast *Colchester Borough Council v Smith* [1991][30] concerned a man occupying agricultural land under an agreement with the council. This agreement allowed him to remain in occupation for the rest of that year without charge at his own risk. It was

27 [1989] Ch 1; [1988] 2 All ER 147.
28 [1990] 39 EG 64.
29 [1951] 1 KB 149; [1950] 2 All ER 342.
30 [1991] Ch 448; [1991] 2 All ER 29.

held that this agreement was a licence, even though he enjoyed exclusive use of the land; the absence of a rent was highly relevant to the decision. Ferris J explained:

> Although in this case the council did, in my judgment, grant exclusive possession to Mr Tillson it did not do so at a rent and only in a limited sense can it be said to have done so for a term. In my view the rejection of Mr Tillson's implied offer to pay a reasonable rent, the expression of the transaction in terms of non-objection to continued occupation as distinct from the grant, the insistence that Mr Tillson must occupy at his own risk and must give up possession at short notice if the land were required for other purposes, all point towards this being an exceptional transaction, not intended to give rise to legal obligations on either side.

Whilst rent may or may not be an essential requirement of a lease it will be an important factor in determining whether or not exclusive possession has been granted to the occupier as it indicates an intention to enter into a legal relationship.

TYPES OF LEASES

FIXED TERM

This is the most commonly used lease. The landlord grants a fixed term of years to the tenant. This could be 5 years, 50 years or even 500 years. There are no limits on how long the term of years is, it simply comes down to what the parties decide. The only requirements are that the period of time is fixed and certain before the lease starts. As we have seen above, uncertainty as to the commencement and duration will result in the lease failing. It should be pointed out, however, that as long as the duration is certain at the point of commencement it does not matter if the lease was uncertain upon creation of the document.

A fixed-term lease may begin at a future date, such a lease being known as a 'reversionary lease'. There are rules, however, in the granting of a reversionary lease under s 149(3) of the LPA 1925, as a lease which takes effect more than 21 years from the instrument creating will be void. The same applies to any contract made after 1925 which agrees to create such a term. For example, a grant of a lease in 2017 commencing 1 May 2045 will be *void*, as would a contract in 2017 to grant in 2017 a lease commencing 1 May 2045.

A lease for a fixed period automatically determines when the fixed period expires. Once the term is fixed neither party can determine it (i.e. terminate it) unless the lease contained provisions for either party to determine the lease at a certain point. This is known as a break clause.

> ## TUTOR TIP – 5
> ....
>
> In addition to notice, there are other ways that leases are determinable:
>
> 1 *A right of re-entry.* This is the right of the landlord to recover or repossess the property following a breach of the lease by the tenant. A lease that incorporates a right of re-entry will be a valid term of years.
> 2 *By any other event.* A break clause is a good example of any other event. A break clause, common in commercial leases, is a point in the lease where either party has the option of bringing the lease to an end early and not to continue it.

PERIODIC TENANCY

A periodic tenancy is a lease that runs on a continuing basis i.e. week by week, month by month, year by year. This can be confusing, as we have seen from the definition under s 205(xxvii) of the LPA 1925 that a term of years absolute implies that the term or duration of the lease must be clear at the outset and the end date must be clear. So how can a periodic tenancy have a certain duration? The answer is in the definition itself, as s 205(xxvii) states that the term must be 'either certain or liable to determination by notice, re-entry, operation of law, or in any other event'. A periodic tenancy does not terminate until appropriate notice is given by either the landlord or the tenant, meaning there is certainty as to when notice can be given and when the lease will then end. Such tenancies are, therefore, capable of being a legal estate under s 1(1)(b).

Periodic tenancies are 'determinable' i.e. they can be brought to an end by either party at any time by the exercising of notice on the other party. Notice is the formal period of time that either party serves on the other party to indicate that they want the lease to be brought to an end. For example, if the landlord serves the tenant with two months' notice, it means that the tenant has had a written warning from the landlord that he wishes the lease to be brought to an end and for the tenant to leave the property in two months' time. As long as the notice period is clear, the duration of the lease need not be clear at the outset and certainty exists. In *Prudential Assurance Co Ltd v London Residuary Body* [1992],[31] Lord Templeman confirmed this, stating: 'the certainty of term rule applies to all leases and tenancy agreements. A tenancy from year to year was saved from being uncertain because each party had the power to determine by notice at the end of any year.'

As we have seen, periodic tenancies can be on a yearly, quarterly, monthly or weekly basis and will continue indefinitely until ended by one of the parties to it serving proper notice.

....

31 [1992] 2 AC 386; [1992] 3 All ER 504.

> **TUTOR TIP – 6**
>
> It is important to be careful with the wording used in a periodic tenancy, as you may create something that you did not intend. The wording needs to be clear and unambiguous, as with *Re Searle* [1912] 1 Ch 610.
>
> For example a landlord who grants 'to Anna from year to year' or 'to Anna as a yearly tenant' will create a yearly tenancy.
>
> However, if the landlord grants the premise 'to Anna for one year and thereafter from year to year' he will then have created a lease for at least two years.

The notice period, unless expressly stated in the tenancy, will depend on the form that the periodic tenancy takes, i.e. one full period for a weekly or monthly tenancy and six months for a yearly one. However, in the case of residential tenancies at least four weeks' notice must be given even if it is a weekly tenancy.[32]

LEASES FOR LIVES

In essence, an individual would be granted a lease of a property until they died, at which time it would revert back to the landlord, the freeholder. However, s 205(xxvii) of the LPA 1925 requires certainty of duration, for the parties to know at the beginning of the lease how long it will last and as we know a person's life is not certain. To combat this, leases for lives are converted into a fixed 90-year lease under s 149(6) of the LPA 1925. The lease will not automatically terminate on the death but when either party dies one month's notice can be served onto the other party to terminate the lease.

> **KEY CASE:** *MEXFIELD HOUSING CO-OPERATIVE LTD V BERRISFORD* [2011] UKSC 52; [2012] 1 AC 955
>
> An occupancy agreement between a mutual housing association and one of its members was expressed to be 'from month to month until determined'. The tenant was entitled to terminate the agreement by giving one month's written notice. The housing association had agreed that it could only end the agreement if (1) the rent fell 21 days in arrear, (2) the tenant breached any of the other terms of the agreement, or (3) the tenant ceased to be a member of the association. The association served the tenant with one month's notice, on the basis that there was a monthly periodic tenancy determinable by such.
>
> The Supreme Court said that in the absence of contrary indication, a tenancy granted 'from month to month' was a monthly tenancy. However, the interpretation of the agreement depended on the terms and the circumstances. The purpose of entering into an agreement with the tenant had been to provide

---

32 Protection from Eviction Act 1977.

her with a home and it was clear that the arrangement created by the agreement was determinable by the association only in the defined circumstances. It was held that the agreement could not take effect as a periodic tenancy.

The arrangement was a lease for an uncertain term, as the association's right to serve notice was tied to events that are uncertain. However, prior to 1926, the common law would have treated an agreement with an uncertain term as a tenancy for life. The agreement was, therefore, treated by the Supreme Court as a tenancy for life which, after 1926, under s 149(6) LPA 1925 means takes effect as a 90-year lease.

The argument in *Mexfield* is subject to formalities. In *Hardy v Haselden* [2011] EWCA Civ 1387, an oral offer could not create the equitable interest that a tenancy for life necessarily is as its creation would have to comply with the formalities of s 53 of the Law of Property Act 1925 or there would have to be a written contract for its creation complying with s 2 of the Law of Property (Miscellaneous Provisions) Act 1989. Furthermore, in *Southward Housing Co-operative Ltd v Walker* [2015] EWHC 1615 (Ch) the High Court held that *Mexfield* applies only where the parties intended to create a lease for life.

TENANCY AT WILL

Where a person, with the consent of the owner, occupies land as a tenant and not merely as a servant or licensee a tenancy at will can be established. A tenancy at will can be determined at any time by either party.

TENANCY AT SUFFERANCE

This arises where a tenant having entered upon land under a valid tenancy stays in the premises and 'holds over' without the landlord's consent or dissent at the end of that valid tenancy. A tenant at sufferance differs from a trespasser in that his original entry was lawful, and differs from a tenant at will as here the tenancy exists without the landlord's consent. A tenancy at sufferance can be determined at any time.

APPLY YOUR LEARNING – TASK 3

Looking at the different types of leases discussed above, which type of lease do you consider Elizabeth and George have and why?

Do you think that there could be a fixed-term lease? Do the words used by Elizabeth's aunt 'for as long as they should wish, whilst ever I do not need the cottage to live in upon my retirement' create a fixed maximum duration?

What about a presumed periodic tenancy? Elizabeth and George are paying rent on a monthly basis and have to give one month's notice if they decide to leave. But what of *Mexfield*, if the agreement were in writing, does the wording used in the agreement restrict the aunt's ability to determine a monthly tenancy? If so, this is a tenancy for an uncertain duration as we cannot know when the aunt will retire. Would this be interpreted as a tenancy for life? In our scenario, we are not concerned with social housing and the right to occupy appears to be intentionally somewhat precarious.

To avoid these problems, the aunt should have either expressly granted a periodic tenancy without any further restriction on her ability to serve notice; or she should have specified a maximum fixed term, subject to a break clause allowing her to terminate the lease upon her retirement.

CREATION OF LEASES

Leases can be created in three different ways:

- legal lease arising from express grant
- legal leases arising by implication
- equitable leases arising by virtue of a contract or an informal grant.

LEASES ARISING FROM EXPRESS GRANT

In order to create a legal lease, there are two points to always check. First, was a deed used and, second, was the lease registered?

Use of a deed

To create a legal estate after 1925 a lease must not only grant a term of years absolute under s 1(1)(b) of the LPA 1925 but must be made by deed in accordance with s 52(1) of the LPA 1925.

It is possible, however, to create a legal lease without a deed by mere writing or even orally, provided for under s 54(2) of the LPA 1925. This is only possible where the 'lease takes effect in possession for a term not exceeding three years (whether or not the lessee is given power to extend the term) at the best rent which can be reasonably obtained without taking a fine'.

(a) **If the lease is for a term not exceeding three years**
    A three-year lease can include tenancies from year to year or other periodic tenancy, even though they will continue indefinitely until determined by notice. The three years rule also includes a fixed term for three years or less, which contains an option for it to be extended beyond the three years.

(b) **The lease takes effect in possession**

The lease must start straightaway. This is contrasted with a reversionary lease, which takes effect in the future, for example where it is granted to start in three months' time.

(c) **At the best rent reasonably obtainable and no 'fine'**

A 'fine' is a lump sum payment, sometimes made in consideration of a reduced rent. It is often called a 'premium' today. If an individual purchases a warehouse flat in the centre of Leeds they may pay £200,000 for the granting of the leasehold. This would be the premium, or fine.

The position is similar in relation to the granting of a sublease and upon assigning a lease. In order to effect a legal assignment of a lease, a deed must be employed under s 52(1) of the LPA 1925 if it is for more than three years. In *Crago v Julian* [1992][33] the husband and wife separated and then agreed to get divorced. The husband at the time was a weekly tenant under a legal lease created orally. He vacated the property and agreed by way of a written undertaking to transfer his interest in the property to his wife. The landlord was not informed nor his permission sought. During the time the wife was in the property she made alterations and improvements to the property believing that the paperwork was in order and that the lease had been transferred to her. Upon discovering the situation, the landlord refused to change the rent book and would not accept rent from her. He ordered her to quit the property and sought possession of the property. The landlord's possession order was granted, as there had been no assignment of the lease by deed to the wife. The husband and wife did not follow the necessary formalities under s 52 of the LPA 1925 and as such she was not classified as a tenant.

> TUTOR TIP – 7
>
> ....
>
> Remember that granting a lease is different from a contract to grant a lease. A contract to grant means that it is something you undertake to do in the future; it does not mean that you have done it now. An estate contract to grant must comply with s 2 of the Law of Property (Miscellaneous Provisions) Act 1989, which related to the regulations for contracts. This, however, does not comply with s 52(1). You can also distinguish between the two by the language that is used between the parties
>
> Granting a lease would be **'I hereby GRANT you a lease of the property'** whilst contracting to grant a lease would be **'I hereby AGREE that I will grant you a lease of the property.'**
>
> The first example is actually doing something, the second is promising that you will do something.

Registration of a legal lease

To complete the formalities for legal leases the Land Registration Act 2002 (LRA 2002) imposed a number of registration requirements under ss 4 and 27.

---

33 [1992] 1 All ER 744; [1992] 1 WLR 372.

Leases over seven years

Legal leases of over seven years created out of either an unregistered freehold or leasehold estates, are compulsorily registrable if they are either for valuable or other consideration, by way of a gift or pursuant to an order of any court under s 4(1)(c) of the LRA 2002. Under s 7 of the LRA 2002 the effect of not complying with the registration requirement is that the grant of the lease is void at law and will only take effect as a contract, again resulting in it becoming an equitable lease.

Legal leases of over seven years granted out of registered land must themselves be registered to be legal and to bind as required under s 27(2)(b)(i) of the LRA 2002. These leases are substantially registerable and will have their own unique title number and register with the Land Registry. As it is registration that confers title, the lessee will not have legal title until the legal lease is registered. Until registration, the lease is only an equitable lease and will probably only have the potential to bind third parties as an overriding interest with the lessee establishing they are a person with an interest in actual occupation under sch 3, para 2 of the LRA 2002.

Leases of no more than seven years

Legal leases of seven years or less do not require registration. As legal leases of seven years or less they qualify as overriding interests under sch 3, para 1 of the LRA 2002. This means that they do not appear on the register but will bind third parties automatically.

In the case of leases under seven years created in unregistered land, again registration will not be required. Instead, the lease will override the first registration of the superior unregistered estate under sch 1, para 1 of the LRA 2002.

It is important to note that these two sections only apply to legal leases as it has been held that equitable leases are not capable of being overriding in the case of *City Permanent Building Society v Miller* [1952].[34]

LEGAL LEASES ARISING BY IMPLICATION

Leases are often the result of an express agreement between landlord and tenant. This has the advantage that the details of the arrangement, including any particular undertakings the parties have agreed to, can be negotiated and clearly accepted. However, provided the lease does not fall under s 52(1) of the LPA 1925 as requiring a deed then it is equally possible for a lease to arise by implication.

If, however, a tenant takes possession with the landlord's consent, as seen above, a tenancy at will or a tenancy at sufferance is created. As soon as rent is paid by the tenant and is accepted by the landlord, such tenancies at will are converted into a monthly or other periodic tenancy as seen in *Martin v Smith* [1874].[35] The effect of this presumption at common law is to create an implied legal lease, providing all four elements are present (Figure 6.4).

---

34 [1952] Ch 840; [1952] 2 All ER 621.
35 [1873–74] LR 9 Ex 50.

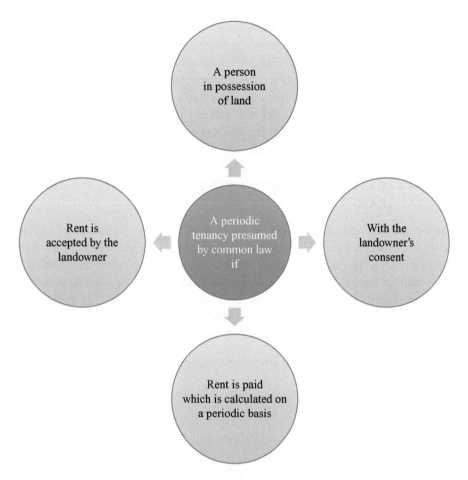

Figure 6.4 Finding a presumed periodic tenancy

The type of periodic tenancy created is determined by the way rent is expressed to be due rather than the way in which it is paid. This principle was established in *Ladies Hosiery and Underwear Ltd v Parker* [1930].[36] For example, a tenancy on a yearly basis will arise by implication, if the tenant is in possession of the property and paying the rent agreed as an annual sum i.e. £12,000 per annum, even if the payments received are monthly in 12 payments of £1,000.

Recent cases, however, have emphasised the importance of discovering the real intention of the parties – see *Cardiothoracic Institute v Shrewdcrest* Ltd [1986][37] and *Javad v Mohammed Aqil* [1991].[38] In *Javad v Mohammed Aqil*, the Court of Appeal conceded that in the total absence of any other 'material surrounding circumstances', the inference 'sensibly and reasonably to be drawn' from the payment of rent is that the parties intended to create a periodic tenancy. Nicholls LJ indicated that it is relatively rare that

36 [1930] 1 Ch 304, 99 LJ Ch 201.

37 [1986] 3 All ER 633; [1986] 1 WLR 368.

38 [1991] 1 All ER 243; [1991] 1 WLR 1007.

the fact of a periodic payment should stand alone from other factors which may help to clarify the situation, such as any agreement made between the parties or their overall intentions at the time of the agreement. He explained that 'a tenancy springs from a consensual arrangement between two parties: one person grants to another the right to possession of land for a lesser term than he, the grantor, has in the land. The extent of the right thus granted and accepted depends primarily upon the intention of the parties.' It is possible however for this formula to be rebutted by evidence to the contrary in relation to the parties' intentions.

EQUITABLE LEASES ARISING BY VIRTUE OF A CONTRACT OR AN INFORMAL GRANT

Whilst we have established that a lease that does not follow the formalities of s 52(1) of the LPA 1925 will fail to create any legal estate, it may not be entirely ineffective, since it might be treated as a contract to grant the lease agreed upon. As we have seen, a lease is clearly distinct from a contract to grant a lease. Both law and equity treat an imperfect lease as a contract to grant a lease, provided it is made for value and is in writing to comply with s 2(1) of the Law of Property (Miscellaneous Provisions) Act 1989 (LP(MPA)A 1989). In doing so it provides a party to the contract with two options:

- The party can seek the common law remedy of breach of contract and damages as the contract has not been performed as promised.
- The principles of equity would apply where *Equity regards as done that which ought to be done.*

Following the equitable principles, if the parties had intended to grant a lease and had simply not followed the correct formalities, the court will construe a lease in equity and on that basis be in a position to order specific performance, i.e. make the parties enter into a legal lease by the landowner granting the tenant a lease and ensure that the lease is granted in a deed.

The availability of equity is still dependent on the normal equitable rules, in that the party seeking specific performance must come with clean hands, so they must not delay enforcement unduly and must not have breached any of the terms of the agreement themselves. Additionally the party must establish that there is a valid contract under s 2(1) of the LP(MP)A 1989 which provides that the contract must be in writing, contain the main terms and be signed by the parties. These principles were followed in the case *of Parker v Taswell* (1858).[39] This will result in an equitable rather than legal lease being created as of the date of the contract, with the equitable lease being held on the same terms as those contained and promised in the contract.

The Walsh v Lonsdale *principle*

Walsh v Lonsdale (1882)[40] took this concept one stage further so that the intended tenant does not actually need to obtain or even seek a decree of specific performance of

---

39 (1858) 2 De G & J 559.
40 (1882) 21 ChD 9.

the contract from the court. The tenant will be able to establish that a decree would have been granted to them if they had applied to the courts providing they can show:

- there is a valid contract for a lease; and
- specific performance would be available to them.

Equity will then simply apply the doctrine of conversion and 'looks on that as done which ought to be done'. The intended tenant does not have a legal lease but a lease in equity, which is regarded as being on terms identical to those in the defective lease.

KEY CASE: *WALSH V LONSDALE* (1882) 21 CHD 9

The landlord agreed in writing to grant by deed a lease of a mill to the tenant for seven years, one term of the lease being that the tenant should on demand pay a year's rent in advance. No deed was executed, but the tenant was let into possession and for a year and a half paid rent quarterly, although not in advance. The landlord then demanded a year's rent in advance, and on tenant's refusal to pay, distrained for it. The tenant then brought an action for damages for wrongful distress, and for specific performance of the agreement.

The tenant argued that distress was a legal not an equitable remedy and that as at law he was only a yearly tenant with no obligation to pay rent in advance, the landlord could not distrain for the rent.

Jessel MR stated:

> The tenant holds under an agreement for a lease. He holds, therefore, under the same terms in equity as if a lease had been granted, it being a case in which both parties admit that relief is capable of being given by specific performance. That being so, he cannot complain of the exercise by the landlord of the same rights as the landlord would have had if a lease had been granted. On the other hand, he is protected in the same way as if a lease had been granted; he cannot be turned out by six months' notice as a tenant from year to year. That being so, it appears to me that being a lessee in equity he cannot complain of the exercise of the right of distress merely because the actual parchment has not been signed and sealed.

As such it was held that since the distress would have been legal had the lease agreed upon been granted by deed, and since equity treated the parties as if this had been done, the distress was lawful in equity; the equitable rule prevailed over the legal rule, so even at law the tenant could not complain over the distress. The relationship of the parties was the same as if the lease had actually been granted.

TUTOR TIP – 8

It is not uncommon for both an implied legal period tenancy and an equitable lease to be arguable.

Since the *Earl of Oxford's Case* in 1615, now encompassed in s 49 of the Supreme Court Act 1981, if there is a conflict between the rules of common law and the rules of equity, the latter always prevail. So in situations where it is possible to argue that both an implied legal period tenancy *and* an equitable lease exist, equity will prevail.

Remember equity will only prevail *if* the preconditions of equity apply. Once equity needs to intervene because the legal formalities to create or assign a lease have not been met, it will need to be shown that:

1 there is a valid contract for a lease; and
2 specific performance would be available to the tenant.

If one or more of these are absent then equity will not grant relief and the tenant would have to fall back on his implied legal periodic tenancy.

CONSIDER THIS – 1

Consider what advice you would give if, when the cottage renovations are completed, Elizabeth's aunt agrees in writing with Elizabeth and George to grant them a lease of the cottage for five years at £400 a month rent. The agreement was signed by all three and the couple moved in and started making the payments. No deed of lease has been executed.

Applying your knowledge from your reading of creation of lease, would you argue (1) a legal lease arising from express grant, (2) a legal lease arising by implication or (3) an equitable lease arising by virtue of a contract or an informal grant?

Equitable and legal leases compared

In *Re Maughan* [1885],[41] Field J stated that 'since the Judicature Acts there is now no distinction between a lease and an agreement for a lease, because equity looks upon that as done which ought to be done.' The case law also confirmed that the same principle applies to imperfect leases, which are enforceable as an agreement for a lease.

---

41 (1885) 14 QBD 956, 54 LJQB 128.

CONSIDER THIS – 2

If no differences exist between a legal and an equitable lease why would parties feel inclined to follow the formalities and requirements of a legal lease? Are there distinctions between the two?

Specific performance

The existence of an equitable lease is always dependent on the availability of specific performance and any party seeking this equitable remedy must 'come with clean hands'. As such the party must not delay enforcement unduly and must have not breached any of the terms of the agreement of the lease themselves.

Additionally if the court lacks jurisdiction to order specific performance, a tenant will not be in a position to enforce the agreement in that court. This was seen in *Foster v Reeves* [1892][42] where Lopes LJ pointed out:

> 'There is only one court, and equity rules prevail in it.' The decision applies to every branch of the High Court, which has concurrent jurisdiction in law and equity, but does not apply to a county court, which is not affected by the Judicature Acts. If this is so, the county court, having no equitable jurisdiction in this matter, is in the same position as that of the common law courts before the passing of the Judicature Acts. The common law courts could not then have entertained the claim, and the county court cannot now entertain it.

In such situations where the courts cannot or will not grant specific performance then the only option to the individual is to sue for breach of contract and damages.

Easements

As we will see in Chapter 12, an agreement for a lease is not within the statutory definition of a conveyance, thus a tenant under an agreement for a lease cannot claim easements or profits which are transferred under s 62 of the LPA 1925.

Assignment and enforceability of covenants

The doctrine of *Walsh v Lonsdale* (1882) does not treat an enforceable agreement for a lease as being as good as a lease as regards third parties. It is only enforceable between the actual parties to the agreement under the principles of privity of contract. As we will see in Chapter 7, privity of estate will exist between the landlord and the new tenant under a pre-1996 lease. There is no privity of contract between the landlord and the new tenant under an agreement for a lease merely by virtue of the assignment, even though it is made by deed. The implication of this is that whilst the benefit of a contract is assignable the burden is not. Thus the assignee can sue the landlord but the landlord can only sue the original tenant and not the new tenant.

---

42 [1892] 2 QB 255.

The Landlord and Tenant (Covenants) Act 1995 changes the position slightly in relation to leases created on or after 1 January 1996 and means that both the benefit and the burden of all covenants pass upon assignment of a legal lease, an agreement for lease or an assignment of an equitable lease except those expressed to be personal.

The effect upon third parties

The rights of a tenant under an agreement for a lease, being equitable, are subject to the same frailties as all equitable interest. In unregistered land a contract for a lease must be registered as an estate contract Class C(iv) entry. If it is not registered it will be void against a purchaser for money or money's worth under ss 4(6) and (7) of the Land Charges Act 1972. Registration is deemed to be actual notice to the world at large.

In registered land, a contract to grant a lease must be protected as a notice against the register for the land under s 32 of the LRA 2002. If the interest is not registered, it is still possible to bind third parties as an overriding interest under sch 3, para 2 of the LRA 2002 if the tenant is in actual occupation.

DETERMINATION OF TENANCIES

A lease or tenancy may come to an end in a number of ways, the most important are set out in Figure 6.5.

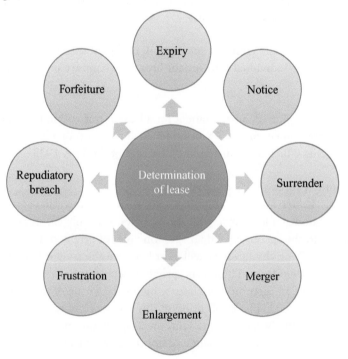

Figure 6.5 Determining a tenancy

EXPIRY

The general rule is that a lease for a fixed period automatically determines when the fixed period expires. Once the term is fixed then neither party can determine it (i.e. terminate it) unless the lease contained provisions for either party to determine the lease at a certain point – this is known as a break clause.

NOTICE

A fixed period lease or tenancy cannot be determined by notice unless it has been expressly agreed by the parties, i.e. a provision within the lease stating that either party can bring the lease to an end upon giving two months' written notice to the other party. With commercial leases where a more substantial term has been granted e.g. 25 years the lease will normally contain a number of break clauses enabling the tenant to determine the lease at various points during the agreed term, for example at the end of the fifth, tenth and fifteenth years. In such cases the length of notice required, the time when it is to be given, and other matters of this kind will have to be expressed within the lease. In the absence of such provisions the lease will continue for the full period agreed.

With periodic tenancies, it is the notice period that makes the tenancy certain. There cannot be any restriction placed upon the parties' right to serve notice as established in *Prudential Assurance Co Ltd v London Residuary Body* [1991].[43] Such provisions cannot prevent the landlord or tenant from serving notice to quit and any attempts to preclude either party from serving notice will be invalid. Equally, no conditions can be placed upon how or when notice is served. For example, any attempts to prevent the tenant from serving notice until such time as the 'landlord shall stipulate' or 'the landlord's new apartment accommodation becomes available' will be invalid due to its uncertainty. In such situations the common law will imply notice periods. In the *Prudential* case, the tenant could not rely on the clause preventing the landlord from terminating the lease until such time as the land was required for road-widening purposes. The timing of this event was uncertain and therefore not a valid fetter on the service of notice.

SURRENDER

Where a tenant surrenders his lease to his immediate landlord, and the landlord accepts surrender, the lease merges in the landlord's reversion and is extinguished. The surrender must be to the immediate landlord and may be by either express or by operation of law. A transfer to a superior landlord does not affect surrender and merely operates as an assignment. Equally a surrender of the lease does not terminate an existing subtenancy as these are protected and preserved under s 139 of the LPA 1925.

---

43 [1991] UKHL 10; [1992] 2 AC 386; [1992] 3 All ER 504.

Express surrender

For a lease where the term exceeds three years, a deed is required in accordance with s 52 of the LPA 1925. For leases of less than three years, for best rent and without a fine, express surrender can be achieved under ss 53(1) and 54(2) of the LPA 1925 if there is evidence in writing, which has been signed by the parties, i.e. a contract.

Surrender by operation of the law

Surrender by operation of law will occur if the parties do some act showing an intention to terminate the lease. The parties must behave in an unequivocal way, which is inconsistent with the continuation of the lease or tenancy. Surrender requires the agreement of both parties. In *Cannan and Grimley, Assignees of Tanner a Bankrupt v Hartley* [1850][44] it was held that surrender cannot be a unilateral act, whilst in *Preston Borough Council v Fairclough* [1983][45] it was held that the tenant simply leaving the property did not constitute an implied surrender if the landlord performed no action to show he had accepted that the lease had come to an end. In order to achieve implied surrender there must be actions by both parties pointing towards surrender. For example, in *Phene v Popplewell* [1862][46] the courts held that a surrender had occurred without formalities when the landlord accepted back the premises, painted out the tenant's name on the signboard and put up a 'to let' sign, as this demonstrated both parties behaving in an unequivocal way.

MERGER

This is the opposite of surrender and occurs where the tenant retains the lease and acquires the reversion, or where a third party occupies both the lease and the reversion. To be effective, the lease and the reversion must be vested in the same person in the same right with no vested estate intervening. This merger often happens when a person holding the lease for a leasehold house purchases the freehold interest when it becomes available. In these cases the leasehold and the freehold merge and the individual is left with a freehold house.

ENLARGEMENT

Enlargement enables a tenant to unilaterally declare that his leasehold interest is 'enlarged' into a freehold estate. The process of enlargement must be done by executing a deed of enlargement and then registered with the Land Registry. Under s 153 of the LPA 1925, enlargement can only be achieved if:

(i) there is not less than 200 years of the lease unexpired;
(ii) the lease was originally granted for at least 300 years;

----

44 [1850] 137 ER 1040.
45 [1983] 8 HLR 70.
46 [1862] 12 CB NS 334.

(iii) no trust or right of redemption (i.e. under a mortgage) exists in favour of the reversioner;
(iv) the lease is not liable to be determined by re-entry for condition broken; and
(v) no rent or money value is payable, i.e. no more than a 'peppercorn rent' payable under the lease.

A fee simple can only be obtained if all five provisions are satisfied. Enlargement is not something that is used greatly in practice, especially as a lease will contain provision for ground rent, even if for a nominal amount such as £5. Additionally, most leases will contain the provision for re-entry as standard.

FRUSTRATION

Frustration is where something serious and unexpected happens which affects the contractual agreement. The event, which is through no fault of either party, results in the performance of the contract being radically different from that originally agreed. For example a three-month lease of a country cottage would be frustrated if, on the first day, through no fault of either the tenant or landlord the cottage is destroyed by a gas explosion. It had been argued that this doctrine has no application to leases as they are not contracts but estates in land: *National Carriers Ltd v Panalpina Ltd* [1981][47] clarified the position. The House of Lords stated that the doctrine of frustration was applicable to leases generally. Factors to be considered in making such a decision are:

- The length of the interruption.
- The likely length of continuance of the lease after the interruption of the user in relation to the term originally granted.

In *National Carriers Limited*, however, the House of Lords were not persuaded that a 20-month period of a ten-year lease where the local authority closed the only access road to the warehouse did radically affect the performance of the contract.

REPUDIATORY BREACH

A repudiatory breach is a breach of the contract by one party that is so fundamental that it is tantamount to that party's rejection of the contract. Both the landlord and the tenant can use an argument of repudiatory breach. In *Hussein v Mehlman* [1992][48] a three-year lease had been granted. The landlord was under a duty to ensure that the structure and the exterior of the property were in a good state of repair in addition to the installing water, gas and electricity at the premises. The landlord did not comply with these covenants and was in serious breach of the lease. The tenants handed back the keys after 15 months and vacated the property, claiming a repudiatory breach on the part of the landlord. The court held that the landlord had no intention of

---

47 [1981] AC 675; [1981] 1 All ER 161.
48 [1992] 2 EGLR 87; [1992] 32 EG 59.

complying with these covenants and believed that the tenants were deprived of an essential part of the lease. They accepted the tenants' argument that there had been a repudiatory breach by the landlord and released the tenants from their obligations under the lease.

In *Chartered Trust plc v Davies* [1997],[49] the tenant of a shopping unit withheld rent claiming his business was adversely affected by the landlord's failure to control and supervise other tenants in the development. The tenant argued that the landlord had breached the covenant not to derogate from his grant and as such constituted a repudiatory breach. The Court of Appeal upheld this.

FORFEITURE

Forfeiture will be explored in detail in Chapter 7 on leasehold covenants. Forfeiture is the ability to bring the lease to an end earlier than originally agreed when the tenant has breached a covenant contained in the lease. The landlord will have the right to forfeit the lease if the tenant breaks a promise and the lease contains an express provision for forfeiture for breach of covenant. In practice, most well-drafted leases will contain such a clause; however, it is important that a landlord checks this and simply does not assume it exists. Even with such a provision in place, a breach renders the lease voidable, allowing the landlord the option to forfeit, rather than allowing the lease to be automatically forfeited and ended.

CONSIDER THIS – 3

The contract between Elizabeth's aunt and Elizabeth and George created a five-year lease. Now let us add a term to it, requiring the couple to maintain the house and its garden.

Nine months on, Elizabeth and George decide that they would like to spend the next year travelling the world and want to bring their lease with Elizabeth's aunt to an end. Although Elizabeth and George had agreed to maintain the garden, they have not done so and the garden is very overgrown.

Assess what options are available to Elizabeth, George and Elizabeth's aunt to terminate the lease. Which option is the most appropriate in the circumstances and why?

---

49 (1997) 75 P & CR D6, 76 P & CR 396; [1997] 2 EGLR 83.

DISCUSSION

Despite the objective test set out by Lord Templeman in *Street v Mountford* [1985] being welcomed by many as a way of combating 'sham' agreements disguising leases as licences, there are a number of possible criticisms.

First, does the decision undermine freedom of contract? Giving the question express consideration, Lord Templeman reasoned why it did not:

> In the present case, the agreement … professed an intention by both parties to create a licence and their belief that they had in fact created a licence. It was submitted on behalf of Mr. Street that the court cannot in these circumstances decide that the agreement created a tenancy without interfering with the freedom of contract enjoyed by both parties. My Lords, Mr. Street enjoyed freedom to offer Mrs. Mountford the right to occupy the rooms comprised in the agreement on such lawful terms as Mr. Street pleased. Mrs. Mountford enjoyed freedom to negotiate with Mr. Street to obtain different terms. Both parties enjoyed freedom to contract or not to contract and both parties exercised that freedom by contracting on the terms set forth in the written agreement and on no other terms. But the consequences in law of the agreement, once concluded, can only be determined by consideration of the effect of the agreement.

Second, are the more problematic questions of just how objectively the objective test can be applied. It is far from easy to always tell exclusive occupation from the necessary exclusive possession. As our consideration of case law suggests, there are many factors to consider. The additional acknowledgement that, even with exclusive possession, it is necessary to also show an intention to enter into a legal relationship also creates further difficulties. There is also *Bruton* to now consider; given the objective of *Street v Mountford* [1985] itself was to distinguish between leases and licences this apparent invention of a new 'non–proprietary' lease does not fit well.

CONSIDER THIS – 4

The criteria identified by Lord Templeman in *Street v Mountford* [1985] were intended to settle long-running uncertainties about distinguishing leaseholds from licences. To what extent has that certainty proved possible in practice and could a degree of debate in individual cases ever be avoided?

END OF CHAPTER SUMMARY

- To be called a lease, the right must possess a number of essential characteristics identified and defined in the case of *Street v Mountford* [1985]. These characteristics are certain duration, exclusive possession and an intention to create legal relations (the payment of rent is relevant to determining this factor).
- Exclusive possession gives rise to exclusory power and the ability to exclude all others including the landlord from the property.
- In order to establish exclusive possession the courts will look at whether there was an intention to create legal relations. A number of situations can negate this including family relationships, acts of friendship, acts of charity, service occupation and policy reasons.
- There are several types of leases, including fixed term, period tenancies, leases for life, a tenancy at will and tenancy at sufferance.
- Leases can be created in three ways. To create a legal lease it must be created by deed in accordance with s 52(1) of the LPA 1925. It may be possible to create a legal lease in writing or orally if it complies with s 54(2) of the LPA 1925.
- A legal lease may arise by implication if the tenant takes possession with the landlord's consent and pays rent, which is then accepted by the landlord. This creates an implied periodic tenancy.
- It is also possible to create an equitable lease by virtue of a contract or an informal grant, providing it complies with s 2 of the LP(MP)A 1989 and the general principles of equity.
- There are many ways of bringing a lease to an end. While the majority of leaseholds will end naturally upon expiry of the agreed term, the most common of bringing a lease to an end earlier than originally agreed is by way of forfeiture.

PREPARING FOR ASSESSMENTS
QUESTIONS

ESSAY QUESTION

It has been stated by some that an equitable lease, an agreement for a lease, is as good as a legal lease.

Analyse this statement and assess how true this is.

PROBLEM QUESTION

Gavin is the registered proprietor of a freehold house, 36 Mexico Way. Twelve months ago Gavin let the property to Adam, an eccentric local artist. Adam does not believe in the need for solicitors, so Gavin and Adam wrote the following on the back of one of his pictures:

> 'Gavin will let 36 Mexico Way to Adam for 6 years and Adam will pay Isaac £1,500.00 per quarter'

Both parties signed the painting and Adam moved in the same day. As Adam does not earn a large amount of money he pays Gavin £500.00 every month. Gavin has been happy with this arrangement. Last week Adam returned from a six week long artist's conference in Spain and found that Nancy was living in the house. Nancy told Adam that she was the new owner of the property. It would appear that Gavin had sold the house to Nancy and the sale had been completed and registered ten days ago. Nancy then handed Adam a written notice requiring him to vacate the property after one week.

Advise Adam as to his rights and what action Nancy could take against him.

FURTHER READING

- Bridge, B, 'Tenancies at Will in the Court of Appeal' (1991) 50(2) CLJ, 232. Comments on the case of *Javad v Mohammed Aqil* and how arrangements between parties may result in an implied tenancy or a presumed periodic tenancy.
- Bright, S, 'Avoiding Tenancy Legislation: Sham and Contracting Out Revisited' (2002) 61(1) CLJ, 146. Explores case law on techniques used to avoid tenancy legislation. Focuses on doctrines of sham and pretence to show that the outward agreement does not represent the true intentions of the parties.
- Gardner, S, 'Equity, Estate Contracts and the Judicature Acts: Walsh v Lonsdale Revisited' (1987) 7(1) OJLS, 60. Examines the apparently well-established rule that the doctrine of *Walsh v Lonsdale* operates on a contract to grant an estate or interest only so long as it is specifically enforceable.
- Harwood, M, 'Leases: Are They Still Not Real?' (2000) 20(4) LS, 503. Reviews the historical treatment of leases as not forming part of real property, and considers whether there should be a reappraisal of the lease to be properly classified as part of real property.
- Hill, J, 'Intention and the Creation of Proprietary Rights: Are Leases Different?' (1996) 16(2) LS, 200. Explores the extent to which a proprietary right can be created when the parties intended that the arrangement would be purely personal in relation to the distinction between lease and licence.
- Lower, M, 'The Bruton Tenancy' [2010] Conv 38. Discusses the development of the concept of the non-proprietary lease. Explains the decision in *Bruton v London & Quadrant Housing Trust* and considers its implications.
- Pawlowski, M and Brown, J, 'Bruton: a new species of tenancy?' (2000) 4(6) L&T Review 119.
- Roberts, N, 'The Bruton Tenancy: A Matter of Relativity' [2012] Conv 87. An interesting article looking at the House of Lords decision in *Bruton v London & Quadrant Housing Trust* and exploring whether 'Bruton tenancies' should be treated as a form of proprietary tenancy.

- Williams, I, 'The Certainty of Term Requirement in Leases: Nothing Lasts Forever' (2015) 74(3) CLJ 592. Assesses the doctrinal basis of the rule that a valid term of years estate has a term which is certain from the outset.
- Williams, P, 'Exclusively Yours – A Look Back at Street v Mountford' (2014) 18(3) L&T Review 92. Argues that Bruton tenancies should be seen as a form of proprietary tenancy, as creating a circumscribed proprietary right in land which is best understood through the concept of relativity of title.

7

CHAPTER 7
LEASEHOLD COVENANTS

CHAPTER AIMS AND OBJECTIVES

In this chapter we will consider the issue of leasehold covenants. Leasehold covenants are promises or obligations made between the tenant (or lessee) and landlord (lessor) in relation to how the property will be used and looked after and how the parties will behave during the lease. Such obligations relate normally to: the payment of rent; who is responsible for repairs; what the tenant can and cannot do at the property whilst in possession; whether the lessee can assign or sublet the property; and what the lessor can do if these promises are broken. Leasehold covenants are extremely important, as the landlord will want to make sure that the property is being looked after by the tenant for the duration of the lease, as at the end of the fixed term the property will revert back to them.

Leasehold covenants regulating the land may not only affect the original parties to the lease but may also affect the successors in title. We will begin by considering the types of leasehold covenants frequently created and how they bind between original landlord and tenant. This will be followed by a consideration of how covenants can bind successors in title and how the Landlord and Tenants (Covenant) Act 1995 has impacted upon the liability of an outgoing landlord and tenant when the lease is assigned. Finally, we will consider the remedies available to a landlord when a tenant breaches the covenants or breaks their promise.

By the end of this chapter, you should be able to:

- understand different types of leasehold covenants that will be created in a lease and why they are relevant;
- understand the relationships between the different parties to the lease and how the law affects these relationships;
- know and understand the statutory principles underpinning the running of covenants both pre- and post-1995;
- know and understand the principles whereby landlords can enforce covenants in leases against tenants/subtenants;
- explain the range of remedies available when a covenant has been breached;
- apply the above to the case studies and learning tasks.

CASE STUDY – ONE

Aaron has recently purchased Primrose Villa, a large house with expansive gardens. As this is one of several properties owned by Aaron, he has considered whether he should lease the property as he does not intend to live in the property himself. Primrose Villa is currently a residential property and it is Aaron's intention for it to remain so. Additionally Aaron wants to ensure that the gardens remain as such and should not be built on.

Aaron has recently spoken to Bilal and is considering granting a 50-year lease in respect of Primrose Villa in return for rent of £1,000 per month. As part of the discussions, in addition to assurances about residential use and non-building, it has been agreed in principle that Bilal will be responsible for repairing, decorating and insuring the property if the lease were to go ahead.

KEEP IN MIND

- The assurances Aaron is seeking should he agree to the lease are ones that would benefit not only himself but future owners. We will need to consider whether and how the benefit of the covenants could pass to a successor.
- Bilal is about to make promises that will last for as long as the lease continues. This is a 50-year lease and so it is more than possible that Bilal will want to move on, assigning whatever remains of the lease to another when he does so. Should this mean that the new tenant takes on responsibility for the leasehold covenants, and would Bilal be removed from any continuing responsibility?
- Alternatively, Bilal may at some point in the future decide he wants to sublet the property. We will need to think about what the impact would be on the covenants.
- The express promises being made all benefit the landlord, but do you think that there are certain obligations that Aaron as a landlord must be assumed to take on and are thereby implied?
- Finally, we know that when dealing with land we expect there to be certainty and evidence of arrangements. How do you think leasehold covenants are entered into?

THE BASICS

Rights and duties are very important in relation to leasehold property, more so than with freehold land. The landlord is loaning the land to the tenant for a set period of time and will want to make sure that the tenant looks after the property during this time, as the property will revert back to the landlord at the end of the lease. The tenant also wants to ensure that they have the full use and enjoyment of the land for the term agreed.

ESSENTIAL TERMINOLOGY

Covenant	A promise contained in a deed.
Covenantor	The person who makes the promise.
Covenantee	The person to whom the promise is made. The covenantee will be the person seeking to enforce the covenant if the promise is broken.
Benefit of a covenant	The ability to enforce the covenant and sue.
Burden of a covenant	The responsibility of the covenant and the ability to be sued.

Every lease, no matter how informal will have a number of provisions which define the obligations of a landlord and a tenant under a lease. The obligations of the parties are known as covenants. A covenant is a promise from one party to the other for the other person's benefit. Covenants fall under three headings:

Express covenants   In many leases the parties will agree express covenants, which cover all the relevant points.

Implied covenants   If the lease is silent then implied terms are presumed in addition to those agreed by the parties.

Usual covenants   If the parties have merely agreed that a lease containing the 'usual covenants' shall be granted, then subject to any contrary agreements by the parties, the lease will contain whatever covenants and conditions may be 'usual' in the circumstances.

TYPES OF COVENANTS

Many of the covenants in Table 7.1 are self-explanatory. There are, however, a number of covenants that require consideration and explanation.

Table 7.1 Examples of landlord and tenant covenants

By the landlord (lessor)	By the tenant (lessee)
• Allow the tenant quiet enjoyment	• To pay rent, taxes and service charges
• Not to derogate from his grant	• To repair
• Obligations as to fitness for habitation	• Permit landlord access to repair
• To repair	• To insure
	• Not to alter the structure
	• Not to assign or sublet without permission
	• To use for a specific purpose
	• Not to deny landlord's title

The landlord's covenants

Quiet Enjoyment

This is normally included in every lease but even it is not expressed it will in any event be implied into every lease. This does not mean quiet enjoyment in the acoustic sense, in this context quiet means uninterrupted use. Essentially the tenant will be free from any disturbance with their use of the property from the landlord. The tenant will be entitled to damages if his enjoyment is substantially interfered with by the acts or failure to act of the landlord. Whether a substantial interference occurred is a question of fact and degree.

A number of cases have helped to illustrate where a landlord has failed to give quiet enjoyment and where the landlord has been seen to interfere with the tenant's right of quiet enjoyment. In *Markham v Paget* [1908][1] the landlord reserved the right to mines and minerals under the property; however, his mining activities caused subsidence of the premises and were held to interfere with the tenant's quiet enjoyment. In *Lavender v Betts* [1942],[2] the landlord removed the doors and windows in an attempt to evict the tenant and was, unsurprisingly, found to be in breach. In *Perera v Vandiyar* [1953][3] the landlord cut off the gas and electricity supply to the property whilst in *Sampson v Floyd* [1989][4] insulting and violent behaviour amounted to a breach. This duty extends to all acts of the landlord and the lawful acts of those claiming under him, for example, controlling his other tenants.[5]

> TUTOR TIP – 1
> ....
>
> Inconvenience does not amount to a breach of the right to quiet enjoyment, as was seen in the case of *Browne v Flower* [1911] 1 Ch 219, 80 LJ Ch 181 where the landlord erected an external staircase outside the property which looked into the tenants' property, infringing upon their privacy.

The right to quiet enjoyment does not extend to conditions that existed before the tenancy was granted.

> **KEY CASE:** *SOUTHWARK BOROUGH COUNCIL V MILLS* [1999] UKHL 40; [2001] 1 AC 1; [1999] 4 ALL ER 449
>
> The tenants lived in a block of flats owned by the council with ineffective sound insulation and argued that the landlord was in breach of the covenant for quiet enjoyment. The court was satisfied that excessive noise could have amounted to a breach.

1 [1908] 1 Ch 697.
2 [1942] 2 All ER 72, 167 LT 70.
3 [1953] 1 All ER 1109; [1953] 1 WLR 672.
4 [1989] 33 EG 41.
5 *Sanderson v Berwick-upon-Tweed Corporation* (1884) 13 QBD 547.

In considering that sound insulation, which was below the standards for new buildings at the time, it was held that the flats had been constructed in 1919 and that a landlord's duty to allow quiet enjoyment does not extend to a positive duty to require an improvement to the building.

Lord Hoffmann explained: '[T]he covenant does not apply to things done before the grant of the tenancy, even though they may have continuing consequences for the tenant'.

The court also considered the liability of the landlord for the nuisance being caused by their other tenants in creating the noise. Lord Millett said that for a landlord to be liable in nuisance for his tenant's acts, it is not enough 'to be aware of the nuisance and take no steps to prevent it. They must either participate directly in the commission of the nuisance, or they must be taken to have authorised it by letting the property.'

Non-Derogation from the Grant

The landlord and those claiming under him must not make the premises substantially less fit for the purpose for which they are let. In *Harmer v Jumbil (Nigeria) Tin Areas Ltd* [1920][6] the property was let for the express purpose of storing explosives, requiring a licence under the Explosives Act 1875. It was held to be a breach of covenant for the landlord to lease the adjoining land, allowing mining works and buildings to be erected in close proximity, so as to endanger the statutory licence.

No action will lie unless the action of the landlord makes the premises materially less fit for purpose, for example if the landlord, having let the premises for some particular trade, lets adjoining premises for purposes that will be in competition to the former lease. In such circumstances the court held that the premises were still fit for that trade, as was seen in *Port v Griffith* [1938].[7] Here the landlord let premises to be used as a wool shop. He then let the adjoining premises for a purpose, which permitted trade competition. It was held that the original premises were still fit to be used as a wool shop by the tenant.

Fitness and Repair

As a general rule, the landlord gives no implied undertaking that the premises are or will be fit for habitation, nor that he is liable to repair them. The position is different, however, for furnished lettings and short leases. Here, there is an implied covenant not to allow the property to become a danger to those who may foreseeably enter it.

At common law, in relation to furnished lettings the landlord impliedly undertakes that they will be fit for human habitation. If this is not the case the tenant may repudiate the tenancy and claim damages for any losses he has suffered.

6 [1921] 1 Ch 200, 90 LJ Ch 140; [1920] 1 ALL ER 113.
7 [1938] 1 All ER 295.

In *Smith v Marrable* [1843][8] the property let was infested with bugs and despite an attempt to remove them the problem remained. It was held to be a breach of an implied condition of law that the landlord undertook to let the premises in a habitable state.

Under the Landlord and Tenant Act 1985 (LTA 1985), for leases of dwelling houses granted on or after 24 October 1961 for a term of less than seven years,[9] a covenant is imposed by s 11 of that Act requiring the landlord to:

■ keep the structure and exterior of the premises in proper repair, and
■ keep in repair and proper working order the installations of the house (e.g. supply of gas, electricity, water and sanitation).

In *Staves & Staves v Leeds City Council* [1991][10] a problem of dampness, attributable to condensation, had caused mould growth on the internal walls. The continual mould and damp caused areas of plaster to perish. The tenant brought an action under s 11 of the LTA 1985 asserting that the local authority were in breach of their implied covenant to keep in repair the structure and exterior of the house. The court held it was impossible for the council to say that they kept the structure of the house in repair when the physical condition of the plaster, due to saturation, was such that it required to be renewed. It concluded that dampness in the plasterwork was part of the structure and exterior, for which the council was liable.

Additionally, the landlord owes a duty to all persons who might reasonably be expected to be affected by defects in the state of the premises. As part of this duty he must take reasonable care to see that they or their property are reasonably safe from injury or damage as per s 4 of the Defective Premises Act 1972.

The tenant's covenants
Waste
A tenant has an obligation not to commit waste i.e. any act or failure to act that alters the nature of the land for the better or the worse. The liability of the tenant here depends upon the nature of his tenancy and includes both voluntary waste (a positive act) and permissive waste by the tenant. A tenant must keep and deliver up the premises in a tenant-like manner which includes repairs where the property may otherwise be permanently altered.

Assigning, Underletting or Parting with Possession
The landlord may wish to and has the right to restrict the tenant's ability to sell, dispose of or assign or sublet the property in an attempt to ensure that the property does not come into the possession of anyone who may not take care of the property. This is known as an alienation covenant. Such covenants come in two forms:

---

8 [1843] 152 ER 693.
9 Section 13 of the LTA 1985.
10 [1991] 23 HLR 107.

- An absolute covenant means the tenant cannot assign, underlet or part with the property on any basis.
- A qualified covenant means the landlord's prior written consent will be required.

A covenant against assigning, underletting or parting with possession is often inserted in leases. If the lease is silent on the matter, the tenant is entitled to assign, underlet or part with possession without the landlord's consent.

With an absolute covenant, it is possible for the tenant to make an approach to the landlord to ask that covenant be waived. Whilst the landlord is entitled to waive it he cannot be compelled to do so even if his attitude is unreasonable.

In relation to a qualified covenant, s 19(1) of the Landlord and Tenant Act 1927 automatically inserts a requirement of reasonableness on the part of the landlord, in that his consent may not be withheld unreasonably. This does not permit the tenant to assign or sublet without seeking the landlord's consent, but if he applies and it is withheld unreasonably, he may then assign or sublet without the consent or seek a declaration from the court of his right to do so. The onus is on the tenant to show that the withholding of consent was unreasonable. The landlord is not entitled to refuse on grounds which have nothing to do with the landlord and tenant relationship. See *International Drilling Fluids v Louisville Investments (Uxbridge) Ltd* [1986] Ch 513; 1 All ER 321. The question of reasonableness is one of fact. The landlord is required to show that his conduct was reasonable, *not* that it was right or justified; see *Ashworth Frazer Ltd v Gloucester CC* [2001].[11] It is also unlawful to refuse on the grounds of sex, race or disability. Under s 1 of the Landlord and Tenant Act 1988, a landlord will be liable for unreasonably withholding or delaying consent.

Payment of Rent
This is a requirement of the tenant. Unless the lease provides otherwise, rent is normally paid in arrears. It is normal, however, for rent to take the form of regular payment of money. It continues to be payable even if the premises cannot be used e.g. owing to destruction by fire or other calamity. However, this rule is usually mitigated by an express provision in the lease.

Unless expressly stated otherwise, the rent will remain the same throughout the duration of the lease although there are normally express clauses in long leases and commercial leases to review and alter the rent at certain periods in the lease, in line with inflation or in line with an express rent review clause.

Repairs
In long leases or leases of the whole premises, the tenant usually covenants to do all repairs; in short leases, the landlord frequently assumes liability for external and structural repairs. If no express provision is made for repairs, the general law relating to waste will still apply to tenants and the landlord will have an implied obligation to

---

11 [2001] UKHL 59; [2001] 1 WLR 2180.

repair in some cases. Where the property is let furnished, it must be fit for human habitation at the beginning of the lease. See *Smith v Marrable* [1843] 152 ER 693. Under s 8 of the Landlord and Tenant Act 1985, low rent properties (not exceeding £80 per annum or £52 elsewhere) must be kept fit for human habitation for their duration, but such low rent is rare. Sections 11 to 14 of the Landlord and Tenant Act 1985 impose duties on leases for dwelling houses granted from 24 October 1961 for a term of less than seven years. The structure, exterior and installations must be kept in repair.

> TUTOR TIP – 2
> ....
>
> Leases normally deal with repairs in a number of clauses which combine the responsibility.
>
> - A requirement for the tenant to keep the subject premises in repair throughout the term.
> - Carry out repairs within specified time if served with a notice to repair by landlord.
> - Redecorate at fixed times throughout the lease and at the end.
> - To yield up the premises in repair.

Following the case of *Proudfoot v Hart* [1890][12] the general standard is 'such repair as having regard to the age, character and locality would make it reasonably fit for the occupation of a reasonably minded tenant of the class likely to take it'. A covenant to repair will normally involve the maintenance and replacement of part (see *Lurcott v Wakely* (1911))[13] and to completely rebuild the premises if destroyed as in *Bullock v Dommitt* [1796].[14]

Insurance
It is normal for the tenant to covenant that they will obtain and pay for buildings insurance, for the full property value and for the full duration of the lease. The alternative is that the landlord will obtain the insurance *but* charge the tenant for it. The latter is more common with a lease of part, thereby ensuring that the whole premises is fully insured.

LEASES CONTAINING THE USUAL COVENANTS

If the parties have merely agreed that a lease containing the 'usual covenants' shall be granted, or if there is an agreement that a lease shall be granted, with no reference being made to the covenants it shall contain, then, subject to any contrary agreement by the parties, the lease must contain whatever covenants and conditions may be 'usual' in the circumstances. The following covenants are always 'usual':

---

12 (1980) 25 QBD 42.
13 (1911) 1 KB 905; [1911–13] All ER Rep 41.
14 [1796] 2 Chit 608.

1   A covenant for quiet enjoyment by the landlord.
2   Covenant by the tenant to pay rent, tenant's rates and taxes.
3   Covenant by the tenant to keep the premises in repair and deliver them up at
    the end of the term in this condition.
4   Covenant to permit the landlord to enter and view the state of the premises, if
    he is liable to repair.
5   A condition for re-entry for non-payment of rent but not for breach of any other
    covenant.

Other covenants may be 'usual', however, by virtue of local custom or trade usage. In
each case this is a question for the courts, taking into account the nature of the
premises, their situation, the purpose for which they are let and the length of the term
etc. In *Flaxman v Corbett* [1930][15] it was suggested that a covenant would be regarded as
'usual' if nine out of ten leases of the same kind would also include the term. In *Chester
v Buckingham Travel Ltd* [1981][16] the courts accepted a wider range of covenants in
commercial leases such as restrictions on alternation and a right of re-entry for the
landlord in the case of any breach of the lease.

> **APPLY YOUR LEARNING** – TASK 1
>
> What covenants would you advise be included in the lease between Aaron and
> Bilal?

THE RUNNING OF COVENANTS

If the tenant breaches an express or implied covenant, then the landlord has a number
of remedies against him. The usefulness of these remedies is, however, sometimes
dependent on whom action can be taken against. It may no longer be the tenant who
made the covenant originally who is occupying the property. They may well have
decided to assign the lease to another or to create a sublease. As such, before exploring
the remedies, we must consider where any liability rests.

The original landlord may also decide to move on, selling the reversion. Similar
questions then emerge and whom the tenant may take action against if the new
landlord breaks express or implied covenants.

When an assignment is made, the answers to these questions are dependent upon when
the lease was granted; leases entered into before 1996 or 'old leases' continue to be
subject to their own set of rules. Leases from 1996, known as 'new leases', are governed
by a very different regime.

15 [1930] 1 Ch 672.
16 [1981] 1 All ER 386; [1981] 1 WLR 96.

PRE-1996 LEASES

Position of the original parties

The original parties to the lease (i.e. the first landlord and tenant) remain liable for the whole duration of the lease for any breaches committed under privity of contract; see *Allied London Investments Ltd v Hambro Life Assurance Ltd* [1984].[17] This is irrespective of them assigning their estate to another as they are taken, under s 79 of the Law of Property Act 1925 (LPA 1925), to covenant not only on behalf of themselves but also successors in title. For the full term for which the lease was granted, they can be sued for damages because of the breaches committed by others; see *Thursby v Plant* [1667].[18]

Following a change of tenant

In Figure 7.1, when T assigns the lease to A1 for the remainder of the duration of the lease, privity of contract remains between L and T, as they entered into a contract with each other. T, as our original tenant, is liable for any breaches of the leasehold covenants by A1.

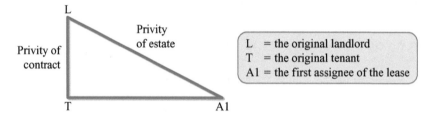

Figure 7.1 How privity of contract and privity of estate works

Privity of estate would have existed between L and T prior to the assignment, as they both held an estate in the same real property. But on the assignment between T and A1, there only will be privity of estate between L and A1, the new tenant. The new tenant, A1 will acquire the burdens and benefits of all the covenants that '*touch and concern*' the demised premises according to the rule that was established in the case of *Re Spencer's Case* [1583].[19] *Re Spencer* established that for A1 to acquire the benefits and burdens of the covenants two points must be established:

- There must be privity of estate between A1 and the person wishing to enforce it or against whom enforcement is sought (L).
- The relevant covenant must '*touch and concern*' the demised premises.

The most helpful explanation of the phrase '*touches and concerns*' can be found in the case of *P & A Swift Investment v Combined English Stores Group plc* [1989].[20] The questions that must be asked are:

....

17 [1984] 269 EG 41.
18 [1667] 83 ER 396.
19 [1583] 5 Co Rep 16a.
20 [1989] AC 632; [1988] UKHL 3.

- Does the covenant cease to be of benefit if it does not pass to the assignee?
- Does the covenant affect the nature, quality, mode of user or value of the land of the reversionary?
- Is the covenant not expressed to be personal?
- If the covenant relates to money, is it connected with something to be done on to something in relation to the land?

KEY CASE: *P & A SWIFT INVESTMENT V COMBINED ENGLISH STORES GROUP PLC* [1988] UKHL 3; [1989] AC 632

'A' company let the premises on a sublease to 'B' company, a subsidiary of 'C' company. C guaranteed B's obligations under the sublease. A conveyed the interest expectant on the reversion to 'P' company without any specific assignment of the benefit of C's covenant. B was wound up and P sued C for the outstanding rent, and obtained judgment.

The main question was whether the benefit of a covenant passes to an assignee – in this case can the assignee enforce the payment of rent by a person who has entered into a surety covenant guaranteeing the performance of the tenant's obligations under the lease, when the assignee of the reversion has not taken an express assignment of the surety covenant?

It was held that a benefit under a covenant could be enforced by the assignee of the reversion without express assignment if the covenant touched and concerned the land and that P could therefore enforce the covenant against C.

Lord Oliver constructed a helpful test that could be applied in deciding whether the covenant passes:

> Formulations of definitive tests are always dangerous, but it seems to me that, without claiming to expound an exhaustive guide, the following provides a satisfactory working test for whether, in any given case, a covenant touches and concerns the land:
>
> (1) the covenant benefits only the reversioner for time being, and if separated from the reversion ceases to be of benefit to the covenantee;
> (2) the covenant affects the nature, quality, mode of user or value of the land of the reversioner;
> (3) the covenant is not expressed to be personal (that is to say neither being given only to a specific reversioner nor in respect of the obligations only of a specific tenant);
> (4) the fact that a covenant is to pay a sum of money will not prevent it from touching and concerning the land so long as the three foregoing conditions are satisfied and the covenant is connected with something to be done on to or in relation to the land.

It is important to remember that the landlord can only sue one party and that party
must be someone with whom they have privity; either of contract or of estate. In
Figure 7.2 that will either be T or A4.

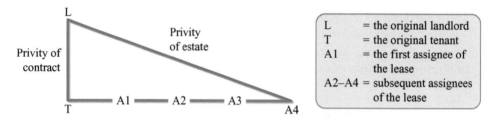

Figure 7.2 Establishing the position when the tenant assigns the lease

T, the original contracting party, is still liable for the full duration of the lease despite
the multiple times the lease has now been assigned. T will therefore wish to protect his
position when disposing of his interest as he does not want to be sued for a breach of
covenant caused by his successors in title, in this case A1, A2, A3 or A4. But what can
he do?

If the landlord seeks to recover damages from the original tenant in respect of a breach
by a successor in title, the tenant (T) can look to protect himself in a number of ways:

1   T can rely on the rule in *Moule v Garrett* (1872)[21] to imply a promise on A4 to
    indemnify against any liability he incurs because of A4 breaking the leasehold
    covenants. In *Moule*, the court held that this is an implied promise on the part of
    each assignee to indemnify the lessee.
2   As the original tenant will not be able to escape liability even for later breaches
    of covenants following the assignment of his term, he will normally seek an
    express indemnity from the new tenant upon assignment.
3   Failing that:

21 (1872) LR 7 Exch 101. 104.

- under s 77(1)(C) of the LPA 1925 (unregistered land assignment) the assignor will be able to rely on an implied indemnity covenant from the assignee if the assignment is for the residue of the lease term and was by deed for valuable consideration.
- or sch 12, para 20 of the Land Registration Act 2002 (registered land assignment) without valuable consideration.

TUTOR TIP – 4

In order to expressly create an indemnity covenant, which is the safest option, the original tenant and the assignee ensure that the following clause is inserted into either the Deed of Assignment or the TR1 transferring the leasehold estate from seller to buyer.

> The transferees hereby jointly and severally covenant by way of indemnity with the transferor that the transferees and the persons deriving title under them will observe and perform the covenants contained mentioned or referred to in the Lease dated [date] so far as they affect the land hereby transferred and are still subsisting and capable of being enforced and will keep the transferor and his/her estate and effects indemnified against all actions, claims, demands and liabilities arising from any future breach or non-observance or non-performance thereof.

How does the indemnity work?

The original tenant will protect himself by what is known as 'indemnity'. T will ensure that A1, the new party, indemnifies him in relation to any future breaches of the lease by A1. A1 will then ensure that A2 indemnifies him. A2 will ensure that A3 indemnifies him. A3 will ensure that A4 indemnifies him. This is known as a chain of indemnity, as seen in top half of Figure 7.3.

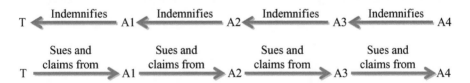

Figure 7.3 How the chain of indemnity works

Therefore if T is sued after he has disposed of his interest he will sue the party who obtained the lease from him (bottom half of Figure 7.3) and therefore there is privity of contract between the parties.

Following a change in landlord

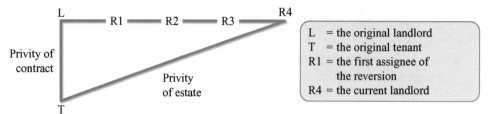

Figure 7.4 Establishing the position when the landlord assigns the lease

The privity of contract remains between L and T and the original parties to the contract. Under s 79 of the LPA 1925, L is taken to covenant on behalf of his successors in title and so has continuing liability even after assignment to another. He may want to rely on the *Moule v Garret* (1872) principle or to secure express indemnities from his successors.

The new landlord R4 will have the benefit of the covenants that T made by virtue of s 141 of the LPA 1925 if the covenants have 'reference to the subject matter' of the lease. Under s 142 of the LPA 1925, R4 will also have the burden of the covenants that have 'reference to the subject matter' of the lease. This is similar to the concept of touching and concerning the land. Purely personal matters will not be affected.

All change

In Figure 7.5, R1 has both the benefit and the burden of covenants that have 'reference to the subject matter' of the lease under ss 141 and 142 of the LPA 1925. A1 has the benefit of covenants that 'touch and concern the land' under *Spencer's Case* (1583). So the current landlord and tenant must both respect the original lease covenants between themselves.

Figure 7.5 Establishing the position when both the landlord and the tenant assign the lease

Following the grant of a sublease

As can be seen in Figure 7.6, there is privity of contract and privity of estate between L and T, which allows L to enforce any covenant against T and vice versa. If either L or T sell or assign their interest the principles stated above will continue to apply.

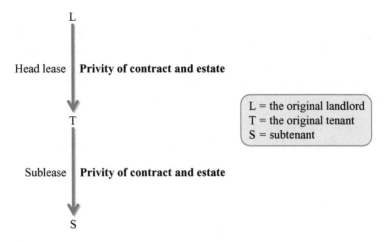

Figure 7.6 How privity of estate and privity of contract work with subleases

In relation to the sublease there is privity of contract and privity of estate between T and S, again this allows T to enforce any covenant against S and vice versa. If either T or S sell or assign their interest the principles stated above will continue to apply.

There is however *no* privity of contract or estate between L and S. This means that L cannot enforce any covenant against S nor can S enforce any covenant against L. If S breaches a covenant T will still be liable to L under the head lease if the same convents are contained in the head lease and the sublease.

CONSIDER THIS – 1

Upon creation of the lease Aaron covenanted with Bilal:

- To pay rent for £1,000 per month in addition to taxes and service charges.
- To insure the property.
- To keep the property in good and substantial repair throughout the term.
- Permit the lessor access to the property to inspect and view the property and to examine its condition.
- Not to alter the structure or carry out any structural alterations to the property.
- Not less than once in every period of five years during the term and in the last three months of the term to redecorate the property, both interior and exterior in a good and workmanlike manner.
- To use the flat for residential purposes only.
- Not to assign or sublet without the lessor's prior written consent.
- Not to deny the lessor's title.
- At the termination of the lease to quietly yield up the property repaired, maintained, decorated and kept in accordance with the lessee's covenants in the lease.

If the lease had been granted before 1996, what would be the consequence of Bilal now considering selling the remainder of the lease to Jude after gaining the written consent of Aaron to proceed with the assignment? To what extent would the covenants pass from Bilal to Jude upon assignment of the lease and under what would Bilal remain liable for the covenants?

Do you think that the position Bilal is in is fair? What could he do to try and mitigate the effects of any liability for Jude's possible future breaches?

POST-1996 LEASES

The traditional principles of privity of estate and contract were considered by the Law Commission in its 1988 report, *Landlord and Tenant: Privity of Contract and Estate.*[22] In this report the Law Commission considered that two general principles should underlie the law relating to the enforceability of leasehold covenants:

- A landlord or tenant should not continue to enjoy rights nor be under any obligations arising from the lease once he has parted with all interests in the property.
- All the terms of the lease should be regarded as a single bargain for letting the property. When the interest of one of the parties changes hands the successor should fully take his predecessor's place as landlord or tenant, without distinguishing between different classes of tenants.

These two principles radically alter two foundations of the traditional rule for the passing of the benefit and burden of leasehold covenants namely:

- The continuing contractual liability of the original tenant to the landlord (or assignees) would cease.
- The limitation of confining liability/enforceability to covenants which 'touch and concern' under privity of estate would be abolished.

Originally the Law Commission wanted its proposals to affect both existing and new tenancies, but this was not followed. Whilst reforming the rules of privity of estate and continuing contractual liability, the Landlord and Tenant (Covenants) Act 1995 (LTCA 1995) does not apply to all leases, only those created on or after 1 January 1996. Additionally, the new rules do *not* apply to tenancies created after 1 January 1996 but which arise from an earlier agreement or court order *or* arising from an earlier option (including rights of pre-emption).

---

22 Law Com No 174, 1988.

Section 2 of the LTCA 1995 abolishes the distinction between covenants which 'touch and concern' and those which are 'personal covenants'. Any covenant entered into by the tenant and written into the lease will be enforceable by/against the current landlord by/against the current tenant under the principle of privity of estate. The effect of this, under s 3 of the LTCA 1995, is that the benefit and burden of *all* covenants in the lease pass *provided* they are not expressly stated to be personal covenants. This position was clarified in the case of *BHP Petroleum v Chesterfield Properties* [2002].[23]

Following a change in tenant

Section 5 of the LTCA 1995 abolishes the liability of the tenant for rent and other leasehold covenants once the premises have been assigned. Under s 5(7) the tenant is released on assignment from the 'tenant covenants' and 'ceases to be entitled to the benefit of the landlord covenants' after the assignment. Quite rightly, this does not apply where an assignment is made in breach of covenant or by operation of law. In such situations the outgoing tenant will remain liable for any breaches of the lease upon assignment. For example, if the tenant is in breach of covenant for non-payment of rent at the time of the assignment he will *still* be liable for that rent after assignment.

The effect of s 5 of the LTCA 1995 is to render obsolete ss 78 and 79 of the LPA 1925, together with the rule in *Moule v Garrett* (1872). Additionally, where the tenant only assigns part of the premises leased to him, then from the time of assignment the tenant 'is released from the tenant covenants ... and ... ceases to be entitled to the benefit covenants ... to the extent that those covenants fall to be complied with in relation to that part of the demised premises' under s 5(3).

From 1 January 1996, former tenants (or guarantors) can only be held to be liable for the debts of a successor if they entered into an authorised guarantee agreement (AGA) under s 16 of the LTCA 1995. An AGA is an agreement whereby the outgoing tenant promises to pay the rent and perform the covenants of the incoming tenant if they fail to do so. Such guarantees enable the landlord to insist that the outgoing tenant guarantees the liabilities of his immediate assignee, but limits the liability to the incoming tenant but not subsequent assignees, so long as it is reasonable to do so. Such guarantees place the onus upon the outgoing tenant to ensure the landlord has a tenant of equal creditworthiness as at the original date of the lease.

Under s 16 of the LTCA 1995, a landlord may require an AGA to be entered into in a number of situations:

- Where there is a covenant against assignment.
- Where there is an express provision in the lease that consent to assignment will only be given if the tenant enters into an 'authorised guarantee'.
- Where the requirement is reasonable.

---

23 [2002] Ch 194; [2001] 2 All ER 914.

Liability for fixed charge payments will only arise under an AGA if the landlord has served a Section 17 'warning notice' on the former tenant or guarantor, within six months of the date on which the debt fell due and before any formal legal action has been commenced. The position of a former tenant/guarantor is strengthened further under the provision of s 19 in situations where they are forced to pay the debt of a successor. This allows them to call for an overriding lease, thus enabling them to take control of the interest, bring the lease, and as such bring their liability, to an end. The terms of the overriding lease will be consistent with the terms of the original lease previously assigned and will be for the residue of that lease plus three days. In order to take an overriding lease the tenant/guarantor must first make full payments of the monies demanded under the Section 17 notice and then make the request for an overriding lease within 12 months of making payment. The landlord is required to grant this within a reasonable time. If there are two such requests for an overriding lease, only one will be granted, the rule being 'first come, first served'.

In situations where an overriding lease is granted, the defaulting assignee becomes a subtenant or undertenant of the former tenant/guarantor, who will then have all the rights of an immediate landlord.

CONSIDER THIS – 2

Returning to Bilal's plans to assign the lease to Jude, what difference would it make to your advice with regard to the passing of the covenants and Bilal's remaining liability, if the lease is created after 1996. Taking into account any alteration in Bilal's liability, what advice would you give Aaron about AGAs?

Following a change in landlord
LTCA 1995 not only abolished the privity of contract rule regarding continuous liability throughout the term of the lease for the original tenant, but also for the landlord. However, unlike for the tenant, the release for the landlord is not automatic. If the original landlord wishes to be released from his obligations under the leasehold covenants, he must serve notice on the current tenant before or within four weeks of the assignment of the reversionary interest under s 7 of the LTCA 1995.

Providing no objections have been raised by the original tenant within 28 days of receiving the request, the landlord will obtain a release from his obligations under the lease under s 8. The original landlord will also be released if the tenant, having initially objected, subsequently withdraws his objection or it is overruled by a county court.

The effect of ss 7 and 8 of the LTCA 1995 are therefore to render ss 141 and 142 of the LPA 1925 and the rule in *Spencer's Case* obsolete. As explained above these new rules apply equally to legal and equitable leases i.e. agreements to create a lease.

CONSIDER THIS – 3

Aaron is now considering selling the freehold reversion to Peter. To what extent will Aaron remain liable under the provisions of the Landlord and Tenant (Covenants) Act 1995 and what steps would he have to take in order to bring this liability to an end?

REMEDIES FOR A BREACH OF COVENANT

A range of remedies including damages, specific performance and forfeiture may be available in relation to a breach of covenant.

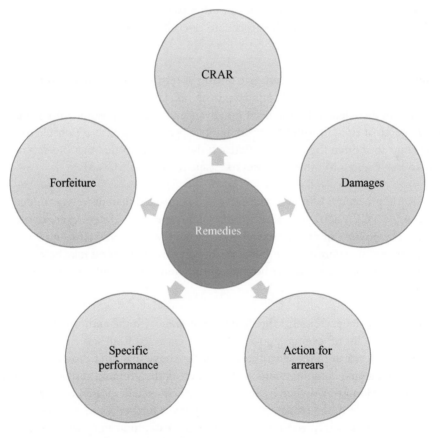

Figure 7.7 Remedies for a breach of covenant

COMMERCIAL RENT ARREARS RECOVERY (CRAR)

Originally the ancient remedy of distress was available to landlords. It allowed the landlord to seize and sell goods found on the leased property to recover the rent arrears. The remedy was an attractive remedy as it did not require the sanction of the court, so was seen as a self-help remedy. Distress was replaced in April 2014, under the Tribunals, Courts and Enforcement Act 2007 (TCEA 2007), with Commercial Rent Arrears Recovery (CRAR). Its replacement has been criticised for being a less effective remedy for a landlord as the circumstances under which is can be used are greatly reduced from its predecessor.

CRAR applies only to wholly commercial premises and there is no equivalent remedy for residential premises or mixed residential/commercial premises. CRAR is available only where the lease is in writing and can only be used to recover 'true' rent in addition to the VAT and interest on that rent. It is not possible therefore to use CRAR to recover other payments owed by the tenant, for example business rates, service charges, repairs, maintenance, insurance or other payments which are often reserved as 'rent' in the lease. Additionally the procedure can only be used if a minimum of at least seven days' rent is outstanding.

In order to comply, landlords must give tenants at least seven clear days' written notice of their intention to use CRAR. Sundays, bank holidays and public holidays are therefore not included. With the need for advance notice it is possible for tenants to remove goods at risk of seizure before the notice period expires. It is possible to apply to the court to shorten the period of notice if the court is satisfied that the debtor is likely to move goods to other premises to escape the effect of CRAR.

The CRAR procedure is more prescriptive and controlled than distress, as under sch 12 of the TCEA 2007 only certificated bailiffs are empowered to exercise the remedy. The power can only be exercised between the hours of 6 a.m. and 9 p.m. on any day, unless the court orders otherwise, though this time period may be extended if the premises are open for trade or business during hours that would otherwise be prohibited.

CRAR can only be exercised at the demised premises with the authorisation of the court. There is a list of 'exempt goods' which are excluded from seizure, together with the first £1,350 worth of the tenant's equipment. Above that limit, however, equipment including computers and vehicles at or on the premises can now be seized. Any item seized must be owned by the tenant, which excludes leased equipment and vehicles. Once seized, the tenant must then be given a further seven days' notice of the proposed sale of the seized goods with details of the date, time and place of the sale. Finally, the landlord has the option of serving a notice on any subtenants requiring them to pay their rent directly to the head landlord, but such a notice will only take effect 14 days after service.

DAMAGES

Damages can be recovered when the tenant is in breach of covenants except for non-payment of rent. The landlord is entitled to recover the contractual measure of damages for the loss suffered. This is based on the principles established in *Hadley v Baxendale* [1854],[24] in which a landlord is entitled to damages where the loss arises naturally from the breach of the contract in order to restore him into the position had the breach not occurred. It is possible to claim damages in conjunction with other remedies and as such appears an attractive and straightforward remedy that appears to compensate the landlord. The remedy is, however, more complicated in situations where the landlord is claiming damages for a breach of a repairing covenant, as there are a number of limitations and pitfalls of this form of redress.

During the lease

Any award of damages for breach of repairing covenants will be limited. *Crewe Services & Investment Corp v Silk* [2000][25] clarified that damages should only compensate the landlord for the decrease in value of the reversion rather than the actual cost of repairs. The rationale here is that the breach suffered must be balanced against the possibility that the landlord may not carry out the repairs, may have difficulty gaining access to the property to do so, or that the tenant may complete the repairs at some future point before the lease term expires.

Pursuing a claim for damages during the lease is further complicated where the original lease term granted was for a term over seven years with three years or more remaining. Under s 1 of the Leasehold Property (Repairs) Act 1938 (LP(R)A) damages are unenforceable against a tenant unless a Section 146 (of the LPA 1925) notice has first been served. Compliance with s 1 is mandatory and the notice must be served one month before damages proceedings are commenced. The notice must formally notify the tenant that he has breached a covenant under the terms of the lease, how the breach can be rectified and advising them of their right to serve a counter notice within 28 days of service of the landlord's notice.

Should a counter notice be issued by the tenant, the landlord is then prevented from continuing a claim for damages without first obtaining leave of the court under s 1(3) of the LP(R)A 1938. This additional requirement is complex, time-consuming and costly. In situations where repairs are urgent it may lead a landlord to conclude that pursuing a remedy of damages is not suitable. As Michael Wheeler QC highlighted in *SEDAC Investments Ltd v Tanner* [1982],[26] this legislation:

---

24 [1854] 156 ER 145.
25 [2000] 79 P & CR 500.
26 [1982] 1 WLR 1342.

makes no provisions whatsoever for the situation where the consequences of the breach ... require urgent attention and where the lessor takes immediate remedial action either of his own volition or, perhaps, because the lessee is unable or unwilling to take the necessary action sufficiently promptly.[27]

End of the lease

Damages for a breach of repairing covenant are more commonly pursued at the end of the lease and are recoverable in line with the reasonable costs of completing the repairs to fulfil the tenant's covenant obligations, less a discount for betterment; see *Joyner v Weeks* [1891].[28] Whilst s 1 of the 1938 Act is no longer relevant, landlords must be aware of s 18(1) of the Landlord and Tenant Act 1927, which restricts the level of damages the landlord is entitled to claim. Such restrictions are twofold. First, it caps the landlord's damages and prevents them exceeding the amount by which the tenant's breach has diminished the value of the reversion. Second, it bars damages completely where the landlord intends to demolish or structurally alter the property which will render any outstanding repairs claimed valueless.

ACTION FOR ARREARS OF RENT

A landlord will be able to bring a civil claim for arrears of rent, though they must be mindful of s 19 of the Limitation Act 1980, which precludes the landlord bringing an action for arrears 'after the expiration of six years from the date on which the arrears became due.'

SPECIFIC PERFORMANCE

Whilst the equitable remedy of specific performance has been available for decades as a solution to many legal disputes, its availability to landlords as a remedy has not. It is only very recently, following the case of *Rainbow Estates Ltd v Tokenhold Ltd* [1999][29] that landlords have been able to consider specific performance to compel tenants to fulfil their obligation under their repairing covenant.

Tokenhold reversed the entrenched position of *Hill v Barclay* [1810][30] which had previously ruled against specific performance on the grounds it had no mutuality and difficulties relating to supervision. General equitable principles mean that specific performance should be mutually available to the parties. *Hill* held that tenants could not be compelled to repair, on the basis that as tenants were not entitled to relief from forfeiture, landlords should not be entitled to specific performance. To do so, the court said, would place the parties in an unequal position and in conflict with general equitable principles.

---

27 [1982] 1 WLR 1342 at 1349.
28 [1891] 2 QB 31.
29 [1999] Ch 64.
30 [1810] 16 Vesey Junior 402.

The *Tokenhold* case ruled that the mutuality argument could no longer be sustained given legislative changes in favour of tenants. Such changes included relief from forfeiture and protection under s 1 of the LP(R)A 1938. Additionally specific performance had been made available to tenants in relation to a landlord's breach of a repairing covenant (see s 17 of the LTA 1985). This statutory ability to use specific performance by tenants reinforced the case law position in *Jeune v Queen's Cross Properties Ltd* [1974][31] which had allowed specific performance against a landlord's repairing obligation, compelling him to carry out 'specific work'. *Tokenhold* therefore redressed the balance in favour of landlords in accordance with general equitable principles.

KEY CASE: *RAINBOW ESTATES LTD V TOKENHOLD LTD* [1999] CH 64

The plaintiff was the freeholder of a listed building of which the defendants were lessees. The defendants had covenanted to keep and maintain the property in good and tenant-like repair throughout the term and to permit the landlord access to examine the condition of the property. The lease, however, contained no provisions for the landlord to enter the premises to carry out any repairs and there was no express forfeiture clause. The property was in a serious state of disrepair and its condition was deteriorating. The landlord brought proceedings in respect of the state of repair of the property and claimed five years' arrears of rent.

The court held that there was no constraint preventing the court from ordering specific performance of a tenant's repairing covenants where damages were not an adequate remedy.

Tokenhold had a number of 'unusual circumstances' which set it apart from other cases. First the leases granted to the defendants omitted forfeiture clauses or express rights of re-entry in favour of the landlord. As such, neither forfeiture or self-help remedies were available to the landlord to remedy the breach. Whilst landlords have implied rights to enter property to comply with their own repairing obligations, express provisions are required to enable a landlord to enter to carry out a tenant's repairing obligations and reclaim the costs from the tenant as a debt due. Given that most well-drafted commercial leases contain such clauses in reality very few landlords would be in a similar position.

Second, pursuing the remedy of damages was not a realistic option. The defendants' financial positions were either limited or unknown and repairs had been assessed in the region of £300,000. In the circumstances damages would be worthless with no prospect of the defendants ever paying.

---

31 [1974] Ch 97.

Third, with the landlord's property in a state of serious dilapidation, action to repair was vital. The situation was compounded by the local authority serving a number of statutory notices pursuant to the Housing Act 1985 and the Environmental Protection Act 1990, including an abatement notice. As non-compliance would result in the council completing repair works and securing a charge over the property until the costs had been recovered, it was imperative that the court made a decision.

Lawrence Collins QC in his judgment, however, warned of the need for 'great caution in granting the remedy against a tenant.' Pointing out that it would only be appropriate in rare cases as landlords would 'normally have the right to forfeit or to enter and do the repairs at the expense of the tenant.'

In its report *Landlord and Tenant: Responsibility for State and Condition of Property* (Law Com No 238), the Law Commission were of the view that specific performance should be available to both a landlord and a tenant for a breach of repairing covenant. Despite these developments, specific performance is still not commonly used. Whilst the Law Commission may have supported it, the courts are not comfortable in granting specific performance to either party, as the case of *Newman v Framewood Manor Management Co Ltd* [2012][32] recently demonstrated. Here the tenant sought specific performance and damages against the landlord in respect of breaches of lease covenants. The Court of Appeal held the original judge had been right to refuse an award for specific performance. Arden LJ ruling the costs involved in complying with such an order would be 'excessive and disproportionate when compared with the loss of amenity' compared to the alternative remedy of damages. Whilst this case relates to a landlord's breach of covenant rather than a tenant's, Arden LJ's comments are still pertinent. Clearly landlords not only have to demonstrate other remedies are not available or not appropriate but additionally that the cost of specific performance can be justified in comparison to the loss incurred by the tenant's breach of repairing covenant. The court may feel it more cost effective for the landlord to undertake repairs at the tenant's expense.

FORFEITURE

Nearly all leases contain a list of things a tenant agrees to do at the property and a list of things they must refrain from doing at the property. In such cases, the landlord will have the right to forfeit the lease if the tenant breaks these and the lease contains an express provision for forfeiture for breach of covenant. In practice, most well-drafted leases will contain such a clause; however, it is important that a landlord checks this and simply does not assume it exists. Even with such a provision in place, a breach renders the lease voidable, allowing the landlord the option to forfeit, rather than allowing the lease to be automatically forfeited and ended.

---

32 [2012] EWCA Civ 159.

Has the breach been waivered?

As soon as the breach has occurred the landlord must ensure they do not waiver the breach and act in a way which would be seen as continuing the lease. Waiver is seen as an act of forgiveness by the landlord of the tenant's actions or behaviour and an acceptance that the lease is continuing. The use of waiver has been criticised by the Law Commission[33] as acting 'as a trap for unwary landlords'[34] and 'has the potential to cause serious injustice to landlords who had not intended to waive their right to forfeit.'[35] It is therefore imperative the landlord does nothing from the date of the breach that may be perceived as an acceptance of the breach as the effect of a waiver may at best delay forfeiture proceedings even for a short period of time or at worst prevent the landlord from proceeding at all.

A waiver occurs when the landlord, with either actual or imputed knowledge of the breach 'does some unequivocal act recognising the continued existence of the lease' as held in *Matthews v Smallwood* [1910][36] as approved in *Cornillie v Saha and Bradford & Bingley* [1996].[37] A waiver is implied if:

- the landlord is aware of the acts or omissions of the tenant giving rise to the right or forfeiture and as such has knowledge of it, and
- the landlord or his agent does some unequivocal act recognising the continued existence of the lease, for example, if he demands or accepts rent falling due.

Both elements must be present to constitute an implied waiver. Examples of 'unequivocal acts' include demanding or accepting rent, entering into negotiations to renew the lease or offer to vary the terms of an existing lease – essentially any act which to the outside looks like the landlord is still accepting the lease. Waiver can occur expressly or impliedly through the landlord's employees or agents without motive or intention, as was found in *David Blackstone Ltd v Burnetts (West End) Ltd* [1973][38] and *Metropolitan Properties Co v Cordery* [1980].[39] Actions constituting waiver include demanding and accepting rent, without prejudice and even by mistake, as demonstrated in *Central Estates (Belgravia) Ltd v Woolgar (No 2)* [1972].[40] Here the tenant took an assignment of a long lease of a house in Pimlico. He supported himself by letting furnished rooms in the house. The tenant was convicted of keeping a brothel. The landlord's agent, aware of the conviction, made an internal note not to demand any further rent from the tenant; however, due to a clerical error the next quarter's rent

---

33 Lord Chancellor's Office: Law Commission Final Report 'Termination of Tenancies for Tenant Default' (31 October 2006) HMSO (Law Com No 303).
34 Law Com No 303 at 1.10.
35 Law Com No 303 at 3.106.
36 [1910] 1 Ch 777 at 786.
37 [1996] 72 P & CR 147.
38 [1973] 3 All ER 782.
39 [1980] 39 P & CR 10.
40 [1972] 1 WLR 1048.

was demanded, accepted and a receipt issued by the agent. Lord Denning MR explained the position regarding the waiver very clearly.

> Was this rent demanded and accepted by the landlords' agents with knowledge of the breach? It does not matter that they did not intend to waive. The very fact that they accepted the rent with the knowledge constitutes the waiver. The position here is quite plain. The agents, who had full authority to manage these properties on behalf of the landlords, did demand and accept the rent with full knowledge. It may be that the instructions did not get down the chain of command from the partner to the subordinate clerk who issued the demands and gave the receipts for rent. That cannot affect, to my mind, the legal position. It comes within the general rule that the knowledge of the agent – and of his clerks – is the knowledge of the principal. A principal cannot escape the doctrine of waiver by saying that one clerk had the knowledge and the other received the rent. They must be regarded as one for this purpose. The landlords' agents knew the position and they accepted the rent with knowledge. That is a waiver.

Whilst it is clear that a mistake or even an automated demand for rent generated by computer error would constitute a waiver, any action by the landlord to demand, sue for or accept rent will not amount to a waiver if the landlord has demonstrated a wish to bring the lease to an end, for instance, by commencing an action for possession as seen in *Civil Service Co-operative Society Ltd v McGrigor's Trustee* [1923].[41] Such actions would not be consistent with the landlord wishing the lease to continue.

Landlords must also apply caution in serving a notice of intention to carry out repairs following the tenant's breach. Whilst the lease may contain the option to serve notice to repair as well as a right of re-entry, a landlord is not entitled to both. Littledale J in *Doe on the joint demise of the Baron and Baroness de Rutzen v Lewis* [1836][42] confirmed the right to forfeiture could be waived by the service of the notice to repair.

A landlord's waiver only extends to the particular breach in question and does not operate as a general waiver for all future breaches of the same covenants. The effect of the waiver also depends on the type of breach; for example, there are continuing breaches and 'once and for all' breaches. For example, a breach of repairing covenant constitutes a continuing breach rather than a 'once and for all' breach. A door that was not painted by this month's deadline may still fail to be painted if I give the tenant another month to get the job done. Time may be allowed for a new home to be found for a pet in breach of the covenants. As a general rule, an act waiving a continuing breach waives forfeiture only up to the date of the act and thus allows the availability of forfeiture the following day should the breach continue, for example see *Cooper v Henderson* [1982].[43]

....

41 [1923] 2 Ch 347.
42 [1836] 111 ER 1170.
43 [1981–82] 5 HLR 1.

Mode of forfeiture

In theory two options are available to undertake forfeiture, though in reality only one is safe for a landlord to use. Forfeiture may be enforced by peaceable re-entry of the property or through the court.

Peaceable re-entry requires nothing more than entering the empty property, changing the locks and displaying re-entry notices with contact details. Whilst this may appear a quick and inexpensive solution it is not advisable. Lord Templeman in *Billson v Residential Apartments* [1991][44] described the practice as a 'dubious and dangerous method of determining a lease'. Even in situations where it is legitimately available to a landlord, peaceable re-entry is neither favoured nor advisable. Additionally, its use has been greatly restricted over the years; for example, peaceable re-entry of occupied dwellings is prevented under s 2 of the Protection from Eviction Act 1977. A landlord may face criminal liability by using or threatening violence to secure entry into the premises under ss 6 and 7 of the Criminal Law Act 1977. To ensure that a landlord does not fall foul of the law, it is advisable in all cases to pursue forfeiture through the courts under s 146 of the LPA 1925, for anything other than non-payment of rent. Whilst a lengthy and complex procedure, it is the safest option.

Once a landlord has established it is available and that it has not been waivered, they must begin the legal process of serving a forfeiture notice upon the tenant under s 146 of the LPA 1925. The basis behind a Section 146 notice is to allow the tenant to remedy the breach where possible in order to avoid the ultimate sanction of forfeiture. The notice must, however, follow the strict requirements and time limits under s 146, as failure to comply will invalidate the notice and bar the landlord from forfeiture.

Under s 146 the notice must:

- specify the breach complained of, and
- advise what the tenant has to do to remedy the breach if this is possible, and
- advise the tenant of what reasonable time they have available in order to remedy the breach and
- advise the tenant to make compensation in money for the breach if the landlord requires such compensation.

In situations where the breach is regarded as incapable of being remedied, the landlord need only specify the breach and then may proceed immediately to forfeit the lease. Breaches which are considered irremediable are those where, for example, the premises have been allowed to be used for immoral purposes by the tenant. Such breaches are seen as irremediable as the landlord suffers lasting damage. For example they may be stigmatised as an owner of a brothel, finding it hard to rent the property in the future and adversely affecting the value of the premises.

---

44 [1992] 1 AC 494; [1991] 3 All ER 265.

The landlord too should not be required to soil his hands by claiming compensation from the tenant's ill-gotten gains from using the premises for illegal or immoral purposes as in *Rugby School (Governors) v Tannahill* [1935].[45] A more recent variation on this theme can be seen in the case of *Van Haarlem v Kasner* [1992][46] where a tenant's conviction for offences committed under the Official Secrets Act was regarded as irremediable. The actions of the tenant broke a covenant that the premises should not be used for illegal activities and much of the tenant's activity as a spy had taken place within the flat.

Reasonable time

The tenant must be given reasonable time to rectify the breach to avoid the ultimate sanction of forfeiture. This is more an art than science, with no definitions or guidance. With remediable breaches, the court simply considers the nature of the breach and the particular circumstances in deciding what amounts to reasonable time. In *Horsey Estate Ltd v Steiger* (1899)[47] two days' notice was held to be insufficient, and 14 days was held to be enough in *Scala House & District Property Co Ltd v Forbes* [1974].[48] Many academic texts talk of three months being a good rule of thumb; however, common sense should be used. For example, if the lease covenant specified a specific timescale, such as the completion of a task within two months, then common sense would suggest it would be reasonable to specify a further two months in the s 146 notice for the tenant to rectify the breach.

Allowing the tenant reasonable time to remedy the breach is imperative, as failure to do so will render forfeiture unlawful as in *Cardigan Properties v Consolidated Property Investment Ltd* [1991].[49] This will have major consequences for a landlord, requiring at the very least the start of fresh proceedings, which will incur delay and additional costs.

Relief

Once the specified reasonable time has elapsed however, the landlord can take steps to forfeit the lease by applying to the court for possession of the property. Even at this stage the tenant may still apply for relief from forfeiture, the effect of which is to allow the tenant to remain in the property and for the lease to continue as before. This is possible either under the landlord's action for forfeiture or as a separate application under s 146(2) of the LPA 1925. It is possible for the tenant to apply for relief from forfeiture under s 146(2) at any time from the moment the notice has been served, until the landlord has secured possession of the property, see *Pakwood Transport v 15 Beauchamp Place* [1978][50] and *Billson v Residential Apartments Ltd (No 1)*

---

45 [1935] 1 KB 87.
46 [1992] 64 P & CR 214.
47 (1889) 2 QB 79.
48 [1974] QB 575.
49 [1991] 1 EGLR 64; [1991] 07 EG 132.
50 [1978] 36 P & CR 112; (1977) 245 EG 309.

[1991].[51] The court does not have the power to grant relief after the landlord has secured possession of the property.

Relief is discretionary and follows the court's general equitable jurisdiction. The court has wide discretion to allow relief, having regard to 'the proceedings and conduct of the parties' and 'all the other circumstances'. There are no hard and fast rules regarding what is taken into account but certain issues will be considered such as:

- the gravity of the breach,
- the conduct of the lessee, i.e. was the breach wilful?
- the disparity between the value of the property and the damage caused.

Relief is only available to the tenant if the landlord's position has not been 'irrevocably damaged' by the breach, see *WG Clark (Properties) Ltd v Dupre Properties Ltd* [1992].[52] Similarly the court will only grant relief where the breach is regarded as irremediable in exceptional cases. It is, for example, established practice not to grant relief where the breach involves immoral use.

Landlords must, however, exercise caution with remediable breaches as it is possible even at a very late stage for the tenant to remedy the breach. In such circumstances whilst the court may allow the lease to continue, the landlord may be awarded costs, expenses, damages and/or compensation as the court sees fit. Additionally, the court may wish to protect the landlord in the future by granting an injunction to restrain similar breaches by the tenant, although from the landlord's point of view the continuation of the lease still means they must deal with an unreliable or problematic tenant.

The position of subtenants

Under s 146(4) of the LPA 1925, as amended by the Law of Property (Amendment) Act 1929, s 1, a subtenant may apply for relief against the forfeiture of his landlord's lease on whatever ground that forfeiture is being enforced. This is the case even if the head lease has been forfeited for non-payment of rent, irrespective of whether the tenant himself can claim relief. If the court decides that the head lease is destroyed by the court order for forfeiture, the ex-subtenant is granted a new head lease for a period no more than they were originally granted. The court has the discretion to decide the terms of the new lease.

It is also possible for mortgagees (lender) to claim under this section to protect their interest when the mortgagor (borrower) is the tenant facing forfeiture. If the mortgagee is successful in applying then the new lease is granted to them, which means that they will be in a position to sell and recoup the outstanding mortgage monies.

---

51 [1991] 3 All ER 265.
52 [1992] Ch 297.

APPLY YOUR LEARNING – TASK 2

Peter has now purchased the freehold reversion from Aaron whilst Jude is the current lessee of Primrose Villa.

Jude has converted Primrose Villa into bed and breakfast accommodation. In order to maximise his potential profits, he has commenced the building of an annex to accommodate an additional six guest rooms over one-third of the garden area.

What remedies if any would Peter have against Jude and to what extend would such remedies be of value in rectifying the breaches?

DISCUSSION

Forfeiture is an important remedy for landlords, allowing them to end the lease, but there must be safeguards to prevent landlords from taking advantage of a breach.

Given the risks associated with re-entry, even if peaceful, landlords should use the court process. Note, that there are two procedures, depending on whether it is for non-payment of rent or breach of other covenants, under s 146 of the LPA 1925.

CONSIDER THIS – 4

Whether the s 146 process is fairly balanced between the needs of landlord and tenant has been questioned. What do you think?

CONSIDER THIS – 5

In addition to the length of time the forfeiture procedure can take, there are a number of criticisms which can be made in relation to the s 146 process. For example:

- The ability of the tenant to avoid the matter reaching court by remedying the consequences of a breach. For repeat offences (e.g. not paying the rent) or for very serious breaches, is this fair?
- The need to include an express forfeiture clause. Is this fair for the landlord who is entering into what is a commercial arrangement?

■ Is the doctrine of 'waiver' fair, it is unclear when the tenant should be able to rely on assurances from the landlord. How about replacing it with a 'default period' the landlord must act within, say six months?

■ Are the orders available to the court wide enough and are the factors to be taken into account set out with sufficient clarity?

All of these points, and some possible solutions, are set out in the Law Commission Report *Termination of Tenancies for Tenant Default*, published on 31 October 2006 (Law Com No 303). The need for a separate procedure for non-payment of rent was also questioned.

END OF CHAPTER SUMMARY

■ A covenant is a promise from one party to the other for the other person's benefit.

■ Covenants under a lease fall under the three headings of express, implied or usual covenants.

■ Privity of contract exists between the original landlord and tenant and all the covenants will be enforceable between them. When the parties sell, assign or transfer their interest in relation to a pre-1996 lease, privity of contract stays with the original landlord and tenant but privity of estate will now exist between the two parties now in a direct relationship of landlord and tenant.

■ Where there is privity of estate then those covenants, which 'touch and concern' the land are enforceable between them.

■ Personal covenants or those which do not touch and concern will not automatically pass to the new tenant on assignment but can only pass if there is a deed expressly assigning the benefit of that covenant.

■ The position differs in relation to post-1996 leases as the Landlord and Tenant (Covenant) Act 1995 takes effect.

■ Section 2 of the LTCA 1995 abolishes the distinction between covenants, which 'touch and concern' and those which are 'personal covenants.' Any covenant entered into by the tenant and written into the lease will be enforceable by/against the current landlord by/against the current tenant under the principle of privity of estate.

■ Outgoing tenants are automatically released from the liability unless they are required to enter into an Authorised Guarantee Agreement upon assignment of the lease under s 16 of the LTCA 1995.

■ Landlords, however, are not automatically released from their obligations under the lease covenants but must serve notice on the current tenant before or within four weeks of the assignment of the reversionary interest under s 7 of LTCA 1995.

■ A range of remedies are available for breach of covenant including damages, specific performance, CRAR and forfeiture.

PREPARING FOR ASSESSMENTS
QUESTIONS

ESSAY QUESTION

In 1988 the Law Commission produced a report and Draft Bill (No 174). This document contained various proposals for the reform of the law of leasehold covenants. The Commission concluded that the illogicalities and injustices of the then current law justified a fundamental restructuring. The Commission's findings resulted in the introduction of the Landlord and Tenant (Covenants) Act 1995.

Consider the law relating to leasehold covenants as it stood prior to 1996 and assess whether the deficiencies in the law specifically relating to enforceability of leasehold covenants were sufficient to justify the introduction of the Act.

PROBLEM QUESTION

In 2000, Samantha purchased the freehold estate to 4 Honour Oak Mews, a large Victorian house, built over three floors. In 2004, Samantha carried out substantial building work to the property and converted each of the three floors of the property into a flat. Samantha found tenants for each of the flats and granted a lease of 99 years by deed to each tenant. All the leases were identical and as part of the terms of the leases, Samantha ensured that the following tenant covenants were included:

- Not to assign the flat without Samantha's prior written consent.
- Not to carry out any structural alterations to the flat.
- To keep the property in good repair.
- To use the flat for residential purposes only.

Each lease also contains an express right of re-entry which is actionable upon breach of any of the tenant covenants.

Samantha had originally leased the basement flat to Eric. Eric was a good tenant and always paid his rent on time. However, in January of this year, Eric told Samantha that he wished to move on. Accordingly, Eric assigned his lease of the basement flat to a new tenant, Tristan, by deed. Samantha's written consent was obtained to the assignment in accordance with the lease. Tristan has now registered the lease.

In February of this year, Samantha sold her reversionary interest in the freehold estate to Claire.

Tristan, the new tenant, is an artist and in March of this year, he decided to open a small gallery in the basement flat to display and sell his work. In order to create the gallery area, Tristan removed one of the structural walls of the flat to open out the floor space. When Tristan opened the gallery, it came to the attention of Claire, the landlord, that Tristan was running a business from the flat and that he had made structural alterations to it.

Claire did not contact Tristan about the changes as she had been happy with him as a tenant especially as he has never missed a rental payment. Last week however, a friend advised Claire that she might be able to evict Tristan on the grounds of his breaches of covenant and be able to sell his flat herself for a significant profit.

Advise Claire as to whether or not she may forfeit Tristan's lease and as to how she should now proceed.

_____

FURTHER READING

- Bignell, J, 'Forfeiture: A Long Overdue Reform? A Discussion of Some of the Deficiencies in the Present Law' (2007) 11(5) L&T Review 140. A discussion of the doctrine of forfeiture is in need of reform in light of the impact on it of interventions by the courts and the legislature.
- Bridge, S, 'Forfeiture: A Long Overdue Reform?' (2007) 11(5) L&T Review 145. Reproduces Law Commissioner Stuart Bridge's Blundell Lecture on the recommendation in the Commission's report *Termination of Tenancies for Tenant Default* that termination by means of forfeiture be abolished and replaced with a statutory scheme.
- Brown, J and Pawlowski, M, 'Specific Performance of Repairing Obligations' [1998] Conv 495. Considers the availability of specific performance to a landlord in a breach of repairing covenant situation where there is no adequate alternative remedy.
- Law Commission, *Forfeiture of Tenancies* (Law Com No 142, 1985). Makes recommendations that the law on forfeiture should be replaced by a new statutory scheme of termination orders.
- Law Commission, *Landlord and Tenant – Privity of Contract and Estate* (Law Com No 174, 1988). Examines the nature and duration of each party's liability under a lease under the rules of privity of contract and estate.
- Law Commission, *Termination of Tenancies for Tenant Default* (Law Com No 303, 2006). The Law Commission's final report, recommending the abolition of the law of forfeiture and its replacement by a new, simpler, fairer and more coherent statutory scheme. The report also sets out a draft of 'Landlord and Tenant (Termination of Tenancies) Bill'.
- Luxton, P, 'The Landlord and Tenant (Covenants) Act 1995: Its Impact on Commercial Leases' [1996] JBL 388. Considers the Landlord and Tenant (Covenants) Act 1995 its impact on commercial leases in the context of privity of contract.

- Riley, A, 'The Landlord and Tenant (Covenants) Act 1995: 20 Years On – Part 1' (2015) 19(3) L&T Review 109.
- Riley, A, 'The Landlord and Tenant (Covenants) Act 1995: 20 Years On – Part 2' (2015) 19(4) L&T Review 139.
- Riley, A, 'The Landlord and Tenant (Covenants) Act 1995: 20 Years On – Part 3' (2015) 19(5) L&T Review 190. These three articles form a comprehensive look at the Landlord and Tenant (Covenants) Act 1995 after 20 years and its effectiveness in doing what it was implemented to do.
- Roberts, P, 'Straighten Things Out' (2007) 0707 EG 138. An article aimed at students, providing an overview of remedies available to landlords in the event of a tenant's default.
- Walter, P, 'The Landlord and Tenant (Covenants) Act 1995: A Legislative Folly' [1996] Conv 432. Examines the Act and considers whether a landlord will attempt to circumvent the rules of privity of contract to ensure tenants retain liability.

8

CHAPTER 8
LICENCES

CHAPTER AIMS AND OBJECTIVES

In this chapter we will explore licences to enter and use land. Licences create neither an estate nor an interest in land. They are not proprietary in nature but rather personal rights giving permission to enter land owned by another for some particular purpose without being a trespasser.

We have already briefly considered licences in Chapter 6 on leaseholds and how they can create rights that have some similarities to leases. However, they are used in a diverse range of circumstances and that makes them very important to consider in their own right. The enforcement of licences is also very interesting, with some licences proving to have more durability than their nature as rights *in personam* may at first suggest.

We will begin by explaining the nature of licences and how they may arise in different situations. Then we will consider enforcement between the original parties and, more controversially, the potential for binding third parties to the agreement.

By the end of this chapter, you should be able to:

- define a licence and explain its nature as a right;
- identify the different types of licences and how they are created;
- understand the impact of licences on the original parties;
- understand the impact of licences on third parties;
- appreciate the connection between licences and constructive trusts and proprietary estoppel;
- apply the above to the case studies and learning tasks.

CASE STUDY – ONE

Sapphire was the owner of Toadstool Hall. The estate comprises a large house, in which Sapphire lived, and a smaller cottage on the grounds, called Mushroom Cottage.

For several years, Mushroom Cottage was used as a holiday rental. However, the property was not well maintained and so fell out of use.

Two years ago, Sapphire allowed her daughter Sophie to move into the Cottage with her partner Sebastian and assured them that the house 'would one day be theirs'. The couple paid no money to Sapphire, but did pay for substantial repairs to the property that included a new roof and new external windows and doors. Sebastian likes to keep chickens and started to use a small space that he thought Sapphire would not miss next to the Cottage a year ago for that purpose. He has erected a fence and assembled a chicken coop.

Toadstool Hall was sold to Sam three months ago, he has asked Sophie and Sebastian to vacate the Cottage and remove the chickens.

In fact Sam is a very private person in general, and also objects to the number of people coming to his front door in order to deliver sales materials and to the owner of the neighbouring property, Moldgreen House, entering part of the grounds of Toadstool Hall set aside to grow apple trees in order to collect some of the crop.

KEEP IN MIND

- A licence creates no estate or interest in land but does act as a defence to trespass.
- As personal rights, an impact upon the new owner of Toadstool Hall may not be expected.
- Many of the arrangements referred to in the case study look to have been either short term or informal.
- But what about Sophie and Sebastian, do you think that what they have done while living at Mushroom Cottage should have any bearing on the situation?
- With regards to the agreement with the owner of Moldgreen House, could that arrangement fall under one of the legal interests in land under s 1 of the Law of Property Act 1925. If so, could it be exercised without a permission to enter the grounds of Toadstool Hall?

MEANING AND THE CREATION OF A LICENCE

A licence is permission given by a landowner, making it lawful to enter that property without being a trespasser and to utilise it in some way. It does not create an estate or interest in land.

KEY CASE: *THOMAS V SORRELL* [1673] EWHC KB J85

Vaughan CJ gave the classic definition, confirming that licences are not property rights but only a personal interest, acting as a defence to trespass:

> A dispensation or licence properly passeth no interest nor alters or transfers property in any thing but only makes an action lawful, which without it had been unlawful.

As a result, there are no particular formalities for the creation of a licence and, even if, say, a deed is used to grant one, that will not alter its nature. While licences may be created expressly, be aware they also frequently come about through implication. For example, a mail carrier, salesperson or even a new neighbour walking up the garden path to knock on the door and say hello may be a lawful visitor without express permission. Outside of private homes, other examples could be entering a shop or a public house or the parent of a child entering their school. Such persons will not be trespassers, provided they do not exceed the implied permission. Such implied permissions can, however, be withdrawn at any time or withheld.

KEY CASE: *ROBSON V HALLETT* [1967] 2 QB 939

The case involved a police officer making inquiries. In deciding whether there was an implied licence, Diplock LJ said:

> When a householder lives in a dwelling house to which there is a garden in front and does not lock the gate of the garden, it gives an implied licence to any member of the public who has lawful reason for doing so to proceed from the gate to the front door or back door and to inquire whether he may be admitted and to conduct his lawful business

After the withdrawal of the licence:

> [T]he sergeant had a reasonable time to leave the premises by the most appropriate route for doing so, namely, out of the front door, down the steps and out of the gate, and, provided that he did so with reasonable expedition, he would not be a trespasser while he was so doing.

APPLY YOUR LEARNING – TASK 1

Sam objects to salespeople coming to the front door of Toadstool Hall. Assuming that they do not wander off and proceed directly to the door, do you think that they have an implied licence or would you consider them to be trespassers?

What difference would it make if Sam had padlocked the gate and they had to climb over it to enter the property, what if Sam put up a sign saying 'No Salespersons or Leafleting'?

In contrast express licences are created in cases where the permission to enter has been expressly directed towards a particular person. For example, when an owner invites a person round to the house for a coffee, a child to retrieve their lost football from the garden or into a cinema to watch a film.

Licences may be created in a number of different circumstances, with four main types as seen in Figure 8.1.

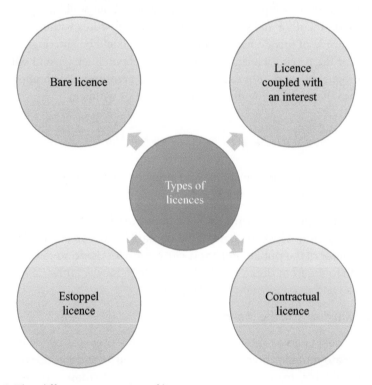

Figure 8.1 The different categories of licence

BARE LICENCE

A bare licence is given gratuitously without any payment or consideration from the licensee (the person with the permission). As a mere permission to enter land, it can be ended by the licensor (the landowner who gave the permission) telling the licensee to leave. There are no special words that must be used to terminate the licence, provided the meaning is clear, but a reasonable period of time to leave the premises must be allowed.

KEY CASE: *ROBSON V HALLETT* [1967] 2 QB 939

Note this relates to the case of the police officer making inquiries, mentioned earlier. It was held that following the withdrawal of a bare licence the former licensee must be given a reasonable period of time in which to leave. Per Lord Parker CJ:

> It seems to me that when a licence is revoked as a result of which something has to be done by the licensee, a reasonable time must be implied in which he can do so, in this case to get off the premises; no doubt it will be a very short time, but he was doing here his best to leave the premises.

APPLY YOUR LEARNING – TASK 2

If the owner of Moldgreen House was given express verbal permission to collect apples one day by Sapphire while chatting over the garden fence, could she have changed her mind and do you think such an informal permission could bind a new owner like Sam?

Assuming that Sam has not put up a sign, the salespeople coming to the door have an implied licence. Sam can revoke that permission, but would they then become trespassers right away?

LICENCE COUPLED WITH AN INTEREST

A licence coupled with an interest, or licence coupled with a grant, is one that is linked with a proprietary interest in the land. For example, to exercise the right to collect firewood under a profit à prendre there must be a licence to go on to land in order to do so.

CONTRACTUAL LICENCE

A contractual licence is a licence given in exchange for a consideration. Use of land may be the primary purpose of the contract. However, for many contractual licences entry to land is a secondary purpose necessary for the primary one, for example when paying to see some 'spectacle' or entertainment. In cases such as *Wood v Leadbitter* [1845],[1] paying for a day at the races, and in *Hurst v Picture Theatres Ltd* [1915],[2] purchasing a cinema ticket, in order to watch the events there had to be a contractual licence to come upon the land.

The contract in question may be very short term such as seeing a football match, something a little longer such as staying for a few nights at a hotel or for a much longer period of time such as lodging at a house or residing in a care home. Sometimes, it can be difficult to determine whether longer-term occupation could amount to the proprietary interest of a lease. As we have seen in Chapter 6 the distinction is based upon whether the interest possesses the characteristics identified in *Street v Mountford* [1985].[3]

---

1 [1845] 13 M&W 838.
2 [1915] 1 KB 1.
3 [1985] AC 809; [1985] 2 WLR 877.

Contractual licences are generally created expressly. However, in some cases the courts have been willing to infer or imply a contract. This can prove problematic, given the need to show that there was an intention to 'enter into legal relations' as required by the law of contract. We saw in Chapter 6 that the principle of intention to create legal relations can be problematic in relation to leases. In establishing exclusive possession the courts will consider a 'combination of factors' and in particular will look at whether there is an intention to create legal relations. Consideration is given to:

■ What circumstances gave rise to exclusive possession?
■ Did the grantor have the power to grant a lease?
■ Was there anything that negated the party's intention to create a lease?

As a lease is a formal document creating a contract between the parties, there must be an intention to create legal relations between the parties. If this cannot be satisfied, the courts may then conclude that the parties have a licence as opposed to a lease. There are a number of situations that can cause difficulty when establishing an intention to create legal relations. Such situations that can cause difficulties are acts of friendship, acts of charity, service occupation, policy reasons and most notably family situations. In relation to licences, too, it is in the family context that courts have implied terms in a bid to resolve disputes.

KEY CASE: *TANNER V TANNER (NO 1)* [1975] 1 WLR 1346; [1975] 3 ALL ER 776

An unmarried mother moved out of her own rent-controlled house after giving birth to twins to live in a house purchased as a home for them by the father of the children.

The court found an implied contractual licence on her part to occupy the premises whilst the children were of school age for so long as is reasonably required by her and the children.

In *Chandler v Kerley* [1978][4] when a woman's former matrimonial home was purchased by her lover, she was found to have an implied contractual licence to continue to live

---

4 [1978] 1 WLR 693; [1978] 2 All ER 942.

there. The licence was terminable on reasonable notice, which would be 12 months. In *Hardwick v Johnson* [1978][5] a mother purchased a house for her son and his wife to live in under an informal arrangement whereby they would make monthly payments. Many payments were missed, for which the mother never pressed. A contractual licence was inferred.

TUTOR TIP – 1

The finding of an intention to enter into legal relations in these cases is debatable; in *Hardwick v Johnson* [1978] Lord Denning rejected the argument of a contract because of the family nature of the arrangement. Today, these cases would more likely be responded to using a common intention constructive trust (see Chapter 9) or an estoppel (see Chapter 16).

The above cases should not, however, be taken as suggesting that the courts will find a contract in the absence of the intention to create legal relations.

KEY CASE: *HORROCKS V FORRAY* [1976] 1 WLR 230; [1976] 1 ALL ER 737

A house was purchased by a man for his mistress and their daughter to occupy. This mistress argued, relying particularly upon the decision in *Tanner v Tanner*, that she had a contractual licence to remain in occupation or at least to do so until the daughter completed her education.

The court noted that a contract requires a meeting of the minds or mutual agreement to be demonstrated with the parties commonly understanding there to be a contract and having an intention to affect a legal relationship.

It held that there was no evidence to support an implication that any such binding promise had been made. The fact that the man had it in mind to seek to provide some security for the mistress was not sufficient to bring into existence a binding contract in the nature of a licence.

It was also noted that, unlike in *Tanner v Tanner* (in which the lady had given up her rent-controlled flat as part of the bargain), no consideration had been given.

APPLY YOUR LEARNING – TASK 5

Consider Sophie and Sebastian. Do you think there was an intention to enter into legal relations between them and Sapphire on the facts provided?

---

5 [1978] 1 WLR 683; [1978] 2 All ER 935.

LICENCE PROTECTED BY ESTOPPEL

The doctrine of propriety estoppel is explored in depth in Chapter 16. The general principle is that where a landowner makes a representation or assurance of rights in the land to another party and that party relies upon that representation to his determent, equity may intervene to uphold their claim.

When a licensee relies upon a representation and has taken detrimental action, for example the expenditure of money on land, that licence may be protected by equity (Figure 8.2). If an estoppel has arisen, a court may grant any remedy appropriate to satisfy it. This could take the form a personal licence, but it could be a proprietary interest in the property. Where a licence is granted, the terms may make it an irrevocable licence if an assumption of a right to occupy has arisen.

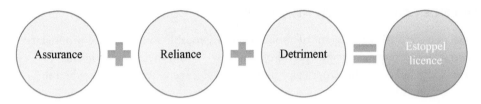

Figure 8.2 The elements of an estoppel licence

KEY CASES: *IRREVOCABLE LICENCES*

RE SHARPE [1980] 1 ALL ER 198; [1980] 1 WLR 219

An aunt loaned her nephew £12,000 in order to purchase property on the understanding that she should live in the house for the rest of her life. She successfully claimed a right under an irrevocable licence to occupy the property until repayment of the loan.

GREASLEY V COOKE [1980] 3 ALL ER 710; [1980]1 WLR 1306

A woman relied upon assurances given that she could remain in a house for life, performing household duties for no payment and caring for members of the family. The owners of the house were estopped (prevented) from denying her right to occupy the house under a licence for as long as she liked.

APPLY YOUR LEARNING – TASK 6

In relation to Sophie and Sebastian living at Mushroom Cottage, could there be an estoppel based upon the assurance and the actions of the couple?

ENFORCEMENT BETWEEN THE ORIGINAL PARTIES

The question of whether a licence can be lawfully revoked by a licensor depends on the type of licence.

BARE LICENCE

As we have already considered, as a mere permission a bare licence is easily revoked. The only limitation is that the former licensee be given a reasonable period of time to leave before they become a trespasser.

LICENCE COUPLED WITH AN INTEREST

A licence coupled with a grant of an interest is irrevocable so long as the proprietary interest (for example, a profit à prendre) continues. This is because the licence is intrinsically linked to the proprietary interest, the licence will only cease when the interest comes to an end.

CONTRACTUAL LICENCE

At common law, a contractual licence can be revoked at any time and any breach of contract remedied by the award of damages.

KEY CASE: *WOOD V LEADBITTER* (1845) 153 ER 351; (1845) 13 M & W 838

A ticket holder who had paid to attend the races was evicted from the racecourse. Whether or not he became a trespasser after being asked to leave was crucial in the outcome of the case. He was attempting to sue the race steward for battery and false imprisonment (for which the substantial damages would be recoverable). If the licence could be revoked, then the force used against him would have been legal.

It was held that the licence could be revoked; while this might be a breach of contract the common law would award damages to compensate for that.

While the common law does not compel the performance of contracts, the remedies available in equity may be used to restrain the breach in the form of an injunction.

CONSIDER THIS – 2

When a contract is breached, the only remedy at law is that of damages. Given what we know about each piece of land being 'unique', do you think there might be a better remedy available in equity when a landowner tries to break with a contractual agreement?

Imagine you have booked your dream wedding venue and it is cancelled with short notice, or that you are asked to leave halfway through a play at the theatre. Would you be satisfied with a return of the money you have lost, or is there a type of loss that cannot be satisfied by money alone?

It is important to note that *Wood v Leadbitter* [1845] was decided before the Supreme Court of Judicature Acts 1873 and 1875 (which fused the historically separate courts of common law and equity). After their passing, both legal and equitable rules and remedies are applied in all courts. Do you think that a different outcome on similar facts could result in equity?

The modern practice is that equity will intervene and protect contractual rights by way of specific performance and injunctions.

KEY CASE: *HURST V PICTURE THEATRES* [1915] 1 KB 1

The purchaser of a ticket for a seat at a cinema show was forcibly turned out of his seat (under a mistaken belief that he had not paid for his seat). Once again, whether he became a trespasser upon being asked to leave was central to whether this amounted to assault and false imprisonment.

This time, however, the rules of equity were applied. The court reasoned that the purchase of a ticket for a seat at a theatre or other similar entertainment gives a right to stay and witness the whole of the performance. In the absence of improper behaviour or breaking the terms of the contract, the licence is irrevocable for the duration of the performance.

Therefore, either specific performance of the contract or an injunction to prevent the breach would have been available meaning that he was not a trespasser and his removal was wrongful.

The contractual licence and any inability to revoke will be implied in accordance with the terms of the contract. In *Hounslow LBC v Twickenham Garden Developments Ltd* [1970][6] a property owner entered into a building contract and granted a licence to the

6 [1971] Ch 233; [1970] 3 All ER 326.

builder to enter on his land and do work there. The owner argued he was entitled to determine the defendant's bare licence to remain on the site independently of the contractual position. The court held that the licence could not be revoked otherwise than in accordance with the terms of that contract.

If the contract is not specific about the period of time it will continue, then the court will imply reasonable notice for its revocation.

KEY CASE: *WINTER GARDEN THEATRE (LONDON) LTD V MILLENNIUM PRODUCTIONS LTD* [1948] AC 173; [1947] 2 ALL ER 331

A licence of a theatre for the purpose of producing plays had been granted. The initial agreement was for six months, but with the option to renew at the end of six months' periods. The licensee contended that the licence was not revocable by the owner.

It was held that the licence was revocable subject to a reasonable notice being given. The one month given to the licensee to withdraw was found to be sufficient.

Specific performance and injunctions are available where the possession under the licence has not yet taken place. In *Verrall v Great Yarmouth BC* [1981][7] the court confirmed that there is no reason it should not order specific performance of a contractual licence of only short duration, or of a licence wrongfully repudiated before the licensee entered into possession. The Conservative council of Great Yarmouth had granted the National Front a contractual licence to hold their annual conference at their hall. The Conservative council became a Labour council after elections and purported to cancel the agreement. The National Front was unable to find alternative premises and successfully secured specific performance of the contract against the Great Yarmouth council.

Despite our selection of cases in which the equitable remedies were awarded, do note that they will not always be given. Equitable remedies are discretionary, and common law damages will be appropriate in many cases.

APPLY YOUR LEARNING – TASK 7

Consider the use of Mushroom Cottage for short-term holiday rentals. Could a guest who had booked the accommodation for a week and paid a deposit have been forced to leave because Sapphire had since 'changed her mind'? If there is no other accommodation available, do you think that they would be happy to simply have their money back or were they planning on enjoying their stay?

---

7 [1981] QB 202; [1980] 1 All ER 839.

LICENCE PROTECTED BY ESTOPPEL

Whether a licence by estoppel can be revoked is dependent on the terms of the licence granted to satisfy the equity. For example, the licence may be irrevocable or determinable only in accordance with certain conditions. The terms of the licence will be determined by the courts as it is the courts who decide whether an estoppel licence exists; they too decide when it will be revoked.

ENFORCEMENT BETWEEN SUCCESSORS IN TITLE

The ability of licences to bind successors in title has proved to be a more dynamic area than may first be thought given that they are, after all, not a proprietary right capable in themselves of binding others.

BARE LICENCE

As we have considered, a bare licence is subject to immediate revocation. As such, a successor in title could not possibly be bound by it.

LICENCE COUPLED WITH AN INTEREST

The licence here is linked with a proprietary interest, for example a profit. It will, therefore, bind the successor in title only if they take subject to the property right itself.

> TUTOR TIP – 2
> ....
>
> Because this type of licence is able to bind successors in title, it may appear to recognise a proprietary type of licence. However, it is in fact the interest it is associated with that does so.

CONTRACTUAL LICENCE

The benefit of the rights under the licence may be assignable or not assignable depending on the express and implied terms of the agreement.

Early case law applied standard contractual conditions in relation to the burden of a licence binding a successor to the original licensor. Contracts, as with licences, create only personal rights and so there was nothing to bind a third-party successor in title.

> **KEY CASE:** *KING V DAVID ALLEN & SONS BILLPOSTING LTD* [1916]
> UKHL 1; [1916] 2 AC 54; (1915) 2 IR 213
>
> ---
>
> A contractual licence giving permission to affix advertisements to the walls of a
> cinema for a period of four years was granted. The cinema was later leased to a
> third party and that company refused the permission granted by the agreement.
>
> It was held that the agreement did not create an interest in land capable of
> binding a third party, but created merely a personal obligation on the parties to
> the contract. As the licensor had put it out of his power to fulfil his obligation
> under the agreement he could only be liable in damages for breach of contract.

A similar outcome was reached in *Clore v Theatrical Properties Ltd* [1936].[8] Here the
contractual licence gave front of the house rights of a theatre. It was held that being a
personal contract it could only be enforced by parties to the contract and had no effect
on a third–party purchaser.

This line of cases was, however, decided before *Winter Gardens* [1948] and its
recognition that equity can intervene in some cases to make a contractual licence
irrevocable by the licensor. After that ruling, there followed a view that such licences
be treated as proprietary interests with the potential to be binding upon third parties,
most notably in the reasoning of Denning, recognising irrevocable contractual licences
as equitable interests in land or a proprietary licence.

> **KEY CASES:** *DENNING'S PROPRIETARY LICENCE*
>
> ---
>
> *ERRINGTON V ERRINGTON AND WOODS* [1952] 1 KB 290; [1952] 1 ALL
> ER 149
>
> ---
>
> A father bought a house for his son and daughter-in-law to live in. He told them
> that the property would be transferred into their names once they paid off the
> mortgage. The daughter-in-law paid the instalments regularly with the result that
> much of the mortgage had been repaid. The father later died, leaving the house
> to his widow. Soon after, the son left his wife. The widow sued her daughter-in-
> law for possession of the house. It was held that the contractual licence could
> not have been withdrawn by the father provided the payments were made.
> Furthermore, in relation to the effect of this on the widow, Denning
> reasoned that:

---

8 [1936] 3 All ER 483.

This infusion of equity means that contractual licences now have a force and validity of their own and cannot be revoked in breach of contract. Neither the licensor nor anyone who claims through him can disregard the contract except a *purchaser for value without notice*

Note here the treatment of the irrevocable licence as an equitable proprietary interest, binding upon the widow, who was not a purchaser.

BINIONS V EVANS [1972] CH 359; [1972] 2 ALL ER 70

The owner of a property agreed with the widow of an employee (Mrs Evans) that she would have the right to reside in a cottage for the rest of her life, provided she kept it in repair. The cottage was later sold subject to that licence but its new owners attempted to seek possession of it. The Court of Appeal found in favour of Mrs Evans for different reasons:

- Lord Denning held that she occupied the property under an irrevocable contractual licence and that a licence of this type takes effect as an equitable interest in land. Clearly, the new owners had notice.
- Alternatively, Denning reasoned that because the new owners had acquired land expressly subject to a contractual licence it would be inequitable for them to now deny it and, therefore, a constructive trust would be imposed protecting the licence.

Denning's recognition of a new proprietary interest in land was soon firmly rejected; after all, one of the purposes of the 1925 legislation was to simplify landownership by reducing and restricting such interests. However, the outcomes in both of the above cases were supported and his argument in *Binions v Evans* [1972] of a constructive trust accepted. As such, a person who acquires land expressly subject to a contractual licence may be bound by the licence through the imposition of a constructive trust.

KEY CASE: *ASHBURN ANSTALT V ARNOLD* [1989] CH 1; [1988] 2 ALL ER 147

A full review of the status of contractual licences and their proprietary status was carried out by the Court of Appeal following a claim that a licence could be binding upon a third party by reason of the decision in *Errington*, or by reason of the doctrine of constructive trust.

Whilst the case was decided upon other grounds, it was clearly stated that a contractual license does not create an interest in land capable of binding third parties; and the decision in *Errington* was to this extent only *per incuriam*. Fox LJ said:

A licence in connection with land while entitling the licensee to use the land for the purposes authorised by the licence does not create an estate in the land … Before the Errington case the law appears to have been well understood. It rested on an important and intelligible distinction between contractual obligations which gave rise to no estate or interest in the land and proprietary rights which by definition, did.

The argument of a constructive trust referenced in *Binions v Evans* was accepted but it was stressed that such a trust would not be imposed merely because land is expressed to be conveyed 'subject to' a licence. A constructive trust required the conscience of the estate owner to be affected. Fox LJ continued:

The far-reaching statement of principle in *Errington* was not supported by authority, not necessary for the decision of the case and per incuriam … Of course, the law must be free to develop. But as a response to problems which had arisen, the *Errington* rule … was neither practically necessary nor theoretically convincing. By contrast, the finding on appropriate facts of a constructive trust may well be regarded as a beneficial adaptation of old rules to new situations.

The constructive trust principle to which we now turn has been long established and has proved to be highly flexible in practice. It covers a wide variety of cases … The test, for present purposes, is whether the owner of the property has so conducted himself that it would be inequitable to allow him to deny the claimant an interest in the property…

We come to the present case. It is said that when a person sells land and stipulates that the sale should be 'subject to' a contractual licence, the court will impose a constructive trust on the purchaser to give effect to the licence (see *Binions v Evans* [1972] 2 All ER 70 at 76, [1972] Ch 359 at 368 per Lord Denning MR). We do not feel able to accept that as a general proposition…

The court will not impose a constructive trust unless it is satisfied that the conscience of the estate owner is affected. The mere fact that that land is expressed to be conveyed 'subject to' a contract does not necessarily imply that the grantee is to be under an obligation, not otherwise existing, to give effect to the provisions of the contract … The words 'subject to' will, of course, impose notice. But notice is not enough to impose on somebody an obligation to give effect to a contract into which he did not enter.

In determining whether the conscience of the third party had been affected, Fox LJ raised as relevant facts the finding that there had been no reduced payment as a result of the conveyance being subject to the agreement creating the licence.

In *Binions v Evans* [1972], the purchasers had paid a reduced purchase price as a result of buying subject to the rights of the widow and that was a key factor in finding a constructive trust. If a purchaser has given an express undertaking to take subject to the rights of contractual licensees then that may give rise to a defined beneficial interest in the property, thereby giving rise to a constructive trust. In *Lyus v Prowsa Developments Ltd* [1982][9] a contract of sale included a clause stipulating that the purchaser would on acquiring the land give effect to a contractual licence. They were found to hold as constructive trustees.

> TUTOR TIP – 3
>
> Do not be caught out by a question raising a licence created with formality, even if under seal (granted by deed) or for valuable consideration. They remain only rights *in personam*. Remember a licence can never be legal as it is not listed in ss 1(1) or 1(2) of the LPA 1925.
>
> In equity the licence may be irrevocable and an injunction could be granted to restrain a breach or if appropriate specific performance. This does not, however, alter the position that a licence is merely personal and does not bind a purchaser. Even if the purchaser has actual notice, they will only be bound if their conscience is affected so as to impose a constructive trust, for example, by the payment of a reduced purchase price.

LICENCE PROTECTED BY ESTOPPEL

While an estoppel claim remains inchoate – that is, a court has not as yet satisfied the estoppel by awarding a particular remedy – the equity by estoppel can bind a third party. For a detailed explanation of this, see Chapter 16. In unregistered land, the equity by estoppel is subject to the doctrine of notice (it cannot be registered under the Land Charges Act 1972). For registered land, s 116 of the Land Registration Act 2002 (LRA 2002) clarifies the status of an equity by estoppel as a proprietary interest. The right can therefore by protected by a notice in the register (s 29 of the LRA 2002) or as an overriding interest by actual occupation (sch 3, para 2 of the LRA 2002).

Where a licence is the remedy awarded by a court in response to a proprietary estoppel, the question is more difficult on its ability to bind a third party.

Section 116 of the LRA, provides that in registered land an equity by estoppel: 'has the effect from the time the equity arises as an interest capable of binding successors in title'. One reading of this is that it confers proprietary status on a licence granted as a response to the creation of an equity by estoppel. A licence awarded by estoppel would then be enforceable against a third party.

---

9 [1982] 2 All ER 953; 1 WLR 1044 (Ch).

This would mean, however, that the position of a licensee under a licence granted as a remedial response to an equity by estoppel is in a better position than a contractual licensee to enforce that licence against a third party. Such an understanding also arguably does not reflect the distinction made in the decision of the court not to award a proprietary right, for example a lease or a right under a constructive trust, as a remedy. It could be argued that after the equity by estoppel has been satisfied it is extinguished and so the position of such a licensee should not be any stronger than the holder of any other licence. The licence awarded would then be incapable of affecting a third party absent unconscionable conduct by that third party. The argument against proprietary standing is well-made in *Megarry & Wade*:

> Although such a licence was once thought to be binding on a third party with notice of it, the recognition that contractual licences do not create property rights [*Ashburn Anstalt*] has cast serious doubt on the correctness of this conclusion. [The licensee] will therefore be vulnerable against a third party purchaser. This is a factor that the court now takes into account when giving relief. It may grant [the licensee] a proprietary right if the licence would not adequately protect his position.[10]

DISCUSSION

This is a complex area that continues to generate debate between lawyers and academics.

For a time it appeared that contracts were able to give rise to a property licence. It is well worth your time to consider the reasoning of Lord Denning in making such arguments. Restrictive covenants, which have now long held proprietary status in equity, were once only recognised as personal contractual arrangements. It is not, therefore, as surprising as it may first seem that Denning attempted to recognise a new interest in land and in *Ashburn Anstalt* that, 'the law must be free to develop'. It is not, however, surprising that there was no rush to create a new interest given the objective of the 1925 legislation to simplify landownership.

Yet, case law recognised that contractual licences may bind if a constructive trust is imposed and that still creates complexity for a purchaser. The uncertainty caused by estoppel for successors in title is also problematic. While s 116 of the LRA 2002 has helped there remains a question mark over the treatment of licences after an inchoate claim is formalised and a licence awarded to satisfy it.

---

10 Harpum, C, Bridge, S and Dixon, M, *Megarry & Wade: The Law of Real Property* (8th edn, Sweet and Maxwell 2012) 738.

CONSIDER THIS – 3

Do you think that licences are to some extent becoming proprietary interests in land? Consider the position between the original parties and successors in title.

END OF CHAPTER SUMMARY

- A licence is a permission given by the licensor to the licensee to enter land.
- The permission can be express or implied; without it the licensee would be a trespasser.
- A bare licence can be revoked immediately by the licensor and will not bind a third-party successor in title.
- A licence coupled with an interest, for example a profit, cannot be revoked whilst the interest remains and will bind a third party if they take subject to the interest.
- Contractual licences cannot be revoked between the original parties otherwise than in accordance with the terms of that contract. Modern case law suggests that such licences do not bind third party successors in title unless a constructive trust is imposed or possibly protected by an estoppel.
- A licence protected by estoppel can bind successors in title. An equity by estoppel is subject to the doctrine of notice in unregistered land and in registered land and can be registered using a notice or have overriding status by actual occupation.

PREPARING FOR ASSESSMENTS
QUESTIONS

ESSAY QUESTION

Vaughan CJ gave the classic definition of a licence in *Thomas v Sorrell* [1673] EWHC KB J85: 'A dispensation or licence properly passeth no interest nor alters or transfers property in any thing but only makes an action lawful, which without it had been unlawful.' To what extent is this still true today?

PROBLEM QUESTION

In 2008 Mr Joseph, a married man, entered into a relationship with Miss Jacob. As a result of this relationship Miss Jacob became pregnant and gave birth to a baby girl in August 2010.

Mr Joseph, purchased a property with the intention of Miss Jacob moving into it and raising their child there. He explained to her because he was still married he would not be living at the property with her and that for tax reasons the property must be registered in his sole name, but assured her that the house was to be hers.

Miss Jacob gave notice on her assured shorthold tenancy in relation to the two-bedroom flat she has lived in for the previous five years and moved into the new property. Miss Jacob did not claim child maintenance for their daughter as Mr Joseph agreed to pay the mortgage on the property. She did, however, decorate the property and keep up to date with the maintenance and repair of the property.

What would be the position in each of the following unrelated situations?

(a) Mr Joseph, having ended the relationship with Miss Jacob, has decided to sell the property. He has asked Miss Jacob to leave and is now seeking possession. She states that she has a lease and as such is refusing to leave. Consider Miss Jacob's claim.

(b) If Miss Jacob cannot establish that she has a lease, what interest does she have and what would be the effect if Mr Joseph sells the property to Mrs Louise. Consider this in the context of the property being registered land.

(c) If Mr Joseph was killed in a plane crash and left the property to his wife in accordance with his will, would Miss Jacob's interest bind Mrs Joseph? Consider this in the context of the property being unregistered land.

FURTHER READING

- Battersby, G, 'Contractual and Estoppel Licences as Proprietary Interests in Land' [1991] Conv 36. Explores the relationship between contractual licences and licences arising by proprietary estoppel following the decision in *Ashburn Anstalt.*
- Bright, S, 'The Third Party's Conscience in Land Law' [2000] Conv 398. Reviews the use of constructive trusts in cases such as *Binions v Evans.*
- Moriarty, S. 'Licences and Land Law: Legal Principles and Public Policies' (1984) 100 LQR 376. Examines estoppel licences as a form of equitable interest binding upon third parties.

9

CHAPTER 9
EXPRESS, RESULTING AND CONSTRUCTIVE TRUSTS

CHAPTER AIMS AND OBJECTIVES

Trusts provide a mechanism to divide the ownership of property, segregating control or management (by the trustee or trustees) from the benefit and enjoyment (by the beneficiary or beneficiaries). They are used in a large variety of contexts where it is better for the management of property to rest elsewhere, for example, where professional expertise is needed in order to make investment decisions on behalf of the beneficiaries or where the beneficiaries are incapable or too inexperienced to make decisions for themselves.

Given the nature of land, it has also been the subject of extensive case law on how resulting, implied and constructive trusts may arise. Both resulting and constructive trusts play a vital role in settling disputes about the ownership of land. Therefore, the consideration of how they arise and how the beneficial interests under them are quantified will add another dimension to our exploration.

By the end of this chapter, you should be able to:

- appreciate trusts as a means to divide the ownership of property at law and in equity;
- identify the requirements for the express creation of a trust of land;
- recognise the need for trusts that arise informally: implied, resulting and constructive;
- explain the implication of a conveyance or transfer of land expressly dealing with the beneficial interests;
- understand the role of trust principles in settling disputes about landownership in equity.

CASE STUDY – ONE

You have been asked to advise on the possibility of express or implied trusts of land based on the following events:

(a) Annabel is the legal owner of Bramble Cottage. Last month she orally declared that she will hold it on trust for her 14-year-old grandson Steven.

(b) Jason and his partner Betty purchased the legal title to Thorn House in joint names three years ago to live in together. Jason contributed three-quarters of the purchase price.

(c) Mavis is the legal sole owner of the legal title to Cedar Way; it was purchased five years ago with her partner Cedric contributing half of the price.

(d) Sebastian and Edward purchased Willow Bay as an investment property to renovate one year ago. Sebastian contributed 90 per cent of the price.

(e) Ralph is the legal owner of Maple Drive. Ten years ago he allowed his partner Sandy to move into the property with him. Sandy has a part-time job and gives money to Ralph to pay the household bills, looks after their two children, and has used some of her savings to substantially improve the house.

EXPRESS TRUSTS

We have already seen that dealings with land often require writing. The creation of an express trust in land is another example of those requirements. Section 53(1)(b) of the Law of Property Act 1925 (LPA 1925) provides: 'A declaration of trust respecting any land or any interest therein must be manifested and proved by some writing signed by the person who is able to declare such trust or by his will.'

The express creation of an *inter vivos* trust of land must, therefore, be evidenced in writing. The trust will not be void in the absence of writing, but will be unenforceable. An express trust may also arise under a valid will.[1]

CONSIDER THIS – 1

Think about the evidential benefits of requiring written evidence signed by the settlor – for example, the avoidance of fraud and confusion in relation to the existence of a binding trust obligation and its terms.

However, injustice may result if the rules are applied too strictly. There is a long history of implying trusts based upon the presumed intentions of the landowner or where they have dealt with the property in an unconscionable manner. Do you think exceptions should be made to the requirement for trusts to be created in writing for implied, as opposed to express, trusts?

---

1 Section 9 of the Wills Act 1837 sets out requirements which must be complied with, including: that it is in writing and signed by the person making the will (the testator), or signed on the testator's behalf in his presence and by his direction. This must be done in the presence of two witnesses who then sign the will in the presence of the testator.

APPLY YOUR LEARNING – TASK 1

Is the oral declaration of Annabel that she holds Bramble Cottage on trust for Steven enforceable in the absence of writing?

Wherever there is co-ownership of land a trust is automatically imposed. In land, the trustees and the beneficiaries are often the same people. Therefore, when Jason and Betty jointly purchased the legal title to Thorn House a trust was created. Chapter 11, 'Co-ownership', explores this complex and important topic in detail. For now, note that at law co-owners have equal rights in the property but in equity they can hold equally or own different shares in the land. A trust would have been implied where the land was conveyed to Jason and Betty, but why is it normal practice to make an express declaration of trust? Could the express trust of land reflect Jason having paid three-quarters of the purchase price?

In the case of Mavis and Cedar Way, we would normally have expected both Mavis and Cedric to have been registered as joint legal co-owners. That this has not been done raises the distinct possibility that there is no written declaration by Mavis of a trust in favour of Cedric. Does it seem fair that Cedric has no enforceable beneficial interests in the house, given that he paid for half of the purchase price?

The situation with Ralph and Maple Drive may pose similar problems – there is unlikely to be any written declaration of trust in favour of Sandy. However, given the actions of Sandy in paying bills and making improvements to the house could it be unconscionable for Ralph to hide behind the lack of written evidence of any agreement between them? If written evidence is not needed, what sort of behaviour or type of contribution could a court accept as indicating an agreement?

RESULTING AND CONSTRUCTIVE TRUSTS

Section 52(2) of the LPA 1925 provides that resulting and constructive trusts do not require written evidence for their implied creation or operation.

A resulting trust will arise where a contribution is made to the purchase price of property by the person claiming a beneficial interest, with the share in the land quantified accordingly. A constructive trust can, by contrast, take into account the 'whole course of dealings' between the parties in quantifying a beneficial interest and is therefore more flexible.

RESULTING TRUSTS

A resulting trust gives effect to the presumed intention of parties, where property has been voluntarily transferred to someone who does not provide any consideration or by a contribution of money to the purchase price. The trust property is said to 'result' back to the transferor or contributor (implied settlor).

KEY CASE: *DYER V DYER* [1788] EWHC EXCH J8; (1788) 2 COX EQ CAS 92

Chief Baron Eyre explained the presumption of a resulting trust from contributions of purchase money:

> The clear result of all the cases, without a single exception, is, that the trust of a legal estate, whether freehold … or leasehold; whether taken in the names of the purchasers and others jointly, or in the name of others without that of the purchaser; whether in one name or several; whether jointly or successive, results to the man who advances the purchase-money.

The contribution must be directly referable to the purchase of the property so, for example, payment of household bills, providing furnishings or work on the house are insufficient.

KEY CASE: *BURNS V BURNS* [1984] CH 317; [1984] 1 ALL ER 244

A couple lived together for a many years in a house registered in the name of the man only. The woman took the man's name, performed household duties and looked after the man and their children. Latterly she returned to work using her earnings to pay for household expenses. All mortgage instalments continued to be met by the man.

The court determined that there was no resulting trust; given there was no contribution to the purchase price of the property.

APPLY YOUR LEARNING – TASK 2

Do you think that the efforts of Sandy in caring for the children, paying household bills and even using her savings to improve the house could be direct contributions to the purchase price for Maple Drive?

TUTOR TIP – 1

For many purchases, a mortgage is necessary in order to generate the necessary funds. This raises the question of what qualifies as a direct financial contribution. Traditionally, resulting trusts are based on the intention presumed to be held on the date of the conveyance of transfer (see *Pettitt v Pettitt* [1970] AC 777; [1969] 2 All ER 385) and so should not take account of later intentions. This is reflected by case law considering the different points at which assistance towards a mortgage may arise.

A Contribution to the Deposit – This qualifies as a direct contribution, for example see *Halifax Building Society v Brown* [1996] 1 FLR 103.

Taking Out and Assuming Liability for a Mortgage – This qualifies as a direct contribution, for example see *Laskar v Laskar* [2008] EWCA Civ 347; [2008] 1 WLR 2695.

Making Mortgage Payments After the Time of Acquisition – This is problematic, given the payments happen after the resulting trust should have 'crystallised' at the time the house was bought. In *Curley v Parkes* [2004] EWCA Civ 1515; [2005] 1 P & CR DG15. Peter Gibson LJ explained:

> The relevant principle is that the resulting trust of a property purchased in the name of another, in the absence of contrary intention, arises once and for all at the date on which the property is acquired. Because of the liability assumed by the mortgagor in a case where monies are borrowed by the mortgagor to be used on the purchase, the mortgagor is treated as having provided the proportion of the purchase price attributable to the monies so borrowed. Subsequent payments of the mortgage instalments are not part of the purchase price already paid to the vendor, but are sums paid for discharging the mortgagor's obligations under the mortgage

This decision may be open to challenge but, given that such later payments are certainly relevant in finding a constructive trust (discussed in the next subsection of this chapter), this type of dispute is resolved by way of a constructive trust. As we shall see, constructive trusts often provide the better solution for the modern social context.

The proportion of the contribution to the purchase price is reflected in the beneficial share under the resulting trust. For example, if A purchases a house with a contribution from B amounting to 20 per cent of the price it is presumed that B has a 20 per cent beneficial interest or share in the property. At law then, A owns the property but in equity A owns only 80 per cent and B 20 per cent.

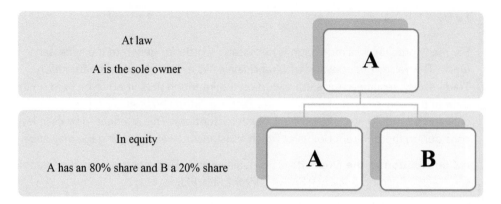

Figure 9.1 Ownership in law and in equity

APPLY YOUR LEARNING – TASK 3

When Sebastian and Edward purchased Willow Bay as an investment property to renovate one year ago, Sebastian contributed 90 per cent of the price.

If the property is vested in one name only, will there be a presumed resulting trust in favour of the other and, if so, what will be the beneficial shares?

If the property is owned jointly in both of their names, given this is a 'commercial' co-ownership case their unequal contributions to the price again means the presumption of resulting trust. See Chapter 11 for a full review of co-ownership.

The presumption of a resulting trust is rebuttable. It may be that a gift is intended when the property is transferred or that the money contributed was a gift or a personal loan. A presumption of advancement, that a gift was intended, is actually presumed in certain relationships replacing the presumption of a resulting trust.[2]

TUTOR TIP – 2

Given that money provided towards the purchase of a house is often a significant amount, it may be difficult to argue a gift was intended even in relationships where one seems more likely (for example, where the contributor is a parent). The solution to this is to evidence a gift or any loan in writing.

---

2 Husbands are presumed to make gifts to wives and fathers to a child. The presumption of advancement, which seems somewhat dated in its assumptions, has been subject to heavy criticism (see, for example, *Pettitt v Pettitt* [1970] AC 777). It was to be abolished by s 199 of the Equality Act 2010 but the section has not been brought into force as at the time of writing.

Following *Stack v Dowden* [2007][3] and *Jones v Kernott* [2011],[4] in 'domestic' cohabitation cases the presumption of resulting trust based on contributions is displaced. Instead, courts use the approach of a constructive trust based on a wider view of the parties' intentions.

TUTOR TIP – 3
....

Stack v Dowden [2007] and *Jones v Kernott* [2011] both concerned cohabitants jointly acquiring the legal title. However, it appears that the two decisions were also intended to have an impact on the beneficial ownership of properties in single legal ownership.

APPLY YOUR LEARNING – TASK 4

Jason and Betty jointly purchased the legal title to Thorn House in both of their names. Their unequal contributions to the price would have, prior to *Stack v Dowden* [2007] and *Jones v Kernott* [2011], meant the presumption of resulting trust. Would that presumption have had a significant impact on the determination of their respective beneficial shares?

Jones v Kernott [2011]:
Lord Walker and Baroness Hale recognised that:

> [I]n the case of the purchase of a house or flat in joint names for joint occupation by a married or unmarried couple, where both are responsible for any mortgage, there is no presumption of a resulting trust arising from their having contributed to the deposit (or indeed the rest of the purchase) in unequal shares.

When Mavis purchased Cedar Way solely in her name she did so with a contribution from Cedric amounting to half of its price. Prior to *Stack v Dowden* [2007] and *Jones v Kernott* [2011], his direct contribution would have meant a presumed resulting trust. Now, his share will be determined by the intentions of the parties by assessing a range of different evidence under a constructive trust.

Gallarotti v Sebastianelli [2012] EWCA Civ 865; [2012] 2 FLR 1231
Two friends purchased a flat with one paying a larger share of the deposit. The property was transferred into one name only. A resulting trust approach was not used given this was a 'domestic' relationship based upon friendship rather than a 'commercial' context of business partners. Whereas only contributions to the acquisition of property will be taken into account in the case of a resulting trust, the common intention constructive trust allowed the court to examine the whole course of conduct of the parties. The considerations applied by the court included how the parties had arranged their finances with respect to the property, what their financial contributions in fact were and that they were flat sharers rather than a family unit.

....

3 [2007] UKHL 17; [2007] 2 AC 432; [2007] 2 All ER 929.
4 [2011] UKSC 53; [2012] 1 AC 776; [2011] 3 WLR 1121.

CONSTRUCTIVE TRUSTS

A constructive trust will be imposed where it would be unconscionable for the owner of property to deny the beneficial interests of another. As they can arise in a wide range of situations, they are difficult to define. While the coverage is wider,[5] in relation to land it is the common intention constructive trusts that have the most significance, most notably in use as an equitable remedy to settle disputes arising from shared homes usually by a cohabiting couple who are unmarried or unregistered.

> TUTOR TIP – 4
> ....
>
> If a married couple divorce, there are extensive powers given to a court to decide about ownership of the home under the Matrimonial Causes Act 1973. Similar provisions are made under the Civil Partnership Act 2004 for the dissolving of a registered partnership.
>
> This means that trust principles (and those of proprietary estoppel) are not normally relevant to the division of assets. However, the same is not true of couples cohabiting outside of a marriage or a registered partnership, or of other non-romantic types of household.

When considering the application of constructive trusts as a remedy, it is helpful to break that consideration down into the two parts: first, establishing the interest and second, quantifying the interests.

Establishing the interest

A constructive trust requires the claimant to establish a common intention. This requires either:

- an express agreement, relied upon by the claimant so that they acted their detriment, or
- an agreement implied by the conduct of the parties.

> **KEY CASE:** *LLOYDS BANK PLC V ROSSET* [1990] UKHL 14; [1991] 1 AC 107; [1990] 1 ALL ER 1111
>
> A house was conveyed into the sole name of Mr Rosset, with the intention that he and his wife would renovate and live in the property together. The wife claimed a beneficial interest under a constructive trust based upon her efforts in supervising the builders and decorating (the husband paid all costs).

---

5 For example, we have already seen that where a vendor and purchaser enter into a valid estate contract for the sale of land, the vendor becomes a constructive trustee of the land for the purchaser.

Lord Bridge explained that there are two routes for a finding the parties' common intention. The first relates to an express agreement:

> The first and fundamental question which must always be resolved is whether, independently of any inference to be drawn from the conduct of the parties in the course of sharing the house as their home and managing their joint affairs, there has at any time prior to acquisition, or exceptionally at some later date, been any agreement, arrangement or understanding reached between them that the property is to be shared beneficially. The finding of an agreement or arrangement to share in this sense can only, I think, be based on evidence of express discussions between the partners, however imperfectly remembered and however imprecise their terms may have been. Once a finding to this effect is made it will only be necessary for the partner asserting a claim to a beneficial interest against the partner entitled to the legal estate to show that he or she has acted to his or her detriment or significantly altered his or her position in reliance on the agreement in order to give rise to a constructive trust or a proprietary estoppel.

The second, in the absence of an express agreement, agreement implied by conduct:

> In sharp contrast with this situation is the very different one where there is no evidence to support a finding of an agreement or arrangement to share, however reasonable it might have been for the parties to reach such an arrangement if they had applied their minds to the question, and where the court must rely entirely on the conduct of the parties both as the basis from which to infer a common intention to share the property beneficially and as the conduct relied on to give rise to a constructive trust. In this situation direct contributions to the purchase price by the partner who is not the legal owner, whether initially or by payment of mortgage instalments, will readily justify the inference necessary to the creation of a constructive trust. But, as I read the authorities, it is at least extremely doubtful whether anything less will do.

Express agreement and detriment

Where there have been express discussions between the parties a trust can arise, despite the absence of written evidence in accordance with s 53(1)(b) of the LPA 1925.

For cases where the property is held in joint names, it is usually taken for granted that the intention to share equitable ownership of the property is not an issue.

APPLY YOUR LEARNING – TASK 5

When Jason and his partner Betty purchased the legal title to Thorn House, they did so in joint names.

Do you think a court would find a common intention to share the beneficial ownership?

In single name cases, following *Stack v Dowden* [2007] and *Jones v Kernott* [2011], the starting point is the assumption that beneficial ownership follows legal title and, therefore, the sole legal owner is assumed to be the sole beneficial owner unless the contrary can be established.

APPLY YOUR LEARNING – TASK 6

Mavis is the legal sole owner of the legal title to Cedar Way, despite Cedric contributing half of the price. What will be the presumed position with beneficial ownership in equity?

There often is no express agreement and, even with assurances, the agreement often lacks supporting evidence. As Waite J observed in *H v M (Beneficial Interest)* [1992]:[6]

> [T]he tenderest exchanges of a common law courtship may assume an unforeseen significance many years later when they are brought under equity's microscope and subjected to an analysis under which many thousands of pounds of value may be liable to turn on fine questions as to whether the relevant words were spoken in earnest or in dalliance and with or without representational intent.

If there is anything at all ambiguous about the assurances relied upon, common intention may not be established.

KEY CASE: *JAMES V THOMAS* [2007] EWCA CIV 1212; [2008] 1 FLR 1598

A woman moved into a house owned solely by the man with whom she had formed a relationship. After they separated, she claimed to have a beneficial interest in the property based on assurances he made. The woman had worked in the business he ran from the property without remuneration, given him money to pay off a tax bill and undertaken work on property. It was decided that the assurances given were insufficient to show common intention.

6 [1992] 1 FLR 229.

Sir John Chadwick:

> [I]t is, to my mind, at least as likely that the observation 'this will benefit us both' (in relation to improvements to the property) was intended to mean – and was understood at the time to mean – that the improvements would have the effect that the property in which they were living as their home would be more comfortable and more convenient: or, to put the point another way, that the improvements to the property would be reflected in an improvement to the quality of their life together. It is, I think, unreal to suggest that an observation in those terms, made in that context, was intended or understood to be a promise of some property interest, either present or in the future. Nor, as it seems to me, can it be said that the observation 'this will benefit us both', when made in the context of a discussion of matters relating to the business, was intended or understood to be a promise of some property interest in The Cottage … [T]here is no reason to think that the observation … was more than a statement of the obvious: what was of benefit to the business was of benefit to both Mr Thomas and Miss James, for whom the business was their livelihood. The second of the assurances said to have been relied upon was that 'He told her that in the event of his death "you will be well provided for" '. I find it impossible to see that as a representation that Miss James was to have a present proprietary interest in the property – or as a representation that she would have a proprietary interest in the property during Mr Thomas's lifetime. It was, as it seems to me, a representation as to what the position would be after Mr Thomas' death. And it must, I think, be seen as a representation made on the basis of a common assumption that the parties would still be living together when that eventuality occurred.

Detrimental reliance is also required, but need not be directly referable to the property itself and need only be 'significant'.

KEY CASES: *DETRIMENTAL RELIANCE*

LLOYDS BANK V ROSSET [1990] UKHL 14; [1991] 1 AC 107; [1990] 1 ALL ER 1111

The reliance must be more than *de minimis*, as was made clear by Lord Bridge. With regard to the wife's efforts which we set out earlier, he reasoned:

> It was common ground that Mrs. Rosset was extremely anxious that the new matrimonial home should be ready for occupation before Christmas if possible. In these circumstances it would seem the most natural thing in the world for any wife, in the absence of her husband abroad, to spend all the

time she could spare and to employ any skills she might have, such as the ability to decorate a room, in doing all she could to accelerate progress of the work quite irrespective of any expectation she might have of enjoying a beneficial interest in the property.

This may be contrasted with two other cases, both of which Lord Bridge referred to approvingly.

EVES V EVES [1975] EWCA CIV 3; [1975] 1 WLR 1338

A couple lived together in a property which was conveyed into the man's name alone. He told the woman that this was because she was under 21 she was too young to have her name on the legal title and that if she had been old enough the house would have been in both their names. The woman did not provide any direct contribution to the purchase price but carried out substantial work on the property including much work in the house and garden and cared for the man and the children. It was held that she was entitled to one-quarter of the beneficial interest under a constructive trust.

GRANT V EDWARDS [1986] CH 638; [1986] 2 ALL ER 42

The facts were similar to those of *Eves* v *Eves*. The excuse given by the man in this case for the conveyance into his name alone was that adding the woman to the legal title might affect her divorce. The woman made substantial contributions to the household expenses which enabled Mr Edwards to meet the mortgage instalments.

While the contributions in both *Eves v Eves* [1975] and *Grant v Edwards* [1986] were substantial enough to show reliance upon the expressed common intention, do note that that conduct would not by itself have supported a claim. In the absence of the 'excuses' both men had given, to infer common intention based on the women's contributions would have failed.[7] In *Lloyds Bank v Rosset* [1990], Lord Bridge explained that:

---

7 Note that the cases *Eves v Eves* [1975] and *Grant v Edwards* [1986] do not mean that the mere giving of an excuse will usually amount to an expressed common intention to share the beneficial ownership. See, for example, *Curran v Collins* [2015] EWCA Civ 404; [2016] 1 FLR 505 in which a partner, when asking her share in a property owned by the man, was told that it would be 'too expensive' for her name to be on the deeds. There was no positive assertion that the property would otherwise have been purchased in joint names, and so no common intention. The lack of any significant contribution from her cast further doubt upon the nature of the assertion and also meant that would be no detrimental reliance in any event.

The subsequent conduct of the female partner in each of these cases, which the court rightly held sufficient to give rise to a constructive trust … supporting her claim to an interest in the property, fell far short of such conduct as would by itself have supported the claim in the absence of an express representation by the male partner that she was to have such an interest.

Referring back to Lord Bridge's explanation of the second route for common intention set out in *Lloyds Bank v Rosset* [1990], when considering what conduct would have sufficed, Lord Bridge doubted whether, 'anything falling short of direct contributions would suffice'.

APPLY YOUR LEARNING – TASK 7

Mavis is the legal sole owner of the legal title to Cedar Way, but Cedric contributed half of the purchase price. There is no suggestion of a loan here – the property was bought to live in. Cedric's direct contributions would be treated as evidence of a common intention that he should have an interest in the house.

Implied agreement from conduct

The conduct that Lord Bridge reasoned would suffice to infer a common intention was in the form of direct contributions towards the acquisition of the property, whether initially or by the payment of mortgage instalments.

The decision of Lord Bridge in *Lloyds Bank v Rosset* [1990] did not, however, rule out that indirect contributions could ever give rise to a constructive trust.

CONSIDER THIS – 2

Do you think only recognising that direct contributions infer a common intention is open to criticism?

Note the case, decided prior to *Lloyds Bank v Rosset* [1990], of *Gissing v Gissing* [1971] AC 886; [1970] 2 All ER 780. A couple divorced after many years of marriage. The legal title of the home was vested in the husband alone. The wife claimed to be entitled to half of the beneficial interest. Although her contributions were held to be insufficient to infer a common intention and as such her claim failed, the reasoning of Lord Diplock is of interest:

> On what then is the wife's claim based? In 1951 when the house was purchased she spent about £190 on buying furniture and a cooker and refrigerator for it. She also paid about £30 for improving the lawn. As furniture and household durables are depreciating assets whereas houses have turned

out to be appreciating assets it may be that she would have been wise to have devoted her savings to acquiring an interest in the freehold; but this may not have been so apparent in 1951 as it has now become. ... There is no suggestion that the wife's efforts or her earnings made it possible for the husband to raise the initial loan or the mortgage or that her relieving her husband from the expense of buying clothing for herself and for their son was undertaken in order to enable him the better to meet the mortgage instalments or to repay the loan. The picture presented by the evidence is one of husband and wife retaining their separate proprietary interests in property whether real or personal purchased with their separate savings and is inconsistent with any common intention at the time of the purchase of the matrimonial home that the wife who neither then nor thereafter contributed anything to its purchase price or assumed any liability for it, should nevertheless be entitled to a beneficial interest in it.

The decision may be read as suggesting that had the contributions indirectly enabled the husband to pay the mortgage, common intention could have been inferred. Looking at the parties' global dealings over the ownership of the property may be fairer, particularly as the parties may not realise the importance of how they share the financial responsibilities.

In the case of *Le Foe v Le Foe* [2001],[8] the court, after considering *Gissing v Gissing* and *Lloyds Bank v Rosset*, inferred from the wife's very substantial, indirect contributions (which allowed the mortgage to be paid by the husband) a common intention to share beneficially. Nicholas Mostyn QC, sitting as a deputy High Court judge, explained that not to look at more global arrangement would mean that, 'these cases would be decided by reference to mere acts of fortune, being the arbitrary allocation of financial responsibility between the parties'.

In *Stack v Dowden* [2007],[9] a case where the property in question was held in joint names so that intention to share was not in issue, there was an *obiter* consideration of the view of Lord Bridge in *Lloyds Bank v Rosset* doubting anything other than direct contributions would do. Lord Walker commented that: 'Whether or not Lord Bridge's observation was justified in 1990, in my opinion the law has moved on, and your Lordships should move it a little more in the same direction'. Baroness Hale, with whom three of their Lordships agreed, criticised the criteria for establishment set out by Lord Bridge, stated that they, 'have set that hurdle rather too high in certain respects'.

8 [2001] 2 FLR 970.
9 [2007] AC 432; [2007] 2 All ER 929.

Post *Stack v Dowden* there was, therefore, a suggestion that the scope to infer a constructive trust from conduct is now wider than the more restrictive formula set out by Lord Bridge, at least in relation to indirect contributions. In *Jones v Kernott* [2012],[10] Baroness Hale and Lord Walker affirmed that common intention between parties can be 'deduced objectively from their conduct'. The criteria set out in *Stack v Dowden* for quantifying the interests under a trust included many non-financial factors. This raises the possibility of a shift towards non-financial considerations being also relevant to initially establishing the existence of a trust. As stated by Baroness Hale in the Privy Council decision *Abbott v Abbott* [2007],[11] 'the parties' whole course of conduct in relation to the property must be taken into account in determining their shared intentions as to its ownership'. However, the decision in *Jones v Kernott* did not clearly remove the requirement for a contribution to imply common intention and the courts have continued to exercise caution and taken a strict line. There is particular difficulty in cases of marriage or cohabitation as, while in a relationship, the motivation for conduct may often be explained by factors other than acquiring an interest in the property.

KEY CASE: *JAMES V THOMAS* [2007] EWCA CIV 1212; [2008] 1 FLR 1598

This is the key case already referred to with regard to finding an expressed common intention. The argument was also considered whether there could be implied common intention based on the conduct of the woman. She had performed work of a heavy nature (for example, she drove a tipper, dug trenches, picked up materials, laid concrete, tarmac and gravel and generally undertook manual work associated with the business of Mr Thomas with whom she was cohabiting).

Sir John Chadwick said:

> The true position, as it seems to me, is that she worked in the business, and contributed her labour to the improvements to the property, because she and Mr Thomas were making their life together as man and wife. The Cottage was their home: the business was their livelihood. It is a mistake to think that the motives which lead parties in such a relationship to act as they do are necessarily attributable to pecuniary self-interest.

She was not entitled to a beneficial interest.

The difficulty is more acute where the party claiming the common intention has personally benefited from the conduct in question.

---

10 [2012] AC 776; [2011] UKSC 53.
11 [2007] UKPC 53; [2008] 1 FLR 1451.

KEY CASE: *MORRIS V MORRIS* [2008] EWCA CIV 257; [2008] FAM
LAW 521

A husband and wife lived together on a farm owned by the husband and his
mother. The wife helped considerably with the farming business for no pay and
later established a very successful riding school at the property, contributing
towards the construction of new buildings for use by the school.

Sir Peter Gibson:

> Certainly, so far as the activities of the claimant in support of the farming
> business conducted by the man with whom she was living are concerned, I
> cannot see that they are of such an exceptional nature as to lead to any
> inference … that the claimant must have acted in the belief that she was
> acquiring an interest in the Farm. As for the financial contributions … paid
> towards the building of the manège served to benefit the claimant in
> conducting a profitable riding school business on the Farm without, it seems,
> paying any proper sums by way of rent for the benefits which she received,
> including the use of the land on which the business was conducted. That was
> for her own financial benefit, even though it can be acknowledged that
> improvements, such as the manège and the indoor riding school building, did
> add to the capital value of the Farm.

At all times, the central concern is intention relating to the property rather than any
ability to impute intention based upon fairness. This was reiterated more recently in
Graham-York v York [2015],[12] by Tomlinson LJ:

> [I]t is irrelevant that it may be thought a 'fair' outcome for a woman who has
> endured years of abusive conduct by her partner to be allotted a substantial
> interest in his property on his death. The plight of Miss Graham-York attracts
> sympathy, but it does not enable the court to redistribute property interest in a
> manner which right-minded people might think amounts to appropriate
> compensation. Miss Graham-York is 'entitled to that share which court considers
> fair having regard to the whole course of dealing between them in relation to the
> property'. It is these last words, which I have emphasised, which supply the
> confines of the enquiry as to fairness.

---

12 [2015] EWCA Civ 72; [2016] 1 FLR 407.

APPLY YOUR LEARNING – TASK 8

Ralph is the legal owner of Maple Drive, but is there an argument that allowing his partner Sandy for ten years to provide money to pay the household bills, look after their two children, and use savings to substantially improve the house could give rise to a common intention constructive trust?

The whole course of conduct will be taken into account, but was the motivation for Sandy really about ownership of a property or about the furtherance of the parties' relationship?

Quantifying the interests

The quantification of the beneficial interests or shares under a trust of land is now dependent on whether it relates to a case of sole legal ownership, with the legal estate held by one person, or to a case of joint legal ownership, with the legal estate co-owned by two persons or more.

TUTOR TIP – 5

If the parties expressly agree what their beneficial interests should be, that will be conclusive. The position is clearly set out in *Goodman v Gallant* [1985] EWCA Civ 15; [1986] 1 FLR 513 by Slade LJ:

> If … the relevant conveyance contains an express declaration of trust which comprehensively declares the beneficial interests in the property or its proceeds of sale, there is no room for the application of the doctrine of resulting implied or constructive trusts unless and until the conveyance is set aside or rectified; until that event the declaration contained in the document speaks for itself.

For a more recent example, see *Pankhania v Chandegra* [2012] EWCA Civ 1438; [2013] 3 FCR 16.

Sole legal ownership

While direct financial contributions may remain necessary to infer a common intention, once an agreement to share the beneficial interest is found then the respective financial contributions are not determinative.

KEY CASE: *MIDLAND BANK V COOKE* [1995] 4 ALL ER 562; [1995] 2 FLR 915

The home was conveyed into the sole name of the husband, but the wife contributed £550 by way of a gift from her parents. The wife later contributed towards household bills and substantial improvements to the home.

She successfully claimed to have beneficial interest in the property, which the trial judge ruled amounted to 6.47 per cent based on her direct contributions. She appealed on the quantification of her interest, where she was held to be entitled to 50 per cent of the beneficial interest based on the 'whole course of dealings'. Per Waite LJ:

> When the court is proceeding, in cases like the present where the partner without legal title has successfully asserted an equitable interest through direct contribution, to determine (in the absence of express evidence of intention) what proportions the parties must be assumed to have intended for their beneficial ownership, the duty of the judge is to undertake a survey of the whole course of dealing between the parties relevant to their ownership and occupation of the property and their sharing of its burdens and advantages. That scrutiny will not confine itself to the limited range of acts of direct contribution … It will take into consideration all conduct which throws light on the question what shares were intended.

The broader approach of *Midland Bank v Cooke* was developed by *Oxley v Hiscock* [2005] and affirmed by the House of Lords in *Stack v Dowden* [2007].

KEY CASES: *OXLEY V HISCOCK* [2004] EWCA CIV 546; [2005] FAM 211

The case again involved a property registered in the name of the husband, but acquired with a direct financial contribution to the purchase price by the wife. The husband argued that her beneficial interest should be determined by the proportion of her contribution; the court explained that the 'whole course of dealings' must be considered. Per Chadwick LJ:

> It must now be accepted that … the answer is that each is entitled to that share which the court considers fair having regard to the whole course of dealing between them in relation to the property. And, in that context, 'the whole course of dealing between them in relation to the property' includes the arrangements which they make from time to time in order to meet the outgoings (for example, mortgage contributions, council tax and utilities, repairs, insurance and housekeeping) which have to be met if they are to live in the property as their home.

KEY CASE: *STACK V DOWDEN* [2007] UKHL 17; [2007] 2 AC 432

This case concerned a joint or co-ownership, but the ruling explored the range of factors that were relevant to the court in quantifying shares in sole ownership cases and for 'unusual' joint ownership ones.

Baroness Hale explained that each case will turn on its own facts, with many more factors than financial considerations relevant to 'divining the parties' true intentions'. These include:

- Advice or discussions at the time of the transfer.
- The reasons why the house was acquired in their joint names.
- The reasons why (if it be the case) the survivor was authorised to give a receipt for capital moneys.
- The purpose for which the home was acquired.
- The nature of the parties' relationship.
- Whether they had children for whom they both had responsibility to provide a home.
- How the purchase was financed, both initially and subsequently.
- How the parties arranged their finances.
- How they paid outgoings on the property and their other household expenses.
- The parties' individual characters and personalities may also be a factor.

While the flexibility of the factors in *Stack v Dowden* is welcomed, that flexibility presents a challenge when predicting beneficial shares.

Joint legal ownership

In the case of joint or co-ownership, the approach in *Stack v Dowden*, as reviewed in *Jones v Kernott* [2011],[13] means that in the 'family' context there is now a presumed beneficial joint tenancy in equity. The implications of this assumption and the nature of a joint tenancy will be explored in Chapter 11 on co-ownership. For now, it is sufficient to note that this means that the parties have equal rights to the whole property and have no different shares in the property.

TUTOR TIP – 6

In the 'commercial' as opposed to the family context, the resulting trusts method of analysing beneficial interests in property is still used.

Laskar v Laskar [2008] EWCA Civ 347; [2008] 1 WLR 2695

---

13 [2011] UKSC 53; [2012] 1 AC 776.

> This case related to an investment property, purchased by a mother and daughter in order to let it out. Lord Neuberger considered whether the presumption of beneficial interest following legal interests set out in *Stack v Dowden* applied to this case. He concluded that it would not be right to apply *Stack* to this case as the property had not been purchased as a home but as an investment.

The joint tenancy is only an assumption, but according to *Stack v Dowden* [2007], it would be unusual for joint purchasers making no express declaration as to entitlement of the beneficial interest in the property to be able to vary that presumption.

APPLY YOUR LEARNING – TASK 9

Jason and Betty purchased the legal title to Thorn House in joint names, with Jason contributing three-quarters of the purchase price.

Following *Stack v Dowden* [2007], it would be presumed that Jason and Betty have equal rights to the whole property. This is despite Jason having put in more money.

As Baroness Hale explained in *Stack v Dowden*:

> [I]t will almost always have been a conscious decision to put the house into joint names. Even if the parties have not executed the transfer, they will usually, if not invariably, have executed the contract which precedes it. Committing oneself to spend large sums of money on a place to live is not normally done by accident or without giving it a moment's thought.

What should Jason have done to evidence an intention that he should have a larger share in equity?

The factors set out by Baroness Hale for divining the parties' true intentions, as set out previously, were met in this case but the court emphasised this would be 'very unusual'. The factors leading to this decision were that the parties contributed unequally to the purchase price; did not pool their resources (keeping separate savings and investments); and had separate responsibility for household outgoings.

KEY CASE: *STACK V DOWDEN* [2007] UKHL 17; [2007] 2 AC 432; [2007] 2 ALL ER 929

The starting point for determining beneficial interests where the legal title was held jointly or co-owned is that beneficial interest will also be held jointly. This presumption may be displaced by evidence that this was not their intention. Per Baroness Hale:

In the cohabitation context, mercenary considerations may be more to the fore than they would be in marriage, but it should not be assumed that they always take pride of place over natural love and affection. At the end of the day, having taken all this into account, cases in which the joint legal owners are to be taken to have intended that their beneficial interests should be different from their legal interests will be very unusual.

This is, therefore, a very unusual case. There cannot be many unmarried couples who have lived together for as long as this, who have had four children together, and whose affairs have been kept as rigidly separate as this couple's affairs were kept. This is all strongly indicative that they did not intend their shares, even in the property which was put into both their names, to be equal (still less that they intended a beneficial joint tenancy with the right of survivorship should one of them die before it was severed). Before the Court of Appeal, Ms Dowden contended for a 65% share and in my view she has made good her case for that.

The presumption in *Stack v Dowden* will not be easily rebutted by conduct.

KEY CASE: *JONES V KERNOTT* [2011] UKSC 53; [2012] 1 AC 776

Baroness Hale and Lord Walker stated:

[A] challenge to the presumption of beneficial joint tenancy is not to be lightly embarked on… If a couple in an intimate relationship (whether married or unmarried) decide to buy a house … in which to live together, almost always with the help of a mortgage for which they are jointly and severally liable, that is on the face of things a strong indication of emotional and economic commitment to a joint enterprise. … even if the parties … fail to make that clear by any overt declaration or agreement

In this case the property had been purchased in joint names but, after the couple split, for 14 years the woman continued to pay the mortgage and bills as well as the cost of bringing up their children. This was sufficient to depart from the presumption of beneficial joint tenancy, the intentions had changed after the split and she was awarded a 90 per cent share.

The evidence will need to be robust for any variation, as highlighted by the contrasting outcomes in two cases.

KEY CASE: *BARNES V PHILLIPS* [2015] EWCA CIV 1056; [2016] HLR 3

The couple purchased a property jointly. After the relationship broke down, the woman took on sole responsibility for mortgage repayments, child maintenance and funded substantial maintenance works to the property.

The court concluded that, 'the weight of the evidence' supported 'an inference that the parties intended to alter their shares in the property'.

KEY CASE: *MONTALTO V POPAT* [2016] EWHC 810 (CH); [2016] ALL ER (D) 118 (APR)

A same-sex couple in a relationship akin to marriage owned beneficial shares in a property. The difficulty was determining the size of those shares. One of the men argued the property was beneficially held equally; the other had paid off the mortgage and asked for a division in line with their monetary contributions.

The court rejected a resulting approach given that there was not an investment property. On the evidence, there had been a common intention that the flat would be held by M and P as tenants in common in equal shares.

In accordance with *Jones v Kernott* [2011], it was a 'heavy burden' to show that a 'changed common intention has come about post acquisition' but 'context is all'. The mortgage had always been a joint liability of the parties, the precise contributions did not alter that shared endeavour. (However, while not altering the intended ownership of the house, the repayment was to be treated as a loan for which the party was entitled to be repaid.)

DISCUSSION

OVERLAP WITH ESTOPPEL

The operation of common intention constructive trusts is closely aligned with the operation of the equitable doctrine of estoppel, explored in Chapter 16. The parallels are in fact so significant that the same facts can give rise to both. This has led to some suggestions that, in these cases, there is little difference and that constructive trusts and estoppel have been assimilated.

CONSIDER THIS – 3

In *Oxley v Hiscock* [2004] 3 WLR 715, Chadwick LJ said that: 'I think that the time has come to accept that there is no difference, in cases of this nature, whether the true analysis lies in constructive trust or in proprietary estoppel.'

Do you agree that common intention trusts are now indistinguishable from proprietary estoppel?

The dictum of Chadwick LJ in *Oxley v Hiscock* reflected what he referred to as a 'recent trend in other Commonwealth jurisdictions towards more generalised principles of unconscionability and unjust enrichment'.[14] It was suggested again in *Yaxley v Gotts* [2000][15] by Robert Walker LJ, who suggested that there was: '[M]uch common ground between the doctrines of proprietary estoppel and the constructive trust … [both are] concerned with equity's intervention to provide relief against unconscionable conduct'. However, in *Stack v Dowden* [2007] distinctions between the approach and the outcomes were set out. Lord Walker himself stated:

> I have to say that I am now rather less enthusiastic about the notion that proprietary estoppel and 'common [intention]' constructive trusts can or should be completely assimilated. Proprietary estoppel typically consists of asserting an equitable claim against the conscience of the 'true' owner. The claim is a 'mere equity'. It is to be satisfied by the minimum award necessary to do justice. … which may sometimes lead to no more than a monetary award. A 'common intention' constructive trust, by contrast, is identifying the true beneficial owner or owners, and the size of their beneficial interests.

TUTOR TIP – 7

The differences between common intention constructive trusts and proprietary estoppel are not always obvious, but there are two which will be helpful for you to keep in mind.

Estoppel Does Not Require a Common Intention – As we have seen, in the absence of an express agreement it is difficult to infer a common intention for a constructive trust. Estoppel can be based on a representation, so may be used where there is insufficient evidence to support a common intention and even for cases of passive assurances.

---

14 Notably, Australia, Canada and New Zealand. In Canada, for example, the courts have adopted the concept of unjust enrichment as the basis for 'remedying the injustice that occurs when one person makes a substantial contribution to the property of another without compensation' (*Peter v Beblow* (1993) 101 DLR (4th) 621). In *Sorochan v Sorochan* (1986) 29 DLR (4th) 1, the three requirements to be for an unjust enrichment were listed: an enrichment; a corresponding deprivation; and the absence of juristic reasoning for the enrichment.

15 [2000] Ch 162; [2000] 1 All ER 711.

The Remedies Are Different – The remedy for a constructive trust is whatever share in the property is found to have been intended. A successful claim in estoppel is far more flexible. It is satisfied by whatever the court determines is the appropriate remedy to 'do justice' between the particular parties. This may involve awarding a beneficial share in the property, a licence to live there for a lifetime, or a return or award of money.

If a share in the property is given as the remedy, it may differ from that which would be awarded under a constructive trust. In *Arif v Anwar and Rehan* [2015] EWHC 124 (Fam); [2016] 1 FLR 359 no common intention could be found, it had been argued that there was an agreement giving a 50 per cent share via a constructive trust, yet estoppel was successfully argued to find a 25 per cent interest in the property.

UNCERTAINTY IN OPERATION

The operation of constructive trusts is sometimes criticised as being too uncertain, arguably becoming even more flexible from *Stack v Dowden* [2007] onwards because of social changes. This can make it particularly difficult for third parties such as mortgage lenders and purchasers. However, too many restrictive rules could reduce the flexibility needed to allow just results for individual cases.

TUTOR TIP – 8
....

The Law Commission published in 2007 the report *Cohabitation: The Financial Consequences of Relationship Breakdown* (Law Com No 307, 2007) considering the financial consequences of the ending of cohabiting relationships by separation or death. It proposed a detailed statutory scheme that would, in the absence of opting out, address particular economic consequences of the contributions made by the parties during the relationship. Those eligible to apply would need to satisfy the eligibility criteria of living together for a specific number of years or having children of the relationship.

Its recommendations relating to the basis on which awards would be made were clear that they would be based only on qualifying contributions with enduring consequences. The applicant would have to show that the respondent retained a benefit, or that the applicant had a continuing economic disadvantage, as a result of contributions made to the relationship. The point is summarised at para 1.31:

> We contended that cohabiting couples should not be entitled to a share of each other's assets at the end of their relationship irrespective of the extent to which they shared their lives during the relationship.

> Applicants should only be able to obtain a remedy on separation if they could show that the effects of the contributions and associated economic sacrifices they had made during the relationship would otherwise be unfairly shared following separation. In many cases, neither party would be able to establish this and no claim would therefore be tenable.

The proposed scheme would have provided some solution to the uncertainty of the application of complex constructive trusts and proprietary estoppel principles and expensive disputes. However, in 2011, the government rejected the proposals, stating that: '[T]he family justice system [was] in a transitional period, with major reforms already on the horizon.'

Here, it is interesting to again note the cohabitation case of *Barnes v Phillips* [2015], referred to above as an 'exceptional' case in which the shares in a property were varied. Account was taken of the failure by the man to make payments due for the maintenance of their children and his taking money from a remortgage for himself, in the woman's favour she had contributed to the children's maintenance as well as paying mortgage instalments and funding repairs to the house.

Lloyd Jones LJ commented:

> Finally, I note, as did Lord Walker and Baroness Hale in *Jones v Kernott* … that in certain other Commonwealth jurisdictions legislation has conferred on the courts a limited power to vary or adjust proprietary rights in the home when an unmarried couple split up. Here, the Law Commission has made recommendations to a similar effect (Cohabitation: The Financial Consequences of Relationship Breakdown (2007), Law Commission No 307). The Government's response to this report is, however, still pending.

END OF CHAPTER SUMMARY

- A declaration of trust comprising land must be evidenced in writing (s 53(1)(b) of the Law of Property Act 1925).
- Absent an express agreement, beneficial interests in land can be acquired informally under a resulting or constructive trust.
- Resulting trusts arise where a contribution is made to the purchase price of property. However, outside of 'commercial' cases since *Stack v Dowden* [2007] a constructive trust approach is used.
- A constructive trust will arise if there is either (1) an express agreement, or (2) common intention is inferred through conduct (and detriment).
- In joint ownership cases, the intention to share is presumed.
- In sole owner cases:
  - Since *Stack v Dowden* there is a strong presumption that the position in equity is the same as at law, meaning the sole legal owner will also be the sole equitable owner.
  - However, direct contributions to the acquisition of the property will readily justify the inference of a common intention.
- Once a common intention to share is found, the beneficial interests must still be quantified.

- In joint ownership cases:

  - When quantifying the beneficial interests, since *Stack v Dowden* there is a strong presumption that the position in equity is the same as at law, meaning equal rights to the whole property and with no different shares in the property.
  - Variation is possible in exceptional circumstances, but will require robust evidence looking at the whole course of dealings.

- In sole owner cases, once a common intention is found, the whole course of dealings will be taken into consideration.

PREPARING FOR ASSESSMENTS QUESTIONS

ESSAY QUESTION

'The requirement for evidence in writing for trusts concerning land is vital for certainty, but just claims must not be unnecessarily thwarted by technical rules.'

Analyse the statement, considering: the role of s 53(1)(c) of the LPA 1925 in avoiding a reliance upon oral assurances when creating express trusts; the justification for resulting and constructive trusts being excepted; and how the rules for implying resulting and constructive trusts ensure that oral assurances are not enough.

PROBLEM QUESTION

Seven years ago, David and Pamela set up home together. They purchased Flowerpot House in joint names, with David paying all of the £15,000 deposit.

Upon first moving in, Pamela redecorated the house throughout and oversaw the fitting of a new bathroom and a kitchen using money in David's savings account.

Three years ago, Pamela was promoted and received a large pay rise. As a result, for two years she paid substantially more towards the mortgage instalments and paid a generous proportion of her earnings into David's account by standing order each month towards household expenses. Both kept separate bank accounts.

After David and Pamela separated a year ago, Pamela stayed on in the house and paid all of the mortgage instalments and bills for the property.

Advise on how they may hold the beneficial interest in Flowerpot House.

CONSIDER THIS – 4

What difference would it make to your answer if:

(a) the legal estate had been vested in David alone; or

(b) Pamela had only moved into the property after David had already been living there for two years before meeting her and she did not make any direct payments towards the mortgage; or

(c) you were advising the couple from the moment they decided to purchase a house together.

FURTHER READING

- Delany, H and Ryan, D, 'Unconscionability: A Unifying Theme in Equity' [2008] Conv 401. Explores the potential for principle of unconscionability to provide a unifying theme capable of explaining the nature of liability in equity. Examines use of the principle in constructive trust and proprietary estoppel cases.

- Dixon, M, 'The Still Not Ended, Never-Ending Story' [2012] Conv 82. Reflects on issues examined in *Jones v Kernott* and discusses the implications for advising clients.

- Gardner, S and Davidson, K, 'The Supreme Court on Family Homes' (2012) 128 LQR 177. Discusses the significance of *Jones v Kernott*.

- Law Commission, *Cohabitation: The Financial Consequences of Relationship Breakdown* (Law Com No 307, 2007).

- Pawlowski, M, 'Beneficial Entitlement No Longer Doing Justice?' [2007] Conv 354. Discusses the ruling in *Stack v Dowden*. Looks at whether indirect financial contributions give rise to a beneficial interest under a constructive trust.

- Pawlowski, M, 'Imputing a Common Intention in Single Ownership Cases' (2015) 29 Trust Law International 3. Considers whether the English courts should impute a common intention of beneficial entitlement at the acquisition stage in single ownership cases, asking whether the Canadian approach of presumptive inference should be used.

- Pawlowski, M and Brown, J, 'Joint Purchasers and the Presumption of Joint Beneficial Ownership – A Matter of Informed Choice?' (2013) 27 Trust Law International 3. Examines the presumption of equality to cases involving joint ownership and how this might be adjusted. Reports the results of a study on whether clients were given sufficient legal advice to appreciate the consequences of joint ownership.

- Piska, N, 'Intention, Fairness and the Presumption of Resulting Trust after Stack v Dowden' (2008) 71 MLR 120. Comments on *Stack v Dowden*, examining the majority's approach and Lord Neuberger's dissenting opinion as to whether the presumption of resulting trust should be the starting point.

- Sparkes, P, 'Non Declarations of Beneficial Co-ownership' [2012] Conv 207. Criticises the ruling in *Stack v Dowden* and suggests legislative intervention to reverse the decisions.

CHAPTER 10
TRUSTS OF LAND

CHAPTER AIMS AND OBJECTIVES

Since the 1925 legislation, every concurrent and successive interest with regard to the same piece of land now must take effect in equity under a trust.[1] For example, whenever a couple jointly own a property or if a house is left to a partner for life with the remainder to a child. Given the prevalence of trusts comprising land and the nature and importance of land, clear schemes for their governance are needed. In relation to land, both the 1925 legislation and the Trusts of Land and Appointment of Trustees Act 1996 (ToLATA 1996) have helped to simplify and strengthen the framework for trusts of land.

By the end of this chapter, you should be able to:

■ explain what is meant by a trust in land;
■ appreciate the need for the reforms brought about by ToLATA 1996, notably:

  ■ no new strict settlements
  ■ all trusts for sale were converted into trusts of land
  ■ all new trusts comprising land are trusts of land;

■ understand that the ToLATA 1996 statutory framework governing trusts of land sets out the powers and duties of trustees and the rights of beneficiaries;
■ apply the above to the case study and the learning outcomes.

---

1 On this point, it may be helpful to refer back to Chapter 2 and the explanation of s 1 of the Law of Property Act 1925 (LPA 1925) and its effect of removing the legal status of certain estates, making them recognisable as only equitable interests under a trust. Before the LPA 1925, successive interests – entails (fee tails), life interests, interests in remainder, and interests in reversion – were all once capable of recognition as legal estates. The same was true for concurrent interests: in most cases there would be no trust.

CASE STUDY – ONE

Joshua died and left a will appointing Oliver and Jack as his executors and trustees. His dispositions included the properties Snapdragon House, Bluebell House and Iris House. The will provided:

- I devise Snapdragon House to my daughters April and August in equal shares.
- I devise Bluebell House to my niece June for life, on her death the remainder to her daughter May.
- I devise Iris House to my grandchild Summer (aged 13) absolutely.

Advise Oliver and Jack.

KEEP IN MIND

Each of the dispositions may, since the 1925 legislation, exist only as an equitable interest under a trust. The disposition (a) creates concurrent interests in land, (b) successive interests in land and (c) a beneficiary who cannot hold land because they are a minor. As trusts are raised, this question requires us to consider the operation of ToLATA 1996.

Before the implementation of ToLATA on 1 January 1997, there were three devices for creating a trust comprising land: a strict settlement, a trust for sale or a bare trust. After ToLATA 1996, only pre-1997 strict settlements continue to exist (still governed by the Settled Land Act 1925). All other trusts comprising land now exist under the 'new' device of the trust of land, governed by ToLATA 1996.

The operation of trusts of land will need to be explored. However, we are not told whether the dispositions were made before 1997. This means we will also need to consider strict settlements as any created before the implementation of ToLATA 1996 may still be in existence.

CONCURRENT INTERESTS (CO-OWNERSHIP)

Where property is purchased by two or more people, that joint or co-ownership is said to be concurrent and always creates a trust.

BEFORE 1997

Before ToLATA 1996, a trust for sale would always arise with co-owned land. The essence of a trust for sale was that it imposed an immediate duty upon the trustees to sell the property. This was the duty of conversion, for the land to be sold and converted into money. However, the presumed desirability of an immediate sale (converting the trust property from land to money) is questionable.[2] The very reason for jointly deciding to buy land in the first place is often to live there. Therefore, trustees had an implied power to postpone the sale under s 25 of the Law of Property Act 1925 (LPA 1925). Beneficiaries could apply to the court for postponement under s 30 of the LPA 1925.

AFTER 1996

The law, as it stood, did not reflect the needs of the beneficiaries so trusts for sale and the doctrine of conversion were abolished under ToLATA 1996 from 1 January 1997. No new trusts for sale could be created and existing trusts for sale were converted into trusts of land.[3]

TUTOR TIP – 1

....

The device of a trust of land under ToLATA will be explored in a separate section of this chapter, for now note that there is no longer a duty to sell and beneficiaries have a right to occupy property that is suitable and available.

APPLY YOUR LEARNING – TASK 1

The first disposition in relation to Snapdragon House left the property to April and August in equal shares. This created a concurrent or co-ownership situation, with both April and August having equitable interests under a trust.

Prior to 1997, this would have taken effect as a trust for sale.

If Joshua died before 1997, what would have happened to a trust for sale post the implementation of ToLATA?

If Joshua died after 1996, what is the device under ToLATA for creating all new trusts concerning land?

SUCCESSIVE INTERESTS

Where property is held by one or more persons for life with the property passing to one or more persons upon their death, there is an entitlement to the property in succession. Successive interests are always equitable under a trust.

....

2 See Law Commission, *Transfer of Land: Trusts of Land* (Law Com No 181, 1989) para 1.3, citing Law Commission, *Trusts of Land* (Working Paper No 94, 1985) paras 3.17–3.18. It was by then common to have owner-occupation and sale was often not contemplated but rather an interest in the house itself as a place to live.

3 Express trusts for sale may still be created after 1996, and express trusts for sale created before 1997 will continue as such. However, they are now trusts of land governed by ToLATA and under s 4 trustees have a power to postpone that cannot be excluded despite anything contrary in the trust instrument.

BEFORE 1997

Before ToLATA 1996, successive interests took effect as either a trust for sale or as a strict settlement.

The strict settlement was, before 1997, assumed to arise wherever consecutive interests were created in relation to a piece of land unless the trust imposed an immediate and binding duty to sell (a trust for sale). Settled land, within the meaning of s 1 of the Settled Land Act 1925 (SLA 1925), is where:

- land stands limited in trust because of successive equitable interests in the same property, but it
- could also include situations such as land limited in trust for a person being an infant.

APPLY YOUR LEARNING – TASK 2

The second disposition left Bluebell House to June for life, remainder to May. This is a successive interest with consecutive owners. The third disposition left Iris House to Summer (aged 13) absolutely. This raised an infant. Neither disposition imposes a duty to sell.

If Joshua died before 1997, would these examples be a strict settlement for the purposes of the SLA 1925?

Following ToLATA, no new strict settlement could be made but any existing strict settlements continued under the SLA 1925. Therefore, while settlements are dwindling in number and may not be covered in some land law courses, we will consider the operation of the SLA 1925. In so doing, it will also become apparent why the difficulties associated with settlements resulted in their removal as a device.

To create a strict settlement *inter vivos* (during the owner's lifetime) two deeds were required; a vesting deed and a trust instrument (s 4(1) of the SLA). The vesting deed conveyed the legal title to the property to the tenant for life, and included a description of the land itself, stated the names of the trustees of the settlement, a statement of extra powers conferred upon the tenant for life, and the name of any person entitled to appoint new trustees (s 5(1) of the SLA 1925). The trust instrument identified the beneficial interests, and included a declaration of the trusts, appointed the trustees of the settlement, states any extra powers conferred upon the trustees, and set out any power to appoint new trustees (s 4(3) of the SLA 1925).

To create a strict settlement by will, the will itself was deemed as a trust instrument and the personal representatives[4] could make a conveyance to the tenant for life (s 6 of the SLA 1925).

---

4 Personal representatives is the collective name for either executors (in charge of an estate under a valid will) or administrators (in charge of an estate without a will).

A strict settlement, therefore, vests the legal ownership of the property in the tenant for life (the person with the right to enjoy the property for a lifetime), and not in the trustees of the settlement. The tenant for life holds all the powers of management, including the right to sell the property, to grant leases and to mortgage it.

APPLY YOUR LEARNING – TASK 3

The second disposition left Bluebell House to June for life, remainder to May. If Joshua died before 1997 then we still have to deal with the strict settlement under the SLA 1925. June, as the tenant for life, should have the legal title vested in her and is entitled to call for it if this has not been done. This gives her powers of management and sale.

Can you foresee any problems putting a tenant for life in this position?

(The third disposition left Iris House to Summer (aged 13) absolutely. This would only be a strict settlement and caught by the SLA 1925 if Joshua died before 1997, meaning that by now Summer will be more than 18 and the property no longer held upon trust for her.)

TUTOR TIP – 2

The Law Commission has helpfully set out why the role played by the tenant for life may be subject to criticism, given the possibility of a conflict of interest. See Law Commission, *Transfer of Land: Trusts of Land* (Law Com No 181, 1989) para 1.3, citing Law Commission, *Trusts of Land* (Working Paper No 94, 1985) para 3.16:

> It has been suggested that there is an inherent conflict involved in the position of the tenant for life. The legal estate and all the powers of dealing with it are vested in him and under s 16 of the Settled Land Act 1925 he is a trustee. Yet he is, at the same time, the principal beneficiary. While it is quite usual for a trustee to be a beneficiary, given the lack of any other restraints on the tenant's powers, the conflict may become real. It seems that where there is a conflict of interests, the tenant for life is not treated like an ordinary trustee. It has been held that the court will not intervene if the tenant for life allows the estate to become derelict, but only if there is evidence that he has refused to exercise his powers. Thus the remaindermen may inherit an estate much diminished in value and have no remedy. Similarly the interests of the remaindermen may be adversely affected by a sale of the settled land at a low price. Again, they may have no effective remedy as they may not discover the sale until years after it took place and, even if they could establish a breach of trust, the tenant for life may be dead and his estate not worth suing

AFTER 1996

Strict settlements created a number of problems. The requirement for both a vesting deed and a trust instrument was unnecessarily complex and cumbersome, particularly given the risk of inadvertent creation of a strict settlement without legal advice, and could cause difficulties in future dealings with the property and conveyancing.[5]

As a result, ToLATA 1996 prevents the creation of any new strict settlements after 1996 (s 2(1)). A trust of land is imposed instead.

TUTOR TIP – 3

A trust of land is the only type of trust you are likely to come across in practice. Strict settlements are increasingly rare.

Prior to ToLATA 1996, the trust for sale was more popular than strict settlement. Since ToLATA 1996 took effect on 1 January 1997, it is no longer possible to create any new strict settlement. Existing strict settlements are often ended when the life tenants die and the property falls into absolute ownership of the person with the interest in remainder (the remainderman).

APPLY YOUR LEARNING – TASK 4

The second disposition left Bluebell House to June for life, remainder to May. The third disposition left Iris House to Summer (aged 13) absolutely.

If Joshua died before 1997, then both of these situations would be a strict settlement under the SLA. If Joshua died after 1996, then from 1 January 1997 ToLATA 1996 prevents any strict settlements being created under the SLA. What 'new' device would be imposed instead in response to both dispositions?

THE TRUST OF LAND

The problems with settled land and trusts for sale, and the complexity of having a dual system mean that the only means to now create a trust comprising land is as a trust of land under ToLATA 1996.[6]

---

5 See Law Commission, *Transfer of Land: Trusts of Land* (Law Com No 181, 1989) para 1.3, citing Law Commission, *Trusts of Land* (Working Paper No 94, 1985) para 3.15.

6 For a consideration of the problems caused by this dual system with both trusts for sale and settled land, see Law Commission, *Transfer of Land: Trusts of Land* (Law Com No 181, 1989) para 1.3, citing Law Commission, *Trusts of Land* (Working Paper No 94, 1985) para 3.2.

The definition of a trust of land is set out in s 1 of ToLATA 1996:

(1)   In this Act—

    (a)   'trust of land' means (subject to subsection (3)) any trust of property which consists of or includes land, and

    (b)   'trustees of land' means trustees of a trust of land.

(2)   The reference in subsection (1)(a) to a trust—

    (a)   is to any description of trust (whether express, implied, resulting or constructive), including a trust for sale and a bare trust, and

    (b)   includes a trust created, or arising, before the commencement of this Act…

The trusts of land covers bare trusts,[7] trusts for sale, concurrent interests (co-ownership) and successive interests. It covers any trust that includes some land, whether express, implied, resulting or constructive.

ToLATA 1996 sets out the powers and duties of the trustees, and the rights of the beneficiaries.

POWERS AND DUTIES OF THE TRUSTEES

Powers

Trustees have all the same powers of an absolute owner, as set out in s 6(1) of ToLATA 1996: 'For the purpose of exercising their functions as trustees, the trustees of land have in relation to the land subject to the trust all the powers of an absolute owner.'

The powers of an absolute owner of land are extensive. Trustees of land, therefore, have the power to manage, sell, mortgage and lease the land.

> TUTOR TIP – 4
>
> There is no longer any duty to sell, unless it is a trust for sale. Even then, trusts for sale now fall under trusts of land and there is a mandatory power to postpone sale (s 4 ToLATA 1996).

Under ToLATA trustees also have the power to:

■ Acquire more land (s 6(3)). Freehold or leasehold property may be acquired for occupation by the beneficiaries, as an investment, or for any other reason.[8]

---

7 The trustee of a bare trust holds the property for an adult beneficiary absolutely and must obey the instructions of the beneficiary in relation to the land.

8 In accordance with the power conferred upon trustees under s 8 of the Trustee Act 2000.

- Transfer the land to beneficiaries (s 6(2)). The beneficiaries must be of full age and capacity and be absolutely entitled. The trustees can do this even though the beneficiaries have not asked for the conveyance or consented to it. The beneficiaries take on the role of trustees.
- Partition the land (s 7). The beneficiaries must be of full age and capacity, be absolutely entitled and all consent. Dividing the land into separate parts allotted among the beneficiaries may be useful to allow occupation by them.
- Delegate any of their powers by power of attorney to a beneficiary or beneficiaries (s 9). The beneficiary or beneficiaries must be of full age and capacity and be entitled to an interest in possession. The trustees must all agree (s 9(3)).

TUTOR TIP – 5

To be absolutely entitled, a beneficiary must have the sole right to instruct trustees with regard to the management of the trust property. A number of beneficiaries may be deemed jointly absolutely entitled if they hold a similar interest in the trust property. However, if other individuals may benefit from the trust in the future with a different interest in the property, there is no absolute entitlement.

CONSIDER THIS – 1

Assuming that Joshua died after 1996 (so any trust created comprising land would be a trust of land), consider the following:

Transfer to the Beneficiaries – The first disposition left Snapdragon House to April and August in equal shares. This is a concurrent or co-ownership situation, so April and August are jointly absolutely entitled. Assuming they are both now over 18 could the trustees transfer the property to them under s 6(2) of ToLATA 1996?

The second disposition left Bluebell House to June for life, remainder to May. This created successive interests, with June and May owning consecutively. This means that they are not absolutely entitled. Even assuming they are both now over 18, could the trustees transfer the property to them?

The third disposition left Iris House to Summer (aged 13) absolutely. When Summer turns 18 the legal title should be conveyed to her (ending the trust) but while she remains a minor s 6(2) of ToLATA 1996 cannot be used.

Partition of the Land – What if the beneficiaries for the first and the second disposition want to occupy the houses and ask for the buildings to be partitioned?

Is the power under s 7 of ToLATA 1996 available to the trustees in relation to the second disposition, Bluebell House? Note what has been said about June and May not being absolutely entitled.

How about in relation to the first disposition, Snapdragon House? Note what has been said about April and August being jointly absolutely entitled. Note, if April and August both agree and the trustees exercise their power by dividing of land into separate parts, the trustees must then give effect to the partition by transferring the legal estate by deed. April would own one property absolutely, and August the other with the trust coming to an end.

(The question of how easily Snapdragon House could be converted in two self-contained properties and the cost of doing so would be among other factors the trustees must consider in deciding whether or not to exercise any their power. The next section considers the restrictions on the use of trustees' powers; they must take reasonable care in exercising any.)

Delegation of Powers – As an alternative to conveying the land to the beneficiaries, the trustees may under s 9 of ToLATA all agree unanimously to delegate their powers to a beneficiary of full age, who is entitled to an interest in possession.

In relation to the first disposition, Snapdragon House, both April and August have an interest in possession. So, assuming they are of full age, there is a power to delegate to them, for example the power to manage or to sell the property.

In relation to the second disposition, Bluebell House, June has the lifetime interest (the lifetime tenant) and so the interest in possession. Could there be any delegation to May?

(Having the power to delegate does not necessarily mean it should be exercised; trustees must take reasonable care in deciding to delegate a function.)

Restrictions on powers

The wide powers of the trustees are always limited in requiring the trustees to exercise them having 'regard to the rights of the beneficiaries' (s 6(5) of ToLATA 1996) and not in contravention of 'rule of law or equity' (s 6(6) of the ToLATA 1996). This means that they are subject to the normal fiduciary duties of trustees.[9]

---

9 Now set out in s 1(1) of the Trustee Act 2000, which provides that: 'Whenever the duty under this subsection applies to a trustee, he must exercise such care and skill as is reasonable in the circumstances, having regard in particular— (a) to any special knowledge or experience that he has or holds himself out as having, and (b) if he acts as trustee in the course of a business or profession, to any special knowledge or experience that it is reasonable to expect of a person acting in the course of that kind of business or profession.'

> **KEY CASE:** *COWAN V SCARGILL* [1985] CH 270; [1984] 2 ALL ER 750
>
> The case concerned the management of a person fund trust. In explaining the duty of a trustee, Sir Robert Megarry VC clearly set out that a fiduciary must act in the interests of the beneficiaries and not out of self-interest:
>
> > The starting point is the duty of trustees to exercise their powers in the best interests of the present and future beneficiaries of the trust, holding the scales impartially between different classes of beneficiaries. This duty of the trustees towards their beneficiaries is paramount. They must, of course, obey the law; but subject to that, they must put the interests of their beneficiaries first

The powers given under ss 6 and 7 of ToLATA 1996 may also be excluded or restricted by the trust instrument, in accordance with s 8(1) of ToLATA 1996. Powers may be made subject to the consent of the beneficiaries (or other persons) under s 8(2) of ToLATA 1996, for example prior to any sale.

> TUTOR TIP – 6
>
> If the consent of more than two persons is required prior to a sale, then the consent of at least two of the named persons will be sufficient in favour of a purchaser (s 10(1) of ToLATA). However, the trustees may be liable for a breach of trust if they do not secure all of the required consents.

RIGHTS OF THE BENEFICIARIES

Consultation

For express trusts created after 1996 and all implied trusts of land,[10] s 11 of ToLATA 1996 imposes duties upon trustees to consult with the beneficiaries before exercising any function:

(1) The trustees of land shall in the exercise of any function relating to land subject to the trust—

    (a) so far as practicable, consult the beneficiaries of full age and beneficially entitled to an interest in possession in the land, and

    (b) so far as consistent with the general interest of the trust, give effect to the wishes of those beneficiaries, or (in case of dispute) of the majority (according to the value of their combined interests).

---

10 It is possible to exclude the operation of s 11 (s 11(2)(a)). For trusts created or arising under a will before 1997, s 11 does not apply (s 11(2)(b)) unless provided for in a deed executed by the settlor or surviving settlors after 1996 (s 11(3)).

The duty to make reasonable efforts to consult with the beneficiaries does not mean the trustees must always comply with the wishes of the beneficiaries or the majority of them. If the trustee does not consider that the wishes are 'consistent with the general interest of the trust', the beneficiaries may make an application to the court under s 14 of ToLATA 1996.

Occupation

Section 12 of ToLATA 1996 confers a right on beneficiaries to occupy trust property. Section 13 of ToLATA 1996 allows the trustees to restrict the occupation where concurrent joint owners are entitled to occupy under s 12.

CONSIDER THIS – 2
_____

In relation to the first disposition, Snapdragon House, both April and August as concurrent or co-owners have the right to occupy the property if it is available and suitable. If one sister were allowed to occupy the property, s 13 would allow the trustees to require her to compensate the other.

The detailed rules relating to occupation under ss 12–13 of ToLATA 1996 will be considered in Chapter 11 on co-ownership.

POWERS OF THE COURT

Section 14 of ToLATA 1996 gives the court the power to settle disputes about the exercise of trustees' powers. For example, a court order may be made in relation to whether to sell the property, decisions about occupation of it by the beneficiaries, or the need to obtain consents. An application can be made by a trustee or by any interested person such as a beneficiary or the mortgagee.

Section 15(1) of ToLATA 1996 gives the criteria or factors that the court must consider in making decisions under s 14. The operation of ss 14–15 of ToLATA will be explored in Chapter 11 on co-ownership.

PROTECTION FOR PURCHASERS

Purchasers of a legal estate are protected by overreaching under s 2 of the LPA 1925, provided the three necessary conditions under s 2(1)(ii) are met:

- The conveyance is made by all trustees, and they are at least two in number. A conveyance by a sole trustee will not overreach the rights of the beneficiaries.
- The equitable interests must be capable of being overreached. It must be a 'general burden' suitable for conversion into money, which the equitable interests under a trust are.
- The requirements for the payment of capital money are complied with. Under s 27(2) of the LPA 1925, the money must be paid to two trustees, except where the payment has been made to a trust corporation or to a sole personal representative.

Overreaching means the purchaser takes free of the equitable interests of a beneficiary, even with actual notice and can displace any claim based upon actual occupation.[11] It also means that the purchaser will not be responsible for the application of the proceeds from the sale (the trust money) by the trustees.

Protection against trustees selling in contravention of any rule in law or equity, depends on whether the purchase is of unregistered or registered land.

In relation to unregistered land, s 16 of ToLATA 1996 provides that, if the correct procedures for overreaching are followed and in the absence of actual notice, purchasers need not be concerned that the trustees have failed to have regard to the rights of the beneficiaries, to consult with the beneficiaries and give effect to their wishes, or to get required consents.

In relation to registered land, s 16 of ToLATA 1996 does not apply.[12] Restrictions are used to warn purchasers of any limitations on the powers of the trustees to deal with the land, and must be complied with. Further, s 26(1) of the Land Registration Act 2002 means the purchaser may presume an owner is free of any limitation that is not entered as a restriction on the registered title.

DISCUSSION

Co-ownership of land is now very common, but the breakdown of a relationship or the ending of a business relation can lead to serious disputes about what to do with the property. Previously, the old trust for sale regime would have meant the courts favoured a sale if required to settle disputes. Now, with the trust of land regime under ToLATA 1996 there is much more flexibility. Under s 15 of ToLATA 1996 there are a wide range of factors to take into consideration, and the list is not exhaustive.

---

11 See *City of London Building Society v Flegg* [1988] AC 54; [1987] 3 All ER 435. Once overreaching has operated to detach the beneficial interest from the land to the proceeds of sale, there is no longer an interest capable of being overriding.
12 S 16(7) ToLATA 1996.

> **CONSIDER THIS** – 3
>
> Do you think the statutory framework and greater flexibility under ToLATA 1996 is more reflective of modern needs and expectations in relation to land?

END OF CHAPTER SUMMARY

- Trusts of land are governed by the Trusts of Land and Appointment of Trustees Act 1996.
- ToLATA 1996 sets out the powers and duties of trustees and the rights of beneficiaries.
- Trustees have wide powers over the land, enjoying the same powers as an absolute owner. They are, however, subject to the normal fiduciary duty to act in the best interests of all the beneficiaries.
- Beneficiaries have rights to be consulted (s 11), to occupy the land (s 12) and can, in the event of a dispute, apply to the court for it to be settled (s 14).
- In settling a dispute, the court will apply factors set out in s 15.
- After 1996, no more settled land under the Settled Land Act 1925 could be created. Existing settlements continue, but are increasingly rare.
- Trusts for sale are now trusts of land. Even with an express trust for sale the trustees have a power to postpone sale.

PREPARING FOR ASSESSMENTS
QUESTIONS

ESSAY QUESTION

Following the implementation of the Trusts of Land and Appointment of Trustees Act 1996, what are the rights of beneficiaries under a trust of land and how do they compare with the old regime?

PROBLEM QUESTION

Suzanne is the legal owner of 14 London Road Bath. The property is held on trust for the benefit of herself and her two younger sisters Megan (aged 20) and Justine (aged 18).

Suzanne has been approached by Angela, a work colleague, and has been asked whether she would be interested in selling 14 London Road to her for £150,000, which is current market value of the property.

In considering the offer, what are Suzanne's duty as trustee as imposed under the ToLATA legislation? What rights do Megan and Justine have as beneficiaries under ToLATA 1996 that Suzanne must take into consideration.

If the sale of 14 London Road were to take place, what must Angela do to ensure that she buys the property free from any interests of the beneficiaries under the trust?

FURTHER READING

- Ferris, G and Battersby, G, 'The General Principles of Overreaching and the Modern Legislative Reforms, 1996–2002' (2003) 119 LQR 94. Considers the law of overreaching, including the scope of s 16 of ToLATA 1996 for protection of purchasers and changes introduced by Land Registration Act 2002 and the Trustee Act 2000.

CHAPTER 11
CO-OWNERSHIP

CHAPTER AIMS AND OBJECTIVES

In this chapter we will consider co-ownership and how law and equity deals with land ownership by more than one person. We will consider the different ways land can be held and why. We will explain how both law and equity regulates co-ownership and how the right of survivorship affects this. We will consider what each co-owner is entitled in relation to the sale proceeds and what should happen where the co-owners do not agree as to what should be done with the estate e.g. whether or not it should be sold.

By the end of this chapter, you should be able to:

- understand the consequences of land being held by more than one person, looking at co-ownership of both the legal estate and the equitable interests and the types of co-ownership available;
- explain the different ways co-owners can hold land in law and in equity and identify in any given situation whether the interests are held as joint tenants or tenants in common and the implications of this for the trustees and the beneficiaries;
- identify and be able to apply to a given problem the methods of severing the joint tenancy into a tenancy in common, the consequences of a severance, and the ways in which co-ownership generally may be terminated;
- understand the rules relating to the disposition of land, considering the position of both the beneficiaries and the purchaser and the protection of their respective interests;
- analyse a given problem and be able to determine the range of possible outcome(s) and the most likely result;
- apply the relevant law when there is a dispute between the trustees and the beneficiaries as to future dealings with the land;
- advise the parties as to the most suitable course of action and determine the possible outcome(s).

CASE STUDY – ONE

Last year Claire, Suzanne, Mick, Neil and Mark decided to buy a house together to live in whilst they are students at a local university. They each contributed £20,000 except for Neil who contributed £50,000. The property was transferred to them on a trust for sale as joint tenants and was registered as such with the Land Registry.

THE BASICS

Co-ownership arises where two or more persons hold an interest in land at the same time. The co-owners are simultaneously in possession of an interest in the same estate in land; see *Bull v Bull* [1955].[1] As we have seen in Chapter 10, when this happens a trust comes into existence. The new legal estate owners become trustees and hold the legal estate upon trust for those who have contributed to the purchase price of the property, the beneficiaries. This means that in any co-owned estate there are two separate interests in it: ownership of the *legal estate* and ownership of the *equitable interest* relating to that legal estate.

THE LEGAL ESTATE

The trustees or managers of the trust own the legal estate. The legal trustees have no interest in the value of the trust. They have only administrative powers and management functions. For example it is the trustees who will sign the legal documentation in relation to the legal estate.

THE EQUITABLE INTEREST

The beneficiaries behind the trust own the equitable interest. The beneficiaries are entitled to the value of the property, therefore when the property is sold it is the

---

1 [1955] 1 QB 234.

beneficiaries who are entitled to the sale proceeds. The trustees may only distribute the proceeds in accordance with the terms of the trust agreed by the parties.

> ### TUTOR TIP – 1
> ....
>
> In the vast majority of situations, the trustees and beneficiaries will, in fact, be the same people. For example when a couple buy a house together they will both sign the purchase deed and therefore will become the legal owners i.e. the trustees. They will also both put up the money to purchase the property and therefore will become entitled to the benefit of the sale proceeds when the property is eventually sold so will also be the beneficiaries.

THE TWO FORMS OF CO-OWNERSHIP

There are two ways that property can be held: either by a joint tenancy or tenants in common.

JOINT TENANCY

Under a joint tenancy the estate is owned collectively. The co-owners are regarded as being a single component owner. They do not have distinct shares despite what they have contributed to the property and therefore all own the whole together, a bit like a joint bank account.

A joint tenancy must have all four unities. Without these four elements there is no joint tenancy.

Figure 11.1 The four unities of a joint tenancy

Unity of possession
As each joint tenant owns the whole of the land, each person is as much entitled to possession of the land as the others. One joint tenant cannot point to a piece of land as his own to the exclusion of the others; see *Bull v Bull* [1955].[2] In fact unity of possession is common to both forms of co-ownership.

....

2 [1955] 1 QB 234.

As we will see later however under the Trusts of Land and Appointment of Trustees Act 1996 where one co-owner is in sole occupation of any part or all of the land, the other cannot evict him; see *Williams and Glynn's Bank v Boland* [1981].[3]

Unity of interest
The principle of unity of interest also flows from the concept that each person is entitled to the whole of the estate. Unity of interest means that the interest of each co-owner must be identical with regards to its extent, duration and the nature. This is because in theory they hold one estate.

There should be no difference in the legal estate owners. i.e. all parties must hold either the freehold or the leasehold interest. If the parties hold the leasehold interest then additionally it must have the same duration for all. There will be no joint tenancy if each holds a different duration. Any rents or profits must be divided equally between the co-owners. If one person receives the rent of the whole or part of the land he must account to the other co-owners.

Unity of title
Each joint tenant must acquire his title from the same act. This could be from a single document (such as the same purchase deed) or from adverse possession, to give two examples. If a later person wants to become a joint tenant, all the existing owners must join in a new document of transfer or grant in order to achieve this.

Unity of time
The rights of each joint tenant must vest in the interest at the same time, i.e. their interest must start at the same moment.

The right of survivorship

Given that joint tenants collectively own the property, the right of survivorship applies (*jus accrescendi*). The right of survivorship follows on logically from the concept of a single composite ownership which continues until there is only one owner or survivor who will then be solely entitled to the land i.e. last man standing. A joint tenant cannot dispose of his interest by will as survivorship overrides this and the rules on intestacy.

This means that where three people purchase a property together and one person dies, the property will automatically pass to the surviving two joint tenants. At the point of death of a second co-owner, the property will automatically pass to the surviving joint tenant.

The property cannot pass to anyone else at the time of death because a joint tenant has no share in the property to pass to anyone. This is a position established by s 3(4) of the Administration of Estates Act 1925. The deceased's will has no effect upon property owned as joint tenants.

In the rare situations where more than one co-owner dies at the same time and it is not possible to tell who dies first, for example in a plane crash, the rule of commorientes

---

3 [1981] AC 487.

applies under s 184 of the Law of Property Act 1925 (LPA 1925). Under the rule, where it is not possible to tell who died first the deaths are presumed to have occurred in order of seniority. Here, the elder of the co-owners is deemed to have predeceased the younger.

TENANCY IN COMMON

The parties to a tenancy in common do, in contrast, have distinct shares in the property. There is no right to survivorship and each person's share is fixed and unaffected by the death of a co-owner. As such a tenant in common is free to dispose of their share as he sees fit; this includes through a will or under the rules of intestacy upon death.

The parties can hold the property in equal shares or in accordance with what they have contributed to the purchase of the property. The share size will depend upon what the parties specify in any agreement. The starting position is equality.

Although all four unities may be present in a tenancy in common, the only essential element is unity is possession.

LEGAL AND EQUITABLE TITLE

Remember that there are two layers to the ownership of land, the legal interest and the equitable interest.

There are a number of rules to draw from primary legislation in relation to the legal interest.

- Under s 1(6) of the LPA 1925 a legal estate is not capable of subsisting in an undivided share.
- Under s 34(2) of the LPA 1925 the number of legal owners is limited to four.

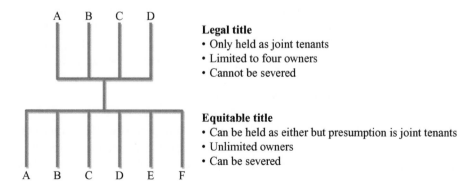

Figure 11.2 Legal and equitable ownership

■ Under s 36(2) of the LPA 1925 there can be no severance of a joint tenancy of a
  legal estate so as to create a tenancy in common in land.

The implication of this is that it is only possible to hold the legal estate as joint tenants
and it cannot be severed in law. Additionally there can only be four owners of the legal
interest; this is normally the first four listed in the purchase deed.

CREATION OF JOINT TENANCIES AND TENANCIES IN COMMON IN EQUITY

EXPRESS CREATION

The express creation of either a joint tenant or a tenancy on common will occur where
the grant or transfer deed expressly states that the land is to be held jointly as joint
tenants *or* the parties state that they wish to hold as tenants in common.

For example,

> **'The transferees hereby declare that they shall hold the property upon trust for
> themselves as joint tenants'**
>
> OR
>
> **'The transferees hereby declare that they shall hold the property upon trust for
> themselves as tenants in common in equal shares'**

If the parties wish to hold the property as tenants in common, they should express in
what proportions their shares are to be held. If the grant simply states that the property
is to be held upon trust as tenants in common equity will then presume that they will
own the property in equal shares. A solicitor acting for co-owners should ensure that
they follow their client's wishes and instructions to avoid serious consequences.
Declaring interests at the outset of a transaction provides clarity about the parties'
intentions and may help to avoid disputes in the future. A solicitor should make clients
aware of the potential consequences of not making a declaration of trust at the time of
acquisition. These may include the possibility of dispute and later costly litigation, and
the possibility that the court will divide the property differently from what they intend.

In *Walker v Hall* [1984][4] Dillon LJ explained that:

> [S]olicitors should take steps to find out and declare what the beneficial interests are
> to be, when the legal estate in a house is acquired by two persons in their joint
> names. The difficulties which otherwise arise … can so easily be avoided by a little

---

4 [1984] 5 FLR 126.

care on the part of the solicitors … I would wish to underline the point as strongly as I can and to suggest that the courts may soon have to consider whether a solicitor acting for joint purchasers is not guilty of negligence if he fails to find out and record what the joint purchasers' beneficial interests in the relevant property are to be

Or more recently in *Carlton v Goodman* [2002],[5] Ward LJ said: 'Perhaps conveyancers do not read the law reports. I will try one more time: always try to agree on and then record how the beneficial interest is to be held. It is not very difficult to do.'

The parties will still need to show that all four unities are present if the property is to be held as joints tenants and the express granting of a tenancy in common will be dependent upon the unity of possession being present.

TUTOR TIP – 2

When registering land, the standard forms prescribed in sch 1 of the Land Registration Rules 2003 must be used to transfer the property. This is Land Registry Form TR1, which can be used for the transfer of both registered and unregistered land.

In order to expressly state how the equitable interest is to be held by the co-owners, the parties simply need to complete the declaration in panel 10 of the TR1. Panel 10 requires confirmation that the transferee is more than one person and an 'X' placed against the relevant intention that:

- they are to hold the property on trust for themselves as joint tenants; or
- they are to hold the property on trust for themselves as tenants in common in equal shares; or
- they are to hold the property on trust.

In circumstances where the parties wish to hold the property as tenants in common in unequal shares, due to their differing contributions, the solicitor will tick the third option and insert into the additional box:

'they are to hold the property on trust for themselves as tenants in common in unequal shares in accordance with a declaration to trust.'

Additionally in relation to unregistered land, upon an application for first registration under form FR1 an identical declaration appears at panel 9. Whilst it is not clear if panels 9 and 10 are compulsory, if they are not completed the Land Registry will still register the transaction and register the parties as joint tenants in line with the presumption that equity follows the law. A wise solicitor acting for co-owners however should ensure that the transfer includes an express declaration of trust, in accordance with their clients' instructions and wishes.

5 [2002] EWCA Civ 545; [2002] 2 FLR 259.

IMPLIED CREATION

If the grant is silent then there is a presumption raised that the new owners will hold the property as joint tenants in equity on the basis that equity follows the law and that equity mirrors the legal position. See *Pettit v Pettit* [1970].[6]

In order to presume a joint tenancy in equity, however, all four unities *must* be present and the presumption must not have been rebutted.

Words of severance

Whilst all four unities may be present, any words of severance used in the initial grant or purchase deed will rebut the presumption of a joint tenancy. If the purchase deed contains a declaration that the parties are to 'hold the property upon trust for themselves equally' this indicates that the parties are wanting to have separate shares in the ownership of the property. Similarly if the parties declare that they want to hold the property in equal shares, again this is an indication that the property is to be held in two distinct halves and not as a collective whole.

> TUTOR TIP – 3
>
> ....
>
> Words indicating that the property is to be held in separate shares:
>
> | In equal shares | *Payne v Webb* (1874–75) LR 19 Eq 26 |
> | Equally | *Lewen v Dodd* [1594] 78 ER 684 |
> | To be divided between | *Peat v Chapman* [1750] 27 ER 1193 |
> | Share and share alike | *Heathe v Heathe* [1740] 2 A & R 121 |

Factors indicating an intention of a tenancy in common

Other factors may be present at the time of purchase which indicate that the parties wish to own the property as tenants in common rather than as joint tenants. For example, the parties may have instructed their solicitor to draft a declaration of trust stating what shares they wished to hold in the property but the document was overlooked and never signed.

> **KEY CASE:** *MALAYAN CREDIT LTD V JACK CHIA-MPH LTD* [1986] 2 WLR 590
>
> _____
>
> The courts were asked to consider whether the property was held as joint tenants or a tenancy in common and if the latter in what proportions; as the lease contained no express declaration as to how the property should be held. Lord Brightman identified a number of factors that if present would give rise to the presumption of tenants in common in equity.

....

6 [1970] AC 777; [1969] 2 All ER 385.

> The argument is that, in the absence of an express agreement, persons who take as joint tenants at law hold as tenants in common in equity only in three classes of case:
>
> 1   Where they have provided the purchase money in unequal shares; in this case they hold the beneficial interest in similar shares;
> 2   Where the grant consists of a security for a loan and the grantees were equal or unequal contributors to the loan; again they would hold the beneficial interest in the same shares; and
> 3   Where they are partners and the subject matter of the grant is partnership.

Unequal contributions

It once was the case that where the parties buy a property and contribute to the purchase price unequally a court would presume a tenancy in common.

For example, a couple purchased a property for £500,000 with one contributing £200,000 and the other £300,000. In such a situation, in the absence of any express or contrary provisions, equity would presume that the parties have purchased the property as tenants in common and that their shares will mirror what they have contributed. In this example the shares of the sale proceeds would be 40:60 respectively.

However, in the context of family homes the presumption has changed following *Stack v Dowden* [2007].[7] The House of Lords explained that the starting point is joint beneficial ownership in joint name cases, in a sole name case sole beneficial ownership with the onus upon the person who seeks to show that the beneficial ownership differs from the legal ownership. The onus of rebutting the presumption will be heavier in joint names cases than in sole name cases, creating what Lord Walker referred to as 'a considerable burden' and Lady Hale said would be 'very unusual'.

Looking back to the example, you can see why a solicitor needs to give proper advice to clients so confirm how they wish to hold in equity, completing panel 10 of the TR1.

Security for a loan

As we will explain in Chapter 13 on mortgages, a mortgage is an interest created over property in the form of a legal charge. The borrower consents to the legal charge being registered against their title in return for the loan of money by the lender. Where there is more than one borrower equity presumes that the property is held as tenants in common. This is to enable the debt owed by each borrower to be secured against an identifiable share which could then pass to the lender should the borrower die before the loan is repaid. This view was expressed in the case of *Morley v Bird* [1798].[8]

---

7   [2007] UKHL 17; [2007] 2 AC 432; [2007] 2 All ER 929.
8   [1798] 30 ER at 1193.

Commercial partners or business tenants

Where commercial partners purchase a property together as part of a business venture, equity will presume that they hold the property as tenants in common. This is because equity takes the view that business partners would not want the right of survivorship to apply to business property. Business tenants who acquire a leasehold interest in land will also be presumed to hold in the same way for similar reasons.

APPLY YOUR LEARNING – TASK 1

Using what you have learnt above considering the five students Claire, Suzanne, Mick, Neil and Mark. How do they hold the legal and equitable interests to the property? Explain why this is the case.

If you had been the solicitor advising the parties, how would you have explained the consequences of them agreeing to hold in equity as joint tenants, particularly given the unequal contributions made?

SERVERANCE OF JOINT TENANCY

It is possible to change a joint tenancy to a tenancy in common in equity. This is called severance. As we know it is only possible for a joint tenancy to exist at law, so any severance will *only* be effective in equity. Once severance occurs, the beneficiaries will have their own distinct separate share of the sale proceeds.

TUTOR TIP – 4
....

As we will see there are various forms of severance; this is, however, subject to only one main restriction. Severance can only be achieved *inter vivos* (between the living). It is therefore not possible for severance to occur by will.

MODES OF SEVERANCE

Written notice

The ability to sever the joint tenancy by written notice comes from s 36(2) of the LPA 1925 which states: 'where a legal estate … is vested in joint tenants beneficially, and any tenant desires to sever the joint tenants in equity, he shall give to the other joint tenants notice in writing of such desire.'

As can be seen from the wording of s 36(2) the written notice only serves to sever the joint tenancy in equity. This is reaffirmed by s 36(2) of the LPA 1925, which clearly states there can be no severance of a joint tenancy of a legal estate.

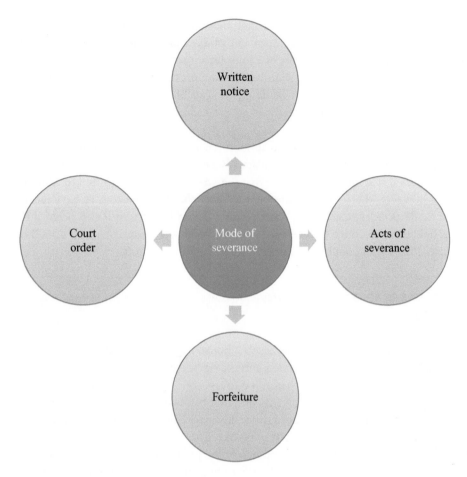

Figure 11.3 Severing a joint tenancy in equity

In order to be effective, there are a number of preconditions to the use of written notice for severance.

1   The notice must be given to *all* joint tenants. Therefore if the notice is only sent to two of the three joint tenants, the written notice to sever will be void.
2   There must be evidence that the notice has been delivered to the joint tenants. This does not mean evidence of the notice being received. In *Kinch v Bullard* [1999][9] a notice *posted* but *not received* was held effective.
3   The notice *must* express the parties' immediate intention to sever the joint tenancy; a wish or desire to serve the joint tenant in the future will not be sufficient. The court will look at whether the parties intended to immediately sever the joint tenancy. See *Harris v Goddard* [1983].[10]

....

9   [1999] 1 WLR 423.
10 [1983] 3 All ER 242; [1983] 1 WLR 1203.

There are no set words or format governing the written notice. It is therefore possible for a letter, writ or originating summons and affidavit in support issued in respect of proceedings to determine the rights of a joint tenant to suffice. In *Hunter v Babbage* (1994)[11] it was held that the wife's affidavit in support of her application for ancillary relief, in the course of divorce proceedings, was capable of being sufficient notice of an intention to sever the joint tenancy.

Whilst written notice must be sent to all joint tenants, it does not need to be signed. It is also possible for it to be achieved unilaterally i.e. no consent of the other joint tenants being required. It is sufficient to show that the written notice was posted to all joint tenants; however, there is no requirement to show that the joint tenants have received it (see *Re 88 Berkeley Road* [1971][12] and *Kinch v Bullard* [1999]). In *Re 88 Berkeley Road* it was held that the notice of severance complied with the requirements of s 36(2) of the LPA 1925 even though it was never received by the plaintiff.

KEY CASE: *RE DRAPER'S CONVEYANCE* [1969] 1 CH 486; [1967] 3 ALL ER 853

In 1951, a husband and wife purchased a house together as joint tenants. Fourteen years later the wife was granted a decree nisi, which was made absolute in 1966. The wife then applied to the court and was granted an order for the matrimonial home to be sold and that the sale proceeds be divided equally between herself and her former husband. The former husband, however, died intestate before the property was sold. The question was whether the court documentation constituted a severance of the joint tenancy or whether the whole property passed to her under the right of survivorship by virtue of the joint tenancy. The courts held that she held it as trustee for herself and the estate as tenants in common in equal shares.

Acts of severance

It is possible to severance a joint tenancy at equity by actions rather than words. This is recognised under s 36(2) of the LPA 1925 and acknowledges that it was possible to sever joint tenancies in this way prior to the 1925 legislation.

---

11 (1994) 69 P & CR 548; [1995] 1 FCR 569.
12 [1971] Ch 648; [1971] 1 All ER 254.

KEY CASE: *WILLIAMS V HENSMAN* (1861) 1 JOHN & H 546; 30 LJ
CH 878

Sir William Page-Wood VC laid down three categories under which it would be
possible to sever a joint tenancy by actions:

> in the first place, an act of any one of the persons interested operating upon
> his own share may create a severance as to that share. The right of each joint-
> tenant is a right by survivorship only in the event of no severance having taken
> place of the share which is claimed under the *jus accrescendi*. Each one is at
> liberty to dispose of his own interest in such manner as to sever it from the
> joint fund – losing, of course, at the same time, his own right of survivorship.

> Second, a joint-tenancy may be severed by mutual agreement.

> And, in the third place, there may be a severance by any course of dealing
> sufficient to intimate that the interests of all were mutually treated as
> constituting a tenancy in common. When the severance depends on an
> inference of this kind without any express act of severance, it will not suffice to
> rely on an intention, with respect to the particular share, declared only behind
> the backs of the other persons interested.

The *Williams v Hensman* rule therefore lays down three categories for severance by
action:

1   Destruction of one of the four unities
2   Mutual agreement
3   Mutual conduct.

Destruction of one of the four unities

As we have seen earlier, in order to have a joint tenancy in equity the four unities of
possession, interest, time and title must be present. It therefore follows that if one of
these is destroyed then it is not possible for a joint tenancy to exist. This is the first of
the *Williams v Hensman* principles.

For example, if a joint tenant sells, gifts or gives away his interest to a third party, the
purchaser would not have the unity of title or time with the other existing joint
tenants. Severance would therefore follow here, as technically under a joint tenancy the
seller has no share to sell unless severance had taken place. A similar situation would
arise if the joint tenant had entered into a contract to sell, lease or mortgage his interest
to a third party. Severance would not occur, however, if the joint tenant had drafted a
will, as joint tenancies operate outside the provisions of wills and intestacy.

TUTOR TIP – 5

How can a joint tenant sell a share when they do not have a distinct share in the property?

Under land law the act of selling is said to be both the 'source' of the partitioning and the 'vehicle' of sale. A joint tenant who enters into a sale of his or her equitable 'share' creates the share to sell by way of severance.

Remember, however, that an act will only sever the joint tenancy in equity as under s 36(2) of the LPA 1925 there can be no severance of a joint tenancy of a legal estate.

The legal interest will also not transfer to the purchaser unless the sale is completed by a purchase deed executed between the seller and purchaser. As we have seen earlier the legal interest can only be created and transferred by deed.

The granting of a lease, mortgage or charge over one joint tenancy's own interest in the property will sever the joint tenancy in equity. This can be a unilateral act and does not require the agreement, consent or even the knowledge of the other joint tenants; see *Mortgage Corporation v Shaire* [2000].[13] It is even possible to sever the joint tenancy by obtaining the mortgage by deception as in the case of *First National Securities v Hegerty* [1984].[14]

The joint tenancy can also be severed when one joint tenant becomes bankrupt. Whilst it may not be the party's intention to do this, the effect of a bankruptcy order is to trigger a transfer and vesting of the joint tenant's interest in the trustee in bankruptcy.

Where the severance of the joint tenancy has occurred unilaterally, the parties are assumed to hold the tenancy in common in equal shares (*Nielson-Jones v Fedden* [1975]).[15]

Mutual agreement

A joint tenancy can be severed by the mutual agreement of the parties either expressly or impliedly. When the severance is by implication, consideration is given to the intentions or conduct of the parties. The agreement is not required to be in any prescribed form. In *Burgess v Rawnsley* [1975] the Court of Appeal held that an oral agreement will suffice and that there are no requirements that the agreement be acted upon.

---

13 [2001] Ch 743; [2000] EWHC Ch 452; [2000] 1 FLR 973.
14 [1984] 3 All ER 641; [1984] 3 WLR 769.
15 [1975] Ch 222; [1974] 3 All ER 38.

KEY CASE: *BURGESS V RAWNSLEY* [1975] CH 429; [1975] 3 ALL ER 142

A widower, Mr Honick became friends with a widow, Mrs Rawnsley. Mr Honick had the opportunity of buying the house he had been a tenant in and following a conversation with Mrs Rawnsley, she agreed to purchase the property with him. Mr Honick instructed his solicitor to have the property conveyed into the *joint* names of himself and Mrs Rawnsley. The reason for the *joint* names was, as the judge found, because Mr Honick: 'firmly believed that he was going to marry [Mrs Rawnsley] and that would be the matrimonial home. ... I have no doubt whatever [said the judge] that that was his reason for purchasing the house in joint names.'

In July 1968, being disappointed in his hopes of marriage, Mr Honick wanted Mrs Rawnsley to sell him her share in the house. After coming to an agreement he advised his solicitor that as Mrs Rawnsley was not going to marry him she had agreed to sell her interest to him for £750. His solicitor then sent Mrs Rawnsley a letter to this effect. Mrs Rawnsley went to the solicitors the next day to advise that she was not willing to sell as she wanted £1,000. Mr Honick died in 1971 leaving the plaintiff, his daughter, as his administratrix.

Lord Denning MR held that there was evidence that Mr Honick and Mrs Rawnsley did come to an agreement that he would buy her share for £750. That agreement was not in writing and it was not specifically enforceable. Yet it was sufficient to effect a severance. Even if there was not any firm agreement but only a course of dealing, it clearly evidenced an intention by both parties that the property should henceforth be held in common and not jointly. Browne LJ added that in his view Mrs Rawnsley's subsequent repudiation of that agreement made no difference.

Mutual conduct

Mutual conduct will be any course of dealing between the joint tenants which demonstrates that the interests of all were mutually treated as constituting a tenancy in common.

In *Burgess v Rawnsley* [1975], Lord Denning MR indicated how far a course of dealings would provide evidence of severance:

[I]t is sufficient if there is a course of dealing in which one party makes clear to the other that he desires that their shares should no longer be held jointly but be held in common. Similarly it is sufficient if both parties enter on a course of dealing which evinces an intention by both of them that their shares shall henceforth be held in common and not jointly.

The desire or the intention to sever however must be an immediate intention as held by Lawton LJ in *Harris v Goddard* [1983][16] otherwise it does not comply with the requirements of s 36(2) of the LPA 1925. In *Harris*, Lawton LJ pointed out that:

> When a notice in writing of a desire to sever is served pursuant to s 36 (2) it takes effect forthwith. It follows that a desire to sever must evince an intention to bring about the wanted result immediately. A notice in writing which expresses a desire to bring about the wanted result at some time in the future is not, in my judgment, a notice in writing within s 36 (2).

There has been some discussion as to whether negotiations by the parties constitute an intention to sever the joint tenancy. Whilst Lord Denning saw no issue with this, others have. Sir John Pennycuick in *Burgess v Rawnsley* [1975] suggested that inconclusive negotiations may not be sufficient to demonstrate mutual conduct. In *Gore and Snell v Carpenter* [1990][17] it was held that negotiations were not sufficient for severance where there was no express agreement to sever as the negotiations did not amount to a sufficient course of dealings for severance. Additionally in *Harris v Goddard* [1983] the prayer in a divorce petition, under s 24 of the Matrimonial Causes Act 1973 for an order relating to the former matrimonial home, was not a desire to sever but instead a package of options.

If the more easy and clear route of written notice is not used then the difficulties and potential expense of failing to do so or to follow the right processes is well demonstrated by the more recent decision in *Quigley v Masterson* [2011].[18] A couple owned a property as joint tenants, both in law and equity. The relationship broke down and the man's solicitors tried to sever the joint tenancy by an unsuccessful attempt to serve the woman with written notice pursuant to s 36(2) of the LPA 1925. He then lost capacity. The man's daughter applied to the Court of Protection and was appointed as his deputy (i.e. she became responsible for managing his personal affairs). On the application form, she wrote: 'It is intended to sell the house which is owned jointly with former partner, who also wishes to sell.' Plans were made to sell the house. However, before steps could be taken in relation to the property, the man died. His family argued that there had been a severance.

There was no effective severance under s 36(2) of the LPA 1925 and no course of conduct on the part of the daughter could be shown (she did not have right to act on her father's behalf until her appointment, making her prior conduct irrelevant). However, the woman had filed documents in the proceedings in which she clearly indicated her belief that she and the man each owned a 50 per cent share in the property. Those documents constituted written notice of severance and consequently that the joint tenancy was severed prior to the man's death.

----

16 [1983] 3 All ER 242; [1983] 1 WLR 1203.
17 [1990] 61 P and CR 456.
18 [2011] EWHC 2529 (Ch); [2012] 1 All ER 1224.

Consider what would have happened in the absence of those documents: the man's family would have received nothing and the woman had sole ownership of the property.

Forfeiture as a means of severance

The rule is that no one may benefit from his crime. As such if one joint tenant kills another he cannot benefit from that other's death by the operation of the right of survivorship. In such circumstances the death of the joint tenant will act as a severance of the joint tenancy. This will allow their severed share to fall into their estate and pass in accordance with their will or the rules of intestacy.

CONSIDER THIS – 1

A year into their studies Claire met Keith and decided to leave university to travel around the world with him. The events that followed were:

- Claire wrote to Suzanne, Mick, Neil and Mark to say that she no longer wanted the property and wanted her share of the money from it to use for her travelling. The letter invited Suzanne, Mick, Neil and Mark to either purchase Claire's share or to agree to sell the property on the open market.
- Following the letter, Mick has changed his will leaving his 'share' in property to his sister.
- Neil and Mark, while not meeting with all of the other owners, met with each other and agreed they would also like to sell and then divide the sale proceeds between themselves equally.

Do you consider that these acts amounted to severances?

THE EFFECT OF SEVERANCE

A successful severance has no impact at law (s 32(2) of the LPA 1925). In equity, if the severance was not mutual then it will have only a unilateral effect. This means that the tenant who severed will have their own separate share as a tenant in common in equity, but the others will continue as joint tenants.

For example, take four people (A, B, C, D) purchasing property together and agreeing hold as joint tenants with the following subsequent events:

- First, A mortgages his 'share' in the house.
- The next day, B dies and it transpires that he told his girlfriend that he was leaving her his 'share' in the house.
- Two days later, upset by the death of the friend all the parties meet and mutually agree to sell the house. They immediately instruct a solicitor.

If advising the parties, you would start by establishing the position at law. There could be no severance at law as there could only ever be a joint tenancy, so the only thing of relevance here is the death of B. The legal ownership is A, C and D as joint tenants.

In equity, things are very different.

A has severed his share by entering into the mortgage. He has 'operated on his own share' and thereby destroyed one of the four unities. At the time he did so, there were four joint tenants in equity and so he will have a quarter, or 25 per cent, separate share as a tenant in common. The other three (B, C and D) continue to hold as joint tenants in equity of three-quarters, or 75 per cent.

B may have been trying to sever, but he has not used a valid route. As such, when he died he did not have a separate share to leave to his girlfriend. Instead, the right of survivorship under the joint tenancy will operate. A still holds a quarter as a tenant in common, but now only C and D hold three-quarters as tenants in common.

When all of the parties agree to the sale, they sever. This means that A holds one-quarter as a tenant in common, C holds three-eighths (37.5 per cent) as a tenant in common and D holds three-eighths as a tenant in common.

APPLY YOUR LEARNING – TASK 2

After the letter from Claire to Suzanne, Mick, Neil and Mark severing her share (she was the only one who successfully did so) tragic events unfold.

In April of this year Claire and Keith are killed in a plane crash. A week later Mick dies in a car accident on his way to work.

How do these tragic events affect how the legal and equitable interests to the property are held and why?

THE TRUSTS OF LAND AND APPOINTMENT OF TRUSTEES ACT 1996

It is not unusual for co-owners of property to have differences over the management of the property. The Trusts of Land and Appointment of Trustees Act 1996 (ToLATA 1996) sets out the duties of trustees under a trust for land and the rights of the beneficiaries, as well as giving the court certain powers to resolve disputes about the ownership of land.

Under ToLATA 1996 there is no obligation to sell the land, although a settler can *expressly* impose such an obligation if he wishes. Apart from this, however, trustees have power to postpone the sale indefinitely under s 4(1) of ToLATA 1996. Before exercising the function of sale, the trustees must first obtain any consent that may be required, as it is a breach of trust not to obtain them. If more than two consents are required, the purchaser is only required to see evidence of two consents under s 10 ToLATA, although the trustees have a duty to consult any beneficiaries under s 11 of ToLATA.

THE POWERS AND DUTIES OF THE TRUSTEE

Section 6(1) For the purpose of exercising their functions as trustees, the trustees of land have in relation to the land subject to the trust all the powers of an absolute owner.

Section 6(3) The trustees of land have power to purchase a legal estate in any land in England or Wales.

Section 6(4) The power conferred by subsection (3) may be exercised by trustees to purchase land:

(a) by way of investment
(b) for occupation by any beneficiary, or
(e) for any other reason.

Section 6(5) Trustees have to have regard to the rights of the beneficiaries.

Section 11 Trustees are required to consult with the beneficiaries:

(a) so far as practicable, consult with beneficiaries of full age and beneficially entitled to an interest in possession in the land, and
(b) so far as consistent with the general interest of the trust, give effect to the wishes of those beneficiaries.

Section 13(1) Trustees have the power to allow just one person to occupy or a number of people in the class of people entitled to occupy. In these circumstances under s 13, trustees have the discretion to exclude or restrict occupation rights of one or more of the beneficiaries (but not all of them).

Section 13(3) Trustees may impose 'reasonable' conditions on any beneficiary in relation to his occupation of land e.g. the beneficiary paying outgoings or expenses in respect of the land or undertaking work.

Section 13(4) The trustees will consider:

(a) the intentions of the persons who created the trust
(b) the purpose under which the land is held
(c) the circumstances and wishes of the beneficiaries entitled to occupy.

What does this mean?

Under the ToLATA 1996 regime the powers of trustees are wider than they were previously. This new approach under s 6(1) avoids listing each power as before, the phrase 'powers of an absolute owner' is also used where the trustees are also the owners of the beneficial interests. The wider power is the very foundation of the new balance that has arisen in trusts of land between the power to sell and the power to retain the property.

Trustees have a duty to exercise their new powers in the interests of the beneficiaries. This duty arises under their *general equitable duties* and under s 6(5) of ToLATA. It should be noted that the trustees have to have regard to these 'rights' of the beneficiaries within s 6(5), not their 'interests', therefore the section is narrower than the general equitable duties of trustees.

The wide powers granted to trustees under ss 6 and 7 are not compulsory and they can be excluded or limited, provided the trust is not charitable, ecclesiastical or public. It is apparent that the whole sections can be excluded, not just powers. This must of course mean that s 6(5), under which trustees must have regard to the rights of the beneficiaries, can also be excluded. This would be unwise, however, as the whole existence of a trust is to look after the interests of the beneficiaries. In any event the general equitable duties that apply to trustees would always apply.

How trustees should deal with the property

All co-owned land is now held on a trust for land. Under the old trust for sale, if trustees could not agree to postpone the sale of the property it would have to be sold as the presumption was to sell; see *Re Mayo* [1943].[19] Under ToLATA 1996, however, there is no obligation to sell, although a settlor can *expressly* impose such an obligation if he wishes. If an express trust for sale is established, ToLATA 1996 ensures that this trust is always subject to an inviolable power to postpone sale indefinitely under s 4(1).

Before exercising this function of sale, trustees must carry out any consultation required by s 11. This mandatory requirement takes priority over even any obligation to sell. The duty to consult may, however, be excluded by the settlor under s 11(2)(a). This rule reverses the former position where consultation had to be expressly included – now they are implied unless excluded.

> TUTOR TIP – 6
> ....
>
> Whilst s 11 places a mandatory requirement upon the trustees to consult with the beneficiaries, a purchaser of the property is under no obligation to check whether this consultation has taken place. This is sensible since the issue of whether the trustees have taken into account the beneficiaries' views would be very difficult for a purchaser to ascertain.

---

19 [1943] Ch 302.

It is possible to place conditions upon a trust for land; for example, it may state that land may not be sold until certain individuals or bodies consent to a sale. If a trust of land is subject to such a consent requirement, the consent must be obtained before the sale can go ahead. This use of consents is not new and can prevent the sale from taking place for considerable periods of time. However, s 8(2) of ToLATA 1996 makes the validity of requiring consents explicit. The requirement of consent, if imposed, must be contained with the 'disposition creating the trust'.

RIGHTS OF A BENEFICIARY

Section 12(1)(a) A person who is holding beneficial interest in a property is entitled to occupy it if it can be shown by the beneficiary concerned that one of the purposes of the trust was to provide a dwelling for him.

Section 12(1)(b) Even if the purposes of the trust do not make the land available for occupation, occupation is still possible if the land is factually available i.e. the property is vacant and available for occupation.

Section 12(2) If more than one beneficiary claims the right to occupy the premises the decision is based on whether the property is available and suitable for occupation and the premises are not suitable for them all to live there.

Section 13(5) The beneficiary in occupation will have to pay the outgoings and expenses.

Section 13(6) Where a beneficiary's occupation has been excluded or restricted then the trustees may require a beneficiary in occupation to *either* pay compensation to the excluded beneficiary *or* forgo any payments or other benefits to which he would otherwise be entitled under the trust so that these benefits would accrue to the excluded beneficiary(ies) instead.

What does this mean?
Under ss 12 and 13 of ToLATA 1996, certain beneficiaries of a trust of land are given express rights to occupy the property. This flows from the recognition that beneficiaries have an interest in the property under the 1996 Act rather than merely in the sale proceeds of it.

A beneficiary is entitled to occupy the land if one of the purposes of the trust is to provide a dwelling for the beneficiary and it is available to occupy. The purpose may be evidenced expressly by the terms of the trust, i.e. if the trust is set up by will which states that a particular beneficiary should have the option of living in the property. The purpose of the trust, however, may be taken from other evidence other than the express provisions of the trust, i.e. the evidence of the beneficiary himself as to what he understood the purposes of the trust were. Even if this is not the case it is still possible to occupy under s 12(1)(b) if the land is factually available i.e. the property is vacant and available for occupation.

Occupation is not possible if it is already legally occupied by a non-beneficiary e.g. a tenant under a continuing tenancy agreement or if it is unsuitable e.g. an office block is excessive for the beneficiary's needs. Indeed, ToLATA 1996 contains explicit instructions to trustees in relation to existing occupation, as under s 13(7)(a) they are not entitled to exercise their power to evict any person who is already in occupation. A person already in occupation therefore effectively has priority other any beneficiaries who may wish to move in. An existing occupant is further protected by the provisions of s 13(7)(b) as an existing occupant may not be manipulated into leaving by the unreasonable use of s 12. For example, a beneficiary widow already in occupation of her deceased's husband's property may not be manoeuvred into leaving by the trustees moving in hostile step-children using their s 12 powers.

Section 12 states that the applicant beneficiary may be a member of a class of beneficiaries identified as being entitled to occupation. There is no requirement to show that he is the only one entitled to occupy the property to succeed in an occupation claim. For example, a gift under a will stating that the *spouse and children* may occupy the family home as they wish will allow the spouse to claim the right of occupation.

Under s 13(3) trustees may impose 'reasonable' conditions on any beneficiary in relation to his occupation of land under s 12. Section 13(5) gives examples of the type of conditions that may be imposed. Any reasonable conditions may be imposed but include:

- the beneficiary paying outgoings or expenses in respect of the land or
- undertaking any other obligation in relation to the land or to any activity which is or is proposed to be conducted there e.g. farm work.

Problems occur when more than one beneficiary claims the right to occupy the premises and the premises are not suitable for them all to live there. Under s 13(1) of ToLATA 1996, the trustees have a power to allow just one person to occupy or a number of people in the class of people entitled to occupy. As such, trustees have discretion to exclude or restrict occupation rights of one or more of the beneficiaries (but not all of them). It is still the case that trustees must exercise this discretion unanimously; see *Re Mayo* [1943]. Under s 13(6) where a beneficiary's occupation has been excluded or restricted then the trustees may require a beneficiary in occupation to *either* pay compensation to the excluded beneficiary *or* forgo any payments or other benefits to which he would otherwise be entitled under the trust so that these benefits would accrue to the excluded beneficiary(ies) instead.

DISPUTE RESOLUTION – POWERS OF THE COURT

Section 14(1) Any person who is a trustee of land or has an interest in property subject to a trust of land, may make an application to the court for an order.

Section 14(2) The court may make any such order as the court thinks fit:

(a) relating to the exercise by the trustees of any of their functions (including an order relieving them of any obligation to obtain the consent of, or to consult, any person in connection with the exercise of any of their functions), or
(b) declare the nature or extent of a person's interest in property subject to the trust.

Section 14(3) The court may not make any order as to the appointment or removal of trustees.

Section 15(1) In determining an application the court should have regard to four criteria:

(a) the intentions of the person(s) who created the trust
(b) the purposes for which the trust property is to be held
(c) the welfare of any minor who occupies or might reasonably be expected to occupy any land as his home
(d) the interests of any secured creditor of any beneficiary.

Section 15(2–3) The court is also to have regard to the circumstances and wishes of certain beneficiaries.

What does this mean?

In situations of dispute, the courts have powers under ss 14 and 15 of ToLATA 1996. These powers are much wider than those previously available to a court in looking at a trust for sale under s 30 of the LPA 1925. Section 14 applies both to former trusts for sale and new trusts of land. Under s 14(2) the court may make any order relating to the trustees' exercise of their functions i.e. the court may make an order for sale or to confirm that the trustees must postpone sale until the occurrence of a specified event and may also make an order relieving them of any obligation to obtain the consent of or to consult any person in connection with the exercise of their functions. Alternatively, the court may determine under s 14(2)(b) the existence or extent of any person's interest in a property e.g. if a person has contributed to the purchase price of a property but no trust deed expressly acknowledging her interest has been made, she may apply to the court for an order acknowledging the extent of her beneficial interest.

Matters for consideration

In determining an application the court should have regard to four criteria set out in s 15(1) of ToLATA 1996 and also the criteria in s 15(3).

(a) The intentions of the person(s) who created the trust

The court may review what was intended by the settlor(s) at the time of creating the trust i.e. in a dispute over a claimed interest based upon a financial contribution to the purchase price – was the person's contribution meant to confer upon her an interest in the property?

(b) The purposes for which the trust property is to be held

A sale will not be ordered by the court if the property was acquired for a particular purpose and that purpose is still continuing.

KEY CASE: *RE BUCHANAN-WOLLASTON'S CONVEYANCE* [1939] CH 738; [1939] 2 ALL ER 302

In 1928 four owners and occupiers of dwelling houses in the immediate vicinity of a piece of open land agreed to purchase it. Their intention was to prevent the open land being built upon in the future. They purchased the land in unequal shares and it was conveyed to them in fee simple as joint tenants. To achieve their intention they entered into a deed of covenant which recited that they had purchased the land so as to secure that it should not be so used as to be a nuisance or annoyance or to cause depreciation in the value of their properties, and which regulated the future user of the land and dealings therewith, providing for the determination of disputed questions arising with reference to it by vote among the joint tenants.

In 1938, one of the parties, having sold his house, asked for the land to be sold contrary to the wishes of the other owners. He then applied to the court to order a sale. Farwell J stated:

> I have no doubt what the purpose of the deed of covenant was. It was to preserve the land as an open space. The parties all intended that nothing should be done with the land which the others thought detrimental to their respective properties. The question is this: Will the Court assist the plaintiff to do an act which would be directly contrary to his contract with the other parties, since it was plainly the intention of the parties to the said contract that the land should not be sold save with the consent of them all?

The Court held that it would not assist the plaintiff in avoiding his contractual obligations and the intention of the trust as set up by the four owners.

Was the property meant to provide a residence as well as an investment for both parties? If it is still required as a residence, the sale of the property may be delayed. However, if that residence in the property linked to another purpose then it may well subsist only for as long as that purpose. For example, if a relationship breaks down the property may well have to be sold.

KEY CASE: *JONES V CHALLENGER* [1961] 1 QB 176; [1960] 1 ALL ER 785

As we have seen, a sale will not be ordered by the court if the property was acquired for a particular purpose and that purpose is still continuing. In the case of *Jones*, a married couple purchased the lease of a house to occupy as the matrimonial home. The lease was assigned to them as trustees to sell the same with power to postpone the sale upon trust for themselves as joint tenants. Three years later, the husband obtained a divorce on the ground of his wife's adultery. After the decree the wife, who had remarried, asked for the house to be sold. The husband still living in the property refused to agree to the sale.

Despite being prior to ToLATA 1996, Devlin LJ's judgment is an excellent example of how consideration of the purpose of the trust is practically applied and a decision reached.

In the case we have to consider, the house was acquired as the matrimonial home. That was the purpose of the joint tenancy and, for so long as that purpose was still alive, I think that the right test to be applied would be that in *In re Buchanan-Wollaston's Conveyance*. But with the end of the marriage, that purpose was dissolved and the primacy of the duty to sell was restored. No doubt there is still a discretion. If the husband wanted time to obtain alternative accommodation, the sale could be postponed for that purpose, but he has not asked for that. If he was prepared to buy out the wife's interest, it might be proper to allow it, but he has not accepted a suggestion that terms of that sort should be made. In these circumstances, there is no way in which the discretion can properly be exercised except by an order to sell, because, since they cannot now both enjoy occupation of the property, that is the only way whereby the beneficiaries can derive equal benefit from their investment, which is the primary object of the trust.

KEY CASE: *RAWLINGS V RAWLINGS* [1964] P 398; [1964] 2 ALL ER 804

This case involved a married couple with an adult son who had always resided shared a marital home. After the marriage broke down, the wife left her husband and son residing in the property. Two years later, an order for sale was awarded to her.

It was held that in the circumstances, the marriage being at an end in fact though not in law, the bungalow was no longer in fact the matrimonial home: the order for sale was correct. It was noted by Salmon LJ that if there were young children the outcome would have been different as one of the purposes of the trust would be to provide a home for them, and whilst that purpose continued a sale would not generally be ordered.

(c) the welfare of any minor who occupies or might reasonably be expected to occupy any land as his home

The courts will not tend to exercise its power of sale where the trust is to provide a family home for the parties and their children, if any. Here the primary object is the provision of a home and the courts will not order sale as long as that purpose remains.

In *Re Evers' Trust* [1980][20] the parties, both previously married and divorced, began to live together. They bought a cottage for themselves, her two children and the couple's child, the cottage being conveyed to them in joint names on a trust for sale for the benefit of themselves as joint tenants, with power to postpone sale. Upon separation, the mother was awarded custody of the child and the father applied for an order for sale of the cottage. The judge ordered that the property be sold, but that sale should be postponed until the child attained the age of 16 or until further order. Upon appeal the court pointed out that the inference was irresistible that the parties had purchased it as a family home for themselves and the three children for the indefinite future and with the underlying purpose of the trust to provide a home for all five of them for the indefinite future. It held that the court has no power to adjust property rights or to redraft the terms of the trust.

(d) the interests of any secured creditor of any beneficiary.

If a beneficiary does not wish the property to be sold but he has mortgaged his share of the property to a creditor, the creditor's interests in a property sale will be taken into account.

Section 15 of ToLATA 1996 does not apply, however, where the application under s 14 is made by a trustee in bankruptcy.

PROTECTING THE PURCHASER

A purchaser should ensure that he pays his purchase monies to at least two trustees and therefore overreach the interests of the beneficiaries. Following *Caunce v Caunce* [1969][21] it was established that a purchaser of unregistered land who pays the capital monies to only *one* trustee for sale takes the legal estate free from the beneficial interests provided he has no notice (actual or constructive) of the existence of the trust, i.e. the purchaser is a bona fide purchaser of the legal estate for value without notice.

In registered land, a beneficial interest behind a trust may become overriding if the beneficiary is in occupation of the land under sch 1 para 2 and sch 3 para 2 of the Land Registration Act 2002. However, if purchase monies are paid to two trustees, at the time of the purchase, the beneficiaries' interests in property will be converted into monetary interests only and therefore will not be overriding 'at the time of the disposition'; see *Williams and Glynn's Bank Ltd v Boland* [1981].[22]

---

20 [1980] 3 All ER 399; [1980] 1 WLR 1327.
21 [1969] 1 All ER 722; [1969] 1 WLR 286.
22 [1981] AC 487; [1980] 2 All ER 408.

APPLY YOUR LEARNING – TASK 3

Following the tragic events involving Claire and Mick, Neil decides that he wants to leave university and return home to his family in Scotland. Mark and Suzanne have both made it clear that they wish to stay in the property until they have finished their studies in two years' time. Neil is unhappy with this and wants the property to be sold now and has stated that as he contributed the largest sum of money his view takes priority. Is this the case?

Using the Trusts of Land and Appointment of Trustees Act 1996, how can this dispute be resolved?

DISCUSSION

Whilst the distinction between a joint tenancy and a tenancy in common is relatively straightforward, the decision as to which option is best for co-owners is more complicated. Gone are the days where married couples hold property as joint tenants because their money is 'joint money' or because an unmarried couple is *not* married they should hold the property as tenants in common.

A number of factors must be considered before advising clients on the best way to hold property. Solicitors in practice today will need to ask a range of questions to obtain information about clients' personal circumstances, how they organise their finances and the purpose for purchasing the property. The myriad of questions may include:

- What contributions are they each putting in to buy the property?
- Are any savings jointly or individually accumulated?
- Are the parties contributing monies from properties they have previously owned individually?
- Are the co-owners obtaining a mortgage and will that be a joint mortgage?
- How will the parties be contributing to the monthly mortgage payments? Will this be equally or will one party be contributing more money each month?
- Will any co-owner be investing in the property by carrying out repairs, alterations or general upgrades and decoration, which will increase the value of the property?
- If the co-owners are a couple, have they previously been married or are they planning on getting married? This may have implications on any will.
- Do they have children from previous relationships and do they want to ensure these children benefit from the property if their parent were to die?
- Do they wish for the property to automatically pass to the other co-owners upon death?

- Do they own any other property currently and/or high-value assets that would put them into the inheritance tax threshold?
- What is the purpose for purchasing the property? Will it be the main family home or is it being purchased for some other purpose?

Obviously this list is not exhaustive but it gives an idea of the type of information a solicitor will need to obtain before advising their clients whether it is better for them to hold the property as joint tenants or tenants in common.

CONSIDER THIS – 2

Consider Case Study Two and the information provided. How would you advise Christine as to the best way for her to hold 13 Lakeview Crescent? Joint tenants or tenants in common? What would be the reasons for this and would you require any additional information to help come to that conclusion?

CASE STUDY – TWO

You have been asked to advise Christine on the best way to hold a property she is buying with her husband Geoffrey. They are buying 13 Lakeview Crescent for £356,000.

Christine has previously been married and has two children by this previous marriage.

They are getting a mortgage in order to purchase 13 Lakeview Crescent in the sum of £256,000. Both will be contributing equally to the monthly mortgage payments. Christine will be contributing £75,000 coming from sale proceeds from a house she previously owned in her sole name. Geoffrey will be contributing £25,000 from savings.

The property will be used as the family home.

END OF CHAPTER SUMMARY

- There are two ways that land as co-owners can be held, joint tenancy and tenancy in common.
- Under a joint tenancy the estate is owned collectively, the co-owners regarded as being a single components owner. Additionally the four unities must be present.
- The right of survivorship applies to joint tenancy and therefore cannot be disposed of by will or intestacy.

- With tenants in common, the co-owners have distinct shares and therefore the right of survivorship does not apply. Whilst the four unities may be present, the unity of possession is required.
- It is possible to sever a joint tenancy by express notice, acts of severance, forfeiture or by a court order. It is only possible for the severance to occur in equity as under s 36(2) of the LPA 1925 there can be no severance of a joint tenancy in law.
- ToLATA 1996 sets out the duties of trustees under a trust of land and the rights of the beneficiaries.
- ToLATA 1996 also gives the courts the power to deal with dispute between the trustees and beneficiaries as to future dealings with the land.

PREPARING FOR ASSESSMENTS
QUESTIONS

ESSAY QUESTION

What rights does a beneficiary have under a trust of land and to what extend are these rights effectively and fairly protected by the Trustees of Land and Appointment of Trustees Act 1996?

PROBLEM QUESTION

Lawson has recently died and in his will he has left his freehold detached five-bedroom house to his trustees upon trust for his second wife Regan and his two children Rosie, aged 31, and Jamie, aged 16, in equal shares. The will states that if they wish to live in the house they may do so.

Advise the trustees in each of the following alternative circumstances:

1   Rosie would like to live in the house with her husband and their three children but Regan and Jamie want it sold.
2   Jamie would like to live in the house with his aunt who is his guardian.
3   Regan would like to continue living in the house but Rosie and Jamie want her to pay rent.

How would your answer differ if Lawson's will had made no provision for the occupation of the house by Regan, Rosie and Jamie?

Figure 11.4 will support you in working through the problem.

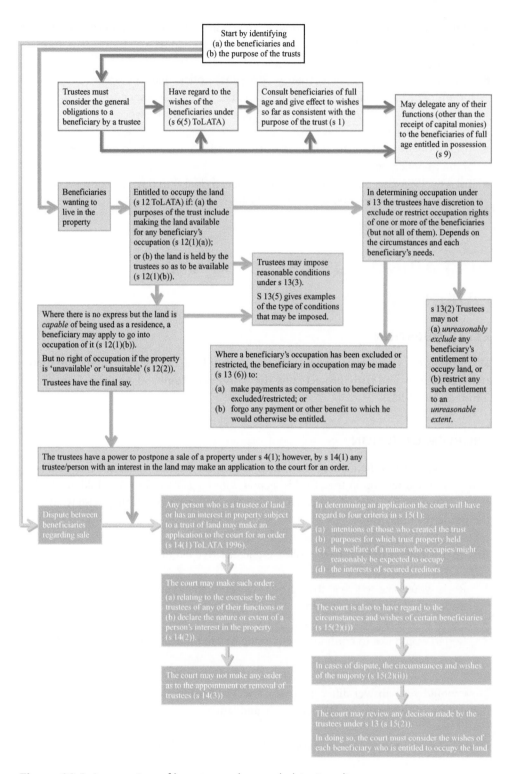

Figure 11.4 An overview of how to resolve a cohabitation dispute

FURTHER READING

- Conway, H, 'Joint Tenancies, Negotiations and Consensual Severance' [2009] Conv 67. This article considers the ruling in *Saleeba v Wilke*, an Australian case, in the context of whether there had been a consensual severance of a joint tenancy by mutual agreement or by way of a course of conduct in circumstances.
- Crown, BB, 'Severance of Joint Tenancy of Land by Partial Alienation' (2001) 117 LQR 477. Provides background to doctrine of severance of joint tenancy in the context of alienation.
- Fox, L, 'Unilateral Demise by a Joint Tenant: Does It Effect a Severance?' [2000] Conv 208. A comparative look at the effect of a grant of a lease by one tenant on a relationship and its effect upon the joint tenancy by comparing case law in England, Ireland, Australia, Canada and California.
- Glover, N and Todd, P, 'The Myth of Common Intent' (1996) 16(3) LS 325. Considers the relevance of intention in determining individuals' beneficial interests in property.
- Gravells, NP, 'Co-ownership, Severance and Purchasers – The Law of Property (Joint Tenants) Act 1964 on Trial?' [2000] Conv 461. Looks at the case of *Grindal v Hooper* (1999) EG 150 (CS) and considers the effectiveness of the severance of the joint tenancy and its impact upon a subsequent sale.
- Percival, M, 'Severance by Written Notice – A Matter of Delivery?' [1999] Conv 61. Note on *Kinch v Bullard*.
- Tee, L, 'Severance Revisited' [1995] Conv 105. A retrospective look at the Law Commission's 1985 working paper on trusts of land.
- Thompson, MP, 'Beneficial Joint Tenancies: A Case for Abolition' [1987] Conv 29. An analysis of trusts for sale following the Law Commission's 1985 working paper on trusts of land following its provisionally recommendation for the abolition of both the strict settlement and the trust for sale.

CHAPTER 12
EASEMENTS

CHAPTER AIMS AND OBJECTIVES

In this chapter, we will consider the issue of easements and profits à prendre. Easements and profits are interests in land and are property rights that a person has over land held by someone else. Easements are much more important than profits à prendre. Such rights can be extremely important and can significantly increase the value of land as they benefit land; for instance, they may give a landowner the right of access over a neighbour's land. By the same notion, the existence of an easement can be a burden on the neighbour's land as it may limit the way that land can be utilised. As we will see, easements are not just confined to rights of way across a neighbour's land but can be created to benefit land in many ways.

We will begin by considering what easements and profits are, what the essential characteristics of easements are, how they are created and how they bind the original parties. This will be followed by a consideration of how easements are protected, how they bind the neighbour's land and how easements can be enforced against successors in title. Finally, we will consider the Law Commission's report and recommendations for changes to the area of easements.

By the end of this chapter, you should be able to:

- understand what an easement is and how it is created;
- know the characteristics of an easement and be able to identify whether a potential interest in land is an easement;
- know and be able to recognise how and when an easement is acquired;
- explain how easements are passed to successors in title;
- know and understand the necessary methods of protecting the easement, both in the context of unregistered and registered land, against a purchaser of the 'servient tenement';
- analyse and apply the law in the context of the law of easements and profits in order to advise the owners/occupiers of either the servient or dominant tenement as to whether a potential easement or profit can be enforced;
- apply the above to the case studies and learning tasks.

CASE STUDY – ONE

In 1995, Lydia purchased land and built a large detached house, Orchard House, on it. The house had very large expansive gardens that required considerable maintenance. Orchard House was not far from the village shop and coffee shop. Lydia often used a shortcut across the rear gardens to visit the coffee shop and to do her shopping.

Following an illness in 2000, Lydia found that the garden had become too much for her. She sold half of the garden area, including the rear gardens nearest to the village, to Debbie. There was already a semi-derelict cottage on the property with a large number of windows. Debbie has now renovated the cottage and moved in.

Since the sale of the land, Lydia has continued to use the shortcut as a means of access to the village shops (she has alternative access that she uses for everyday access to Orchard House). Debbie did not object at first but then last December Debbie put up a fence to stop Lydia from using the shortcut. Angry at her new neighbour, Lydia has had a particularly high boundary wall constructed which is blocking the light to all of the cottage's downstairs windows at the front. Debbie is furious.

KEEP IN MIND

- The use of the 'shortcut' when Lydia first started using it would not have been an easement, after all she was just walking over her own gardens at the time.
- If Lydia had wanted to be sure that Debbie would have to allow her to keep using it, she could have expressly reserved it as an easement in the sale to her. If Debbie was aware of the regular use of the shortcut, do you think she should have to honour it?
- Easements do not always take the form of rights of way – there are many categories for us to explore. The right to light is one; can you see where one might be raised in this question?
- Debbie could have insisted on a right-to-light easement was expressly granted when purchasing the property. Do you think she might simply have assumed that the existing windows in the cottage would continue to get light? If so, should Lydia honour that and what, if any, difference should it make that Debbie is the buyer rather than the seller of the land?

THE BASICS

An easement is a right annexed to land to use other land in different ownership in a particular manner and for its benefit or to prevent the owner of the other land from using his land in a particular manner. An easement does not involve the taking of any part of the natural resources of that land or any part of its soil. It is a proprietary interest in land. The benefit of an easement may therefore run with the land passing to successors in title of the land. The easement may also bind subsequent owners of the servient land and once created is irrevocable, unlike licences.

A profit à prendre is a right to take part of the soil or natural produce on the 'servient land'. Profits, unlike easements, can exist 'in gross', i.e. the owner of the profit need not be the owner of any adjoining or neighbouring land, or indeed, any land at all.

The 'dominant' land is the land that enjoys the easement or profit, while the 'servient' land is that which is subject to the easement or profit.

ESSENTIAL TERMINOLOGY	
An easement	A right attached to land to use land owned by others in a particular manner or to prevent the owner of the other land from using his land in a particular manner. The right is attached to benefit the land in some way.
A profit	A right to take part of the soil or produce of the 'servient tenement'.
Grantor	The person whose land is affected by the easement.
Grantee	The person whose land benefits from the easement.
Dominant tenement or dominant land	This is the land owned by grantee. This is the land that enjoys the easement.
Servient tenement or servient land	This is the land owned by the grantor. This is the land that is subject to the easement.
Reservation	Opposite of a grant and occurs where the landowner reserves for himself an easement or a profit over a portion of land he is conveying to a third party for the benefit of the land he retains.

In the example in Figure 12.1, B grants an easement to A for A to have a right of way along the driveway in order to gain access to the main road (Figure 12.1).

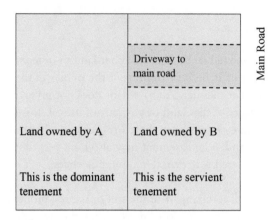

Figure 12.1 An example right of way easement

THE EASEMENT MAY BE POSITIVE OR NEGATIVE IN NATURE

A positive easement is a positive right over another's land. A positive right will almost always have a negative impact on the owner of the servient land, however; at worst he will be restricted from interfering with the right granted. An easement can be restrictive in nature; for example, an easement of support from one property to another.[1] A semi-detached house will have a right of support from its adjoining house. If an easement of support is granted in favour of the dominant land, the dominant land takes from the servient property an undertaking that the servient land will not be used in such a way as to take away support from the dominant land, for example, by removing a supporting wall or by excavating thereby causing next door's garden to collapse.

AN EASEMENT SHOULD NOT CONFER A RIGHT OF EXCLUSIVE POSSESSION

An easement should not grant the dominant land rights over the servient land as would amount to a right of exclusive possession of the servient land by the dominant landowner. The servient landowner must not have his ability to use the servient land taken away by the easement.

AN EASEMENT IS A PROPRIETARY RIGHT SO IT MAY BE PASSED ON TO FUTURE OWNERS

An easement is not a purely contractual right between the parties who created it. An easement is a proprietary right, which means that if created correctly it will benefit and bind successors in title of both the dominant and servient land.

---

1 For example, see *Bradburn v Lindsay* [1983] 2 All ER 408; [1983] 2 EGLR 143 and the removal of a party wall supporting a semi-detached house after one of the properties fell in disrepair and was demolished. Damages were awarded for the necessary resulting repairs.

A PUBLIC RIGHT OF WAY IS NOT AN EASEMENT

A right of way in favour of members of the public, for example a public footpath, is not an easement. This is because the public do not own a parcel of dominant land. Such rights of way therefore should not be referred to as easements as they are statutorily created rights.

APPLY YOUR LEARNING – TASK 1

Using the introduction and essential terminology above consider how, if Debbie's right to light is an easement, the above terms would apply.

In respect of that easement, does Debbie own the dominant or the servient tenement? Is Lydia the grantee or is she the grantor?

THE CHARACTERISTICS AND QUALITIES OF AN EASEMENT

To be an easement, the right must possess a number of essential characteristics. These characteristics were first identified and defined in the case of *Re Ellenborough Park* [1955][2] by Evershed MR. The essential qualities of an easement are:

- there must be a dominant and servient tenement;
- the easement must accommodate the dominant tenement, that is, be connected with its enjoyment and for its benefit;
- the dominant and servient owners must be different persons; and
- the right claimed must be capable of forming the subject matter of the grant.

KEY CASE: *RE ELLENBOROUGH PARK* [1956] CH 131; [1955] 3 ALL ER 667

In 1855, Ellenborough Park and the surrounding property in Weston-super-Mare was sold off in parts for building purposes. At the time of the sale, the freehold land was open and unbuilt on and surrounded the park, which was retained by the sellers. The sale of the building plots granted each purchaser and their successors:

---

2 [1956] Ch 131; [1955] 3 All ER 667.

> [T]he full enjoyment … at all times hereafter in common with the other persons to whom such easements may be granted of the pleasure ground [Ellenborough Park] … but subject to the payment of a fair and just proportion of the costs charges and expenses of keeping in good order and condition the said pleasure ground.
>
> All purchasers covenanted to pay a fair proportion of the expenses of making the pleasure ground and then at all times keeping it in good order and condition and well stocked with plants and shrubs. The sellers covenanted to keep Ellenborough Park as an ornamental pleasure ground.
>
> Properties were subsequently built on the building plots. Eventually, the right granted in 1855 was challenged with arguments that the property owners surrounding the park had only a personal advantage (a licence) and not a proprietary easement.
>
> The case reached the Court of Appeal, Evershed MR giving the single judgment of the court. He identified as the substantial question in the case what the characteristics and qualities are 'as understood by, and known to our law'. He concluded these were the:
>
>> [F]our characteristics formulated in Dr Cheshire's Modern Real Property (7th Edition) p 456 et seq. They are (i) there must be a dominant and a servient tenement; (ii) an easement must accommodate the dominant tenement; (iii) dominant and servient owners must be different persons; and (iv) a right over land cannot amount to an easement unless it is capable of forming the subject-matter of a grant.
>
> It was held that the right to use the pleasure ground was a right known to the law and recognised as an easement. As such the purchasers of plots and their successors in title had legal and effective easements to use Ellenborough Park.

ONE: THERE MUST BE A DOMINANT AND SERVIENT TENEMENT

A proprietary easement cannot exist on its own 'in gross' benefiting a particular person. It must be attached to and benefit a defined dominant piece of land and burden a defined servient land.[3]

TWO: THE EASEMENT MUST ACCOMMODATE THE DOMINANT TENEMENT

It follows from the requirement that easements be attached to the dominant land itself that it must not confer only a personal privilege/advantage on the current landowner. In order to accommodate the dominant land, the owner must be benefited in their capacity as the owner of that land.

---

3 See *London and Blenheim Estates Ltd v Ladbroke Retail Parks Ltd* [1993] 4 All ER 157; [1994] 1 WLR 31.

A canal company granted by deed the sole and exclusive right or liberty of putting or using pleasure boats for hire on their canal to the plaintiff. It was held that it was not possible to create rights unconnected with the use and enjoyment of land but then try and annex them to the land. It was held that what had been granted to the plaintiff merely operated as a licence or covenant and was only binding on them and not anyone else.

Evershed MR reasoned:

> It is clear what the plaintiff was trying to do was to set up, under the guide of an easement, a monopoly which had no normal connection with the ordinary use of the land, but which was merely an independent business enterprise. So, far from the right claimed subserving or accommodating the land, the land was but a convenient incident to the exercises of the right.

What may be of benefit to the dominant land?

Enhanced Land Value – If the benefit of a right granted increases the market value of the dominant land, then that is an indicator that the right may be an easement. It is not conclusive evidence, however. There must be a 'sufficient nexus between the enjoyment of the right and the use of the dominant land' as was argued in *Re Ellenborough Park* [1956].

The Benefit of Trade Conducted on the Dominant Land – Does the creation of the right have a positive effect upon the trade or business that is carried out on the dominant land? For example, the owner of a public house, a business that had operated on the land for several years, could claim an easement to having an advertising signboard on the servient land. The sign benefited the trade the land was now well-established as being normally used for. The commercial advantage must be an enhancement of the use of the dominant land, as shown in *Moody v Steggles* [1879].

An enhancement to the enjoyment of a dwelling – As Evershed MR explained in *Re Ellenborough* [1956] itself 'the use of a garden undoubtedly enhances, and is connected with, the normal enjoyment of a house to which it belongs.'

The owners of a public house argued that a right to affix a signboard to the wall of the defendants' house was an easement. The court held that this was an easement benefiting the dominant land.

How does this case differ from *Hill v Tupper*?

As we have seen the easement must accommodate the dominant tenement and it was held in *Hill v Tupper* [1863] that the granting of the sole and exclusive right of putting or using pleasure boats for hire on their canal to the plaintiff was not a benefit to the land but only a personal advantage on its current owner while he set up a business.

The defendants in *Moody* also tried to claim that the easement did not relate to the land but to the business of the occupant of the land and was therefore personal. The courts, however, disagreed, stating the land was and had been under commercial use for a number of years and the business and the land had become intrinsically linked. As Fry J explained:

> [T]he house can only be used by an occupant, and that the occupant only uses the house for the business which he pursues, and therefore in some manner (direct or indirect) an easement is more or less connected with the mode in which the occupant of the house uses it … In *Hoare v. Metropolitan Board of Works*, which is still more like the present case, the easement was to have a signboard supported by a pole fixed into the common, an easement which could be useful only so long as the occupant used the house for some purpose which rendered an invitation to the public desirable.

TUTOR TIP – 1

Students struggle with the concept of whether the easement 'accommodates the land'. Substitute the word 'accommodate' with the word 'assist' or 'help' and this will make it easier to understand and apply this part of the *Re Ellenborough Park* test.

To accommodate the land, the dominant and servient land must be sufficiently proximate. They need not be neighbouring, but the further apart they are the more difficult it will be to show the connection between the right and the dominant land. In *Bailey v Stephens* [1862],[4] Byles J commented that, 'you cannot have a right of way over land in Kent appurtenant to an estate in Northumberland'.

THREE: THE DOMINANT AND SERVIENT LAND MUST BE OWNED OR OCCUPIED BY DIFFERENT PERSONS

The dominant and the servient land must be owned and/or occupied by different people. The case study appears to relates to two adjoining freehold properties. It is clear that they are now both owned and occupied by different people. However, where there is a leasehold, easements may then occur whereby both the dominant and the servient land are *owned* by one person (the landlord) but the dominant land is in *occupation* by a different person (the tenant of the lease).

4 (1862) 12 CBNS 91; 142 ER 1077.

For example, Abigail is the freehold owner of a block of ten flats. She rents the top one to Barclay. He, and the other tenants, all need a right of way over the land that is retained by the landlord Abigail to use the shared stairwell in order gain access to their flats. Abigail owns the freehold of the retained land and the freehold of the Barclay's flat but there will be separate occupation of the parcels of land concerned. Abigail as landlord will own the stairwell (the servient land) and Barclay as the tenant will occupy the flat (the dominant land).

FOUR: THE EASEMENT MUST BE CAPABLE OF FORMING THE SUBJECT MATTER OF A GRANT

This means that an easement must at least be capable of being granted by deed. In order for that to be achieved a number of elements are required:

1 **There must be a capable grantor**
   The servient owner must be capable of making the grant of an easement. *Nemo dat quod non habet* or no one [can] give what he does not have. In order to create a legal easement over their land the servient landowner must hold a legal estate in that land. A servient landowner cannot grant a legal easement over their land if they only own an equitable estate. Additionally, a licensee cannot grant a legal easement, as they have no estate vested in them. They are therefore not in a position to grant anything other than a licence in respect of the land. As the easement must be created out of the estate of the servient owner, the estate of the servient owner must be established to see if it is capable of supporting the grant of the easement claimed. The extent of the grant of an easement will be defined by the extent to which the owner of the servient land was capable of granting it.

> TUTOR TIP – 2
> ....
>
> **WHAT CAN A GRANTOR GRANT?**
>
> | **What do they hold?** | **What can they grant?** |
> | --- | --- |
> | Legal estate | Can grant legal and equitable rights and licences |
> | Equitable estate | Can grant equitable rights and licences |
> | Licence | Can grant a licence only |

2 **There must be a capable grantee**
   The dominant owner must be capable of receiving the grant. For example, a company without the power to acquire easements may not take the benefit of an easement, as was seen in *National Guaranteed Manure Co Ltd v Donald* (1859).[5]

---

5 (1859) 4 Hurl & N 8, 157 ER 737.

3   **The right must be sufficiently definite**
    The right must be certain, capable of clear description and a precise definition.
    If the grantor and grantee do not know clearly what the right is or what land it
    affects how can the easement be created *and* work properly in practice? In
    particular, the servient landowner must know what their obligation is and how it
    affects their land. In order for an easement to succeed as an easement, it
    cannot be too wide in scope, its extent is too vaguely described or its duration
    unclear. There must also have been an intention to create an easement as such.

    (a) **Not too wide in scope**
         The easement cannot be too wide in scope so that it is totally restrictive
         upon the servient land. For example, an easement for the uninterrupted
         general passage of light and air would be too wide.[6] Whilst such a right
         would ensure that the dominant land had an uninhibited receipt of light
         and air, this could prevent any building to take place on the servient land,
         which would be too restrictive upon the servient land. As such a right to
         light and air on the dominant land will only be allowed through defined
         apertures, i.e. existing window as defined in *Harris v Pinna* (1886).[7] Similarly,
         an attempt to grant a right to the uninterrupted flow of air over a parcel of
         servient land for the benefit of a windmill on the dominant land was held to
         be too wide in scope by *Webb v Bird* [1861].[8]

         More recent is the case *of Hunter v Canary Wharf Ltd* [1997],[9] where a
         group of local residents argued that they had an easement to receive a
         television signal, which they claimed the Canary Wharf Tower was
         interfering with. The House of Lords held that this easement was too wide
         and too vague to be capable of being an easement. The courts are
         unhappy with the impact of negative easements upon the use of servient
         land and are, therefore, resistant to adding to the list.

         Thinking more about this case, if the right had been upheld then the
         commercial impact of preventing the erecting of buildings that could
         interfere with this type of signal (mobile phones, broadband etc.) would be
         massive. As we shall see, even if an easement is not expressly granted it is
         possible to rely on something called prescription. Prescription enables an
         individual to claim an easement by demonstrating long continuous use of
         the right. This type of easement would, therefore, be problematic if it could
         be recognised.

    (b) **Its extent is too vaguely described**
         As with being too wide in scope, the easement cannot be too vague.
         Hunter v Canary Wharf Ltd [1997], as demonstrated above, is an example of

---

6 This also applies to water and passage, which must be through defined channels.
7 (1886) 33 Ch D 238, 50 JP 486.
8 [1861] 10 CBNS 268, 30 LJCP 384.
9 [1997] AC 655; [1997] 2 All ER 426.

an easement that failed for being too wide and too vague in nature. The classic example is the *William Aldred's Case* (1610).[10] Here it was held that there is no common law right to a good view. This cannot exist as an easement as it was too vague and subjective. For example, I may consider that my sight of the motorway in the distance is part of my good view from the garden. Others may well disagree. Without sufficient clarity, how could my neighbour be sure what it is they are required not to interfere with? It could be argued too that a right of privacy is also too vague and subjective and would also fail as an easement.

(c) **Its duration is unclear**

The terms for the easement must be set. Its duration must be certain. Its creation therefore works in the same way as an estate in land. Either it must be granted in perpetuity, in the same way that a freehold estate is forever, or for a clear and set period of time as with leasehold. If the term of the easement cannot be determined from the wording of the grant or the circumstances surrounding it, this could result in the easement failing at law.

(d) **There was no intention to create an easement**

A permission, which the parties intend to simply be a licence, will not be an easement. In *Green v Ashco Horticulturist Limited* [1966][11] Cross J held that a tenant's intermittent use of access through the landlord's premises with his landlord's permission from time to time was not such use which could have been the subject of a legal grant.

4 **The right must be recognisable as an easement**

To be capable of being an easement, the right must be within the general nature of rights traditionally recognised as easements. There is now a fairly authoritative body of what kind of right an easement may be. As easements are a proprietary right over another's land, the courts are reluctant to recognise rights as easements that have not been previously recognised as such. We have already considered most of the common types set out below and will explore parking and storage shortly. The right to use of facilities on servient land includes, for example, the use of lavatories[12] and recently a decision has been made that it can extend to the use of sporting facilities.[13]

---

10 (1610) 77 ER 816.

11 [1966] 2 All ER 232; [1966] 1 WLR 889.

12 *Miller v Emcer Products* [1956] Ch 304; [1956] 1 All ER 237.

13 *Regency Villas Title Ltd v Diamond Resorts (Europe) Ltd* [2015] EWHC 3564 (Ch); [2016] 4 WLR 61; [2015] All ER (D) 101 (Dec). The use of 'the swimming pool, golf course, squash courts, tennis courts ... and any other sporting or recreational facilities on the ... adjoining estate' was held to be an easement. While a recreational right that is wholly extraneous to the use of dominant land and independent of its use would be personal, here the benefit was to the dominant land (holiday accommodation). The rights were not too wide or vague, did not amount to rights of joint occupation or deprive the servient owner of possession.

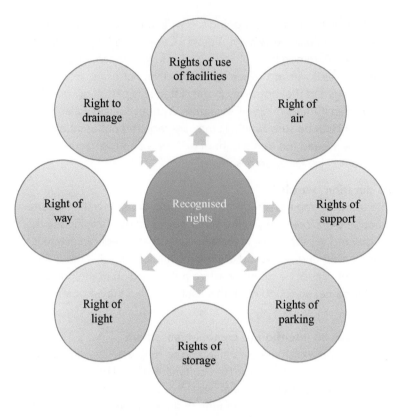

Figure 12.2 The recognised categories of easement

5   **There must be no positive burden on the servient land**
    There must be no positive burden on the servient land.[14] The courts are
    unwilling to recognise or impose easements requiring expenditure on the part
    of the servient land as easements are designed to enable people to gain
    benefits and not impose obligations. There must be no positive act undertaken
    by the owner of the servient tenement, nor any acts of repair required of him or
    payment of money. In *Duke of Westminster v Guild* [1984][15] an easement to use
    a drain did not impose an obligation of repair of the drain upon the servient
    land, though the courts have come close to recognising positive easements in
    Cardwell v Walker [2004][16] and the maintenance of an electricity supply.

---

14 The exception to this rule is the 'spurious easement' noted in Chapter 14 on Freehold Covenants. This relates
    to the maintenance of boundary fencing enclosing livestock such as cattle. It is called spurious as it clearly does
    not fit the *Re Ellenborough* definition of an easement, looking more like a positive covenant. The rule, as set out
    in *Crow v Wood* [1971] 1 QB 77; [1970] 3 All ER 425, is very limited in its application. The case itself relating
    to fences and walls against moorland sheep.
15 [1985] QB 688; [1984] 3 All ER 144.
16 [2003] EWHC 3117 (Ch); [2004] 2 P & CR 122.

6   **The right must not exclude the reasonable use of the servient land**
     The easement must not preclude the grantor from possession of the servient
     land. Any right which requires exclusive possession or joint occupation of the
     servient land by the dominant landowner may not be an easement.
     An attempt to create a right of storage, for example, is problematic. As we have
     seen, an easement cannot be too wide in scope so that it is totally restrictive
     upon the servient land, and for a right of storage to operate the dominant
     landowner would have possession, possibly of an area of the servient land for
     storage. This could be problematic, as the benefit should not include exclusive
     possession. Yet, they can exist, as established in *Wright v Macadam* [1949],[17]
     provided they are not too excessive. Of course, this raises the question of what
     that means. In the case itself, the right was to store coal in a shed and it is difficult
     to see what use of that area of the servient land was left for its owner. There are,
     however, limits, as can be seen in *Copeland v Greenhalf* [1952].[18]

This list is not set in stone, however, and it is not the case that new categories of
easements cannot be created or developed. Most recently, the developments around
parking of cars demonstrate a willingness to expand in light of changes in society. It is,
however, highly unlikely that a new negative easement would be recognised by a
court.

KEY CASE: *COPELAND V GREENHALF* [1952] CH 488; [1952] 1 ALL
ER 809

A strip of land belonging to another person was used by a wheelwright who
owned a house opposite it. The strip was used by the wheelwright to store
vehicles upon, with the wheelwright claiming that his long use meant he had
acquired an easement to do so.

The court found that the breadth of the right was too wide, per Upjohn J:

> I think that the right claimed goes wholly outside any normal idea of an
> easement, that is, the right of the owner or the occupier of a dominant
> tenement over a servient tenement. This claim (to which no closely related
> authority has been referred to me) really amounts to a claim to a joint user of
> the land by the defendant.

Over recent years there have been a number of cases as to whether the right of parking
constitutes an easement. Again, the issue is to what extent the servient landowner is
restricted in the use of his land by the easement. Both *Kettel v Bloomfold Ltd* [2012][19]

---

17 [1949] 2 KB 744; [1949] 2 All ER 565.
18 [1952] Ch 488; [1952] 1 All ER 809.
19 (2012) L&TR 30; [2012] All ER (D) 04 (Jul).

and *R Square Properties Ltd v Nissan Motors (GB) Ltd* [2014][20] the courts held that a right to park constituted an easement. In *Kettel*, Cooke J justified it on the basis that: 'Each tenant was not granted "sole use" of the car parking space, but rather the sole right to use it for parking. This was not the language of exclusive possession.' In *R Square Properties Ltd*, the decision of Mr Stuart Isaacs QC, sitting as a deputy judge of the Chancery Division, was that a company's exclusive right to use parking spaces on an industrial estate constituted an easement, as the servient landowner had not been completely deprived of the reasonable use of the land by the right. This was upheld by Patten LJ.

APPLY YOUR LEARNING – TASK 2

Lydia is attempting to claim she has a right of way easement across a defined path. Ignoring for now the formalities for creating an easement, let's consider the nature of this right:

- There is dominant and servient land.
- The right accommodates the dominant tenement; the shortcut is not only of personal value to Lydia.
- The dominant and servient land are in separate ownership and/or occupation.
- The right lies in the grant.

    - It is within the nature of rights recognised as easements and sufficiently definite.
    - It imposes no positive obligation upon Debbie.
    - It does not exclude reasonable use of the servient land.

Now consider whether Debbie's claim to a right to light to the windows in the cottage could have the qualities and characteristics of an easement according to *Re Ellenborough Park* [1956].

CONSIDER THIS – 1

What difference could it make to your response if:

- Lydia was claiming a right to 'wander at will' around the land now belonging the Debbie, and
- Debbie is claiming a general right to light, rather than to the pre-existing windows in the cottage?

---

20 [2014] EWCA Civ 1769.

ACQUISITION OF AN EASEMENT OR PROFIT

Easements and profits may exist as legal rights; they are included interests listed in s 1 of the LPA 1925. However, to exist in law, as with any right or interest in land, certain conditions must be satisfied:

- The easement or profit must be held for an interest equivalent to an estate in fee simple *or* a term of years absolute per s 1(2)(a) of the LPA 1925.
- The easement or profit must be created expressly by deed, be implied, or be acquired through the operation of statute or prescription.
- If granted out of registered land, the easement or profit must be completed by registration in accordance with s 27(2)(d) of the Land Registration Act 2002 (LRA 2002). It will not operate at law until this is done under s 27(1).

If these legal requirements are not met or the grant was not out of a legal estate, then the easements or profits may be equitable. If a deed was not used, then the easement will arise in equity only if enforceable under the Rule in *Walsh v Lonsdale* (1882).[21] However, to be specifically enforceable equitable easements and profits must comply with s 2 of the Law of Property (Miscellaneous Provisions) Act 1989 and the formalities of a contract. This means:

- the document must be in writing;
- it must contain the main terms of the agreement;
- it must be signed by both parties.

DISTINGUISHING BETWEEN A GRANT AND A RESERVATION

An easement or a profit may come into existence as either a grant or a reservation. It is very important that you can spot the difference between the two. If an easement is not created expressly, there are many more ways to argue an implied grant has occurred than are available for a failure to reserve one.

Grant

A grant arises where a landowner gives an adjoining landowner the right of an easement over his land and may be expressly or impliedly granted. For example, the landowner sells part of his land but grants a right of way to the purchaser over the land he (the landowner) retains.

Reservation

A reservation occurs where the landowner reserves for his land an easement over a portion he is conveying to a third party for the benefit of the land he (the landowner) has retained.

---

21 (1882) 21 Ch D 9.

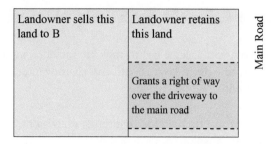

Figure 12.3 An example of a grant upon the sale of part of a property

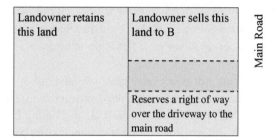

Figure 12.4 An example of a reservation upon the sale of part of a property

APPLY YOUR LEARNING – TASK 3

Is the right of way that Lydia is attempting to claim over the land she sold a grant or a reservation?

What about the right to light Debbie claims was part of the sale of the land she purchased?

GRANT OF AN EASEMENT

Express words of grant

If the easement or profit is made expressly, express words of grant will be used in an independent deed or in a deed of sale i.e. a transfer or TR1.[22] The deed *must* comply with s 52(1) LPA. An example of the wording used could be

'A hereby grants to B a right of way over the area of A's land coloured red on the plan attached for the benefit of the land coloured blue'

---

22 Public utility companies will often have easements over land owned by private individuals in order to gain access to the service media, for example the running of pipes and wires under people's properties to deliver gas, electricity water etc. Statute gives to such companies the right to easements over private land even though the utility companies do not own a correlating dominant tenement.

Implied grant

An implied grant will be considered in situations where there is no evidence of an express grant in a deed. When we are considering whether or not an easement has been implied, we are looking at a sale of a piece of land where the person who has been sold the parcel is arguing that he should have been granted an express right when he bought it. In essence, that a right was or should have been granted to him in the transfer deed but it was overlooked.

The law will help a buyer in this situation if it means that not granting the easement would mean that the seller would be derogating from his grant i.e. he is unable to use the land for the purpose it was purchased for. On every sale of land, an owner gives an implied guarantee to a buyer that he has good title to the land. This is his grant. Clearly if the land cannot be accessed without, for example, a right of way over the land the owner retains, this guarantee of title is undermined by not granting the right of way that is needed. This is known as a derogation from the grant[23] to the buyer as he has gone back on the guarantee to the buyer. Hence: 'A grantor having given a thing … is not to take away the means of enjoying it with the other'.[24]

> TUTOR TIP – 3
>
> ....
>
> Remember that you can only argue an implied grant of an easement *if* you have first established that the right is capable of being an easement under the *Re Ellenborough* tests.

An implied grant of an easement can be established in one of four ways, as set out in Figure 12.5.

Necessity

Arguing an implied grant of an easement in a transfer by means of necessity will only be successful in situations where the land cannot be used but for the easement over the land retained by the transferor. It is insufficient for it to be highly desirable.[25] As such, it usually concerns the need for an easement of right of way as without the easement the land concerned will be 'landlocked' by other land, i.e. there will be no legal right to get to and from the land.

The use of the easement *must* be essential to the use of the land, not just more convenient; even access by boat has stopped entitlement to an implied easement of necessity.[26] The necessity must also arise at the date of the transfer to the buyer, otherwise they have not derogated from their grant, as held in *Union Lighterage Co v London Graving Dock Co* [1902].[27]

----

23 A grantor may not derogate from his grant – *Aldridge v Wright* [1929] 2 KB 117 at 130.
24 Bowen LJ in *Birmingham, Dudley and District Banking Co v Ross* (1888) 38 Ch D 295 at 313.
25 *Pryce v McGuiness* [1966] Qd R 591.
26 *Manjang v Drammeh* [1990] 61 P & CR 194.
27 [1902] 2 Ch 557.

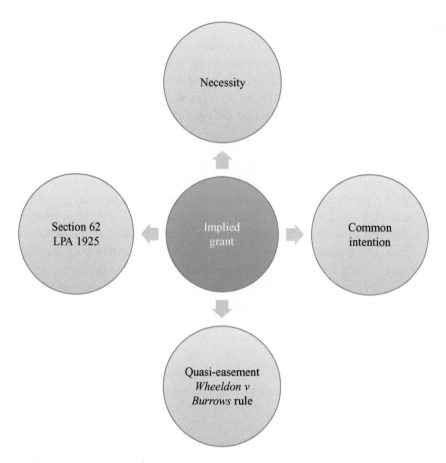

Figure 12.5 Circumstances for implying the grant of an easement

It is, therefore, difficult to argue necessity. Furthermore, even if successful there will only be a duty to provide reasonable access and not necessarily the route that would be preferred.[28]

Common Intention

There may be implied grant of an easement to give effect to a common intention of the seller and the buyer. In *Pwllbach Colliery Co Ltd v Woodman* [1915][29] Lord Parker advised that:

....

28 *Pearson v Spencer* (1861) 1 B&S 571; 121 ER 827.
29 [1915] AC 634; 84 LJKB 874.

The law will readily imply the grant or reservation of such easements as may be necessary to give effect to the common intention of the parties to a grant of real property, with reference to the manner or purposes in and for which the land granted or some land retained by the grantor is to be used.

It can be argued in situations where there is a clear purpose for which the property sold was to be used but the parties at the time of the sale of the land simply forgot or did not realise that the inclusion of an express grant of an easement was required, an implied easement under the principle of common intention may be granted. There was a common intention that the land sold should be used for a particular purpose and an easement was required over the land retained by the seller to give effect to this purpose then it may be granted.

KEY CASE: *WONG V BEAUMONT PROPERTY TRUST LTD* [1965] 1 QB 173; [1964] 2 ALL ER 119

An easement may be implied even though the parties did not realise it was necessary at the time of the grant. In *Wong*, Beaumont Property Trust, the landlord, granted a lease of the basement premises to Wong to use as a restaurant. The basement premises had no windows. The lease contained covenants on the part of the tenant stating that he would comply with all public health requirements and would eliminate all noxious smells. In order to comply with this covenant, Wong was required to install a ventilation system, which had to go through the premises above the restaurant, which were retained by the landlord. Both the landlord and the tenant at the time of granting the lease had intended that the premises should be used as a restaurant and that the tenant would have to comply with local authority public health requirements. It was held that an easement to install and use a ventilation duct was therefore required for the tenant to comply with his obligations under the lease though the parties did not realise that this was necessary at the time the lease was granted. As Lord Denning MR noted:

> That was 'a definite and particular manner' in which the business had to be conducted. It could not be carried on in that manner at all unless a ventilation system was installed by a duct of this kind. In these circumstances it seems to me that, if the business is to be carried on at all – if, in the words of Rolle's Abridgment, 15 the lessee is to 'have any benefit by the grant' at all – he must ... be able to put a ventilation duct up the wall.

OTHER EXAMPLES OF COMMON INTENTION

CORY V DAVIES [1923] 2 CH 95

A row of terraced houses was built with a drive in front and an exit to the road at each end; one owner barred the exit. No express grant of an easement had been made in favour of all the house owners over all parts of the drive. But it was held that the original parties had a common intention that the drive should be used in this way.

STAFFORD V LEE (1993) 63 P & CR 172

An area of land fronting a private drive was sold with no right over the driveway, retained by the seller, expressly granted. The plot when sold was, however, illustrated on the plan as adjoining two other plots both of which had houses erected on them. New owners of the plot obtained planning permission for a house, but wanted to use the driveway retained by the sellers. It was held that the plan formed part of the agreement and showed a common intention of the original parties at the time of the grant.

Nourse LJ explained:

> [T]he significant … feature of the plan is that it delineates, as the land conveyed, a plot adjoining and of comparable area to other enclosures, each adjoining the other, which … are seen to be plots of land on which dwellings have already been constructed.

The parties could only have intended the lot be used for the construction of another dwelling. The result was an implied vehicular use over the driveway for residential use, including traffic for the construction of the house.

KENT V KAVANAGH [2006] EWCA CIV 162; [2006] 3 WLR 572

Semi-detached houses had a boundary running down the middle of a narrow pathway that they had always shared. The lease of the two properties made no reference to their rights and a dispute emerged. It was held that as the path could not be used by either tenant without passing over the half that lay on the land of the other tenant the common intention must have been that the path be shared.

DAVIES V BRAMWELL [2007] EWCA CIV 821; [2008] 1 P & CR D4

The common intention of the parties was that servicing and repair of cars would take place in the garage on the land sold. This required a ramp for access to the garage which, to be used safely, meant vehicles would have to be driven across the seller's retained property. Common intention was again found.

Quasi-Easements or the Rule in Wheeldon v Burrows

Quasi-easements or the rule in *Wheeldon v Burrows* [1879][30] operates where there is a subdivision of land. It is continuing a practice that was used when the land was under single ownership and is to continue upon the subdivision. It is known as a quasi-easement as it could never be a right when the land was under single ownership. Figure 12.6 illustrates the position under single ownership, and Figure 12.7 after subdivision.

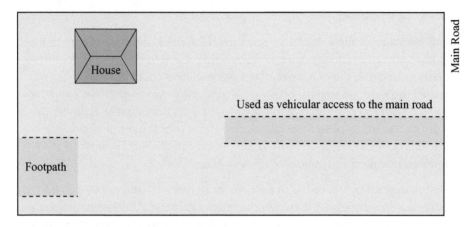

Figure 12.6 Quasi-easement: under single ownership

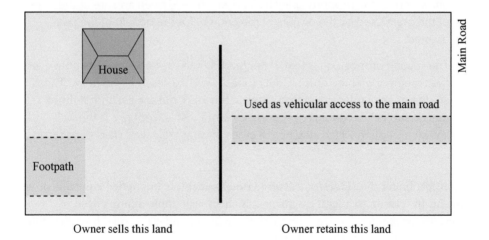

Figure 12.7 Quasi-easement: after subdivision

So, when the land is subdivided and sold to B, the rule will operate to give B, here the new owner of the house, such rights that the original owner used while he owned the land so as to make proper use of it.

---

30 (1879) 12 Ch D 31.

KEY CASE: *WHEELDON V BURROWS* (1879) 12 CH D 31

A workshop and an adjacent piece of land belonging to the same owner were put up for sale by auction. The piece of land was sold but the workshop was not. A month after the piece of land was conveyed to the purchaser the vendor agreed to sell the workshop to another person, and in due time conveyed it to him, the workshop back windows overlooking and receiving their light from the piece of land first sold.

It was held that, as the seller had not reserved the right of access of light to the windows when the land was sold, no such right passed to the purchaser of the workshop, and that the purchaser of the piece of land could build so as to obstruct the windows of the workshop. Second, whatever might have been the case had both lots been sold at the same sale by auction, there was, under the circumstances, no implied reservation of any right over the piece of land first sold. As a general rule for an implied right to be established Thesiger LJ at 49 explained that two propositions must exist that:

> [O]n the grant by the owner of a tenement of part of that tenement as it is then used and enjoyed, there will pass to the grantee all those continuous and apparent easements (by which, of course, I mean quasi easements), or, in other words, all those easements which are necessary to the reasonable enjoyment of the property granted, and which have been and are at the time of the grant used by the owners of the entirety for the benefit of the part granted.

> The second proposition is that, if the grantor intends to reserve any right over the tenement granted, it is his duty to reserve it expressly in the grant. Those are the general rules governing cases of this kind, but the second of those rules is subject to certain exceptions. One of those exceptions is the well-known exception which attaches to cases of what are called ways of necessity.

It is possible under the *Wheeldon v Burrows* rule to establish an implied equitable or legal easement. In relation to a legal easement it is effectively implied into a deed of conveyance or transfer. To argue an implied easement under this rule, however, four components must be established (Figure 12.8).

Continuous – The right must have been used 'continuously' and over a substantial period of time as seen in *Hansford v Jago* [1921].[31] Whilst this requires the right to have been used regularly it does *not* have to be consistently used i.e. used every day or on every occasion.

---

31 [1921] 1 Ch 322; 90 LJ Ch 129.

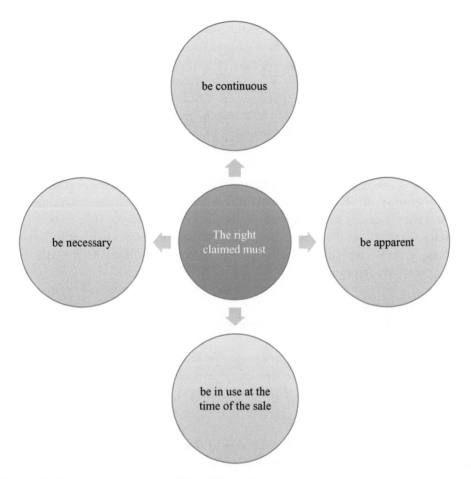

Figure 12.8 Requirements for a Wheeldon v Burrows quasi-easement

Apparent – The right claimed must be apparent and visible to the purchaser prior to purchase of the land. To argue this, the right must be capable of being seen upon 'a careful inspection by a person ordinarily conversant with the subject' as established in *Pyer v Carter* [1857].[32]

In use at the time of the sale – The right claimed must have been in use at the time of the purchase e.g. an easement of support for a building erected after the purchase of the land cannot be a right claimed under this rule, although an established means of access may not fail the test because it has fallen out of use for a short period of time before the sale to the purchaser. In *Costagliola v English* [1969],[33] the right of way being claimed had not been used for approximately ten months prior to the sale due to the fact that the landowner had an alternative access available. Here it did not negate a claim of an implied grant under the *Wheeldon v Burrows* rule.

32 [1857] 156 ER 1472.
33 (1969) 210 EG 1425.

The right claimed however *must* have been in use under the same ownership *and* occupation as was demonstrated in *Kent v Kavanagh* [2006].[34] In *Kent* it was held that there was not an implied easement of a right of way on foot over that half of the path, which ran between two properties. Whilst the land had been under the same ownership part of the land had been occupied by a tenant. Chadwick LJ held that it was 'an unnecessary and artificial construct to hold that the grantor, as common owner and the landlord of the land conveyed, is himself using the rights over the retained land which his tenant enjoys under the lease.'

Necessary – The right claimed must be 'necessary to the reasonable enjoyment of the property granted'. In *Ward v Kirkland* [1967][35] it was held that the right to maintain the wall was not reasonably necessary to the enjoyment of the property. The cases in relation to the need for the right to be necessary have been split as to whether or not this component is a separate element or simply required to establish that the right used is continuous and apparent.

Section 62(1) of the LPA 1925
Section 62(1) of the LPA 1925 largely underpins the rule in *Wheeldon v Burrows*.

> A conveyance shall be deemed to include and shall by virtue of the Act operate to convey, with the land, all … easements, rights and advantages, whatsoever, appertaining to or reputed to appertain to the land … at the time of the Conveyance.

It is called a word-saving provision and is very similar in nature to s 78 of the LPA 1925, which implies into every creation of a freehold covenant words that deem that it is made for the benefit of successors in title as we will see in Chapter 14. The effect of s 62 of the LPA 1925 is to automatically imply into a conveyance or transfer deed of any land all easements benefiting the land at the time of the transfer, although the provisions of s 62(1) can be excluded expressly in the transfer deed or conveyance. It is not possible to use s 62 by a purchaser in equity as was shown in the case of *Borman v Griffith* [1930][36] which related to a purchase which was a contract for a lease for more than two years.

TUTOR TIP – 5

Section 62 is *only* activated by a formal conveyance of land and therefore will only operate on the transfer of a legal estate. It is important to note s 205(1)(ii) of the LPA 1925, which defines a conveyance as including: 'a mortgage, charge, lease, assent, vesting declaration, vesting instrument, release and every other assurance of property or of an interest therein by any instrument, except a will.'

34 [2006] EWCA Civ 162; [2007] Ch 1.
35 [1967] Ch 493; [1966] 1 WLR 601.
36 [1930] 1 Ch 493.

Section 62 of the LPA 1925 can also have an unintended effect by creating rights that, while in use before the sale of the benefited land, were not previously categorised as easements, for example upgrading a licence to an easement upon transfer, although it must be noted that upon converting a prior permission to an easement, the right must still satisfy all the characteristics of an easement as seen in *Wright v Macadam* [1949].[37] Therefore, purely personal rights will not be upgraded, neither, too, will rights that are too vague or insubstantial to form the basis of an easement. This was seen in *Green v Ashco Horticulturist Limited* [1966][38] where a bare permission had been given by the landlord to the tenant to use an access across his premises. The access was rarely exercised and the permission was given in each instance. The courts held that the right was too fragile to be capable of being converted into an easement under s 62.

The use of s 62 is much wider than the rule in *Wheeldon v Burrows* [1879] as it can be used for both easements and profits and with s 62 there is no requirement to demonstrate that the right claimed is, 'reasonably necessary to the enjoyment of the land'. Although, in order to benefit the land there is usually a test that the right is continuous and apparent.

Unlike the rule for necessity and common intention, which require a common owner and a subdivision, s 62 of the LPA 1925 will only operate where there had previously been separate ownership *or* occupation of the land concerned, though unlike the rule in *Wheeldon v Burrows* it does not have to be separate ownership *and* occupation, as demonstrated in *International Tea Stores Co v Hobbs* [1903].[39] Here Mr Hobbs, the defendant, was the owner of two properties; he granted a lease of one to the plaintiff then subsequently granted a bare licence. The tenant then purchased the freehold reversion of the property from Mr Hobbs. It was then claimed that the licence had been upgraded into an easement under s 62 by virtue of the transfer of the freehold from Mr Hobbs to the tenant. The court held that because a tenant occupied one property at the time the bare licence was created, s 62 could succeed. The precise nature of the role of diversity of occupation was also discussed in the case of *Sovmots Investments v Secretary of State for the Environment* [1977][40] in which it was held that s 62 does not apply to compulsory purchases of land under statute.

APPLY YOUR LEARNING – TASK 4

Is it possible for Debbie to argue that her right to light has been created by an implied grant? If so, which of necessity, common intention, the rule in *Wheeldon v Burrows* and s 62 is likely to be successful?

---

37 [1949] 2 KB 744; [1949] 2 All ER 565.
38 [1966] 2 All ER 232; [1966] 1 WLR 889.
39 [1903] 2 Ch 165; 72 LJ Ch 543.
40 [1979] AC 144; [1977] 2 All ER 385.

RESERVATION OF AN EASEMENT

As the law dislikes any derogation from grant, it is a general rule of application that a reservation can only be claimed by express provision. There are two exceptions, however, and it is possible to argue an implied reservation of an easement by either:

- necessity.
- common intention.

The rule in *Wheeldon v Burrows* cannot be argued for a reservation of an easement nor does s 62 apply. It should also be noted that common intention is applied more strictly for reservations with a higher burden of proof to establish it.[41]

The Court of Appeal was willing to imply a reservation in a case where the intention was arguably obvious.

KEY CASE: *PECKHAM V ELLISON* [2000] 79 P & CR 276

The case concerned two neighbouring houses that had formed part of a terrace of council houses owned by the local authority. Since the houses were built in the 1940s, the tenants of number 16 (along with all the other owners of houses in the terrace) had used a path over number 15 to get to their back door. Later, the tenants of both houses bought them from the local authority. Number 15 was sold first with no express reservation of any right of way over the path leading to the back door of number 16. The question was whether there had been, because of the exceptional circumstance, an implied reservation. It was held that there had been a common intention to reserve a right of way.

APPLY YOUR LEARNING – TASK 5

Is it possible for Lydia to argue that her 'easement' has been created by an implied reservation? Do you think she could argue necessity or common intention?

---

41 *Re Webb's Lease* [1951] Ch 808; [1951] 2 All ER 131.

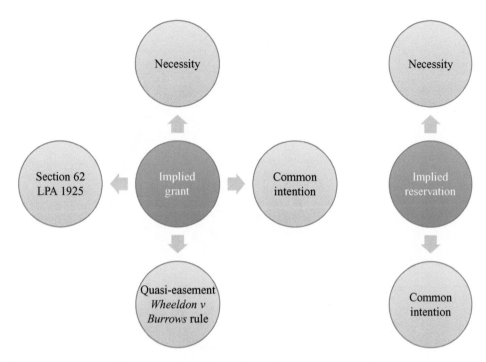

Figure 12.9 Limited circumstances for implying the reservation of an easement

PRESCRIPTION

Prescription recognises rights that have been used and built up over a long period of time but have done so without the normal formalities. Legal easements and profits are established by prescription by showing that the person has exercised the easement or profit claimed for a very long time.

The basis of acquiring a right by prescription, however, is not just long use, but also a history of continuous use *as of right*. The right must be exercised *nec vi, nec clam, nec precario* as established in *Union Lighterage Co v London Graving Dock Co* [1902].[42]

NEC VI – WITHOUT FORCE

The basic position is that there must be no level of violence used in the enforcement of the right. Equally, though, if the enforcement of the right is met with protest by the servient owner, the right will be taken to have been exercised with force.

---

42 [1902] 2 Ch 557; 71 LJ Ch 791.

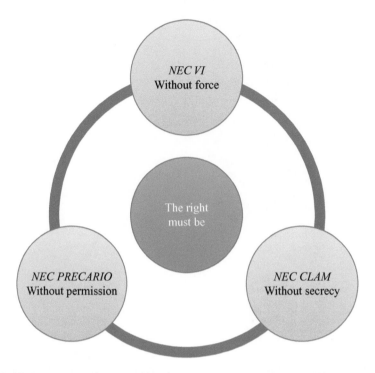

Figure 12.10 Prescription: use as of right

NEC CLAM – WITHOUT SECRECY

The exercise of the right must be obvious. The case of *Union Lighterage Co v London Graving Dock Co* [1902] the defendant fixed the side of a dock to the soil of a wharf by means of underground rods, which remained undetected for 20 years. Here it was held that there was no right established by long use due to the secrecy of the use of the right.

NEC PRECARIO – WITHOUT PERMISSION

The person claiming the right must not have sought permission to use the right. If the right is exercised as a result of permission by the servient landowner the right is not exercised as of right and therefore will not be a right capable of being granted by prescription. Therefore, a licence to graze cannot be claimed as a prescriptive profit.

Under common law there must be some level of acquiescence by the servient landowner in the rights exercised by the dominant owner. This compliance or submission is distinct, however, from granting permission and will be more akin to passive assent or agreement without protest i.e. having knowledge of the action being taken by the dominant landowner the servient landowner simply allowed it to continue without protest. The case of *Dalton v Henry Angus & Co* (1881)[43] is helpful in

....

43 (1881) 6 App Cas 740.

explaining what acquiescence is and what must be demonstrated on the part of the servient landowner. Acquiescence by the servient landowner requires:

- **A Knowledge of the Acts Done** – The question to ask is would the reasonable person be aware the third party, the dominant landowner, is asserting the rights claimed?
- **A Power to Stop the Acts** – Does the person have sufficient control over the servient land to stop the acts i.e. is he in *possession of the land as a freeholder*?
- **An Abstinence From Exercising Such Power** – Once it has been established that the servient landowner had knowledge of the acts on the land and having the power to stop them, it must be shown that the servient landowner did not stop the right continuing. Mere tolerance of the acts on the basis of good neighbourliness may not be enough to be construed against the servient landowner. The general principle is that the courts do not want to stifle neighbourly civility or for acts of cooperation between neighbours to be used against people to their detriment.

WHAT IS MEANT BY LONG USER?

Once it has been established that the right claimed has been exercised without force, secrecy or permission, the requisite time period must be established.

There are three different routes of prescription available. If you find this confusing, you are in good company as we will shortly explore a Law Commission report into reforming easements and having multiple overlapping routes is one of the things they would like to see reformed.

Common law prescription

The use claimed must have been a continuous use from 'time immemorial'. The phase 'time immemorial' means that the right must have been 'ancient beyond memory or record'. In law if the right claimed could be shown as being used prior to 1189, it *must* have been rooted in a valid original grant. The year 1189 is seen as the date of legal memory according to the Statute of Westminster 1275. This is, somewhat artificially, classed as the start of legal memory and if it can be established that the right existed before then the right has existed since 'time immemorial' and will therefore succeed. In reality, however, this is impossible to establish and as such the courts moved to a position where *if* a use of the right claimed could be established for a period of 20 years or more there would be a presumption that the use had commenced before 1189.

The difficulty is that the presumption is often easy to rebut by showing that the right could not have existed in 1189 and, given that most extant houses were not even built at that time, a right to light to a particular window or a right to support from a neighbouring property could not have existed. Equally, properties may have been in the same ownership. So, other routes are also available.

Lost modern grant

The courts developed the doctrine of the 'modern lost grant' or as Lush LJ described it in *Dalton v Henry Angus Co* (1877)[44] as the 'revolting fiction of a lost grant'. Under this, 20 years' enjoyment is presumed as evidence that there was a grant (modern, as it happened sometime after 1189) and it has since been lost. The period of 20 years does not have to be immediately prior to the claim, it can be any 20 years of continuous uninterrupted use.

The Prescription Act 1832

The Prescription Act 1832 further supplements the common law rules on the acquisition of rights under the 'lost modern grant'.

Easements other than light – s 2

Under s 2, if the easement claimed has been enjoyed as of right and without interruption for at least 20 years prior to the commencement of court action then the court can grant a legal easement. Unlike under lost modern grant, it is not possible to choose any time period of uninterrupted use. However, the advantage is that an interruption to the right will only defeat a claim if the claimant had notice of the interruption *and* of the person making the interruption *and* then submitted to or acquiesced to that interruption for at least a year.

Additionally, if the easement claimed as of right has been used and enjoyed without interruption for 40 years it cannot be defeated unless it can be demonstrated that it was used with permission or had been expressly granted.

Easements in respect of light – s 3

Rights in respect of light are governed by s 3. The long user must establish a continuous period of use of 20 years without interruption. Again, they must establish that this right has been used and enjoyed without written consent. If this can be established the right becomes absolute and indefeasible.

Profits – s 1

The position in respect of profits is simply to that of rights other than light under s 4. The only difference is the length of time that must be proven. Under s 1, the profit claimed must have been enjoyed as of right and without interruption for at least 30 years prior to the commencement of court action. Then the court can grant a legal profit though, as with easements under s 4, it is possible to defeat them.

If the profit claimed as of right has been used and enjoyed without interruption for 60 years, however, it cannot be defeated and is deemed absolute and indefeasible, unless it can be demonstrated that it was used with permission or had been expressly granted.

---

44 (1877) 3 QBD 85.

Continuous use does not have to be established by the same owner of the dominant land for the period of time claimed.

Example

Anna owned the dominant land and used the right claimed for eight years, then Benedict owned the dominant land and used the right claimed for six years and currently Clare has owned the dominant land and used the right claimed for eight years. A period of 20 years can therefore be established by the accumulative use of the three owners of dominant land.

In order to prove this however each person will have to provide a statutory declaration stating:

■ the period of time they owned the dominant land;
■ that they used the right being claimed, and
■ that the right was exercised without force, secrecy or permission.

PROTECTION OF EASEMENTS AND PROFITS

THE BENEFIT OF PROFITS AND EASEMENTS

In unregistered land, legal easements and profits are annexed to the dominant land. Under s 62(1)(2) of the LPA 1925 legal easements and profits are automatically transferred on with any conveyance of a legal estate in the land as we have seen earlier. Profits in gross, however, are expressly assigned only by independent deeds. The grant of a new easement in unregistered land will not trigger a first registration, but once a first registration does take place the easement will be registered on the title register of the dominant land under section A the Property Register.

In registered land a legal easement or profit expressly created must be registered in order to bind under s 27(2)(d) of the LRA 2002. Once registered, however, it is integral to the dominant land and will pass for the benefit of future owners. If it has not been registered it will only be capable of passing as an interest in equity.

Equitable easement cannot be registered in the register for the dominant land either on first registration of the dominant land or subsequently, as the LRA 2002 only makes provision for the registration of legal interests under s 2.

THE BURDEN OF PROFITS AND EASEMENTS

In unregistered land, legal easements and profits bind the world and bind the purchaser of the servient land. As we have discussed earlier, the grant of an easement in unregistered land will not trigger a first registration of either the dominant or servient land; however, all legal easements and profits are classified as overriding interests upon first registration under sch 1, para 3 of the LRA 2002.

An equitable easement or profit must be registered as a Class D(iii) land charge to bind purchasers for money or money's worth. Estoppel easements are not capable of being registered under the Land Charges Act 1972 (LCA 1972) and therefore will only bind a third-party purchaser for value with actual or constructive notice of the circumstances giving rise to the estoppel.

In registered land a legal easement or profit expressly created is listed under s 27(2)(d) of the LRA 2002 and therefore must be registered under ss 32 and 38 of the LRA 2002 in order to bind under. If it is not registered, expressly created legal easements will only be equitable.

An easement created by prescription, or which is implied by the common law or statute does not need to be registered to be legal and is instead an overriding interest under sch 3, para 3 of the LRA 2002 if it is obvious on a reasonably careful inspection or has been exercised in the year preceding the transfer to the new owner, though it is possible to register an implied or prescriptive easement as appurtenant to the registered estate in the dominant land under r 73A of the Land Registration Rules 2003.

Equitable easements must be registered to be binding and must be registered as a notice on the register of the servient land under s 32 of the LRA 2002. Unregistered equitable easements will not bind third parties or subsequent owners of the servient land, nor are they capable of being overriding interests.

> **TUTOR TIP – 7**
> ....
>
> The same registration rules apply to profits as they do easements. However, you need to be aware of s 3(1)(d) of the LRA 2002, which makes profits in gross registerable in their own right.

EXTINGUISHMENT OF EASEMENT/PROFIT

Easements and profits can be extinguished in one of three ways:

- Merger of dominant and servient tenements.
- Express release.
- Implied release.

MERGER OF DOMINANT AND SERVIENT TENEMENTS

It is not possible to have an easement over your own land and therefore when both the dominant and servient land come into the same ownership the easement will be extinguished.

EXPRESS RELEASE

As we know a legal interest is created expressly in a deed and the transfer of a legal interest is completed in a deed *and* the release of a legal interest is undertaken in a deed. Both the servient and dominant landowners will enter into a deed of release to extinguish the legal easement or profit.

If should be remembered, however, that as it is registration that gives a legal interest its power, an application must be made to the Land Registry to cancel any entries in the register relating to the easement.

IMPLIED RELEASE

It is possible to extinguish an easement or profit by implication i.e. where there is an abandonment of the right and a clear intention by the parties that the right should be released.

Abandonment is not easy to infer or establish. The conduct and the action of the parties must be clear and demonstrate that the use of the right has come to an end; for example, the dominant landowner stops using the right of way and blocks up the point of access from his land to the servient land by building a wall across the access point. Simply discontinuing exercising the use of the right without doing anything additional is insufficient to establish such an intention and unlikely to lead to a finding of abandonment.

In *Gotobed v Pridmore* [1971][45] Buckley LJ held that to establish abandonment of an easement the conduct of the dominant landowner must be such to, 'make it clear that he had at the relevant time a firm intention that neither he or any successors in title of his should thereafter make use of the easement.'

In *Benn v Hardinge* [1992][46] the claimant Mr Benn had owned the dominant land for 20 years. Mr and Mrs Hardinge were the owners of the servient land, which was situated to the south of Mr Benn's land. A track ran along part of the boundary of the claimant's land, with part of the track running between two entrances, A and B, to two of his fields. Neither the claimant nor his predecessors in title had ever sought to use either entrance B or the track leading to it from A for any purpose since they had alternative

45 [1971] EGD 114.
46 (1992) 66 P & CR 246; (1992) Times, 13 October.

access and it appeared that this right had not been exercised in approximately 175 years.
Mr Benn however now wished to use the track and entrance B when other parts of his
land became waterlogged.

The court held that whilst the right had been given up there was not a clear intention
to show that the right had been abandoned or had come to an end. Abandonment
could not be presumed merely because no one used it, even if that had been for a
period of 175 years. Mr Benn was therefore entitled to exercise the right of way along
the track.

DISCUSSION

The Law Commission has identified a number of recommended reforms in *Making
Land Work: Easements, Covenants and Profits à Prendre*.[47] The reforms extend over a
number of different aspects and it is very important that you read the document. What
follows is a summary of possible amendments, split into three parts:

- The nature and definition of easements.
- The creation of easements.
- Abandonment.

NATURE

There must be a dominant tenement and a servient tenement.

- It is suggested this should be retained. Recognising easements 'in gross' would
  result in too many being created, and there would be no way of limiting their impact
  to that strictly necessary to the need of the dominant land.

The easement must accommodate the dominant tenement.

- It is suggested this should be retained, although some consultees suggested it
  caused problems for developers wanting to create easements in favour of land not
  yet in their ownership.

The dominant and servient tenements must be owned by different persons.

- The logic is that no one needs an easement over their own land, and so cannot have
  given one to themselves!
- It is suggested, however, that this be changed because of the complexities
  created by the registered land system.

---

47 Law Commission, *Making Land Work: Easements, Covenants and Profits à Prendre* (Law Com No 327, 2011).

■ Where there is a developer building a large estate (perhaps hundreds of houses),
the fact that the easements can only be created on the sale of plots (when the
developer ceases to be the legal owner and so the estates are owned by different
persons) means there are lots of easements all being created at the same time,
and not necessarily in the right order. Things after, can and do go wrong.

The easement must be capable of forming the subject matter of a grant.

■ This relates to the need for clear easements that are not excessive in their impact on
the enjoyment of the servient land. In particular:

- An easement cannot amount to exclusive possession – that must be a lease if for a
  set duration, or a freehold if forever. Some of the cases relating to storage, like the
  coal-shed case, are discussed and it is determined that post *Street v Mountford*
  [1985] it should never be possible to claim such ownership through an easement.
- There is also the 'ouster' principle i.e. is the interference taking away the
  reasonable enjoyment? This is a flexible concept and can be hard to predict in
  practice. This is criticised; the report concludes that provided the negotiation
  has not reached the point of agreeing to exclusive possession, parties should
  be free to agree to anything they wish.
- This would mean that an easement that stops short of exclusive possession,
  even if it deprives the owner of much of the use of his land, or indeed of all
  reasonable use of it, would be valid.
- Taking an example, even an exclusive right to park would be okay provided
  the owner of the servient land could make some limited use of his property.

IMPLIED CREATION

The first point is that there is no suggestion that the option of implied easements should
be removed altogether. The relevance of the principle of non-derogation is important.

There is an overall suggestion that the distinction between implied grant and implied
reservation (treated far more harshly) should be removed – there is no real reason to
assume that the seller of land is in a better position to understand the need for formality
than the buyer.

- Necessity – currently available for grants and reservations.
- Common intention/intended use – currently available for grants and reservations,
  but harder to establish for reservations. It is suggested that grants and
  reservations should receive the same treatment.
- *Wheeldon v Burrows*/quasi-easements – currently available for grants only. It is
  suggested that it should be made available for reservations too.

There is also a suggestion that rather than having the three methods of implication set
out above, there should be one single statutory test.

Various simple tests were suggested, but the consultation found that all the current principles are important so all the elements of those tests would need to be retained.

The one decided upon was whether the easement was necessary and reasonable to the enjoyment of the land at the date of sale.

Factors to consider are set out as:

- The use of the land at the time of the grant.
- The presence on the servient land of any relevant physical features.
- Any intention for the future use of the land, known to both parties at the time of the grant.
- So far as relevant, the available routes for the easement sought.
- The potential interference with the servient land or inconvenience to the servient owner.

Section 62 of the LPA 1925 is given particular attention, and it is suggested that it be removed in terms of its ability to create new easements ('statutory magic').

- It is considered unfair that friendly permission be converted into legal rights, simply because the landlord was not aware of the need to exclude s 62.
- The idea is the new 'one test' set out above would catch those situations where a right a tenant had enjoyed was 'forgotten' to be incorporated into a conveyance to them – removing the need for the blunt instrument and inflexible approach of s 62.
- The ability to make leasehold easements into freehold easements (i.e. where a tenant buys the land they once leased) would remain – it seems clear that unless said otherwise formal legal easements agreed to by the parties would form part of such a sale.

PRESCRIPTION

The lack of documentation makes proof very difficult, as well as causing issues with determining the scope of the easement.

There was a suggestion that prescription could be removed, but that idea was rejected in the consultation, after other options were considered and rejected as unworkable.

However, it is suggested that the common law prescription rules be removed as they are a total fiction – everyone knows it is not really the case that the paperwork has been lost!

Instead, the suggestion is to have one statutory period of 20 years. It would have no provision for interruption, there would be no need to wait for litigation to claim the right and get it registered and there would be no automatic loss of the right if there is a delay in claiming it.

This continues to raise the issue (currently faced in the lost modern grant) of a buyer finding they are subject to an easement that has not been used much for a few years but was used continually for 20 years before.

One proposal was to require registration, but it was decided that overriding status is still needed.

However, it is stressed that sch 3 of the LRA 2002 already confirms easements can override only if known of, visible or used in the past year.

ABANDONMENT

As abandonment is hard to show (note that 175 years of non-use was insufficient), it is proposed that for new easements the Lands Chamber should have a power to discharge them.

After 20 years on non-use, there would be a rebuttable presumption of abandonment.

CONSIDER THIS – 2

To what extent to you agree with the reforms suggested by the Law Commission?

END OF CHAPTER SUMMARY

- An easement is a right annexed to land to use other land in different ownership in a particular manner and for its benefit or to prevent the owner of the other land from using his land in a particular manner.
- A profit is a right to take part of the soil or some natural produce on the 'servient land'. Profits, unlike, easements can exist 'in gross'.
- To be called an easement, the right must possess a number of essential characteristics first identified and defined in the case of *Re Ellenborough Park* [1956].
- Easements and profits may exist as legal or equitable interests.
- To exist in law the easement or profit must be held for an interest equivalent to an estate in fee simple *or* a term of years absolute per s 1(2)(a) of the LPA 1925; *and* must be created by deed, statute or prescription.
- It is possible to create an easement by an implied grant. This will be considered in situations where there is no evidence of an express grant in a deed.
- An implied grant can be argued in one of four ways: necessity, common intention, quasi-easements and under s 62 of the LPA 1925.

- Prescription recognises rights that have been used and built up over a long period of time but have done so without the normal formalities. Legal easements and profits can be established by prescription in accordance with the Prescription Act 1832.
- Easement must be protected by either registration or be virtue of their overriding status.
- Easements and profits can be extinguished by the merger of dominant and servient tenements, express release or by abandonment.

PREPARING FOR ASSESSMENTS QUESTIONS

ESSAY QUESTION

In *Re Ellenborough Park* [1956] Ch 131, the court approved four rules, which could be used to establish whether or not a claimed right may stand as an easement. The rules established in *Re Ellenborough Park* certainly help to flesh out the reference in s 1(2)(a) of the Law of Property Act 1925, however, they also give rise to much complexity in their application.

With reference both to the case of *Re Ellenborough Park* and further case law, discuss the extent to which the rules established by *Re Ellenborough Park* may be used to clearly and effectively define an easement.

PROBLEM QUESTION

In 2008, Amelie purchased two adjoining freehold properties: The Cottage Kitchen and The Pudding Plot. Both properties were registered with HM Land Registry.

The Cottage Kitchen property comprises a large residence with an attached barn, which was converted for use as a bakery in 1980. Amelie used outbuildings at The Pudding Plot to park her delivery vans.

Until recently, both properties had direct access to a busy main road which runs along the front boundaries. The access point from The Pudding Plot to the main road, however, was quite dangerous to use as visibility there was restricted. In order to avoid using this difficult access point, whenever Amelie wished to go to and from the main road to The Pudding Plot, Amelie would use the access point located at The Cottage Kitchen by driving over a track which ran through The Cottage Kitchen from The Pudding Plot.

In 2013, Amelie decided that she needed to raise some capital for her business. Amelie moved her vans off The Pudding Plot and sold the plot to Leon. The transfer deed made no reference to easements.

Leon built a residence on The Pudding Plot and Leon went to and from this property by using the track which ran over The Cottage Kitchen to the safe access point. In

2015, Leon landscaped the garden around his residence and blocked off the direct access point from The Pudding Plot to the main road.

Last month, Amelie and Leon had an argument and now Amelie is refusing to let Leon use the track across The Cottage Kitchen to gain access to and egress from his property.

Advise Leon.

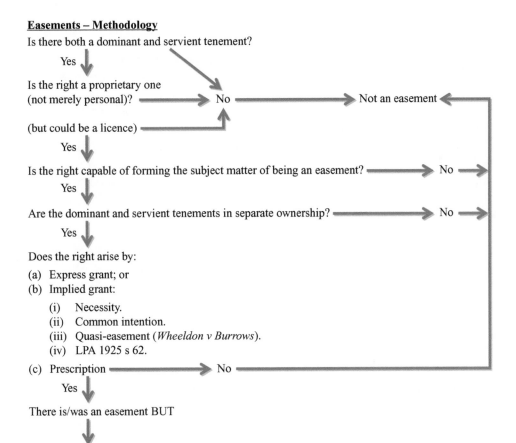

Easements – Methodology

Is there both a dominant and servient tenement?

Yes ↓

Is the right a proprietary one (not merely personal)? ⟶ No ⟶ Not an easement ⟵

(but could be a licence) ⟶

Yes ↓

Is the right capable of forming the subject matter of being an easement? ⟶ No ⟶

Yes ↓

Are the dominant and servient tenements in separate ownership? ⟶ No ⟶

Yes ↓

Does the right arise by:

(a) Express grant; or
(b) Implied grant:

    (i)   Necessity.
    (ii)   Common intention.
    (iii) Quasi-easement (*Wheeldon v Burrows*).
    (iv) LPA 1925 s 62.

(c) Prescription ⟶ No ⟶

Yes ↓

There is/was an easement BUT

↓

Has the easement been protected?

(a) Equitable easements over unregistered land must be protected with a land charge under the LCA 1972, Class D(iii).
(b) An express legal easement over registered land must be registered to bind under s 27 of the LRA 2002. If not, it is equitable.
(c) Equitable easements over registered land must be recorded with a notice under s 32 of the LRA 2002.
(d) Implied legal easements are overriding (unless or until registered) under Sch 3 para 3 of the LRA 2002.

↓

Has the easement been abandoned?

Figure 12.11 Is there an easement? Putting it all together

FURTHER READING

- Barnsley, DG, 'Equitable Easements 60 Years On' (1999) 115 LQR 89. A consideration of equitable easements from how they are created, how they work in registered land, how the benefit is transferred and how they are protected against purchaser for value of legal estate.
- Bogusz, B, 'The Doctrine of Lost Modern Grant: Back to The Future or Time to Move On?' [2013] Conv 198. Looks at the doctrine of lost modern grant in the light of Comments on the Law Commission's proposal to introduce a modified version of the doctrine.
- Burns, FR, 'Prescriptive Easements in England & Legal "Climate Change" ' [2007] Conv 133. Examines prescriptive easements and discusses whether they are still relevant today.
- Dixon, M, 'Editor's Notebook' [2011] Conv 167. Discusses a number of cases, including *Magrath v Parkside Hotels Ltd* [2011] on issues relating to the creation of easements, in light of the forthcoming Law Commission recommendations.
- Dixon, M, 'Editor's Notebook' [2012] Conv 1. Reflects on and discusses the Law Commission's June 2011 report *Making Land Work: Easements, Covenants and Profits à Prendre*.
- Douglas, S, 'How to Reform s 62 of the Law of Property Act 1925' [2015] Conv 13. Considers s 62 in the light of the Law Commission report *Making Land Work: Easements, Covenants and Profits à Prendre*. Reviews the criticisms made of the powers of s 62 and discusses potential problems with the suggested reforms.
- Gardner, S, 'The Grant of an Easement Under the Law of Property Act 1925 s 62' (2016) 132 LQR, 192. Considers the Court of Appeal decision in *Wood v Waddington* [2015].
- Harpum, C, 'The Acquisition of Easements' (1992) 51 CLJ 220. Examines the circumstances in which a quasi-easement will be upgraded into an easement under s 62 of 1925 Act.
- Pulleyn, S, 'Equitable Easements Revisited' [2012] Conv 387. Assesses whether a document in accordance with Law of Property Act 1925 s 53(1)(a) creates a valid easement in equity or whether such an easement can only be created with a specifically enforceable contract.
- Sara, C, 'Prescription – What Is It For?' [2004] Conv 13. Analyses the rationale behind the common law doctrine of prescription.
- Tee, L, 'Metamorphoses and s 62 of the Law of Property Act 1925' [1998] Conv 115. Considers the problems caused by case law on effect of s 62 in deeming conveyances to include all easements and rights appertaining to land.
- West, J, 'Wheeldon v Burrows Revisited' [1995] Conv 346. Looks at the practical implications of *Wheeldon v Burrows* and how this works in practice.

13

CHAPTER 13
MORTGAGES

CHAPTER AIMS AND OBJECTIVES

In this chapter we will explore mortgages, which most people must get to afford to purchase land. We will begin by explaining the role played by mortgages and the methods for their creation, both today and historically. This will be followed by a consideration of how the rights of borrowers are protected in such arrangements. We will next consider the remedies available to a lender, where the borrower fails to fulfil their obligations. Finally, we will explain the rules governing the priority of mortgages.

By the end of this chapter, you should be able to:

- understand the meaning of mortgages;
- identify how legal mortgages are created;
- identify how equitable mortgages are created;
- explain the rights of a mortgagor;
- explain the rights of a mortgagee;
- understand priority of mortgages;
- apply the above to the case studies and learning tasks.

CASE STUDY – ONE

Jason purchased a 25-year lease of an ice-cream parlour with assistance of a 15-year legal mortgage of £50,000 from a local dairy.

As the deal was completed in difficult financial times, Jason agreed to pay interest at a rate of 15 per cent above the base rate of the Bank of England.

Incorporated into the mortgage deed was a clause stating that the interest could be raised each year in line with the rises of the Retail Prices Index and it was agreed in the deed that the mortgage could not be redeemed during the 15-year term.

Under the terms of the mortgage, Jason also promised that, for the whole of the mortgage term, he would sell only ice cream produced by the dairy.

Advise Jason as to the enforceability of the initial interest rate, the proposed annual uplift to the interest rate, the restriction upon the redemption and the trade clause requiring him to purchase all his products from the dairy during the mortgage term.

> **KEEP IN MIND**
>
> ■ The purpose of the mortgage is to secure the loan; you would normally expect to be able to pay it off and the property to then be free of it.
> ■ Could the terms agreed to be viewed as unfair? Does it matter that this was in a commercial context?

WHY HAVE MORTGAGES?

The cost of buying property is high – for many people house prices will be between five to ten times greater than their annual salary. With such a high cost few people can afford to buy a house outright. Most people have to seek help by borrowing the money to purchase their home or land and this is commonly done by way of obtaining a mortgage from a bank or building society which is secured against the land in case the borrower becomes unable to repay the mortgage. As we will see in this chapter mortgages are not just used to purchase a home since sometimes a businessman will obtain a loan on the security of his home in order to acquire or inject capital into his business. It is possible to have more than one mortgage over the land and we will consider the rules for priority of mortgages i.e. who is entitled to their money first.

ESSENTIAL TERMINOLOGY	
Mortgage	A disposition of some interest in land or property as a security for the payment of a debt, or the discharge of some other obligation for which it is given. The mortgage is the security and not the loan itself.
Mortgagee	The person who receives the security, i.e. the lender/creditor.
Mortgagor	The person who gives the security, i.e. the borrower/debtor.
Legal charge	Confers rights in the land or property on a chargee (lender) as security (as before).
Redemption	The right of the mortgagor to repay the loan and claim back the land or property free from incumbrance (also spelled encumbrance), exercisable after the date fixed for repayment has passed.
Equity of redemption	The totality of the equitable rights of the mortgagor, including the right to redeem. Its value equals the market value of the land less the amount of debt outstanding on the land at any time.
Power of sale	The legal right of the mortgage company to sell the property if you breach your repayment obligations.

MEANING AND THE CREATION OF A LEGAL MORTGAGE

We must begin by considering what Jason has entered into when he granted a mortgage. This will enable him to begin to comprehend what his responsibilities are, what the lender may expect, and what will happen in the case of a default.

A mortgage is a security interest created over property, normally for the payment of debt. The borrower gives the mortgage, and is therefore referred to as the 'mortgagor'. The lender obtains the interest, and so is called the 'mortgagee'. Should the mortgagor default on repaying the debt, then ultimately the mortgagee can sell the property and use the proceeds to recover what is owed. Any type of property can be mortgaged, but it is most commonly real property and only land is considered in this chapter.

This security is vital for real property given the large sums of money which need to be borrowed in order to, for example, purchase a first house. As a mortgage is a legal interest in land, it will bind third parties and give security in the event of the mortgagor becoming insolvent. The mortgagee, as a secured creditor, has an interest which prevails against other creditors and may demand the property be sold to repay the debt.

Today, a borrower does not in fact give a mortgage to the lender but rather a legal charge. Whereas a mortgage of land transfers an estate to the mortgagee, a charge only attaches a secured right to the land. However, as we shall see, while the modern mortgages by legal charge are different from historic mortgages their everyday effect remains the same.

MORTGAGES BEFORE 1926

Before 1926 the standard means for creating a mortgage was a conveyance of an estate to the mortgagee i.e. the entire freehold or leasehold estate or a sublease one day shorter than that of the mortgagor. The mortgagee then owned the land, but subject to a right for the mortgagor to recover or 'redeem' it by repaying the debt on a particular date. This is called the legal right to redeem. While ownership was given to the lender, the borrower would usually retain possession.

At common law, if the mortgagor did not repay on the exact legal date of redemption as specified in the mortgage deed then they permanently lost all rights to the property. This outcome applied irrespective of the debt owed compared to the value of the property, the briefness of any delay to making payment, or the fault of the borrower.

Equity has intervened to prevent injustices caused by the strictness of the law. It allows the mortgagor the opportunity to redeem after the legal redemption date provided the debt will be repaid within a reasonable time. The result of this equitable right to redeem is that legal date for redemption is no longer as important. There is therefore no need to agree a legal date for redemption which is a long time into the future – the borrower will anyway be given more time in equity to repay and recover the property. It is in fact better for the lender to set a short period as until the legal date passes the mortgagee cannot be said to be in default.

> ### TUTOR TIP – 1
> ....
>
> You may be confused, having heard reference to mortgages for say 25 or 30 years. In fact, this period of time does not relate to the legal date for redemption.
>
> The convention is now to set the legal date for redemption at six months but it is not normally the real date when the borrower is expected to repay in full, with the principal and interest repayable in monthly instalments over many years. It does, however, mark the date after which the lender can use remedies against the mortgagor should they default.

While in law the legal estate belonged to the mortgagee, equity regards the mortgagor as the real owner. This is the equity of redemption which, while crucially including the equitable right to redeem explained above, manifests itself in a number of important ways. The equity of redemption, the borrower's 'equity' in the property determined by the value of the property less the outstanding debt, can be sold to another, leased, settled or itself mortgaged (enabling successive mortgages over the same property).

MORTGAGES POST-1925

The Law of Property Act 1925 (LPA 1925) prohibits the creation of a mortgage by transfer of the mortgagor's estate, the legislators having accepted equity's interpretation of the mortgagor as the true owner.

Mortgages of freehold

In relation to a mortgage of a freehold, s 85(1) of the LPA 1925 permits only two methods. Either:

- a demise for a term of years absolute (creation of a long lease), or
- a charge by way of legal mortgage.

Use of a legal charge is the easier of the options and so most often used. Also, while both methods may still be used for unregistered land, a registered title may now only be mortgaged by way of a legal charge (s 23(1) of the Land Registration Act 2002 (LRA 2002)).

Demise for a Term of Years Absolute

A purported conveyance of the freehold to create a mortgage is converted under the LPA 1925 to a long lease for 3,000 years (s 85(2) of the LPA 1925).

Charges by Way of Legal Mortgage (Legal Charge)

A charge by way of legal mortgage, or legal charge, is created by deed and must expressly state that the borrower thereby charges the property by way of a legal mortgage (s 87(1) LPA 1925). While it does not give the mortgagee ownership of an estate in the land, he does acquire rights over the property as if he had a mortgage by demise i.e. as if a mortgage for 3,000 years was granted his favour (s 87(1)(a) of the LPA 1925).

Mortgages of leases

In relation to a mortgage of a leasehold, s 86(1) of the LPA 1925 permits two methods: either (1) a sublease (demise), or (2) a charge by way of legal mortgage. Remember that a registered title may now only be mortgaged by way of a legal charge (s 23(1) of the LRA 2002).

Sublease (Sub-Demise)

A purported assignment of a lease to make a mortgage is converted under s 86(2) of the LPA 1925 to a sublease granted for ten days less than the mortgagor's lease.

Charges by Way of Legal Mortgage (Legal Charge)

A charge by way of legal mortgage can be used in relation to both freehold and leasehold land. It puts the mortgagee in the same position as if they had taken a mortgage by sublease (s 87(1)(b) of the LPA 1925).

Mortgages post-2002

Under s 23(1)(a) of the LRA 2002 a mortgage of registered land, whether freehold or leasehold, can now only be created by a registered charge removing the possibility of creating a mortgage by demise or sub-demise.

Charges by way of legal mortgage must be created by deed (s 52(1) of the LPA 1925) and completed by entry onto the charges register of the register of title (s 27(1)–(2) of the LRA 2002).

Section 25(1) of the LRA 2002 may provide requirements as to form and content of the charge, but no such rules have been made. However, the Land Registry does provide an example form (form CH1) and will approve forms developed by lenders.

While it is still possible to create a mortgage by demise or sub-demise over unregistered land, in practice it is rare. Also, note that a first legal mortgage is a trigger event for first registration of the land (ss 4(1)(g) and 6(2)(a) of the LRA 2002).

TUTOR TIP – 2

It is very important that borrowers understand the seriousness and the effect of signing a mortgage deed. The implications are far greater than the bank lending an agreed amount of money and the borrower agreeing how and when they will repay it.

By signing the mortgage deed, the borrower is granting the mortgagee a charge over the property. A charge is a financial debt or liability affecting the property in favour of the mortgage company.

The borrower is agreeing to adhere to certain terms and conditions imposed by the mortgage company for the agreed term in consideration of him receiving the mortgage monies. The terms and conditions are normally contained in a very lengthy booklet received at the same time as the mortgage offer. These terms and conditions will be in addition to paying the amount owed under the mortgage by monthly instalments, in addition to any interest due.

The mortgage deed also contains a power of sale in favour of the mortgage lender in the event of non-payment of monthly instalments. As we will see later in this chapter, a power of sale is the legal right of the mortgage company to sell the property if you breach your repayment obligations or, indeed, any terms set out in the mortgage conditions.

EQUITABLE MORTGAGES

An equitable mortgage can be created if the mortgagor has only an equitable interest in the property or when legal formalities were not complied with i.e. executed by deed and registered if necessary.

The equitable mortgage would still need to conform with s 2 of the Law of Property (Miscellaneous Provisions) Act 1989. Before the LP(MP)A 1989, it had been possible to create an equitable mortgage by deposit of title deeds with the lender. While traditionally that act was seen as a contract through part performance, the effect of s 2 of the LP(MP)A 1989 is to remove the doctrine of part performance with only a written and signed agreement containing the terms of the agreement now acceptable.

RIGHTS OF A MORTGAGOR

By entering into a mortgage, Jason has secured a loan against the property but that is all he has done and the lender cannot prevent him from redeeming it. The scenario raises some requirements set by the lender which may go against that principle.

The equity of redemption, recognising the mortgagor as the true owner, gives rise to rights protecting their interests. There may be no clogs and fetters on the equity of redemption, voiding any attempt to exclude or restrict the mortgagor's right to redeem or to apply unfair terms.

RESTRICTING THE EQUITABLE RIGHT TO REDEEM

A mortgage cannot be made irredeemable, but any attempt to restrict the mortgagor's ability to repay the debt and redeem the mortgage may also be challenged.

> **KEY CASE:** *BROWNE V RYAN* [1901] 2 IR 653
>
> The reasoning why fairness requires that there be must be a right to redeem was explained by Walker LJ:
>
>> [T]he mortgagor is entitled to get his property as free as he gave it, on payment of principal, interest, and costs, and provisions inconsistent with that right cannot be enforced. The equitable rules 'once a mortgage always a mortgage', and that the mortgagee cannot impose any 'clog or fetter on the equity of redemption' are merely concise statements of the same rule.

The right to redeem must be genuine.

> **KEY CASE:** *FAIRCLOUGH V SWAN BREWERY LTD* [1912] AC 565, 81 LJPC 207; [1911–13] ALL ER REP 397
>
> The mortgaged property was a leasehold and the agreed date for redemption was set at six weeks before the end of the mortgagor's lease. This term was held to be oppressive, and therefore in equity the mortgagor could redeem earlier. This case represents an extreme postponement, really amounting to making the mortgage irredeemable, which is never permitted. As Lord Macnaghten said:
>
>> The encumbrance on the lease the subject of the mortgage according to the letter of the bargain fails to be discharged before the lease terminates, but at a time when it is on the very point of expiry, when redemption can be of no advantage to the mortgagor … For all practical purposes this mortgage is irredeemable.

However, a term postponing the right to redeem will only be a clog if it is oppressive or unconscionable. Being unreasonable is not enough.

> **KEY CASE:** *KNIGHTSBRIDGE ESTATES TRUST LTD V BYRNE* [1939] CH 441; [1938] 4 ALL ER 618
>
> A postponement for 40 years was upheld – there was a fair bargain. The case concerned two commercial organisations negotiating at arm's length and the rate of interest was low to reflect repayment by instalments over a long period of time.

The mortgaged property was freehold, meaning the right to redeem was not illusionary. Sir Wilfred Greene MR explained: '[E]quity does not reform mortgage transactions because they are unreasonable. It is concerned to see two things – one that the essential requirements of a mortgage transaction are observed, and the other that oppressive or unconscionable terms are not enforced.'

APPLY YOUR LEARNING – TASK 1

Do you think that the postponement of the ability to redeem the mortgage on the ice-cream parlour for 15 years would be considered as a clog on the equitable rights to redeem? The right to redeem is not illusionary, given that the lease is for 25 years but could it be viewed as oppressive or unconscionable? Jason has borrowed the money for commercial purposes, but he is a small business so the organisations may not be equally matched and there is no suggestion that he has received any reciprocal advantage such as low interest.

OPTIONS TO PURCHASE

A clause allowing the mortgagee an option to purchase the mortgaged property will be a clog on the equity of redemption.

KEY CASE: *SAMUEL V JARRAH TIMBER AND WOOD PAVING CORPORATION LTD* [1904] UKHL 2; [1904] AC 323

An option to purchase was held to be a clog, despite the view of the court that the bargain itself was not oppressive and the parties were of equal bargaining power. A mortgage on some stock gave the mortgagee the right to buy the property, which would thereby have prevented the mortgage from being redeemed and was therefore a clog.

For a more recent example, see *Jones v Morgan* [2001][1] where again there was no suggestion of any unfairness.

A distinction is made where the option to buy the property is a separate transaction to the mortgage. So, in *Reeve v Lisle* [1902],[2] an option was upheld which was agreed several days after the mortgage. It was an independent transaction subsequent to the mortgage.

1 [2001] EWCA Civ 995, 82 P & CR D36; [2001] Lloyd's Rep Bank 323.
2 [1902] AC 461, 71 LJ Ch 768.

COLLATERAL ADVANTAGES

The mortgagee may seek to obtain additional advantages beyond repayment of the debt, for example buying its product (a 'solus tie'). Such ties are generally not a problem if they cease upon redemption provided the terms are not oppressive or unconscionable. But if such an arrangement purports to endure beyond the return of the loan this could potentially be a clog on the equity of redemption under which property should be redeemed in its original state.

In *Noakes v Rice* [1902][3] the mortgagee, a brewery, imposed a condition that the mortgagor, the landlord of a public house, sell only its beer for the entire duration of his lease even after the mortgage had been redeemed. This was found to be a clog, with the continuation beyond repayment of the loan a key factor in the term being oppressive or unconscionable. In *Bradley v Carritt* [1903][4] it was again held that terms could not be enforced after redemption.

However, the courts have since upheld terms which continue after redemption.

KEY CASE: *G&C KREGLINGER V NEW PATAGONIA MEAT AND COLD STORAGE CO LTD* [1913] UKHL 1; [1914] AC 25

The mortgagor agreed that the mortgagee would for five years have the right to buy their sheepskins at market value. The mortgage was redeemed before the five years expired, and the mortgagor argued that the term continuing was unfair. The court upheld the agreement, it being neither unfair nor unconscionable. It was a business agreement between two commercial parties negotiating at arm's length, freely entered into. One reason given for the court distinguishing this case was finding the undertaking to be separate to the mortgage, but this idea of an independent agreement was a somewhat forced distinction and arguably the real reason was an unwillingness to meddle with contracts fairly entered into.

Lord Parker said:

> My Lords, after the most careful consideration of the authorities I think it is open to this House to hold, and I invite your Lordships to hold, that there is now no rule in equity which precludes a mortgagee, whether the mortgage be made upon the occasion of a loan or otherwise, from stipulating for any collateral advantage, provided such collateral advantage is not either (1.) unfair and unconscionable, or (2.) in the nature of a penalty clogging the equity of redemption, or (3.) inconsistent with or repugnant to the contractual and equitable right to redeem.

---

3 [1902] AC 24, 66 JP 147.
4 [1903] AC 253, 72 LJKB 471.

These types of collateral advantage may be challenged on the basis of the common law doctrine of restraint of trade, where the mortgage is taken over premises already owned and used by a business.[5] This looks to the reasonableness of the terms. So, for example, in *Esso Petroleum Co Ltd v Harper's Garage (Stourport) Ltd* [1967][6] an agreement to purchase only the lender petrol for 21 years was found to be an unreasonable restraint of trade.

APPLY YOUR LEARNING – TASK 2

Could the clause requiring Jason to purchase all of his ice cream for 15 years from the lender be a collateral advantage? It is to subsist only for the duration of the mortgage, but could it be viewed as unfair or unconscionable? This being a business arrangement may mean it is not, but again we are dealing with a small business where there is no obvious reciprocal advantage.

Unfair terms

Any terms which are oppressive or unconscionable may be struck down by equity; it is not enough for a term to be unreasonable.

In *Cityland Holdings Ltd v Dabrah* [1968][7] the mortgage secured a debt of £2,900 and took the form of a premium to pay £4,553 by monthly instalments over a six-year period. The agreement provided that upon a default by the mortgagor, the full premium would become payable. Default occurred with the added premium due representing 57 per cent of the amount of the loan. The court considered this to be a penal rate and varied to the equivalent of an annual interest rate of 7 per cent.

But the fairness of terms is very much dependent on the particular facts of the case.

KEY CASE: *MULTISERVICE BOOKBINDING LTD V MARDEN* [1979] CH 84; [1978] 2 ALL ER 489

An interest rate calculated against the Swiss currency, with the result that the borrower's liability was substantially increased, was upheld. This time, the agreement between two commercial parties and the link to the Swiss franc was not intended to take advantage. It may have been a bad deal for the borrower, but there was no suggestion of sharp practice. A term cannot be unconscionable, per Browne-Wilkinson J: 'unless one of the parties to it has imposed the objectionable terms in a morally reprehensible manner.'

---

5 There must be an existing right to trade in order for there to have been interference.
6 [1967] UKHL 1; [1968] AC 269; [1967] 1 All ER 699.
7 [1968] Ch 166; [1967] 2 All ER 639.

Under the Consumer Credit Act 1974, statutory controls now provide protection where the borrower is an individual.

APPLY YOUR LEARNING – TASK 3

Do you think the interest rate which Jason agreed to may be successfully challenged, and what about the annual uplift linked to the retail prices index? The index link was not intended to take advantage of the mortgagor. But paying 15% above the base rate may be unfair.

Statutory protection

Borrowers also have various statutory safeguards, which may be used to provide additional protection.

Consumer Credit Act 1974 (as amended)

Sections 140 A–D of the Consumer Credit Act 1974, as amended by the Consumer Credit Act 2006, empower the courts to reopen consumer credit bargains after considering all of the circumstances. Section 140 A states:

(1) The court may make an order under s 140B in connection with a credit agreement if it determines that the relationship between the creditor and the debtor arising out of the agreement (or the agreement taken with any related agreement) is unfair to the debtor because of one or more of the following—

   (a) any of the terms of the agreement or of any related agreement;
   (b) the way in which the creditor has exercised or enforced any of his rights under the agreement or any related agreement;
   (c) any other thing done (or not done) by, or on behalf of, the creditor (either before or after the making of the agreement or any related agreement).

(2) In deciding whether to make a determination under this section the court shall have regard to all matters it thinks relevant (including matters relating to the creditor and matters relating to the debtor).

The court is not, therefore, limited to reviewing the original terms of the agreement at the time it was entered into but may consider the behaviour of the lender throughout the term of the mortgage.

TUTOR TIP – 3
....

Be careful when trying to apply the Act – many mortgages of land are excluded from protection under the Consumer Credit Act 1974. Notably, first legal residential mortgages are regulated instead by the Financial Conduct Authority under the Financial Services and Markets Act 2000.

Financial Conduct Authority guidance

The Financial Conduct Authority (FCA), formerly the Financial Services Authority, has powers to regulate consumer credit under the Financial Services and Markets Act 2000 (FSMA 2000), as amended by the Financial Services Act 2012. Any regulated mortgage, which the vast majority of first mortgages of residential property will be, must comply with FCA standards. FCA standards are designed to protect consumers, by delivering fair treatment and transparency and preventing excessive or hidden charges. The FCA monitors compliance and takes disciplinary proceedings if necessary.

The FCA rules are extensive, covering expectations and requirements both pre and post agreement of a mortgage, and in any dispute it is vital that you are aware of them. A complete record of FCA instruments is contained in the *FCA Handbook*.[8]

UNDUE INFLUENCE OR MISREPRESENTATION

A mortgage may be set aside for undue influence or misrepresentation. This can come from the mortgagee but is commonly exerted by a third party such as a husband putting pressure on or dominating a wife. There has been an explosion of cases over the past 30 years where mortgagors (mainly wives) have sought to set aside mortgages granted to guarantee someone else's debt (usually their husband or ex-husband's debt) on the grounds that they acted under the undue influence of their husband.

The first stage of consideration in such cases is whether there has been undue influence or misrepresentation. The second stage is whether the mortgagee is affected by the conduct of that third party.

Establishing undue influence or misrepresentation

A misrepresentation must be proved by showing a false statement of a fact has been made and relied upon. As explained by Patten LJ in *Royal Bank of Scotland v Chandra* [2011][9] in distinguishing misrepresentation from undue influence:

> The two are not the same, although in certain cases they may overlap. Undue influence is concerned with the abuse of a relationship of trust and confidence by the husband exercising control over the will of the wife in order to procure her consent to the guarantee. In a case of misrepresentation that consent has been procured not by the exercise of some form of pressure or domination but by the making of a false statement which the wife in the relationship of trust has relied upon.

Undue influence has two classes, as clarified in *Royal Bank of Scotland plc v Etridge (No 2)* [2001].[10] Class 1 is actual undue influence, where evidence proves undue influence.

8 Financial Conduct Authority, *FCA Handbook*, available online at: www.handbook.fca.org.uk.
9 [2011] EWCA Civ 192; [2011] 2 P & CR DG1.
10 [2001] UKHL 44; [2002] 2 AC 773.

Class 2 is presumed undue influence where the relationship of the parties being one of trust and confidence means undue influence is presumed if the terms of the agreement cannot readily be explained by the relationship of the parties. Trust and confidence may be inferred from the specific category of relationship, such as solicitor and client, doctor and patient, or child and parent, or from acts showing a relationship of trust has occurred, for example, between husband and wife.

Effect on the lender

For undue influence or misrepresentation on the part of a third party to affect the lender, it needs to be shown that either:

- the third party was acting as an agent of the bank (very exceptionally arguable), or
- the lender was put on inquiry with actual or constructive notice of the wrongdoing.

For the lender to be open to attack it is necessary that they are first put on notice of a vitiating factor. The source of this notice or information will be the mortgage application made by the potential borrowers. Lenders must therefore protect themselves if the reason for the mortgage application is not one of financial benefit to all legal owners of the property.

For example, a husband raises money against the family home for his sole benefit (a common real-life occurrence). This could fall under Class 2, presumed undue influence. The situation will support the wife in establishing a relationship of trust and confidence, with a presumption that the husband abused the relationship and exerted undue influence. For the lender, the crucial factor is that they have been put on notice of the potential for undue influence to be exerted and must take extra care.

KEY CASE: *BARCLAYS BANK PLC V O'BRIEN* [1993] UKHL 6; [1994] 1 AC 180; [1993] 4 ALL ER 417

Since this case, the doctrine of notice has become the main argument. In *O'Brien* the husband arranged an increase in the mortgage and the wife signed the documentation without reading it. The court considered that the fact that the security was against the matrimonial home was not sufficient in itself to put the bank on notice of this.

In order to establish whether the mortgage lender had notice the court looked at the nature of the transaction to alert the mortgagee that consent to the mortgage may not have been given freely.

Following this case the doctrine of notice requires that a lender takes reasonable steps to satisfy himself that agreement has been properly obtained wherever he is put on inquiry, which in this case was suggested to include wives and other non-commercial emotional relationships.

Lord Browne-Wilkinson set out the reasonable steps to be taken by creditors to avoid being fixed with constructive notice:

> Therefore in my judgment a creditor is put on inquiry when a wife offers to stand surety for her husband's debts by the combination of two factors: (a) the transaction is on its face not to the financial advantage of the wife; and (b) there is a substantial risk in transactions of that kind that, in procuring the wife to act as surety, the husband has committed a legal or equitable wrong that entitles the wife to set aside the transaction.

> It follows that unless the creditor who is put on inquiry takes reasonable steps to satisfy himself that the wife's agreement to stand surety has been properly obtained, the creditor will have constructive notice of the wife's rights.

> What, then are the reasonable steps which the creditor should take to ensure that it does not have constructive notice of the wife's rights. … It is plainly impossible to require of banks and other financial institutions that they should inquire of one spouse whether he or she has been unduly influenced or misled by the other. But in my judgment the creditor … can reasonably be expected to take steps to bring home to the wife the risk she is running by standing as surety and to advise her to take independent advice. … [F]or the future in my judgment a creditor will have satisfied these requirements if it insists that the wife attend a private meeting (in the absence of the husband) with a representative of the creditor at which she is told of the extent of her liability as surety, warned of the risk she is running and *urged* to take independent legal advice. If these steps are taken in my judgment the creditor will have taken such reasonable steps as are necessary to preclude a subsequent claim that it had constructive notice of the wife's rights. I should make it clear that I have been considering the ordinary case where the creditor knows only that the wife is to stand surety for her husband's debts. I would not exclude exceptional cases where a creditor has knowledge of further facts which render the presence of undue influence not only possible but probable. In such cases, the creditor to be safe will have to *insist* that the wife is separately advised. [Emphasis added.]

Reasonable steps include, as considered in *Royal Bank of Scotland plc v Etridge (No 2)* [2001], steps such as ensuring the wife has obtained proper legal advice which included the core practical elements such as the nature of the undertaking, its implications, the risks and that the decision is hers alone. A bank fulfils this duty by relying upon confirmation from a solicitor acting for the wife that he has met with and appropriately advised the wife.

If undue influence or misrepresentation is successfully pleaded, it will render the mortgage voidable. Where only some of the mortgage obligations were influenced, only part of the security will be voided and second, where the wife has herself received a benefit, restitution will first be required.

KEY CASE: *ROYAL BANK OF SCOTLAND (NO 2) V ETRIDGE* [2001] UKHL 44; [2002] 2 AC 773; [2001] 4 ALL ER 449

The case of *Royal Bank of Scotland plc. v Etridge (No 2)* was significant for lenders and changed the way legal advice was given in such situations. The guidance set down is there not only to ensure the parties were aware of the risks involved in entering into the transaction but also to protect the lender from claims of undue influence. The view was taken that in *every* case where a wife/husband stands as surety for her partner's debts, the lender *must* take certain precautions.

1   The lender must communicate directly with the wife, making it clear that they will require written confirmation from her solicitor confirming that they have advised on the transaction, its effect and its practical implications and that this confirmation will be evidence against any future arguments invalidating the mortgage. The lender must also take reasonable steps to satisfy itself that the wife has had fully explained to her in a meaningful way the practical implications of the transaction. These included:

2   The wife must be made aware that she is free to choose her legal representation. The solicitor must make it clear that when advising the wife, he is acting solely in her interests. If the solicitor at any stage in the advice found that there was a conflict of interest he must cease to act for her.

3   In order for the advice to be given the solicitor must be furnished with sufficient information to advise fully, including financial information concerning the application, information about the husband, obviously with the husband's consent.

4   The wife's solicitor should:

(a)   advise on the nature of the documents and their practical consequences for her if she signs them;

(b)   point out the seriousness of the risks involved. She should be told the amount of his potential liability, the purpose of the proposed new facility, its amount and principal terms and that the bank might change its terms without reference to him;

(c)   advise that she has a choice whether to sign the documentation and check whether she wishes to proceed and whether she is content for her solicitor to write to the lender confirming their explanation of the documents and their practical implementation.

RIGHTS OF THE MORTGAGEE

Where there is default on the mortgage, the mortgagee has a number of rights to enforce payment: action on the personal covenant to pay; taking possession; sale; appointing a receiver; and foreclosure. The next case study considers what actions the lender may take in response to a default, and how that is balanced against the needs of the borrower.

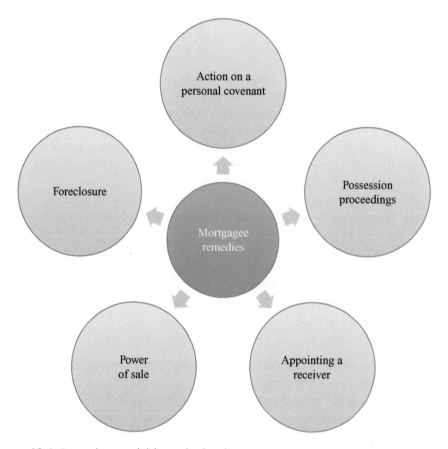

Figure 13.1 Remedies available to the lender

CASE STUDY – TWO

Lee purchased the freehold of a house two years ago, by means of a deposit of £8,000 and the balance of £80,000 with the aid of a loan from a building society secured by a legal mortgage.

Last year, Lee lost his job and has made no mortgage repayments for eight months and the Society are about to issue proceedings for possession, prior to sale.

Lee is now in his final year of a part-time law degree. He believes that he will do well in the examinations, and is sure to secure a highly paid job shortly afterwards allowing him to pay off the sums owed and to meet future payments.

He is concerned that, should the Society sell the property, they will not secure the best value for the property and he will lose the equity he has in it.

Advise Lee.

KEEP IN MIND

- A sale of the property will raise funds to pay the lender back, but you would expect there to be limits before such a right could be exercised by the lender.
- The lender will want possession of the property in order to affect a sale, but this could result in conflict with the borrower. A court order for possession helps to safeguard the lender against any culpability.
- In deciding whether to give the lender immediate possession, do you think the ability to repay the debt in time might be a relevant consideration?

ACTION ON THE PERSONAL COVENANT TO PAY

The mortgagee may sue to recover the principal sum and interest in arrear, the mortgagor being personally responsible for the contractual agreement entered into. Ordinarily the mortgagor will prefer to use the stronger rights he enjoys as a secured creditor, but this remedy is often used in cases of negative equity. Where the value of the mortgaged property is less than the debt owed, sale alone will not repay the sums due and so personal action will be used as an additional option.

Action must be brought within 12 years from that date when the right to receive the money accrued for the principal sum or capital (s 20(1) of the Limitation Act 1980). In the cases of arrears of interest, an action is barred after six years (s 20(5) of the Limitation Act 1980).

TAKING POSSESSION

The right to take possession is not dependent upon any default by the mortgagor. This is by virtue of the mortgagee historically having an estate in land vested in him and nowadays a charge by way of legal mortgage which gives rights equivalent to a mortgage by demise.

KEY CASE: *FOUR-MAIDS LTD V DUDLEY MARSHALL (PROPERTIES) LTD* [1957] CH 317

In this case Harman J explained something that may surprise people:

> The right of the mortgagee to possession in the absence of some contract has nothing to do with default on the part of the mortgagor. The mortgagee may go into possession before the ink is dry on the mortgage unless there is something in the contract … whereby he has contracted himself out of that right. He has the right because he has a legal term of years in the property.

However, in practice this right will not usually be exercised unless there is a default. Normally possession proceedings will be done in advance of selling the property to ensure that the lender will be able to sell the property with vacant possession to recover the monies owed. Indeed, it often is not possible to take possession without some default, particularly in relation to dwelling houses.

It is important to note that possession proceedings do not necessarily mean the end to the mortgage. As such some mortgagees use this method to keep the mortgage alive as lenders make their money from the interest on the monies borrowed. This can be advantageous in relation to commercial property. For example, a mortgagee in possession may sublet or run the business over which a mortgage exists as a method of securing recovery of the monies owed in addition to any outstanding interest on the loan. The mortgagee must exercise caution, however, as they may find themselves having to account to the mortgagor for any money he has or should have received whilst in possession and it could also mean that the mortgagee will have to make up a shortfall to the mortgagor. In *White v City of London Brewery Co* [1889][11] a brewery (and mortgagee) took possession of the commercial premises and let it on condition that their beer was sold. They were made to account for the money they would have received had they let the premises as a free house. It was held that the brewery was liable to account to mortgagor for the actual and presumed profits.

Court proceedings

The mortgagee will normally want the security of having a court order before taking possession. Possession can be taken without court proceedings; for example in *Ropaigealach v Barclays Bank plc* [1998][12] a court order was not needed for a residential property standing empty whilst undergoing repairs, but situations where peaceful entry is possible are limited. The risks of using this self-help remedy are very high, given that it is a criminal offence to take possession of premises from another with the use or threat of violence (s 6(1) of the Criminal Law Act 1977).

---

11 [1889] 42 CHD 237.
12 [1998] EWCA Civ 1960; [2000] QB 263; [1999] 4 All ER 235.

At common law, the courts have long claimed inherent jurisdiction to adjourn an application for possession for a short period of time. But given that the mortgagee is *prima facie* entitled to possession, the courts have no jurisdiction to refuse or suspend an order and any adjournment will be only temporary so as to enable the whole of the debt to be repaid. For example, in *Birmingham Citizens Permanent Building Society v Caunt* [1962][13] only a 28-day adjournment was allowed. Russell J explained, at 912, that possession proceedings: 'may be adjourned for a short time to afford the mortgagor a chance of paying off the mortgagee in full or otherwise satisfying him; but this should not be done if there is no reasonable prospect of this occurring.'

The court's inherent jurisdiction was too limited to really assist mortgagors and this, following a report from the Payne Committee,[14] resulted in statutory protection introduced by s 36 of the Administration of Justice Act 1970 (AJA 1970), as amended by the AJA 1973. Do note that, as confirmed in *Ropaigealach v Barclays Bank plc* [2000], the section applies only where a court order is sought.

Section 36 of the AJA 1970 provides:

(1) Where the mortgagee under a mortgage of land which consists of or includes a dwelling-house brings an action in which he claims possession of the mortgaged property, not being an action for foreclosure in which a claim for possession of the mortgaged property is also made, the court may exercise any of the powers conferred on it by subsection (2) below if it appears to the court that in the event of its exercising the power the mortgagor is likely to be able within a reasonable period to pay any sums due under the mortgage or to remedy a default consisting of a breach of any other obligation arising under or by virtue of the mortgage.

(2) The court—

(a) may adjourn the proceedings, or
(b) on giving judgment, or making an order, for delivery of possession of the mortgaged property, or at any time before the execution of such judgment or order, may—

(i) stay or suspend execution of the judgment or order, or
(ii) postpone the date for delivery of possession, for such period or periods as the court thinks reasonable.

(3) Any such adjournment, stay, suspension or postponement as is referred to in subsection (2) above may be made subject to such conditions with regard to payment by the mortgagor of any sum secured by the mortgage or the remedying of any default as the court thinks fit.

---

13 [1962] Ch 883; [1962] 1 All ER 163.
14 *Report of the Committee on the Enforcement of Judgment Debts* Cmnd 3909 (1969).

A court has the power to adjourn proceedings or to suspend or postpone the execution of an order if it appears to the court that the mortgagor is likely to be able to repay 'any sums due' within a 'reasonable period'.

Taking sums due first, the difficulty was that most mortgages provided that in the event of a default with payments, the entire debt became payable. The courts interpreted any sums due as therefore including the principal or capital sum lent; even if the mortgage was intended to be paid in instalments (see *Halifax Building Society v Clark* [1973][15]). Clearly, repayment of the whole debt at once was often not possible within a reasonable period.

This unsatisfactory outcome was responded to by AJA 1973 s 8(1) which redefined 'any sums due' and reversed the decision in the *Halifax Building Society v Clark* [1973] case. Under s 8(1), if:

> the mortgagor is entitled or is to be permitted to pay the principal sum secured by instalments or otherwise to defer payment of it in whole or in part, but provision is also made for earlier payment in the event of any default by the mortgagor or of a demand by the mortgagee or otherwise, then for purposes of s 36 of the Administration of Justice Act 1970 … a court may treat as due under the mortgage on account of the principal sum secured and of interest on it only such amounts as the mortgagor would have expected to be required to pay if there had been no such provision for earlier payment.

As such the court has the discretion to refuse an order for immediate possession if the mortgagor can show that he is likely to catch up with the instalments, though it should be noted that the courts will also want assurances that future payments can also be met. This leaves the question of what is meant by a reasonable period.

Whilst not given specific time limits a number of cases had provided an element of guidance as to the court's ability to postpone an order for possession. *Royal Trust of Canada v Markham* [1975][16] confirmed that the court had no powers under s 36(2) to suspend a possession order indefinitely. Additionally, the mortgagor must present evidence to the court that they were likely within a reasonable period to be able to pay the amount due under the mortgage. The court also believed that they may have no discretion to postpone or suspend an order where there was no realistic chance of the mortgagor meeting the accrued arrears let alone future payments. See *First National Bank v Syed* [1991][17] where the court held that they could not use their discretion where the mortgagor had offered a repayment structure of the arrears which were clearly beyond their means.

---

15 [1973] Ch 307.
16 [1975] 3 All ER 433; [1975] 1 WLR 1416.
17 [1991] 2 All ER 250, 10 Tr LR 154.

The case of *Cheltenham & Gloucester Building Society v Norgan* [1996] has, however, provided the most helpful and comprehensive guidance when determining 'reasonable time'.

KEY CASE: *CHELTENHAM & GLOUCESTER BUILDING SOCIETY V NORGAN* [1995] EWCA CIV 11; [1996] 1 WLR 343; [1996] 1 ALL ER 449

Repayment over the whole of the remaining term of the mortgage was accepted as the starting point for a reasonable period for repayment. There are various considerations which are relevant in deciding what is a reasonable period, which Evans LJ listed as including:

(a) How much can the borrower reasonably afford to pay, both now and in the future?
(b) If the borrower has a temporary difficulty in meeting his obligations, how long is the difficulty likely to last?
(c) What was the reason for the arrears which have accumulated?
(d) How much remains of the original term?
(e) What are relevant contractual terms, and what type of mortgage is it, i.e. when is the principal due to be repaid?
(f) Is it a case where the court should exercise its power to disregard accelerated payment provisions (section 8 of the Act of 1973)?
(g) Is it reasonable to expect the lender, in the circumstances of the particular case, to recoup the arrears of interest

  (1) over the whole of the original term, or
  (2) within a shorter period, or even
  (3) within a longer period, i.e. by extending the repayment period? Is it reasonable to expect the lender to capitalise the interest or not?

(h) Are there any reasons affecting the security which should influence the length of the period for payment? In the light of the answers to the above, the court can proceed to exercise its overall discretion, taking account also of any further factors which may arise in the particular case.

The need to show a realistic prospect of meeting the repayments makes it vital the mortgagors produce a detailed budget to satisfy the court. There is also a Pre-Action Protocol for Possession Claims based on Mortgage or Home Purchase Plan Arrears in Respect of Residential Property,[18] which describes the behaviour the court will normally expect of the parties prior to the start of a possession claim. It does not alter the parties' rights and obligations, but does aim to ensure that a lender and a borrower act fairly and reasonably with each other in resolving the matter, to encourage greater

---

18 Eighty-first update to the Civil Procedure Rules.

pre-action contact in order to seek agreement between the parties, and to communicate with information that is clear, fair and not misleading and the borrower is able to understand.

TUTOR TIP – 4

The guidance is helpful not only to the courts in making a decision but to mortgagors as to what evidence to present to the court for determination.

1   In demonstrating how much they can afford to repay, both now and in the future mortgagors should provide detailed budget planner with details of all income and expenditure and finance commitments in order to demonstrate their offer of repayment is realistic.
2   The courts will look more favourably if the mortgagor can show why the arrears have arisen and that those issues are outside of their control, for example redundancy or illness. Further credit will be given if the mortgagor is able to show that the problem was temporary and when it is likely to end i.e. evidence of a job offer.
3   The courts look more favourably on mortgagors that have run into difficulties further into their mortgage term. A mortgagor who runs into difficulties 15 years into a 25-year term will have greatly reduced the outstanding debt and have demonstrated a long period of stability in their ability to repay. This of course will be helped further in situations where the reasons for their arrears have been outside of their control.

APPLY YOUR LEARNING – TASK 4

Lee will wish the court to suspend any possession proceedings initiated by the building society to give him time to pay off the arrears. Under s 36 of the AJA 1970, as amended by s 8 of the AJA 1973, the court is able to suspend possession proceedings for a reasonable time period if satisfied that in such time, the mortgagor will be able to repay the arrears and also continue to meet the regular instalments as they fall due. The starting point for a reasonable period is the remainder of the term of the mortgage. What are the factors in the scenario which may be relevant?

Lee will have to produce a detailed budget showing his ability to meet the arrears and the future instalments. The difficulty is that his ambitions following his degree appear to be based on a hope that looks highly speculative, particularly given he has not even completed his degree yet. Coupled with the problem that he does not have significant equity in the house and the size of the arrears will keep rising, his case does not look strong. See *Town & Country Building Society v Julien* (1992) 24 HLR 312 and *Cheltenham & Gloucester Building Society v Norgan* [1996] for the issues with speculative windfalls and future highly paid employment.

Problems for mortgagees – deserted spouse, civil partner or cohabitee

The mortgagee's ability to obtain an order for possession is further complicated in situations where a non-owning spouse, civil partner or cohabitee occupies the property. The mortgagee must be mindful of the rights granted to such parties under the Family Law Act 1996 (FLA 1996), as amended by the Civil Partnership Act 2004. The provisions only extend to properties which have been or which were intended to be the family home.

Where a mortgagee wishes to commence possession proceedings, they are only required to notify those with whom they have a contractual arrangement, i.e. the mortgagors. As the non-owning spouse or civil partner will not be a party to the mortgage deed, the mortgagee will have no contractual relationship with them. In order for them to have a 'voice' in the possession proceedings they must either make an application to be joined in proceedings under s 55 of the FLA 1996 or if they have previously registered a Class F land charge (for unregistered land) or a Matrimonial Homes Act charge (for registered land) then the mortgagee is required to serve notice of the proceedings on them under s 56.

> **TUTOR TIP – 5**
> ....
>
> As a general rule, most family law solicitors will automatically register a Class F land charge or a Matrimonial Homes Act charge against a matrimonial home after an initial appointment for divorce/separation, once they have established that their client is a non-owning spouse or civil partner. This is done not only to protect their client in relation to any future financial negotiations and settlements but also to ensure that the non-owning spouse will receive notification should a possession proceeding situation arise at a later point. A right protected in this way will bind late purchasers of the legal estate.

The position differs depending whether the non-owning partner is a spouse/civil partner, or a cohabitee.

Position of spouses and civil partners

Under s 30 of the FLA 1996, a spouse or civil partner has a right not to be evicted or excluded from the matrimonial home if already in occupation; and a right, with the leave of the court, to enter and occupy if not already in occupation. Despite there being no contractual relationship between them and the lender, under s 30(3) any payments made to the lender in respect of the mortgage by the non-owning spouse or civil partner must be accepted by the lender and regarded as being good payment by the mortgagor. This can be extremely useful where there are mortgage arrears as the non-owning party is not only able to make good the deficit but may be able to establish a beneficial interest in the property.

Once a non-owning party is a party to any possession proceedings they will be treated in the same way as the mortgagor. As such, both their legal representative and the court should have regard to the guidance set out in *Cheltenham & Gloucester Building Society v Norgan* [1996]. The non-owning party will be able to ask the court to suspend any order for possession proving they can demonstrate an ability to meet the arrears *and* continue to meet future instalments, again building up an equitable interest in the property. In relation to non-owning spouses and civil partners the FLA 1996 gives the courts the power to grant a postponement of a possession order and an occupation order that can last indefinitely.

Position of cohabitees

Prior to the FLA 1996, an unmarried cohabitant had no protection under the spousal rights of occupation legislation in the Matrimonial Homes Act 1983. However, the FLA 1996 confers protection on cohabitants and other 'associated persons', although the statutory rights of occupation are more limited than that of spouses and civil partners. Again, the cohabitant may be joined as a party to the proceedings under s 55 of the FLA 1996, in order for them to have a 'voice' in any possession proceedings. Under s 36(13), a cohabitant in possession of such an order will now be eligible to require the lender to accept payments made by her/him as if made by the original mortgagor in the same way as a spouse or civil partner may do so under s 30(3) of the FLA 1996. This is, however, only possible during the continuance of the court order.

Under s 36 of the FLA 1996, the court has discretion to permit a cohabitant the right not to be evicted or excluded from the dwelling house if in occupation and the right to enter into and occupy the dwelling house for the period specified in the order. The rights conferred on cohabitants are less favourable than they are for married couples or civil partnerships. For a spouse or civil partner, the occupation order can last indefinitely, but under a s 36 order the courts may only grant an occupation order for six months subject to one only extension of another six months. Thus the maximum period of protection is for one year. Unlike spouses and civil partners, under s 36(6) the courts must follow a list of matters to take into account:

- The housing needs and housing resources of each of the parties and of any relevant child.
- The financial resources of each of the parties.
- The likely effect of any order, or of any decision by the court not to exercise its powers on the health, safety or well-being of the parties and of any relevant child.
- The conduct of the parties in relation to each other and otherwise.
- The nature of the parties' relationship.
- The length of time during which they have lived together as husband and wife.
- Whether there are or have been any children who are children of both parties or for whom both parties have or have had parental responsibility.
- The length of time that has elapsed since the parties ceased to live together.

Under s 41(2) of the FLA 1996 the court must also have regard to 'the fact that the cohabitants have not given each other the commitment involved in marriage'.

Postponement for sale by the mortgagor

The best option for the mortgagor may be to sell the property himself. They may believe they will get more money if they sell the property themselves rather than the mortgagee forcing a sale. Originally, the courts were only willing to postpone an order for possession if there was evidence of a purchaser and a sale within a short period of time. A more flexible approach has since developed.

KEY CASE: *NATIONAL & PROVINCIAL BUILDING SOCIETY V LLOYD* [1996] 1 ALL ER 630

Where sale of the property would cover the debt, it was held that the key issue is whether there is clear evidence that a sale could take place whether that be in 'six or nine months or even a year'. The court confirmed there was no rule of law to the effect that the power under s 36 of the AJA 1970 to adjourn or suspend a possession order would only be exercised, in the case of the sale of mortgaged property, if the sale would be taking place within a short period of time.

For an interesting application of these considerations, see *Bristol & West Building Society v Ellis* (1996).[19] The extent to which the debt is secured by the value of the property is an important factor in deciding the length of any postponement. A court may also be more generous with the time allowed if the value of the property far exceeds the debt. Where there is negative equity no postponement with a view to sale will be given. If there is no reasonable chance of repayment then the mortgagee's right to possession is immediate; see *Cheltenham & Gloucester plc v Krausz* [1997].[20]

APPLY YOUR LEARNING – TASK 5

Assuming that he is not in negative equity, Lee may successfully get possession postponed so he can sell the property himself and avoid a forced sale. Does it matter that Lee does not have evidence of a purchaser, or could he still get a postponement? Note *National & Provincial BS v Lloyd* [1996] where it was held that the mortgagor should be given a 'proper opportunity of making good his default to capital repayment'. What type of evidence could be relevant in deciding whether there is a likelihood of an early sale?

---

19 (1996) 73 P & CR 158. It was held there was insufficient evidence to show there could be sale at a price to discharge Mrs Ellis's overall debt to Bristol & West within any reasonable period, and certainly not one of up to three to five years. As such the court lacked the evidence to enable it to exercise its discretion and must grant an order of immediate possession.

20 [1997] 1 All ER 21; [1997] 1 WLR 1558.

Liabilities of the mortgagee in possession

Once the mortgagee takes possession of the property, he is responsible for the physical state of the property and liable account for rents and profit.

KEY CASE: *WHITE V CITY OF LONDON BREWERY CO* (1889) 42 CH D 237; 58 LJ CH 855

The mortgagee (a brewery) took possession of mortgaged property (a public house). It leased the property to a third party, with a tie-in requiring them to sell their beer. This reduced the rental value. It was held that the mortgagee must account not only for the income which was received during possession but also the income which could have been received had the rent not been reduced due to the restriction.

The duties of a mortgagee in possession mean that normally possession is only sought with a view to quickly selling the property. If the property is to be kept, for example where the property is commercial and generating an income from being leased out, then the appointment of a receiver is often favourable for the mortgagee.

APPOINTING A RECEIVER

Once his power of sale has become exercisable (which we will explore shortly), the mortgagee has a statutory power to appoint a receiver under s 101(1)(iii) of the LPA 1925.

A receiver taking control of the mortgaged property and managing it can use rent and income to repay the outstanding loan. As the receiver is appointed by the lender as an agent of the borrower (s 109(2) of the LPA 1925) the lender is distanced from the borrower and any liabilities rest with the receiver. As such the receiver is deemed to be the agent of the borrower, not the lender. The implications of this are that the lender bears no liability for any negligence on the part of the receiver; see *Chatsworth Properties v Effiom* [1971].[21] The Court of Appeal in *Medforth v Blake* [1999][22] defined a receiver's main duty as that of trying to engineer a situation where the debt and interest under the mortgage could be repaid. Additionally in situations where the receiver took on the conduct of the borrower's business, he had a duty to try to carry it on profitably and with due diligence.

This does not mean, however, that the lender has no duty in respect of appointing a receiver.

---

21 [1971] 1 All ER 604; [1971] 1 WLR 144.
22 [2000] Ch 86; [1999] 3 All ER 97.

THE POWER OF SALE

In most cases a mortgage will contain an express power of sale but otherwise, by s 101(1)(i) of the LPA 1925, a power is implied where the mortgage is made by deed (as is required to be legal). To use the power of sale the mortgagee must show that the power of sale has arisen and that the power of sale is exercisable.

This power arises as soon as the legal (contractual) date for redemption has passed; remember that this is normally set at six months in. It is not, however, exercisable unless any one of the criteria in s 103 of the LPA 1925 is satisfied:

> A mortgagee shall not exercise the power of sale conferred by this Act unless and until—
>
> (i) Notice requiring payment of the mortgage money has been served on the mortgagor or one of two or more mortgagors, and default has been made in payment of the mortgage money, or of part thereof, for three months after such service; or
> (ii) Some interest under the mortgage is in arrear and unpaid for two months after becoming due; or
> (iii) There has been a breach of some provision contained in the mortgage deed or in this Act, or in an enactment replaced by this Act, and on the part of the mortgagor, or of some person concurring in making the mortgage, to be observed or performed, other than and besides a covenant for payment of the mortgage money or interest thereon.

APPLY YOUR LEARNING – TASK 6

Can the building society issue proceedings against Lee with a view to sale? The lender will have a power to sell the property under s 101 of the LPA 1925. The mortgage is assumed to have been made by deed; the legal date for redemption will have passed (this is usually six months after the date of the mortgage) and we must assume that there is nothing to the contrary contained in the mortgage deed.

The power to sell must have become exercisable to avoid any action by Lee for damages. It appears from the information provided that Lee is in arrears of interest by more than two months per s 103(ii) of the LPA 1925.

CONSIDER THIS – 1

It is something of an anomaly that mortgagors only enjoy the protection of s 36 of the AJA 1970 when a mortgagee brings court proceedings for possession. When a mortgagee exercises a contractual or an implied statutory right to sell under s 101(1) of the LPA 1925, there is no requirement for a court order (*Ropaigealach v Barclays* [2000] QB 23). The subsequent purchaser can recover possession of the property, with the exercise of the power of sale overreaching any interest of the mortgagor (s 2(1)(iii) of the LPA 1925) and thus rendering them a trespasser on the property.

Despite the entry into force of the Human Rights Act 1998 (HRA 1998), this means of avoiding the statutory protection for mortgagors under s 36 continues. In *Horsham Properties v Clark* [2008] EWHC 2327, the mortgagors had defaulted on their mortgage repayments and the mortgagee exercised their contractual and implied statutory power of sale under s 101(1) of the LPA 1925. The mortgagors claimed the sale to a third party and the subsequent claim for possession by the new owners breached the HRA 1998, specifically the right to peaceful enjoyment of possessions.

Briggs J held that the exercise of the contractual provisions was part of a private bargain between the parties, and not because of a state action or intervention. If s 101 of the LPA 1925 had been relied upon, Briggs J concluded that would still be acceptable under the HRA 1998. The statutory power seeks to implement rather than override the bargain between the lender and borrower, creating an ordinary default position which the parties were free to overlap or replace in their own agreement.

Duties on sale

If the power of sale is exercised, the mortgagee has a duty to the mortgagor to take reasonable care to achieve the best price reasonably obtainable. Best price means, as explained in *Cuckmere Brick Co Ltd v Mutual Finance Ltd* [1971],[23] the 'true market value at the date of the sale'.

The decision when to sell is that of the mortgagee. There is no need for him to wait until market conditions improve (*Cuckmere Brick Co Ltd v Mutual Finance Ltd*). Nor is there a duty to sell immediately because non-exercise of the power will occasion loss or damage to the mortgagor as the value of the property declines (*China and South Sea Bank Ltd v Tan Soon Gin* [1990][24]). However, despite this general principle case law has recognised that a decision to delay a sale may be open to challenge in very exceptional circumstances if it will result in the debts of the mortgagee rising.

....

23 [1971] Ch 949; [1971] 2 All ER 633.
24 [1990] 1 AC 536; [1989] 3 All ER 839.

In *Palk v Mortgage Services Funding plc* [1993][25] the defaulting mortgagors had found a buyer for the mortgaged property but the sale price would not fully cover the debt. The mortgagee refused to sell the property, wanting to wait until the housing market improved. If done, the mortgagors would fall into increasing debt of some £30,000 each year. The court ordered a sale, relying on s 91 of the LPA 1925, which gives courts discretion to order a sale upon request by either mortgagor or mortgagee.

Proceeds of sale

After the sale, s 105 of the LPA 1925 regards the mortgagee as a trustee for proceeds of sale and directs how the sale proceeds must be distributed. The proceeds of sale in the hands of a mortgagee must be applied in the following order:

- Paying off any mortgagee earlier in priority.
- Discharge any costs of sale and any formerly attempted sale.
- Pay off the total capital, interest and costs debt owed to the selling mortgagee.
- Pay off any subsequent mortgagees.
- Pay any balance to the mortgagor.

APPLY YOUR LEARNING – TASK 7

Assuming that a forced sale occurs, how will the duties of the lender help to safeguard Lee and how would proceeds of the sale be applied as between him and the building society?

FORECLOSURE

Under ss 88(2) and 89(2) of the LPA 1925 the right to foreclose is established. However, the remedy is rarely used. It extinguishes any claim based on the equity of redemption by the mortgagor over the property, with the court declaring the estate belongs to the mortgagee. As a result, any 'equity' which the mortgagor had built up in that property is lost.

In any action for foreclosure the court may exercise its discretion under s 91(1) of the LPA 1925 to order sale instead of foreclosure. This is advantageous for the borrower because, when the property is sold, they will be able to retain the difference between the debt and the proceeds from sale. The mortgagee would therefore be expected to make a request.

---

25 [1993] Ch 330; [1993] 2 All ER 481.

PRIORITY OF MORTGAGES

Where there are two or more mortgages over one piece of land and the mortgaged property is sold, rules of priority give the order in which mortgages will be settled. Section 105 of the LPA 1925 requires prior (earlier) mortgages to be paid first. The question is which mortgage ranks higher? The order is normally dependent on the date order in which the mortgages were created, but due to the effects of registration this is now in accordance with the date of registration.

Priority in unregistered land

Compulsory registration came into effect on 1 December 1990 and as such the creation of a legal charge will trigger a first registration of the legal estate. In relation to mortgages created before this date, s 85(1) of the LPA 1925 confirms a first mortgagee's right to take possession of the title deeds as its security. Where a mortgagee takes possession of the title deeds, the mortgage is not capable of registration as a land charge under s 2(4) of the Land Charges Act 1972 (LCA 1972).

A mortgagee will lose priority in unregistered land if it allows the mortgagor to retake possession of the title deeds, thus enabling the mortgagor fraudulently to represent to a new lender or purchaser that there are no mortgages currently on the property. In situations where a mortgagee releases the title deeds to the mortgagor where monies remain outstanding they should immediately register a Class C(i) puisne mortgage.

As with legal mortgages, where an equitable mortgage has protected itself by deposit of the title deeds there is no requirement to register a land charge. If the mortgagee is unable to take possession of the title deeds, the interest must be protected by way of land charge under the LCA 1972. An equitable mortgage is registered as a Class C(iii) 'general equitable charge'. Section 4(5) of the LCA 1972 deems that non-registration of a charge registerable under Class C will make it void as against a purchaser of the land charged. The result of this will be that a later mortgagee will take free of the prior interest. Section 97 of the LPA 1925 however states, 'every mortgage affecting a legal estate in land … whether legal or equitable … shall rank according to its date of registration as a land charge pursuant to the Land Charges Act'.

EXAMPLE

1 January	A creates a puisne mortgage
8 January	B creates a puisne mortgage
10 January	A registers his mortgage
12 January	B registers his mortgage

Under the LCA 1972 s 4(5), B has priority as when he created his mortgage, A had not registered his interest, as such B would have no knowledge of the mortgage. This would result in A's interest being void as against B. Under s 97 of the LPA 1925, however, mortgages are declared to rank in order of their registration. As A registered before B, A would have priority over B.

The accepted view is that the LCA 1972's doctrine applies and B will have priority as A's unregistered charge is void as against him. A's right to recovery of the debt is not lost altogether but will rank behind B's.

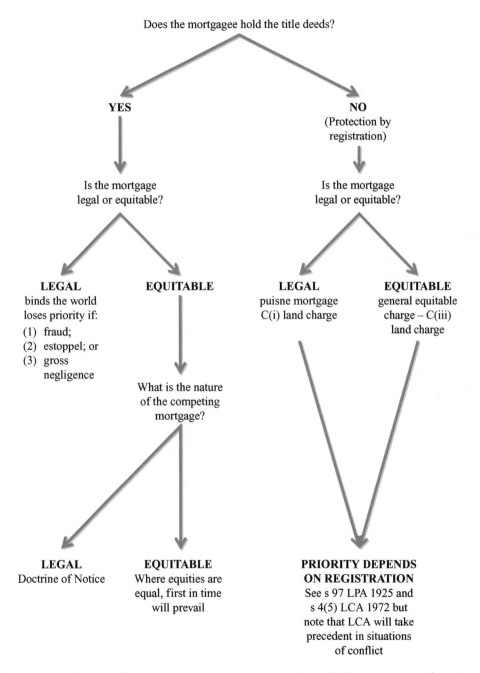

Figure 13.2 Priority of mortgages in relation to unregistered title: mortgage of a legal estate

Priority in registered land

Section 29 of the LRA 2002 has the effect that a mortgage granted on a registered estate[26] shall upon its registration (required by s 27(1) of the LRA 2002 in order to have legal status) only be subject to an earlier interest that is recorded on the register and any overriding interest. In practice, the priority of legal mortgages for registered land is thereby determined by the date of registration not the date of creation. (See also s 48(1) of the LRA 2002 and r 101 of the Land Registration Rules 2003.)

An equitable mortgage must be protected by entering a notice on the register under s 32 of the LRA 2002. Once recorded, it will have priority over all subsequent (later) mortgages.

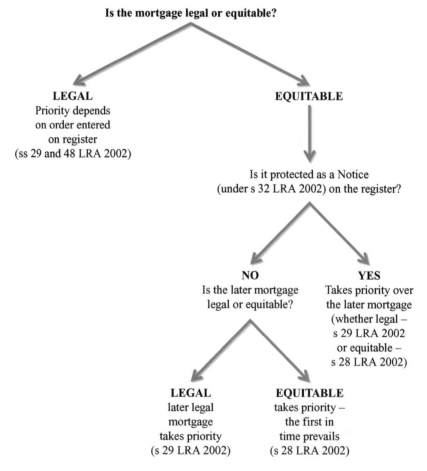

Figure 13.3 Priority of mortgages in relation to registered title: mortgage of a legal estate

---

26 The same is true for a registrable disposition of a registered mortgage under s 30 of the LRA 2002. However, you are unlikely to be asked to consider the selling of the mortgage debt itself during your course.

But what if an equitable mortgage is not recorded by using a notice at the time and a late mortgage is protected on the register? If the later mortgage is legal (i.e. registrable) then s 29 will operate and the equitable mortgage will have no binding effect against it. If the later mortgage is equitable (i.e. only recordable with the entry of a notice), then s 29 does not apply. So, as between equitable mortgages they are governed by s 28 of the LRA 2002, which means that priority is by the date of creation.

The Law Commission, in its latest consultation as at the date of writing[27] as explained in Chapter 5, has proposed that the special rules for priority under s 29 could be extended so that they also apply to determine the priority between competing interests that cannot be registered but can be recorded.

DISCUSSION

The protection afforded to mortgagors was once much more limited; now there is a range of both hard and soft law, out-of-court procedures encouraging settlement, and a greater willingness on the part of courts to intervene where necessary.

> **CONSIDER THIS – 2**
>
> How would you respond if challenged that the rights of the commercial lender to have the loan repaid as agreed are being unfairly undermined?

END OF CHAPTER SUMMARY

- Legal mortgages historically gave possession of the property to the mortgagor; today they normally take the form of a charge by way of legal mortgage and in registered land all mortgages take effect as charges.
- A first legal mortgage over an unregistered estate triggers a first registration. All mortgages created over a registered estate must be entered on the register to take effect at law.
- Where there are two or more mortgages over one piece of land, prior mortgages have priority. The order used to normally depend on the date order in which the mortgages were created, but now is usually according to the date of registration.
- The legal redemption date is normally set at six months, but the equitable right to redeem continues long after.

---

27 Law Commission, *Updating the Land Registration Act 2002: A Consultation Paper* (Consultation Paper No 227, 2016).

- The equity of redemption gives a number of rights to the mortgagor, including protection against irredeemable mortgages or postponement of redemption, collateral advantages and unfair terms.
- A mortgage can be set aside if obtained through misrepresentation or undue influence, provided the mortgagee was put on inquiry and did not take reasonable steps.
- If a mortgagor fails to repay there are different actions available to the mortgagee:

  - Sue on the covenant – may be used in conjunction with one of the other actions where there is negative equity (the property is worth less than the debt).
  - Sale – they will have to get the market value.
  - Possession – the mortgagor can prevent possession if they satisfy the court that they can repay arrears within a reasonable time and continue to meet the regular instalments as they fall due. The starting point for a reasonable period is the remainder of the mortgage term.
  - Appoint a receiver – relevant where the property is leased out to tenants and generating an income.
  - Foreclosure – the mortgagor's rights are destroyed (so any positive equity is lost) and the mortgagee becomes the outright owner but the court may order a sale instead.

PREPARING FOR ASSESSMENTS QUESTIONS

ESSAY QUESTION

Equity will not allow a clog on the equity of redemption. Analyse the statement, considering postponement of redemption, requiring redemption within a limited period, charging of excessive interest, and collateral advantages.

PROBLEM QUESTION

At the height of a property boom, Terry and Rachel purchased a freehold property for £300,000 with the assistance of a legal mortgage from a bank.

Last year, Terry was made redundant from his job as a store manager for a retail company. Terry has been unable to find alternative employment and Rachel's work is not well paid. The couple are now experiencing financial problems and are six months in arrears with their mortgage payments. In addition, Rachel has discovered that she is pregnant. The baby is due in September. Rachel will be on maternity leave for six months from August at half her normal salary.

The bank is now seeking immediate possession and sale of the property.

The debt currently owed to the bank including the outstanding mortgage loan, arrears and all charges is in the region of £175,000. The bank intends to market the property for £210,000 given the current economic conditions. However, Terry and Rachel have found a potential buyer for the property who will pay £240,000.

Advise Terry and Rachel as to the building society's right of possession and sale in relation to the property in the light of the above information.

_____

FURTHER READING

■ Brown, S, 'The Consumer Credit Act 2006: Real Additional Mortgage Protection?' [1990] Conv 431. Considers whether the Consumer Credit Act 2006 increases the protection available to mortgagors. Details the background to the Act, its main provisions and the factors determining when a mortgage will be governed by its rules.

■ Dixon, M, 'Combating the Mortgagee's Right to Possession: New Hope for the Mortgagor in Chains?' (1998) 18 Legal Studies 279. Explores the extent of the court's jurisdiction to suspend or deny a mortgagee's right to possession.

■ Dixon, M, 'Editor's Notebook: Mortgagees Powers and Duties' [2010] Conv 111. Considers proposals for the reform of the law of mortgages in the light of increased use of remedies by lenders in the economic downturn and asks what controls might be employed.

■ Haley, M, 'Mortgage Default: Possession, Relief and Judicial Discretion' (1997) 17 Legal Studies 483. Explores the history of exercise of the court's discretion to grant relief from possession by a mortgagee.

■ Mujih, EC, 'Over Ten Years After Royal Bank of Scotland plc v Etridge (No 2): Is the Law on Undue Influence in Guarantee Cases Any Clearer?' (2013) 24(2) ICCLR 57. Examines how the law on undue influence, particularly in relation to the taking of guarantee on matrimonial homes, has developed since *Etridge* and whether ten years on the case has clarified the law in this area.

■ Thompson, MP, 'Wives, Sureties and Banks' [2002] Conv 174. Constructive notice; legal advice; mortgagees powers and duties; spouses; surety; undue influence; examines the guidance from case law relating to the precautions which mortgagee should take to avoid transaction being set aside, where party grants mortgage to secure another's debts. Considers the cases *Royal Bank of Scotland plc v Etridge (No 2)* [2001] UKHL 44 and *Barclays Bank plc v O'Brien* [1994] 1 AC 180.

14

CHAPTER 14
FREEHOLD COVENANTS

CHAPTER AIMS AND OBJECTIVES

In this chapter we will consider the issue of freehold covenants. Covenants are a form of private control over the use of land whereby one landowner promises another to perform or to abstain from doing something over his land. These promises are normally extracted when a landowner sells off part of his property and seeks to regulate how the transferred land is used. Covenants over freehold land are extremely common. The arrangement regulating the land will not only affect the original parties entering into it but can also have an effect on the successors in title.

We will begin by considering how covenants are created and how they bind the original parties to the agreement. This will be followed by a consideration of how covenants can bind their successors in title both at common land and in equity. We will next explain the remedies available when a person breaches the covenants or breaks their promise. Finally, we will explore how covenants can be changed or removed.

By the end of this chapter, you should be able to:

- understand what a covenant is and how they are created;
- identify the difference between positive covenants and restrictive covenants;
- understand how covenants may be enforced in freehold land by and against the original parties;
- explain how the ability to enforce covenants (the benefit) passes to successors in title both at common law and in equity;
- explain how the responsibility of covenants (the burden) passes to successors in title both at common law and in equity;
- understand how covenants are protected in both registered and unregistered and;
- explain the range of remedies available when a covenant has been breached;
- understand how covenants can be changed or removed;
- apply the above to the case studies and learning tasks.

CASE STUDY – ONE

Harry purchased the freehold property known as Mayfield House in 2005. The property was registered with HM Land Registry. In 2010, Harry sold part of it (known as The Annex) to Tom.

Harry wanted to ensure that Tom would bear half all future costs of maintaining a driveway providing shared access for both Harry and Tom. Additionally, Harry wanted to control how Tom could use the land once it had been transferred to him. In the transfer deed from Harry to Tom the following was stated.

> For the benefit and protection of the adjoining or neighbouring land of the Vendor and with the intent to bind the land hereby conveyed into whosesoever hands the same may come the Purchaser for himself and his successors in title HEREBY COVENANTS with the Vendor

> 1 To pay an equal proportion of the cost of maintaining repairing clearing restoring and reinstating the driveway as indicated between the points marked A and B on the said plan.
> 2 To erect and forever maintain a timber fence on the south and north boundaries of the land hereby conveyed.
> 3 Not to use the land hereby conveyed for any purpose other than that of a single residential house.
> 4 Not to park any caravans or commercial vehicles on the land.

Harry sells Mayfield House to Christopher in 2013 and in 2015 Tom sells The Annex to Sidney.

KEEP IN MIND

- It is normal for landowners selling part of their land to impose covenants into the deed of transfer as has happened here. Looking at promises made by Tom, think about the advantages for Harry.
- Now consider that the reason that Harry finds the terms beneficial to him is because they improve his enjoyment of the property he has retained for himself, Mayfield House.
- Do you think this link with land means that the covenants should survive a change in the ownership of the properties?
- After all, any new owner of Mayfield House would be pleased to have the ability to enforce these covenants and Tom could arguably have some appreciation that the promises he made for the benefit of freehold land are expected to endure or 'run' with it.

■ For Tom's successors in title to the burdened The Annex, it is more difficult to say they should take on the promises of another. Can you think of any arguments for saying that the burden of covenants should 'run' with the affected land? Taking another look at the covenants above, note that some of them require the owner of The Annex to spend money or to undertake labour. Should that make a difference?

COVENANTS AND HOW ARE THEY CREATED

A covenant is simply a promise contained in a deed. The deed may be standalone, but covenants normally arise in either a transfer deed (normally using a Land Registry TR1 document), or in a conveyance or assignment (for unregistered land).

TUTOR TIP – 1

Be aware that just because a covenant is created in a deed, that does not mean it is a legal right. As covenants are not listed under s 1(2) of the Law of Property Act 1925 (LPA) they simply do not have the potential to be legal no matter how we go about creating them.

It is when a landowner is selling or giving property to another that they have the most potential and the greatest incentive to require the new owner to enter into any agreement that they see fit with regards to the future use. For example, consider a seller retaining part of his land to continue living there himself and the clear advantages of controlling what his new neighbour does. Stopping them from, say, building upon a specified area above a certain height, as it would spoil the view from the retained land, or from running a busy business next door may be desirable.

Extract 1 at the end of this chapter shows how the covenants would appear on the register once registered at the Land Registry.

Providing the new landowner agrees to the terms, there are no restraints upon what limits and duties may be placed over the burdened servient land for the benefit of the dominant land. For example, A could contract to sell part of his land to B and plant and maintain a cherry tree, an apple tree and a willow tree along the boundary separating the two pieces of land. Providing the covenant was correctly created by deed and registered, if B (the covenantor) does not plant the trees then B would be liable to A (the covenantee) for a breach of covenant.

Covenants will be either positive or restrictive (negative) in nature. The ability to distinguish between the two types is of vital importance, as we shall see as our discussion of this topic progresses. A positive covenant generally will require a positive physical action by the person making the promise. For example, a requirement to plant and maintain the trees along the boundary or to keep parts of the property not built upon in a clean and tidy condition. Alternatively, the person will be required to make some form of financial contribution to comply with their promise, for example making a payment towards the maintenance or upkeep of a shared facility, such as the maintenance of a shared driveway. A positive covenant will therefore require the person making the promise to do something positive in order to comply with it.

KEY CASE: *HAYWOOD V BRUNSWICK PERMANENT BENEFIT BUILDING SOCIETY* (1881) 8 QBD 403; 46 JP 356

Cotton LJ who established a test for deciding whether a covenant was positive by asking whether the person was required to 'put his hand into his pocket'.

By contrast a restrictive or negative covenant will require the person making the promise not to do something, i.e. not to use the property in a particular way or to act in a certain way. If a covenant can be complied with by doing nothing then it is a restrictive covenant, for example not to construct more than a certain number of buildings on the land or limiting the materials that can be used to construct the building.

TUTOR TIP – 2

Look at the substance of a covenant rather than the form. A covenant which states **'Do not let the driveway fall into disrepair'** may on first glance appear to be a restrictive covenant as the words 'do not' are used. If however we ask whether the person is required to put his hand in his pocket, as Cotton LJ stated in the *Haywood* case, we can see that the covenant is actually a positive covenant.

Although it is drafted in negative terms in order to comply with the covenant the person *must* do something positive. To stop the driveway falling into disrepair they would need to take positive action and pay money to keep the driveway in good repair. You must look at the effect of the words, or their substance, before deciding whether any covenant is a positive or restrictive covenant.

It is important to understand the key terminology relating to covenants before we start to analyse the case study. The terms that follow are vital when applying the legal tests that determine whether the different covenants raised can be enforced against the various parties.

ESSENTIAL TERMINOLOGY

A covenant	A promise contained in a deed.
Covenantor	The person who makes the promise.
Covenantee	The person to whom the promise is made. The covenantee will be the person seeking to enforce the covenant if the promise is broken.
Dominant tenement or dominant land	This is the land owned by the covenantee. This is the land that has the *benefit* of the covenant.
Servient tenement or servient land	This is the land owned by the covenantor. This is the land which has the *burden* of the covenant.
Benefit of a covenant	The ability to enforce the covenant and sue.
Burden of a covenant	The responsibility of the covenant and the ability to be sued.
Positive covenants	A positive covenant will require the person making the promise to positively do something, i.e. an act of maintenance or repair.
Restrictive covenants	A negative or restrictive covenant will require the person making the promise not to do something, i.e. not to use the property in a particular way.

APPLY YOUR LEARNING – TASK 1

Using the essential terminology above, apply the key terms to the case study. For now, consider only the position of the original parties to the covenants.

Start by identifying which of the properties, Mayflower House and The Annex, is the dominant and which is the servient tenement.

Next, make a note of who owns each property. Does this make Harry or Tom the covenantor (the person with the benefit of the covenants) and who is the covenantee (the person with the burden of the covenants)?

Finally, for each of the covenants determine whether they are positive or restrictive in nature.

TUTOR TIP – 3

When noting down the facts of a scenario, it can be useful to use a diagram. You can do this in relation to the learning task above.

Here is an example of one approach, based on the following facts. Alf is the owner of a large freehold estate, called Squirrels' Leap. He sells a large part of its grounds to Barclay (The Plot). In the transfer, Barclay covenants, on behalf of himself and his

> successors in title, with Alf for the benefit of Squirrels' Leap to: (a) not to use the property for more than one private dwelling house, (b) to erect a fence or wall along common boundary, (c) not to park caravans, boats or other commercial vehicles on the property, and (d) not to keep chickens or other domestic poultry at the property.
>
> Squirrels' Leap (Dominant Tenement)
>
> Alf (Covenantee)

THE ORIGINAL PARTIES AND ENFORCEABILITY OF THE COVENANTS

Under contract law, during the life of the covenant, the original covenantee takes the benefit of the covenant and the original covenantor takes on the burden.

LAW OF PROPERTY ACT 1925 S 56(1)

The deed between the original parties represents a contract and as such there is privity of contract between them. This means the original covenantee may always enforce any express covenant against the original covenantor. At common law however, there was a strict rule that no one could sue under a deed if they were not named as a party to the deed. This could be an issue if, for example, Harry wanted the covenants by Tom to be enforceable not only by himself but also by other neighbouring properties, let's say by Barbara, the owner of Springfield House.

The common law rule is relaxed by s 56(1) of the LPA 1925, which states: 'A person may take … the benefit of any … covenant over or respecting land … although he may not be named as a party to the conveyance or other instrument.'

The effect of this was that privity of contract was extended to a person who was not a party to the covenant to sue upon it. This means that the benefit of our covenants could be extended to Barbara. Case law has, however, influenced and effected the interpretation of s 56.

In *Re Ecclesiastical Commissioners for England's Conveyance* [1936][1] it was held that the effect of this section was that a person expressed in the conveyance to be one for whose benefit the covenant was made was regarded as an original covenantee even though he had not been a party to the deed. The House of Lords decision in *Beswick v Beswick* [1968],[2] however, restricted the interpretation of s 56 so no one other than the original *named* beneficiary or covenantee under a covenant could sue on it.

---

1 [1936] Ch 430.
2 [1968] AC 58.

The current position under s 56 is that a person not specifically named in a covenant may sue for the performance of the covenant provided three things are satisfied:

1   The claimant is referred to in the covenant under a generic description.
2   The covenant is expressed to be made *with* the third party and not just for his benefit.
3   The third party existed and was identifiable at the date of the covenant.

This was confirmed in the case of *Amsprop Trading Ltd v Harris Distribution Ltd* [1997].[3] The third requirement is potentially problematic. For example, returning to Barbara, the benefit of Tom's covenants can be extended to her as the current owner of Springfield House. However, if Barbara sells the house on to Paul he will not be able to use s 56 because he was not as yet in existence and identifiable at the date of the covenant.

CONTRACTS (RIGHTS OF THIRD PARTIES) ACT 1999

For contracts made after 11 May 2000, s 1(1) of the Contracts (Rights of Third Parties) Act 1999 (C(RTP)A 1999) allows a third party who is not a party to a contract to enforce its terms in his own right, providing:

1   there is an express term in the contract to that effect; or
2   the term in question purports to confer a benefit on him.

Under s 1(3): 'The third party must be expressly identified in the contract by name, as a member of a class or as answering to a particular description but need not be in existence when the contract is entered into'.

This means that people in Paul's position will be able to enforce covenants made for the benefit of 'successors in title'; there is no requirement that the person be in existence at the time the contract is made.

> TUTOR TIP – 4
> ....
>
> The C(RTP)A 1999 applies only to the benefit of a covenant and not a burden. It is relevant where any person for whose benefit the covenant is made, including a successor in title, is enforcing a covenant.
>
> It cannot be used in situations where either:
>
> ■ the original covenantee is trying to enforce the burden of a covenant against a successor in title of the original covenantor; or
> ■ a successor in title of the original covenantee is trying to enforce the burden of a covenant against a successor in title of the original covenantor.

3 [1997] 2 All ER 990; [1997] 1 WLR 1025.

APPLY YOUR LEARNING – TASK 2

Harry sold Mayfield House to Christopher in 2013 and in 2015 Tom sold The Annex to Sidney. Consider what would happen if Sidney has now decided to develop The Annex and commenced the building of four detached houses on it. In order to undertake this work, Sidney has removed the south boundary fence to enable construction vehicles to gain access to the site. The weight of the construction vehicles has caused extensive damage to the shared driveway including a number of potholes. As the work is ongoing, Sidney also parks these vehicles on the land overnight and at weekends.

Christopher is unhappy with this and wants to know whether he can take action, as he believes Sidney is breaching the covenants that were imposed on The Annex by Harry when Tom first purchased the land in 2010.

Could Christopher claim the benefit of the covenants using s 56(1) of the LPA 1925 as a person in existence and identifiable at the time of the covenant? What about under s 1(1) of the C(RTP)A 1999 as a person falling under s 1(3) of the Act?

Our consideration of the position between the original parties to the covenant while still in possession takes us only so far. Both the dominant land and the servient land change ownership: in our scenario Mayfield House now belongs to Christopher and The Annex to Sidney.

The rules we have explored under the C(RTP)A 1999 can be used to transfer the benefit of covenants, but many covenants predate that Act coming into force. In any event, the rules we will shortly consider under s 78(1) of the LPA 1925 are often preferable in annexing the benefit of covenants to the dominant land. We have also not yet considered the passing of the burden of covenants.

ENFORCEABILITY OF COVENANTS BY SUCCESSORS IN TITLE

In order to embark on an action successfully and to enforce a covenant a successor in title to the original party must show:

1   That the benefit of the covenants has run to himself from the covenantee.
2   That the burden of the covenants has passed to successor in title of servient land from the covenantor.

If the burden does not pass to the successor in title of servient land, action may be taken against the original covenantor.

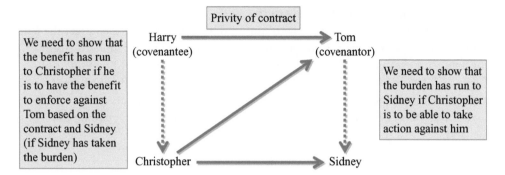

Figure 14.1 Passing of the benefit and the burden to successors in title

For the successor in title to the covenantee (Christopher) to be able to action against the original covenantee (Tom), we only need to show that he has taken the benefit. However, he will be limited to seeking damages from Tom as Tom is no longer in possession of The Annex. To be able to take action against the successor in title to the covenantee (Sidney as the new owner of The Annex), he will need to show that both the benefit *and* the burden of the covenant have passed.

The burden runs with the land more easily in equity; the courts will always act to mitigate the harshness of the common law and do what is fair and just. However, we must begin with the position at law given that equity follows it.

PROVING THE PASSING OF BENEFIT AT COMMON LAW

First, you must demonstrate that somebody has the ability to sue under the covenant. At common law, the benefit of both positive and restrictive covenants may pass either by express assignment or by implied assignment. To demonstrate express assignment there must be a transfer deed from one owner of the dominant land to the new owner of the dominant land. For the covenant to pass by implied assignment four conditions must be satisfied.

KEY CASE: *SMITH AND SNIPES HALL FARM LTD V RIVER DOUGLAS CATCHMENT BOARD* [1949] 2 KB 500

The Court of Appeal laid down four conditions to establish whether the benefit of a covenant would pass at common law by implication. All four conditions *must* be proved for the test to be satisfied.

- The covenant must touch and concern the land.
- There must have been an intention that the benefit of the covenant should run with the land.
- The covenantee must have a legal estate in the dominant land.
- The new owner must take a legal estate in that land.

The covenant must touch and concern the land

The covenant must 'touch and concern' the land, that is 'it must either affect the land as regards its mode of occupation, or it must such as per se, and not merely from collateral circumstances, affects the value of the land' (per Tucker LJ in *Smith and Snipes Hall Farm Ltd v River Douglas Catchment Board* [1949]). The basis of the requirement is that obligations that are purely personal to covenantee and covenantor are not enforceable as it is inappropriate for them to the passing of the land.

KEY CASE: *SMITH AND SNIPES HALL FARM LTD V RIVER DOUGLAS CATCHMENT BOARD* [1949] 2 KB 500

The Court of Appeal laid down four conditions to establish whether the benefit of a covenant would pass at common law by implication. All four conditions MUST be proved for the test to be satisfied.

- The covenant must touch and concern the land.
- There must have been an intention that the benefit of the covenant should run with the land.
- The covenantee must have a legal estate in the dominant land.
- The new owner must take a legal estate in that land.

Applying this in practice, the questions that must be asked to determine whether the covenant touches and concerns the land are:

- Does the covenant cease to be of benefit if it does not pass to the successor in title?
- Does the covenant affect the nature, quality, mode of user or value of the land of the reversionary?
- Is the covenant expressed to be personal?
- In relation to money, is compliance of the covenant connected with something to be done on, to or in relation to the land?

There must have been an intention that the benefit of the covenant runs with the land

It is not enough that the covenant touches and concerns the land. It must also be shown that the original parties intended the covenants would run with the land and would affect successor in title. This can be evidenced both expressly and impliedly.

A good place to start is to look at how the original covenants were drafted in the deed and what words were used. For example:

> For the benefit and protection of the adjoining or neighbouring land of the Transferor and with the intent to bind the land hereby conveyance into whosesoever hands the same may come the Transferee for himself and his successors in title HEREBY COVENANTS with the Transferor.

If there are no express provisions contained in the deed then consider what was implied by the deed. Were the promises meant to be long-term ones?

To a large extent, the difficulties of establishing such an intention has been greatly diminished by the Court of Appeal decision in *Federated Homes v Mill Lodge Properties Ltd* [1979].[4] This case gave a wide interpretation to s 78(1) of the LPA 1925, which provides:

> A covenant relating to any land of the covenantee shall be deemed to be made with the covenantee and his successors in title and the persons deriving title under him or them, and shall have effect as if such successors and other persons were expressed. For the purposes of this subsection in connection with covenants restrictive of the user of land 'successors in title' shall be deemed to include the owners and occupiers for the time being of the covenantee intended to be benefited.

Brightman LJ considered that:

> [I]f the condition precedent of s 78 is satisfied, that is to say, there exists a covenant which touches and concerns the land of the covenantee, that the covenant runs with the land for the benefit of his successors in title, persons deriving title under him and other owners and occupiers.

Thus the covenant is deemed to run with the land by virtue of this statutory provision unless the deed expressly provides that the benefit is not intended to run with the land.

The original covenantee must have held a legal estate in the land

It makes sense that a covenant that touches and concerns the land will only be capable of passing at common law if the original covenantee held a legal estate.

The successor in title must have acquired a legal estate in land

The benefit of a covenant will only pass at common law if the successor in title holds a legal estate in the land. The case of *Smith and Snipes Hall Farm Ltd v River Douglas Catchment Board* [1949] clarified the effect of s 78 of the LPA 1925 and confirmed that the

---

4 [1979] EWCA Civ 3; [1980] 1 All ER 371.

successor in title did not have to have an identical estate to the original covenantee *provided* it would be shown that the successor had derived a legal estate from the original covenantee. Therefore the original covenantee could have held the freehold estate and their successor in title have acquired the leasehold estate and would still be successful.

TUTOR TIP – 6

Once successfully established the benefit of the covenants attaches itself to the whole of the land. Therefore should the land be divided up later into smaller pieces of land and sold to different people, any one of those owners or their successors in title will be able to enforce the covenant. This was established in *Federated Homes v Mill Lodge Properties* [1979].

APPLY YOUR LEARNING – TASK 3

Following step one above, apply the four conditions laid down in the case of *Smith and Snipes Hall Farm Ltd v River Douglas Catchment Board* [1949] to see whether the benefit of the covenants have successfully passed from Harry to Christopher at common law.

PROVING THE PASSING OF BURDEN AT COMMON LAW

Once you have successfully proven that somebody has the ability to sue, you must consider who he or she can sue. We have established that the original covenantor will always remain liable under privity of contract. The question is whether it is possible to sue their successor in title? In order to prove this you must show that the burden of the covenant has passed to the successor in title.

At common law the burden of a covenant cannot run with the land as stated in *Austerberry v Oldham Corporation* (1885).[5] This was affirmed in *Rhone v Stephens* [1994].[6]

KEY CASES: *AUSTERBERRY V CORPORATION OF OLDHAM* [1885] 29 CH D 750

RHONE V STEPHENS [1994] UKHL 3; [1994] 2 AC 310; [1994] 2 ALL ER 65

Cotton, Lindley and Fry LJJ in *Austerberry* all agreed that there was no authority which allowed the burden of a covenant to run with property at common law. Cotton LJ stated that he was:

5   (1885) 29 ChD 750.
6   [1994] UKHL 3; [1994] 2 AC 310; [1994] 2 All ER 65.

not prepared to say that any covenant which imposes a burden upon land does run with the land, unless the covenant does, upon the true construction of the deed containing the covenant, amount to either a grant of an easement, or a rent-charge, or some estate or interest in the land. A mere covenant to repair, or to do something of that kind, does not seem to me, I confess, to run with the land in such a way as to bind those who may acquire it.

He went on to say that, 'no case has been decided which does establish that such a burden can run with the land.'

This decision was affirmed in *Rhone v Stephens* by the House of Lords. Lord Templeman believed that the 'rule in *Austerberry v Oldham Corporation*, 29 Ch D 750 has stood the test of time and ought to be applied.' His rationale was that, 'At common law a person cannot be made liable upon a contract unless he was a party to it.'

The case is also interesting as it clarified the position in respect of s 79 LPA 1925. Section 79 is the counterpart to s 78, discussed above, which in *Federated Homes* was interpreted to automatically attach the benefit of covenants to the land in the absence of any other evidence. The plaintiff in *Rhone v Stephens* argued that s 79 reversed the decision in *Austerberry* but the House of Lords refused to allow s 79 to have the same effect in relation to the burden of covenant.

> Without casting any doubt on those long standing decisions I do not consider that it follows that s 79 of the Act of 1925 had the corresponding effect of making the burden of positive covenants run with the land. In *Jones v. Price* [1965] 2 QB 618, 633, Willmer L.J. repeated that: 'a covenant to perform positive acts … is not one the burden of which runs with the land so as to bind the successors in title of the covenantor: see *Austerberry v. Oldham Corporation.*'

The position is therefore clear. The burden of a covenant cannot pass at common law.

A number of cases have attempted to circumvent the effect of the *Austerberry* ruling by finding ways to enable a covenantee to take direct action against a covenantor's successor in title for a breach of certain covenants. At present there are five different situations that have been successful (Figure 14.2).

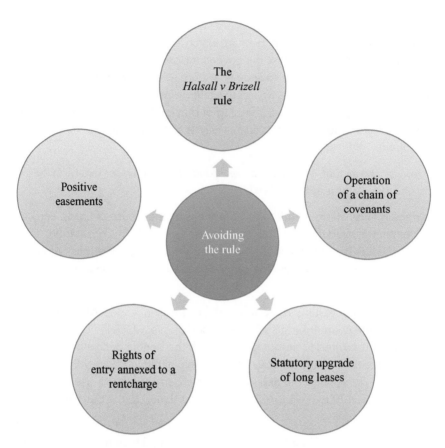

Figure 14.2 Avoiding the rule that the burden of covenants cannot run at law

The rule in Halsall v Brizzell (1957)[7]

This has been named the 'mutual benefit and mutual burden' rule. Lord Denning considered in circumstances where a covenantor has the benefit of a covenant, which was coupled with an obligation to contribute towards the cost, it was unfair that the responsibility to pay did not pass to a successor in title. Lord Denning considered it wrong that the positive element of the covenant could pass but that the obligation to pay towards it could be avoided.

An example of it used in practice would be in relation to a covenant to repair a driveway. You have the benefit of it, the right to drive over it in order to get to your property so you should also have the responsibility of paying towards its upkeep and repair.

The benefit and burden principle has been narrowed, however, by subsequent decisions and the position was succinctly summarised in *Davies v Jones* [2009][8] as follows:

---

7 (1957) ChD 169.

8 [2009] EWCA Civ 1164; [2010] 1 P & CR 22.

1   the benefit and burden must be conferred in the same transaction;
2   the benefit must be conditional upon (and relevant to) the burden; and
3   the successor in title must have been afforded the opportunity to renounce the
    benefit (and in doing so be released from the burden).

It is against this background that we come to the Court of Appeal decision in *Goodman
v Elwood* [2013],[9] which illustrates the use of the benefit and burden principle to enable
the burden of a positive covenant to run.

The operation of a chain of covenants

If B covenants with A to repair a fence and he then sells his land on to C, and if C does
not then repair the fence, i.e. breaches the covenant, A can pursue B for breach of
contract because he cannot pursue C in common law as the burden has not run. To
ensure that B has some form of redress for being sued for a breach of covenant he did
not cause, on the sale to C, B will have taken an indemnity covenant from C to the
effect that if B is pursued by A for breach and damages are recovered, under the
indemnity covenant taken from C, B will sue C for recovery.

How does the indemnity work? – B will ensure that C, new party, indemnifies him in
relation to any future breaches of the covenants. This is known as a chain of indemnity.

Therefore if B is sued after he has disposed of his interest he will sue C who currently
holds title as there is now privity of contract between the parties.

In this way, because C knows he may be sued by B if B is pursued for his breach of
covenant, C will take care not to breach the covenant even though the burden does
not run. This is a way of enforcing covenants against onward successors in title from B
indirectly.

A chain of indemnity is not without its problems. First, the original covenantor will
only be protected if the chain is maintained. If C fails to obtain an indemnity from D
and then D breaches a covenant it is not possible to claim from the party that has
breached the covenant. Additionally the chain can be affected if someone dies or
cannot be traced. Second, whilst damages may be available they may not be best
solution to the breach or the breach may be difficult to quantify.

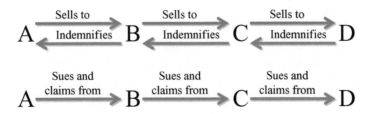

Figure 14.3 The workings of a chain of indemnity covenants

9 [2013] EWCA Civ 110.

Statutory upgrade of long leases

By virtue of s 153 of the LPA 1925, a lease granted for a term for more than 300 years with no rent payable and having more than 200 years left to run may be enlarged into a freehold. This is known as enfranchisement. Following the lessee's right to purchase all or part of the freehold, the freehold is then subject 'to all the same covenants ... as the tenant would have been subject to if it had not been so enlarged.'

Right of re-entry

This will only be applicable *if* the original covenantor made a covenant subject to the right of re-entry. A right of re-entry is a legal interest in land and therefore is capable of binding successors in title. As such the right runs with the land and a successor in title will be bound. This is not an absolute right, however, since the courts have jurisdiction to grant relief against forfeiture where there is a breach.

It is also possible to have indirect enforceability by way of an estate rentcharge to which a right of re-entry is annexed. A rentcharge is a periodic payment charged on land other than rent payable under a lease or interest. Whilst the creation of new rentcharges was prohibited by the Rentcharges Act 1977, estate rentcharges were preserved under s 2(4) of the Act. An estate rentcharge is a rentcharge created to enable the 'rent owner' to enforce the performance of covenants by purchasers of the land, or to collect service charges from them. See *Smith Brothers Farms Ltd v Canwell Estate Co Ltd* [2012][10] in relation to the creation and validity of rentcharge as estate charges.

An estate rentcharge is one way to circumvent the rule that positive covenants are not normally enforceable against purchasers of freehold property. The right of entry attached to the estate rentcharge enables the rent owner to take possession of the property, if the covenant is not complied with. Whilst a very effective solution it is rarely used in practice.

Positive easements

A successor in title may attempt to argue that a covenant to maintain a fence is not actually a covenant but is in fact a positive easement. In the law relating to easements, an exception has been made to enable owners of the dominant tenement to enforce the owner of the servient tenement to maintain a fence. If argued successfully, the burden of an easement would run with the servient land and the covenantor's successor in title could enforce it on that basis.[11]

These positive easements are known as 'spurious easements' because they do not fit with the normal requirement that an easement require no expenditure on the part of the servient land. Despite this, in *Crow v Wood* [1971][12] a fencing covenant has been held to be a positive easement rather than a positive covenant. It should be noted,

----

10 [2012] 2 All ER 1159.

11 Note that easements are a legal proprietary interest in under s 1 of the LPA 1925.

12 [1971] 1 QB 77; [1970] 3 All ER 425.

however, that this case relates to agricultural property and the maintenance of a fence for the enclosure of livestock. The case of *Sugarman v Porter* [2006][13] also makes it clear that the wording must be such as to create an easement. Here, it was held that, while relating to fencing, the wording created only a covenant.

> ### TUTOR TIP – 7
> ....
>
> Given the limited options available for a freehold estate, it is worth exploring other possibilities. As considered in Chapter 7, leasehold covenants run far more readily and so creating a lease rather than selling the freehold is one option for a landowner. The use of commonhold is another possibility. This will be considered in Chapter 17.

APPLY YOUR LEARNING – TASK 4

Given that the *Austerberry* case will not allow the burden of any covenants to run with the land is Christopher able to successfully use any of the five exceptions to demonstrate that the burden of the covenants have passed from Tom to Sidney at common law?

Note the covenants again:

1   To pay an equal proportion of the cost of maintaining repairing clearing restoring and reinstating the driveway as indicated between the points marked A and B on the said plan.
2   To erect and forever maintain a timber fence on the south and north boundaries of the land hereby conveyed.
3   Not to use the land hereby conveyed for any purpose other than that of a single residential house.
4   Not to park any caravans or commercial vehicles on the land.

Also keep in mind that we already know that Sidney had been making use of the driveway (note, *Davies v Jones* [2009]).

PROVING THE PASSING OF THE BURDEN IN EQUITY

If it is not possible to establish that both the benefit and the burden of a covenant has passed at common law then equity may be able to assist. In the nineteenth century the limitations of the common law to enforce covenants prompted equity to intervene by means of injunction. Equity's initial interference grew out of the doctrine of notice. *Tulk v Moxhay* (1848)[14] developed the current status of equitable recognition of covenants.

....

13   [2006] EWHC 331 (Ch); [2006] 2 P & CR 274; [2006] All ER (D) 117 (Mar).
14   (1848) 2 Ph 774, 18 LJ Ch 83.

While we have established that the contract the original covenantor made continues to be enforceable against them even after they sell the land at law, the remedy against them is limited to damages given they no longer own the land. What we need is a route to seek remedies against the current owner of the burdened land, which could include injunctions and specific performance. In recognising the running of the burden in equity, *Tulk* provides such an argument.

KEY CASE: *TULK V MOXHAY* (1848) 2 PH 774; 18 LJ CH 83

The courts were asked to consider whether Mr Moxhay, the covenantor's successor in title, who intended to build on the land in Leicester Square was bound by the following covenant to:

> keep and maintain the said piece or parcel of ground and square garden, and the iron railing round the same, in its present form, and in sufficient and proper repair, as a square garden and pleasure ground, in an open state and uncovered with any buildings, in a neat and ornamental order; and shall not nor will take down, nor permit or suffer to be taken down, or defaced, at any time or times hereafter, the equestrian statue now standing or being in the centre of the said square garden, but shall and will continue and keep the same in its present situation ...

It was held that although the burden would not pass at common law, a purchaser on notice of a covenant could be bound by it in equity and an injunction could be granted to stop him from infringing the covenant.

The case established a number of preconditions in order for the servient owner to be subject to the burden of the restrictive covenant in equity.

- The covenant must be negative.
- The covenant must accommodate the dominant land.
- The covenantor's successor in title must have acquired the servient land subject to the burden of the covenant.

A transferee of the land of the covenantor will only therefore be bound by the *burden* of a *restrictive covenant* if all conditions are fulfilled.

The case of *London and South Western Railway v Gomm* [1882][15] clarified that equity would only enforce a restrictive covenant if was made for the protection of other *land* and not the covenantee personally. Therefore you must establish that the covenant benefits the dominant land. This was a move away from a contractual to a proprietary interpretation and resulted in restrictive covenants resembling easements as being a right in favour of the dominant land over the servient land.

---

15 [1882] 20 Ch D 562.

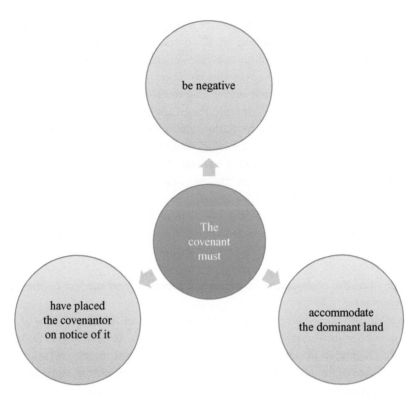

Figure 14.4 Requirements for the burden of a restrictive covenant to run in equity

The covenant must be negative

It is not possible for the burden of a positive covenant to pass. As we have seen above this has been reaffirmed recently in *Rhone v Stephens* [1994]. The acid test for establishing whether a covenant is positive was proposed in *Haywood v Brunswick Permanent Benefit Building Society* (1881),[16] where Cotton LJ asked whether the covenantor was required to 'put his hand into his pocket'. If so, the covenant was a positive one. The Court of Appeal in the *Haywood* case also held that the rule in *Tulk v Moxhay* (1848) had no application to positive covenants. As such equity would only enforce those covenants 'restricting the mode of user of the land'.

The covenant must accommodate the dominant land

Only covenants that can be said to accommodate the dominant land become proprietary interests capable of binding successors in title. A restrictive covenant in equity accommodates the dominant tenement if the following criteria are present:

- The original covenantee was the owner of land to be benefited at the date when the covenant was granted. This would not be possible if he owned no land at that date.
- The dominant tenement must have enjoyed sufficient proximity with the servient tenement. Whilst the land to be benefited is often adjoining the servient

---

16 (1881) 8 QBD 403.

tenement, such closeness is not necessary though it is worth noting that the further apart the two pieces of land are the harder it will be to successfully argue the dominant tenement has sufficient proximity. In the case of *Formby v Barker* [1903][17] it was considered that covenants binding land in Hampstead (the servient land) were too remote to benefit land in Clapham (the dominant land).

■ The original parties must have intended the burden to run with the land. This intention would usually have been made clear in the deed but this is not essential since s 79(1) of the LPA 1925 has the effect that the burden of the restrictive covenant will be taken as intended to run with the land unless there is an express intention to the contrary. As Robert Walker LJ explained in *Morrells of Oxford Ltd v Oxford United Football Club Ltd* [2001][18]: 'Section 79 is concerned with simplifying conveyancing by creating a rebuttable presumption that covenants relating to land of the covenantor are intended to be made on behalf of successors in title, rather than be intended as purely personal.'

The assignee of the covenantor acquired the servient land subject to the burden of the covenant

If the servient land comprises registered land then the covenant should have been entered as a notice (unilateral agreed) in accordance with s 32 of the LRA 2002. If it has not been registered in this way the covenantor's successor in title will take the servient land free of the restrictive covenant. If the land comprises unregistered land, then the restrictive covenant should have been registered as a Class D(ii) land charge. If it has not been protected in this way then it will be void as against a purchaser of a legal estate for value. Post-1925 covenants under s 79 of the LPA 1925 are deemed to be made by the covenantor on behalf of himself and his successors unless a contrary intention is expressed in the deed.

Table 14.1 Registering the burden of a restrictive covenant

Registered land	Unregistered land
The covenantee must enter a notice in the register of the servient tenement	Covenants created after 1925 must be registered as a Class D(ii) land charge
If the covenant is not registered, it will not bind a person taking a registrable disposition of the land for valuable consideration	If a covenant is capable of being registered as a land charge and it is not, it will be void as against a purchaser for money or money's worth
The covenantor's successor in title will therefore take free of the restrictive covenant as it cannot be an overriding interest; see *Hodges v Jones* [1935] Ch 657 at 671	The covenantor's successor in title will therefore take free of the restrictive covenant

17 [1903] 2 Ch 539.
18 [2000] EWCA Civ 226; [2001] Ch 459; [2001] 2 WLR 128.

APPLY YOUR LEARNING – TASK 5

Of the remaining covenants that would not pass from Tom to Sidney at common law, which ones can now pass in equity?

PROVING THE PASSING OF BENEFIT IN EQUITY

As you are aware, to successfully enforce a covenant a successor in title to the original party must show that the benefit of the covenants has run to himself from the covenantee *and* the burden of the covenants has passed to successor in title of servient land from the covenantor. To sue in equity, the claimant must show that both elements have passed. To demonstrate that the benefit of a covenant has passed in equity two conditions must be satisfied:

- It must be shown that the covenant touches and concerns the land of the covenantee.
- The benefit of the covenant must have passed to the covenantee's successor in title.

The covenant touches and concerns the land of the covenantee

This is the same principle as we saw in relation to the running of the benefit at common law at step one. The covenant must 'touch and concern' the land. Again we follow the test laid down in the case of *P & A Swift Investment v Combined English Stores Group plc* [1989].[19] The basis of the requirement is that obligations that are purely personal to covenantee and covenantor are not enforceable. The questions that must be asked to determine whether the covenant touches and concerns the land are:

- Does the covenant cease to be of benefit if it does not pass to the successor in title?
- Does the covenant affect the nature, quality, mode of user or value of the land of the reversionary?
- Is the covenant expressed to be personal?
- In relation to money, is compliance of the covenant connected with something to be done on to or in relation to the land?

The benefit of the covenant must have passed to the covenantee's successor

This can be achieved in one of three ways:

- annexation
- assignment
- building scheme.

----

19 [1989] AC 632.

Annexation

The wording of the original covenant must show an intention that the benefit was to run with land into whosever's hands the land may pass. The benefit passing on by annexation will be proof that a covenant has fastened, as if superglued, itself to the dominant land. If it can be shown that the covenant has been annexed to a parcel of land, it will not require further annexation on a future sale of the dominant land. Once annexed to the land, it will be stuck to the land for the benefit of all successors in title to all or part of the land.

Annexing a covenant to a piece of land may be evidenced in one of three ways.

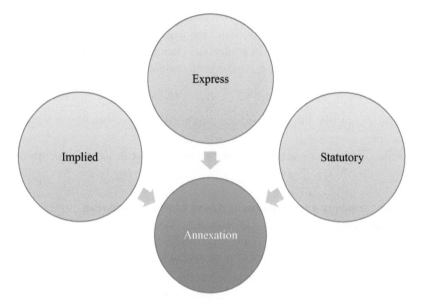

Figure 14.5 Evidence for establishing annexation

Express Annexation – If the original covenant contained words which expressly acknowledged that the benefit of the covenant should benefit successive owners of the dominant land then the covenant can be said to be expressly annexed or superglued to the dominant land.

An example of express wording would be:

> **'B covenants with A and his successors in title for the benefit of A's retained land into whosever hands the same may come…'**

The wording of the covenant should clearly show that the covenant was made for the benefit of the land whoever may own it as opposed to for the personal benefit of the first covenantee.[20] It must identify the land to be benefited[21] and must benefit more

....

20 *Rogers v Hosegood* [1900] 2 Ch 388.
21 *Renals v Cowlishaw* [1878] 9 Ch D 125.

than a small part of the total land.[22] If this can be established, the new covenantee will take the benefit of the covenant and will be about to enforce it.

Implied Annexation – Annexation may be implied if intention can be found in the general wording of the deed creating the covenant and the surrounding circumstances that the benefit of the covenant should run.

Annexation will be implied if the benefit of the covenant was so obviously intended to run that to ignore it would be 'not only an injustice by a departure from common sense'.[23] To be successful, however, the dominant land must be defined and the covenant must be intended to benefit the land not the covenantee.[24]

KEY CASE: *MARTEN V FLIGHT REFUELLING LTD* [1962] CH 115

In *Marten v Flight Refuelling Ltd* it was held that there was no express annexation in the deed containing the original covenant. Nevertheless, the judge found that annexation was so obviously intended by the original parties, it would be wrong not to ignore the evidence provided the covenant was to benefit a clearly definable piece of land and it was intended that it would attach to the land.

Statutory Annexation – You will remember s 78(1) of the LPA 1925 from the consideration of the benefit of covenants at common law. Section 78(1) states:

> A covenant relating to any land of the covenantee shall be deemed to be made with the covenantee and his successors in title and the persons deriving title under him or them, and shall have effect as if such successors and other persons were expressed.

Brighton LJ in *Federated Homes Ltd v Mill Lodge Properties Ltd* [1979][25] held that s 78(1) automatically annexes the benefit of the covenant to the dominant land:

> If the condition precedent of s 78 is satisfied – that is to say, there exists a covenant which touches and concerns the land of the covenantee – that covenant runs with the land for the benefit of his successors in title

---

22 *Re Ballard's Conveyance* [1937] 2 All ER 691.
23 *Rogers v Hosegood* [1900] 2 Ch 388.
24 *Marten v Flight Refuelling Ltd* [1962] Ch 115.
25 [1979] EWCA Civ 3; [1980] 1 All ER 371.

There is a note of caution however as concern was voiced in *Roake v Chadha* [1984][26] that an automatic annexation would deny express words to the contrary in a deed creating the covenant. It was held that s 78(1) of the LPA 1925 could not be used to annex the benefit of a covenant when the express wording in the deed creating the covenant precluded such annexation. In *J Sainsbury plc v Enfield London Borough Council* [1989][27] it was further highlighted that the annexation would not be automatic and that one had to construe the covenant in the light of all the circumstances to see whether or not the benefit was to be annexed.

Assignment

If the covenant is not annexed to the land the covenant remains separate from the land. In order for the benefit to pass there must be an express assignment of the covenant. The assignment must be simultaneous with the transfer of the dominant land to the new owner. This is usually achieved by adding a clause within the purchase deed (normally the TR1). In order to be effective an express assignment is required every time the property changes hands and the assignment must be with the transfer of the dominant land to the new owner. To be successfully assigned the covenant must benefit the dominant land at the date of the covenant and the dominant tenement must be certain and identifiable.[28]

TUTOR TIP – 8

Annexation   The attachment of the benefit to the land happens at the time of the creation of the covenant. Once annexation to the land it stays forever.

Assignment   The transfer of the benefit to the land following its creation. As such the benefit must be assigned from transferor or transferee every time the land is transferred.

Since the decision in *Federated Homes*, assignment is now far less important.

Building Scheme

Where a building scheme exists both benefit and the burden of the covenants will pass with the land. A building scheme normally arises where a developer is building a new housing estate and has imposed restrictions on the purchaser of each plot. The intention is that once all the plots have been sold each purchaser and his successors will be able to enforce the restrictions directly against other purchasers and their successors in title rather than the developer, who at that point has no connection to any of the land. The requirements of a building scheme were first set out in the case of *Elliston v Reacher* (1908)[29] and are based on the notion of mutual enforceability.

---

26 [1984] 1 WLR 40.
27 [1989] 1 WLR 590.
28 *Miles v Easter* [1933] Ch 611 at 625.
29 (1908) 2 Ch 374.

KEY CASE: *ELLISTON V REACHER* [1908] 2 CH 665; [1908–10] ALL E REP 612

In order to establish that the benefit and burden of a covenant passes under a building scheme, a number of facts must be proved:

1   The plaintiff and the defendant must have derived their title from a common vendor.
2   Before selling the common vendor (normally the developer) must have laid out the estate in plots.
3   The common vendor must have intended the restrictions to be for the benefit of all the plots.
4   The purchasers from the common vendor must have purchased on the understanding that the covenants were to be enforceable by every other purchaser.
5   The area to which the scheme relates must be clearly defined.

Providing all five points can be established, equity will allow the benefit of the covenants imposed on the other plots to run automatically to all the successors of the original purchasers, without the need for annexation or assignment as described above.

TUTOR TIP – 9

Normally when the dominant and servient land merges into the same ownership the covenant will lapse. This does not apply in relation to building scheme covenants. In *Texaco Antilles Ltd v Kernochan* [1973] AC 609; [1973] 2 All ER 118 it was stated that in a building scheme the covenants revive automatically if the plot of land is subsequently redivided later.

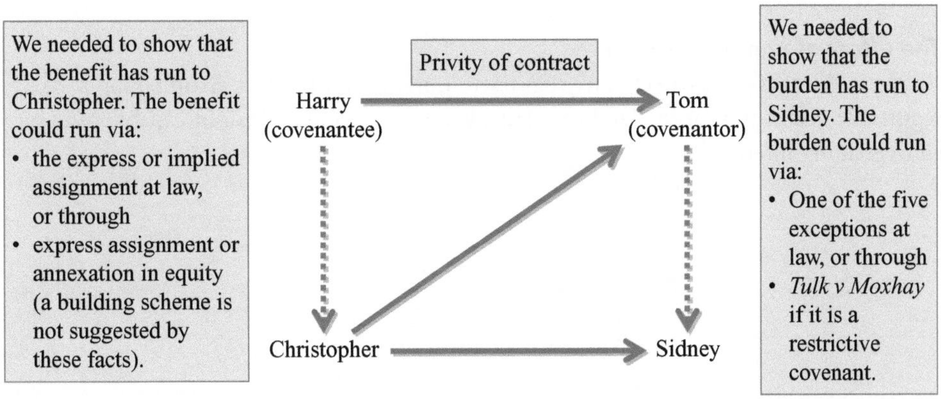

We needed to show that the benefit has run to Christopher. The benefit could run via:
- the express or implied assignment at law, or through
- express assignment or annexation in equity (a building scheme is not suggested by these facts).

Privity of contract

Harry (covenantee) ⟶ Tom (covenantor)

Christopher ⟶ Sidney

We needed to show that the burden has run to Sidney. The burden could run via:
- One of the five exceptions at law, or through
- *Tulk v Moxhay* if it is a restrictive covenant.

Figure 14.6 Showing that the benefit and burden has passed to successors in title

PROTECTION OF COVENANTS

UNREGISTERED LAND

Covenants created prior to 1925

Covenants created before 1925 are not capable of registration. Working under the doctrine of notice principle, they will bind all persons *except* the bona fide purchaser for value *without notice* of the covenant. Notice may be actual or constructive.

Covenants created after 1925

Covenants created after 1925 must be registered either as a land charge or a local land charge. Restrictive covenants must be registered as a Class D(ii) land charge and registered against the estate owner of the servient land. If a covenant is capable of being registered as a land charge and it is not, it will be void as against a purchaser for money or money's worth.

REGISTERED LAND

The covenantee must enter a notice in the register of the servient land. Notices are governed under s 32 of the Land Registration Act 2002 (LRA 2002) which states that 'an entry in the register in respect of a burden of an interest affecting a registered estate or charge'. Notices may be entered either by the registered proprietor or the person who claims the right to be protected. Applications must be made as either an:

- **Agreed Notice** – This means that the registered has consented to the entry or the person applying for the notice can prove to the Land Registry that the claim is valid, or a
- **Unilateral Notice** – Entered onto the register without the registered owner's consent. With a unilateral notice the person applying does not have to show that they have a valid claim or provide supporting evidence for their claim. It is in effect a hostile act, carried out in order to protect the owner of the interest and ensure that any potential purchaser knows that it exists.

The effect of non-registration

If the covenant is not protected by registration, it will not bind a person taking a registrable disposition of the land for valuable consideration and is not capable of being an overriding interest.[30]

---

30 *Hodges v Jones* [1935] Ch 657; 104 LJ Ch 329.

REMEDIES

AT COMMON LAW

If you are able to prove the benefit and burden of the covenant at common law, the claimant may claim damages from the defendant and the court cannot refuse.

IN EQUITY

If you are able to prove the benefit and burden of the covenant in equity, you would be entitled to ask for:

- injunctive relief (for restrictive covenants)
- specific performance (for positive covenants)
- damages under s 50 of the Supreme Court Act 1981

As we have seen it is easier to prove that the benefit and burden of a covenant runs in equity and as such is available to more people. There are therefore more remedies available under equity of a breach of covenant. Equitable remedies are, however, at the discretion of the court.

Modern approach to equitable remedies

The courts are uncomfortable with granting an injunction for a breach of covenant as it is seen as draconian and restrictive. The courts have taken the approach of awarding equitable damages in the place of an injunction in situations where:

- the injury to the claimant's legal rights is small;
- the damage can be estimated in money and can be adequately compensated by a *small* money payment; and
- the court considers that an injunction would be too oppressive.[31]

What constitutes a 'small money payment'?

In *Wrotham Park Estate Co Ltd v Parkside Homes Ltd* [1974][32] Brightman J awarded compensation stating that it was in the sum of what 'might reasonably have been demanded ... as a quid pro quo for relaxing the covenant' i.e. what sum would have been paid if the covenantor had approached the covenantee to release the covenant. In this case it was felt that 5 per cent of the developer's anticipated profit might reasonably be demanded. In *Amec Developments Ltd v Jury's Hotel Management UK Ltd* (2000)[33] £375,000 was awarded in place of an injunction where a Jury's hotel was built four metres over a building line in breach of a covenant.

---

31 *Shelfer v City of London Electric Light Co* [1895] 2 Ch 388.
32 [1974] 2 All ER 321; [1974] 1 WLR 798.
33 (2000) 82 P & CR 286; [2001] 1 EGLR 81.

Proportionality – would an injunction be 'too oppressive'?

In considering whether the grant of an injunction would be oppressive to the defendant, all the circumstances of the case have to be considered. In *Jaggard v Sawyer* [1994][34] the question asked was 'Did the defendant act openly and in good faith in ignorance of the covenant or flagrantly in full knowledge of the breach?' At one extreme, the defendant may have acted openly and in good faith and in ignorance of the plaintiff's rights, and thereby inadvertently placed himself in a position where the grant of an injunction would either force him to yield to the claimant's extortionate demands or expose him to substantial loss. At the other extreme, the defendant may have acted with his eyes open and in full knowledge that he was invading the plaintiff's rights and hurried on his work in the hope that by presenting the court with a fait accompli he could compel the plaintiff to accept monetary compensation.

An example of the latter can be seen in *Wakeham v Wood* (1981).[35] The defendant had acted flagrantly in breach of a covenant to build and in doing so obstructed the plaintiff's view of the sea. The Court of Appeal would not allow the defendant to 'buy his way out of his wrong' and granted an injunction.

DISCHARGE OF RESTRICTIVE COVENANTS

Restrictive covenants may be brought to an end in one of four ways.

EXPRESS DISCHARGE

Unless discharged a restrictive covenants run forever. A covenant may be discharged or extinguished by a covenantee expressly releasing it. As covenants are created by a deed it is usual for them to be extinguished by deed also.

IMPLIED DISCHARGE

It is possible in certain circumstances for a restrictive covenant to be impliedly discharged. A restrictive covenant may cease to be enforceable if:

- Over a long period of time, a covenantee has ignored the breaches of the covenant.
- Changes in the neighbourhood have made the covenant valueless. For example a covenant restricting the property being used for business use where the surrounding properties are now predominately used as offices and for businesses.

---

34 [1994] EWCA Civ 1; [1995] 2 All ER 189; [1995] 1 WLR 269.
35 (1981) 43 P & CR 40, 125 Sol Jo 608.

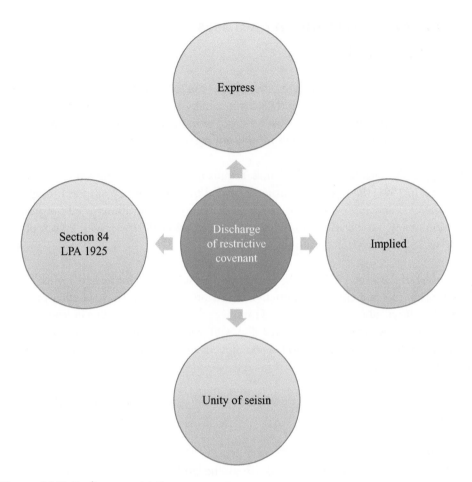

Figure 14.7 Ending a restrictive covenant

In *Chatsworth Estates Co v Fewell* [1931],[36] Farwell J considered that: 'The Court [was] entitled to consider the change in the neighbourhood irrespective of the plaintiffs' acts or omissions.' For example, would changes to the neighbour mean that it was inequitable to enforce them, regardless of the plaintiff's actions?

UNITY OF SEISIN

Where the dominant tenement and the servient tenement come into the hands of the same person, the covenant is discharged. As we know from earlier however this does not apply in relation to building scheme covenants. In *Texaco Antilles Ltd v Kernochan* [1973] it was stated that in a building scheme the covenants revive automatically if the plot of land is subsequently redivided later.

---

36 [1931] 1 Ch 224, 100 LJ Ch 52.

SECTION 84 LAW OF PROPERTY ACT 1925

Under s 84(1) of the LPA 1925:

> The Lands Tribunal shall … have power from time to time, on the application of any person interested in any freehold land affected by any restriction arising under covenant or otherwise as to the user thereof or the building thereon, by order wholly or partially to discharge or modify any such restriction…

The Upper Tribunal (formerly the Lands Tribunal) discretion is exercised sparingly, however. In 1991, the Law Commission reported that in its survey of cases brought between 1981 and 1990, 14 out of 32 (or 44 per cent) of applications faced outright rejection of any modification or discharge. For the period 1991–98, with 20 out of 42 cases (or 48 per cent) facing outright rejection.

Section 84 of the LPA 1925 may be relied upon by successors in title and against successors in title and covers *all* restrictive covenants in freehold land, whether pre or post 1925. It will also cover a restricted number of restrictive covenants in leases,[37] but will not cover restrictions made upon a disposal for no or nominal consideration for public purposes.[38] It also applies to bilateral covenants and those made in the context of a building scheme.

An application can be made on one of the following grounds under s 84(1) of the LPA 1925:

- The restrictions are obsolete.
- The restrictions impede reasonable user of the land for public or private purposes *and* the restrictions are of no real value/contrary to the public interest.
- With the covenantee's consent, either expressly or impliedly.
- Discharge would not injure the covenantee.

The restrictions are obsolete

A restriction may be discharged/modified if: 'by reason of changes in the character of the property or the neighbourhood or other circumstances of the case … the restriction ought to be deemed obsolete'.[39]

In applying a test of obsoleteness consideration must be given to whether the original object of the restriction can still be achieved. In *Re Truman, Hanbury, Buxton & Co. Ltd.'s Application* [1955][40] the court was asked to consider whether a restrictive covenant that the 'trade of hotelkeeper, innkeeper, victualler of wines, spirits or beers is not to be carried on upon the said land' was now obsolete given some residential

---

37 S 84(12) of the LPA 1925.
38 S 84(7) of the LPA 1925.
39 S 84(1)(a) of the LPA 1925.
40 [1955] 3 WLR 704.

houses fronting a main road to London had now been converted into shops. The applicant, a firm of breweries, contended that the changes consequent on the building of the shops rendered the restrictive covenant obsolete so far as that particular road was concerned. The court held however the object of the covenant was still capable of fulfilment and afforded a real protection to those entitled to enforce it so that it was not possible to say that the covenant had become obsolete; accordingly, the appeal should be dismissed.

The restrictions impede reasonable user of the land for public or private purposes and the restrictions are of no real value/contrary to the public interest

The restriction may be discharged/modified if its 'continued existence ... would impede some reasonable user for public or private purposes' and in impeding that user. Section 84(1)(aa)(1A) of the LPA 1925:

- it does not secure to persons entitled to the benefit of it any practical benefits of substantial value; or
- it is contrary to the public interest.

The types of practical benefits considered would be such things as:

- a good view over surrounding landscape
- preservation of a house value
- prevention of an increase in traffic movement
- environmental pleasure
- privacy and seclusion and peace and quiet.

It is possible for the local authority to act as the custodian of the local community by stepping in to oppose the removal of a covenant that serves to protect the scenic countryside.

Re Lloyd's and Lloyd's Application [1993][41] set down the following question in relation to the issue of public interest – 'Is the enforcement of the restrictive covenant contrary to the public interest?'

Discharge would not injure the covenantee

The restriction may be discharged/modified if: 'the proposed discharge or modification will not injure the persons entitled to the benefit of the restriction'.[42]

This section was added in an attempt to safeguard against the vexatious litigant and stop the dominant owners being able to defend the continuance of the covenant, if to remove it would not cause them any harm.

---

41 (1993) 66 P & CR 112; [1993] JPL 689.
42 S 84(1)(C) of the LPA 1925.

Powers

Under s 28 of the LPA 1969 the Upper Tribunal have the power to discharge or modify a covenant, imposing an alternative covenant in addition to awarding compensation to the covenantee. A defendant in an action where a restrictive covenant is being enforced through the courts may ask for a stay of proceedings to allow an application to be made to the Upper Tribunal.

KEY CASE: *APPLICATION UNDER S 84 LAW OF PROPERTY ACT 1925 BY HAMDEN HOMES LTD LP/38/1999 MEMBER: NJ ROSE – DECISION GIVEN 12 DECEMBER 2001*

It is clear from the case law that covenants preserving an environmental purpose in the community will generally be upheld and this has more relevance than other factors such as the age of the covenant. The tribunal case of Hamden Homes is a good example of what is taken into consideration in relation to what is obsolete and what would impede some reasonable user of the land.

In *Hamden Homes Ltd* the applicant, a developer, sought to modify a 1930 restrictive covenant restricting the erection of more than one house on each plot and requiring that all houses should be detached. The applicant sought modification of the covenant to enable a pair of semi-detached houses to be built in the rear garden of the original detached house, though planning permission had been granted for the erection of two pairs of semi-detached properties and a terrace house.

The application was dismissed. The tribunal held the covenant would be obsolete if its only purpose were to prevent the erect of one pair of semi-detached houses. However, given the planning permission was for five properties this constituted a much higher density than any of the immediately surrounding land. The tribunal believed the original covenant's purpose was to prevent over-intensive development and that the covenant was not obsolete.

Additionally, the tribunal believed that the proposed development would severely diminish the view from some of the adjoining properties and would thereby cause injury to the owners and therefore failed under s 84(1)(c) of the LPA 1925.

DISCUSSION

The Law Commission has considered reforms to freehold covenants. The report *Making Land Work: Easements, Covenants and Profits à Prendre* (Law Com No 327, 2011) followed a comprehensive review of the general law of easements, covenants and profits à prendre.

It acknowledged that the current system in relation to freehold covenants was seriously defective. It identified that as covenants take effect primarily as contracts, liability between the original parties persists due to privity of contract and whilst the benefit and burden of a restrictive covenant can pass to future owners upon the sale of the land to which it relates (according to complex rules), the burden of positive covenants could not.

It recommended that land obligation should function within the land registration system in the same way as an easement does, with the benefit and burden capable of registration so that there would be no difficulty in identifying the benefiting parties. The original parties to the land obligation would not be liable for breaches of it occurring after they parted with the land.

The Law Commission believed it was possible for land obligation to exist for the benefit of an estate in land, subject to some conditions as to the nature of the obligation. The obligation could either be negative or positive; the former would restrict the burdened owner from doing something on his own land; the latter would oblige the burdened owner to do something in relation to his own land.

The Law Commission believed that it was possible for a land obligation to be a positive obligation and by treating them in this way conveyancers would no longer have to use devices such as chains of indemnity covenants or estate rentcharges, to secure the performance of positive obligations. Additionally positive obligations could also be 'reciprocal payment' obligations to make a contribution towards the cost of work on and ancillary obligations, which would enable the imposition of administrative provisions such as the manner and timing of payment.

The Law Commission believed that by making the changes land obligations have the potential to facilitate the sharing of facilities and obligations between neighbours, bilaterally or in small groups. They would not be suitable for truly interdependent properties such as flats where a management arrangement is needed; in such cases commonhold or leasehold will continue to be appropriate.

Conveyancing practice would remain largely unchanged – except that complicated workarounds would become a thing of the past. In providing a new right, which is in tune with what conveyancers need to achieve, with what the land registration system is designed to offer and with the existing law of easements, this reform has the potential to benefit a great many people.

It recommended that existing restrictive covenants would be unaffected by reform, and there would be no need for them to be converted into the new interest.

CONSIDER THIS – 1

1   Do you think the rules relating to the running of the benefit are sufficiently clear and could they be simplified?
2   Is it fair that the burden of restrictive covenants cannot normally run?

END OF CHAPTER SUMMARY

- There is privity of contract between the original parties. This means the original covenantee may always enforce any express covenant against the original covenantor.
- In order for a successor in title to enforce a covenant they must show that the benefit has run to himself from the covenantee and must demonstrate that the burden of the covenants has passed to successor in title of servient land from the covenantor.
- In order to obtain the common law remedy of damages for a breach of covenant you must prove the benefit and burden of the covenant pass at common law.
- If you are able to prove the benefit and burden of the covenant in equity then you would be entitled to ask for the equitable remedies of injunctive relief (for restrictive covenants), specific performance (for positive covenants) or damages under s 50 of the Supreme Court Act 1981.
- The courts have taken the approach to award equitable damages in the place of an injunction where possible.
- In unregistered land, a post-1925 restrictive covenant must be registered as a Class D(ii) land charge and registered against the estate owner of the servient land.
- In registered land, the covenantee must enter a notice in the register of the servient land under s 32 of the LRA 2002.
- Restrictive covenants may be discharged expressly, implied, by unity of seisin or under s 84 of the LPA 1925.

PREPARING FOR ASSESSMENTS QUESTIONS

ESSAY QUESTION

To what extent do you consider that Law Commission recommendations to replace the law relating to restrictive covenants will provide a better means to attach obligations to land and enable positive obligations to be enforced against successors in title?

Table 14.2 Guidance on answering questions on freehold covenants

Freehold Covenants – Revision and Methodology

To answer a question on restrictive covenants in a logical, structured manner follow the instructions below.

1 Identify the dominant and servient land and the covenantee and covenantor.
2 Is the covenant a positive or restrictive covenant? Remember the 'acid test'. Covenants that require the expenditure of money are generally positive covenants.
3 Now follow the arrows around the quadrants dealing with each matter within each quadrant.

Common Law – The Running of the Benefit
Follow *P & A Swift Investments v Combined English Stores Group plc* [1989]

a The covenant must 'touch and concern' the land;
b There must be an intention that it will run with the land;
c Covenantee and assignee of covenantee must hold a legal estate in land;
d Must be an intention that it bind successors in title – LPA 1925 s 78 (see below);
e LPA 1925 s 56: successors in title may take even though not expressly named.

Equity – The Running of the Benefit
a Annexation – LPA 1925 s 78 – *Federated Homes v Mill Lodge Properties* [1980];
b Assignment – *Roake v Chadha* [1983] 3 All ER 503;
c Building Schemes – *Elliston v Reacher* [1908] 2 Ch 374

(i) There must be a common vendor;
(ii) Laid out in lots as a general scheme of development;
(iii) Restrictions will benefit all lots;
(iv) Parties have purchased on this basis
(v) Area of the scheme is clearly defined.

4 Has the restrictive covenant been protected?
Covenants created prior to 1925
Covenants created after 1925

Common Law – The Running of the Burden
The burden of covenants cannot run at common law *Austerberry v Oldham Corporation* (1885) as affirmed in *Rhone v Stephens* [1994]
Can the rule be circumvented?

a Benefit and burden rule – *Halsall v Brizzell* (1957).
b Positive easement – *Crow v Wood* [1971].
c Chain of indemnity covenants.
d Rights of re-entry.
e Enlargement of long leases – LPA 1925 s 153.

Equity – The Running of the Burden
Tulk v Moxhay (1848) 2 Ph 774

a Only applies to restrictive covenants.
b Must touch and concern the dominant land.
c Dominant land must be retained – *Formby v Barker* [1903].
d Must show an intention to annex the burden to the servient land – LPA 1925 s 79.
e Must show it was intended that the benefit would run in equity.

Protected by doctrine of notice
Unregistered land: D(ii) – s 2 Land Charges Act 1972
Registered land: Entry as a notice under s 32 LRA 2002: unilateral or agreed notice.

Consider the Law Commission report *Making Land Work: Easements, Covenants and Profits à Prendre* (Law Com No 327, 2011). In doing so, analyse the ease with which the benefit of a freehold covenant currently passes to a successor in title of the covenantee and how the burden of a freehold covenant passes to the successor in title of the covenantor and the need for any reform.

PROBLEM QUESTION

In 2003 David was the registered proprietor of a large plot of freehold land called Millionaire Field. In 2012 he subdivided the land into three separate plots and transferred each plot to Helen, George and Tina.

David made sure each transfer was identical. The covenants included:

- Only one dwelling house to be erected on the land. No other buildings shall be erected.
- The land is not to be used for any trade or business purposes.
- The boundary fences are not to be more than six feet high.
- The landscaped gardens are to be maintained.

The covenants were expressly made: 'for the benefit of the owners for the time being of land now or formerly part of Millionaire Field'.

In 2013 both Helen and George decided to sell their land. Helen sold her property to Lia and George sold his to Matt.

Lia has built a pool and pool-house on her plot. She is concerned about privacy and has installed a state of the art security system which includes an eight-foot-high fence around the borders of her land.

Matt has a recording studio in his home that he uses to produce his records. His business friends also use his studio to record their own albums and he sometimes has 30 people or more at his house. Their cars drive over the landscapes, which are now ruined. Tina is fed up with her neighbours and a row between the three of them has erupted.

Advise Tina.

FURTHER READING

- Bullock, A, 'Federated Homes Revisited' [2005] 155 NLJ 238. Explains the law on the statutory annexation of the benefit of restrictive covenants affecting land before and after the entry into force of s 78 of the LPA 1925 and considers the Court of Appeal's decision in Crest Nicholson Residential (South) Ltd v McAllister [2004] EWCA Civ 410.
- Clark, P, 'The Benefit of the Freehold Covenants' [2012] 2 Conv 145. Considers s 78 of the LPA 1925, the decision in Crest Nicholson Residential (South) Ltd v McAllister [2004] and the effect on conveyancing practice and the drafting of covenants.
- Cooke, E, 'To Restate or Not to Restate? Old Wine, New Wineskins, Old Covenants, New Ideas' [2009] Conv 448. A progress report on the Law Commission's project on easements, covenants and profits à prendre, and in particular on the development of our ideas about positive obligations since the publication of the Consultation Paper in March 2008.
- Dixon, M, 'Is There Any Value in Restrictive Covenants? Enforceability and Remedies' [2007] 71 Conv 70. A consideration of remedies for breach of restrictive covenants in the light of Small v Oliver & Saunders (Development) Ltd [2006] EWHC 1293 (Ch).
- Gravells, N, 'Enforcement of Positive Covenants Affecting Freehold Land' (1994) 110 LQR 346. A consideration of enforcement of positive covenants in the light of Rhone v Stephens [1994] 2 WLR 429.
- Martin, J, 'Remedies for Breach of Restrictive Covenants' [1996] Conv 329. A comprehensive review of the range of remedies available for a breach of restrictive covenant.
- O'Connor, P, 'Careful What You Wish For: Positive Freehold Covenants' [2011] Conv 191. Discusses the general rule that positive covenants do not run with freehold title and the recommendations in favour of allowing continuing positive obligations to be imposed on landowners, and the abolition of the Austerberry rule.
- Sutton, T, 'On the Brink of Land Obligations Again' [2013] Conv 17. Reviews the proposals in the Law Commission's June 2011 report entitled Making Land Work: Easements, Covenants and Profits à Prendre.
- Todd, P, 'Annexation After Federated Homes' [1985] Conv 177. Explores the implications on annexation of following the decision in Federated Homes Ltd v Mill Lodge Properties Ltd [1979].

EXTRACT 1 EXTRACT OF PROPRIETORSHIP AND CHARGES REGISTERS

Entry No.	B. PROPRIETORSHIP REGISTER TITLE – ABSOLUTE
1	(27 Dec 2015) Proprietor(s): SIDNEY of The Annex, New Town, Shires SH6 NT4
2	(27 Dec 2015) The Conveyance to the proprietor contains a covenant of indemnity in respect of the covenants referred to in the Charges Register.

Entry No.	C. CHARGES REGISTER
1	(21 Jun 2010) A Transfer of part of land in this title dated 17 June 2010 made by Harry to Tom contains covenants for the benefit of Mayfair House, details of which are set below: For the benefit and protection of the adjoining or neighbouring land of the Vendor and with the intent to bind the land hereby conveyed into whosesoever hands the same may come the Purchaser for himself and his successors in title HEREBY COVENANTS with the Vendor

1 To pay an equal proportion of the cost of maintaining repairing clearing restoring and reinstating the driveway as indicated between the points marked A and B on the said plan.
2 To erect and forever maintain a timber fence on the south and north boundaries of the land hereby conveyed.
3 Not to use the land hereby conveyed for any purpose other than that of a single residential house.
4 Not to park any caravans or commercial vehicles on the land.

CHAPTER 15
ADVERSE POSSESSION

CHAPTER AIMS AND OBJECTIVES

In this chapter, we will consider adverse possession (you may have heard the concept referred to as 'squatters' rights') as a means of acquisition of title to an estate in land. The first consideration will be the reasons for recognising the doctrine in land law. Next, we will explore the requirements as they apply to both unregistered and registered land. Finally, the effect of adverse possession in unregistered land and registered land will be compared and the changes made by the Land Registration Act 2002 (LRA 2002) in response to difficulties in its operation explained.

By the end of this chapter, you should be able to:

- understand the justifications for the doctrine of adverse possession;
- identify the requirements for adverse possession, namely the meaning of 'factual possession' and 'intention to possess';
- explain the effect of adverse possession in unregistered and registered land;
- appreciate the role of the LRA 2002 in responding to concerns about the operation of the doctrine and the rules introduced;
- apply the above to the case study and learning tasks.

CASE STUDY – ONE

Nigel is the owner of the unregistered freehold title to a large country estate, Daffodil Acres. Nigel intends to redevelop the house and its surrounding gardens in due course into a luxury spa and health retreat but for now he has no use for it.

In 1998 Jane, the owner of adjoining land, grew tired of seeing an increasingly untidy concrete parking area on the estate unused and decided to start using the area herself. Jane removed a padlock to a gate leading to the main road and replaced it with a lock of her own and she put a 'Private Property, Keep Out' sign on the gate. Next, she tidied the planted areas surrounding the concrete and repaired damage to the surface. Jane began to routinely park her car and fenced the area off from the rest of Daffodil Acres.

In 2005 Naresh, who had nowhere to live, broke into the main house which was empty and had been vandalised and began to live there. Naresh has made the house watertight and secure.

Advise Nigel.

What difference would it make if Daffodil Acres were registered land?

KEEP IN MIND

- Is it ever justified for Nigel to lose his property with no compensation?
- Nigel has failed to evict the squatters for a number of years. Is that a sufficient reason?
- Why is unregistered and registered property treated differently when it comes to the effect of long use of land by squatters?
- Do the current rules create a fair balance between the original owner of property and squatters who have made use of the land?

JUSTIFICATIONS FOR ADVERSE POSSESSION

To evaluate whether Nigel's lack of active use of Daffodil Acres, combined with others making productive use, justifies depriving him of his title we need to consider the possible reasons for the regime.

One justification for adverse possession is protection against stale claims. Titles to an estate in land are relative, meaning that an owner's claim may be defeated by the better (older) claim of another. The difficulty with this is that once a person's earlier claim has been slept on for a long time it may become difficult to prove and could leave owners who have relied upon their possession vulnerable to uncertain stale claims. To reduce these concerns, it has long been required that a court case must be brought within a certain time.

Section 15(1) of the Limitation Act 1980 (LA 1980) provides that:

> No action shall be brought by any person to recover any land after the expiration of twelve years from the date on which the right of action accrued to him or, if it first accrued to some person through whom he claims, to that person.

The approach of limiting the recovery of land to a 12-year period from the date of adverse possession[1] still applies to unregistered land and to registered land where it was

---

1 Under sch 1, para 8 of the LA 1980 the right of action accrues to the landowner once a person takes adverse possession of the land.

adversely possessed for 12 years by the time the LRA 2002 came into force on 13 October 2003. For registered land, we shall see that other provisions apply but those still allow adverse possession based on long use.

Another justification is that it makes conveyancing possible. Remember that under the unregistered land system there is no guarantee of ownership, with the title documents giving only a 'paper title'. The basis for title is ultimately possession, and the 12-year limitation period is in line with the requirements for a good root of title dating back at least 15 years.

Adverse possession then has advantages where the person taking possession genuinely believed they own the land. For example, where documents proving ownership or the 'paper title' have been lost, or there is some flaw in that title, or some uncertainty about exact boundaries. In relation to registered land, uncertainty as to the state of the title is removed and so different rules now operate following the LRA 2002.

Another justification is that land is a limited and vital commodity which must be used effectively and remain marketable. So, where an owner ignores the land but another makes use, even if the other person did so knowing they were trespassing adverse possession may still apply.

THE REQUIREMENTS FOR ADVERSE POSSESSION

Given the serious implications of an adverse possession claim for Nigel, it is to be expected that there will be robust requirements for Jane and Naresh to satisfy.

The burden of proof and the requirements for a claim of adverse possession are helpfully set out by Slade J in *Powell v McFarlane* [1979]:[2]

> In the absence of evidence to the contrary, the owner of land with the paper title is deemed to be in possession of the land, as being the person with the prima facie right to possession. The law will thus, without reluctance, ascribe possession either to the paper owner or to the persons who can establish a title as claiming through the paper owner.

> If the law is to attribute possession of land to a person who can establish no paper title to possession, he must be shown to have both factual possession and the requisite intention to possess (*'animus possidendi'*).

---

2 (1979) 38 P & CR 452.

So, there is a presumption that the original owner or true owner is in possession and to attribute possession to another requires clear proof of both factual possession and also an intention to possess.

> **APPLY YOUR LEARNING** – TASK 1
>
> Nigel, as the owner of the paper title, is presumed to have possession of the whole of Daffodil Acres. Jane or Nigel will have to show adverse factual possession and intention to possess.

FACTUAL POSSESSION

The adverse possessor must have taken physical possession by 'dispossession' or 'discontinuance' of possession by the paper owner.

Discontinuance occurs where the paper owner has abandoned the land. For example, in *Hounslow v Minchinton* (1997)[3] the paper owner (a local council) excluded itself from a strip of land by building a fence preventing them entering the area other than via the other's land. But the more used category is dispossession where the paper owner is effectively driven out of possession by another.[4] Therefore, as put by Lord Browne-Wilkinson in the House of Lords case *JA Pye (Oxford) Ltd v Graham* [2002]:[5] 'The question is simply whether the defendant squatter has dispossessed the paper owner by going into ordinary possession of the land for the requisite period with the consent of the owner.'

Possession requires clear physical control of the land excluding all others from it, including the paper owner. What is required depends on the particular circumstances of the case, such as the nature of the land in question and its expected use.

Fencing an area of previously open ground is good proof (see *Seddon v Smith* [1877][6]). Occupying a building is also a clear act. The evidence of possession is, however, often less clear. While what is needed depends on the land and its suitability for use, it must be more than trivial. A number of cases illustrate the test for possession, and show that the onus of proof falls on the adverse possessor.

---

3 (1997) 74 P & CR 221; [1997] NPC 44.

4 In *Rains v Buxton* (1880) 14 Ch D 537 at 539–540 Fry J explained the distinction: '[T]he difference between the dispossession and discontinuance of possession might be expressed in this way – the one is where a person comes in and drives out the others from possession, the other case is where the person in possession goes out and is followed into possession by other persons.'

5 [2002] UKHL 30; [2003] 1 AC 419; [2002] 3 All ER 865.

6 [1877] 36 LTR 168.

In *Tecbild Ltd v Chamberlain* (1969)[7] the acts relied on to establish adverse possession included children playing on the land and ponies being tethered and grazed. These were too trivial.

KEY CASE: *POWELL V MCFARLANE (1979) 38 P & CR 452; [1977]
LS GAZ R 417*

A teenager started to graze a cow on the defendant's land. He also used the field in other ways such as cutting and taking away hay to feed the cow, clearing brambles and cutting trees, repairing the fence, installing a water supply, keeping a goat and more cows, and organising shoots. These actions were again found to be too trivial and insufficient to amount to factual possession. Powell was not in possession of the land but simply took the benefit of various profits. Although the later acts of placing and enforcing notices for intruders to keep out and using the land to run a business including the parking of vehicles and lorries did suffice, they had not lasted 12 years.

Slade J made an important statement about the requirements to show factual possession (which was referred to approvingly by Lord Browne-Wilkinson the House of Lords in *JA Pye (Oxford) Ltd v Graham*):

> Factual possession signifies an appropriate degree of physical control. It must be a single [exclusive] possession, though there can be a single possession exercised by or on behalf of several persons jointly. Thus an owner of land and a person intruding on that land without his consent cannot be both in possession of the land at the same time. The question what acts constitute a sufficient degree of exclusive physical control must depend on the circumstances, in particular the nature of the land and the manner in which land of that nature is commonly used or enjoyed. Everything must depend on the particular circumstances, but broadly, I think what must be shown as constituting factual possession is that the alleged possessor has been dealing with the land in question as an occupying owner might have been expected to deal with it and that no-one else has done so.

In *Red House Farms (Thorndon) Ltd v Catchpole* (1976)[8] the nature of the land was crucial to an outcome which you may not at first predict from the acts argued to show possession. The act over a large area of land was shooting wildfowl. It was held sufficient, given that the land was unsuitable for any other significant use or for fencing.

In *Buckinghamshire Council v Moran* [1990][9] cultivating land and putting up a fence with a gate which was kept locked was clear evidence.

---

7 (1969) 20 P & CR 633, 209 EG 403.
8 (1976) 121 Sol Jo 136; [1977] 2 EGLR 125.
9 [1990] Ch 623; [1989] 2 All ER 225.

In *Roberts v Crown Estate Comrs* [2008][10] the Crown Estates Commissioners were held to be in possession of an area of foreshore based on acts such as fishing and dredging the river bed.

The possession must be openly exercised, it must not be concealed from the paper owner. This ensures an opportunity, should the owner visit the property, to notice and challenge the possession.

There must be no break in the period of time of the possession, although the possession over land is transmissible and can pass to successors who may continue to complete the limitation period. This transfer of an uncompleted adverse possession may be with the cooperation of the previous possessor, for example to a purchaser or under a will. For unregistered land only, it may also be through the dispossession of the first squatter. The second squatter acquires the benefit of any time that had already run against the paper owner, but the first squatter may recover possession from the second until expiry of the limitation period from the date when they were dispossessed.

10 [2008] EWCA Civ 98; [2008] Ch 439.

The possession must be adverse to the paper owner's title. So, it must not be with the permission. For example, occupation under a lease or a licence would not suffice,[11] although, once the permission ends continued possession may from that point be adverse. In *JA Pye (Oxford) Ltd v Graham* [2003] use of a field had been permitted under a licence. The licence was then not renewed but the adverse possessor continued to use the land along with the rest of their farm property. He was found to be in adverse possession. What began as adverse possession may be ended by the paper owner giving a licence; this is irrespective of whether the squatter wants to accept or not (see *BP Properties Ltd v Buckler* [1987][12] and *Colin Dawson Windows Ltd v King's Lynn and West Norfolk BC* [2005]).[13]

CONSIDER THIS – 2

Would it make a difference in the scenario concerning Daffodil Acres if Nigel found out about Jane's use of the concrete area after a year, and wrote to her saying she was welcome to continue her use of the land until such time as he was ready to develop it?

Could Jane simply ignore the offer?

Prior to the LA 1980, if the paper owner argued they had no immediate use for the land, then a person claiming to adversely possess would often be found to have an implied licence (see *Wallis's Cayton Bay Holiday Camp Ltd v Shell-Mex & BP Ltd* [1975][14]). However, sch 1, para 8(4) of the LA 1980 overturns the doctrine of implied licences to possess:

> For the purpose of determining whether a person occupying any land is in adverse possession of the land it shall not be assumed by implication of law that his occupation is by permission of the person entitled to the land merely by virtue of the fact that his occupation is not inconsistent with the latter's present or future enjoyment of the land.

In *Leigh v Jack* [1879][15] it had been suggested that the possession needed to be inconsistent with the paper owner's future use. This has since been strongly rejected.

---

11 Tenants and trustees cannot be in adverse possession, tenants as they have permission under a lease and trustees as they hold the property for the benefit of the beneficiary preventing any possession becoming adverse.
12 (1987) 55 P & CR 337; [1987] 2 EGLR 168.
13 [2005] EWCA Civ 9; [2005] 2 P & CR 19.
14 [1975] QB 94.
15 [1879] 5 Ex D 264. The case concerned land planned to be used in the future to build a highway. Per Bramwell LJ, at 273: 'In order to defeat a title by dispossessing the former owner, acts must be done which are inconsistent with his enjoyment of the soil for the purposes for which he intended to use it: that is not the case here, where the intention of the plaintiff and her predecessor in title was not either to build upon or to cultivate the land, but to devote it at some future time to public purposes.'

KEY CASE: *JA PYE (OXFORD) LTD V GRAHAM* [2002] UKHL 30; [2003] 1 AC 419

Any requirement that possession be inconsistent with the paper owner's intended future use of land in order to be adverse was rejected. Lord Browne-Wilkinson called any argument based on the intention of the paper owner 'heresy'. If the adverse possessor is aware of the future purpose then Lord Browne-Wilkinson did not rule out that could be relevant to intention, but he considered it improbable it would have such an impact:

> The highest it can be put is that, if the squatter is aware of a special purpose for which the paper owner uses or intends to use the land and the use made by the squatter does not conflict with that use, that may provide some support for a finding as a question of fact that the squatter had no intention to possess the land in the ordinary sense but only an intention to occupy it until needed by the paper owner. For myself I think there will be few occasions in which such inference could be properly drawn in cases where the true owner has been physically excluded from the land. But it remains a possible, if improbable, inference in some cases.

APPLY YOUR LEARNING – TASK 3

Do you think that Nigel's planned future use of Daffodil Acres will prevent a finding of adverse possession?

INTENTION TO POSSESS

The physical or factual possession must be coupled with an intention to possess. In *JA Pye (Oxford) Ltd v Graham* [2003] Lord Browne-Wilkinson once more endorsed the ruling of Slade J in *Powell v McFarlane* [1979] using the definition set out in that case of intention to possess. The definition does not require the taking of possession with the intention of excluding the owner or acquiring ownership of the property, but only to possess so far as he can: 'intention, in one's own name and on one's own behalf, to exclude the world at large, including the owner with the paper title ... so far as is reasonably practicable and so far as the process of law will allow'.

Therefore, a claim of possession will not be defeated because he is aware that the paper owner could recover the land or that he would have been willing to pay for the use.

Intention is normally inferred from acts, unequivocal actions asserting possession to the world. As put by Peter Gibson LJ in *Prudential Assurance Co Ltd v Waterloo Real Estate*

Inc [1999]:[16] '[T]he claimant must, of course, be shown to have the subjective intention to possess the land, but he must also show by his outward conduct that that was his intention.'

Returning once more to Slade J in *Powell v McFarlane* [1979], he explained that where the question is whether a trespasser has acquired possession: 'In such a situation the courts will, in my judgment, require clear and affirmative evidence that the trespasser, claiming he has acquired possession, not only had the requisite intention to possess, but made such intention clear to the world.'

This is well illustrated by the reasoning of Slade J in applying this to the acts of the teenager which preceded the later more drastic and unquestionable actions. Those early acts, in his judgment, did not show an intention to possess to the exclusion of the paper owner (although, age appears to have been a major consideration in drawing that conclusion).

However, physical control does not always prove an intention to possess property. Intention is a separate consideration, as stressed and explained by Lord Browne-Wilkinson in *JA Pye (Oxford) Ltd v Graham* [2003]:

> [T]here has always … been a requirement to show an intention to possess in addition to objective acts of physical possession. Such intention may be, and frequently is, deduced from the physical acts themselves. But there is no doubt in my judgment that there are two separate elements in legal possession. So far as English law is concerned intention as a separate element is obviously necessary. Suppose a case where A is found to be in occupation of a locked house. He may be there as a squatter, as an overnight trespasser, or as a friend looking after the house of the paper owner during his absence on holiday. The acts done by A in any given period do not tell you whether there is legal possession. If A is there as a squatter he intends to stay as long as he can for his own benefit. But if he only intends to trespass for the night or has expressly agreed to look after the house for his friend he does not have possession. It is not the nature of the acts which A does but the intention with which he does them which determines whether or not he is in possession.

APPLY YOUR LEARNING – TASK 4

Do the physical acts of possession by the squatters you identified in relation to Daffodil Acres show an intention to possess, making their intention clear to the whole world? Remember, it does not matter that Jane and Naresh accepted they could not exclude Nigel if he decided to retake the land.

---

16 [1999] 2 EGLR 85; [1999] 17 EG 131.

TIME

A signed, written acknowledgement by the squatter of the paper owner's title will stop time under the LA 1980 limitation period running (ss 29(2) and 30(1) of the LA 1980).[17] It may be a direct or an indirect acknowledgement so, for example, a written offer by the squatter to purchase the land from the owner would suffice (*Edginton v Clark* [1964][18]).

The paper owner bringing and pursuing legal proceedings is also effective in stopping time under the LA 1980. However, a demand from the owner that the squatter leave does not stop time running (*Mount Carmel Investments Ltd v Peter Thurlow Ltd* [1988][19]). Nor does the mere issuing of proceedings which are not pursued and later dismissed (*Markfield Investments Limited v Evans* [2001][20]).

The paper owner may also interrupt adverse possession by physically retaking exclusive possession from the squatter or, as we discussed above, by giving their permission for the occupation whether or not the squatter agrees. With regards to physically interrupting the use of the land by the squatter, despite being the paper owner, it is still necessary for the acts to be unequivocal.

KEY CASE: *ZARB V PARRY* [2011] EWCA CIV 1306; [2012] 1 WLR 1240

The event argued as interrupting possession involved entry by the paper owner on to a strip of land which an adjoining landowner was wrongfully occupying. He began banging posts into it, cut down a tree, pulled up fencing, used tape to mark off the land he claimed was his, and clearly stated he was taking the land. However, following a confrontation when the adverse possessors returned, his efforts at retaking possession were abandoned before he had wholly taken control. It was, however, suggested by the court that it would have been a 'close run thing' if he had continued in his efforts to erect a fence.

TUTOR TIP – 1

As we shall consider, the LRA 2002 removes the application of the limitation period to registered land.

This means that pursuing legal claims before 12 years expires is no longer a consideration for registered property, as the paper owner will not lose their right to make a claim for possession by mere passage of time. It may possibly also have the

---

17 An oral acknowledgement may be evidence that the squatter did not have intention to possess: *Pavledes v Ryesbridge Properties Ltd* (1989) 58 P & CR 459.
18 [1964] 1 QB 367.
19 [1988] 3 All ER 129; [1988] 1 WLR 1078.
20 [2001] 2 All ER 238; [2001] 1 WLR 1321.

effect that the provisions relating to written acknowledgement of title cease to apply. However, even if this is the case such acknowledgement would be evidence of a lack of intent to possess.

The giving of permission will still prevent possession being adverse and possession may be retaken by the paper owner.

APPLY YOUR LEARNING – TASK 5

Where Daffodil Acres is unregistered, Nigel could have stopped the limitation period by pursuing legal proceedings before the 12 years expires and his claim is barred.

What could Nigel have done in order to interrupt possession by Jane and Naresh, which applies to both unregistered and registered land? Consider the giving of permission and retaking of possession.

THE EFFECT OF ADVERSE POSSESSION

The rules which apply to Daffodil Acres vary considerably because the land is unregistered.

UNREGISTERED LAND

Unregistered land is still governed by the LA 1980 and the limitation period. The adverse possessor has a freehold estate simply by taking possession, but remember that title is relative and the paper owner has a better title until the expiration of the limitation period. Once the limitation period is complete, the title of the paper owner who was entitled to possession is destroyed (s 17 of the LA 1980) meaning the adverse possessor then has a stronger title than anyone else.

However, the adverse possessor will take that ownership subject to (1) any legal third party rights such as easements and profits, or (2) equitable rights such as restrictive covenants whether or not registered as a land charge or potentially protected by the doctrine of notice (not being a 'purchaser').

APPLY YOUR LEARNING – TASK 6

Daffodil Acres is unregistered. Jane appears to have been in adverse possession since 1998 and Naresh since 2005. Has the 12 year limitation period under the LA 1980 passed, meaning Nigel cannot make a claim against either of them?

REGISTERED LAND

For registered land, the position varies depending on whether the limitation period for adverse possession was completed before the LRA 2002 came into force on 13 October 2003.

Adverse possession is not an easy fit with the concept of indefeasibility of title under the registered land system and the justifications relating to curing uncertainty of ownership are removed by identification of ownership in the register. Concerns were explored and reforms put forward in the Law Commission report *Land Registration for the Twenty-First Century: A Conveyancing Revolution* (Law Com No 271, 2001). These were enacted by the LRA 2002, which has made it much harder for squatters to make claims.

Before the LRA 2002 came into effect the limitation period ran against a registered owner in the same manner as it did an unregistered landowner. At the end of 12 years, per s 15 of the LA 1980, the original owner was barred from taking action. But, given he remained the registered proprietor, instead of being extinguished at the end of the appropriate limitation period his estate was deemed by s 75(1) of the LRA 1925 to be held on trust for the squatter. The squatter could then apply for registration as the owner under s 75(2) of the LRA 1925:

(1)   The Limitation Acts shall apply to registered land in the same manner and to the same extent as those Acts apply to land not registered, except that where, if the land were not registered, the estate of the person registered as proprietor would be extinguished, such estate shall not be extinguished but shall be deemed to be held by the proprietor for the time being in trust for the person who, by virtue of the said Acts, has acquired title against any proprietor, but without prejudice to the estates and interests of any other person interested in the land whose estate or interest is not extinguished by those Acts.

(2)   Any person claiming to have acquired a title under the Limitation Acts to a registered estate in the land may apply to be registered as proprietor thereof.

Under the LRA 2002, provided the limitation period was completed before 13 October 2013 a beneficial equitable title will be protected as an overriding interest if the squatter remains in actual occupation (sch 3, para 2 of the LRA 2002).

CONSIDER THIS – 3

Where the title to Daffodil Acres is registered, if Jane's occupation of the concrete area had started in 1990 could Nigel now take action against her?

Following the LRA 2002, s 15 of the LA 1980 no longer applies in relation to registered land (s 96(1) of the LRA 2002). There is, therefore, no 12-year limitation period after which the paper owner ceases to be able to claim possession. The adverse possessor is required to actively make their claim. After being in possession of the land for ten years, a squatter can apply to the Registrar for registration of the estate according to s 97 of the LRA 2002, which gives effect to sch 6, para 1(1).

Notification of the application is then given by the Registrar to the registered proprietor (and other interested parties) under sch 6, para 2(1):

> The registrar must give notice of an application under paragraph 1 to—
>
> (a) the proprietor of the estate to which the application relates,
> (b) the proprietor of any registered charge on the estate,
> (c) where the estate is leasehold, the proprietor of any superior registered estate,
> (d) any person who is registered in accordance with rules as a person to be notified under this paragraph, and
> (e) such other persons as rules may provide.

The notice will allow a person receiving it 65 business days to respond. They may object to the application, for example on the grounds there has not been ten years of adverse possession. They may also use a counter notice, even if they do not dispute that the factual basis is made out, which then requires the application to be dealt with under sch 6 of the LRA 2002. A counter notice causes the squatter's application to be rejected unless one of three conditions are met under sch 6, para 5(1):

> (1) If an application under paragraph 1 is required to be dealt with under this paragraph, the applicant is only entitled to be registered as the new proprietor of the estate if any of the following conditions is met.
> (2) The first condition is that—
>
>> (a) it would be unconscionable because of an equity by estoppel for the registered proprietor to seek to dispossess the applicant, and
>> (b) the circumstances are such that the applicant ought to be registered as the proprietor.
>
> (3) The second condition is that the applicant is for some other reason entitled to be registered as the proprietor of the estate.
> (4) The third condition is that—
>
>> (a) the land to which the application relates is adjacent to land belonging to the applicant,
>> (b) the exact line of the boundary between the two has not been determined under rules under section 60,
>> (c) for at least ten years of the period of adverse possession ending on the date of the application, the applicant (or any predecessor in title) reasonably believed that the land to which the application relates belonged to him, and
>> (d) the estate to which the application relates was registered more than one year prior to the date of the application.

If no objection or counter notice is received, the squatter will be registered as proprietor (sch 6, para 4 of the LRA 2002). Where there is an objection or counter notice, the normal result is that application will be rejected even if the squatter can show ten years of adverse possession. The three conditions or grounds which the squatter must show following a counter notice are not normally present.

APPLY YOUR LEARNING – TASK 7

Where Daffodil Acres is registered, both Jane and Naresh appear to have been in adverse possession for ten years and can apply for registration as proprietors.

The Land Registry would then write to Nigel. You would expect Nigel to respond (even if he accepts the fact of adverse possession) with a counter notice. What does that mean in terms of the Land Registry going ahead with or refusing the registration applications?

The third of the grounds following a counter notice, reasonable belief by a squatter owning adjoining land that the disputed area belongs to him (a boundary dispute), is an important one. In *Zarb v Parry* [2011][21] it was held that the fact that a boundary is known to be disputed by the adverse possessor (for example if, as in this case, the squatter was informed in writing) does not necessarily make a squatter's belief of ownership 'unreasonable'. In *IAM Group plc v Chowdrey* [2012][22] it was found that, when deciding whether or not a squatter's belief is reasonably held, the squatter should not be imputed with knowledge of any of its agents (for example, as in this case, their solicitor).

CONSIDER THIS – 4

What would be the implications in relation to Daffodil Acres if Jane had believed that she owned part of the disputed concreted area?

The land is unregistered, so provided she has adversely possessed the area for 12 years her title cannot be challenged by Nigel.

However, when the question is varied to make the land registered, the rules are very different.

Before the LRA 2002, registered land was still subject to the 12-year limitation period. If Jane was a squatter for at least 12 years prior to the LRA 2002 coming into effect on 13 October 2003 then she would have adverse possession of the land. But she only took possession in 1998 and so would not have been.

---

21 [2011] EWCA Civ 1306.
22 [2012] EWCA Civ 505.

Under the current system, which applies to registered land only from 13 October 2003, Jane does not automatically acquire adverse possession of the land by merely occupying it for a long time. She must apply to the Land Registry with proof of adverse possession of the land for ten years. Once that application is made the Land Registry will next notify the paper owner of the land who may object or respond with a counter notice. Normally, that will defeat the application but there are exceptions, and a reasonably held belief of a mistaken boundary is an important one. Of course, this then requires a careful consideration of whether Jane's wrongly held belief was reasonable.

In the event of a refusal to register (following an objection or counter notice), the registered proprietor then has two years in which to take action to remove the squatter or to reach some agreement on their occupation. Schedule 6, para 6(1) of the LRA 2002 states:

Where a person's application under paragraph 1 is rejected, he may make a further application to be registered as the proprietor of the estate if he is in adverse possession of the estate from the date of the application until the last day of the period of two years beginning with the date of its rejection.

But, after that time has elapsed the squatter may rely upon sch 6, para 7 of the LRA 2002, which states: 'If a person makes an application under paragraph 6, he is entitled to be entered into the register as the new proprietor of the estate.'

APPLY YOUR LEARNING – TASK 8

In relation to Daffodil Acres, this means that should Nigel successfully respond with a counter notice to an application for registration by Jane or Naresh he then has two years in which to evict them. Otherwise, they will be registered as the new owners.

The registration of a squatter does not affect the priority of any interest affecting the estate (sch 6, para 9(2) of the LRA 2002). Therefore, when a squatter is registered as proprietor they will take subject to any legal and equitable interests affecting the land.

ADVERSE POSSESSION AND LEASES

A person claiming adverse possession against leasehold property has no rights against the freehold property owner without satisfying additional requirements.

Where the leasehold estate is unregistered, once 12 years of adverse possession has expired the claim of the leasehold estate owner is extinguished. However, the limitation period does not start to run against the freehold estate owner until the lease ends. When the lease expires, the landlord may assert their better title. It is also possible for the lease to be ended by the landlord forfeiting it in response to a breach of leasehold covenants or, more controversially, for the disposed tenant to surrender his lease to the landlord (see *Fairweather v St Marylebone Property Co Ltd* [1963][23]).

Where the leasehold estate is registered, once the squatter completes ten years of adverse possession against the tenant he can apply to be registered as the owner. Once registered, there is then no option for the disposed tenant to surrender his lease as he no longer owns it. The new owner will be subject to all of the terms of the lease. Should the adverse possessor then complete another ten years occupying the land, he will be able to apply to be registered as the owner of the title to the freehold estate.

CONSIDER THIS – 5

Assume that in 2000 Nigel made the house habitable and granted a 22-year legal lease to Naresh. The lease included a covenant 'Not to use the house nor permit the same to be used for any purpose other than as a private dwelling house in the occupation of one family'. In 2003 Katy entered into adverse possession of the property and was herself dispossessed by Natalie in 2008. Natalie has over time allowed several friends to occupy the property with her.

Advise Nigel what he can do to remove Natalie or to enforce the covenant against her.

Keep in mind that, where the land is unregistered, Natalie would need to show 12 years of occupation for the limitation period to operate in her favour. Her period of adverse possession was begun by Katy in 2003, with Natalie then continuing it. This means that the leasehold title of Naresh is now barred, but Katy could still bring an action for possession. The freehold title of Nigel is not barred, unless Natalie's adverse possession continues for 12 years after the lease expires. Clearly, we are nowhere near that point yet. But until the lease does expire, Nigel has no right to possession which he can enforce against Natalie. He would need to show that the lease contains a right of re-entry or forfeiture right, allowing him to bring a lease to an end in the event of a breach by the tenant. Assuming this is so – it normally is in any well-drafted document – the covenant not to use the house in occupation of one family is being broken. This would allow an action for forfeiture against Naresh. If, however, there is no forfeiture right then if Naresh can be located it is possible for him to surrender the lease.

---

23 [1963] AC 510; [1962] 2 All ER 288.

> Where the land is registered, at the end of ten years of adverse possession Natalie may make an application to be registered as proprietor of the lease. Notice of the application will then be given to Naresh and to Nigel, who are likely to serve a counter notice. She does not appear to meet any of the three grounds which must be shown following a counter notice. If she then remained in possession for another two years, a second application could be made and she would become the registered proprietor. But does she have the requisite ten years? In registered land, only a successor in title can claim her predecessor's period of occupation as part of her own and the land was not transferred to her with her instead taking it from Katy.

HUMAN RIGHTS

The possible loss of Nigel's title is potentially very controversial, although the requirements in place provide significant safeguards to balance those concerns. Adverse possession is undoubtedly an interference with the right to peaceful enjoyment of one's property under Article 1, Protocol 1 of the European Convention on Human Rights. However, it is only a violation of the right if it cannot be justified.

When a claim was made against the operation of UK law before the European Count of Human Rights the claim was rejected by the Grand Chamber. The court ruled that the system was proportionate and permissible. In *J A Pye (Oxford) Ltd v United Kingdom* (2007),[24] it is notable that the case was made against registered land governed by the pre-LRA 2002 rules, where the justification for adverse possession and safeguards are at their weakest.

CRIMINAL LAW AND ADVERSE POSSESSION

Rights from adverse possession must derive from a civil wrong, but what if the act is also criminal?

By s 6 of the Criminal Law Act 1977 it is an offence to use or threaten violence in order to enter property and by s 7 for a trespasser not to leave having been asked to do so by the displaced residential owner or a protected intending occupier. With the enacting of s 144 of the Legal Aid, Sentencing and Punishment of Offenders Act 2012 (LASPOA 2012) there is now a further new offence outlawing squatting in residential buildings, having entered as a trespasser.

---

24 (2007) 46 EHRR 1083.

In *R (Best) v The Chief Land Registrar* [2015][25] it was explained that there was nothing in case law meaning acts of criminal trespass barred any subsequent claim of adverse possession (although there could be cases in which it would) and s 144 of the LASPOA 2012 did not effect that position. The case itself concerned an entry into an abandoned residential house. An application to the Land Registry was cancelled, on the basis that the occupation had been a criminal offence.[26] The decision by the Court of Appeal was that the Land Registry decision was wrong, and the application must be considered.

APPLY YOUR LEARNING – TASK 9

Will Naresh be unable to claim adverse possession of the house, given s 144 the LASPOA 2012?

DISCUSSION

Adverse possession is argued by some as being outmoded, particularly since the Human Rights Act 1998.

CONSIDER THIS – 6

Why might adverse possession be argued to interfere with a paper owner's human rights, what are the possible justifications and do you think the safeguards on its use are satisfactory in light of those reasons?

END OF CHAPTER SUMMARY

- Adverse possession is justified as protecting against stale claims to title, ensuring land is utilised and making conveyancing possible.
- Some of these justifications are weaker in relation to registered land, where ownership of land is established not by possession but by registration of title.
- Adverse possession requires that the squatter has (1) factual possession of the land, (2) the necessary intention to possess the land, and (3) does so without the paper owner's consent.

---

25 [2015] EWCA Civ 17; [2016] QB 23.

26 The Land Registry did so in reliance upon the decision in *R (Smith) v Land Registry* [2009] EWHC 328 (Admin); [2009] All ER (D) 208 (Mar), which held that criminal obstruction of a public highway could not establish adverse possession.

- Before the LRA 2002, under the LA 1980 a limitation period of 12 years applied to both unregistered and registered land. Adverse possession for 12 years will extinguish the claim of the paper owner.
- The LRA 2002 creates a new regime that applies only to registered land for cases from 13 October 2003. Adverse possession of registered land for 12 years of itself will no longer affect the registered proprietor's title. After the expiry of ten years, the squatter is entitled to apply to be registered as proprietor. The registered proprietor is notified of the application and given the opportunity to object, making it harder to lose land to a squatter.
- If the application is not opposed, the squatter is registered as proprietor. If the application is opposed, it will be rejected unless one of the three exceptions is shown. If after the application is rejected the squatter then remains in adverse possession for a further two years, they are able to reapply to be registered as proprietor and will be so registered whether or not anyone objects.

PREPARING FOR ASSESSMENTS
QUESTIONS

ESSAY QUESTION

The Land Registration Act 2002 makes it more difficult to claim a legal title through adverse possession. To what extent do you agree that reform was needed and do you consider that the rules now achieve a fair and effective balance between the rights of the paper owner and those of the adverse possessor?

PROBLEM QUESTION

A property developer has large property portfolio, including a barn on a registered estate.

The developer was ready to start work on converting the barn into residential living accommodation but has now learned that the barn is being occupied by Ava. Ava claims to have 'squatter's rights' to remain, having lived in it since 2000.

Advise the developer whether Ava might successfully apply to be registered as proprietor of the barn.

FURTHER READING

- Dixon, M, 'Criminal Squatting and Adverse Possession: The Best Solution?' [2014] JHL 94. Reflects on the criminal offence of squatting in a residential building, introduced by the Legal Aid, Sentencing and Punishment of Offenders Act 2012, and details the approach taken *in R (Best) v Chief Land Registrar* [2014] EWHC 1370 (Admin) as to how the offence interacts with a squatter's rights under the law of adverse possession.
- Dixon, M, 'Adverse Possession, Human Rights and Land Registration: And They All Lived Happily Ever After?' [2007] 71 Conv 552. Examines the European Court of Human Rights ruling in *JA Pye (Oxford) Ltd v United Kingdom* (44302/02) on the compatibility of adverse possession principles as applied to registered land prior to the entry into force of the Land Registration Act 2002 with the European Convention on Human Rights 1950.
- Dixon, M, 'Adverse Possession and Registered Land' [2009] 73 Conv 169. Highlights matters for consideration in relation to adverse possession claims against registered land under the Land Registration Act 2002, sch 6.
- Dixon, M, 'Human Rights and Adverse Possession: The Final Nail?' [2008] 72 Conv 160. Analyses the Court of Appeal decision in *Ofulue v Bossert* [2008] EWCA Civ 7 on whether the European Court of Human Rights ruling in *JA Pye (Oxford) Ltd v United Kingdom* (44302/02) applies to all cases of adverse possession. Also considers whether adverse possession would only be established where the claimant's possession was inconsistent with the registered proprietor's intended use of the land.
- Dockray, M, 'Why Do We Need Adverse Possession?' [1985] Con 273. Considers the social and economic justifications for adverse possession, including certainty of title.

CHAPTER 16
PROPRIETARY ESTOPPEL

CHAPTER AIMS AND OBJECTIVES

Proprietary estoppel has already been considered in earlier chapters when we considered its impact in relation to negotiations occurring prior to enforceable land contracts in Chapter 3, the revocability and nature of licences in Chapter 8, and its overlap in family contexts with constructive trusts in Chapter 9. This chapter does not aim to repeat those points, but is rather a general discussion of estoppel as a doctrine. It explains points which are relevant both to questions raising it as one argument in relation to any of those separate topics or to those focusing on it as topic on its own.

We will explore how a person may establish how the doctrine of estoppel applies to the situation they find themselves in, when an estoppel has arisen what types of rights and interests a court may order to satisfy it, and what the implications are for third parties.

By the end of this chapter, you should be able to:

- explain the meaning of proprietary estoppel;
- identify the elements for establishing a claim, namely:

  - a representation
  - detrimental reliance
  - unconscionability;

- appreciate the range of remedies a court may grant to satisfy the equity;
- understand the implications of an equity before it is satisfied (an 'inchoate equity') for purchasers;
- apply the above to the case study and the learning outcomes.

CASE STUDY – ONE

Tulip Cottage is a cosy property for which Catherine inherited the legal freehold title from her grandmother. The cottage remained empty for some years, and ended up being in a somewhat tired state and requiring repair.

Then Catherine met Marcus and, after a whirlwind romance, they moved in to Tulip Cottage together. At the time she declared to Marcus, 'You can stay here with me, forever'. There were several other occasions, during the seven years in which they lived happily together, upon which she made assurances along the lines of them building a home for life together.

Marcus spent a considerable proportion of his wages, from working in a job that he hated, contributing towards the redecoration and repair of the cottage, and gave up the opportunity of pursuing his long-held ambition to make his career as a stage actor. All seemed well, but then Catherine met Wayne and ended her relationship with Marcus.

For a time, it seemed the pair could continue to keep living together as friends. But Catherine now wants to move in Wayne and this has caused serious quarrelling between her and Marcus. Marcus has been forced to move out, renting a small single room in a shared house. He has no significant savings and is unsure what he can do. Please advise him.

KEEP IN MIND

This question requires you to consider not only estoppel, but also why other possible remedies may not be so suitable. Think back to Chapter 8, on licences. A contractual licence could be argued on the basis that his various contributions amount to a consideration. However, be aware that the terms here seem quite imprecise for a contractual undertaking and Denning's creativity in terms of recognising these more 'family' type situations as contracts has not always found favour. What is now clear is that a contractual licence is not an interest in land. Now consider Chapters 9 and 10, on trusts of the family home. Could he argue a constructive trust has arisen? The difficulty is that Catherine's statements never show an intention that he should have any ownership in the house, it was more about assuring him of a secure home.

The better argument is proprietary estoppel and it is the principles of that remedy which we will apply to the scenario as we work through this chapter. You need to consider that, while we might feel sorry for Marcus, in order to have a claim against Catherine we need to show his position is linked to the assurances made by Catherine. Any remedy we suggest would also need to reflect what he could reasonably expect.

THE MEANING OF PROPRIETARY ESTOPPEL

Marcus has no legal title to Tulip Cottage, so we need to explore informal routes for him making some claim based on Catherine's assurances. Proprietary estoppel is a means of protecting a person's right over land which, though not created as a formal property right or (normally) agreed by contract, it would be inequitable or unconscionable for the landowner to deny. In such cases, estoppel is used to prevent the legal owner asserting his strict legal rights, per Denning MR in *Crabb v Arun District Council* [1975][1]:

> to mitigate the rigours of strict law … It will prevent a person insisting on his strict legal rights … when it would be inequitable for him to do so having regard to the dealings which have taken place between the parties.

A court in considering how to satisfy the estoppel, may give a remedy which enforces a property right, hence the term 'proprietary' estoppel.

Given the increased formalities required to create or transfer estates and interests in land, the ability of estoppel to protected informal arrangements is clearly important. Three areas where informal arrangements may arise are:

- imperfect gifts of an estate or interest in land;
- a common expectation that a party will acquire an estate or interest; or
- acquiescence to a mistaken unilateral belief about entitlement to an estate or interest.

This threefold classification, while not suggesting it is possible to fit the different factors in cases neatly under one or other of these elements, is nonetheless an invaluable means for a structured consideration and has support from its adoption by Lord Walker in *Cobbe v Yeoman's Row Management Ltd* [2008][2]. The suggested categories and the cases reviewed under each by Lord Walker were taken from the authors of Gray and Gray. Now in its fifth edition, *Elements of Land Law* contains an updated review of the wide variety of circumstances where estoppel may assist.[3]

---

1 [1976] Ch 179; [1975] 3 All ER 865.
2 [2008] UKHL 55; [2008] 4 All ER 713.
3 K Gray and SF Gray, *Elements of Land Law* (5th edn, OUP 2009) 1202–1208.

IMPERFECT GIFTS

> **KEY CASE:** *DILLWYN V LLEWELYN* (1862) 4 DE GF & J 517
>
> A son spent a large sum of money building a house, having relied upon a signed memorandum with his father promising that he would have rights in the land. Unfortunately, the memorandum was not in the form of a deed. While such an imperfect gift would not normally be enforced, the promise made and the expenditure of the son in reliance gave rise to a claim in estoppel.

COMMON EXPECTATION

> **KEY CASE:** *RAMSDEN V DYSON* (1866) LR 1 HL 129, 12 JUR NS 506
>
> A landowner was alleged to have encouraged the expectation of a long lease by a tenant, who claimed to have relied upon that belief and spent a lot of money building on the land. While the majority of the House of Lords did not accept the claim on the facts, the principle of how estoppel may apply to such common promises or expectations was set out by Lord Kingsdown:
>
>> If a man, under a verbal agreement with a landlord for a certain interest in land, or, what amounts to the same thing, under an expectation, created or encouraged by the landlord, that he shall have a certain interest, takes possession of such land, with the consent of the landlord, and upon the faith of such promise or expectation, with the knowledge of the landlord, and without objection by him, lays out money upon the land, a Court of equity will compel the landlord to give effect to such promise or expectation.

ACQUIESCENCE TO A MISTAKEN BELIEF

The case of *Ramsden v Dyson* is also useful authority for the relevance of acquiescence, a failure to act or silence, in relation to a mistaken belief. Lord Cranworth explained:

> [I]f a stranger begins to build on my land supposing it to be his own, and I perceiving his mistake, abstain from setting him right, and leave him to persevere in his error, a court of equity will not allow me afterwards to assert my title to the land on which he had expended money on the supposition that the land was his own.

A landowner's uncomplaining acquiescence will be an assurance upon which a party may reasonably rely if, according to Pattern J in *Lester v Woodgate* [2010]:[4]

---

4 [2010] EWCA Civ 199; [2010] 2 P & CR 21.

the landowner becomes aware of the work and knows that the other party is carrying it out in the belief that he owns the land in question or has rights over it but fails to object, [and in such a case] his silence will be treated as a species of equitable fraud sufficient to found an estoppel.

ESTABLISHING PROPRIETARY ESTOPPEL

Historically, the requirements routinely applied were very restrictive of the help available. They would have been of little assistance to Marcus.

KEY CASE: *WILLMOTT V BARBER* (1880) 15 CH D 96; 49 LJ CH 792

Five requirements were laid down to be satisfied in an estoppel claim. While the context in which Fry J formulated his five *probanda* related to mistaken belief, the criteria were routinely applied by the courts in relation to the other areas:

> In the first place the plaintiff must have made a mistake as to his legal rights. Secondly, the plaintiff must have expended some money or must have done some act (not necessarily upon the defendant's land) on the faith of his mistaken belief. Thirdly, the defendant, the possessor of the legal right, must know of the existence of his own right which is inconsistent with the right claimed by the plaintiff. If he does not know of it he is in the same position as the plaintiff, and the doctrine of acquiescence is founded upon conduct with a knowledge of your legal rights. Fourthly, the defendant, the possessor of the legal right, must know of the plaintiff's mistaken belief of his rights. … Lastly, the defendant, the possessor of the legal right, must have encouraged the plaintiff in his expenditure of money or in other acts which he has done, either directly or by abstaining from asserting his legal right. Where all these elements exist, there is fraud of such a nature as will entitle the Court to restrain the possessor of the legal right from exercising it, but, in my judgment, nothing short of this will do.

The modern test preferred by the courts[5] is far less restrictive and more flexible to assist people in the position Marcus finds himself in.

---

5 But note a small number of cases using the *Willmott v Barber probanda* such as *Coombes v Smith* [1986] 1 WLR 808 and *Matharu v Matharu* [1994] 2 FLR 597.

> **KEY CASE:** *TAYLORS FASHIONS LTD V LIVERPOOL VICTORIA TRUSTEES CO LTD* [1982] QB 133
>
> The position was clarified by Oliver J who made some important general observations that, in the light of the more recent cases of proprietary estoppel:
>
> > requires a very much broader approach which is directed rather at ascertaining whether, in particular individual circumstances, it would be unconscionable for a party to be permitted to deny that which, knowingly, or unknowingly, he has allowed or encouraged another to assume to his detriment than to enquiring whether the circumstances can be fitted within the confines of some preconceived formula serving as a universal yardstick for every form of unconscionable behaviour.

So today the elements upon which a claim is based are set out as:

- a representation or assurance
- detrimental reliance upon that representation; and
- unconscionability of the behaviour.[6]

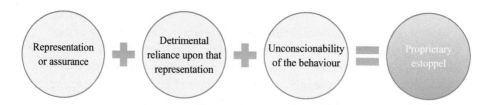

Figure 16.1 Establishing a claim by way of proprietary estoppel

However, it is clear that the particular circumstances or context of each case is critical. It is unavoidable that for each of these elements one should expect varying and sometimes difficult to predict decisions, nor are they neat headings under which particular considerations in a case will always exclusively fall. That said, it does provide an approach for principled and objective application of judicial opinion to individual disputes.

---

6 In *Thorner v Major* [2009] UKHL 18; [2009] 1 WLR 776 Lord Walker explained that whilst there was no universal definition of proprietary estoppel, most scholars agreed that: 'the doctrine is based on three main elements, although they express them in slightly different terms: a representation or assurance made to the claimant; reliance on it by the claimant; and detriment to the claimant in consequence of his (reasonable) reliance (see Megarry & Wade, Law of Real Property, 7th edn (2008) para 16-001; Gray & Gray, Elements of Land Law, 5th edition (2009) para 9.2.8; Snell's Equity, 31st edn (2005) paras 10-16 to 10-19; Gardner, An Introduction to Land Law (2007) para 7.1.1).'

This point was made by Robert Walker LJ in *Gillett v Holt* [2000].[7] Walker used the three elements in *Taylors Fashions Ltd v Liverpool Victoria Trustees Co Ltd* for the purpose of analysis and structured decision-making, but noted they cannot be treated as watertight compartments:

> although the judgment is, for convenience, divided into several sections with headings which give a rough indication of the subject-matter, it is important to note at the outset that the doctrine of proprietary estoppel cannot be treated as subdivided into three or four watertight compartments. … [I]n this court it repeatedly became apparent that the quality of the relevant assurances may influence the issue of reliance, that reliance and detriment are often intertwined, and that whether there is a distinct need for a 'mutual understanding' may depend on how the other elements are formulated and understood. Moreover the fundamental principle that equity is concerned to prevent unconscionable conduct permeates all the elements of the doctrine. In the end the court must look at the matter in the round.

A REPRESENTATION

The representation may be that the claimant already has a property right, or that they will acquire one in the future.

KEY CASE: *PASCOE V TURNER* [1979] 2 ALL ER 945; [1979] 1 WLR 431

This case demonstrates promises relating to existing rights. The defendant had been assured that 'the house is yours and everything in it'. In reliance on that assurance she used her savings to pay for improvements to the house. Her claim was established based on proprietary estoppel.

KEY CASE: *RE BASHAM* [1987] 1 ALL ER 405; [1986] 1 WLR 1498

This case confirms the availability of proprietary estoppel where the relevant expectation was that rights would be acquired in the future (for example, under a will). The claimant and her husband cared for her stepfather and passed up jobs and the chance to move in the belief that she was to inherit his property. The stepfather had made clear promises, but in fact never made a will. The claimant successfully claimed the house through proprietary estoppel. Any need for the expectation to relate to an existing (rather than a future) right was dismissed.

The representation must be such that it could be relied upon. This entails a number of considerations.

....

7 [2001] Ch 210; [2000] 2 All ER 289.

An expectation of rights in some particular property

KEY CASE: *LAYTON V MARTIN* [1986] 2 FLR 227; [1986] FAM LAW 212

A claimant could not rely on a written representation offering her, 'what emotional security I can give, plus financial security during my life, and financial security on my death'. The claim failed as the promise did not relate to a right in some specific property. (As opposed to circumstances such as those in *Pascoe v Turner* [1979] 1 WLR, in which an assurance that 'the house is yours and everything in it' created an expectation of rights in identified property.)

Scott J reasoned that a representation that 'financial security' would be provided was not a representation that the plaintiff would have, 'some equitable or legal interest in any particular asset or assets.'

However, in a later case a similar type of promise to leave non-specific property was successfully relied upon. There is therefore some uncertainty regarding this point. In *Re Basham* [1986][8] the promise was to leave the whole of a residuary estate to the claimant and not any specified property.

Case law other than for leaving the whole of a residuary estate is, in line with the reasoning of *Layton v Martin* [1986], that general promises to support a claimant are not enough as they do not relate to identified property. For example, in *Lissimore v Downing* [2003][9] a man who said to his girlfriend 'I bet you never thought all of this would be yours in a million years' and described her as 'the Lady of the Manor' made no representations referable to 'a certain interest in property'. Or in *James v Thomas* [2007][10] where assurances that 'you will be well provided for' and that her work on the house 'will benefit us both' were insufficient. In both cases, there was no evidence of any identification of the property affected.

By comparison, in *Southwell v Blackburn* [2014],[11] a case on cohabitation upheld a finding that an assurance to a woman 'would always have a home and be secure in this one' suggested her partner 'was taking on a long-term commitment to provide her with a secure home' and that 'he led her to believe that she would have the sort of security that a wife would have'. More recently in *Liden v Burton* [2016],[12] reassurances by a partner that payments by a woman were 'towards the house' could be reasonably understood and meaning 'towards ownership of the house' they lived in together.

This shows, as we shall see repeatedly, that context really is everything.

---

8 [1986] 1 WLR 1498.
9 [2003] 2 FLR 208.
10 [2007] EWCA Civ 1212; [2008] 1 FLR 1598.
11 [2014] EWCA Civ 1347; [2015] 2 FLR 1240.
12 [2016] EWCA Civ 275; [2016] Fam Law 687.

KEY CASE: *THORNER V MAJOR* [2009] UKHL 18; [2009] 1 WLR 776

The approach taken was to once more require specific property. Lord Hoffmann clearly stated that: '[A] a claim, under the principle known as proprietary estoppel, requires the claimant to prove a promise or assurance that he will acquire a proprietary interest in specified property.'

This might be satisfied provided the property specified is identifiable. The property in question was farmland, and the extent of the farm may have varied over the years, but the nature of what the claimant was to receive was clear.

Lord Walker considered the issue of the identity of the farm in depth and made some useful distinction between this case and the more general assurances in *Layton v Martin* [1986]:

> In my opinion it is a necessary element of proprietary estoppel that the assurances given to the claimant (expressly or impliedly, or, in standing-by cases, tacitly) should relate to identified property owned (or, perhaps, about to be owned) by the defendant ...

> In this case the deputy judge made a clear finding of an assurance by Peter that David would become entitled to Steart Farm. ... Both Peter and David knew that the extent of the farm was liable to fluctuate (as development opportunities arose, and tenancies came and went). There is no reason to doubt that their common understanding was that Peter's assurance related to whatever the farm consisted of at Peter's death ...

> The situation is to my mind quite different from a case like *Layton v Martin* [1986] 2 FLR 227, in which the deceased made an unspecific promise of 'financial security'. It is also different (so far as concerns the award of the whole of the deceased's residuary estate) from *Re Basham* [1986] 1 WLR 1498

This view was echoed by Lord Neuberger:

> In this case, the extent of the farm might change, but, ... there is, as I see it, no doubt as to what was the subject of the assurance, namely the farm as it existed from time to time. Accordingly, the nature of the interest to be received by David was clear: it was the farm as it existed on Peter's death. ... [T]he property the subject of the equity could be conceptually identified from the moment the equity came into existence, but its precise extent fell to be determined when the equity crystallised, namely on Peter's death.

Of course, even where there is no doubt about the physical identity of the property over which an assurance is alleged to have been made, the nature of the promised right in that property it must still be sufficient to rely upon.

The representation must be clear and unequivocal

In previous chapters we considered the development and the purpose of increased formality in the creation and transfer of estates and interests. Designed to provide greater certainty and to prevent disputes about what has been agreed and when, s 2 of the Law of Property (Miscellaneous Provisions) Act 1989 (LP(MP)A 1989) requires land contracts be in writing, to set out the agreement, and to be signed by the parties thereby showing negotiations have moved to the point of binding agreement.

> TUTOR TIP – 1
> ....
>
> Implied, resulting and constructive trusts are expressly excepted from the requirements of s 2 of the LP(MP)A 1989 by s 2(5) but estoppel is not. However, it has been suggested that proprietary estoppel cases fall within the exceptions created for resulting, implied or constructive trusts. In *Yaxley v Gotts* [1999], Robert Walker LJ reasoned:
>
>> [T]he species of constructive trust based on 'common intention' is … closely akin to, if not indistinguishable from, proprietary estoppel. Equity enforces it because it would be unconscionable for the other party to disregard the claimant's rights. Section 2(5) expressly saves the creation and operation of a constructive trust.
>>
>> I cannot accept that the saving should be construed and applied as narrowly … To give it what I take to be its natural meaning … would not create a huge and unexpected gap in s. 2. It would allow a limited exception, expressly contemplated by Parliament, for those cases in which a supposed bargain has been so fully performed by one side, and the general circumstances of the matter are such, that it would be inequitable to disregard the claimant's expectations, and insufficient to grant him no more than a restitutionary remedy.
>
> However, in *Cobbe v Yeoman's Row* [2008] Lord Scott expressed doubt about the availability of estoppel as an exception:
>
>> Section 2 of the 1989 Act declares to be void any agreement for the acquisition of an interest in land that does not comply with the requisite formalities prescribed by the section. Subsection (5) expressly makes an exception for resulting, implied or constructive trusts … Proprietary estoppel does not have the benefit of this exception. The question arises, therefore, whether a complete agreement for the acquisition of an interest in land that does not comply with the s 2 prescribed formalities, but would be specifically enforceable if it did can become enforceable via the route of proprietary estoppel. It is not necessary in the present case to answer this question, for the second agreement was not a complete agreement and, for that reason, would not have been specifically enforceable so long as it remained incomplete. My present view, however, is that proprietary estoppel cannot be prayed in aid in order to render enforceable an agreement that statute has declared to be void. The proposition that an owner of land can be estopped from asserting that an agreement is void for want of compliance with the requirements of section 2 is, in my opinion, unacceptable. The assertion is no more than the statute provides. Equity can surely not contradict the statute.

Setting aside the ongoing uncertainty about the availability of estoppel in 'failed contract' cases, assuming the doctrine is available then the absence of an agreement in compliance with s 2 of the LP(MP)A 1989 must still be an important consideration. As Lord Justice Lewison explained in *Shirt v Shirt* [2012]:[13] 'Formal requirements for the disposition of interests in land exist for a good reason. They are designed in part at least to prevent expensive disputes about half-remembered conversations which took place many years before a dispute crystallised.'

A factor in determining whether there is sufficient clarity in what is expected must then be the absence of such formality. Certainly in a commercial context, a business person would seek legal advice and so vague assurances outside of formal contract may struggle to create a clear enough expectation. In a domestic context, purchasers of property should also expect to do so with professional guidance and have an awareness of the vulnerability of a planned purchase prior to exchange of contracts. In informal family contexts, however, a strict requirement for terms to be precise and reduced to writing could result in inequitable outcomes.

The relevance of context is illustrated in two contrasting cases, one commercial and the other a family setting.

KEY CASE: *COBBE V YEOMAN'S ROW MANAGEMENT LTD* [2008] UKHL 55; [2008] 1 WLR 1752

This case relates to a claimant who agreed to seek planning permission for property owned by the defendant company. It was agreed that if the claimant secured planning permission, he would then purchase the property at an agreed price with the details of the agreement to be settled then. The claimant won planning permission, after investing a considerable amount of effort and time in the process. The defendant company refused to honour the agreement and enter into a formal contract. Given the commercial context, the House of Lords looked for a 'certain interest in land'.

Per Lord Scott:

> [The] requirement that there be an expectation of 'a certain interest in land' ... presents a problem for Mr Cobbe's proprietary estoppel claim. The problem is that when he made the planning application his expectation was, for proprietary estoppel purposes, the wrong sort of expectation. It was not an expectation that he would, if the planning application succeeded, become entitled to 'a certain interest in land'. His expectation was that he and Mrs Lisle-Mainwaring, or their respective legal advisers, would sit down and agree the outstanding contractual terms to be incorporated into the formal written

---

13 EWCA Civ 1029; [2013] 1 FLR 232.

agreement, which he justifiably believed would include the already agreed core financial terms, and that his purchase, and subsequently his development of the property, in accordance with that written agreement would follow. This is not, in my opinion, the sort of expectation of 'a certain interest in land' that Oliver J in the *Taylors Fashions* case or Lord Kingsdown in *Ramsden v Dyson* had in mind.

…To the extent that he had an expectation of a 'certain interest in land', it was always a contingent one, contingent not simply on the grant of planning permission but contingent also on the course of the further contractual negotiations and the conclusion of a formal written contract.

But in a family context, a different outcome may be reached as discussed by Lord Walker:

In the commercial context, the claimant is typically a business person with access to legal advice and what he or she is expecting to get is a contract. In the domestic or family context, the typical claimant is not a business person and is not receiving legal advice. What he or she wants and expects to get is an interest in immovable property, often for long-term occupation as a home. The focus is not on intangible legal rights but on the tangible property which he or she expects to get. The typical domestic claimant does not stop to reflect (until disappointed expectations lead to litigation) whether some further legal transaction (such as a grant by deed, or the making of a will or codicil) is necessary to complete the promised title.

KEY CASE: *THORNER V MAJOR* [2009] UKHL 18; [2009] 1 WLR 776

This is the case already referred to above relating to a farm, and was in a family context. The claimant (a second cousin) worked on a farm for nearly 30 years without payment relying on assurances that the property would be left to him. While, as put by Lord Scott, it is trite law that 'a representation, if it is to found a claim based on proprietary estoppel, must be clear and unequivocal' the assurance was 'clear enough' given the context, including the relationship between and the character of the parties.

Per Lord Rodger:

Even though clear and unequivocal statements played little or no part in communications between the two men, they were well able to understand one another. So, however clear and unequivocal his intention to assure David that he was to have the farm after his death, Peter was always likely to have expressed it in oblique language. Against that background … I would hold that it is sufficient if what Peter said was 'clear enough'. To whom? Perhaps

> not to an outsider. What matters, however, is that what Peter said should have
> been clear enough for David, whom he was addressing and who had years of
> experience in interpreting what he said and did, to form a reasonable view
> that Peter was giving him an assurance that he was to inherit the farm and that
> he could rely on it.

More recently in *Ghazaani v Rowshan* [2015][14] the authority on this point was reviewed
in the High Court. Judge Behrens observed that:

> Despite the observations of Lord Scott in … *Cobbe* it is probably still possible to
> have a proprietary estoppel in the case of a contract which does not satisfy s 2 of
> the LP(MP)A 1989. However this will necessarily be an exceptional case.

Owing to the exceptional circumstances, an oral agreement was held to be sufficient to
order that the property be transferred.

Revocable assurances

Taylor v Dickens [1998][15] concerned an elderly lady who said that she would leave her
estate to the gardener and later changed her mind (without telling him) after he had
stopped charging her for his work. Judge Weeks rejected a claim of estoppel, as:

> [I]t is not sufficient for A to believe that he is going to be given a right over B's
> property if he knows that B has reserved the right to change his mind. In that case,
> A must show that B created or encouraged a belief on A's part that B would not
> exercise that right.

KEY CASE: *GILLETT V HOLT* [2001] CH 210; [2000] 3 WLR 815

Despite the inherent nature of wills as revocable, it was confirmed that this will
not prevent a binding reliance in some circumstances, such as where assurances
are repeated over a long period of time. Per Robert Walker LJ:

> [T]he inherent revocability of testamentary dispositions … is irrelevant to a
> promise or assurance that 'all this will be yours' … Even when the promise or
> assurance is in terms linked to the making of a will … the circumstances may
> make clear that the assurance is more than a mere statement of present
> (revocable) intention, and is tantamount to a promise …

---

14 [2015] EWHC 1922 (Ch); [2015] All ER (D) 263 (Jul).
15 [1998] 3 FCR 455; [1998] 1 FLR 806.

… [I]t is notorious that some elderly persons of means derive enjoyment from the possession of testamentary power, and from dropping hints as to their intentions, without any question of an estoppel arising. But in this case Mr Holt's assurances were repeated over a long period, usually before the assembled company on special family occasions, and some of them (such as 'it was all going to be ours anyway' on the occasion of the Beeches incident) were completely unambiguous.

APPLY YOUR LEARNING – TASK 1

The particular property, Tulip Cottage, is identified. Given this is a family context, do you think the assurances about a home for life are clear enough?

DETRIMENTAL RELIANCE

Reliance

There must be an alteration to the claimant's position as a result of the representation. In proving reliance, the representation is not required to be the sole reason for the changed position but must have had an 'influence', as confirmed in *Amalgamated Property Co v Texas Commerce International Bank* [1982][16] by Goff J:

[T]he question is not whether the representee acted, or desisted from acting, solely in reliance on the encouragement or representation of the other party; the question is rather whether his conduct was so *influenced* by the encouragement or representation … that it would be unconscionable for the representor to enforce his strict legal rights.

Reliance may be demonstrated by expenditure of money or work on property, or by other methods. Once it is established that representations were made, any detrimental act is then taken as indication of reliance thereby shifting the burden of proof to the defendant to establish the claimant did not rely on the assurance.

KEY CASE: *GREASLEY V COOKE* [1980] 3 ALL ER 710; [1980] 1 WLR 1306

A live-in maid who was assured that she could remain in the property for the rest of her life by the family and continued to look after the property (without payment) and to care for an ill family member was presumed to have done so in reliance on the promise, given her possible detriment in not looking for an alternative job. Denning MR reasoned

---

16 [1982] QB 84; [1981] 3 All ER 577.

> No one can say what she would have done if Kenneth and Hedley had not
> made those statements. It is quite possible that she would have said to
> herself, 'I am not married to Kenneth, I am on my own. What will happen to
> me if anything happens to him? I had better look out for another job now:
> rather than stay here where I have no security'.

On the basis of that determinant, there was a rebuttable presumption of reliance,
per Denning MR:

> [The statements] were calculated to influence her – so as to put her mind at
> rest – so that she should not worry about being turned out … So, instead of
> looking for another job, she stayed on at the house looking after Kenneth and
> Clarice. There is a presumption that she did so, relying on the assurances
> given to her by Kenneth and Hedley. The burden is not on her, but on them,
> to prove that she did not rely on their assurances.

Proof of detriment requires a claimant to show that his conduct was something he
would not have done without the promise.

KEY CASE: *COOMBES V SMITH* [1986] 1 WLR 808; [1987] 1 FLR 352

The claimant moved into the property after she became pregnant with the child
of the defendant and left her husband to be with him (in fact, they never actually
lived together). The court found no detriment – her actions where those which
could be expected of any woman in her position. Deputy Judge Jonathan Parker
QC said:

> The reality is that the plaintiff decided to move … because she preferred to
> have a relationship with, and a child by, the defendant rather than continuing to
> live with her husband. It seems to me to have been as simple as that. There is
> no evidence that she left her husband in reliance on the defendant's assurance
> that he would provide for her if and when their relationship came to an end

---

An interesting contrast is provided by the case *Wayling v Jones* [1993].[17] A gay couple
lived together for more than 16 years. The claimant was promised that he would inherit
the business (a hotel). The claimant worked for the defendant for minimal pay, but the
defendant never actually altered his will. While the claimant admitted that he would
have remained even if the promise was never made, he confirmed that should the
defendant have told him the promise was withdrawn, he would then have left. It is this
last point which was used by the Court of Appeal to find reliance. While there may
have been mixed motives, there was evidence enough.

---

17 (1993) 69 P & CR 170; [1996] 2 FCR 41.

KEY CASE: *CAMPBELL V GRIFFIN* [2001] EWCA CIV 990; (2001) 82 P & CR D43

The claimant lodged with a couple and, after five years, the relationship moved from that of friendship to one more akin to family. The couple then became increasingly ill and he provided the couple with care. He was given assurances that he could live in the house for the rest of his life. The difficulty was that, in court, he agreed that he would have helped the couple in spite of the assurance because of friendship which had developed. But his behaviour was found to have been influenced by an enduring belief in a close relationship which was in turn maintained by that assurance continuing. Robert Walker LJ said:

> By 1990 at latest there was a much closer, family-type relationship, with assurances of a home for life being given from about 1987. By 1990 Mr Campbell was doing much more for the Ascoughs than could be ascribed to even the most friendly lodger. He had become part of the family, and there was a strong presumption that the assurances given to him … were influencing his conduct.

The facts that Mr Campbell agreed, under skilful cross-examination, that he would not in any event have ignored his elderly landlord

> '…if he had been lying on the floor, and had not eaten for two days'

is not sufficient to rebut that presumption. … In cases of this sort it is inevitable that claimants should be asked hypothetical questions of the 'what if' variety but the court is not bound to attach great importance to the answers to such hypothetical questions. As Lord Denning MR said in *Greasley v Cooke* [1980] 1 WLR 1306, 1311,

> 'No one can say what she [the claimant] would have done if Kenneth and Hedley [the two brothers who owned the property] had not made those statements.'

… [I]t would do no credit to the law if an honest witness who admitted that he had mixed motives were to fail in a claim which might have succeeded if supported by less candid evidence. As Balcombe LJ said in *Wayling v Jones* [at p.178]

> 'The promises relied upon do not have to be the sole inducement for the conduct: it is sufficient if they are an inducement.'

In my judgment the assurances given by the Ascoughs were an inducement to Mr Campbell's conduct, from 1990 at latest.

Detriment

We have already seen that detriment need not be financial – it can be behaving in a particular way, such as the example of providing care we considered. The range of actions which may be detrimental is wide, for example in *Jones (AE) v Jones (FW)* [1997][18] giving up a home and a job to move closer and in *Ottey v Grundy* [2003][19] giving up aspirations for a career in acting and modelling.

However, the detrimental behaviour must be something 'substantial'. The detriment is assessed at the point at which the party who gave the assurance seeks to go back on it. As explained by Robert Walker LJ in *Gillett v Holt* [2001]:[20]

> The overwhelming weight of the authorities shows that detriment is required. But the authorities also show that it is not a narrow or technical concept. The detriment need not consist of the expenditure of money or other quantifiable financial detriment, so long as it is something substantial. The requirement must be approached as part of a broad inquiry as to whether repudiation of an assurance is or is not unconscionable in all the circumstances.

> There are some helpful observations about the requirement for detriment in the judgment of Slade LJ in *Jones v Watkins* [1987].[21] There must be sufficient causal link between the assurance relied on and the detriment asserted. The issue of detriment must be judged at the moment when the person who has given the assurance seeks to go back on it. Whether the detriment is sufficiently substantial is to be tested by whether it would be unjust or inequitable to allow the assurance to be disregarded – that is, again, the essential test of unconscionability. The detriment alleged must be pleaded and proved.

The detriment must be more than *de minimis*, so carrying household chores, answering the telephone, and recording programmes was not sufficiently substantial in *Century (UK) Ltd SA v Clibbery* [2004].[22]

A balancing exercise

In assessing the significance (or not) of the detriment, the court must weigh against any detriment countervailing benefits to the claimant over the course of the relationship.

In *Henry v Henry* [2010],[23] the promise was inheritance of property if the claimant cultivated it and looked after the owner until she died. In its assessment of whether there was detrimental reliance (more than simple reliance), the court considered that he had benefited substantially (living rent-free and selling produce of the land as his livelihood). However, those gains were outweighed by the detriments of giving up opportunities to a more attractive life for himself and his family elsewhere.

....

18 [1997] 1 WLR 438.
19 [2003] EWCA Civ 1176; [2003] WTLR 1253.
20 [2001] Ch 210; [2000] 2 All ER 289.
21 26 November 1987, unreported.
22 [2004] EWHC 1870 (Ch); [2004] All ER (D) 541 (Jul).
23 [2010] UKPC 3; [2010] 1 All ER 988.

In order to weigh the detriment of behaving in a particular way, it is necessary to consider whether a 'better' opportunity existed elsewhere. Per Morgan J in *Creasey v Sole* [2013]:[24]

> In order to determine whether [the claimant] acted to his detriment in reliance on some promise or assurance, it is necessary to consider what alternative course or courses might have been open to him. If the arrangement which he had with his parents was profitable to him but he gave up the opportunity of a more profitable alternative, then a decision, in reliance on a promise or assurance, to stay with the arrangement could be said to be detrimental to him.

KEY CASE: *DAVIES V DAVIES* [2014] EWCA CIV 568

This case usefully highlights once again that this balancing exercise is not an exclusively financial evaluation or an 'exercise in forensic accounting'. In assessing the decision to work at a parent's farm for many years in place of another job, any difference in remuneration is not the only factor a court should consider in deciding whether a better opportunity was sacrificed. For example, in this case, the person claiming estoppel had loved her other job. She had enjoyed getting to meet people and working more social hours to suit her family life and she would have been able to work substantially less hours for the same money as paid to her at the farm and have avoided a difficult working relationship with her parents. The Court of Appeal found that the judge at first instance had not erred and his conclusion that there was a net detriment to her.

Any benefit which is taken into consideration in the balancing exercise must, just as with the detriment, be because of the assurance. In *Southwell v Blackburn* [2014], the cohabitation case referred to earlier, Mrs Blackburn had undoubtedly benefited from financial support for her and her children but that flowed from the relationship rather than the promise and was no more than, 'an inherent and intrinsic element in the Respondent's decision to rely upon the Appellant's assurance of security'.

APPLY YOUR LEARNING – TASK 2

What is the relevance of Marcus giving up opportunities and spending a large amount of his money on the house over a long period of time?

Would it make a difference if Marcus had only spent money paying half the household bills and for holidays away together, and if his work on the house was limited to painting and wallpapering the house to make it more pleasant?

---

24 [2013] EWHC 1410 (Ch); [2013] WTLR 931.

UNCONSCIONABILITY

Unconscionability has applied in relation to the other elements of making out a case of estoppel. It may then be questioned whether it is truly a separate element, or rather an underpinning consideration uniting the evaluation of those points into an overall conclusion on conscionability. Lord Walker said in *Cobbe v Yeoman's Row Management* [2008]:

> That argument raises the question whether 'unconscionability' is a separate element in making out a case of estoppel, or whether to regard it as a separate element … Here it is being used (as in my opinion it should always be used) as an objective value judgment on behaviour (regardless of the state of mind of the individual in question). As such it does in my opinion play a very important part in the doctrine of equitable estoppel, in unifying and confirming, as it were, the other elements. If the other elements appear to be present but the result does not shock the conscience of the court, the analysis needs to be looked at again.

SATISFYING THE EQUITY

Assuming that Marcus can establish his claim in relation to Tulip Cottage, what would he actually be entitled to?

Once an estoppel has been established, the claimant is entitled to a remedy and the court must consider how to 'satisfy the equity' by awarding whatever is most appropriate. This may range from a property right capable of binding third parties, such as the transfer of a legal estate, to a mere personal right such as a licence to occupy or monetary compensation.

KEY CASE: *JENNINGS V RICE* [2002] EWCA CIV 159; [2003] 1 FCR 501

Robert Walker LJ clarified that the courts must 'take a principled approach and cannot exercise a completely unfettered discretion according to the individual judge's notion of what is fair in any particular case'. Two principles were outlined:

- A court will ascertain the maximum extent of the claimant's equity (the claimant's expected interest) and then award only the minimum to do justice.
- The remedy must be proportionate, taking into account not only the expectations but the actual detriment and all the other circumstances relevant to doing justice between the parties.

As he explains: 'The equity arises not from the claimant's expectation alone, but from the combination of expectations, detrimental reliance, and the unconscionableness of allowing the [promisor] … to go back on the assurance'. He also reasons that: 'the essence of the doctrine of proprietary estoppel is to do what is necessary to avoid an unconscionable result, and a disproportionate remedy cannot be the right way of going about that'.

A recent example of the challenges for a court determining what to do with the expectation as the starting point comes from a return to the situation we explored earlier in *Davies v Davies* [2014]. Remember, this was the case involving a daughter working on the family farm. This time, the case related to the award she was given to satisfy her equity.

KEY CASE: *DAVIES V DAVIES* [2016] EWCA CIV 463

The daughter was awarded £1.3 million at first instance. Her parents now appealed the amount of the award.

As we already know, she worked and lived on the farm for many years, receiving little remuneration, and also sacrificed an alternative career. The representations she was given varied substantially across the years. There was a draft partnership agreement but this was never signed. The working relationship between the parties was very acrimonious at times, causing the parents to change their will several times and the daughter on a number of occasions to temporarily cease living and working on the farm.

The judge at first instance found that at times the parents had allowed her to have an expectation of not only an entitlement to a share in the property and the business but to inherit it upon their deaths. While not ordering that the farm be transferred to her, a substantial monetary award was required to satisfy her equity.

The Court of Appeal unanimously allowed the appeal, reducing the award to £500,000. It considered that the approach of the judge at first instance, 'had taken far too broad a brush and failed to analyse the facts that he found with sufficient vigour in deciding to award the Claimant £1.3 million.' In applying *Jennings v Rice* [2002] regarding unclear expectations, Lewison LJ suggested that one means of approaching the position of expectation in a case such as this would be to adopt a: '[S]liding scale by which the clearer the expectation, the greater the detriment and the longer the passage of time during which the expectation was reasonably held, the greater would be the weight that should be given to the expectation.'

This is not to say that it is the level of detriment which necessarily dictates the remedy. The expectation remains the start for any consideration. Too much emphasis on the detriment may be inappropriate, for example where the representation was reasonably clear on the nature and terms of the right in property, or unhelpful where the detriment was something difficult to quantify such as providing care or a lost opportunity in life.

Arden LJ, in applying Robert Walker LJ's reasoning in *Jennings v Rice* [2002] in relation to proportionality, considered detriment relevant where the claimant's expectations are more than could be fairly derived from the detriment suffered. As he explained in *Suggitt v Suggitt* [2012]:[25]

> [T]his principle does not mean that there has to be a relationship of proportionality between the level of detriment and the relief awarded. What Walker LJ holds in this paragraph is that if the expectations are extravagant or 'out of all proportion to the detriment which the claimant has suffered', the court can and should recognise that the claimant's equity should be satisfied in another and generally more limited way

The flexibility available to the court is best demonstrated by a consideration of the range of remedies awarded in different cases.

Transfer or grant of an estate or interest

An order to transfer or grant an estate or interest will be made only where the claimant's expectation comes from a representation or assurance promising the particular right.

It is rare for a court to order the transfer of a freehold, but it will do where it is the only remedy that will satisfy the expectation.

KEY CASE: *DILLWYN V LLEWELYN* [1862] EWHC CH J67

The estoppel was raised by a father signing a memorandum (not complying with the formalities for a deed) purporting to transfer land to his son 'for the purpose of furnishing himself with a dwelling-house'. The son built his home on the land, and claimed estoppel. The court concluded that the only remedy was to award the son the freehold as, 'no one builds a house for his own life only.'

In *Pascoe v Turner* [1979][26] the claimant's expectations could, in other circumstances, have been possibly met through a licence for life or a conveyance of the freehold. The assurance was that 'the house is yours and everything in it'. In choosing between

---

25 EWCA Civ 1140; [2012] WTLR 1607.
26 [1979] 1 WLR 431.

the remedies, the court felt that the plaintiff would pursue his attempts to evict her by any legal means at his disposal with a ruthless disregard of the obligations binding on conscience. Only awarding her the freehold could prevent this. This was the minimum required to do equity.

Other cases show the courts' ability to grant entitlement in keeping with the representation or assurance.

In *JT Developments Ltd v Quinn* (1990)[27] the claimant had been assured he could rely on obtaining a new lease on the same terms as a tenant of a neighbouring shop. In reliance, he carried out work on the property. An order to grant the lease was made.

In *Sleebush v Gordon* [2004][28] the claimant had lived in a property, which was purchased by her husband, but lived as a tenant in common with his mother. She and her husband had paid off the mortgage based on assurances from the mother that the property belonged to them. She was awarded the whole beneficial ownership of the property.

In *ER Ives Investment Ltd v High* [1967][29] the claimant has an oral agreement (no deed was ever used) with a neighbouring landowner that he would be granted a right of way. The neighbouring landowner then sold his property. The new owners allowed the claimant to use the right of way and to build a garage on his property which could be reached only with the promised easement. The neighbouring property was then sold on again, and its new owner claimed he was not bound by the right. The court found that the elements of estoppel were present, and the claimant was entitled to the grant of an easement.

A right to occupy

This remedy recognises a licence to occupy property, on whatever terms the expectation requires. This may include that the licence is irrevocable.

In *Greasley v Cooke* [1980] the maid, who you will recall had cared for the property and looked after an ill family member, was promised she could remain in the property for the rest of her life and so her remedy awarded was an entitlement to do so rent-fee.

KEY CASE: *INWARDS V BAKER* (1965) 2 QB 29; [1965] 2 WLR 212

A father encouraged his son to build a bungalow on his land. The house was built at the son's own expense and with his own hands, money and time. The son lived at the house for a number of years until, after the father died and left all his property to his partner, and she sought to remove him.

---

27 [1991] 2 EGLR 257; (1990) 62 P & CR 33.
28 [2004] EWHC 2287 (Ch); [2005] 1 P & CR DG6.
29 [1967] 2 QB 379.

It was held that the son was entitled to remain in the property. Lord Denning MR explained:

> [I]n this case, even though there is no binding contract to grant any particular interest to the licensee, nevertheless the Court can look at the circumstances and see whether there is an equity arising out of the expenditure of money. All that is necessary is that the licensee should, at the request or with the encouragement of the landlord, have spent the money in the expectation of being allowed to stay there. If so, the Court will not allow that expectation to be defeated where it would be inequitable so to do. In this case it is quite plain that the father allowed an expectation to be created in the son's mind that this bungalow was to be his home. It was to be his home for his life or, at all events, his home as long as he wished it to remain his home. It seems to me, in the light of that equity, the father could not in 1932 have turned to his son and said: 'You are to go. It is my land and my house'. Nor could he at any time thereafter so long as the son wanted it as his home.

In *Inwards v Baker* there was never any commitment to transfer the land to the son and so no expectation of a transfer of the freehold estate. But he was assured he would be able to live in the house for the rest of his life. This made an award of a remedy of a lifetime right to occupy appropriate in these circumstances.

The implications of an 'irrevocable' licence for third parties purchasing land is a point upon which there remain differing views. There is case law to support the ability of such a licence, when it arises through estoppel, to bind. For a detailed analysis of authority on this point see Chapter 8.

Monetary compensation

Monetary compensation is an appropriate remedy where the detriment is disproportionate in relation to the value of the expectation claimed or where circumstance makes it impossible for an expectation of occupation to be met.

In *Dodsworth v Dodsworth* [1973][30] a sister allowed her brother and his wife to live with her on their return from Australia saying that they could remain in the house for as long as they wished. They spent over £700 on improvements. The court did not grant a right of occupancy but did order an award of the money spent.

In *Campbell v Griffin* [2001] the lodger who had provided care for the owners beyond that which a lodger normally would was found to have done so in reliance on a promise that he had a home for life. But the court considered that it would be disproportionate to give full effect to his expectation of a lifetime right to occupy and instead ordered compensation of £35,000.

---

30 (1973) 228 EG 1115; [1973] EGD 233.

In *Baker v Baker* [1993][31] an elderly man gave up secure accommodation and contributed to the purchase of a house with his son and daughter. The relationship broke down, so that the court considered occupation was not a possibility with a clean break the best course of action. Compensation was awarded for loss of accommodation, calculated to be sufficient to provide for an appropriate alternative.

KEY CASE: *HUSSEY V PALMER* [1972] EWCA CIV 1; [1972] 3 ALL ER 744; [1972] 1 WLR 1286

The claimant was invited to live with her daughter and son-in-law and paid £607 towards an extension to the house. After a falling-out, she left the property. When the issue reached court, estoppel could have been used to give her the remedy of a right of occupation but, possibly because the breakdown in relations meant it was not realistic for them to live together, she was given a share in the beneficial interest proportionate to the amount she contributed.

In *Burrows and Burrows v Sharp* [1991][32] the claimants agreed to pay the mortgage on a flat purchased by Mrs Sharp. They were to be left it when she died. After the relationship broke down the court could have ordered a right of occupation but it was not practical and compensation for their expenditure was instead awarded.

APPLY YOUR LEARNING – TASK 3

What remedy do you think might be appropriate for Marcus? He may claim his expectation was a lifetime right to occupy, but remember a court will not make an order which is disproportionate and, given the circumstances, it may not be practical. Remember, we are dealing with the end of a relationship, where there is quarrelling and a desire to move in another person. What might be a better alternative remedy?

---

31 [1993] 2 FLR 247.
32 [1991] Fam Law 67.

THE PROPRIETARY STATUS OF A CLAIM

The final question is the status of any claim by Marcus.

AFTER A REMEDY IS GRANTED

Once a court determines an estoppel has arisen, whatever it awards to satisfy the equity will be crystallised by a court order. The ability to bind a third party then depends on the normal rules relating to the right or interest granted. Specifically, whether it is proprietary (such as a freehold, leasehold, beneficial interest or easement) or a personal right (such as payment of a sum of money or a licence). Do note, however, that irrevocable licences raise considerable uncertainty about their impact on third parties. See Chapter 8 on licences for an exploration of the challenges.

BEFORE A REMEDY IS GRANTED

Before the courts satisfy the equity, it is as yet uncrystallised. Such an 'estoppel equity' or 'inchoate equity' once created significant uncertainty about what this means for third-party purchasers. One view is that while the claim remains inchoate, there is no proprietary right as of yet which can bind. The other is that, given a proprietary remedy may be given, it is to be treated as such and be capable of binding purchasers once it has arisen (of course, the actual remedy given by a court to satisfy the equity may still only be personal).

Registered land

The Land Registration Act 2002 (LRA 2002) has clarified the position in relation to registered land. Section 116 provides that:

> It is hereby declared for the avoidance of doubt that, in relation to registered land…
>
> (a)   an equity by estoppel…
>
> has effect from the time the equity arises as an interest capable of binding successors in title…

This means a claim may be protected by a notice in the register (s 29 of the LRA 2002) or override if there is actual occupation (sch 3, para 2 of the LRA 2002).

Unregistered land

In unregistered land, case law has determined that whether an inchoate claim binds a purchaser will normally be decided in accordance with the doctrine of notice. For actual notice, the cases *ER Ives Investment Ltd v High* [1967] and *Lloyds Bank v Carrick* [1996][33] illustrate the point. While less certain, it also seems constructive notice will probably be enough after *Bristol & West Building Society v Henning* [1985].[34]

----

33 [1996] 4 All ER 630.

34 [1985] 1 WLR 778.

> **TUTOR TIP – 2**
> ....
>
> Holding third parties to be bound by an equity by estoppel when they are not the party who made the representations may seem harsh, particularly when it is so often an overriding interest safeguarded by actual occupation. However, it may not be the case that the remedy to which the equity gives rise would be the same for the original party and the third party. In *Henry v Henry* [2010] EWCP 3 the Privy Council noted that:
>
> > The Board does not rule out the possibility that cases may arise in which the particular circumstances surrounding a third party purchase may, notwithstanding the claimant's overriding interest, require the court to reassess the extent of the claimant's equity in the property.
>
> See also *Thompson v Foy* [2009] EWHC 1076 (Ch); [2010] 1 P & CR 308.

DISCUSSION

The flexibility of estoppel may be seen as risking undermining some of the aims of the 1925 legislation in creating greater simplicity and certainty in dealings with land.

> **CONSIDER THIS – 1**
>
> What are the justifications for the availability of proprietary estoppel in relation to land, and to what extent are any risks to the aims of the 1925 legislation avoided?

Note that the nature of land means there is a need for certainty and that comes in the form of writing, whether the requirement for a deed to grant legal estates and interests or for enforceable land contracts to be in a particular form. Estoppel avoids the needs for formalities, and may reintroduce a degree of ambiguity. Why is it still necessary to recognise it and what do the cases in this chapter tell us about courts safeguarding against possible pitfalls?

END OF CHAPTER SUMMARY

- Proprietary estoppel arises where a representation or assurance is made to another that he has or will have rights in land, causing that person to act to their detriment in reliance.
- The claimant must prove: representation, reliance, detriment and unconscionability.

- The representation can be active or passive. It must relate to identifiable property and be sufficiently clear given the context (commercial or family).
- Reliance requires it to be shown that the claimant changed their position because of the promise.
- Detriment is not limited to money or working on the property, but it must be substantial.
- The court has discretion in what remedy it gives to satisfy the equity.

PREPARING FOR ASSESSMENTS QUESTIONS

ESSAY QUESTION

In *Yeoman's Row Management Ltd v Cobbe* [2008] UKHL 55, the House of Lords restricted the application of proprietary estoppel to where particular requirements are satisfied and stated that it is not 'a sort of joker or wild card to be used whenever the Court disapproves of the conduct of a litigant who seems to have the law on his side'. In doing so, it was influenced by the desire to promote certainty in commercial transactions.

To what extent does this secure certainty in a commercial context, and how does it differ from the approach in a domestic or family context?

PROBLEM QUESTION

Since childhood, Billy has farmed Turnpike Farm with his father. He was told by his father that the farm and the business would be left to him. Billy has dedicated his entire working life to the farm, despite his low wage, because of assurances that it would one day be his.

Billy's sister Tess has built a small cottage on the farm, having been told by her father that the plot would be hers when he died.

The father recently died, and the will leaves the entirety of his estate to his brother.

Advise Billy and Tess.

FURTHER READING

- Battersby, G, 'Contractual and Estoppel Licences as Proprietary Interests in Land' [1991] Conv 36. Considers the relationship between contractual licences and licences arising by proprietary estoppel, including the case *Ashburn Anstalt v WJ Arnold & Co* [1989] Ch 1.

- Dixon, M, 'Defining and Confining Estoppel: The Role of Unconscionability' (2010) 30 LS 408. Examines how unconscionability can be shown for the purpose of establishing a proprietary estoppel claim and how a clear and principled account can limit the risk of estoppel being overused and undermining the aims of the 1925 legislation. Considers the cases *Thorner v Major* [2009] UKHL 18 and *Cobbe v Yeoman's Row Management Ltd* [2008] UKHL 55.
- Gardner, S, 'The Remedial Discretion in Proprietary Estoppel – Again' (2006) 492 LQR 122. Explores case law on the correct approach to estoppel relief, including *Jennings v Rice* [2002] EWCA Civ 159.
- Handley, KR, 'Unconscionability in Estoppel by Conduct: A Triable Issue or Underlying Principle' [2008] Conv 382. Examines the role played by the concept of unconscionability in estoppel cases. Reviews English and Australian case law on the principles to be applied. Includes *Taylors Fashions Ltd v Liverpool Victoria Trustees Co Ltd* [1982] QB 133 (Ch D); *Gillett v Holt* [2001] Ch 210 and *Cobbe v Yeoman's Row Management Ltd* [2006] EWCA Civ 1139.
- Mee, J, 'Proprietary Estoppel and Inheritance: "Enough Is Enough?" ' [2013] Conv 280. Questions the increased use of proprietary estoppel to uphold claims by people who acted to their detriment on the basis of expectation of inheritance and calls for restraint. Refers to the decisions in *Suggitt v Suggitt* [2012] EWCA Civ 1140 and *Bradbury v Taylor* [2012] EWCA Civ 1208.
- Samet, I, 'Proprietary Estoppel and Responsibility for Omissions' (2015) 78(1) MLR 85. Explores the 'acquiescence' category of proprietary estoppel as a rare example of responsibility for pure omissions in private law. Concludes that in proprietary estoppel the law is justified in imposing a duty on the right-holder to alert a stranger when his actions are based on a mistake. This 'duty to speak' is, however, relatively weak. The current law, in which owners who failed to correct the mistake of the relying party incur similar liability to owners who actively encouraged the other party to rely, is untenable.
- Thompson, MP, 'The Flexibility of Estoppel' [2003] Conv 225. Reviews *Jennings v Rice* [2002] EWCA Civ 159.

CHAPTER 17
COMMONHOLD

CHAPTER AIMS AND OBJECTIVES

In Chapter 14, while exploring freehold covenants, we identified the problems caused by the burden of positive covenants (such as keeping property in good repair) not transferring with freehold property when it is sold. Single properties are often interdependent with other buildings and shared facilities, requiring proper maintenance and repair.

The only arrangement for the long-term enforcement of positive obligations was long leasehold ownership of interdependent properties.[1] In 2002, however, a new way was created of owning freehold properties that have communal facilities, commonhold. Common parts are owned by a commonhold association, which has the responsibility of managing the area.

We will explore the benefits of commonhold, the legal rules that apply to the creation of a commonhold, and the reasons why there are so very few commonhold schemes.

By the end of this chapter, you should be able to:

- explain the meaning of commonhold;
- appreciate why this new way of owning land was introduced;
- identify the requirements to create a commonhold;
- understand the operation of a commonhold;
- understand the ways to terminate commonhold;
- apply the above to the case study and the learning outcomes.

CASE STUDY – ONE

Alan is the owner of an old disused mill which he plans to convert into several self-contained apartments. Alan is concerned that the communal areas in the development should be kept properly maintained and repaired in the future.

Advise Alan of the ways in which he can make sure that any positive covenants entered into by the first purchasers of the individual apartments will transfer to future owners.

---

1 See Chapter 6 on leaseholds for an explanation of how both negative and positive leasehold covenants may be enforced by and against an assignee of a lease.

THE MEANING OF COMMONHOLD

To advise Alan on the possible use of commonhold, we need to understand its key characteristics.

Commonhold combines the freehold ownership of individual properties (a unit) in a development with collective ownership of the freehold of common parts as a limited company. A commonhold consists of units (such as flats, houses, offices or shops) and common parts (such as the grounds, roof and stairs). The limited company, known as a commonhold association, manages the common parts of the development and oversees the individual units. Membership of the commonhold association is restricted to unit-holders within the commonhold, giving each owner a vote on what work needs to be done in accordance with the community statement. When unit-holders sell property, the new unit-holder is affected by the rights and duties under commonhold.

THE BENEFITS OF COMMONHOLD

What are the possible benefits of using commonhold for Alan?

The inability to transfer the burden of positive covenants with freehold land means there is reliance upon the use of long leaseholds for residential flats and other interdependent properties. Leases have a number of issues: their value reduces as the term runs down, the need for a landlord and the potential for inconsistent and poor drafting. By contrast, with commonhold: ownership is on a freehold basis, the commonhold association provides a democratic way of unit-holders owning the common parts and managing the commonhold, and the commonhold documentation is standardised.

THE REQUIREMENTS FOR COMMONHOLD LAND

For Alan to use commonhold, there are a number of requirements he must first satisfy, set out in s 1(1) of the Commonhold and Leasehold Reform Act 2002 (CLRA 2002):

Land is commonhold land if—

(a) the freehold estate in the land is registered as a freehold estate in commonhold land,

(b) the land is specified in the memorandum of association of a commonhold association as the land in relation to which the association is to exercise functions, and

(c) a commonhold community statement makes provision for rights and duties of the commonhold association and unit-holders (whether or not the statement has come into force).

First, all of the land held as commonhold must be freehold and already registered.[2] Second, a commonhold association must be set up as a limited company. It will be registered at Companies House and have a memorandum and articles of association governing it.[3] Third, the commonhold association must produce a community statement. This document, which has a prescribed form, identifies the extent of the commonhold and also the rights and duties of the association and the unit-holders. Duties imposed by the community statement may include, under s 31(5) of the CLRA 2002, to:

■ pay money
■ undertake works
■ grant access
■ give notice
■ refrain from entering into transactions of a specified kind in relation to a commonhold unit
■ refrain from using the whole or part of a commonhold unit for a specified purpose or for anything other than a specified purpose

---

2 Title must also be absolute, under s 2 of the CLRA 2002.

3 In accordance with the Companies Act 2006.

- refrain from undertaking works (including alterations) of a specified kind
- refrain from causing nuisance or annoyance
- refrain from specified behaviour
- indemnify the commonhold association or a unit-holder in respect of costs arising from the breach of a statutory requirement.

An application is made, according to s 2 of the CLRA 2002, by the registered freeholder to the Land Registry who shall register a freehold estate in land as a freehold estate in commonhold land. This is, however, subject to the consent of certain people specified under s 3(1) of the CLRA 2002. Notably, registered proprietors of: the freehold estate, a leasehold estate granted for more than 21 years, or a charge (mortgage).

APPLY YOUR LEARNING – TASK 2

In the scenario with Alan, there is no suggestion of anyone from whom consent would be required.

What if part of the mill was being rented out for use as a storage area, by a lease granted for 30 years?

CONSIDER THIS – 1

What if rather than being a new development, the apartments had already been built and sold on a leasehold basis. How easy do you think it would be to get everyone to agree to create a commonhold for such an existing development?

The move to commonhold will convert any leases into commonhold (s 7(3)(d) of the CLRA 2002). This reflects the principle that all land held as commonhold must be freehold. That same principle means that unit-holders within a commonhold are not able to lease a residential unit for more than seven years.

TERMINATION OF COMMONHOLD

Should Alan create the commonhold, it is possible for it to be wound up in the future. A commonhold may be brought to an end voluntarily by members. Under s 43 of the CLRA 2002, at least 80 per cent of members must agree. Where the agreement is less than 100 per cent, the matter must go to court in accordance with s 45 of the CLRA 2002 so that the court may determine the terms and conditions of the termination statement.

It is also possible for a court to order compulsory winding-up on the grounds of insolvency. Under s 51 of the CLRA 2002 the court will normally grant a succession order, with another association taking over. Only if the circumstances of the insolvent commonhold association make a succession order inappropriate will the court decline to do so. In that event, the commonhold would be terminated.

DISCUSSION

Despite the advantages of commonhold, very few commonhold schemes have been created. In relation to the many existing long-lease developments, converting to commonhold is made difficult by the ability of any owner of a lease granted for more than 21 years to refuse to consent. Even for new development, uncertainty about a new form of ownership has acted as a barrier. From a developer's point of view, leasehold may be more attractive than commonhold as with a leasehold they retain ownership of the land and will therefore have future income from lease extensions. Also, limiting unit-holders to granting leases of no more than seven years is off-putting for purchasers. There are also difficulties with enforcement of the community statement, including the risk of a falling-out between neighbours when action is taken.

END OF CHAPTER SUMMARY

- Commonhold is a new means of ownership, providing an alternative to long leaseholds for interdependent properties.
- Unit-holders own the freehold to their individual unit, the common parts are owned by a commonhold association.
- The commonhold association, made up of unit-holders, manages the commonhold.
- Commonhold avoids the problems caused by the burden of positive convents not transferring with freehold property.
- The take-up of commonhold has been disappointing.

PREPARING FOR ASSESSMENTS

ESSAY QUESTION

A developer is building a new block of flats and is considering commonhold over leasehold. Advise on how commonhold responds to the difficulties of enforcing positive covenants between freehold owners, the requirements to setup a commonhold and the advantages and disadvantages of choosing commonhold over leasehold.

FURTHER READING

- Clarke, D, 'The Enactment of Commonhold – Problems, Principles and Perspectives' [2002] Conv 349. Explores the main provisions of the Commonhold and Leasehold Reform Act 2002
- Smith, P, 'The Purity of Commonholds' [2004] Conv 194. Examines the impact of the purity principle, whereby commonholds must remain separate from leaseholds.
- Wong, S, 'Potential Pitfalls in the Commonhold Community Statement and the Corporate Mechanisms of the Commonhold Association' [2006] Conv 14. Reviews key principles and limitations of commonhold, including freehold ownership of individual units, self-management through the commonhold association, and standardised documentation.

18

CHAPTER 18
THE CONVEYANCING OF LAND

CHAPTER AIMS AND OBJECTIVES

In this chapter we will consider the practical application of land law and the process of buying and selling land.

This is a brief introduction as this topic is a whole book in itself. On an undergraduate law degree, you are very unlikely to be asked in any detail about all the stages and various searches listed here beyond the depth already covered in Chapters 4 and 5 on unregistered and registered land. It is useful, however, to read through the content to help appreciate the relevance and importance of that knowledge in practice. It will also allow you to see some of the challenges to be overcome and appreciate why ideas such as e-conveyancing have ultimately failed, at least as of yet, to be successfully taken forward,[1] beyond some elements being available through online systems.

By the end of this chapter, you should be able to:

- understand the outline of a conveyancing transaction;
- understand the distinction between the registered and unregistered land systems;
- apply the above to the case studies and learning tasks.

CASE STUDY – ONE

Your firm has been instructed to act on behalf of Emma Jane Wilton and Lindsay Steven Wilton. The couple are selling 18 Bankhouse Road Huddersfield for £249,000 and purchasing 10 Coastal Path South Stacks Anglesey. The purchase price for the property is £300,000 but this includes £1,000-worth of garden furniture.

The clients do not need a mortgage to fund the transaction and confirm that they have sufficient savings to cover the difference in price.

---

1 Given the view adopted by the Law Commission in its recent consultation (explored in Chapter 5) that these difficulties mean it would be better that the requirement of simultaneous completion and registration be removed altogether from the Land Registration Act 2002, this does not look likely to change soon. Law Commission, *Updating the Land Registration Act 2002: A Consultation Paper* (Consultation Paper No 227, 2016).

INITIAL MATTTERS

When commencing a conveyancing transaction, whether it be a sale or a purchase *the* most important thing to do at the start is obtain clear and detailed instructions from your client. It is important to ascertain who your clients are and what they want to achieve. This may sound obvious, but unless the solicitor obtains full instructions how can they manage their clients' expectations and deliver what the client wants?

WHAT INFORMATION SHOULD BE OBTAINED?

The property

It is important to obtain the full details of the property to be bought and sold. What is the sale price and does that include fixtures and fittings within that price or will an additional fee be payable for these?

The clients

Who is your client? Does the person you are obtaining instructions from match up with the parties who legally own the property and will have to transfer title on completion? Are there any third parties living in the property who may have an equitable or beneficial interest in the property that could affect the sale? In such cases, as we explain in other chapters, this may require the need to overreach on completion and ensure that the purchase monies are paid to two trustees. It is important to ascertain who is entitled to the sale proceeds upon completion not only in relation to those with beneficial interests but also other third parties such as mortgagees who may have registered legal charges secured again the property.

If the clients are purchasing the property, then how many people are purchasing and what contributions will they be making to the purchase price? Is anyone contributing to the purchase price but not intending to be a legal owner of the property? If so it is possible that they will acquire a beneficial interest in the property. Will the clients be obtaining purchase funds from a third party, for example, a mortgage company? Who will be living at the property but not contributing towards the purchase price? It is possible that such people will acquire rights of occupation which would affect a mortgage company's ability to obtain a possession order in the future.

Timescales

A large number of complaints from clients relate to the transaction taking too long. It is vital that solicitors find out from the clients at the start of the transaction what their expectations are in terms of completion dates. It may be the client has an unrealistic target for completion, that even if everything was favourable the date could not be met. However, if the solicitor does not ask this question, how will they know and how can they manage their clients' expectations of when a realistic completion will be? Remember that the conveyancing transaction is dependent upon many third parties doing their jobs, for example: the other side providing requested information; the mortgage company producing a mortgage offer; and the local authority producing replies to the local authority search. Timescale will also be important in situations where clients are selling and buying property and wish for the transactions to be completed simultaneously. This is known as a 'chain transaction'. A chain transaction will obviously be more complicated, with more delays due to the fact that more people are involved.

Costs

Another big area of complaints from clients is in relation to costs. Clients need to be properly advised as to the costs involved in the transaction, so that disbursements are not a surprise – some clients even lack of awareness of the taxes incurred in buying or selling property. Solicitors are required under the Solicitors Code of Conduct 2011 to deal with such matters. Indeed, there is a requirement under the Code to ensure that the client receives the best possible information about the likely overall costs of their matter both at the time of engagement and as matters progress (see Outcome 1.13 of the Solicitors Code of Conduct 2011). It is important that solicitors are transparent about not only their fees but also of the disbursements and taxes involved in a transaction from the very start. This can be achieved by giving a client a full breakdown at an initial interview *and* they with a follow up client care letter.

FIRST STEPS

Once initial instructions have been taken from the client the solicitor needs to get the transaction moving. They will send a client care letter to their client, confirming the instructions received, initial advice given, an estimate of the timescale involved and a breakdown of the fees and disbursements involved in accordance with the Solicitors Code of Conduct. They will write to the estate agent and the solicitor acting for the other side to confirm that they have been instructed and confirming the property address and the agreed purchase price.

Preparing the sale pack

The seller's solicitor will prepare the sale pack to send to the buyers. This will consist of evidence to demonstrate the seller's legal title to sell the property together with a draft contract of sale. See Extract 1 at the end of this chapter.

Where the property is registered land, the solicitor will obtain up-to-date Official Copy Entries for the title. See Extract 2 at the end of this chapter. As we have seen in Chapter 5, the registers give details of the registered proprietor of the property, i.e. in whom the legal title to the land is currently vested. Additionally, the registers will contain details of all legal easements, legal charges, registered covenants and any other third-party rights.

As we have seen in Chapter 4, for unregistered land, proof of ownership is based upon title deeds. See Extract 3 at the end of this chapter. These documents are required not only to show in whom legal title is vested but also to identify what legal and equitable rights have been created and may bind the land on completion. If no legal charges affect the property the legal owners will normally be in possession of the title deeds. If there is a legal charge, as we have seen in Chapter 13, s 85(1) of the Law of Property Act 1925 (LPA 1925) confirms a first mortgagee's right to take possession of the title deeds as its security and as such the lender should be in possession of the deeds. In such situations, the seller's solicitor will need to request and obtain the title deeds from the lender in order to ascertain legal title and to draft the contract for sale.

Draft contract

There are two main stages to a conveyancing transaction: completion, which is when the legal title to the land transfers from the seller to the buyer and exchange of contracts. Exchange of contracts is the point that the parties become legally bound to buy and sell the property. The contract will contain the details of sellers, buyers, the price agreed, the completion date and any additional terms agreed between the parties.

It is the seller solicitor's job to draft the contract of sale. This is because the seller is in possession of the title deeds and they will need to demonstrate their client has legal title to the property and can show what rights and interests the property is being sold subject to.

As with any contract, the terms of the contract for the sale of land are governed by s 2 of the Law of Property (Miscellaneous Provisions) Act 1989 (LP(MP)A 1989), which specifies that a contract must be in writing, contains the main terms agreed and is signed by the parties. Given the complexity of land transactions and the risks involved, most solicitors will use a standardised contract especially designed for the sale of land. Most residential transactions use a contract incorporating standard conditions, currently the Standard Conditions of Sale (fifth edition). See Extract 1 at the end of this chapter. Where such conditions are incorporated it is still possible for these to be excluded or varied by the parties. The decision to do this is dictated by their client's instructions and any specific issues relating to the land. Any exclusions or variations to the standard conditions are set out in the special conditions and will prevail over the standard conditions.

Under Standard Condition 3.1.1, the seller contracts to sell the property free from incumbrances save for any listed under Standard Condition 3.1.2, which are:

- those specified in the contract
- those which are discoverable by inspection of the property
- those which the seller does not and could not know about
- entries made before the date of the contract in public registers
- public requirements.

You will see from Extract 1 that the front page of the standardised contract has been left blank for the seller's solicitor to insert the relevant information.

Date

This is the date of the contract, i.e. the date that contracts are exchanged. At this point neither the seller nor the buyer knows precisely when this will be and therefore it is left blank until exchange of contracts takes place.

Seller

The sellers should be those people who currently have legal title vested in them. For registered land this information will be obtained from section B of the proprietorship register of the Official Copy Entries. In relation to unregistered land, the most recent conveyance, assent or deed of gift should be used as this shows evidence as to who currently holds legal title. Additionally, the sellers' addresses must be inserted. This is important as if any documents have to be served later in the transaction an address for service is available.

Buyer

As the sellers' solicitor will be drafting this, they may not have the details of the buyers or their current address. This is therefore left blank for the buyer's solicitor to insert as they amend the contract.

Property

The property may be described by a single postal address, which will be acceptable if the property is a standard residential dwelling and is easily identifiable from this description. If it cannot then it is advisable to attach a detailed scaled plan. It is important to get the description accurate as a misdescription in the contract will entitle the buyer to rescind the contract or seek abatement in the purchase price. For best practice on registered land, it is advisable to obtain the property details from the property register, section A of the Official Copy Entries. The information together with the unique title number for the land makes identification clear and accurate.

The description of the land is more complicated in relation to unregistered land, particularly as the land being transferred will trigger a first registration upon completion. Best practice will be to describe the property from a conveyance in the bundle of title deeds, which accurately described the property, and normally has a plan attached to the conveyancing identifying the boundaries. An example of a property clause for unregistered land would be:

> All that freehold property situate and known as 22 Spanish Way Huddersfield West Yorkshire more particularly described in a Conveyance dated the 17th April 1972 made between Adam Haddock (1) and Raymond Mitty (2) ('the 1972 Conveyance') as delineated edged red on the plan attached to the 1972 conveyance.

Title number/root of title

This is the unique number allocated to the land and which can be obtained from the Official Copy Entries. If the property is unregistered then the root of title document will be used. As you will remember from Chapter 5, a seller need only produce a document going back at least 15 years, in accordance with s 23 of the Law of Property Act 1969 (LPA 1969), in order to establish what is referred to as a 'good root of title'. This will normally be a deed of conveyance. If there is not one in the title deeds, it is possible to use a mortgage deed, a voluntary conveyance or a post-1925 assent.

Incumbrances

As we have seen, under Standard Condition 3.1 the property is sold free from any incumbrances save for those specified in the contract. It is important for the seller to examine the title documents or registered title to ascertain whether any, for example restrictive covenants, have been registered. If so these should be disclosed here.

Title guarantee

There are three options for title guarantee: full title guarantee, limited title guarantee and no title guarantee. By offering full title guarantee the seller is confirming that they have the power to sell the land, and owns the whole legal and equitable interest in the property. Additionally they are confirming that the land is free from incumbrances (an incumbrance is a right to or interest in the land, for example, a mortgage or an easement) except for those disclosed or of which he is not and could not be expected to be aware.

With limited title the seller is confirming that he/she has the ability to transfer title to the buyer but, as they are selling the transaction in a professional capacity, they cannot guarantee the extent of the incumbrances the property is subject to, as they have no knowledge as to the extent to which they affect the property. This is normally because the seller is either a personal representative, a mortgagee in possession or selling the property on trust for others.

In the case of no title guarantee, the seller cannot guarantee the extent of the incumbrances the property is subject to, as they have no knowledge as to the extent to which they affect the property and as such has no choice but to give no title guarantee. This may be in situations where seller has little or no knowledge of the property or where the disposition is by way of a gift. This is not commonly used in practice.

Completion date

Although the parties will agree the completion date in advance it will not be written into the contract until exchange of contracts. If the contract is silent on the completion date however, Standard Condition 6.1.1 sets completion at 20 working days after the date of the contract.

Contract rate

The contract provides for compensation to be paid if one party defaults beyond the contractual date for completion. This rate forms the basis of working out that compensation. Unlike damages, the innocent party does not have to prove loss just that the contract has been breached by non-completion. Standard Condition 1.1.1(e) states that the contract rate will be 'the Law Society's interest rate from time to time in force'.

This is currently 4 per cent above the base rate of the Bank of England. Most solicitors use this. Solicitors acting in chain transactions however should take care to ensure that the contract rate in the purchase is *not* higher than that on the sale.

Deposit

Under Standard Conditions 2.2.1 the buyer is required to pay a deposit of 10 per cent of the purchase price at exchange of contracts. It is possible to negotiate a reduction in the deposit if the seller is agreeable. This is usual in situations where the purchase price is very high and a lesser deposit would still be an adequate amount to compensate the seller if the buyer were to default. Alternatively a lesser deposit is agreed where the buyer is funding the deposit from the deposit from their related sale, the sale price of which is less than the purchase price. In such situations the seller will be protected in the case of default by Standard Condition 6.8.3 which states that the buyer will be required to pay the balance 10 per cent deposit upon the service of a notice to complete.

Additionally, under Standard Conditions of Sale 2.2 the deposit is protected between exchange and completion by being held as 'stakeholder'. This means the seller's solicitors are required to hold the deposit as on behalf of both the seller and buyer until completion successfully takes place. If so, it can be released to the seller together with the balance purchase monies. If not then the deposit may be given to the innocent party in accordance with the terms of the contract. If the seller is purchasing another property in England and Wales then under Standard Condition 2.2.5 they are able to use all or part of the deposit as a deposit for their onward purchase, provided provisions have been made at the top of the chain for the deposit to be held as stakeholder.

Vacant possession

Under the open contract rule it is an implied term that the seller must give vacant possession of the property to the buyer upon completion. Under the Standard Conditions of Sale (fifth edition), Special Condition 4 has two options, one of which must be deleted, either

4a   vacant possession will be given or
4b   the property is being sold subject to a lease or a tenancy agreement.

Most transactions will be with vacant possession but if the property is being sold subject to a tenancy agreement or a lease the details of that document and parties to it will be inserted in Special Condition 4. Additionally, it is important to remember the effect of sch 4 of the Family Law Act 1996. This states that the seller will secure the cancellation of any occupation enjoyed by the spouse and will give vacant possession. As such those individuals will be required to sign the contract to confirm that any right registered will be cancelled in addition to giving their consent to the sale of the property. Finally, if any occupiers over the age of 18 live in the property, they too will be required to sign the contract confirming that they agree to the sale and will vacate the property on or before the completion date. Their details are inserted at Special Condition 7 'Occupiers Rights'.

Completion time

Standard Condition 6.1.2 states that completion must take place by 2 p.m. on the day of completion otherwise completion is deemed to have taken place the next working day. In order to achieve completion, the seller must give vacant possession by 2 p.m. and the buyer must ensure that the balance purchase monies are cleared funds in the seller's solicitor's client bank account. This can cause problems where a client is both buying and selling as completion of the sale is required before completion of the purchase can be concluded. In such situations it is normal for the solicitor to vary the Standard Conditions on the sale contract and bring the completion time forward, usually by a couple of hours. This is achieved by amending Special Condition 5.

Defects in title

Defects in title should be disclosed as a special condition, for example the disclosure of a missing conveyance, or evidence proving ownership, otherwise the seller is implying that the property is being sold free from defects and flaws. Such defects relate only to title, as the seller has no duty to disclose physical defects in the property. The buyer is obliged to investigate the physical condition of the property as Standard Condition 3.2.1. states that they accept the property in its physical condition as at exchange of contracts.

Responsibility of the property between exchange and completion

Standard Condition 5.1.1 states that the buyer will bear the risk of the property from exchange of contracts. This includes assuming the risk of loss and damage of the property and why buyers should obtain buildings insurance from exchange of contracts. It is possible to consider excluding Standard Condition 5.1.1 and placing the responsibility and liability back with the seller until completion. If Standard Condition 5.1.1 remains, solicitors should advise buyers of their responsibility from exchange of contracts.

Indemnity covenants

As we have seen in Chapters 7 and 14, covenants are created by deed between the original parties and represents a contract. As such there is privity of contract between the original parties. It means the original covenantee may always enforce any express covenant against the original covenantor. The original covenantor will protect himself by what is known as indemnity. In relation to a conveyancing transaction the seller ensures the buyer indemnifies him in relation to any future breaches of freehold or leasehold covenants. The buyer will then of course repeat this process when they sell the property. The indemnity will be created in the transfer deed, the TR1 on completion; however, to ensure that the buyer will do this the seller will include it as a clause in the contract so that the buyer is contractually obliged to do so when the contracts are exchanged. The clause would look something like this:

> In the transfer to the Buyer the Buyer shall enter into a covenant to observe and perform the Specified Incumbrances and to indemnify the Sellers in respect of any future breach, non-observance or non-performance thereof.

INVESTIGATING TITLE

The buyers' solicitor will carry out an investigation of title on behalf of the buyers. The solicitor is looking to ensure that the property has a good and marketable title and that the property is free from any incumbrances, which could adversely affect the property or their clients' use of it. Why? The buyers need to be mindful of the phrase *Caveat Emptor* – Let the buyer beware. As we have seen earlier, the sellers are under a very limited duty to disclose defects and incumbrances affecting the property under Standard Condition 3.1.2. Additionally if the buyer is buying with the assistance of a mortgage, the lender will normally instruct the buyers' solicitors, as many of the checks and investigations will be the same. The lender will also require the property to have a good and marketable title in accordance with the Council of Mortgage Lenders Handbook. The process of investigating title is slightly different depending on whether the property is registered or unregistered land as the documentation differs although things to look for will be the same.

REGISTERED LAND

In order to investigate title for registered land, the solicitor must examine the office copy entries. As we have seen in Chapter 5 each title to land is registered separately at the Land Registry. Registration of the title provides a state guarantee, meaning any subsequent purchaser can then rely on the accuracy of the register of title as a record of ownership. The buyer will take the property subject to those entries registered, in addition to any overriding interests affecting the property.

The first consideration is to ensure that the information is valid and up to date. This is done by comparing the property address, the title number on the register and the title number on the plan to ensure that they correspond. Additionally, the Official Copy Entries should be no more than 12 months old upon receipt from the seller's solicitors. Best practice is never to accept official copies entries from the sellers' solicitors that are more than six month old. Looking at the example in Extract 2 at the end of this chapter, this can be done by looking at the top of the Official Copy Entries. You will see two dates. The first is the edition date. This is the date that the Land Registry last updated the registers or made any amendments to the registers. The second date you will see consists of a date and a time. This represents the precise moment that the Official Copy Entries were produced, in effect it is a screen shot of the registers at that precise date and time. This is the date the solicitor is interested in. It is this date that must be within 12, but preferably six, months.

Once this has been completed the solicitors will examine the registers, looking at what benefits and burdens the land. Any missing documents or additional information required will be raised as questions, called requisitions, to the sellers' solicitor to ensure that what the owner does at the property on a day-to-day basis is legally possible.

A: Property Register

The Property Register will confirm whether the estate is freehold or leasehold and if the latter will include basic details of the lease, for example the parties, the date it was created and the term agreed. The full postal address for the property will be indicated; this together with the official plan will clearly identify the property.

As we have seen from Chapters 5 and 12, all legal easements must be registered. In order to bind, the benefit of a legal easement or profit must be registered under s 27(2)(d) of the Land Registration Act 2002 (LRA 2002) whilst the burden must be registered under ss 32 and 38 of the LRA 2002 in order to bind. Once this has been done legal easements and profits will appear in the property register. It is important to ascertain how the easement affects the property i.e. where the easement is and whether it is essential for the day-to-day use of the property. If, for example, another property needs a right of way to pass and repass then how does the burden affect the use and enjoyment of the property? On a more practical note homeowners will need to know answers to many practical and financial questions relating to the easement. For example, with a right of way landowners will want to know:

- Where is the right of way?
- How many people use the right of way?
- Has the use of the right of way ever been refused?
- Has the current owner blocked or refused to allow others use of the right of way?
- Is the right of way currently in a good state of repair?
- What are the maintenance costs for the right of way and who is required to contribute to it?
- When was it last maintained and what were the costs?
- Did everyone required to contribute do so or were there disputes with payment?
- What are future maintenance costs?

B: Proprietorship Register

The proprietorship register will, first, advise what classification of title has been allocated by the Land Registry to the estate. As explained in Chapter 5, there are different grades of title the Land Registry may grant, with the assessment process principally determined by the quality of the documents proving title. When a title is first registered, applicants must provide all the deeds and documents relating to the title to be examined by the Land Registry. In unregistered conveyancing, as explained Chapter 4, showing a full documentary title commencing with a good root of title at least 15 years old should normally establish ownership. In a minority of cases, there may be questions about the strength of an applicant's claim to ownership. There are currently seven grades of title prescribed by ss 9 and 10 of the LRA 2002, three classifications for freehold and four for leasehold.

In relation to conveyancing transactions, the lender will require the title classification to be title absolute in order to protect their security. A lender may accept a good leasehold

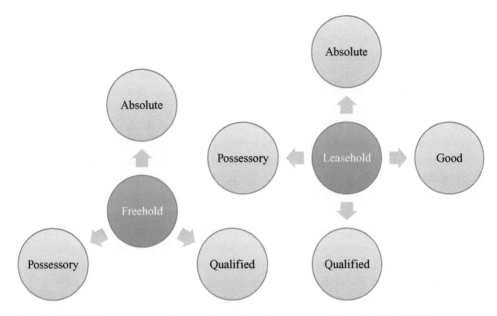

Figure 18.1 The seven grades of title under the Land Registration Act 2002

title, particularly if the solicitor can clarify that the good leasehold title is very common in the geographical area that the property is located.

The registered proprietor and the effect of restrictions

The main purpose of conveying property is for the legal title to be transferred from the sellers to the buyers in exchange for an agreed sum of money. From the buyers' perspective it is essential that they establish who currently holds legal title and therefore to whom the purchase monies should be given. Additionally, the buyers will need to ensure that there is nothing that will affect the proprietor's ability to do this. As we have seen in Chapter 5, under s 40 of the LRA 2002, restrictions are entries that prevent or regulate the registration of any dealings with a property. For example, there may be a restriction identifying that the property is held as tenants in common and as such stating there can be no dealings with a sole proprietor; or a mortgage company who in addition to registering a registered charge have also entered a restriction requiring their consent before the registered proprietors can have any dealings with the register. Any restrictions will have to be complied with if the buyers are going to successfully ensure that the legal title is transferred from the current owners to themselves.

C: Charges Register

The Charges Register contains the particulars of any interests to which the land is subject (i.e. where the land has the burden), such as mortgages, restrictive covenants, easements and leases. This will normally raise a number of requisitions that will need to be answered by the sellers' solicitor.

Restrictive covenants

As we identified in Chapter 14, covenants are a form of private control of land use and involve the landowners seeking to regulate how the land is used after they have sold the land and have transferred title to someone else. The arrangement regulating the land will not only affect the original parties entering into it but can also have an effect on the successors in title and are commonly found in freehold land. From a buyer's perspective they will wish to establish what restrictions affect the land and ensure that they will not affect their future use and enjoyment of the land. For example, a restrictive covenant prohibiting any commercial vehicles being parked overnight at the property will affect a buyer's future use and enjoyment of the property if they are a delivery driver who uses the delivery van outside of working hours.

In addition to establishing what restrictive covenants affect the land, the buyer will seek to ensure that the current owner has not breached any of the covenants. As a successor in title the buyer will be responsible for complying with covenants and could be liable for any breaches. Any breaches of covenants identified by the buyer will require resolving before contracts are exchanged between the parties.

Charges

In Chapter 13 we explained that mortgages of registered land do not take effect as legal charges unless and until they have been registered with the Land Registry; see ss 27(1) and 2(f) of the LRA 2002. Priority for registered land is determined by the date of registration not the date of creation under s 48(1) of the LRA 2002. Each registered charge will appear as two entries in the charge register. The first entry will identify when the charge was created and registered, the second will confirm whom the registered charge is in favour of. When a register charge appears, the buyers' solicitor should raise a requisition asking the sellers' solicitor to provide an undertaking that the outstanding monies will be paid off from the proceeds of sale and provide the necessary documentation to enable the Land Registry to remove the entries upon registration of the transaction following completion.

APPLY YOUR LEARNING – TASK 1

Looking at the Official Copy Entries in Extract 2, which requisitions would need to be raised for 10 Coastal Path? Are there any missing documents that would be required? Are there any easements that you will need additional information about and are there any restrictive covenants that may affect the clients' use and enjoyment of the property?

UNREGISTERED LAND

With investigation of title for unregistered land, the principles are the same as with registered land:

1   proof of title to the land being purchased, and
2   identifying third party rights in that land.

As title to land has not yet been registered with the Land Registry, however, the required information is simply presented in current and historical title deeds relating to the property rather than in organised registers. It would, however, be an onerous task to examine every document relating to the property so consequently s 23 of the LPA 1969 requires a buyer to investigate a period of 15 years. The implication of this is that a seller need only produce documents going back at least 15 years in order to establish what is referred to as a 'good root of title'.

In practice this means the seller identifying a document which is at least 15 years old as the 'root document' i.e. the starting point for the root period. Acceptable documents as the root document are:

1   a conveyance
2   a legal mortgage
3   a voluntary conveyance
4   an assent post-1925

TUTOR TIP – 1
....

Whilst any of the above documents will be acceptable, a conveyance is always best, even if it is older than other acceptable documents. For example the bundle of documents relating to 18 Bankhouse Road include:

20 July 1990   Assent
17 June 1990   Legal mortgage
5 December 1985   Conveyance

On the face of things the assent is an acceptable document and is at least 15 years old, as too is the legal mortgage. However the conveyance is a 'better' document to use as the buyer's solicitor in 1985 would also have been required to investigate a period of at least 15 years so the legal and equitable title to the property between 1970 and 1985 should be sound.

Think of the list of acceptable documents as a list of preference. First, look for a conveyance that is at least 15 years old *even* if there are other, newer, documents available. If no conveyance is available then look for a legal mortgage that is at least 15 years old even if there is newer voluntary conveyance or assent available, and so on.

APPLY YOUR LEARNING – TASK 2

Considering the documents available in relation to Mr and Mrs Wilton's sale property which document do you think is the most appropriate to use as the root of title document and why?

Although s 23 of the LPA 1969 only requires an investigation of at least 15 years, buyers must be mindful that they will be deemed 'on notice' of any interests contained mentioned or referred to in the root of title documents. So, taking our example above, if the conveyance dated 5 December 1985 makes reference to a legal easement, a right of way across the back of the garden, created in an earlier conveyance, the buyers will be on notice of that easement and the burden affecting the land. As such they should raise suitable requisitions regarding that easement as part of their investigations. This is essentially looking behind the root document. If the 1985 conveyance makes reference to covenants created in an earlier document, the buyer must raise requisitions as to what the covenants are, how they affect the land and whether they have been breached. Additionally, as restrictive covenants will only bind successors in title if they have been correctly registered as Class D(ii) entries, the buyer should also undertake a full land charges search to ascertain whether they have been registered. You will remember the effect of s 198 of the LPA 1925. Registration of the land charge operates as actual notice of the interest to the world under s 198. Meaning that any purchaser is bound by a registered right irrespective of whether they search the Land Charges Register.

TUTOR TIP – 2

When to look behind the root
1   Does the root document make reference to an earlier plan that identifies the boundaries of the property or identified the position of an easement benefiting or burdening the property?
    Then you must look behind the root and raise necessary requisitions.
2   Does the root document make reference to an earlier document, which may affect the property?
    Then you must look behind the root and raise necessary requisitions.
3   Does the root document make reference to rights or interests created in an earlier document, which may affect the property?
    Then you must look behind the root and raise necessary requisitions.

What to consider with each document in bundle
In addition to establishing whether the document created any new rights or interests, each document, including the root document, *must* be examined in details to confirm a number of procedure points:

1 *Does the document correctly and clearly identify the property to be purchased?*
Additionally is the description consistent throughout from the root document
to the most recent? If not this will require additional requisitions to ascertain
what has happened. Has land been removed or added?

2 *Are there any breaks in the chain of ownership?*
Ensure that the root is unbroken from the root document to the present day by
checking that the chain of ownership is not broken, i.e. A sells to B, B sells to C,
C sells to D, D sells to the current owner.
If there is a break the buyers need to establish why and obtain the missing
documents. It could be as simple as a change in the names of the owners, in
which case a change of name deed or a marriage certificate will be required.

3 *Has each document been correctly executed by the parties to it?*

4 *Has stamp duty been correctly paid?*
In purchasing an unregistered title, documents that have not been produced to
HM Revenue and Customs and/or have had the necessary duty on them paid,
will not be accepted by the Land Registry until any fines/interest are paid. This
might mean a delay in registration, which could be disastrous.
Stamp duty was payable to HM Revenue and Customs (Inland Revenue before
18 April 2005) within 30 days of completion of the transaction. In the event that
the stamp duty was not paid within 30 days of completion, a penalty would
have to be paid plus the amount of the unpaid duty together with interest
thereon calculated on a daily rate. In addition to this every document had to be
produced to the HM Revenue and Customs even if no duty was payable on the
transaction. A 'PD' (particulars delivered) stamp would evidence this.

If there is no evidence of a PD stamp and of the necessary payment of stamp duty,
the buyers' solicitor must requisition the sellers' solicitor to ask them to resolve the
defect by paying any outstanding stamp duty, plus interest plus the requisite penalty.

5 *Would the document have triggered first registration?*
As we saw in Chapter 5, s 4 of the LRA 2002 specifies the triggers for a first
compulsory registration, including:

- Transfer (whether as a gift, for consideration, by means of an assent, or in
  pursuance of a court order) of an unregistered legal freehold or of a leasehold
  that has more than seven years to run from the date of the grant.
- The grant of a leasehold of more than seven years.
- The grant of a lease of any duration to take effect in possession after a period
  of more than three months beginning with the date of the grant (such future
  leases are known as 'reversionary leases').
- The creation of a protected first legal mortgage (one that ranks in priority
  ahead of any other mortgages affecting the mortgaged estate) of a freehold
  estate or leasehold estate of more than seven years.

6 *Is there evidence of a land charges search shortly before every transfer of title?*
It is good practice for the seller to include previous land charges. In
unregistered land transactions these are carried out shortly before the

transaction is completed and is undertaken against all current (outgoing) legal owners for the full period of their ownership. Checks should be made to ensure:

- A search was carried out.
- The search was made against all legal owners involved in the transaction *and* was carried out against their full names and correct spellings.
- If the person changed their name or was known as many different names, was the search carried out against all of these names?
- The search was made for the full period of the person's ownership of the property.
- That the transaction completed within the priority period of the search.
- Did the search result reveal any adverse entries? If so what were they?

APPLY YOUR LEARNING – TASK 3

Looking at the bundle of unregistered documents in Extract 3 (documents A, B and C) do you think the purchasers of 18 Bankhouse Road Huddersfield will need to look behind the root of title? If so, why and what documents would be requested?

SEARCHES

Searches should be carried out by the buyers' solicitor in every transaction. This is extremely important, remember *Caveat emptor* – let the buyer beware. This is based upon the principle that the buyer alone is responsible for checking the quality and suitability of goods before a purchase is made. The buyer will take the property in whatever physical condition it is in and subject to any adverse entries registered on public registers against it. Both the buyers (and the mortgage company) are looking to ensure that the property is good and marketable.

The searches to be carried out will depend on the property itself and where the property is. There are a number of searches, however, that a solicitor should carry out in every case.

LOCAL AUTHORITY SEARCH

Under the Standard Conditions of Sale, a purchase of a property is subject to all local land charges. These will not appear on the title register of the property; as you will remember from Chapter 4, local land charges are overriding interests under sch 3, para 6 of the LRA 2002. Information regarding local land charges will, however, appear in the local authority registers because they have a duty to disclose them. For anything held in public registers, the buyer is deemed on notice of them under s 198 of the LPA 1925. The local authority search is split into two parts, the LLC1 form, which is a search the Register of Local Land Charges and the CON 29R, which is a set of standardised inquiries.

LLC1 form

This form is split into 12 sections, generally relating to financial issues affecting the property, for example if there are monies owed to the local authority and what the property can be used for, such as planning permissions.

Such entries are enforceable by the local authority and relate to the property, not the owners or occupiers at the property. Therefore if the purchaser buys the property subject to an adverse entry they will be responsible for that adverse entry, not a previous owner. There is no priority period for this search and no form of protection other than a very limited right to compensation for an error or omission contained in the search.

What does the LLC1 search reveal?

Compulsory Purchase Orders – The council are buying the property. The buyer cannot proceed as the property is being sold to the council.

Conservation Area – This will confirm whether the property is within a conversation area. Important, as it will restrict the development and building in an area. Normally building work can be carried out without planning permission if the work is within permitted developments i.e. under a certain size without the need for planning permission. If in a conservation area, planning permission must be successfully obtained in every instance.

Listed Buildings – Buildings can be deemed to be of special historical or architectural merit and as such there are very strict requirements in relation to building work and development. The buyer must be informed and advised of what his responsibilities are for owning such a building. It is important to ensure that any work previously carried out did not breach listed building requirements and that any conditions for the property have not been breached already.

Financial Charges – This is where money is due to the local authority and a buyer will not wish to proceed in these situations unless the council can confirm that the monies have already been paid and that no further action is required *or* an undertaking from the seller's solicitor that they will pay the monies on completion and provide evidence of the same.

Tree Preservation Order – Again there will be rules and requirements of what can be done to a tree with a TPO. The buyer should be advised of this.

Planning Permissions – The search will reveal planning permission applications, both those that have been successful and those rejected. A solicitor should obtain copies of the planning permissions and buildings regulations consents from the seller's solicitor at the seller's expense. The conditions of the permissions should also be checked to ensure that they have not been breached.

CON 29R – required questions

There are preprinted inquiries about critical matters such as road schemes, outstanding notices, compulsory purchase, slum clearance and planning applications and consents. This should accompany the LLC1 form and should be undertaken with every property.

Planning Applications and Permissions and Buildings

This will again confirm what permission has been applied for, what has been rejected and approved. Information will also be given in relation to certificates and pending applications, lists building issues and conservation areas consents relating to the property. Look out for question 1.2 as this relates to Development Plans Provisions, i.e. what the land and area is primarily used for, residential use, business? If this is at odds with what the property is currently used for more information is required.

Maintenance of Roads, Footways and Footpaths

This is very important as it advises whether the local authority have adopted the roads abutting the property. If they have, the buyers have a right to pass and repass over them, as it is a public highway. It also means that the local authority are responsible for the maintenance and cost of the road. Additionally the question will confirm whether there are any public paths or byways over the property your client wishes to purchase or adjacent to it.

If the road is not adopted, there are two considerations:

1   If the property is new, then the property may be the subject of a s 38 agreement. This is an agreement between the developer and the local authority in which the developer confirms they will build the roads to a required standard, at which point the local authority will inspect them and if they meet that standard the local authority will adopt them, taking over responsibility for maintenance and repairs.
2   If the road is not adopted and there is no agreement in place the buyer will need evidence that there is a legal right of way over the private road. The solicitor will raise a requisition with the seller's solicitors for evidence of this. Additionally the maintenance responsibility is with those using the private road. As such the maintenance questions discussed in an earlier section will need to be raised with the sellers. One point to consider here is that it is still possible that the local authority can adopt the road in the future and as such the frontages to the road could be liable for substantial road-making charges under s 219 of the Highways Act 1980.

Other Matters

This is split into 15 sections, all questions start with 'Do any of the following matters apply to the property?' The questions relate to a vast array of issues including land to be acquired for road works, drainage agreements and consents, nearby road schemes, railway schemes and traffic schemes, contravention of Building Regulations, notices under Planning Acts, whether the property is within a conservation area, if the property is the subject of compulsory purchase, contaminated land and radon gas issues. When studying the results of this section the solicitor is looking for an answer of 'no' to each of the questions.

CON 29O – optional questions

This will depend on the type of property being purchased and its location. In relation to residential property the most common optional question will be question 22, Common Land, Town & Village Greens.

Question 22 – Commons Registration.
This search must be undertaken if the property abuts a village green or common land, if the property has never been built on i.e. a new development or the property is a recent development. The search will confirm whether any of the land to be purchased is registered under the Commons Registration Act 1965; once registered it is difficult to remove the land from the register. The search will disclose if the land to be purchased is a village green or common land. If so it could mean that the property is subject to adverse rights by third parties i.e. the right to graze sheep on the land. It will probably mean that no development or fencing off of the land is possible.

CON 29DW – water and drainage search

This search should be carried out in every transaction and will be required if the clients are obtaining a mortgage. A plan should accompany the search submitted to the regional water company. There is no priority period for the search results. This search will advise and illustrate whether:

- the property is connected to foul and surface water sewers and water pipes
- there are any public pipes within the boundaries of the property, which will be of importance to your client if they intend to extend the property
- the connection is in the road and therefore under a public highway
- the property is connected via a length of private pipe and therefore whether they will be responsible for the maintenance and repair of any sewer pipes
- the property is on a rateable or meter payment basis.

The search result should include an extract map illustrating where sewage and water pipes are located. It is important to establish whether the property connects straight into the public pipes or whether there is any length of private pipes. Further inquiries of the sellers and the water company may have to be made.

If the property is new, then the property may be affected by a s 104 agreement (under the Water Industry Act 1991) and bond. This is similar to the s 38 agreement (under the Highways Act 1980) used in connection with roads. The search will indicate whether there is or likely to be an agreement and bond. This agreement will be between the developer and the water company, again with the developer confirming that it will build the sewages and pipes to the required standard, with the water company adopting the sewages and pipes if it does. Developers may be required to deposit a bond, a sum of money, until the adoption has been completed in case the works are not completed to the requisite standard or the development goes bankrupt before adoption has been completed.

If the property is not new and not connected to the sewage system further inquiries will have to be made, as the property may be connected to a cesspool or a septic tank. Additional requisitions will need to be made in terms of whether the tank and all pipes to it are within the boundaries of the property, in addition to asking general maintenance questions.

CON 29M – mining search

The Coal Authority has a list of areas in which this search should be undertaken. If in doubt, carry out the search. The current mining search also deals with information relating to brine extraction, important for some areas of Greater Manchester and Cheshire. The search is submitted to the Coal Authority.

The search reveals past, present and possible future influences or mining. The search confirms whether the property has been subject to a claim for subsidence. If so, further inquiries of the seller should be made including inquiring how this has affected their buildings insurance; together with obtaining copies of the claim report and schedule of works (i.e. how the claim was remedied). This will have to be disclosed to your client and the mortgage lender for approval and consent to proceed.

The search will also reveal whether there are mine shafts within the locality of the property. More information will be required from the seller as to the problems they have encountered and information from the Coal Authority as to how the shaft has been dealt with, i.e. has it been capped and made safe.

If the property is in Devon or Cornwall, a tin mining search should be carried out. The search is made to the Cornish Chamber of Mines and will reveal similar information to the coalmining search.

Limestone search

Again another regional search, mainly in relation to properties in the West Midlands, a search is carried out with the relevant local authority and will reveal similar information to that of the coal search.

Environmental search

Many homes are built on or near land that was previously used for other purposes, for example industrial, manufacturing or landfill sites. Such areas are known as brownfield sites. As the industry no longer exist on that spot, there may be little evidence to show where it once was. A side effect of such brownfield sites, however, is that there may be contamination of the ground on which a home has been built. In relation to former landfill sites it is important to know what has been disposed of at the former site. Even when a home has not been built directly on an old industrial site, contamination from nearby land, rivers and watercourses can spread into nearby ground, affecting properties.

Under s 78A(2) of the Environmental Protection Act 1990, contaminated land is defined as any land which appears to 'be in such a condition, by reason of substances in, on or under the land, that significant harm is being caused or there is a significant possibility of such harm being caused' to either the land or water environment.

Once identified, unless the remediation works are carried out voluntarily, the enforcing authority, normally the local authority, is under a duty to find and serve remediation notice on appropriate persons to deal with the contamination and pay the related clean-up costs. This hierarchy of liability is split into class A and class B persons. The enforcing authority initially looks for Class A person[s]; those who cause or knowingly permit the presence of the substances on or in the land. If a Class A person cannot be found after reasonable inquiry, the enforcing authority can look to Class B person[s], the owner or occupier of the land. Therefore buyers, as the landowner, could be liable to contribute towards remediation costs.

Some searches will also provide a certificate confirming that the property is not likely to fall within the s 78 definition of contaminated land.

Many environmental searches provide differing information but many should provide the following information of the property and within a 500-metre radius of the property:

- whether the property is on a flood plain
- whether the property is at risk of flooding
- risk of subsidence
- pollution levels
- risk of radon gas
- historical land use
- whether there is historic landfill
- whether there is current landfill
- industry within radius
- issues of contamination.

Company search

This search would either be made through Companies House or through a search agent. If the seller is a company a search must be carried out to ensure that the company does exist and that the name and company number correspond. It is vital to ensure that the company is not in administration, liquidation or receivership, as this would prevent a buyer from purchasing from a company in this state.

When purchasing registered land the effect of the LRA 2002 is that a purchaser is not bound by any charge over the land that is not on the registers of title. It is prudent, however, to carry out the search to ensure the company is not about to become insolvent.

In unregistered land, a company search is vital. The search checks that the land being purchased is not subject to any fixed or floating changes, which your client could buy the property subject to. Where floating charges are indicated, a letter of non-crystallisation is required to ensure that the charge has not attached itself to the property being purchased.

Chancel repair search

Chancel land and chancel repair liabilities can trace their roots back to medieval times, when every parish had its own priest or rector. The rector by the nature of his status had a number of rights, including certain taxes or income from the land of the parish. The cost of repairs to the church was split between the rector and the parishioners, with the parishioners traditionally being responsible for the western end of a church (the area where they sat) and the rector was responsible for repairs to the chancel (the eastern end of a church).

Since these times, although the land may have been broken into many thousands, in some cases, of small parcels, the liability for these repairs has continued to exist and has on occasion been enforced or claimed by the church. Whilst the chancel repair liabilities are normally confined to rural communities this is not always the case. Buyers must be wary of ancient settlements that have grown considerably in size. Chancel land accounts for approximately 40 per cent of all land in England and Wales and its liability today may be substantial.

Determining whether any particular property is subject to chancel repair liability is fraught with uncertainty. There is no single register that can be used to identify such liabilities, and existing records are often incomplete and hard to interpret. Investigations may involve a careful search of the ordnance survey map of the vicinity of the property, checking deeds and registers of title for any clues in addition to undertaking a chancel liability search with a private company.

KEY CASE: *ASTON CANTLOW AND WILMCOTE WITH BILLESLEY PAROCHIAL CHURCH COUNCIL V WALLBANK* [2003] UKHL 37; [2004] 1 AC 546; [2003] ALL ER 1213

Mr and Mrs Wallbank owned a farm, which was partially a rectory property. As such the couple were liable as lay rectors to pay for all necessary repairs to the chancel of the local church under the Chancel Repairs Act 1932. In 1991 Mr and Mrs Wallbank received a bill for £6,000 in relation to repairs for the chancel of the local church. They refused to pay arguing it was a breach of their right to peaceful enjoyment of their possessions under the Human Rights Act 1998.

Aston Cantlow and Wilmcote with Billesley Parochial Church Council appealed against a decision that it was unlawful for it to enforce the Wallbanks' obligation to pay for repairs to the chancel (the space around the altar) of a church. Mr and Mrs Wallbank contended that the church council was a 'public authority' which had acted unlawfully under s 6(1) of the Human Rights Act 1998 by requiring them to pay for the repairs, thereby interfering with their right to the peaceful enjoyment of their possessions under sch 1 part II art 1 of the 1998 Act.

Mr and Mrs Wallbank lost the case and the House of Lords ruled that the final cost for repairs would be £189,969 plus VAT due to the fact that the church had slowly disintegrated during this period of time as the repairs could not be carried out. Additionally there were legal costs of around £400,000.

Chancel repair liability was protected as an overriding interest even if not specifically noted on the title at the Land Registry. Following the LRA 2002, it was believed that chancel repair liability would only retain its overriding status until 13 October 2013 after which time a purchaser of land (for valuable consideration) would take free of chancel repair liability if it had not been protected by notice in the register. The Land Registry, however, have cast doubt on this assumption and for now it seems that chancel repair liabilities continue to retain their overriding status until a subsequent transfer of title has occurred after 13 October 2013. This means that church councils can continue to apply to register chancel repair liability for years, decades and centuries to come where ownership has not changed since 13 October 2013.

Legislation has been proposed to make provision for ending the liability of lay rectors for the repair of chancels, and for connected purposes. The Chancel Repair Bill 2015–2016 received its first reading in the House of Lords on 3 June 2015; at the time of writing, however, it had not been scheduled for a second reading.

Search of the Index Map (SIM)
This search is only carried out where the land is unregistered and will reveal whether the property has already been registered or is subject to a pending registration or a caution against first registration. If adverse entries are noted further inquiries must be made with the seller's solicitor before proceeding.

Rivers, canals and railways
If the property is near any of these, additional checks and searches should be made with these authorities to see how they affect the property and what changes are planned in the future that could affect the property.

PRE-EXCHANGE REPORT TO CLIENT

Once all requisitions have been questioned, all necessary documents obtained, search results in, and a satisfactory survey and mortgage offer issued, a buyer will be in a position to prepare for exchange of contracts. Buyers should not legally commit themselves to buying a property until they are happy with the legal position and physical condition of the property. The report to client is therefore an important part of this process. It is better if the solicitor meets with the clients face to face in order to advise them on a number of issues.

The solicitor will advise the client on title matters, including what rights reservations and restrictions the property is being sold subject to and how that will affect them on a day-to-day basis. The solicitor will explain information obtained from the requisitions on title which resulted from the investigation on title. The solicitor will explain the searches undertaken and what information was discovered from these.

By this point the solicitor will have obtained a satisfactory mortgage offer and will explain to the client the implications of signing the mortgage deed and consenting to the lender placing a legal charge over the property. In particular they will explain the lender's power of sale and what it means for more than one buyer to be joint and severally liable. Finally, the solicitors will take the clients through the contract and explain agreed terms and conditions and the implications of exchanging contracts.

This task is obviously much easier from the seller's point of view given the principle of *caveat emptor*; however, their solicitors will still be under an obligation to explain the significance and implications of the contract.

Once the report to client is complete, the solicitor will ask their clients to sign the contract in readiness for exchange of contracts. By signing the contract here, it does not mean that the parties are legally bound and the completion date has become fixed.

EXCHANGE

Once the solicitor has reported to their client and has a signed contract, they will be in a position to exchange contracts on their client's behalf. There are a number of different ways of exchanging contracts.

- In person. This is where the parties normally meet at one office and physically exchange contracts.
- By post. This is not recommended if there is a linked transaction, due to the time lag.
- By telephone. This is the most common way of exchanging and in reality the only way that solicitors exchange contracts for residential property.

FORMULA A

This is used when one solicitor holds both signed contracts and the deposit. The seller confirms that he holds the signed contract and the deposit. Both solicitors will agree that the seller's solicitor will insert the agreed completion date into each contract. The exchange is formally agreed by the buyer's solicitor releasing the buyer's contract and the seller agrees to hold the seller's contract to the buyer's order. The seller undertakes to forward the seller's contract to the buyer's solicitor that day. The formula is rarely used.

FORMULA B

This is the most common way of exchanging. Each solicitor holds their own contract, and they go through the contract on the phone ensuring that both copies are identical. They agree the completion date and undertake to send the contract in the post that evening together with the deposit.

FORMULA C

This is the safest way of exchanging contracts in a chain of transactions i.e. a related sale and purchase,[2] but the most complicated and undertakings are used.

On the sale side, the solicitor will contact the other side and ensure that all information is agreed, the completion date is agreed, how much deposit will be provided upon exchange and that they are ready to exchange. The solicitor will then contact the other side on their purchase, again ensuring that the contracts are identical, that the completion date is agreed, confirm how much deposit they will be able to provide upon exchange and ensure they too are ready to exchange.

As this formula uses undertaking between solicitors it is important that the solicitor then obtain his client's authority to proceed and exchange contracts, pointing out to them that once this authority has been given it cannot be revoked. This is because once undertakings have been given in relation to an exchange, they must be adhered to.

The solicitor will then call the other solicitor on the sale transaction and request the release of the contract to them, asking that sale solicitor to undertake to exchange provide they call them back before an agreed time, e.g. 3 p.m. The implication of this is that provided the solicitor calls back before 3 p.m. the sale solicitor must exchange contracts. Conversely, if the solicitor is contacted after 3 p.m. the release has disappeared and there is no obligation to exchange. This is known as formula C part I. The parties are not locked in at this point and are not contractually bound to buy or sell.

---

2 For example, where the seller of a house is doing so in order to move into another property he is purchasing. We do not want to contractually commit to completing on a set date in regard to his house, only to find that there has been a change of mind or some delay in relation to house he is buying.

The solicitor will then be in a position to deal with his or her related transactions. In relation to the purchase if the sellers of this property are also buying then the solicitor will release their contract to them, this time giving an undertaking themselves that they will exchange contracts with the other side providing they are contacted again before 2 p.m. If this transaction is the top of the chain then the parties are in a position to exchange contract by using formula B, thus making their respective clients contractually liable to either buy or sell.

Once the purchase contract has successfully exchanged the solicitor will be in a position to contact the solicitor on the other side of the sale transaction and finish off the exchange of contracts, providing they have contacted them before 3 p.m. Once this happens formal C part II has occurred and now both parties are contractually bound to either buy or sell the property.

APPLY YOUR LEARNING – TASK 4

Given Mr and Mrs Wilton are buying and selling which formula would be the most appropriate and the safest way to exchange contracts and why?

CONSEQUENCES OF EXCHANGE OF CONTRACTS

Once contracts have been exchanged the parties are legally bound to buy and sell. The seller still retains the legal title to the property. This does not pass to the buyer until completion with unregistered land and registration with registered land. The seller is still responsible for the outgoings and expenses. The buyer obtains some responsibility for the property – insurance, obligation to purchase on the agreement date and the beneficial ownership in the property passes to them.

It is normal practice not to register the contract unless there is a dispute between the parties, the buyer is suspicious that the seller wants to sell the property to another party or there is going to be a long period of time between exchange and completion. A contract to purchase unregistered land is an estate contract and as such the buyer's solicitor should register a Class C(iv) entry with the Land Charges Department against the current estate owners. When the land being purchased is registered land then a notice against title will be required in accordance with s 32 of the LRA 2002.

PROBLEMS AFTER EXCHANGE OF CONTRACTS

Death

This will not affect the validity of the contract. The contract still retains the obligations and the contract is still enforceable; the deceased's personal representatives are bound to complete. If there is only one seller and he dies the sale must wait until a grant of representation has been obtained to enable the personal representatives to sell the property. There will of course be some delay and the original completion date missed. In such circumstances the buyer will be entitled to compensation in accordance with the terms and conditions of the contract.

If one of the sellers dies, the procedure will depend on how the property is held. If the parties held the property as joint tenants, then the production of a death certificate will be sufficient for the transaction to proceed as the principle of survivorship will apply. If the property was held as tenants in common and there are still two surviving co-owners, then the sale can proceed as normal. Remember that the overreaching principle applies if there are two trustees, which enables the buyer to obtain a valid receipt. Evidence of death will still, however, be required. If the property was held as tenants in common and there is only one owner left, the buyer should insist on evidence of death and that a second trustee be appointed in order that the overreaching principle will apply.

If the buyer dies, then the contract is still valid and a grant of representation must be obtained. The personal representatives will have to join in the contract and documentation. The issue here is that the mortgage offer will be invalid upon death and, therefore, there will be an issue in relation to the funding of the transaction. The surviving buyer remains bound by the contract and will still have to complete. There are likely to be delays whilst these issues are dealt with and the seller will therefore have a right to compensation in accordance with the terms of the contract.

Bankruptcy

If the court makes a bankruptcy order, then the control of the bankrupt's estate passes to the official receiver. A trustee in bankruptcy is appointed and the individual's assets vest automatically in the trustee under s 306 of the Insolvency Act 1986. The buyer must deal with the trustee from this point onwards; the buyer, however, is only affected by bankruptcy entries shown on an official search or on Official Copy Entries but if you do have notice then you must wait to take the transfer from him. The buyer should ask to see a copy of the bankruptcy order together with evidence of the trustee's appointment.

If the title is registered then a creditor's notice will alert the buyer to the fact that a petition has been presented. A bankruptcy entry will alert the buyer that the order has been made. The information will also be registered at the Land Charges Department at Plymouth and will be applicable if the property is unregistered. Any disposition by the seller after the petition has been presented is void without a court order. The bankruptcy order will sever any joint tenancy and the trustee must now execute the document with the other co-owner. If the bankrupt is the buyer, then a trustee must still be appointed but the mortgage offer will no longer be valid.

Any disposition by the seller company after the petition has been presented is void. Purchasing from a liquidator will also require evidence of the liquidation and of the liquidator's appointment. If you are buying from or selling to a company being wound up, you should deal with the liquidator of the company and must ensure that the formalities of the liquidator's appointment have been observed. The appointment of an administrative receiver will normally crystallise a floating charge so it becomes fixed on the company's property. The buyer will need to ensure that the property is released from this charge.

PRE-COMPLETION

A number of steps are taken between exchange and completion; these differ depending on whether the solicitor is acting for the buyer or seller.

STEPS FOR THE BUYER

Drafting the transfer document

As the buyer is required to register the transaction with the Land Registry following completion, it is the buyer's solicitor's responsibility to draft the transfer deed. This document is required to ensure that the legal title passes from the seller to the buyer upon registration of the transactions following completion. Today the transfer deed is a standardised document, containing all the necessary information to ensure that the Land Registry can successfully transfer title to the new owners. As you will remember from Chapter 2, the transfer of legal title must be executed by a deed and must comply with s 52(1) of the LPA 1925. The TR1 (for the transfer of whole) and TP1 (for the transfer of part) meet these legal requirements. The draft transfer will be sent to the seller's solicitor for approval together with the Completion Information and Undertakings Form (TA13).

Pre-completion searches

Land Charges Department Search – K15

We have explored land charges searches in some detail in Chapter 3. The land charges search is undertaken when the land is unregistered and will reveal any equitable interests registered against the estate owners. At this point the search is carried out against the owner of the property i.e. the seller, for the period of time he has owned the property. As discussed previously, the search should be carried out against every name and variation of the spelling of the name the owner has been known as. The search is submitted for the Land Charges Department at Plymouth and is valid for 15 working days from the issuing of the search result. The transaction must be completed within this priority period to ensure the buyer only takes the property subject to the entries revealed on the search certificate. It is therefore advisable to undertake this search just before completion. Any adverse entries must be dealt with before completion can take place. The possible adverse entries and how to deal with them were considered in Chapter 3.

Bankruptcy Search – K16

A bankruptcy search is carried out against the buyer if he is obtaining a mortgage, as a bankrupt is not legally entitled to obtain credit whilst the subject of a bankruptcy order. Additionally, a mortgage company will not lend to a bankrupt or pending bankrupt.

The search is carried out against all the buyers and against their full names. As with the land charges search it is important to search against all known spellings, variations and aliases. Additionally, as with the land charges search the search result will give the searcher a priority period of 15 working days from the date of the search results certificate. The solicitor must therefore complete the transaction within this 15 working day period to receive the protected by the search results.

Official Search – OS1 or OS2

An OS1 (transfer of whole) or OS2 (transfer of part) search is carried out against the *title* for the property you are purchasing. The search searches the registers from the date of the Official Copy Entries supplied by the sellers' solicitor at the start of the transaction to ensure that nothing has changed or altered since that time. The search result will give a priority period of 30 working days from the date of the search and the solicitor must lodge a valid and complete registration application at the Land Registry within the priority period. During this priority period the registers are 'frozen' to prevent anyone else from being added, amending or deleting entries on the registers. Proving the registration is completed within this priority period the buyer will take the land subject to the entries specified on this search result.

If the solicitor does not complete the registration application before the end of the priority period any other applications which were 'waiting in the wings' during the entire priority period jump ahead of buyer's registration application and bind the property. So, for example, if a legal charge was waiting in the wings this will then be registered ahead of the buyer's new mortgage, which would replace in the buyer's lender only getting a second charge over the property. To allow this to happen is professional negligence and very serious.

Deal with finances

The buyer's solicitor will draft a bill of costs and a completion statement. The completion statement will list all monies in and out for the transaction from start to finish. This will include search fees, registration fees, stamp duty, legal costs, discharge of existing mortgages of any property being sold plus the mortgage advance for the new property. This will enable the solicitor to ascertain whether the clients are to receive monies upon completion or whether monies are required from the client for completion. The mortgage advance will be requested from the lender by completing and submitting the Certificate of Title. Additionally the Certificate of Title confirms that the solicitor has complied with the lender's instructions under the Council of Lenders Handbook and that the property has a good and marketable title.

APPLY YOUR LEARNING – TASK 5

In relation to Mr and Mrs Wilton's purchase only, which pre-completion searches would you undertake and why?

STEPS FOR THE SELLER

Approve the transfer document

Upon receipt of the draft transfer deed from the buyer's solicitors. Once approved the solicitor will ensure the document is signed by their client and retained once signed until completion has successfully taken place.

Complete and return the Completion Information and Undertakings Form (TA13)

The Completion Information and Undertakings Form (TA13) contains a set of questions designed to ensure that certain key information is obtained prior to completion. The questions also serve to confirm the mechanics of how the day of completion will work. For example: where should the balance completions monies be sent, how much should be sent, where can the buyer obtain the keys once the seller has received the money, what documents will be forwarded by the seller's solicitor upon completion? This document is also important as the seller is required to give an undertaking to discharge any mortgages on completion from the sale proceeds.

Deal with finances

The seller's solicitors will request a final redemption statement from any current lenders with charges secured against the property. This will enable the solicitor to ensure there are sufficient monies from the proceeds of sale to discharge the mortgages before giving any undertakings to the buyer's solicitor.

The solicitor will request the estate agent's account, if he has authority to pay this on this client's behalf upon completion.

The seller's solicitor will draft a bill of costs and a completion statement. The completion statement will list all monies in and out for the transaction from start to finish. This will include legal costs, payment of the estate agent if instructed to do so and the discharge of existing mortgages. This will enable the solicitor to ascertain how much monies the client is to receive upon completion.

DAY OF COMPLETION

The day of completion is essentially ensuring that the buyer and seller can meet their contractual obligations. For the buyer, this is ensuring that the balance of the purchase monies has been received as clear funds by the seller's solicitor before the contractual completion time. For the seller this is ensuring that the property has been vacated before the contractual time for completion. Once this has happened the seller's solicitor will be in a position to release the keys to the buyer.

The seller's solicitor will then be in a position to redeem any existing mortgages and request the completed DS1 from each lender to enable the Land Registry to remove the lender's entries on the charges register. The seller's solicitor will then be in a position to send the executed transfer deed together with any other agreed documentation, for example planning permission consents and building regulation consents for existing works at the property together with any guarantees and warranties.

The buyer's solicitor will ensure that stamp duty land tax is paid online and the SDLT5 certificate is obtained as confirmation of payment to enable the registration application to be lodged within the necessary priority period. Once the executed transfer document has been received from the seller's solicitor together with the completed DS1, the solicitor will be in a position to submit the registration application to the Land Registry. For registered land this simply involves a re-registration using an AP1 form. This is submitted to the Land Registry before the expiry of the priority period together with other supporting documentation including:

- new mortgage deed and certified copy
- executed transfer deed and certified copy
- registration fee
- SDLT5
- DS1 for existing mortgages.

For first registration applications, registration is completed using an FR1 form within two months of completion. The supporting documentation will include the root documentations, identified upon investigation of title, which will enable the Land Registry to create the title register of title for the property (divided into the property register, proprietorship register and charges register) upon first registration.

LATE COMPLETION AND DELAYED COMPLETION

Standard Condition 6.1.1 of the contract for sale declares that time is not of the essence. This means that the completion date is not a strict and binding date on either party and will not allow the innocent party to immediately withdraw from the contract if breached.

Any delay in completion will result, however, in a breach of contract which will enable the innocent party to seek compensation for loss. This is where the contract rate comes into play under Standard Condition 7.2.2.

As we will remember from earlier in this chapter Standard Conditions 6.1.2 and 6.1.3 stipulate a time and date for completion. If the time limit is breached but completion takes place on the contractual date, completion is deemed to take place the next working day and one day's compensation will arise. If there is a delay in completion but completion does take place, the innocent party is entitled to compensation for each day's delay.

If there is delay by both parties, the party whose total period of default is the greater is to pay compensation to the other under Standard Condition 7.2.1. For example if both parties delay but the seller delays by five days and the buyer delays by seven days, the seller will be entitled to two days' compensation.

HOW TO MAKE THE DEFAULTING PARTY COMPLETE THE TRANSACTION

As we have previously said, time is not of the essence so the innocent party cannot simply walk away from the contract; nor are the full range of remedies available to them at this stage. The innocent party must therefore make time of the essence. To do this a notice to complete must be served on the defaulting party giving a final date for completion. The notice will inform the defaulting party that unless completion takes place by the new date specified on the notice, the innocent party will be entitled to all remedies including a repudiation of the contract.

The notice to complete can be served upon the defaulting party under Standard Condition 6.8.1 any time on or after the date fixed for completion. Any party who is ready willing and able to complete may give the other party notice to complete. It is important that the innocent party is ready, able and willing to complete *but for* the default of the other party as the notice is binding upon *both* parties once served not just the party in default.

Under Standard Condition 6.8.2 the parties must complete the agreement within ten working days of giving the notice to complete. The ten-working-day period excludes the day on which the notice is served. Standard Condition 6.8.3 also makes it clear that a buyer who delays completion and has paid less than a 10 per cent deposit at exchange must pay the remaining monies required to make up the full 10 per cent deposit and must pay the monies immediately on receipt of the notice.

If there is still no completion after the notice to complete is served, the standard contract sets out the available range of remedies. Under Standard Condition 7.4, where the buyer is in default the seller may rescind the contract, in addition keeping the deposit and any accrued interest, reselling the property and claiming damages. Under Standard Condition 7.5, if the seller defaults the buyer can rescind the contract *and* if there is rescission, the buyer can demand the repayment of the deposit with interest and claim damages.

In relation to damages, the general rule is that the innocent party is entitled to seek to recover the losses arising from natural breach of the contract; however they will have to establish that losses claimed have stemmed naturally from the breach (see *Hadley v Baxendale* [1854]).[3] Whilst substantial damages can be claimed especially where the contract has not been completed, the innocent party must mitigate their position, taking reasonable steps to reduce or even avoid the loss where they can (see *Raineri v Miles* [1981]).[4] The defaulting party is entitled to have any claim for compensation from delay offset by any claim paid under this contract (Standard Condition 7.2.3).

> ## TUTOR TIP – 3
> ....
>
> Know the difference between compensation and damages.
>
> **Compensation** is calculated by applying the contract rate to the purchase price/balance purchase monies for the period of delay. There is automatic contractual right to compensation, not dependent on having suffered damage.
>
> **Damages** for loss for breach of contract follow general common law rules. This is loss within the contemplation of the parties or naturally flowing from the breach.

DISCUSSION

Despite being the twenty-first century, the conveyancing process is very much paper-based. Many other countries have, however, already ditched paper and moved towards an electronic system of buying and selling property. These include Ontario Canada and New Zealand whilst other countries such as Ireland, Scotland and Australia are quickly moving in that direction.

It has been considered in England and Wales. In 1998 the Law Commission published a report entitled *Land Registration for the 21st Century – A Consultative Document*.[5] This report proposed the biggest shakeup in land law in nearly 80 years with a complete overhaul of land registration in England and Wales and the 'wholesale replacement'[6] of the Land Registration Act 1925. The primary reason for this overhaul was the 'progressive move towards electronic conveyancing'[7] described as a revolution. The 1998 proposals led to the Land Registration Act 2002, which now governs registered land and Part 8 of the LRA 2002 created the legal framework to enable the 'transfer and creation of interests in registered land by electronic means.'[8]

....

3 [1854] 9 Ex 341.
4 [1981] AC 1050.
5 Law Com No. 254.
6 Law Com No. 254. Para 1.1.
7 Law Com No. 254. Para 1.2.
8 Law Com No. 271. Para 1.12.

It was envisaged that a pilot scheme for electronic conveyancing would be up and running by the end of 2005 with electronic conveyancing being used by all legal profession by 2010. Yet this did not happen and the plans to move from a paper to an electronic system were instead shelved by the 2010 target date.

Things have moved on significantly since the Law Commission's 1998 report – in particular there have been substantial advances in technology. So is now a good time to revisit this issue and consider a move from a paper-based to an electronic system of conveyancing in England and Wales?

CONSIDER THIS – 1

Do you consider that we need a system of electronic conveyancing in England and Wales at all?

END OF CHAPTER SUMMARY

- Conveyancing is the practical application of land law, where the legal title of land is bought and sold.
- A solicitor will obtain initial instructions from their clients to ascertain the details of their proposed sale or purchase. The solicitor will advise on client care, money and finances, taxation, and timescales and expectations.
- The seller's solicitor will obtain the title documents and from this draft the contract.
- The buyer's solicitor will investigate the title for his clients to ensure that it has a good and marketable title.
- The buyer's solicitor will carry out a number of searches including a local authority search, water and drainage search, and an environmental search to check the quality and suitability of the property before a purchase is made.
- Once all information is received and is satisfactory the parties will be able to exchange contracts using one of the prescribed Law Society Formulas.
- Between exchange and completion, the buyer will draft the transfer deed to enable the legal title to be transferred from seller to buyer, request the balance of the purchase monies and undertake the final pre-completion searches.
- On the day of completion, the seller will give vacant possession of the property and the buyer will transfer the balance of the purchase monies required under the contract.
- The buyer will be able to pay stamp duty land tax and submit their registration application once they have received the SDLT5 from HM Revenue and Customs and the DS1 discharge notices from the seller confirming that any existing mortgages have been paid off.
- The buyer will hold legal title to the property once the registration application has been successfully completed.

PREPARING FOR ASSESSMENTS QUESTIONS

ESSAY QUESTION

Undertaking pre-exchange searches, such as the local authority search, water and drainage search, and environmental search, are a vital part of the investigation process for a buyer's solicitor.

Analyse the importance of these searches and explain why you would advise your client to undertake them.

PROBLEM QUESTION

You are acting for Mr and Mrs Turner in relation to their purchase of Plot 16 New Meadow Estate, Minton, North Yorkshire. They do not have a related sale. The property is being sold by the developers, Cravenside Development Ltd. The land which is owned by the developers was formerly recreation land and in a small village. The development is registered under title number LS84759.

The purchase price for Plot 16 is £363,000 and Mr and Mrs Turner are buying with the assistance of a mortgage in favour of Marware Bank plc in the sum of £283,000.

1   Explain with reasons which Law Society Formula will be used to exchange contracts and why.
2   List the pre-completion searches you would undertake for this transaction and give reasons for your answer.
3   List the steps the solicitor will take between exchange and completion and give reasons for your answer.

FURTHER READING

- The Council of Mortgage Lenders' Handbook: www.cml.org.uk/lenders-handbook. The CML Lenders' Handbook provides comprehensive instructions for conveyancers acting on behalf of lenders in residential conveyancing transactions.
- *The Law Society Conveyancing Handbook* (23rd edn, Law Society 2016) General Editor: Frances Silverman, Consultant Editors: Annette Goss, Russell Hewitson, Peter Reekie, Anne Rodell and Michael Taylor. This book presents up-to-date guidance on good practice in residential conveyancing and is a reliable and up-to-date source of reference to answer the common queries arising from day-to-day transactions.

EXTRACT 1 STANDARD CONDITIONS OF SALE (FIFTH EDITION)

Note: © The Solicitors Law Stationery Limited and The Law Society of England and Wales (National Conditions of Sale 25th Edition, Law Society Conditions of Sale 2011)

CONTRACT

Incorporating the Standard Conditions of Sale (Fifth Edition)

For conveyancer's use only
Buyer's conveyancer:
Seller's conveyancer:
Law Society Formula: [A / B / C / Personal exchange]
The information above does not form part of the Contract

Date :

Seller :

Buyer :

Property (freehold/leasehold) :

Title number/root of title :

Specified incumbrances :

Title guarantee (full/limited)

Completion date :

Contract rate :

Purchase price :

Deposit :

Contents price (if separate) :

Balance :

The seller will sell and the buyer will buy the property for the purchase price.

WARNING	Signed
This is a formal document, designed to create legal rights and legal obligations. Take advice before using it.	
	Seller/Buyer

SPECIMEN

STANDARD CONDITIONS OF SALE (FIFTH EDITION)
(NATIONAL CONDITIONS OF SALE 25TH EDITION, LAW SOCIETY'S CONDITIONS OF SALE 2011)

1. GENERAL

1.1 Definitions

1.1.1 In these conditions:
(a) 'accrued interest' means:
  (i) if money has been placed on deposit or in a building society share account, the interest actually earned
  (ii) otherwise, the interest which might reasonably have been earned by depositing the money at interest on seven days' notice of withdrawal with a clearing bank less, in either case, any proper charges for handling the money
(b) 'clearing bank' means a bank which is a shareholder in CHAPS Clearing Co. Limited
(c) 'completion date' has the meaning given in condition 6.1.1
(d) 'contents price' means any separate amount payable for contents included in the contract
(e) 'contract rate' means the Law Society's interest rate from time to time in force
(f) 'conveyancer' means a solicitor, barrister, duly certified notary public, licensed conveyancer or recognised body under sections 9 or 23 of the Administration of Justice Act 1985
(g) 'lease' includes sub-lease, tenancy and agreement for a lease or sub-lease
(h) 'mortgage' means a mortgage or charge securing the repayment of money
(i) 'notice to complete' means a notice requiring completion of the contract in accordance with condition 6.8
(j) 'public requirement' means any notice, order or proposal given or made (whether before or after the date of the contract) by a body acting on statutory authority
(k) 'requisition' includes objection
(l) 'transfer' includes conveyance and assignment
(m) 'working day' means any day from Monday to Friday (inclusive) which is not Christmas Day, Good Friday or a statutory Bank Holiday.

1.1.2 In these conditions the terms 'absolute title' and 'official copies' have the special meanings given to them by the Land Registration Act 2002.

1.1.3 A party is ready, able and willing to complete:
(a) if he could be, but for the default of the other party, and
(b) in the case of the seller, even though the property remains subject to a mortgage, if the amount to be paid on completion enables the property to be transferred freed of all mortgages (except any to which the sale is expressly subject).

1.1.4 These conditions apply except as varied or excluded by the contract.

1.2 Joint parties
If there is more than one seller or more than one buyer, the obligations which they undertake can be enforced against them all jointly or against each individually.

1.3 Notices and documents

1.3.1 A notice required or authorised by the contract must be in writing.

1.3.2 Giving a notice or delivering a document to a party's conveyancer has the same effect as giving or delivering it to that party.

1.3.3 Where delivery of the original document is not essential, a notice or document is validly given or sent if it is sent:
(a) by fax, or
(b) by e-mail to an e-mail address for the intended recipient given in the contract

1.3.4 Subject to conditions 1.3.5 to 1.3.7, a notice is given and a document is delivered when it is received.

1.3.5 (a) A notice or document sent through a document exchange is received when it is available for collection.
(b) A notice or document which is received after 4.00pm on a working day, or on a day which is not a working day, is to be treated as having been received on the next working day.
(c) An automated response to a notice or document sent by e-mail that the intended recipient is out of the office is to be treated as proof that the notice or document was not received.

1.3.6 Condition 1.3.7 applies unless there is proof:
(a) that a notice or document has not been received, or
(b) of when it was received.

1.3.7 A notice or document sent by the following means is treated as having been received as follows:
(a) by first-class post: before 4.00pm on the second working day after posting
(b) by second-class post: before 4.00pm on the third working day after posting
(c) through a document exchange: before 4.00pm on the first working day after the day on which it would normally be available for collection by the addressee
(d) by fax: one hour after despatch
(e) by e-mail: before 4.00pm on the first working day after despatch.

1.4 VAT

1.4.1 The purchase price and the contents price are inclusive of any value added tax.

1.4.2 All other sums made payable by the contract are exclusive of any value added tax and where a supply is made which is chargeable to value added tax, the recipient of the supply is to pay the supplier (in addition to any other amounts payable under the contract) a sum equal to the value added tax chargeable on that supply.

1.5 Assignment and sub-sales

1.5.1 The buyer is not entitled to transfer the benefit of the contract.

1.5.2 The seller cannot be required to transfer the property in parts or to any person other than the buyer.

1.6 Third party rights
Unless otherwise expressly stated nothing in this contract will create rights pursuant to the Contracts (Rights of Third Parties) Act 1999 in favour of anyone other than the parties to the contract.

2. FORMATION

2.1 Date

2.1.1 If the parties intend to make a contract by exchanging duplicate copies by post or through a document exchange, the contract is made when the last copy is posted or deposited at the document exchange.

2.1.2 If the parties' conveyancers agree to treat exchange as taking place before duplicate copies are actually exchanged, the contract is made as so agreed.

2.2 Deposit

2.2.1 The buyer is to pay or send a deposit of 10 per cent of the purchase price no later than the date of the contract.

2.2.2 If a cheque tendered in payment of all or part of the deposit is dishonoured when first presented, the seller may, within seven working days of being notified that the cheque has been dishonoured, give notice to the buyer that the contract is discharged by the buyer's breach.

2.2.3 Conditions 2.2.4 to 2.2.6 do not apply on a sale by auction.

2.2.4 The deposit is to be paid:
(a) by electronic means from an account held in the name of a conveyancer at a clearing bank to an account in the name of the seller's conveyancer or (in a case where condition 2.2.5 applies) a conveyancer nominated by him and maintained at a clearing bank or
(b) to the seller's conveyancer or (in a case where condition 2.2.5 applies) a conveyancer nominated by him by cheque drawn on a solicitor's or licensed conveyancer's client account

2.2.5 If before completion date the seller agrees to buy another property in England and Wales for his residence, he may use all or any part of the deposit as a deposit in that transaction to be held on terms to the same effect as this condition and condition 2.2.6.

2.2.6 Any deposit or part of a deposit not being used in accordance with condition 2.2.5 is to be held by the seller's conveyancer as stakeholder on terms that on completion it is paid to the seller with accrued interest.

2.3 Auctions

2.3.1 On a sale by auction the following conditions apply to the property and, if it is sold in lots, to each lot.

2.3.2 The sale is subject to a reserve price.

2.3.3 The seller, or a person on his behalf, may bid up to the reserve price.

2.3.4 The auctioneer may refuse any bid.

2.3.5 If there is a dispute about a bid, the auctioneer may resolve the dispute or restart the auction at the last undisputed bid.

2.3.6 The deposit is to be paid to the auctioneer as agent for the seller.

3. MATTERS AFFECTING THE PROPERTY

3.1 Freedom from incumbrances

3.1.1 The seller is selling the property free from incumbrances, other than those mentioned in condition 3.1.2.

3.1.2 The incumbrances subject to which the property is sold are:
(a) those specified in the contract
(b) those discoverable by inspection of the property before the date of the contract.
(c) those the seller does not and could not reasonably know about
(d) those, other than mortgages, which the buyer knows about
(e) entries made before the date of the contract in any public register except those maintained by the Land Registry or its Land Charges Department or by Companies House
(f) public requirements.

3.1.3 After the contract is made, the seller is to give the buyer written details without delay of any new public requirement and of anything in writing which he learns about concerning a matter covered by condition 3.1.2.

3.1.4 The buyer is to bear the cost of complying with any outstanding public requirement and is to indemnify the seller against any liability resulting from a public requirement.

3.2 Physical state

3.2.1 The buyer accepts the property in the physical state it is in at the date of the contract unless the seller is building or converting it.

3.2.2 A leasehold property is sold subject to any subsisting breach of a condition or tenant's obligation relating to the physical state of the property which renders the lease liable to forfeiture.

3.2.3 A sub-lease is granted subject to any subsisting breach of a condition or tenant's obligation relating to the physical state of the property which renders the seller's own lease liable to forfeiture.

3.3 Leases affecting the property

3.3.1 The following provisions apply if any part of the property is sold subject to a lease.

3.3.2 (a) The seller having provided the buyer with full details of each lease or copies of the documents embodying the lease terms, the buyer is treated as entering into the contract knowing and fully accepting those terms.
(b) The seller is to inform the buyer without delay if the lease ends or if the seller learns of any application by the tenant in connection with the lease; the seller is then to act as the buyer reasonably directs, and the buyer is to indemnify him against all consequent loss and expense.
(c) Except with the buyer's consent, the seller is not to agree to any proposal to change the lease terms nor to take any step to end the lease.
(d) The seller is to inform the buyer without delay of any change to the lease terms which may be proposed or agreed.
(e) The buyer is to indemnify the seller against all claims arising from the lease after actual completion; this includes claims which are unenforceable against a buyer for want of registration.
(f) The seller takes no responsibility for what rent is lawfully recoverable, nor for whether or how any legislation affects the lease.
(g) If the let land is not wholly within the property, the seller may apportion the rent.

4. TITLE AND TRANSFER

4.1 Proof of title

4.1.1 Without cost to the buyer, the seller is to provide the buyer with proof of the title to the property and of his ability to transfer it, or to procure its transfer.

4.1.2 Where the property has a registered title the proof is to include official copies of the items referred to in rules 134(1)(a) and (b) and 135(1)(a) of the Land Registration Rules 2003, so far as they are not to be discharged or overridden at or before completion.
Where the property has an unregistered title, the proof is to include:
(a) an abstract of title or an epitome of title with photocopies of the documents, and
(b) production of every document or an abstract, epitome or copy of it with an original marking by a conveyancer either against the original or an examined abstract or an examined copy.

4.2 Requisitions

4.2.1 The buyer may not raise requisitions:
(a) on any title shown by the seller before the contract was made
(b) in relation to the matters covered by condition 3.1.2.

4.2.2 Notwithstanding condition 4.2.1, the buyer may, within six working days of a matter coming to his attention after the contract was made, raise written requisitions on that matter. In that event, steps 3 and 4 in condition 4.3.1 apply.

4.2.3 On the expiry of the relevant time limit under condition 4.2.2 or condition 4.3.1, the buyer loses his right to raise requisitions or to make observations.

4.3 Timetable

4.3.1 Subject to condition 4.2 and to the extent that the seller did not take the steps described in condition 4.1.1 before the contract was made, the steps for deducing and investigating the title to the property are to be taken within the following time limits:

Step		Time Limit
1.	The seller is to comply with condition 4.1.1	Immediately after making the contract
2.	The buyer may raise written requisitions	Six working days after either the date of the contract or the date of delivery of the seller's evidence of title on which the requisitions are raised, whichever is the later
3.	The seller is to reply in writing to any requisitions raised	Four working days after receiving the requisitions
4.	The buyer may make written observations on the seller's replies	Three working days after receiving the replies

The time limit on the buyer's right to raise requisitions applies even where the seller supplies incomplete evidence of his title, but the buyer may, within six working days from delivery of any further evidence, raise further requisitions resulting from that evidence.

4.3.2 The parties are to take the following steps to prepare and agree the transfer of the property within the following time limits:

Step		Time Limit
A.	The buyer is to send the seller a draft transfer	At least twelve working days before completion date
B.	The seller is to approve or revise that draft and either return it or retain it for use as the actual transfer	Four working days after delivery of the draft transfer
C.	If the draft is returned the buyer is to send an engrossment to the seller	At least five working days before completion date

4.3.3 Periods of time under conditions 4.3.1 and 4.3.2 may run concurrently.

4.3.4 If the period between the date of the contract and completion date is less than 15 working days, the time limits in conditions 4.2.2, 4.3.1 and 4.3.2 are to be reduced by the same proportion as that period bears to the period of 15 working days. Fractions of a working day are to be rounded down except that the time limit to perform any step is not to be less than one working day.

4.4 Defining the property
The seller need not:
(a) prove the exact boundaries of the property
(b) prove who owns fences, ditches, hedges or walls
(c) separately identify parts of the property with different titles further than he may be able to do from information in his possession.

4.5 Rents and rentcharges
The fact that a rent or rentcharge, whether payable or receivable by the owner of the property, has been, or will on completion be, informally apportioned is not to be regarded as a defect in title.

4.6 Transfer

4.6.1 The buyer does not prejudice his right to raise requisitions, or to require replies to any raised, by taking any steps in relation to preparing or agreeing the transfer.

4.6.2 Subject to condition 4.6.3, the seller is to transfer the property with full title guarantee.

4.6.3 The transfer is to have effect as if the disposition is expressly made subject to all matters covered by condition 3.1.2 and, if the property is leasehold, is to contain a statement that the covenants set out in section 4 of the Law of Property (Miscellaneous Provisions) Act 1994 will not extend to any breach of the tenant's covenants in the lease relating to the physical state of the property.

4.6.4 If after completion the seller will remain bound by any obligation affecting the property which was disclosed to the buyer before the contract was made, but the law does not imply any covenant by the buyer to indemnify the seller against liability for future breaches of it:
(a) the buyer is to covenant in the transfer to indemnify the seller against liability for any future breach of the obligation and to perform it from then on, and
(b) if required by the seller, the buyer is to execute and deliver to the seller on completion a duplicate transfer prepared by the buyer.

4.6.5 The seller is to arrange at his expense that, in relation to every document of title which the buyer does not receive on completion, the buyer is to have the benefit of:
(a) a written acknowledgement of his right to its production, and
(b) a written undertaking for its safe custody (except while it is held by a mortgagee or by someone in a fiduciary capacity).

4.7 **Membership of company**
Where the seller is, or is required to be, a member of a company that has an interest in the property or has management responsibilities for the property or the surrounding areas, the seller is, without cost to the buyer, to provide such documents on completion as will enable the buyer to become a member of that company.

5. RISK, INSURANCE AND OCCUPATION PENDING COMPLETION

5.1.1 The property is at the risk of the buyer from the date of the contract

5.1.2 The seller is under no obligation to the buyer to insure the property unless:
(a) the contract provides that a policy effected by or for the seller and insuring the property or any part of it against liability for loss or damage is to continue in force, or
(b) the property or any part of it is let on terms under which the seller (whether as landlord or as tenant) is obliged to insure against loss or damage.

5.1.3 If the seller is obliged to insure the property under condition 5.1.2, the seller is to:
(a) do everything necessary to maintain the policy
(b) permit the buyer to inspect the policy or evidence of its terms
(c) if before completion the property suffers loss or damage:
 (i) pay to the buyer on completion the amount of the policy monies which the seller has received, so far as not applied in repairing or reinstating the property, and
 (ii) if no final payment has then been received, assign to the buyer, at the buyer's expense, all rights to claim under the policy in such form as the buyer reasonably requires and pending execution of the assignment hold any policy monies received in trust for the buyer
(d) cancel the policy on completion.

5.1.4 Where the property is leasehold and the property, or any building containing it, is insured by a reversioner or other third party, the seller is to use reasonable efforts to ensure that the insurance is maintained until completion and if, before completion, the property or building suffers loss or damage the seller is to assign to the buyer on completion, at the buyer's expense, such rights as the seller may have in the policy monies, in such form as the buyer reasonably requires.

5.1.5 If payment under a policy effected by or for the buyer is reduced, because the property is covered against loss or damage by an insurance policy effected by or on behalf of the seller, then, unless the seller is obliged to insure the property under condition 5.1.2, the purchase price is to be abated by the amount of that reduction.

5.1.6 Section 47 of the Law of Property Act 1925 does not apply.

5.2 **Occupation by buyer**

5.2.1 If the buyer is not already lawfully in the property, and the seller agrees to let him into occupation, the buyer occupies on the following terms.

5.2.2 The buyer is a licensee and not a tenant. The terms of the licence are that the buyer:
(a) cannot transfer it
(b) may permit members of his household to occupy the property
(c) is to pay or indemnify the seller against all outgoings and other expenses in respect of the property
(d) is to pay the seller a fee calculated at the contract rate on a sum equal to the purchase price (less any deposit paid) for the period of the licence
(e) is entitled to any rents and profits from any part of the property which he does not occupy
(f) is to keep the property in as good a state of repair as it was in when he went into occupation (except for fair wear and tear) and is not to alter it
(g) if the property is leasehold, is not to do anything which puts the seller in breach of his obligations in the lease, and
(h) is to quit the property when the licence ends.

5.2.3 The buyer is not in occupation for the purposes of this condition if he merely exercises rights of access given solely to do work agreed by the seller.

5.2.4 The buyer's licence ends on the earliest of: completion date, rescission of the contract or when five working days' notice given by one party to the other takes effect.

5.2.5 If the buyer is in occupation of the property after his licence has come to an end and the contract is subsequently completed he is to pay the seller compensation for his continued occupation calculated at the same rate as the fee mentioned in condition 5.2.2(d).

5.2.6 The buyer's right to raise requisitions is unaffected.

6. COMPLETION

6.1 **Date**

6.1.1 Completion date is twenty working days after the date of the contract but time is not of the essence of the contract unless a notice to complete has been served.

6.1.2 If the money due on completion is received after 2.00pm, completion is to be treated, for the purposes only of conditions 6.3 and 7.2, as taking place on the next working day as a result of the buyer's default.

6.1.3 Condition 6.1.2 does not apply and the seller is treated as in default if:
(a) the sale is with vacant possession of the property or any part of it, and
(b) the buyer is ready, able and willing to complete but does not pay the money due on completion until after 2.00pm because the seller has not vacated the property or that part by that time.

6.2 **Arrangements and place**

6.2.1 The buyer's conveyancer and the seller's conveyancer are to co-operate in agreeing arrangements for completing the contract.

6.2.2 Completion is to take place in England and Wales, either at the seller's conveyancer's office or at some other place which the seller reasonably specifies.

6.3 **Apportionments**

6.3.1 On evidence of proper payment being made, income and outgoings of the property are to be apportioned between the parties so far as the change of ownership on completion will affect entitlement to receive or liability to pay them.

6.3.2 If the whole property is sold with vacant possession or the seller exercises his option in condition 7.2.4, apportionment is to be made with effect from the date of actual completion; otherwise, it is to be made from completion date.

6.3.3 In apportioning any sum, it is to be assumed that the seller owns the property until the end of the day from which apportionment is made and that the sum accrues from day to day at the rate at which it is payable on that day.

6.3.4 For the purpose of apportioning income and outgoings, it is to be assumed that they accrue at an equal daily rate throughout the year.

6.3.5 When a sum to be apportioned is not known or easily ascertainable at completion, a provisional apportionment is to be made according to the best estimate available. As soon as the amount is known, a final apportionment is to be made and notified to the other party. Any resulting balance is to be paid no more than ten working days later, and if not then paid the balance is to bear interest at the contract rate from then until payment.

6.3.6 Compensation payable under condition 5.2.5 is not to be apportioned.

6.4 **Amount payable**
The amount payable by the buyer on completion is the purchase price and the contents price (less any deposit already paid to the seller or his agent) adjusted to take account of:
(a) apportionments made under condition 6.3
(b) any compensation to be paid or allowed under condition 7.2
(c) any sum payable under condition 5.1.3.

6.5 **Title deeds**

6.5.1 As soon as the buyer has complied with all his obligations under this contract on completion the seller must hand over the documents of title.

6.5.2 Condition 6.5.1 does not apply to any documents of title relating to land being retained by the seller after completion.

6.6 **Rent receipts**
The buyer is to assume that whoever gave any receipt for a payment of rent or service charge which the seller produces was the person or the agent of the person then entitled to that rent or service charge.

6.7 **Means of payment**
The buyer is to pay the money due on completion by a direct transfer of cleared funds from an account held in the name of a conveyancer at a clearing bank and, if appropriate, an unconditional release of a deposit held by a stakeholder.

6.8 **Notice to complete**

6.8.1 At any time after the time applicable under condition 6.1.2 on completion date, a party who is ready, able and willing to complete may give the other a notice to complete.

6.8.2 The parties are to complete the contract within ten working days of giving a notice to complete, excluding the day on which the notice is given. For this purpose, time is of the essence of the contract.

6.8.3 On receipt of a notice to complete:
(a) if the buyer paid no deposit, he is forthwith to pay a deposit of 10 per cent
(b) if the buyer paid a deposit of less than 10 per cent, he is forthwith to pay a further deposit equal to the balance of that 10 per cent.

7. REMEDIES

7.1 **Errors and omissions**

7.1.1 If any plan or statement in the contract, or in the negotiations leading to it, is or was misleading or inaccurate due to an error or omission by the seller, the remedies available to the buyer are as follows.
(a) When there is a material difference between the description or value of the property, or of any of the contents included in the contract, as represented and as it is, the buyer is entitled to damages.
(b) An error or omission only entitles the buyer to rescind the contract:
 (i) where it results from fraud or recklessness, or
 (ii) where he would be obliged, to his prejudice, to accept property differing substantially (in quantity, quality or tenure) from what the error or omission had led him to expect.

7.1.2 If either party rescinds the contract:
(a) unless the rescission is a result of the buyer's breach of contract the deposit is to be repaid to the buyer with accrued interest
(b) the buyer is to return any documents he received from the seller and is to cancel any registration of the contract.

7.2 **Late completion**

7.2.1 If there is default by either or both of the parties in performing their obligations under the contract and completion is delayed, the party whose total period of default is the greater is to pay compensation to the other party.

7.2.2 Compensation is calculated at the contract rate on an amount equal to the purchase price, less (where the buyer is the paying party) any deposit paid, for the period by which the paying party's default exceeds that of the receiving party, or, if shorter, the period between completion date and actual completion.

7.2.3 Any claim for loss resulting from delayed completion is to be reduced by any compensation paid under this contract.

7.2.4 Where the buyer holds the property as tenant of the seller and completion is delayed, the seller may give notice to the buyer, before the date of actual completion, that he intends to take the net income from the property until completion. If he does so, he cannot claim compensation under condition 7.2.1 as well.

7.3 **After completion**
Completion does not cancel liability to perform any outstanding obligation under this contract.

7.4 **Buyer's failure to comply with notice to complete**

7.4.1 If the buyer fails to complete in accordance with a notice to complete, the following terms apply.

7.4.2 The seller may rescind the contract, and if he does so:
(a) he may:
 (i) forfeit and keep any deposit and accrued interest
 (ii) resell the property and any contents included in the contract
 (iii) claim damages
(b) the buyer is to return any documents he received from the seller and is to cancel any registration of the contract.

7.4.3 The seller retains his other rights and remedies.

7.5 **Seller's failure to comply with notice to complete**

7.5.1 If the seller fails to complete in accordance with a notice to complete, the following terms apply.

7.5.2 The buyer may rescind the contract, and if he does so:
(a) the deposit is to be repaid to the buyer with accrued interest
(b) the buyer is to return any documents he received from the seller and is, at the seller's expense, to cancel any registration of the contract.

7.5.3 The buyer retains his other rights and remedies.

8. LEASEHOLD PROPERTY

8.1 **Existing leases**

8.1.1 The following provisions apply to a sale of leasehold land.

8.1.2 The seller having provided the buyer with copies of the documents embodying the lease terms, the buyer is treated as entering into the contract knowing and fully accepting those terms.

8.2 **New leases**

8.2.1 The following provisions apply to a contract to grant a new lease.

8.2.2 The conditions apply so that:
'seller' means the proposed landlord
'buyer' means the proposed tenant
'purchase price' means the premium to be paid on the grant of a lease.

8.2.3 The lease is to be in the form of the draft attached to the contract.

8.2.4 If the term of the new lease will exceed seven years, the seller is to deduce a title which will enable the buyer to register the lease at the Land Registry with an absolute title.

8.2.5 The seller is to engross the lease and a counterpart of it and is to send the counterpart to the buyer at least five working days before completion date.

8.2.6 The buyer is to execute the counterpart and deliver it to the seller on completion.

8.3 **Consent**

8.3.1 (a) The following provisions apply if a consent to let, assign or sub-let is required to complete the contract
(b) In this condition 'consent' means consent in the form which satisfies the requirement to obtain it.

8.3.2 (a) The seller is to apply for the consent at his expense, and to use all reasonable efforts to obtain it
(b) The buyer is to provide all information and references reasonably required.

8.3.3 Unless he is in breach of his obligation under condition 8.3.2, either party may rescind the contract by notice to the other party if three working days before completion date (or before a later date on which the parties have agreed to complete the contract):
(a) the consent has not been given, or
(b) the consent has been given subject to a condition to which a party reasonably objects. In that case, neither party is to be treated as in breach of contract and condition 7.1.2 applies.

9. CONTENTS

9.1 The following provisions apply to any contents which are included in the contract, whether or not a separate price is to be paid for them.

9.2 The contract takes effect as a contract for sale of goods.

9.3 The buyer takes the contents in the physical state they are in at the date of the contract.

9.4 Ownership of the contents passes to the buyer on actual completion.

SPECIAL CONDITIONS

1 (a) This contract incorporates the Standard Conditions of Sale (Fifth Edition).

    (b) The terms used in this contract have the same meaning when used in the Conditions.

2 Subject to the terms of this contract and to the Standard Conditions of Sale, the seller is to transfer the property with either full title guarantee or limited title guarantee, as specified on the front page.

3 (a) The sale includes those contents which are indicated on the attached list as included in the sale and the buyer is to pay the contents price for them.

    (b) The sale excludes those fixtures which are at the property and are indicated on the attached list as excluded from the sale

4 The property is sold with vacant possession.

    (or)

4 The property is sold subject to the following leases or tenancies:

5 Conditions 6.1.2 and 6.1.3 shall take effect as if the time specified in them were ___ rather than 2.00 p.m.

6 **Representations**

Neither party can rely on any representation made by the other, unless made in writing by the other or his conveyancer, but this does not exclude liability for fraud or recklessness.

7 **Occupier's consent**

Each occupier identified below agrees with the seller and the buyer, in consideration of their entering into this contract, that the occupier concurs in the sale of the property on the terms of this contract, undertakes to vacate the property on or before the completion date and releases the property and any included fixtures and contents from any right or interest that the occupier may have.

Note: this condition does not apply to occupiers under leases or tenancies subject to which the property is sold.

Name(s) and signature(s) of the occupier(s) (if any):

Name

Signature

Notices may be sent to:

Seller's conveyancer's name:

    E-mail address:*

Buyer's conveyancer's name:

    E-mail address:*

*Adding an e-mail address authorises service by e-mail see condition 1.3.3(b)

EXTRACT 2 OFFICIAL COPY OF REGISTER OF TITLE

| **Official copy of register of title** | Title number AGS150716 | Edition date 31.05.2012 |

-- This official copy shows the entries on the register on 30 Nov 2016 at 13:02:42.

-- This date must be quoted as the 'search from date' in any official search application based on this copy.

-- The date at the beginning of an entry is the date on which the entry was made in the register

-- Issued on 30 Nov 2016

-- Under s.67 of the Land Registration Act 2002, this copy is admissible in evidence to the same extent as the original.

A: Property Register

This register describes the land and estate comprised in the title.

WALES : ANGLESEY

1. (30.09.1987) The **Freehold** land shown edged with red on the plan of the above Title filed at the Registry and being 10 Coastal Path South Stacks Lane, Holyhead Anglesey LL65 1YH.

2. (30.09.1987) The mines and minerals together with ancillary powers of working are excepted.

3. The land has the benefit of rights granted by but is subject to the following rights reserved by a Conveyance of the land in this title dated 2 July 1953 made between (1) Daniel James Schofield and (2) Andrew Booth : -

   "TOGETHER with .... a right of way at all times and for all purposes over and along the path marked "Joint Way" on the said Plan and also SUBJECT TO AND RESERVING a right of way for the owners and occupiers of the adjoining property on the West side of the property hereby conveyed as heretofore used and enjoyed for the purpose of gaining access to such adjoining property such way being marked on the said Plan also "Joint Way" SUBJECT NEVERTHELESS to the payment by the owners of such adjoining properties of a proportionate part of the expense of maintaining and keeping in repair the said Joint Ways."

   NOTE : - Copy Conveyance plan in Certificate. Copy plan filed.

4. The land has the benefit of the rights granted by a Deed of Grant dated 28th August 1977 made between (1) Robert Peston and Elizabeth Peston (the First Owners) (ABCD Bank plc (the Bank) and George Whitely (the Second Owner)

   NOTE : - Copy in Certificate. Copy filed under ANG170716

Title number AGS150716
B: Proprietorship Register

This register specifies the class of title and identifies the owner. It contains any entries that affect the right of disposal.

Title absolute

1. (17.04.2010) **PROPRIETOR :** Paul John Smith of Highspy Cottage High Street Anglesey(LL65 5WJ)

2. (17.04.2010) The price stated to have been paid on 10 April 2010 was £215,000.

3. (30.09.1987) The Transfer to the proprietor contains a covenant to observe and perform the covenants referred to in the Charges register and indemnity in respect thereof.

4. (17.04.2010) **RESTRICTION :** Except under an order of the registrar no disposition by the proprietor of the land is to be registered without the consent of the proprietor of the Charge dated 10 April 2010 in favour of Derbyshire Building Society referred to in the Charges register.

C: Charges Register

This register contains any charges and other matters that affect the land.

1. (30.09.1987) A conveyance of the land in this title dated 2 July 1953 made between (1) Daniel James Schofield and (2) Andrew Booth:- contains the following restrictive covenants:

   "THE Purchaser hereby covenants with the Vendor as follows:

   (1) that no building shall be erected on the land hereby conveyed otherwise than in accordance with plans and specifications approved in writing by the Vendor or his successors in title

   (2) not use the land hereby conveyed for any trade or business purposes

   (3) not to use the land hereby conveyed or any building erected thereon in any manner so as to create any nuisance or annoyance to the owners or occupiers of land now owned by the Vendor and adjoining or near to the land hereby conveyed or any part thereof."

   (4) not to keep at the property any animals save for dog, cats and other domestic pets.

2.   (30.09.1987) A Conveyance of the land in this title and other land dated the 14 September 1868 made between (1) David Mirfin and (2) Robert Edwards contains restrictive covenants but neither the original deed nor a certified copy or examined abstract thereof was produced on first registration.

Title number AGS150716

3.   (17.04.2010) **REGISTERED CHARGE** dated 10 April 2010 to
        secure the moneys including the further advances mentioned.

4.   (17.04.2010) **PROPRIETOR** : DERBYSHIRE BUILDING SOCIETY of **Duffield
        Hall Duffield Derby DD 21 4YU**

5.   (31.05.2012) **REGISTERED CHARGE** dated 20 May 2012 to
        secure the moneys including the further advances mentioned.

6.   (31.05.2012) **PROPRIETOR** : **Financial Solutions Ltd** (Co Regn. No
        987235) of **Financial House, Main Road Sheffield S1 8WA**

End of register

EXTRACT 3 BUNDLE OF DOCUMENTS FOR 18 BANKHOUSE ROAD

DOCUMENT A

THIS CONVEYANCE is made the 27th day of May One thousand nine hundred and eighty three BETWEEN THOMAS WILLIAM and FLORENCE ANNA WILLIAM both of 18 Bankhouse Road Huddersfield in the County of Yorkshire (hereinafter called 'the Vendors') of the one part and JOSEPH ATTEY and CAROL ATTEY of 197 Albert Road Sheffield in the County of Yorkshire (hereinafter called 'the Purchasers') of the other part

(1) WHEREAS the Vendors are seized of the land and buildings described in the Schedule hereto for an estate in fee simple in possession subject as hereinafter mentioned but otherwise free from incumbrances and they hold the same upon trust for sale for themselves as beneficial joint tenants.

(2) The Vendors in pursuance and exercise of the said trust for sale have agreed to sell the land and buildings to the Purchasers at the price of FIFTEEN THOUSAND SEVEN HUNDRED AND FIFTY POUNDS

NOW THIS CONVEYANCE WITNESSETH as follows:−

1   In consideration of the sum of FIFTEEN THOUSAND SEVEN HUNDRED AND FIFTY POUNDS now paid by the Purchaser to the Vendors (the receipt of which the Vendors hereby acknowledge) the Vendors as Beneficial Owners hereby convey unto the Purchasers ALL the land and buildings described in the said Schedule hereto TO HOLD the same UNTO the Purchasers in fee simple as beneficial joint tenants SUBJECT NEVERTHELESS to and with the benefit of the rights exceptions reservations covenants and conditions contained mentioned or referred to in a Conveyance made the Twenty fifth day of August One thousand nine hundred and seventy six between Hayden Aled Jones on the one part and the Vendors of the other part (hereinafter referred to as 'the 1976 Conveyance') so far as the same are still subsisting and capable of taking effect and relate to or affect the said land and buildings hereby conveyed.

2   WITH the object and intention of the affording to the Vendors a full and sufficient indemnity the Purchasers hereby jointly and severally covenant with the Vendors that the Purchasers and their successors in title will at all times hereafter duly observe perform fulfil and keep the said rights exceptions reservations covenants and conditions and indemnify and keep indemnified the Vendors and their respective estates and effects from and against all actions proceedings costs claims and demands whatsoever in respect thereof for the future breach or non-observance or non-performance thereof.

3   The Purchasers hereby declare that the trustees for the time being of this deed shall have full and unrestricted power to mortgage charge lease dispose of or deal with (whether by sale gift or otherwise howsoever) all or part or parts of the said land and buildings with all the powers in that behalf of an absolute owner.

4   IT IS HEREBY CERTIFIED that the transaction hereby effected does not form
      part of a larger transaction or of a series of transactions in respect of which the
      amount or value or the aggregate amount or value of the consideration
      exceeds Twenty five thousand pounds.

IN WITNESS whereof the respective hands and seals of the parties hereto have been
hereunto been set and affixed the day and year first above written.

THE SCHEDULE above referred to

ALL THAT freehold property comprising land and buildings situate at 18 Bankhouse
Road Huddersfield in the County of Yorkshire more particularly described in a
Conveyance made the Twentieth day of January One thousand nine hundred and sixty
six and made between Simon Garth of the one part and Hayden Aled Jones of the
other part and shown edged red on the plan annexed to the 1966 Conveyance

SIGNED SEALED AND DELIVERED
by the said THOMAS WILLIAM   *Thomas William* (signed) LS
in the presence of:
A.D. Aspley (signed)
Solicitor
Aspley & Co Leeds

SIGNED SEALED AND DELIVERED   *Florence Anna William* (signed) LS
by the said FLORENCE ANNA WILLIAM
in the presence of:
A.D. Aspley (signed)
Solicitor
Aspley & Co Leeds

SIGNED SEALED AND DELIVERED
by the said JOSEPH ATTEY   *Joseph Attey* (signed) LS
in the presence of:
George Jackson (signed)
Solicitor
Jackson & Co
Sheffield

SIGNED SEALED AND DELIVERED
by the said CAROL ATTEY   *Carol Attey* (signed) LS
in the presence of:
George Jackson (signed)
Solicitor
Jackson & Co
Sheffield

DOCUMENT B

Mortgage Deed

The account number:	JE/894647832
The date:	27th May 1983
The Borrower:	JOSEPH ATTEY and CAROL ATTEY
The Borrower's address:	18 Bankhouse Road Huddersfield HD4 8JS
The Lender:	Kirklees Building Society of 4 Bank Street Wellington Huddersfield Yorkshire HD3 7AM
The property:	18 Bankhouse Road Huddersfield HD4 8JS
The title number:	Not applicable

1. This mortgage deed incorporates the mortgage conditions. The borrower has received a copy of them.

2. The borrower charges the property by way of legal mortgage with the payment of all money payable by the borrower to the lender under the mortgage conditions.

3. The mortgage secures further advances.

Signed, sealed and delivered by the borrower in the presence of the witness.

The Borrower		The witness (signature, name and address)
Joseph Attey (signed)	LS	George Jackson (signed) Solicitor Jackson & Co Sheffield
Carol Attey (signed)	LS	George Jackson (signed) Solicitor Jackson & Co Sheffield

DOCUMENT C

WE LINDSAY STEVEN WILTON and EMMA JANE WILTON of 94 Seafront
Lane Anglesey as the Personal Representatives of CAROL ATTEY who died on the
12th May 1989 and whose Will was proved by us on the 30th June 1989 in the
Huddersfield District Probate Registry HEREBY ASSENT to the vesting in ourselves
as tenants in common in equal shares of all that land and buildings known as 18
Bankhouse Road Huddersfield more particularly described in a Conveyance made the
Twentieth day of January One thousand nine hundred and sixty six and made between
Simon Garth of the one part and Hayden Aled Jones of the other part and shown edged
red on the plan annexed to the said Conveyance.

AS WITNESS our hands this 20th July 1989.
Signed by the said Lindsay Steven Wilton   *Lindsay Steven Wilton* (Legal Seal)
in the presence of
George Jackson (signed)
Solicitor
Jackson & Co
Sheffield

Signed by the said Emma Jane Wilton   *Emma Jane Wilton* (Legal Seal)
in the presence of
George Jackson (signed)
Solicitor
Jackson & Co
Sheffield

INDEX

Page numbers in *italics* denote tables, those in **bold** denote figures.